THE HURT
BUSINESS

Dear Sports Fan,

No other sport has defined the sportswriter quite like boxing. Whether it is James Baldwin, Joyce Carol Oates, Mark Kram or Norman Mailer, the four corners of the ring, together with the duelling and violence have provided a unique canvas on which to craft their art. And it's all here – 100 years of the greatest fighters and the greatest writers who have followed 'the sweet science'.

The Hurt Business is one of six books that begin our Aurum classics sports list. Publishing sports writing that does justice to the story being told has always been our priority at Aurum. This new series, which covers sports ranging from cricket to boxing, rugby to baseball, gives us the opportunity to celebrate both our own books that, over the years, have come to obtain classic status, and also bring back into print neglected books that deserve to be acclaimed as such. I hope that you will enjoy them all whether you are coming to the subject, the sport, or the writer for the first time.

At Aurum Press we take great care in shaping our sports list to be as diverse and inspiring as possible and we would love to hear what you think of the classics. Let us know on twitter at #aurumsportsclassics. Every month new tweets will be entered into a draw to win a set of all the titles. You can also email me at aurumclassics@aurumpress.co.uk to find out more about our forthcoming titles.

I would also be delighted to hear your suggestions for other forgotten classics, which you think merit re-publishing for a new generation.

Yours sincerely,

Robin Harvie

July 2013

EDITED BY **GEORGE KIMBALL** & **JOHN SCHULIAN** FOREWORD BY **COLUM McCANN**

THE HURT
BUSINESS

AMERICAN WRITERS ON BOXING

First published 2013 in the UK by
Aurum Press Limited
74-77 White Lion Street
London N1 9PF
www.aurumpress.co.uk

First published in the United States by Literary Classics of the
United States as *At the Fights*.

Some of the material in this volume is reprinted with the
permission of holders of copyright and publishing rights.
Acknowledgements begin on page 501.

Every effort has been made to contact the copyright holders of
material in this book. However, where an omission has occurred,
the publisher will gladly include acknowledgement
in any future edition.

A catalogue record for this book is available from the British
Library.

ISBN 978 1 78131 179 0

1 3 5 7 9 10 8 6 2

2013 2015 2016 2017 2014

Printed and bound in Great Britain by CPI Group (UK) Ltd,
Croydon, CR0 4YY

Contents

Last Call

George Kimball was blessed with the kind of voluble charm you find in an Irish bar, and let me tell you he'd been in a few. No amount of drink, however, could rein in his galloping intelligence or his love of the language and good company. He was equally engaging in drier precincts, which made him the perfect editing partner for me. When we began doing interviews to hustle this book, George waxed eloquent and I provided grace notes. But slowly, inexorably, his voice became a sandpaper whisper. It was the chemo, extracting its price for keeping him upright.

Now I had to do the talking, a reluctant solo act trying to score points with strangers armed with questions. Again and again I found myself telling them about the nobility of prizefighters, who willingly risk death every time they step into the ring. But it was always George I thought of, the truest nobleman of my lifetime.

The cancer doctors gave him six months to live in 2005. He spent the next six years making liars of them. Not only did he publish *Four Kings*, a masterful book about boxing's last golden era, he covered fights online and wrote essays, poetry, songs, and even a play. He edited books, too, obviously, and worked on a documentary. Somehow he made time to get to the theater and concerts and dinner, and to France and Ireland as well. He savored the world that was slipping away from him and, with friends old and new, proved forevermore that once he wrapped his arms around someone, he never let go.

Those of us who knew him—and probably some who didn't—will keep the Kimball legend alive with tales of his wild times and all the nights he dropped his glass eye in a drink some unsuspecting soul had asked him to keep an eye on. At such moments George wore the sublimely demented look I first saw in the Lion's Head, the legendary Greenwich Village writers' bar, as he tried to light a friend's sport coat on fire. His friend was wearing it.

The booze and drugs were behind George by 2009, when he and I began digging for the treasures that grace this book. The only remnant of his old life was the unfiltered Lucky Strikes he smoked ceaselessly. "What are they going to do," he'd say, "give me cancer?" He had it by then, of course—the esophageal variety—and he knew that death would win no matter how hard he fought. But he was damned if he wasn't going to go the full twelve rounds. He was fighting for money he would leave his wife and two grown children and for one last grand achievement to cement his legacy in sports writing. *At the Fights* was that achievement.

For six months we searched everywhere we could think of, touting our best discoveries, bumping heads over differences in taste, and all the while mailing envelopes fat with stories to be considered back and forth across the country. George was in New York, I was in L.A., and we didn't see each other until that March day in 2010 when our bosses at The Library of America told us our manuscript had passed muster. We celebrated over lunch at a little joint in the East Sixties. George was so happy it didn't matter that he was too sick to swallow his soup.

The question from that point forward was whether he would live long enough to see our book published. He raised it himself, and answered it in word and deed. He reveled in the interviews we did. He embraced readings with Pete Hamill in Manhattan and made his last triumphant returns to Boston, his stomping grounds as a newspaperman, and Kansas University, where he had twice lost decisions to academia. But it wasn't until the publication party, with everyone from his 89-year-old mother to Gay Talese gathered at the New York Athletic Club, that I knew for certain what I'd long suspected. The book had helped to keep him alive.

That was in April 2011. Three months later George was dead, at sixty-seven, and a great emptiness set in on those of us who had worked with him, howled at the moon with him, loved him. Our solace comes from the same source that I hope will bring you joy: these five hundred-plus pages of great boxing writing. On every one of them, George's heart still beats.

—John Schulian

COLUM McCANN

Foreword

Boxing. You can press the language out of it. The sweathouse of the body. The moving machinery of ligaments. The intimate fray of rope. The men in their archaic stances like anatomy illustrations from an old-time encyclopedia. The moment in a fight when the punches slow down and the opponents watch each other like time-lapse photographs—the sweat frozen in mid-air, the blood still spinning, the maniacal grins like the teeth themselves have gone bare-knuckle.

Writers love boxing—even if they can't box. And maybe writers love boxing *especially* because they can't box. The language is all cinema and violence: the burst eye socket, the ruined cartilage, the dolphin punch coming up from the depths.

What you have with a fight is what you have with writing, and they each become metaphors for each other—the ring, the page; the punch, the word; the choreography, the keyboard; the feint, the suggestion; the bucket, the wastebasket; the sweat, the edit; the pretender, the critic; the bell, the deadline. There's the showoff shuffle, the mingled blood on your gloves, the spitting your teeth up at the end of the day.

Literature recreates the language of the epic. And what's more epic and mythological than a scrap? For those of us who can't fight, we still want to be able to step into a fighter's body. We want to walk off woozy to the corner and have our faces slapped a little bit, then suddenly get up to dance, and hear the crowd roar, and step out once more with a little dazzle.

Boxers get told to imagine punching a spot behind your opponent's head, to reach in so far so they can extend the destruction to the back of the head. Writers do the same thing—they try to imagine a spot behind your brain and punch you there. Boom. Headspin.

Skin-slip on the canvas. Ten, nine, eight. Get the fuck up off this page. Four three two one Mississippi. Get the fuck up. Now.

Mailer. London. Liebling. Oates. Baldwin. Remnick. Who stole their title, The Heart of Darkness? Soccer has never really made great literature, nor has tennis, or football. Baseball and chess get a bit of literary attention, but never on the level of boxing. And I don't know a good poem yet about curling. Let's face it, the Great Book says that in the beginning was the word. And then the word was made flesh. And then it dwelt amongst us.

What's most beautiful about boxing are the lives behind it. They're so goddamn literary. Every boxer you ever met was fathered by Hamlet, and if not the Dane, well, at least Coriolanus. There's always the Gatsby moment and the gorgeous pink rag of a suit. Every promoter you've ever seen has Shylock on his shoulder. You know there's a little bit of Prufrock in that grey-haired trainer hanging out the window with all the other lonely men in shirt-sleeves. And that boxing wife or girlfriend you see at home, sitting at the kitchen table, peeling potatoes, watching the clock, well, she has a little Molly Bloom to her, doesn't she? Later on, when her ruined boy comes home, cuckolded by defeat, she will take that bit of seed-cake from his mouth.

But maybe the appeal of boxing and its own peculiar genius is that it can be used as a recurring metaphor for just about anything. Boxing is so malleable, certainly in terms of its language, that it can stand in at a moment's notice. Boxing as economics. Boxing as supermarket shopping. Boxing as astrophysics. Boxing as a love affair. *Man, she knocked me out.* If you want to talk about the recent financial ruin, stroll along Wall Street and just listen to the brokers in their pin-stripe dressing gowns—their takedowns, their sucker punches, their catch-weights, their glass jaws, their haymakers, their throw-in of the towel on a Friday afternoon.

Boxing is our everyman, our everymove, our everything. And language understands it. Words power the punch. They also power the recovery. They paint the viciousness and then they paint the grace, or the loss, or both at once. It's like making love with ruin, like saying: *I just entered you, won't you stay around just a little longer?* We've all seen the peeling posters on the gym wall. We've witnessed the pull of the string and the click of the lightbulb. We've heard the rear door slowly close and felt the darkness coming down. We've walked down through the foggy alleyway, carrying the wound, going home.

Every now and then, though, boxing moves beyond the human and just becomes plain indescribable, and you have to let the silence. You have to let it. You have to. Let it. Fall.

Colum McCann won the 2009 National Book Award for fiction for Let the Great World Spin.

Disarming Candor

America had seen great and celebrated fights before, but it can be fairly argued that the 1910 confrontation in which Jack Johnson defended his heavyweight crown against Jim Jeffries in a bout fraught with social and racial implications also produced the birth of American boxing *writing*.

The coverage of its predecessors had borne even less resemblance to the often brilliant prose the sport would inspire over the next hundred years than did Johnson–Jeffries, contested under the Queensberry Rules, to the bare-knuckle, eye-gouging contests that prevailed as "boxing" for most of the nineteenth century.

The battle between the defiant Johnson, the first African American to hold the world's heavyweight title, and the undefeated Jeffries, who claimed he had been lured from retirement "for the sole purpose of proving that a white man is better than a Negro," produced boxing's first full-fledged media circus. Among the celebrity press corps dispatched to cover the fight were the novelists Jack London and Rex Beach, along with boxers-turned-wordsmiths John L. Sullivan and Bob Fitzsimmons, Johnson's old rival Joe Choynski, and Abe Attell, the former featherweight champion who would acquire subsequent notoriety for his bagman's role in the 1919 Black Sox scandal. The bout was fought in a wooden stadium so hastily constructed—and so speedily dismantled—that it never had a proper name. In the run-up to the centennial celebration in Reno it took a team of boxing archaeologists months to pinpoint its precise location.

More than six hundred writers of varying stripes augmented the ringside crowd of twenty thousand spectators, nearly double Reno's 1910 population. Western Union transmitted more than a million words of copy, a record that would stand until Lindbergh touched down at Orly seventeen years later. In the century since its publication Jack London's report for the *New York Herald*, the opening piece in this anthology, has been cited as a classic example of turn-of-the-century journalism by his admirers and as damning evidence of his bizarre racial animus by his detractors, but his account has come to symbolize the Johnson–Jeffries fight, for he may have been more responsible than anyone (including the principals themselves) for it happening at all.

Almost by accident, the novelist had been in Sydney two years earlier when Johnson defeated Canadian Tommy Burns to win the world's heavyweight championship. London's description of that day's proceedings incorporated his oft-quoted admission, "he was a white man and so am I. Naturally, I wanted to see the white man win." His dispatch from ringside at Rushcutters Bay famously concluded: "Jim Jeffries must now emerge from his alfalfa farm and remove that golden smile from Jack Johnson's face. . . . Jeff, it's up to you."

That challenge would be the first salvo in a relentless, year-long campaign for a Great White Hope, one that eventually pressured Jeffries out of retirement. Jeffries, who had vowed before hanging up his gloves that he would retire "when there are no more white men left to fight," reluctantly agreed to the fight after being persuaded that the honor of the Caucasian race rested on his shoulders, but in Reno he proved to be no more a match for Johnson than had been Burns. The result produced an explosive and immediate aftershock, prompting nationwide riots and several deaths. (Nearly all the victims were African Americans.) In cities such as Baltimore and as far away as Cuba, newsreel footage showing Johnson's victory was banned from local theaters.

Despite the bout having served as a catalyst for racial discontent, the trappings of legitimacy had been conferred upon boxing in the United States, particularly along its Eastern seaboard, where it had heretofore subsisted, when it existed at all, as an outlaw sport. The year after Johnson–Jeffries, the New York state legislature passed the Frawley Act, which legalized boxing on a limited basis. This legal status was temporarily revoked following America's 1917 entry into World War I, but in 1920 boxing returned to New York in a fully legalized form with the passage of the Walker Act and its concomitant creation of the New York State Athletic Commission, which would soon become the sport's most influential regulatory agency.

This flurry of boxing activity in the decade following the Johnson–Jeffries fight led Tex Rickard, the nation's foremost promoter, to shift his base of operations to the Big Apple, and, in due course, manager Jack "Doc" Kearns, along with his hard-hitting prospect, Jack Dempsey, followed Rickard and the money trail to New York. Rickard eventually assumed control of Madison Square Garden and made it the epicenter of the fight game, while Kearns later managed light-heavyweight champions Joey Maxim and Archie Moore. ("If you gave Doc enough steel wool," Archie once said of Kearns, "he'd knit you a stove.") The colorful manager plays an eponymous role in "Kearns by a Knockout," A. J. Liebling's marvelous account of Maxim's 1952 fight with Sugar Ray Robinson. Moore merits two entries of his own—Liebling's reflections on his 1955 fight against Rocky Marciano and a Jimmy Cannon blues riff cleverly disguised as a column.

When Rickard abdicated as Garden president in 1929 he was succeeded not by his longtime *consigliore* and financial wizard Mike Jacobs, but by the bungling "Boy Bandit" Jimmy Johnston. Boxing has always attracted unsavory types, but the shameful manipulation of Primo Carnera (described herein in Paul Gallico's "Pity the Poor Giant") occurred on Johnston's watch. Jacobs continued to operate out of his Forty-Ninth Street ticket office, and in 1935, in partnership with a trio of newspapermen, founded the Twentieth Century Sporting Club.

Two years later Jacobs, having signed Joe Louis to a promotional contract, snatched "The Cinderella Man," heavyweight champion Jim Braddock, from under the Garden's nose, promising him 10 percent of his successor's future earnings to forego an already arranged defense against the German Max Schmeling and fight Louis instead.

Louis took the title from Braddock. Thus it was that on June 22, 1938, in one of boxing's iconic episodes, Louis avenged his only previous defeat by knocking out Hitler's favorite heavyweight at Yankee Stadium in a geopolitically charged bout broadcast all over the world.

The arrangement with Louis (who would rule the heavyweight roost from 1937 to 1947, and is the subject of vital entries by Bob Considine, Richard Wright, and Red Smith in this volume) provided the key to the bloodless 1938 coup in which Jacobs assumed control of the Garden. While his critics contended that Uncle Mike's relationship with the mob was a bit too cozy, both Smith and Budd Schulberg maintained that, particularly in comparison to his predecessor and successor, Jacobs effectively kept the gangsters at arm's length during his reign.

Jacobs suffered a debilitating stroke in 1946, and the Twentieth Century Club was dissolved when he sold his interest to the International Boxing Club in 1949. As the excerpt from Barney Nagler's *James Norris and the Decline of Boxing* details, it was Norris who invited the foxes into the henhouse and allowed Frankie Carbo and Blinky Palermo unfettered control of the sport throughout the 1950s. It took the Kefauver Committee's investigation of organized crime and subsequent federal prosecution to pry boxing loose from their stranglehold, but anyone laboring under the delusion that corruption disappeared when Carbo and Blinky were packed off to the sneezer need only reference the chapter from Thomas Hauser's *The Black Lights* included here and consider the shadow Don King casts across the boxing landscape even today.

———————

A wise man once pointed out that while one might play baseball, football, or basketball, nobody "plays" boxing. Even when dressed up as "the manly art of self-defense" (early trainers, the spiritual antecedents of Whitey Bimstein, George Gainford, Angelo Dundee, and Freddie Roach, often advertised themselves as "professors" of the sweet science), boxing is not without its moral ambiguities. In no other sport this side of dueling is it an objective to inflict pain, or even physical harm, on one's opponent.

Despite the grim and sometimes murky milieu they must negotiate, boxers have in many cases stepped out of the confines of the twenty-foot squared circle that is their place of work to emerge figures of awe, fascination, and pathos, none more so than Muhammad Ali, who, among the more majestic figures of the twentieth century in any sport, occupied a class of his own.

Thirty years after he last threw a punch in anger, Ali is as beloved today as he was controversial in an earlier era. As a historic figure who transcended sport, Ali has been the object of more great prose by more writers of importance than any boxer before or since. Given the nature of his impact and enduring influence it seems fitting that he is the subject of six essays in this volume, by Murray Kempton, George Plimpton, Dick Schaap, Norman Mailer, Mark Kram, and Budd Schulberg.

From Jack Johnson's era through Ali's, boxing's fortunes were largely intertwined with those of its standard-bearer, the heavyweight champion of the world—and in the fallow periods that fell between Louis and Rocky Marciano and between Marciano and Ali, the genius of Sugar Ray Robinson was there to take up the slack. Robinson (for whom the designation "the greatest, pound-for-pound" was conceived; would that it had been retired with him) had his great rivalries, with Jake LaMotta, with Bobo Olson, and with Carmen Basilio, but he didn't have them all at once. Although Ali's departure presaged another heavyweight lull, any vacuum was filled in short order by the quartet of Sugar Ray Leonard, Marvelous Marvin Hagler, Thomas Hearns, and Roberto Duran, who between 1980 and 1989 engaged in a riveting round-robin series of nine fights that captured the imagination of the public.

Notable exceptions to the anonymity enveloping the post-Ali heavyweights can be found in Larry Holmes and Lennox Lewis, both underappreciated in their time, and in the remarkable reinvention of George Foreman, who, twenty years after his loss to Ali in Zaire, returned in a warm and fuzzy guise to reclaim the title. Foreman's transformation from thug to beloved pitchman is explored in Richard Hoffer's "Still Hungry After All These Years," while the ungracefully aging Holmes depicted in Carlo Rotella's "Champion at Twilight" could be a creaking Lear on the cliffs of Dover.

Briefly burning as a heavyweight comet was the tragicomic Michael Gerard Tyson, who will be remembered less for his seemingly limitless promise and ultimately squandered talent than for two other life-defining moments, one out of the ring and one in it, explored in Joyce Carol Oates's "Rape and the Boxing Ring" and David Remnick's "Kid Dynamite Blows Up."

In a memorable (at least to me) occasion late in Tyson's career, the latest in a seemingly endless succession of consultants attempting to remake his image had come up with the bright idea of having the Baddest Man on the Planet invite several boxing writers to his Las Vegas mansion at tea-time. The host, who had been carefully prepped and, in all likelihood, administered a double-dose of which-ever psychotropic had been prescribed at the time, was on his best behavior and, to most of us, unfailingly polite, but he did notice that our number included an East Coast columnist with whom he had verbally jousted in the past.

"You wrote that I was a 'rapist and a recluse,'" said Iron Mike, eye-ing him with an accusatory glare.

The scribe nervously looked around to see who had his back before he responded, "Yes?"

"Well," said Tyson, "I am *not* a recluse."

Perhaps beyond the simple beauty of a sport that pits one man against another, *sans* teammates, unprotected by armor, and bereft of any weapon save his own fists, the appeal boxing holds for many who write about it for a living comes in the disarming candor of its prac-titioners. Perhaps the fact that it *is* such a brutal sport produces this brutal frankness—or did, in any case, before old-school press agents like Harold Conrad and Irving Rudd and Murray Goodman gave way to the spin doctors of today.

Could any boxer in any era have been more perfectly packaged than was the young Oscar De La Hoya? As the CEO of Golden Boy Promotions, Oscar presides today over an empire that includes the onetime bible of Boxing, *The Ring*, as well as a stable of champions rivaling those of Don King and Bob Arum, but in the decade following his gold-medal winning performance in the 1992 Barcelona Olym-pics, Arum meticulously constructed that image of perfection, one the promoter (having appropriated the appellation from its previous owners, Art Aragon and Donny LaLonde) christened the Golden Boy. To teenaged girls, De La Hoya was a heart-throb, to parents he was the most perfect son since Ma and Pa Kent raised Clark, and many boxing fans believed him to be the best fighter of his era. So did televi-sion executives, who enthusiastically lapped up the Kool-Aid, as did a preponderance of boxing writers. Mark Kriegel's "The Great (Almost) White Hope" at the time represented a dissenting opinion.

The handwriting should have been on the wall when Oscar the Boxer responded to every hiccup along the way by firing another trainer. (De La Hoya changed cornermen more regularly than some people do underwear.) He had already earned tens of millions of dollars by the time he sued Arum in 2006 to have their promotional contract dissolved.

Thus liberated and free for the first time in a dozen years to speak his mind without one of Arum's worrisome publicists hovering over his shoulder, Oscar announced his newly won emancipation by boasting to a stunned group of boxing writers that he had just defeated "one of the biggest Jews ever to come out of Harvard" in court.

As for the target of Oscar's slur, Arum had indeed been a Harvard-trained federal prosecutor before he decided to go into a more honest line of work. He promoted most of the Ali fights that King didn't, as well as seven of the nine bouts involving the Leonard–Hagler–Hearns–Duran nexus.

It is perhaps fitting, then, that Arum should get in the last word here. Nearly thirty years have passed since the promoter, having been caught by a reporter in a position that seemed diametrically opposed to the one he had expressed twenty-four hours earlier, offered the two-sentence defense that may well qualify as his own epitaph—and possibly boxing's as well:

"Yes, but yesterday I was *lying*. Today I'm telling the *truth!*"

An Introduction by JOHN SCHULIAN

The Fist and the Pen

C all it boxing, prizefighting, the sweet science, the fight game, or, if you like your synonyms hard-boiled, the fight racket. By any name, it is the best friend a writer ever had. It doesn't matter whether the writer is a newspaper wage-slave feverishly trying to make his deadline after a title fight or a big-name author who has parachuted in to survey toe-to-toe gladiators and the exotica surrounding them. There is an undeniable jolt to watching violence in the ring, an almost electrical charge composed of equal parts beauty and savagery, and it can stir the poet in a writer who doesn't realize he has poetry in him.

But inspiration comes from more than the blood that spatters a writer's notebook. It comes from quiet moments with fighters who have led unruly lives. And from cornermen whose scrambled syntax bears wisdom that sounds as though it were handed down from the ancient Greeks. And from managers and promoters who care for nothing but the bottom line as long as it isn't *their* skulls getting dented. The whole blessed lot of them can be found in creaking, half-empty arenas or glittering casinos with celebrities at ringside and lithe beauties ready to play for pay. What we have here is more than a mere sport. It is life in all its sweet, stinking varieties.

So it is that boxing has given us compelling, improbably lustrous writing rich in the humanity that thrives even though death's shadow hangs over everyone who steps into the ring. Humanity is the heart and soul of the book you hold in your hands, a rock to cling to in a sport that is bruised, bloody, and maligned, and probably always will be. As my old friend George Kimball and I put this collection together, we had no master plan to seek out stories of courage, coarse dignity, and hardscrabble nobility. They were simply there, in abundance, as organic to boxing as the shenanigans of the scoundrels and out-and-out thieves who seem the creation of Dickens by way of Elmore Leonard.

The sweet and sour of it all coalesced for me one night in 1982, in the bowels of Houston's Astrodome. Tex Cobb, a rowdy, laugh-a-minute heavyweight dreamer, had just absorbed fifteen rounds of abuse from champion Larry Holmes without landing a single decent punch. Now Cobb stood before a press conference, scuffed up and lumped up, and he had an arm around promoter Don King's shoulder, holding him tight as he described how King had cut his purse by $200,000 before he entered the ring. That lesson in accounting, Cobb said, certified the promoter as a "lying, thieving motherfucker." And King just chortled as he blissfully puffed on a cigar the size of a bowling pin. He'd won, as always. He had the money. But Tex Cobb had the moment.

As I think about it, the floodgates of memory open. There's Muhammad Ali catching a reporter whose mind has wandered, his eyes wide with mock anger as he wags a finger and says, "Pay attention, white boy." (The white boy was me.) There's Tommy Hearns two days away from his epic battle with Marvelous Marvin Hagler, publicly yearning for female companionship, all but unhinged by the boxing trope that women weaken legs. And there are Sugar Ray Leonard and Ron Stander at the opposite ends of the fight game. Leonard, his Olympic gold medal around his neck and the world at his feet, is insisting he won't turn professional. (We know how that turned out.) And Stander, a journeyman heavyweight who has been a pro for too long, is drinking beer in his dressing room as he waits to go to the hospital where the gashes in his face will be stitched up, souvenirs of yet another loss. First thing he does when I walk in, he thanks me for writing about him.

How could I not? How could I ignore him or any of the other indelible characters I met in the fight game? And I've got to believe that every other writer who has spent any time around them came away feeling the same. However ambivalent we might have been about boxing—who can ignore its brutality?—we embraced its people because they opened their world to us with a generosity of spirit unknown in other sports. They taught us how to deal with pain, emotional as well as physical, and though they sometimes stretched truth to the point of breaking, they made us laugh, too. In what other sport—hell, on what other planet—could there be heard the oratorical merriment of Don King vilifying rival promoter Bob Arum as "that snake in the grass, that low and scurrilous cad"?

I missed boxing when I stopped writing about sports full-time, but I didn't realize just how much until seeing *Million Dollar Baby* before it won the Academy Awards that immortalized it. There were tears in my eyes when I saw the forlorn gym that the old-timers played by Clint Eastwood and Morgan Freeman worked out of. It was far different than the gym that a Baltimore fight promoter I had known operated above a strip joint, and the one I had visited on Chicago's South Side, with a blue tarpaulin where a vast portion of its roof should have been. Yet they were all really the same place, and realizing it revived a passion that could only be satisfied one way.

I talked *Sports Illustrated* into letting me write about F.X. Toole, whose pluperfect short stories inspired the movie and who was a great story himself, a cut man who didn't become a published author until he was nearly seventy. Toole had died two years before *Million Dollar Baby* made it onto the screen, but Dub Huntley, the trainer who educated him in the ways of the sweet science, brought him back to life for me. Small and soft-spoken, with thick glasses that made his eyes a blur, Dub had never won a championship as a fighter or worked in a champion's corner. His career had been one of long odds and busted luck, but here he was, like Eastwood and Freeman in the movie, still looking for a kid who could change all that. It's what the guys who are the lifeblood of boxing do. They dream and they invite writers along with them, and if they are among the lucky few who make it to the mountaintop, they are the same guys they were before.

Freddie Roach, the sublimely profane Einstein of contemporary trainers, is that way. So was Angelo Dundee in the days of Ali and Leonard, and Ray Arcel before him. And then Arcel did it all over again with one last pupil, Roberto Duran. No wonder A. J. Liebling said that boxing "is joined onto the past like a man's arm to his shoulder." As if to prove it, Freddie Brown, a potato-nosed trainer whom Liebling counted among his "explainers" in the '40s and '50s, worked Duran's corner with Arcel thirty years later.

The knowledge Liebling gleaned from such wise men provided the spine for what he wrote in the least likely of publications, *The New Yorker*, and the glories of his prose, a mixture of sidewalk vernacular and highfalutin' references, have endured like no one else's. The most common knock on Liebling was that he worked for a weekly, which meant readers had to wait, something his competitors from New York's daily press never made them do. Jimmy Cannon's street-smart take on a fight or a fighter was there the next day in the *Post* and, later, the *Journal-American*. The same went for Red Smith, whose elegant *Herald Tribune* columns were chamber music compared to Cannon's blues in the night. For a while, W. C. Heinz played the newspaper game, too, but then he turned to magazines like *True*, *Sport*, and the *Saturday Evening Post*, where he applied the techniques of fiction to the reporting of fact. His meticulous, understated approach was the perfect counterpoint to the whimsy that was John Lardner's calling card in some of the same magazines as well as in his *Newsweek* column. Each of them was a champion, and each is represented here with a sample of how they took boxing as close to literature as it would go without someone calling the cops.

The sport had already inspired memorable prose, of course, and we've gathered the best of it from star sportswriters like Heywood Broun and Paul Gallico and literary heavyweights like Jack London and H. L. Mencken. But the true golden age of boxing writing came in the late '50s and the '60s, when, for one thing, newspapers realized that their sports departments could be more than havens for drunks, hacks, and bribe-takers. Larry Merchant stoked the fires of revolution as sports editor and columnist of the *Philadelphia Daily News* by preaching hard-nosed reporting and disdain for clichés. Then he devoted himself solely to writing at the *New York Post* and became a star with irreverent, imaginative columns like the one you'll find here about musician David Amram's night at the fights. In the same ten-year span that the sports page was being transformed, a new magazine called *Sports Illustrated* raised the standards of reporting and writing still higher, particularly when it enlisted Liebling and Budd Schulberg to cover boxing. The next thing anyone knew, first-rate sportswriting could be found in serious magazines like the suddenly hip *Harper's* as well as gentlemen's magazines like *Playboy*. What a shock the literary set must have got when one of our selections, James Baldwin's meditation on the 1962 Patterson–Liston fight, appeared in *Playboy*'s raunchy cousin, *Nugget*.

Never had there been a better time to be an aspiring sports-writer. The only hurdles you had to scale were geography and the lack of a magazine subscription. I speak from experience because I was stranded in Salt Lake City, where one local columnist was aptly named Hack, when I found my salvation at *Sports Illustrated*, its pages brimming with seemingly untold thousands of words by writers holding their subjects to the light. I remember a passage about a heavyweight contender's father riding the rails to California from East Texas during the Depression, unshaven, unwashed, and so desperate that he imagined setting fire to the homes he saw in the distance just for warmth. This was unlike anything I'd read about any other sport. This was life in the guise of a boxing story. In that moment I began to see sportswriting as more than a compendium of wins and losses; it was a laboratory for stories that could be compassionate, hard-edged, and profoundly human, stories with the feel of fiction and the funk of reality. And I hoped that I might someday write one like Mark Kram wrote about that ragged man in the boxcar door.

The brooding, soulful Kram was one of the premier stylists during *SI*'s glory years in the '60s and '70s, and for me he was also a hero, the first of many over the course of my career. He died in 2002, leaving behind an abundance of great stories to choose from, but one stands taller than the rest: his classic account of the "Thrilla in Manila," the final collision between Ali and Joe Frazier. Its selection says something about the way we put this book together. Most of the stories in it grow out of fights and their immediacy, passion, and pain. Many are eyewitness accounts of classic bouts. With rare exceptions—in particular John Lardner's unforgettable evocation of Stanley Ketchel, the king of go-to-hell middleweights—we leave longing looks into the distant past for somebody else.

As well as re-introducing you to writers and stories you may have already enjoyed, we wanted to surprise you with pieces that surprised us. Consider Leonard Gardner, author of perhaps the best boxing novel, *Fat City*, venturing into journalism to deconstruct the first Duran–Leonard fight. Coupled with Gardner's gem is what may be the only light-hearted story Duran ever inspired, by Vic Ziegel, that rare New York sports columnist who aimed for the funny bone instead of the jugular. In short, it was our good fortune as editors to be up to our ears in stories worth remembering, stories that made boxing-writing heroes of William Nack and Richard Hoffer, Bill Barich and Carlo Rotella and so many more. Their words brought to life the sport that touches readers more deeply than any other. I know, because in my time away from boxing, what they wrote was usually my only connection to the world I used to be part of.

There was a Sunday morning in 1993, however, when the fight game touched me in a way that those writers will understand and readers should know about. My mother had followed my father to the grave, and somehow Johnny Lira, a lightweight contender when I was a newspaper sports columnist in Chicago, had found out. He was no saint, Johnny Lira. His résumé included gangs, street fights, guns, jail, and perhaps the most artless jewelry warehouse robbery ever attempted. But when a criminal court judge gave him one last chance, he grabbed it and never let go, a man of his word. I wrote about him a lot, even helped him get out of a contract with a manager who had a stranglehold on his career. Now he was on the phone.

"You got any brothers or sisters?" he asked.

"No, I'm an only child."

"So you're an orphan."

It took me a moment to answer. I'd never thought of myself that way. "Yeah, I guess I am."

"Well, I'm your brother now," Johnny Lira said.

Jack London

The first major American writer to take boxing seriously, Jack London (1876–1916) wrote both fiction and nonfiction about the sport, though his principal legacy is as the originator of the term "The Great White Hope." In London's day the gulf between boxing champions at the highest level and the accomplished amateur was not nearly as pronounced as it would shortly become, and fight coverage was written from the posture of an acknowledged "expert," in contrast to that of the literary dilettantes who would later chronicle Ali–Foreman in Zaire. On assignment for the *New York Herald*, London was the most prominent of the "celebrity" reporters in attendance for the historic 1910 Jack Johnson–James Jeffries championship match, and while his account remains the most enduring, it is worth noting that his dispatches from Reno did not include the words—"Naturally, I wanted to see the white man win"—most often cited to summarize his views on race in general and Johnson in particular. (That passage had been published two years earlier, in connection with Johnson's defeat of Tommy Burns at Rushcutter's Bay in Sydney, Australia; similarly, London's plea for a "Great White Hope"—"Jim Jeffries must now emerge from his alfalfa farm and remove that golden smile from Johnson's face. . . . Jeff, it's up to you. The White Man must be rescued"—was written more than a year before the fight in Reno was arranged.)

Although London's racial bias seems all the more puzzling in the context of his commitment to socialist causes, the racial animus reflected in coverage of Johnson was not uncommon among newspapers of the era—particularly in Australia, where his views were not considered inflammatory. Its racial references notwithstanding, London's coverage of the Johnson–Burns fight revealed a grudging admiration for the fistic skills of the new heavyweight champion. Moreover, it cemented his reputation as the foremost boxing writer of his era. By the time the Reno fight came along, the plum assignment was his for the asking.

Johnson vs. Jeffries

RENO, Nev., July 4.—Once again has Johnson sent down to defeat the chosen representative of the white race, and this time the greatest of them all. And, as of old, it was play for Johnson. From the opening to the closing round he never ceased his witty sallies, his exchanges of repartee with his opponent's seconds and with the spectators. And, for that matter, Johnson had a funny thing or two to say to Jeffries in every round. The golden smile was as much in evidence as ever, and neither did it freeze on his face nor did it vanish. It came and went throughout the fight spontaneously, naturally.

It was not a great battle, after all, save in its setting and its significance. Little Tommy Burns down in far-off Australia put up a faster, quicker, livelier battle than did Jeff. The fight today, and again I repeat, was great only in its significance. In itself it was not great. The issue, after the fiddling of the opening rounds, was never in doubt. In the fiddling of those first rounds the honors lay with Johnson, and for the rounds after the seventh or eighth it was more Johnson; while for the closing rounds it was all Johnson.

Johnson played, as usual. With his opponent not strong in the attack, Johnson, blocking and defending in masterly fashion, could afford to play. And he played and fought a white man in a white man's country, before a white man's crowd. And the crowd was a Jeffries crowd. When Jeffries sent in that awful rip of his the crowd would madly applaud, believing it had gone home to Johnson's stomach, and Johnson, deftly interposing his elbow, would smile in irony at the spectators, play-acting, making believe he thought the applause was for him—and never believing it at all.

The greatest battle of the century was a monologue delivered to twenty thousand spectators by a smiling negro who was never in doubt and who was never serious for more than a moment at a time.

As a fighter Johnson did not show himself a wonder. He did not have to. Never once was he extended. There was no need. Jeff could not make him extend. Jeff never had him in trouble once. No blow Jeff ever landed hurt his dusky opponent. Johnson came out of the great fight practically undamaged. The blood on his lip was from a recent cut received in training which Jeff managed to reopen.

Jeff failed to lead and land. The quickness he brought into the fight quickly evaporated, and while Jeff was dead game to the end, he was not so badly punished. What he failed to bring into the ring with him was his stamina, which he lost somewhere in the last seven years. Jeff failed to come back. That is the whole story. His old-time vim and endurance were not there. Something has happened to him. He lost in retirement, outside of the ring, the stamina that the ring itself never robbed him of. As I have said, Jeff was not badly damaged. Every day boys take worse lacings in boxing bouts than Jeff took today.

Jeff today disposed of one question. He could not come back. Johnson in turn answered another question. He has not the yellow streak. But he only answered that question for to-day. The ferocity of the hairy-chested caveman and grizzly giant combined did not intimidate the cool-headed negro. Many thousands in the audience expected this intimidation and were correspondingly disappointed. Johnson was not scared, let it be said here and beyond the shadow of a doubt. Not for an instant did he show the flicker of fear that the Goliath against him might eat him up.

But the question of the yellow streak is not answered for all time. Just as Johnson has never been extended, so has he never shown the yellow streak. Just as a man may rise up, heaven alone knows where, who will extend Johnson, just so may that man bring out the yellow streak, and then again, he may not. So far the burden of proof all rests on the conclusion that Johnson has no yellow streak.

And now to the battle and how it began. All praise to Tex Rickard, the gamest of sports, who pulled off the fight after countless difficulties, and who, cool, calm and quick with nervous aliveness, handled the vast crowd splendidly at the arena, and wound up by refereeing the fight.

Twenty thousand filled the great arena and waited patiently under the cloud-flecked wide Nevada sky. Of the many women present, some elected to sit in the screened boxes far back from the ring, for all the world like olden Spanish ladies at the theatre. But more, many more women, sat close to the ringside beside their husbands or brothers. They were the far wiser.

Merely to enumerate the celebrities at the ringside would be to write a sporting directory of America—at least a directory of the 400 of sportdom and of many more hundreds of near four hundreds. At

1:56, Billy Jordan cleared the ring amid cheers, and stood alone, the focal point of 20,000 pairs of eyes, until the great Muldoon climbed through the ropes to call tumultuous applause and ringing cheers from the 20,000 throats, for the State of Nevada, the people of Nevada and the Governor of Nevada.

Beginning with Tex Rickard, ovation after ovation was given to all the great ones, not forgetting Fitzsimmons, whom Billy Jordan introduced as "the greatest warrior of them all." And so they came, great one after great one, ceaselessly, endlessly, until they were swept away before the greatest of them all—the two men who were about to do battle.

It was 2:30 when Johnson entered. He came first, airy, happy and smiling, greeting friends and acquaintances here, there and everywhere in the audience, cool as ice, waving his hand in salute, smiling, smiling ever smiling, with eyes as well as lips, never missing a name nor a face, placid, plastic, nerveless, with never a signal flown of hesitancy nor timidity. Yet was he keyed up, keenly observant of all that was going on, even hearing much of the confused babble of tongues about him—hearing, ay, and understanding, too. There is nothing heavy nor primitive about this man Johnson. He is alive and quivering, every nerve fiber in his body and brain, withal that it is hidden, so artfully, or naturally, under that poise of facetious calm of his. He is a marvel of sensitiveness, sensibility and perceptibility. He has a perfect mechanism of mind and body. His mind works like chain lightning and his body obeys with equal swiftness.

But the great madness of applause went up when Jeffries entered the ring two minutes later. A quick superficial comparison between him and the negro would lead to a feeling of pity for the latter. For Jeff was all that has been said of him. When he stripped and his mighty body could be seen covered with mats of hair, all the primordial adjectives ever applied to him received their vindication. Nor did his face belie them. No facile emotion played on that face, no whims of the moment, no flutterings of a light-hearted temperament. Dark and somber and ominous was that face, solid and stolid and expressionless, with eyes that smouldered and looked savage.

The man of iron, grim with determination, sat down in his corner. And the care-free negro smiled and smiled. And that is the story of the fight. The man of iron, the grizzly giant, was grim and serious. The man of summer temperament smiled and smiled. That is the story of the whole fight. It is the story of the fight by rounds.

At the opening of the first round they did not shake hands. Knowing the two men for what they are, it can be safely postulated that this neglect was due to Jeff or to the prompting of Jeff's corner. But it is not good that two boxers should not shake hands before a bout. I would suggest to these protagonists of a perishing game, if they wish to preserve the game, that they make the most of these little amenities that by custom grace their sport, and give it the veneer of civilization.

Both men went to work in that first round very easily, Johnson smiling, of course, and Jeff grim and determined. Johnson landed the first blow, a light one, and Jeff, in the clinches, gave a faint indication of his forthcoming tactics by roughing it, by crowding the negro around and by slightly bearing his weight upon him. It was a very easy round, with nothing of moment. Each was merely feeling the other out and both were exceedingly careful. At the conclusion of the round Johnson tapped Jeffries playfully on the shoulder, smiled good-naturedly and went to his corner. Jeff, in the first, showed flashes of cat-like quickness.

Second round, Jeff advanced with a momentary assumption of his famous crouch, to meet the broadly smiling Johnson. Jeff is really human and good-natured. He proved it right here. So friendly was that smile of Johnson, so irresistibly catching that Jeff, despite himself, smiled back. But Jeff's smiles were doomed to be very few in this fight.

And right here began a repetition of what took place down in Australia when Burns fought Johnson. Each time Burns said something harsh to Johnson, in the hope of making him lose his temper, Johnson responded by giving the white man a lacing. And so to-day, of course, Jeff did not talk to Johnson to amount to anything, but Corbett, in the corner, did it for Jeff. And each time Corbett cried out something particularly harsh, Johnson promptly administered a lacing to Jeff. It began in the second round. Corbett, in line with his plan of irritating the negro, called out loudly: "He wants to fight a little, Jim."

"You bet, I do," Johnson retorted, and with that he landed Jeff a stinging right uppercut.

Both men were tensely careful, Jeff trying to crowd and put his weight on in the clinches, Johnson striving more than the other to break out of the clinches. And at the end of the round, in his corner,

Johnson was laughing gleefully. Certainly Jeff showed no signs of boring in, as had been promised by his enthusiastic supporters.

It was the same story in the third round, at the conclusion of which the irrepressible negro was guilty of waving his hands to friends in the audience.

In the fourth round Jeff showed up better, rushing and crowding and striking with more vim than hitherto shown. This seemed to have been caused by a sally of Johnson's and Jeff went at him in an angry sort of way. Promptly Jeff rushed, and even ere they came together, Johnson cried out:

"Don't rush me, Jim. You hear what I'm telling you?"

No sign there of being intimidated by Jeffries' first dynamic display of ferocity. All he managed to do was to reopen the training cut in Johnson's lip and to make Johnson playful. It was most anybody's round, and it was certainly more Jeff's than any preceding one.

Round five brought Jeff advancing with his crouch and showed that the blood from Johnson's lip had turned his smile to a gory one. But still he smiled and, to balance things off, he opened Jeff's lip until it bled more profusely than his own. From then until the end of the fight Jeff's face was never free from blood, a steady stream later flowing from his right nostril, added to by the opened cut on his left cheek. Corbett's running fire of irritation served but to make Johnson smile the merrier and to wink at him across Jeff's shoulder in the clinches.

So far no problems had been solved, no questions answered. The yellow streak had not appeared. Neither had Jeff bored in, ripped awfully, nor put it over Johnson in the clinches. Yet one thing had been shown. Jeff was not so fast as he had been. There was a shade of diminution in his speed.

Johnson signalized the opening of the sixth round by landing stinging blows to the face in one, two, three order. Johnson's quickness was startling. In response to an irritating remark from Corbett, Johnson replied suavely, "Too much on hand right now," and at the same instant he tore into Jeff. It was Johnson's first real, aggressive rush. It lasted but a second or two, but it was fierce and dandy, and at its conclusion it was manifest that Jeff's right eye was closing fast. The round ended with Johnson fighting and smiling strong, and with Jeff's nose, lip and cheek bleeding and his eye closed. Johnson's round by a smile all the way through.

The seventh round was a mild one, opening with Jeff grim and silent, and with Johnson leading and forcing. Both were careful, and nothing happened, save that once they exchanged blows right niftily. So far, Jeff's roughing, and crowding and bearing on of weight had amounted to nothing. Also, he was doing less and less of it.

"It only takes one or two, Jim," Corbett encouraged his principal in the eighth round. Promptly Johnson landed two stingers. After a pause he landed another. "See that?" he chirped sweetly to Corbett in the corner. Jeff showed signs perceptibly of slowing down in this round, rushing and crowding less and less. Johnson was working harder and his speed was as flash light as ever. Jeff's slowing down was not due to the punishment he had received, but to poorness of condition. He was flying the first signals of fatigue. He was advertising, faintly, it is true, that he had not come back.

The ninth round was introduced by a suggestion from Corbett, heroically carrying out the policy that was bringing his principle to destruction. "Make that big stiff fight," was Corbett's suggestion. "That's right; that's what they all say," was Johnson's answer, delivered with true Chesterfieldian grace across his adversary's shoulder. In the previous rounds Johnson had not wreaked much damage with the forecasted punch, the right uppercut. In this round he demonstrated indisputably that he could drive the left hand in a way that was surprising. Be it remembered that it had been long denied that he had any sort of a punch in that left of his. Incidentally, in this round he landed a blow near to Jeff's heart that must have been discouraging.

The tenth round showed Johnson, with his deft, unexpected left, as quick as ever, and Jeff's going slower and slower.

The conclusion of the first ten rounds may be summed up as follows: The fight was all in the favor of Johnson, who had shown no yellow, who had shown condition, who had shown undiminished speed, who had not used his right uppercut much, who had developed a savage left, who held his own in the clinches, who had not the best of the infighting and the outfighting, who was unhurt and who was smiling all the way. Jeff was in bad shape; he was tired, slower than ever, his few rushes had been futile, and the sports who had placed their money against him were jubilant. There were men who proclaimed they saw the end.

I refused to see this end, for I had picked Jeff to win, and I was hoping hugely—for what, I did not know; but for something to happen, for anything, that would turn the tide of battle. And yet I could not hide from myself the truth that Jeff had slowed down.

The eleventh round looked better for Jeff. Stung by a remark of Corbett's, Johnson rushed and provoked one grand rally from Jeff. It was faster fighting, and more continuous than at any time in the preceding ten rounds, culminating in a fierce rally, in which Jeff landed hard.

Round twelve found Johnson, if anything, quicker and more aggressive than ever.

"Thought you were going to have me wild?" Johnson queried sweetly of Corbett.

As usual, every remark of Corbett's brought more punishment to Jeffries. And by the end of this round the second of two great questions was definitely answered. Jeff had not come back.

The thirteenth round was the beginning of the end. Beginning slowly enough, but stung by Corbett, Johnson put it all over him in the mouth fighting, and all over Jeff in the outfighting and infighting. From defense to attack, and back again, and back and forth, Johnson flashed like the amazing fighting mechanism he is. Jeff was silent and sick, while, as the round progressed, Corbett was noticeably silent.

A few entertained the fond hope that Jeff would recuperate. But it was futile. There was no come back to him. He was a fading, failing, heartsick, heartbroken man.

"Talk to him, Corbett," Jeff's friends appealed, in the fourteenth round. But Corbett could not talk. He had long since seen the end.

Yet through this round Johnson went in for one of his characteristic loafing spells. He took it easy, and played with the big gladiator, cool as a cucumber, smiling broadly as ever, yet as careful as ever.

"Right on the hip," he grinned once, as Jeff, in a desperate, dying flurry, managed to land a wild punch in that vicinity.

Corbett, likewise desperate, ventured a last sally. "Why don't you do something?" he cried to the loafing, laughing Johnson. "Too clever, too clever, like you," was the response.

Round fifteen, and the end. It was pitiful. There happened to Jeff the bitterness that he had so often made others taste, but which for the first time, perforce, he was made to taste himself. He who had never been knocked down was knocked down repeatedly. He who had never been knocked out was knocked out. Never mind the technical decision. Jeff was knocked out. That is all there is to it. An ignominy of ignominies, he was knocked out and through the ropes by the punch he never believed Johnson possessed—by the left, and not by the right.

As he lay across the lower rope while the seconds were told off, a cry that had in it tears and an abject broken plea went up from many of the spectators.

"Don't let the negro knock him out, don't let the negro knock him out," was the oft-repeated cry.

There is little more to be said. Jeff did not come back. Johnson did not show the yellow streak, and it was Johnson's fight all the way through. Jeff was not old Jeff at all. Even so, it is to be doubted if the old Jeff could have put away this amazing negro from Texas, this black man with the unfailing smile, this king of fighters and monologists.

Corbett and Berger and the others were right. They wanted Jeff to do more boxing and fighting in his training. Nevertheless lacking the come back as he so potently did, this preliminary boxing and fighting would have profited him nothing. On the other hand, it would have saved his camp much of the money with which it backed him.

It was a slow fight. Faster, better fights may be seen every day of the year in any of the small clubs in the land. It is true these men were heavy-weights, yet for heavy-weights it was a slow fight. It must be granted that plucky Tommy Burns put up a much faster fight with Johnson a year and a half ago. Yet the American fight follower had to see this fight to-day in order to appreciate just what Burns did against this colored wonder.

Johnson is a wonder. No one understands him, this man who smiles. Well, the story of the fight is the story of a smile. If ever a man won by nothing more fatiguing than a smile, Johnson won to-day.

And where now is the champion who will make Johnson extend himself, who will glaze those bright eyes, remove that smile and silence that golden repartee?

Irvin S. Cobb

For an otherwise proper gray lady, *The New York Times* certainly worked itself into a tizzy over the Jack Dempsey–Georges Carpentier fight at Boyle's Thirty Acres in Jersey City, New Jersey. Coverage of Dempsey's fourth-round knockout consumed not just the sports section on July 3, 1921, but almost the entire paper. The highlight of this deluge was the story that Irvin S. Cobb (1876–1944) wrote from ringside before and during the fight, capturing the spectacle in and out of the ring in vivid colors and only briefly caving in to the heat of the moment. On loan from *The Saturday Evening Post*, Cobb was the country's reigning journalistic star as well as a novelist, screenwriter, actor, and radio commentator. He basked in adulation as the Mark Twain of his time, and a hotel, a bridge, and a brand of cigars were named after him. Almost a century later, he would be nearly forgotten were it not for the story he hammered out at ringside, tearing each page from his typewriter so it could be telegraphed to the *Times*.

Cobb Fights It Over Again

IT is recorded that, once upon a time, Aaron Burr, being challenged by Alexander Hamilton, bade Hamilton to meet him over in Jersey and there destroyed his enemy. Yesterday afternoon, also New Jersey history, in a way of speaking, repeated itself, which is a habit to which history is addicted. Challenger and challenged met, and again the challenger lost the issue.

Posterity has appraised the loser of that first duel as of more value than the winner who survived. One is moved, to wonder whether in the present instance the analogy will continue. Carpentier, an alien, a man who does not speak our language, was the favorite of the crowd before the fight started and while it progressed, and, if I am one to judge, was still its favorite when he came out of it summarily defeated though he was. Dempsey, a native born, will never forget, I am sure, the vast roar of approbation which arose from thirty acres of close-packed humanity about him when for a half-minute it seemed that he was slipping toward defeat. The thing never happened before when an American champion fought before an American audience. But then we never had for a champion a man whose war record—his lack of one rather—was stained with a taint.

Even so, and to the contrary notwithstanding, he showed himself a better man, as a fighter, than the Dempsey who whipped Willard two years ago at Toledo. Carpentier was the soul of the fight, but Dempsey was the body of it. Considering the thing purely in its pugilistic aspects, he won on merit—won because he was bigger and stronger, because he had more endurance than the Frenchman, and because, as it turned out, he was almost as fast upon his feet, when the needs of the moment demanded speed, and almost as clever a boxer as his opponent was. And to top all, he had a short arm blow, using either arm at will to deliver it, the like of which has not been seen on this Continent since Stanley Ketchel passed out.

LOSES LIKE A GENTLEMAN

It was that drum-fire on his body which wasted Carpentier's substance of resistance, so that when the decisive jolts reached his jaw he had naught left in him with which to weather the blast. He fought fairly, did Carpentier, and like a gentleman he was licked fairly. As a gentleman and a fighter he bulks tonight as the man the majority of the audience hoped to win and for whom, as a gallant soldier and a brave man, they wish good luck through all his days.

As for Dempsey, unless this country should go to war again, it seems probable that he will continue to be our leading fighter for quite some time to come.

Let us consider the matter chronologically, as it were.

At noon of the day when a championship battle is to be fought two hours later almost anything that happens is news. A prominent music hall performer, entering unostentatiously, accompanied only by his private photographer, his personal press agent and his official announcer—one such just came in as I did—constitutes a thrill. A slew-jawed functionary sowing powdered resin broadcast upon the canvas carpet of the ring amounts to a positive sensation. The sight of a near or Hudson seal society leader eating a proletariat ham sandwich in a box is worth a bulletin. And the mere appearance of a moving picture star is a riot. Such being the case, one begins one's preliminary story thus:

Not since the good old days when the courtesies of the press always were extended to the profession with food and drinks free and no questions asked, have I seen so many distinguished journalists gathered in one spot. We sit, we in whose hands the present destiny of English literature rests, in concentric rows about the fighting platform, like so many drops that have coagulated at the bottom of a huge funnel. Terracing up beyond and behind and on every side of us rise the banked tiers of the biggest ampitheatre this world has seen since the Caesars sat in the Circus Maximus having their Christian martyrs fried on one side. It is the biggest arena ever built of match work and pine planking. Assuredly were the weather as sultry as usually it is in these latitudes it would be the hottest. But the whimsical gods of the weather have been mighty good to us this July day. Under a London-colored sky, as gray and almost as thick as a fog, the centre of population of the United States which for this date has shifted from somewhere in Indiana to New Jersey's chief city, finds a measure of comparative comfort.

Even at this early stage of the proceedings one figures that the crowd, enormous as it promises to be, will be well handled. Every other man in sight appears to be either an assistant manager, a deputy promoter, an usher or a constable. The khaki of young traffic cops' uniforms shows against the blue background of serried ranks of their brother gendarmes who have shifted to the darker plumage of the matured of the species and become plain, flat-footed policemen.

Through a hundred entrances the multitude flows in steadily, smoothly, without jamming or confusion. The trickling streams run down the aisles and are absorbed by capillary attraction in the seats. If it takes all sorts of people to make up the world then all the world must be here already. That modest hero of the cinema, Tom Mix, known among friends as the Shrinking Violet of Death Valley, starts a furore by his appearance at 12:15, just as the first of the preliminary bouts is getting under way. His dress proclaims that he recently has suffered a personal bereavement. He is in mourning. He wears a sea-green sport suit, a purple neckerchief, a pair of solid-gold-filled glasses and a cowboy hat the size of a six-furlong track. Actress ladies in makeup and also some few in citizens' clothes jostle against society leaders and those who follow in their wake.

The arts, the sciences, the drama, commerce, politics, the bench, the bar, the great newly risen bootlegging industry—all these have sent their pink, their pick and their perfection to grace this great occasion. A calling over of the names of the occupants of the more highly priced reservations would sound like reading the first hundred pages of Who's Ballyhoo in America. Far away and high up behind them, their figures cutting the skyline of the mighty wooden bowl, are perched the pedestrian classes. They are on the outer edge of events if not actually in it.

Conspicuous at the front, where the lumber-made cliffs of the structure shoal off into broad flats, is that type which is commonest of all alongside a fight ring. He is here in numbers amounting to a host. There must be thousands of him present. He is the soft-fleshed, hard-faced person who keeps his own pelt safe from bruises, but whose eyes glisten and whose hackles lift at the prospect of seeing somebody else whipped to a souffle. He is the one who, when his favorite pug is being hammered to a sanguinary Spanish omelet, calls out: "That's all right, kid—he can't hurt you." I see him countlessly repeated. For the anonymous youths who in the overtures are achieving a still greater namelessness by being put violently to sleep he has a listless eye. But wait until the big doings start. Then will his gills pant up and down as his vicarious lusting for blood and brute violence is satisfied.

Bout after bout is staged, is fought out, is finished. Few know who the fighters are and nobody particularly cares. Who is interested in flea-biting contests when he came to see a combat between young bull-elephants? Joe Humphreys, the human Cave of the Winds, bulks as a greater figure of interest as he vouches for the proper identities of these mute, inglorious preliminary scrappers than do the scrappers themselves.

It's 1 o'clock now. Where an hour ago there were wide vacant stretches of unoccupied seating space, now all is covered with piebald masses—the white of straw hats, the black of men's coats, with here and there bright patches of cola-like peonies blossoming in a hanging garden, to denote the presence of many women in gay Summer garb. The inflowing tides of humanity have inundated and swallowed up the desert. Still there has been no congestion, no traffic jams. How-ever the fight may turn out the handling of the crowd has been com-petent. Tex Rickard is the world's greatest showman.

The hour of one has arrived. Harry Stevens, the official caterer, can't figure within ten thousand of what the full attendance will be and so prepares to slice another ham. One thing is sure—today Boyle's Thirty Acres has given to Tex Rickard a richer harvest than any like area of this world's surface ever yielded.

At this moment—one-sixteen—atmospheric troubles impend. A drizzle has begun to fall. It is a trickle as yet but threatens to develop into an authentic downpour. The air has grown sodden and soggy with moisture thickened to the saturation point. It is as though one breathed into a wet sponge. I figure this sort of thing, continuing or growing worse, will slow up the two chief clouters when their turn comes.

Governor Edwards of New Jersey comes at one-thirty; the first good solid knock-down in the ring at one-thirty-six. Both are heartily approved with loud thunders of applause. Not everyone can be the anti-dry sport-loving governor of a great commonwealth, but a veri-table nobody can win popular approval on a day like this by shoving his jaw in front of a winged fist. There are short cuts to fame though painful.

The shower has suspended, but the atmosphere is still as soppy as a wet shirt. This certainly is a stylish affair. I have just taken note of the fact that the corps of referees all wear white silk blouses and white trousers like tennis players and that the little fat boy who holds up big printed cards with numerals on them to show the number of the next round is done up in spotless white linen like an antisepti-cally bandaged thumb. The humidity with which the air is freighted is beginning now to be oppressive. Even the exertion of shoving a pencil across paper brings out the perspiration and the two ambitious novices up in the ring are so wet and so slick with their own sweat that they make you think of a pair of fresh-caught fish flapping about in a new sort of square net.

At intervals a zealous member of Governor Edwards's staff rises up, majestic in his indignation, and demands to know why some presumptuous commoner is permitted to stand or stoop in front of his Excellency. One almost would think the Governor was a new laid egg and that this gentleman laid him. No less a personage than Tad Dorgan, himself a famous fight impresario, is ejected from the sacred precincts. At the ringside the police guards are having trouble with total strangers, who, lacking the necessary credentials, nevertheless have managed to slip inside the boundaries of the press division.

Along here the sun shows a watery, cocked eye through the misty heavens and coats are peeled off. Bleared heat can be just as hot as the other kind—if not hotter. But it clouds over again as the big hour draws nearer. For the most part time drags. These six and eight round appetizers lack savor. The crowd manifests its feelings. It didn't come here for sardines; it craves raw beef. For one tame bout there is a cho-rus of hoots.

It's 3 o'clock. Prompt on the appointed hour, for once in the history of championship goes, the men are brought forth on time. Carpentier comes first, slim, boyish, a trifle pale and drawn looking, to my way of thinking. He looks more like a college athlete than a professional bruiser. A brass band plays the "Marseillaise"; ninety-odd thousand men and women stand to greet him—or maybe the better to see him—and he gets a tremendous heartening ovation. Dempsey follows within two minutes. A mighty roar salutes him too, as he climbs into the ring and seats himself within the arc of a huge floral horseshoe; but so near as may be judged the applause for him, an American born, is not so sincere or spontaneous as the applause which has been visited upon the Frenchman.

He grins—but it is a scowling, forbidding grin—while photogra-phers flock into the ring to focus their boxes first on one and then on the other. Dempsey sitting there makes me think of a smoke-stained Japanese war idol; Carpentier, by contrast, suggests an Olympian runner carved out of fine-grained white ivory. Partizans howl their approval at the champion. He refuses to acknowledge these. One fig-ures that he has suddenly grown sulky because his reception was no greater than it was.

A little crowd of ring officials surround Dempsey. There is some dispute seemingly over the tapes in which his knobby brown hands are wrapped. Carpentier, except for one solicitous fellow-country-man, is left quite alone in his corner.

Dempsey keeps his eyes fixed on his fists. Carpentier studies him closely across the eighteen feet which separates them. The Gaul is losing his nervous air. He is living proof to give the lie to the old fable that all Frenchmen are excitable.

Overhead aeroplanes are breezing, and their droning notes come down to be smitten and flung up again on the crest of the vast upheaval of sound rising from the earth. A tiresome detail of utterly useless announcements is ended at last.

As the fighters are introduced, Dempsey makes a begrudged bow, but Carpentier, standing up, is given such an ovation as never before an alien fighter received on American soil. It is more plain by this test who is the sentimental favorite. The bettors may favor Jack; the populace likes Georges.

Without handshaking, they spring together; Carpentier lands the first blow. Dempsey, plainly enraged, is fast; Carpentier is faster still. But his blows seem to be wild, misplaced, while Dempsey, in the clinches into which they promptly fall, plants punishing licks with swift, short-armed strokes. The first half minute tells me the story. The Frenchman is going to be licked, I think, and that without loss of time. A tremendous roar goes up as Dempsey brings the first blood with a glancing lick on the side of his opponent's nose; it increases as the Frenchman is shoved half through the ropes. The first round is Dempsey's all the way. He has flung Carpentier aside with thrusts of his shoulders. He has shoved him about almost at will.

But midway of the second round Carpentier shows a flash of the wonderful speed for which he is known. With the speed he couples an unsuspected power. He is not fighting the defensive run-away-and-come-again fight that was expected of him. He stands toe to toe with Dempsey and trades 'em. He shakes Dempsey with a volley of terrific right-handed clouts which fall with such speed you do not see them. You only see that they have landed and that Dempsey is bordering on the state technically known as groggy.

It is a wonderful recovery for the Frenchman. His admirers shriek to him to put Dempsey out. To my mind the second round is his by a good margin. Given more weight I am sure now that he would win. Yet I still feel sure that Dempsey's superiority in gross tonnage and his greater aptitude at in-fighting will wear the lesser man down and make him lose.

The third round is Dempsey's, from bell to bell. He makes pulp of one of Carpentier's smooth cheeks. He pounds him on the silken skin over his heart. He makes a xylophone of the challenger's short ribs. The Frenchman circles and swoops, but the drubbing he gets makes him uncertain in his swings. Most of his blows go astray. They fly over Dempsey's hunched shoulders—they spend themselves in the air.

In the fourth round, after one minute and sixteen seconds of hard fighting—fighting which on Carpentier's part is defensive—comes the foreordained and predestined finishment. I see a quick flashing of naked bodies writhing in and out, joining and separating. I hear the flop, flap, flop of leather bruising human flesh. Carpentier is almost spent—that much is plain to every one. A great spasmodic sound—part gasp of anticipation, part groan of dismay, part outcry of exultation—rises from a hundred thousand throats. Carpentier totters out of a clinch; his face is all spotted with small red clots. He lunges into the air, then slips away, retreating before Dempsey's onslaught, trying to recover by footwork. Dempsey walks into him almost deliberately, like a man aiming to finish a hard job of work in workmanlike shape. His right arm crooks up and is like a scimitar. His right fist falls on the Frenchman's exposed swollen jaw; falls again in the same place even as Carpentier is sliding down alongside the ropes. Now the Frenchman is lying on his side.

Dempsey knows the contract is finished—or as good as finished. Almost nonchalantly he waits with his legs spraddled and his elbows akimbo harkening to the referee's counting. At the toll of eight Carpentier is struggling to his knees, beaten, but with the instinct of a gallant fighting man, refusing to acknowledge it. At nine he is up on the legs which almost refuse to support him. On his twisted face is the look of a sleep-walker.

It is the rule of the ring that not even a somnambulist may be spared the finishing stroke. Thumbs down means the killing blow, and the thumbs are all down now for the stranger.

For the hundredth part of a second—one of those flashes of time in which an event is photographed upon the memory to stay there forever, as though printed in indelible colors—I see the Frenchman staggering, slipping, sliding forward to his fate. His face is toward me and I am aware that on his face is no vestige of conscious intent. Then the image of him is blotted out by the intervening bulk of the winner. Dempsey's right arm swings upward with the flailing emphasis of an oak cudgel and the muffed fist at the end of it lands again on its favorite target—the Frenchman's jaw.

The thud of its landing can be heard above the hysterical shrieking of the host. The Frenchman seems to shrink in for a good six inches. It is as though that crushing impact had telescoped him. He folds up into a pitiably meagre compass and goes down heavily and again lies on the floor, upon his right side, his face half covered by his arms as though even in the stupor following that deadly collision between his face and Dempsey's fist, he would protect his vulnerable parts. From where I sit writing this I can see one of his eyes and his mouth. The eye is blinking weakly, the mouth is gaping, and the lips work as though he chewed a most bitter mouthful. I do not think he is entirely unconscious; he is only utterly helpless. His legs kick out like the legs of a cramped swimmer. Once he lifts himself half-way to his haunches. But the effort is his last. He has flattened down again and still the referee has only progressed in his fateful sum of simple addition as far as "six."

My gaze shifts to Dempsey. He has moved over into Carpentier's corner and stands there, his arms extended on the ropes in a posture of resting. He has no doubt of the outcome. He scarcely shifts his position while the count goes on. I have never seen a prizefighter in the moment of triumph behave so. But his expression proves that he is merely waiting. His lips lift in a snarl until all his teeth show. Whether this be a token of contempt for the hostile majority in the crowd, or merely his way of expressing to himself his satisfaction is not for me to say.

The picture lingers in my mind after the act itself is ended. Behind Dempsey is a dun background of gray clouds, swollen and gross with unspilt rain. The snowy white horizontals of the padded guard ropes cut across him at knee and hip and shoulder line; otherwise his figure stands out clear, a relaxed, knobby figure, with tons of unexpended energy still held in reserve within it. The referee is close at hand, tolling off the inexorable tally of the count—"Seven, eight, nine"—but scarcely is one cognizant of the referee's presence or of his arithmetic either. I see only that gnarled form lolling against the ropes and, eight feet away, the slighter, crumpled shape of the beaten French man, with its kicking legs and its sobbing mouth, from which a little stream of blood runs down upon the lolled chin.

In a hush which instantaneously descends and as instantaneously is ended, the referee swings his arm down like a semaphore and chants out "ten."

The rest is a muddle and mass of confusion—Dempsey stooping over Carpentier as though wishful to lift him to his feet; then Dempsey encircled by a dozen policemen who for some reason feel called upon to surround him; two weeping French helpers dragging Carpentier to his corner and propping him upon a stool; Carpentier's long, slim legs dangling as they lift him and his feet slithering in futile fashion upon the resined canvas; Dempsey swinging his arms aloft in tardy token of appreciation for the whoops and cheers which flow toward him; all sorts of folks crowding into the ring; Dempsey marching out, convoyed by an entourage of his admirers; Carpentier, deadly pale, and most bewildered looking with a forlorn, mechanical smile plastered on his face, shaking hands with somebody or other, and then the ring is empty of all save Humphreys the orator, who announces a concluding bout between Billy Miske and Jack Renault.

As I settle back now to watch with languid interest this anticlimax, three things stand out in my memory as the high points of the big fight, so far as I personally am concerned.

The first is that Carpentier never had a chance. In the one round which properly belonged to him he fought himself out. He trusted to his strength when his refuge should have been in his speed.

The second is that vision of him, doubled up on his side, like a frightened, hurt boy, and yet striving to heave himself up and take added punishment from a foe against whom he had no shadow of hope.

The third—and the most outstanding—will be my recollection of that look in Dempsey's lowering front when realization came to him that a majority of the tremendous audience were partisans of the foreigner.

H. L. Mencken

H. L. Mencken (1880–1956), the Sage of Baltimore and the uncommon scold of the entire nation, was many things over the course of his storied career, all of them fueled by his biting, hyperbolic prose. He laid waste to rubes, boobs, and freebooting politicians as a columnist for his hometown's *Evening Sun*; set cultural agendas as literary critic and co-editor of the *Smart Set* magazine; championed a new breed of writers as co-founder and editor of the *American Mercury*; and wrote *The American Language*, the book that remains the best defense of English as it is spoken by Americans in all its slangy glory. What Mencken was *not* was a boxing writer. But when the New York papers geared up to cover the Dempsey–Carpentier fight in July 1921, the *World* imported him from Baltimore, and not surprisingly, his view of the fight ran contrary to nearly everybody else's. And who but Mencken would have compared the thump of Dempsey's punch to "the bump of a ferryboat into a slip"?

Dempsey vs. Carpentier

IN the great combat staged there in that colossal sterilizer beneath the harsh Jersey sun there was little to entertain the fancier of gladiatorial delicacies. It was simply a brief and hopeless struggle between a man full of romantic courage and one overwhelmingly superior in every way. This superiority was certainly not only in weight nor even in weight and reach.

As a matter of fact, the difference in weight was a good deal less than many another championship battle has witnessed, and Carpentier's blows seldom failed by falling short. What ailed them was that they were not hard enough to knock out Dempsey or even to do him any serious damage. Whenever they landed Dempsey simply shook them off. And in the intervals between them he landed dozens and scores of harder ones. It was a clean fight, if not a beautiful one. It was swift, clear-cut, brilliant and honest.

Before half of the first round was over it must have been plain to even the policemen and Follies girls at the ringside that poor Carpentier was done for. Dempsey heaved him into the ropes, indeed, at the end of the first minute and thereafter gave him such a beating that he was plainly gone by the time he got to his corner. Blow after blow landed upon his face, neck, ribs, belly and arms. Two-thirds of them were upper cuts at very short range—blows which shook him, winded him, confused him, hurt him, staggered him. A gigantic impact was behind them. His face began to look blobby; red marks appeared all over his front.

Where was his celebrated right? Obviously he was working hard for a chance to unlimber it. He walked in boldly, taking terrific punishiment with great gallantry. Suddenly the opportunity came and he let it fly. It caught Dempsey somewhere along the frontiers of his singularly impassive face. The effect upon him was apparently no greater than that of a somewhat angry slap upon an ordinary ox. His great bulk hardly trembled. He blinked, snuffled amiably and went on. Five seconds later Carpentier was seeking cover behind the barricade of his own gloves, and Dempsey was delivering colossal wallops under it, over it and headlong through it.

He fought with both hands, and he fought all the time. Carpentier, after that, was in the fight only intermittently. His right swings reached Dempsey often enough, but as one followed another they hurt him less and less. Toward the end he scarcely dodged them. More and more they clearly missed him, shooting under the arms or sliding behind his ears.

In the second round, of course, there was a moment when Carpentier appeared to be returning to the fight. The crowd, eager to reward his heroic struggle, got to its legs and gave him a cheer. He waded into Jack, pushed him about a bit, and now and then gave him a taste of that graceful right. But there was no left to keep it company, and behind it there was not enough amperage to make it burn. Dempsey took it, shook it off, and went on.

Clout, clout, clout! In the space of half a minute Carpentier stopped twenty-five sickening blows—most of them short, and all of them cruelly hard. His nose began to melt. His jaw sagged. He heaved pathetically. Because he stood up to it gamely, and even forced the fighting, the crowd was for him, and called it his round. But this view was largely that of amateurs familiar only with rough fights between actors at the Lambs club. Observed more scientifically, the round was Jack's. When it closed he was as good as new—and Carpentier was beginning to go pale.

It was not in the second, but in the third round that Carpentier did his actual best. Soon after the gong he reached Jack with a couple of uppers that seemed to have genuine steam in them, and Jack began to show a new wariness. But it was only for a moment. Presently Carpentier was punching holes through the air with wild rights that missed the champion by a foot, and the champion was battering him to pieces with shorts that covered almost every square inch of his upper works. They came in pairs, right and left, and then in quartets, and then in octets, and then almost continuously.

Carpentier decayed beneath them like an Autumn leaf in Vallombrosa. Gently and pathetically he fluttered down. His celebrated right by this time gave Jack no more concern. It would have taken ten of them to have knocked out even Fatty Arbuckle. They had the effect upon the iron champion of petting with a hot water bag. Carpentier went to his corner bloody and bowed. It was all over with the high hopes of that gallant France. He had fought a brave fight; he had kept the faith—but the stars were set for Ireland and the Mormons.

The last round was simply mopping up. Carpentier was on the floor in half a minute. I doubt that Dempsey hit him hard in this round. A few jabs, and all the starch was out of his neck. He got up at nine, and tried a rush. Jack shoved him over, and gave him two or three light ones for good measure as he went down again. He managed to move one of his legs, but above the waist he was dead. When the referee counted ten Dempsey lifted him to his feet and helped him to his stool.

With his arms outstretched along the ropes, he managed to sit up, but all the same he was a very badly beaten pug. His whole face was puffy and blood ran out of his nose and mouth. His façade was one great mass of hoof-prints. Between them his skin had the whiteness of a mackerel's belly. Gone were all his hopes. And with them, the hard francs and centimes, at ruinous rates of exchange, of all the beauty and chivalry of France. Many Frenchmen were in the stand. They took it as Carpentier fought—bravely and stoically. It was a hard and a square battle, and there was no dishonor in it for the loser.

But as a spectacle, of course, it suffered by its shortness and its one-sidedness. There was never the slightest doubt in any cultured heart, from the moment the boys put up their dukes, that Dempsey would have a walk-over.

As I say, it was not only or even mainly a matter of weight. Between the two of them, as they shook hands, there was no very noticeable disparity in size and bulk. Dempsey was the larger, but he certainly did not tower over Carpentier. He was also a bit the thicker and solider, but Carpentier was thick and solid too. What separated them so widely was simply a difference in fighting technique. Carpentier was the lyrical fighter, prodigal with agile footwork and blows describing graceful curves. He fought nervously, eagerly and beautifully. I have seen far better boxers, but I have never seen a more brilliant fighter—that is, with one hand.

Dempsey showed none of that style and passion. He seldom moved his feet, and never hopped, skipped or jumped. His strategy consisted in the bare business: (*a*) of standing up to it as quietly and solidly as possible; and (*b*) of jolting, bumping, thumping, bouncing and shocking his antagonist to death with the utmost convenient despatch.

This method is obviously not one for gladiators born subject to ordinary human weaknesses and feelings; it presents advantages to an antagonist who is both quick and strong; it grounds itself, when all is said, rather more on mere toughness than on actual skill at fighting. But that toughness is certainly a handy thing to have when one hoofs the fatal rosin. It gets one around bad situations. It saves the day when the vultures begin to circle overhead.

To reinforce his left Dempsey has a wallop in his right hand like the bump of a ferryboat into its slip. The two work constantly and with lovely synchronization. The fighter who hopes to stand up to them must be even tougher than Jack is, which is like aspiring to be even taller than the late Cy Sulloway. Carpentier simply fell short. He could not hurt Dempsey, and he could not live through the Dempsey bombardment. So he perished there in that Homeric stewpan, a brave man but an unwise one.

The show was managed with great deftness, and all the antecedent rumors of a frame-up were laid in a manner that will bring in much kudos and mazuma to Mons. Tex Rickard, the manager, hereafter. I have never been in a great crowd that was more orderly, or that had less to complain of in the way of avoidable discomforts.

Getting out of the arena, true enough, involved some hot work with the elbows; the management, in fact, put in small fry after the main battle in order to hold some of the crowd back, and so diminish the shoving in the exits, which were too few and too narrow. If there had been a panic in the house, thousands would have been heeled to death. But getting in was easy enough, the seats though narrow were fairly comfortable, and there was a clear view of the ring from every place in the monster bowl. Those who bought bleacher tickets, in fact, saw just as clearly as those who paid $50 apiece for seats at the ringside.

The crowd in the more expensive sections was well-dressed, good-humored and almost distinguished. The common allegation of professional moralists that prize fights are attended by thugs was given a colossal and devastating answer. No such cleanly and decent looking gang was ever gathered at a Billy Sunday meeting, or at any other great moral outpouring that I have ever attended. All the leaders of fashionable and theatrical society were on hand, most of them in checkerboard suits and smoking excellent cigars, or, if female, in new hats and pretty frocks.

Within the range of my private vision, long trained to esthetic alertness, there was not a single homely gal. Four rows ahead of me there were no less than half a dozen who would have adorned the "Follies." Behind me, clad in pink, was a creature so lovely that she caused me to miss most of the preliminaries. She rooted for Carpentier in the French language, and took the count with heroic fortitude.

Heywood Broun

If Heywood Broun's name strikes a chord with today's readers, it may be because his son, Heywood Hale Broun, delivered witty sports commentary during the early days of color television while attired in plaid sport coats that could have doubled as test patterns. But the elder Broun (1888–1939) had made an even bigger dent on the national consciousness in the '20s and '30s. A political columnist, theater critic, book reviewer, magazine writer, and novelist, he was also one of the driving forces behind the creation of the American Newspaper Guild, which unionized reporters and other underpaid serfs. After beginning his career as a baseball writer, Broun dipped into sports only occasionally, but he obviously felt a kinship to the great Jewish lightweight Benny Leonard. A. J. Liebling said that the following essay, about Leonard's 1922 fight with Rocky Kansas, proved that Broun was a "radical in politics [but] a conservative in the arts." It's hard to say what Leonard thought of such distinctions, but after he retired from the ring, he gave Broun an exercise machine.

The Orthodox Champion

THE entire orthodox world owes a debt to Benny Leonard. In all the other arts, philosophies, religions and what nots conservatism seems to be crumbling before the attacks of the radicals. A stylist may generally be identified to-day by his bloody nose. Even in Leonard's profession of pugilism the correct method has often been discredited of late.

It may be remembered that George Bernard Shaw announced before "the battle of the century" that Carpentier ought to be a fifty to one favorite in the betting. It was the technique of the Frenchman which blinded Shaw to the truth. Every man in the world must be in some respect a standpatter. The scope of heresy in Shaw stops short of the prize ring. His radicalism is not sufficiently far reaching to crawl through the ropes. When Carpentier knocked out Beckett with one perfectly delivered punch he also jarred Shaw. He knocked him loose from some of his cynical contempt for the conventions. Mr. Shaw might continue to be in revolt against the well-made play, but he surrendered his heart wholly to the properly executed punch.

But Carpentier, the stylist, fell before Dempsey, the mauler, in spite of the support of the intellectuals. It seemed once again that all the rules were wrong. Benny Leonard remains the white hope of the orthodox. In lightweight circles, at any rate, old-fashioned proprieties are still effective. No performer in any art has ever been more correct than Leonard. He follows closely all the best traditions of the past. His left hand jab could stand without revision in any textbook. The manner in which he feints, ducks, sidesteps and hooks is unimpeachable. The crouch contributed by some of the modernists is not in the repertoire of Leonard. He stands up straight like a gentleman and a champion and is always ready to hit with either hand.

His fight with Rocky Kansas at Madison Square Garden was advertised as being for the lightweight championship of the world. As a matter of fact much more than that was at stake. Spiritually, Saint-Saens, Brander Matthews, Henry Arthur Jones, Kenyon Cox, and Henry Cabot Lodge were in Benny Leonard's corner. His defeat would, by implication, have given support to dissonance, dadaism, creative evolution and bolshevism. Rocky Kansas does nothing according to rule. His fighting style is as formless as the prose of Gertrude Stein. One finds a delightfully impromptu quality in Rocky's boxing. Most of the blows which he tries are experimental. There is no particular target. Like the young poet who shot an arrow into the air, Rocky Kansas tosses off a right hand swing every once and so often and hopes that it will land on somebody's jaw.

But with the opening gong Rocky Kansas tore into Leonard. He was gauche and inaccurate but terribly persistent. The champion jabbed him repeatedly with a straight left which has always been considered the proper thing to do under the circumstances. Somehow or other it did not work. Leonard might as well have been trying to stand off a rhinoceros with a feather duster. Kansas kept crowding him. In the first clinch Benny's hair was rumpled and a moment later his nose began to bleed. The incident was a shock to us. It gave us pause and inspired a sneaking suspicion that perhaps there was something the matter with Tennyson after all. Here were two young men in the ring and one was quite correct in everything which he did and the other was all wrong. And the wrong one was winning. All the enthusiastic Rocky Kansas partisans in the gallery began to split infinitives to show their contempt for Benny Leonard and all other stylists. Macaulay turned over twice in his grave when Kansas began to lead with his right hand.

But traditions are not to be despised. Form may be just as tough in fiber as rebellion. Not all the steadfastness of the world belongs to heretics. Even though his hair was mussed and his nose bleeding, Lenny continued faithful to the established order. At last his chance came. The young child of nature who was challenging for the championship dropped his guard and Leonard hooked a powerful and entirely orthodox blow to the conventional point of the jaw. Down went Rocky Kansas. His past life flashed before him during the nine seconds in which he remained on the floor and he wished that he had been more faithful as a child in heeding the advice of his boxing teacher. After all, the old masters did know something. There is still a kick in style, and tradition carries a nasty wallop.

Gene Tunney

There have always been prizefighters who could surprise you with what they did with their hands when they weren't punching people. In the bare-knuckle era, one champion, Jem Mace, played the violin and another, Jem Ward, painted pictures. More recently, José Torres turned to writing journalism and books when he was no longer king of the light-heavies, and Paul Thorn, a middleweight journeyman, lost to Roberto Duran but reinvented himself as a blues singer.

The champion of boxing's arts and letters division, however, is Gene Tunney (1898–1978), who wrested the heavyweight title from Jack Dempsey in 1926 and didn't let it go in their controversial rematch the following year. Once billed as the Fighting Marine, Tunney was accused of going soft because he lectured on Shakespeare at Yale and became friends with such literary figures as F. Scott Fitzgerald, Thornton Wilder, and George Bernard Shaw. Instead of apologizing, Tunney married a socialite and wound up the CEO of two companies and a member of the board of a dozen others. And when he sat down to write about the notorious "long count" in the second Dempsey fight, he won his battle with the language by unanimous decision.

My Fights with Jack Dempsey

I.

THE laugh of the Twenties was my confident insistence that I would defeat Jack Dempsey for the heavyweight championship of the world. To the boxing public, this optimistic belief was the funniest of jokes. To me, it was a reasonable statement of calculated probability, an opinion based on prize-ring logic.

The logic went back to a day in 1919, to a boat trip down the Rhine River. The first World War having ended in victory, the Army was sending a group of A.E.F. athletes to give exhibitions for doughboys in the occupation of the German Rhineland. I was light heavyweight champion of the A.E.F. Sailing past castles on the Rhine, I was talking with the Corporal in charge of the party. Corporal McReynolds was a peacetime sports writer at Joplin, Missouri, one of those Midwestern newspapermen who combined talent with a copious assortment of knowledge. He had a consummate understanding of boxing, and I was asking him a question of wide interest in the A.E.F. of those days.

We had been hearing about a new prizefight phenomenon in the United States, a battler burning up the ring back home. He was to meet Jess Willard for the heavyweight championship. His name was Jack Dempsey. None of us knew anything about him, his rise to the challenging position for the title had been so swift. What about him? What was he like? American soldiers were interested in prizefighting. I was more than most—an A.E.F. boxer with some idea of continuing with a ring career in civilian life.

The Corporal said yes, he knew Jack Dempsey. He had seen Dempsey box a number of times, had covered the bouts for his Midwestern newspaper. Dempsey's career had been largely in the West.

"Is he good?" I inquired.

"He's tops," responded Corporal McReynolds. "He'll murder Willard."

"What's he like?" I asked.

The Corporal's reply was vividly descriptive. It won't mean anything to most people nowadays, but at that time it was completely revealing to anyone who read the sports pages. McReynolds said: "He's a big Jack Dillon."

I knew about Jack Dillon, as who didn't thirty years ago? He was a middleweight whose tactics in the ring were destructive assault— fast, shifty, hard-hitting, weaving in with short, savage punches, a knocker-out, a killer. Dillon even looked like Dempsey, swarthy, beetle-browed, and grim—a formidable pair of Jacks.

I thought the revelation over for a moment, and recalled: "Jack Dillon was beaten by Mike Gibbons, wasn't he?"

"Yes," replied the Corporal. "I saw that bout. Gibbons was too good a boxer. He was too fast. His defense was too good. Dillon couldn't lay a glove on him."

Mike Gibbons was the master boxer of his time, the height of defensive skill, a perfectionist in the art of sparring.

I said to the Corporal: "Well, maybe Jack Dempsey can be beaten by clever boxing."

His reply was reflective, thought out. "Yes," he said, "when Dempsey is beaten, a fast boxer with a good defense will do it."

This, coming from a brainy sports writer, who knew so much about the technique of the ring and who had studied the style of the new champion, aroused a breathless idea in me. My own ambition in the ring had always been skillful boxing, speed and defense—on the order of Mike Gibbons.

As a West Side kid fooling around with boxing gloves, I had been, for some reason of temperament, more interested in dodging a blow than in striking one. Fighting in preliminary bouts around New York, I had learned the value of skill in sparring. In A.E.F. boxing I had emphasized skill and defense—the more so as during this time I had hurt my hands. Previously I had been a hard hitter. Now, with damaged fists, I had more reason than ever to cultivate defensive sparring.

Sailing down the Rhine, I thought maybe I might be a big Mike Gibbons for the big Jack Dillon. It was my first inkling that someday I might defeat Jack Dempsey for the Heavyweight Championship of the World, which all assumed Jack was about to acquire.

This stuck in mind, and presently the time came when I was able to make some observations firsthand. I was one of the boxers on the card of that first Battle of the Century, the Dempsey–Carpentier fight. I was in the semifinal bout. This place of honor and profit was given to me strictly because of my service title. The ex-doughboys were the heroes of that postwar period, and the light heavyweight championship of the A.E.F. was great for publicity. I was ballyhooed as the "Fighting Marine."

Actually, I had no business in the bout of second importance on that occasion of the first Million Dollar Gate. I was an A.E.F. champ, but we service boxers knew well enough that our style of pugilism was a feeble amateur thing, compared with professional prizefighting in the United States. The best of us were mere former prelim fighters, as I was. There were mighty few prominent boxers in Pershing's A.E.F. In World War II you saw champs and near-champs in uniform, but the draft was not so stern in such matters during the war against the Kaiser's Germany.

In the semifinal bout of the Dempsey–Carpentier extravaganza, I, with my bad hands, fought poorly. Nobody there could have dreamed of me as a possible future conqueror of the devastating champ—least of all Jack himself, if he had taken any notice of the semifinal battlers. I won on a technical K.O. from my opponent, but that was only because he was so bad—Soldier Jones of Canada, who, like myself, was in the big show only because he too had an army title—the war covering a multitude of sins.

After the bout, clad in a bathrobe, I crouched at one corner of the ring, and watched the Manassa Mauler exchange blows with the Orchid Man of France. As prize-ring history records, the bout was utterly one-sided; the frail Carpentier was hopelessly overmatched. But it afforded a good look at the Dempsey style.

The Corporal on the boat sailing down the Rhine had been exact in his description of Dempsey. The Champ was, in every respect, a big Jack Dillon—with all the fury and destruction implied by that. No wonder they called him the Man Killer. But, studying intently, I saw enough to confirm the Corporal's estimate that when Dempsey was defeated it would be by a skillful defensive boxer, a big Mike Gibbons. Correct defense would foil the shattering Dempsey attack.

This estimate was confirmed again and again during subsequent opportunities. I attended Dempsey fights, and studied motion pictures of them. More and more I saw how accurate defense could baffle the Man Killer's assault. The culmination was the Shelby, Montana, meeting of Dempsey and Tom Gibbons, the heavyweight younger brother of Mike. Tom, like Mike, was a consummate boxer, and Dempsey couldn't knock him out. For the first time in his championship and near-championship career, the Man Killer failed to flatten an opponent. The public, which had considered Tom Gibbons an easy mark, was incredulous and thought there must have been something peculiar about it. For me there was nothing peculiar, just final proof that good boxing could thwart the murder in the Dempsey fists. There was a dramatic twist in the fact that the final proof was given by a brother of Mike Gibbons.

2.

At the Dempsey–Carpentier fight, I had seen one other thing. Another angle flashed, as at a corner of the ring I watched and studied. Famous in those days was the single dramatic moment, the only moment when the Orchid Man seemed to have a chance. That was when, in the second round, Carpentier lashed out with a right-hand punch. He was renowned for his right, had knocked out English champions with it. He hit Dempsey high on the jaw with all his power.

I was in a position to see the punch clearly and note how Carpentier threw it. He drew back his right like a pitcher with a baseball. The punch was telegraphed all over the place. Yet it landed on a vulnerable spot. How anybody could be hit with a right launched like that was mystifying to one who understood boxing. Dempsey went back on his heels, jarred. Carpentier couldn't follow up, and in a moment Jack was again on the relentless job of wrecking the Orchid Man with body blows. But it was a vivid demonstration that the champion could be hit with a right.

Dempsey was no protective boxer. He couldn't do defensive sparring. He relied on a shifty style, his own kind of defense, and couldn't be hit just any way. His weakness was that he could be nailed with a straight right. Later on, I saw this confirmed in other Dempsey battles. It was dramatized sensationally at the Polo Grounds when the powerful but clumsy Firpo smashed him with a right at the very beginning of the first round, and later blasted Dempsey out of the ring with right-hand punches—the Wild Bull of the Pampas almost winning the championship.

To me it signified that the strategy of defensive boxing might be supplemented by a right-hand punch—everything thrown into a right. It would never do for me to start mixing with the Champ in any knock-down, drag-out exchange of haymakers. He'd knock me out. It would have to be a surprise blow, and it could easily be that. Both Carpentier and Firpo, who had nailed the Champ, were noted for their right—all they had. But Jack would never suspect a Sunday punch from me, stepping in and trying to knock him out with a right.

I was catalogued not only as a defensive boxer but also as a light hitter, no punch. I might wear an opponent down and cut him to pieces, but I couldn't put him to sleep with a knockout slam. That had been true—previously. I had been going along with the handicap of bad hands. I could hit hard enough, but didn't dare for fear of breaking my hands. So I was a comparatively light hitter—and typed as one.

Finally, in desperation, I had to do something about my fragile hands. I went to a lumber camp in Canada for one winter and worked as a woodsman, chopping down trees. The grip of the ax was exercise for my damaged mitts. Months of lumber camp wood chopping and other hand exercises worked a cure. My hands grew strong and hard, my fists rugged enough to take the impact of as powerful a blow as I could land. In subsequent bouts I had little trouble with my hands. This I knew, and others might have been aware of the change, but I was tagged as a feather duster puncher—and that was that. The old philosophy of giving a dog a bad name.

Prizefight publicity often resorts to the ballyhoo of a secret punch, a surprise blow, nearly always a fraud—but I really had the chance. At the beginning of the first round I would step in and put everything I had in a right-hand punch, every ounce of strength. I might score a knockout, or the blow would daze the champion sufficiently to make it easier to outbox him the rest of the way.

I was, meanwhile, fighting my way to the position of challenger. I won the light heavyweight championship from Battling Levinsky and subsequently fought Carpentier, the Orchid Man, and went through a series of savage bouts with Harry Greb, one of the greatest of pugilists. In our first bout, Greb gave me a murderous mauling. In our last, I beat him almost as badly. After a long series of matches with sundry light heavies and heavies I went on to establish myself as heavyweight contender by defeating Tom Gibbons. It was dramatic irony that I earned my shot at the title at the expense of Tom, brother of my model, Mike.

Public opinion of my prospects with Dempsey was loud and summary. The champion is always the favorite, and Dempsey was one of the greatest champions, as destructive a hitter as the prize ring has ever known. He was considered unbeatable, and I was rated as a victim peculiarly doomed to obliteration, pathetic, absurd.

It was argued that I was a synthetic fighter. That was true. As a kid prelim battler, my interest had been in romantic competition and love of boxing, while holding a job as a shipping clerk with a steamship company. As a marine in France, my love of boxing and a distaste for irksome military duties after the armistice brought me back as a competitor in A.E.F. boxing tournaments. We gave our best to entertain our buddies and, incidentally, to avoid guard duty. After the war, when I had grown up, my purpose simply was to develop the sparring ability I had as a means of making money—seeing in the heavyweight championship a proud and profitable eminence.

They said I lacked the killer instinct—which was also true. I found no joy in knocking people unconscious or battering their faces. The lust for battle and massacre was missing. I had a notion that the killer instinct was really founded in fear, that the killer of the ring raged with ruthless brutality because deep down he was afraid.

Synthetic fighter, not a killer! There was a kind of angry resentment in the accusation. People might have reasoned that, to have arrived at the position of challenger, I must have won some fights. They might have noted that, while the champion had failed to flatten Tom Gibbons, I had knocked him out. But then the Dempsey–Gibbons bout was ignored as rather mystifying, one of "those things."

The prizefight "experts" were almost unanimous in not giving me a chance. The sports writers ground out endless descriptions of the doleful things that would happen to me in the ring with Dempsey. There were, so far as I know, only a few persons prominent in sports who thought I might win, and said so. One was Bernard Gimbel, of the famous mercantile family, a formidable amateur boxer and a student of ring strategy. The others included that prince of sports writers, the late W. O. McGeehan, and a few lesser lights in the sports-writing profession. They picked me to win, and were ridiculed. The consensus of the experts was echoed by the public, though with genuine sadness on the part of some.

Suspicion of a hoax started following a visit by a newspaperman to my training camp at Speculator, New York. Associated Press reporter Brian Bell came for an interview. He noticed a book lying on the table next to my bed. Books were unexpected equipment in a prizefight training camp. He was curious and took a look at the volume—*The Way of All Flesh*. That surprised him. The Samuel Butler opus was, at that time, new in its belated fame, having been hugely praised by George Bernard Shaw as a neglected masterpiece. It was hardly the thing you'd expect a prizefighter to be reading, especially while training for a bout with Jack Dempsey.

Brian Bell knew a story when he saw one. He later became one of the chief editors of the Associated Press. Instead of talking fight, he queried me about books. I told him I liked to read Shakespeare. That was the gag. That was the pay-off. The A.P. flashed the story far and wide—the challenger, training for Jack Dempsey, read books, literature—Shakespeare. It was a sensation. The Shakespeare-Tunney legend was born.

3.

The story behind it all went back to a day in 1917 when a young marine named Gene Tunney was getting ready to embark with his company bound for the war in France. We were stowing things in our kits, when I happened to glance at the fellow next to me. I noticed that among the belongings he was packing were two books. That surprised me.

In the marines you kept the stuff you took to the minimum. You carried your possessions on your back in the long marches favored by the Marine Corps. Every ounce would feel like a ton. Yet here was a leatherneck stowing away two books to add to his burden. I was so curious that I sneaked a look at the two books and saw—Shakespeare. One was *Julius Caesar*, the other, *A Winter's Tale*. He must be a real professor, I thought.

The leatherneck in question was the company clerk. I had known him when in recruit camp—a young lawyer in civilian life, quiet and intelligent. Now, my respect for him went up many notches. He must be educated indeed to be taking two volumes of Shakespeare to carry on his back on the long marches we would have in France.

We sailed in the usual transport style, piled in bunks in a stuffy hold. The weather was rough, and virtually the whole division of marines became seasick. The few good sailors poked unmerciful fun at their seasick comrades. I happened to be one of the fortunate, and joined in the ridicule of the miserable sufferers.

Sickest of all was the company clerk. He writhed in misery. He would lie on deck all day, an object of groaning filth. At night he was equally disgusting in his bunk. This was the tier next to mine, and I saw more of him than most. The high respect I had formed for him went down those many notches. He might be educated, he might take Shakespeare to war with him, but he was a mess at sea.

We put in at Brest, and promptly the order came—prepare to march. We were to put on a show at the dock for inspection by the brass hats. I started to get ready, and then came the appalling discovery. I couldn't find the tunic of my uniform. I knew I had stowed it in my kit, but it was gone. I hunted everywhere. In the Marine Corps it was practically a capital offense for a leatherneck to be without an article of issue, and here I was without my tunic for the long march upon arrival in France.

I heard a marine asking: "Whose is this?" He was on a cleaning job, and was holding up a disreputable object that he had fished from under the bunks. "Somebody's blouse," he announced with a tone of disgust, "and look at it."

I did—it was my blouse, a mess of seasick filth.

The explanation was easy to guess. The company clerk in the tier of bunks next to mine had done it. Having befouled all of his clothes, he had, in his dumb misery, reached into my bunk and taken my blouse. He had worn it until it was too filthy to wear—after which he had chucked it under the bunks.

There was nothing I could do. There was no time to get the blouse cleaned, and there was no use blaming it on the company clerk. It was strictly up to me to have possession of every article of issue in good shape. I could only inform our company commander that I didn't have my tunic—and take the penalty, extra guard duty and kitchen police.

When, ashore, the company clerk came out of his seasickness and realized what had happened, he was duly remorseful. He was a decent fellow, his only real offense having been seasickness. He told me how sorry he was, and asked what he could do to make up for the trouble he had got me into. What could he give me? That was the way things were requited among the marines—handing something over to make up for something. What did he have that I might want? He hadn't anything I could take, except those two books. I told him, "Give me one of them and call things square." He did. He retained *Julius Caesar* and gave me *A Winter's Tale*. He knew what he was about, as anyone who knows Shakespeare will attest.

Having the book, I tried to read it but couldn't make any sense of it. I kept on trying. I always had a stubborn streak, and figured the book must mean something. But it didn't, so far as I could make out. I went to the company clerk. He had given me the book, and it might mean something to him. It did, and he proceeded to explain.

He coached me, led me through *A Winter's Tale*, which turned out to be interesting. That was practically my introduction to Shakespeare —the hard way. After training on *A Winter's Tale*, I read such works as *Hamlet, Macbeth, Othello*, with ease.

I had always liked reading—and this had a practical side. I found that books helped in training for boxing bouts. One of the difficulties of the prizefight game is that of relieving tension in training camp, getting one's mind off the fight. The usual training camp devices were jazz phonograph records and the game of pinochle. I didn't like jazz, and the mysteries of pinochle were too deep for me. So I resorted to reading as a way to ease the dangerous mental strain during training. I found that books were something in which I could lose myself and get my mind off the future fight—like *The Way of All Flesh*, which Brian Bell of the Associated Press found me reading while training for Dempsey.

Hitherto, as just another prizefighter, my personal and training camp habits had been of little news interest, and nobody had bothered to find out whether I read books or not. Now, as the challenger for the heavyweight title, I was in a glare of publicity, and the disclosure that I read books, literature, Shakespeare, was a headline. The exquisite twist was when one of Dempsey's principal camp followers saw the newspaper story. He hurried to Jack with a roar of mirth. "It's in the bag, Champ. The so-and-so is up there reading a book!"

The yarn grew with the telling—training for Dempsey on Shakespeare. It simplified itself down to the standing joke—Tunney, the great Shakespearean. This put the finishing touch to the laugh over my prospects in the ring with Dempsey.

It made me angry and resentful. I was an earnest young man with a proper amount of professional pride. The ridicule hurt. It might have injured my chances. To be consigned so unanimously to certain and abject defeat might have been intimidating, might have impaired confidence. What saved me from that was my stubborn belief in the correctness of my logic. The laugh, in fact, helped to defeat itself and bring about the very thing that it ridiculed. It could only tend to make the champion overconfident.

For a boxer there's nothing more dangerous than to underestimate an opponent. Jack Dempsey was not one to underestimate. It was not his habit of mind to belittle an antagonist. He was far too intelligent for that. In fact, Jack rather tended to underestimate himself. With all his superb abilities in the ring, he was never arrogant or cocky, never too sure of himself. But not even Jack Dempsey could escape the influence of opinion so overwhelming, such mockery as "It's in the bag, Champ. The so-and-so is up there reading a book." That could help my strategy of a surprise blow to knock him out or daze him for the rest of the fight.

4.

When we finally got into the ring at Philadelphia things went so much according to plan that they were almost unexciting to me. During the first minute of sparring, I feinted Dempsey a couple of times, and then lashed out with the right-hand punch, the hardest blow I ever deliberately struck. It failed to knock him out. Jack was tough, a hard man to flatten. His fighting style was such that it was difficult to tag him on the jaw. He fought in a crouch, with his chin tucked down behind his left shoulder. I hit him high, on the cheek. He was shaken, dazed. His strength, speed, and accuracy were reduced. Thereafter it was a methodical matter of outboxing him, foiling his rushes, piling up points, clipping him with repeated, damaging blows, correct sparring.

There was an element of the unexpected—rain. It drizzled and showered intermittently throughout the fight. The ring was wet and slippery, the footing insecure. That was bad for a boxer like me, who depended on speed and sureness of foot for maneuvering. One false step with Jack Dempsey might bring oblivion. On the other hand, the slippery ring also worked to the disadvantage of the champion. A hitter needs secure footing from which to drive his punches, and any small uncertainty underfoot may rob him of his power. So the rain was an even thing except that it might have the therapeutic value of a shower for a dazed man, and Dempsey was somewhat dazed during the ten rounds. Jack was battered and worn out at the end, and I might have knocked him out if the bout had gone a few rounds more. The decision was automatic, and I was heavyweight champion of the world.

The real argument of the decade grew out of my second bout with Dempsey, at Chicago, the following year—the "long count" controversy. It produced endless talk, sense and nonsense, logic and illogic. To this day in any barroom you can work up a wrangle on the subject of the long count. How long was Tunney on the floor after Dempsey knocked him down? Could he have got up if the count had been normal?

To me the mystery has always been how Dempsey contrived to hit me as he did. In a swirl of action, a wild mix-up with things happening fast, Jack might have nailed the most perfect boxer that ever blocked or side-stepped a punch, he was that swift and accurate a hitter. But what happened to me did not occur in any dizzy confusion of flying fists. In an ordinary exchange Dempsey simply stepped in and hit me with a left hook.

It was in the seventh round. I had been outboxing Jack all the way. He hadn't hurt me, hadn't hit me with any effect. I wasn't dazed or tired. I was sparring in my best form, when he lashed out.

For a boxer of any skill to be hit with a left swing in a commonplace maneuver of sparring is sheer disgrace. It was Dempsey's most effective blow, the one thing you'd watch for—you'd better, for the Dempsey left, as prize-ring history relates, was murder. I knew how to evade it, side-step or jab him with a left and beat him to the punch. I had been doing that all along.

I didn't see the left coming. So far as I was concerned, it came out of nowhere. That embarrassed me more than anything else—not to mention the damage done. It was a blow to pride as well as to the jaw. I was vain of my eyesight. My vision in the ring was always excellent. I used to think I could see a punch coming almost before it started. If there was anything I could rely on, it was my sharpness of eye—and I utterly failed to see that left swing.

The only explanation I have ever been able to think of is that in a training bout I had sustained an injury to my right eye. A sparring partner had poked me in the eye with thumb extended. I was rendered completely blind for an instant, and after some medical treatment was left with astigmatism which could easily have caused a blind spot, creating an area in which there was no vision. Our relative positions, when Dempsey hit me, must have been such that the left swing came up into the blind spot, and I never saw it.

With all his accuracy and power Dempsey hit me flush on the jaw, the button. I was knocked dizzy. Whereupon he closed for the kill, and that meant fighting fury at its most destructive. When Dempsey came in for a knockout he came with all his speed and power. I didn't know then how many times he slugged me. I had to look at the motion pictures the next day to find out. There were seven crashing blows, Dempsey battering me with left and right as I fell against the ropes, collapsing to a sitting position on the canvas.

Of what ensued during the next few seconds, I knew nothing. I was oblivious of the most debated incident of the long count and had to be told later on what happened.

The story went back to the Dempsey–Firpo fight, to that wild first round during which Firpo hit the floor in one knock-down after another. This was in New York, where the rule was that a boxer scoring a knock-down must go to a neutral corner and remain there until the referee had completed the count. In the ring with the Wild Bull of the Pampas, Dempsey undoubtedly through excitement of battle violated that rule, as the motion pictures showed clearly afterward.

Jack confesses he remembers nothing that took place during that entire fight. Firpo landed a terrific first blow. Dempsey, after suffering a first-blow knock-down, apparently jumped up to the fray by sheer professional instinct—the fighting heart of a true champion. Instead of going to a corner, Jack would stand over Firpo and slug him as he got up. After one knock-down, Jack stepped over his prostrate opponent to the other side, to get a better shot at him—the referee was in the way. After another knock-down, Dempsey slugged Firpo before the South American had got his hands off the floor, when he was still technically down. The Champ might well have been disqualified for that—not to mention the fact that he was pushed back into the ring when Firpo battered him out. The referee, however, in his confusion permitted all the violations.

The Dempsey–Firpo brawl aroused a storm of protest and brought about a determination that in the future Dempsey should be kept strictly to the rules. In our Chicago bout the regulation applied—go to a neutral corner upon scoring a knock-down. The referee had been especially instructed to enforce this. He was told that, in case of a knock-down, he was not to begin a count until the boxer who had scored the knock-down had gone to a neutral corner.

This was the reason for the long count. Dempsey, having battered me to the canvas, stood over me to hit me the moment I got up—if I did get up. The referee ordered him to a neutral corner. He didn't go. The referee, in accordance with instructions, refrained from giving count until he did go. That imposed on Jack a penalty of four seconds.

It was that long before he went to the corner and the referee began the count.

When I regained full consciousness, the count was at two. I knew nothing of what had gone on, was only aware that the referee was counting two over me. What a surprise! I had eight seconds in which to get up. My head was clear. I had trained hard and well, as I always did, and had that invaluable asset—condition. In the proverbial pink, I recovered quickly from the shock of the battering I had taken. I thought—what now? I'd take the full count, of course. Nobody but a fool fails to do that. I felt all right, and had no doubt about being able to get up. The question was what to do when I was back on my feet.

I never had been knocked down before. In all the ring battles and training bouts I had engaged in, I had never previously been on the canvas. But I had always thought about the possibility, and had always planned before each bout what to do if I were knocked down, what strategy to use upon getting up. That depended on the kind of opponent.

I had thought the question out carefully in the case of Jack Dempsey. If he were to knock me down, he would, when I got up, rush me to apply the finisher. He would be swift and headlong about it. Should I try to clinch and thus gain some seconds of breathing space? That's familiar strategy for a boxer after a knock-down. Often it's the correct strategy—but not against Dempsey, I figured. He hit too hard and fast with short punches for it to be at all safe to close for a clinch. He might knock me out.

Another possibility was to get set and hit him as he rushed. That can be effective against a fighter who, having scored a knock-down, comes tearing in wide open, a mark for a heavy blow. If you are strong upon getting to your feet, you can sometimes turn the tables by throwing everything into a punch. Bob Fitzsimmons often did it. But that wouldn't do against Dempsey, I reckoned. He was too tough and hit too hard. He would welcome a slugging match. After having been knocked down, I might not be in any shape to take the risk of stepping in and hitting him.

For my second bout with Dempsey the plan that I decided upon, in case I was knocked down, was based on the thing I had learned about Jack. Word from his training camp had indicated that his legs were none too good. I had learned that his trainers had been giving him special exercises for footwork, because he had slowed down in the legs. That was the cue—match my legs against his, keep away from him, depend on speed of foot, let him chase me until I was sure I had recovered completely from the knock-down.

The plan would work if my own legs were in good shape, after the battering I had taken. That was what I had to think about on the floor in Chicago. My legs felt all right. At the count of nine I got up. My legs felt strong and springy.

Jack came tearing in for the kill. I stepped away from him, moving to my left—circling away from his left hook. As I side-stepped swiftly, my legs had never been better. What I had heard about Dempsey's legs was true. As I circled away from him, he tried doggedly, desperately, to keep up with me—but he was slow. The strategy was okay— keep away from him until I was certain that all the effects of the knock-down had worn off. Once, in sheer desperation, Jack stopped in his tracks and growled at me to stand and fight.

I did—but later, when I knew that my strength, speed, and reflexes were completely normal. I started to close with him and hit him with the encyclopedia of boxing. Presently Dempsey's legs were so heavy that he couldn't move with any agility at all, and I was able to hit him virtually at will. He was almost helpless when the final bell rang— sticking it out with stubborn courage.

5.

I have often been asked—could I have got up and carried on as I did without those extra four seconds of the long count? I don't know. I only say that at the count of two I came to, and felt in good shape. I had eight seconds to go. Without the long count, I would have had four seconds to go. Could I, in that space of time, have got up? I'm quite sure that I could have. When I regained consciousness after the brief period of black-out, I felt that I could have jumped up immediately and matched my legs against Jack's, just as I did.

The long count controversy, with all the heated debate, produced a huge public demand for another Dempsey–Tunney fight, number three. Tex Rickard was eager to stage it. He knew, as everybody else did, that it would draw the biggest gate ever. The first Dempsey–Tunney fight grossed over a million seven hundred thousand; the second, over two million and a half. Rickard was sure a third would draw three million. I was willing, eager. I planned to retire after another championship bout, wanted to get all that I could out of it.

But Jack refused. He was afraid of going blind. The battering he had taken around the eyes in his two fights with me alarmed him. The very thing that kept him from being hit on the jaw, his style of holding his chin down behind his shoulder, caused punches to land high. He dreaded the horror that has befallen so many ring fighters and is the terror of them all—the damage that comes from too many punches around the eyes, blindness.

Jack Dempsey was a great fighter—possibly the greatest that ever entered a ring. Looking back objectively, one has to conclude that he was more valuable to the sport or "The Game" than any prizefighter of his time. Whether you consider it from his worth as a gladiator or from the point of view of the box office, he was tops. His name in his most glorious days was magic among his people, and today, twenty years after, the name Jack Dempsey is still magic. This tells a volume in itself. As one who has always had pride in his profession as well as his professional theories, and possessing a fair share of Celtic romanticism, I wish that we could have met when we were both at our unquestionable best. We could have decided many questions, to me the most important of which is whether "a good boxer can always lick a good fighter."

I still say yes.

Sherwood Anderson

As he approached middle age, Sherwood Anderson (1876–1941) was the president of the Anderson Manufacturing Company of Elyria, Ohio, solidly entrenched as a pillar of the community with a wife and three children. Whether as the result of what was described at the time as a "mental breakdown," reportedly accompanied by temporary amnesia, or what today might be regarded as a midlife crisis of epic proportions, in 1912 he abruptly chucked it all to embark upon a life as a man of letters. Although at the time unpublished—his only prior professional writing experience had been in a stint as an advertising copywriter—Anderson had been quietly honing his skills as a writer of fiction even before his breakdown, and his first novel, *Windy McPherson's Son*, was published the year he turned forty. His best-known and most enduring work, *Winesburg, Ohio*, came three years later. Over his final twenty years he would, while going through three more wives, publish fourteen novels, five volumes of essays, three story collections, two memoirs (to be joined by a posthumous autobiography), a biography of Theodore Dreiser, and a dramatic adaptation of *Winesburg*. Even Anderson's death, which came less than five years after the 1936 fight he recounts in "Brown Bomber," was the stuff of literature: he contracted a fatal dose of peritonitis after accidentally swallowing part of a toothpick embedded in a martini olive.

The 5,300-seat Hippodrome was at the time by far the largest venue on Broadway. Just a year before Joe Louis fought Jorge Brescia there, elephants had strutted on its stage in Billy Rose's extravagant circus musical, *Jumbo*. While Anderson is correct in noting that Louis was accustomed to performing before larger crowds in outdoor baseball venues, so, in fact, was Brescia. Since his arrival in the United States three years earlier, the latest "Wild Bull" from Argentina had been fattened for the kill: four of his eight professional bouts had taken place on Louis's undercards; in three others, Primo Carnera was the featured act. Brescia was 8–0 as a pro when he fought Louis, but, once exposed, won just eight of twenty bouts thereafter. He retired from the ring in 1940—a year after the Hippodrome was demolished, and nine months before Anderson's fateful encounter with his last martini.

Brown Bomber

IT wasn't one of the Bomber's big fights, one of the million or half-million-dollar gates. There was no big gate, no National nor American League baseball park, big build-up, to get the big gate. The fellow he was to fight, neither Fred nor myself had ever heard of. His name was Jorge Brescia, and he was described, in the city newspapers . . . they took little or no account of the fight until the day before . . . as another possible 'Wild Bull of the Pampas.' The fight took place in a theater, a big one. They said it would seat seven thousand.

In the late afternoon we went, Fred and myself, to the theater, and got an official program. 'Look . . . eleven bones for a ring-side seat. Not for me.' We took the program with us into a bar. 'At that, I'd like to see him in action,' said Fred. Fred makes little, very human drawings for some of the bigger magazines. There were some men standing at the bar and Fred punched me. One of the men was talking, a big fellow with a cauliflower, almost a calabash, ear. He pounded on the bar with a big fist.

'Yeah,' he said, 'I tell you I know. I was up to his camp. They wanted me for one of his punching-bags. The sucker. Say, if I was five years younger, I'd take him on myself. I tell you this Argentine boy's liable to take him. You listen to me. That smoke's a sucker for a right.'

Fred and I had our drink. The papers said it was five to one on the Bomber, even money he'll take the Argentine in five rounds. I was looking through the program. 'Look, Fred.' I held it up. There was a piece about the Argentine fighter. I read aloud. 'There is Nordic blood in his veins, his grandfather being a native of Alsace-Lorraine, which accounts for his calmness under fire and his methodical way of fighting. He worked as a clerk for the Argentine Government while he was doing his amateur fighting.' I paused. I am quite sure my voice trembled a little.

'What's the matter?' Fred said.

I read on.

'And is one of the best-versed boys in literature in the fighting game.'

'Do you suppose he has read me?' I said.

'I don't suppose he's that bad,' said Fred.

We went far up, to the top gallery, top row. Three-fifty for a seat up there, and we must have got the last two. You couldn't sit any farther from the ring. We were tops. Back of us there was an open space where men could stand. We had got in pretty early and only the standing-room space was filled.

It was filled with Negro men, and already they were excited. You could feel the excitement in the air, a kind of quiet tenseness. 'Say, it means a lot to them, doesn't it?' Fred whispered.

Although the upper gallery was, as yet, but half-filled, we had some trouble getting our seats. There was a kind-hearted usher and he had picked two cripples out of the standing-room crowd and had put them into our places. They were a white man and a Negro, both crippled, both one-legged, both on crutches, and they were both pretty well spiffed. The usher stood looking at our ticket stubs. He scratched his head, looked again. He had a resigned air . . . 'Well, it has to be done. Hey, soldiers, you two guys got to get out of there.'

We were in a bad fix, and for a moment I thought Fred was going to weaken and surrender the seats. 'They're one-legged. They're on crutches,' he whispered. All the others up there, whites and blacks, had turned and were staring at us. The cripples had on the kind of caps the American Legion boys wear when they go to their annual conventions. The convention had just been held. I figured they had got their bonus and were on a bust.

They stood up, and for a moment I thought the white one was going to pitch forward, down over the heads of the people in the rows of seats below. A big Negro man reached over the little wooden fence back of our top row of seats and steadied him and the Negro soldier saved the situation. He grinned.

'Come on. Take your seats. You paid for them. Anyway, we're too drunk to see anything down there,' he said, pointing.

Another Negro man had reached over the fence to steady him. They made their way painfully out. The white man had bottles sticking out of a half-dozen of his pockets. His crutches knocked one of the bottles out of a side pocket and it rolled down the steps into one of the aisles. A Negro man brought it back to him. 'Come on, buddy,' said the white soldier to his Negro companion. 'You quit worrying now. The Bomber'll get him all right. Let's get out of here and be on our way,' he said.

It was time for the preliminary bouts and they weren't so good. The spot lights had come on, flooding the ring, far down there, making all clear, and the man who sat at my left, a little wizened white man, began a conversation. He whispered.

'You see,' he said, 'you can see more from up here than from a ring-side seat. I usually get a ring-side, but I wanted to try it up here,' he said. He seemed to want to apologize for not having spent more money. 'I'm a dentist,' he said. 'I can blow myself for a ring-side seat if I want.'

They were announcing the first preliminary bout and there was a small figure of a man, who spoke into a loud-speaker. He had on a dinner jacket. It seemed the bouts were put on by a man named Mike Jacobs, a very, very handsome man, if you judged by the big photograph of him that filled a whole page in the fight program. For some reason Mike was in bad with the crowd. At the mention of his name, loud groans arose all over the theater. There were the usual introductions, of men more or less famous in the fighting game. The names were all strange to me. As each man was introduced, he did a little half dance, ran to the center of the ring, put both hands above his head, whirled like a chicken when you cut its head off. He seemed to be shaking hands with himself, up there, above his head. It was a ceremony, something you do, no matter whether or not the cash customers applaud. The first two preliminary boys introduced to the crowd were sitting in their corners, each celebrity having done his dance, and the man in the dinner jacket ran from one to the other and seemed to whisper something into his ears. 'Do you suppose he tells them both he hopes they win?' Fred asked. He said he liked these little ceremonies of the ring. It made him think of the way big-league ball-players sent the ball flying gaily from man to man about the diamond when they have retired a batter.

As for the preliminary bouts, they weren't much. We were all waiting for the Bomber. There were boys from Texas, Pennsylvania, Long Island, Detroit, and one, named Eduardo Primo, from the Argentine. He got his all right. If the man who was to fight the Bomber was a Wild Bull of the Pampas, Fred said this one was a steer. He stood with his legs spread far apart while a Negro boy, a dancing, swift-moving one, kept lashing out at him. Round after round he stood, seeming never to move, taking it and taking it. He achieved something. His face was cut and his eyes swollen, but to the end he stood firmly upright on his legs.

We, up there in our top gallery, weren't caring. Our top gallery was full, packed, while, down below, the aristocrats of sport were sitting —millionaires, Fred said—in the ring-side seats, then the seven-fifty ones—fellows probably who owned stores or small factories—then the five-fifties. 'We might have been that good if you had loosened up,' Fred complained.

He was really glad to be where he was. I knew that. We were near the Negro men . . . big ones, small ones, young ones, old ones . . . these evidently Negro workmen, some in overalls, jammed in there behind the little fence at our backs. In the twenty or thirty rows of seats below us, more Negroes who had brought their women . . . these a little more 'upper class,' Fred thought . . . some of the women handsomely gowned . . . a few white men and white women. There was a middle-aged white woman who sat in the row just below us, and she was, as we were, nervous as she waited. She was a fat woman of forty-eight, with the hands of a working woman. She kept rubbing them together. She would be such a woman as might keep a rooming house for young unmarried clerks, somewhere on a side street in the city, in a section that had once been fashionable but now had gone down . . . her man perhaps gone off with a younger woman. Fred said afterward that he didn't think it was that. 'What you trying to do, work the poor woman for one of your sad short stories ?' he said. 'Her old man's dead,' he said. 'They lived together a long and faithful life. He was true to her to the end,' he said.

She was nervous, as we were. She said she had heart disease. She kept turning to whisper to us, like the rest of us giving little or no attention to the preliminary bouts.

Men were standing up in the ring and whaling away. Black eyes, swollen lips, and ugly cauliflower ears were being acquired, we looking occasionally, not caring. They would be men hoping to rise in the pugilistic world, hoping to suddenly attract attention, get into the big money.

'I got heart disease and I climbed the five flights of stairs to get up here. I ain't caring about this man he's fighting tonight, but I want him to have another chance at that Schmeling,' she said. She was voicing something we all felt. It was the thing that had made us all, whites and blacks, that night, so tense, so nervous. 'I don't want anyone else to get him until he gets in there again with that Schmeling.'

She had put her finger on it, touched the spot. The Schmeling had got our Joe, the Brown Bomber, with a right, and all the newspapers had been saying that the Argentine fighter, Brescia, had a powerful right. There had been the whole romance of the Alabama Negro Boy . . . the young Negro lad just a workman in a Ford plant at Fond Du Lac, in Michigan . . . Joe Louis Barrow . . . the Barrow might have been got from some Southern white family who had owned, say, his grandfather . . . it had been dropped . . . But better even than Joe Louis was the other name, probably given him by some newspaper man—'The Brown Bomber.'

And then, suddenly up and up. Riches flooding into him, perhaps. It wasn't that we cared about. He was one of ours. He was a fellow who could do a thing superbly.

And then that Schmeling had got him, with a right. Why, it must have been an accident, the one blow stunning him like that. The fellow in the bar had said that the Bomber was a sucker for a right. When Fred and I were sitting in the bar, I had taken a clipping out of my pocket. It was from a German Nazi magazine, *Der Weltkampf.* 'Max Schmeling's victory over Joe Louis is a "Cultural Achievement" for the white race,' it said. 'It clearly demonstrates the superiority of the white intelligence.' It was that way of putting it, taking it, that had touched us on the raw. It had got us all, white men and Negro men. There had been, Fred had said, something mighty nice about the way the American Negroes had taken the rise of the Bomber. There had been in them no such nonsense about 'culture' . . . 'Superior intelligence.' It was a man doing brilliantly, superbly, the thing he could do, was born to do. We all wanted something set right.

He came into the ring, and if we had been tense before, we grew more so. We leaned forward, silently waiting. He, the Bomber, seemed small. Fred spoke of it. It must have been because the Argentine was tall. By the program he was only three-quarters of an inch taller than Joe.

Or it might have been because he stood up straight, boxed from that position, while the Bomber was in a half crouch. The Bomber is yellow, a quite light and quite shiny silky lemon yellow. They wore some kind of a white thing in their mouths, I presume, to protect the teeth. It seems to be a part of a fighter's manager's job to put it in.

How quickly the round passed, the first one, not many blows struck. Fred thought they must be doing what he spoke of as 'feeling each other out.' The Argentine seemed to get increasingly tall and strong-looking. He kept retreating and the Bomber kept after him, crouching forward, very swift-seeming and cat-like. He was all grace. There were, to be sure, a few blows struck, or attempted, the Bomber getting in two or three and getting a hard one back. He kept after his man.

Round two . . . I can't remember. Among us, in our gallery, there was the same steady tenseness. It made your legs ache, under the knees. Fred was biting his nails. 'Quit it,' I said, but he didn't hear me. It all happened in the third, a sudden swift right, from the Argentine. It might be like the one Schmeling had landed, thus accomplishing the 'cultural achievement.'

The sudden swift flying of fists, so swift that I, at least, couldn't follow. The white man had been retreating and retreating, but suddenly he had pounced.

He had got the Bomber with that right, and for just a moment, our Bomber seemed as he must have seemed that night in the ring with Schmeling.

They were standing close now, whaling away at each other, and in that awful moment the Bomber did seem gone. We had all got to our feet, but up in our gallery there was no sound, while down there, close to the ring, the ring-side seat fellows were madly dancing and shouting. Their words flew up to us . . .

'The right! The right!'

'He's got him with the right!'

There was the sick feeling that mankind, the human race, had turned out to be what the pessimists are always saying it is—'But what about the old stars and stripes?' I found myself asking. I went Bolshevik and so did Fred. He was dancing nervously and making punches at the air with his fists. I was afraid he would sock in the neck the woman who had the heart disease. He didn't.

And then, swiftly . . . hurrah . . . Oh, such a deep sigh of relief! The Bomber had got clear. He wasn't hurt, not too badly. He had got clear, but at once, with a quick, graceful leap, came in again. There were two blows struck, a right and a left. I read about it later in a newspaper. I don't believe I saw them. To me it was like when you put a charge of dynamite under a rock and touch it off. The white man straightened. He stood stiffly, and then he went down, and presently . . . I never saw the referee counting . . . time just passed, and there was the Bomber, so strangely gentle and boyish-seeming, helping to carry the Argentine to his corner.

In our gallery, joy. There was dancing, laughing, shouting. 'My Country, 'Tis of Thee.' I'll never know how Fred and I got out of the jam, away from the happy, dancing whites and Negroes. The woman who had heart disease just sat silently in her seat, such a placid, satisfied look on her face.

When we were in the street, Fred said he was tired. 'Let's have us each a couple of sidecars.' He said he would pay for them. 'Look, isn't the country saved?' He was having himself a good time. 'This Argentine,' he added . . . this when we had got into a bar . . . he quoted . . . 'This Argentine . . . "He's one of the best-versed men in literature, in the fighting game!" I reckon you, being a literary man, that you're mighty sorry for him,' Fred said, grinning at me.

Paul Gallico

Rather than following the footsteps of his father, a noted concert pianist, Paul Gallico (1897–1976) emerged as a virtuoso of his own chosen instrument, the typewriter. A lyrical stylist of the sports pages, he hired on at the *New York Daily News* after graduating from Columbia, rapidly rose to become sports editor, and along the way established an annual amateur boxing tournament he called the Golden Gloves. A pioneer in the field of participatory journalism that would serve George Plimpton so well, Gallico boxed with Jack Dempsey, caught Dizzy Dean's fastball, golfed with Bobby Jones, and drank with Babe Ruth, but with his fortieth birthday fast approaching he unburdened himself with his 1938 valedictory, *Farewell to Sport* (which included this reflection on the sad career of Primo Carnera), and moved to Europe and a new life as a writer of fiction, which, apart from a turn as a World War II correspondent, he remained for the rest of his days. His short story "The Snow Goose" won an O. Henry Award and is still anthologized; he also wrote plays, children's books, and a number of novels, among them *The Poseidon Adventure* (1969), which deserved better than the notably bad film Hollywood made of it.

Pity the Poor Giant

THERE is probably no more scandalous, pitiful, incredible story in all the record of these last mad sports years than the tale of the living giant, a creature out of the legends of antiquity, who was made into a prizefighter. He was taught and trained by a wise, scheming little French boxing manager who had an Oxford University degree, and he was later acquired and developed into the heavyweight champion of the world by a group of American gangsters and mob men; then finally, when his usefulness as a meal ticket was outlived, he was discarded in the most shameful chapter in all boxing.

This unfortunate pituitary case, who might have been Angoulaffre, or Balan, or Fierabras, Gogmagog, or Gargantua himself, was a poor simple-minded peasant by the name of Primo Carnera, the first son of a stone-cutter of Sequals, Italy. He stood six feet seven inches in height, and weighed two hundred and sixty-eight pounds. He became the heavyweight champion, yet never in all his life was he ever anything more than a freak and a fourth-rater at prizefighting. He must have grossed more than two millions of dollars during the years that he was being exhibited, and he hasn't a cent to show for it today.

There is no room here for more than a brief and hasty glance back over the implications of the tragedy of Primo Carnera. And yet I could not seem to take my leave from sports without it. The scene and the story still fascinate me, the sheer impudence of the men who handled the giant, their conscienceless cruelty, their complete depravity towards another human being, the sure, cool manner in which they hoaxed hundreds of thousands of people. Poor Primo! A giant in stature and strength, a terrible figure of a man, with the might of ten men, he was a helpless lamb among wolves who used him until there was nothing more left to use, until the last possible penny had been squeezed from his big carcass, and then abandoned him. His last days in the United States were spent alone in a hospital. One leg was paralyzed, the result of beatings taken around the head. None of the carrion birds who had picked him clean ever came back to see him or to help him.

No one who was present in Madison Square Garden the night that Primo Carnera was first introduced to American audiences will ever forget him as he came bounding down the aisle from the dressing-room and climbed into the ring. It was a masterpiece of stage management.

He wore black fighting trunks on the side of which was embroidered the head of a wild boar in red silk. He disdained the usual fighter's bathrobe and instead wore a sleeveless vest of a particularly hideous shade of green, and on his head a cap of the same shade, several sizes too large for him and with an enormous visor that made him look even larger than he was. Leon See, the Frenchman, then his manager, was a small man. The bucket-carriers and sponge-wielders were chosen for size too—diminutive men; everything was done to increase the impression of Primo's size.

Carnera was the only giant I have ever seen who was well proportioned throughout his body for his height. His legs were massive and he was truly thewed like an oak. His waist was comparatively small and clean, but from it rose a torso like a Spanish hogshead from which sprouted two tremendous arms, the biceps of which stood out like grapefruit. His hands were like Virginia hams, and his fingers were ten thick red sausages.

His head was large, even for the size of his body, and looking at him you were immediately struck with his dreadful gummy mouth and sharp, irregular, snaggle teeth. His lips were inclined to be loose and flabby. He had a good nose and fine, kind brown eyes. But his legs looked even more enormous and tree-like than they were, owing to the great blue bulging varicose veins that wandered down them on both sides and stuck out far enough so that you could have knocked them off with a baseball bat. His skin was brown and glistening and he invariably smelled of garlic.

This was the horror that came into the Madison Square Garden ring and sent a sincere shudder through the packed house. That is to say, he was horrible until he commenced to fight, when he became merely pitiful and an object demanding sympathy. Behind what passed for the wild battle blaze in his eyes and the dreadful gummy leer, emphasized by the size of the red rubber mouthpiece (tooth-protector) with which they provided him, there was nothing but bewilderment and complete helplessness. The truth was that, handi-capped by rules and regulations, a sport he did not understand and was not temperamentally fitted for, and those silly brown leather bags laced to his fingers, never at any time could he fight a lick. His entire record, with a few exceptions, must be thrown out as one gigantic falsehood, staged and engineered, planned and executed by the men who had him in tow and who were building him up for the public as a man-killer and an invincible fighter.

But I think the most dreadful part of the story is that the poor floundering giant was duped along with the spectators. He was permitted, in fact encouraged, to believe that his silly pawings and pushings, when they connected, sent men staggering into uncon-sciousness and defeat. It was not until late in his career, when in spite of himself he learned something through sheer experience and num-ber of fights, that he ever knocked anyone out on the level. But he never could fight, and never will. In spite of his great size and strength and his well-proportioned body, he remained nothing but a glandular freak who should have remained with the small French traveling circus from which Leon See took him.

This big, good-natured, docile man was exhibiting himself in a small wandering cirque in the south of France as a strong man and Greco-Roman wrestler, engaging all comers and local talent in the nightly show, having found that it paid him more and offered a better life than that of his chosen profession of mosaic-worker. Here he was discovered by a former French boxing champion who signed him up and apprenticed him to one Monsieur Leon See to be taught the rudiments of *la boxe*. It is highly probable that the time spent as a wrestler set his muscles and prevented him from ever becoming a knockout puncher. But Monsieur Leon See was taking no chances. He taught and trained Carnera strictly as a defensive boxer.

Now, it must be understood that Leon See was one of the most intelligent, smart and wily men that ever turned a fighter loose from his corner. He was not much more scrupulous than the bevy of public enemies who eventually took Carnera away from him simply by muscling him, but he was much more far-seeing and he had certain well-thought-out notions and theories about the ridiculous game of boxing. Among them was the excellent and sensible thought that the human head was never intended by nature to be punched, and that secondly, from the manner of its construction out of hundreds of tiny, delicately articulated bones, the closed fist was never meant to be one of man's most effective weapons. In this last idea, Monsieur See was not alone. The coterie of tough guys and mobsters who eventually relieved him of his interest in Carnera rarely used the fist, reckoning it, as did See, an inefficient weapon. The boys always favored the pistol or Roscoe, also known as the Difference, the Equalizer, the Rod, and the Heat.

See was a keen student of the human body—for a prizefight manager—and he knew something about men. He was aware that abnormalities of size were usually compensated for by weaknesses elsewhere. He found out—exactly how is not known—that Primo Carnera would never be able to absorb a hard punch to the chin. He may have had some secret rehearsal in a gymnasium somewhere in Paris and, having ordered some workaday heavyweight to clout Primo one just to see what would happen, saw that the giant came all undone, wobbled and collapsed. Be that as it may, Monsieur See knew. And never at any time while he was connected with Carnera would he permit anyone to punch Primo in the head—neither his sparring partners nor his opponents. Since both received their pay from practically the same source, this was not so difficult to arrange as might be imagined. But See also had something else. He was a Frenchman and so he had a heart. He loved big Carnera.

Years later See proved to be right. When Carnera through exigent circumstances was forced to fight without benefit of prearrangement, and the heavyweights began to sight along that big, protruding jaw of his and nail him for direct hits, he was slaughtered. He was brave and game and apparently could take punches to the body all the night long. But one hard, true tap on the chin and he fell down goggle-eyed. For a long time during the early years, however, nobody was permitted to hit him there, and Carnera himself began to think he was invincible.

Primo's first trip to the United States was arranged through an American contact man and importer of foreign fighting talent, a character from Tin-Ear Alley named Walter Friedman or, as Damon Runyon nicknamed him, Walter (Good-Time Charley) Friedman. See was smart enough to know that without an American "in," without cutting in an American manager, he would not get very far in America. What he was not quite smart enough to know was how deep his "in" took him, that the ramifications of Friedman's business and other connections were to lead through some very tough and rapacious parties.

Carnera's first fight in New York involved him with a lanky Swede named Big Boy Peterson. In this fight poor Carnera was hardly able to get out of his own way and caused his opponent the most frightful embarrassment through not being able to strike a blow that looked sufficiently hard to enable him to keep his end of the bargain, if there was one. Eventually Peterson succumbed to a push as Carnera lumbered and floundered past him, and to make assurance doubly sure, the Swede hit himself a punch on the jaw as he went down. Someone had to hit him.

Now, this was a shameless swindle from start to finish, one way or another. If Peterson was making an honest effort to fight he never should have been permitted to enter the ring. The press unanimously announced beforehand that it would probably be a sell and a fake, and when it was over, suggested strongly that it had been. But it said so in a gay and light-hearted manner as though the whole thing were pretty funny (as indeed it was), and there was no one on the New York State Athletic Commission either sufficiently intelligent or courageous enough to throw Primo and his handlers and fixers right out of the ring and thence out of the country. The Peterson fight in Madison Square Garden, the stronghold of professional boxing, was a sort of a test case by the Carnera crowd to see how much they could get away with. On that score it was a clean-cut success. They found out that they could get away with anything. And so they proceeded to do just that. Primo's first American tour was organized, a tour that grossed something like $700,000, of which handsome piece of money Carnera received practically nothing. He was barnstormed across the country in the most cold-blooded, graceless, shameful series of fixed, bought, coerced, or plain out-and-out tank acts ever. If one of them was contested on its merits it was only because the opponent by no possible stretch of the imagination, on his own efforts, could harm Carnera or even hit him.

Where the fight could not be bought—that is to say, where the fighter was unwilling to succumb to a tap on the elbow for a price—guns were produced by sinister strangers to threaten him, and where neither threats nor money were sufficient to bag the fight, he was crossed or tricked, as in the case of Bombo Chevalier, a big California Negro who was fascinated by the size of Carnera's chin, and nothing would do but he was going to hit it, just to see what would happen. Between rounds one of Chevalier's own attendants rubbed red pepper or some other inflammatory substance into his eyes so that he lost all interest in tapping anybody's chin.

In Newark, New Jersey, a Negro was visited in his dressing-room before the bout by an unknown party not necessarily connected with Carnera's management, and was asked to inspect shooting irons, and in Philadelphia another Negro, Ace Clark, was amusing himself readying up Carnera for a knockout—he had already completely closed one of Primo's eyes—when somebody suggested he look down and see what the stranger beneath his corner was holding under his coat, and what caliber it was.

Every known build-up fighter was lined up for this tour, including faithful old hands like K. O. Christner, Chuck Wiggens, and poor Farmer Lodge. Political and gangster friends in the cities visited volunteered with their private heavyweights for quick splashes that might look well on the record-books. It was all for the cause. The more money Carnera made, the more the boys would have to cut up amongst themselves. It was all just one big happy family. It seemed almost as though every scamp in the boxing game contributed his bit somehow to that Carnera build-up.

Friedman, as has been indicated, was the go-between, and although Leon See was quite capable of all the planning necessary to keep Carnera in the victory columns, nevertheless it would have been considered bad form, and downright dangerous, if See had not cut the local boys in. And, at that, I suspect the said local boys showed the amiable and gifted Frog a few things about building up a potential heavyweight champion that made the two Stribling fights arranged by Monsieur See, one in Paris and the other in London and both ending in fouls, look like Holy Gospel.

As adviser and co-director of this tour, Broadway Bill Duffy was cut in. Bill was then in the night-club and fight-managing business, but in his youth he had been convicted of a little alfresco burgling and had been sent away for a spell. He was still to achieve the highest pinnacle of fame that can come to an American—to be named a Public Enemy. It is a curious commentary upon the conduct of boxing around New York that Duffy was allowed to operate as a manager and a second when there was a rule on the books of the State Athletic Commission, if indeed it was not written directly into the boxing law, that no one ever convicted of a felony was to be eligible for any kind of a license.

Duffy usually split even on things with his dearest friend, Owen Madden, better known as Owney, who had also been away for a time in connection with the demise of a policeman. Owney was out on parole at the time—he was sent back later—making beer (and very good beer it was, too) and acting as silent partner in the operation of a number of prizefighters. Also in this crowd was a charming but tough individual known as Big Frenchy De Mange who made news one evening by getting himself snatched and held for ransom by Mad-Dog Vincent Coll. The Mad Dog was subsequently rubbed out in an East Side drug-store telephone booth. But the subject, after all, is Primo Carnera and not gangsters and racket men, though pretty soon it was all one subject and all one sweet and fragrant mess. The boys had their connections in every town. The Philadelphia underworld collaborated through the medium of the always friendly and helpful Maximilian Boo-Boo Hoff, and the same courtesies were extended all the way through to the Pacific Coast, where occurred the Bombo Chevalier incident, which was too nauseous even for the local commission there to stomach. There was an investigation resulting in the suspension of a few unimportant people. But Carnera and his swindle went merrily onwards.

And it continued until he won the heavyweight championship of the world by ostensibly knocking out Jack Sharkey, then world's champion, in the sixth round, with a right uppercut. I say ostensibly because nothing will ever convince me that that was an honest prizefight, contested on its merits.

Sharkey's reputation and the reputation of Fat John Buckley, his manager, were bad. Both had been involved in some curious ring encounters. The reputation of the Carnera entourage by the time the Sharkey fight came along, in 1933, was notorious, and the training camps of both gladiators were simply festering with mobsters and tough guys. Duffy, Madden, et Cie., were spread out all over Carnera's training quarters at Dr. Bier's Health Farm at Pompton Lakes, New Jersey. A traveling chapter of Detroit's famous Purple Gang hung out at Gus Wilson's for a while during Sharkey's rehearsals. Part of their business there was to muscle in on the concession of the fight pictures.

If that fight was on the level, it wasn't like either of the companies operating the two pugs. If it was honest, the only explanation was that the boys were going sissy. As far as Primo knew, the right uppercut with which he tagged Sharkey in the sixth round was enough to kill a steer. He had knocked out many men with the same punch. Now he was the heavyweight champion of the world, and even if he didn't have any money to show for it, Italy and Mussolini were going to be very pleased. I have often wondered how long he remained innocent, how long it was before he began to catch on.

For instance, it must have been a terrible surprise and considerable of an eye-opener to Carnera the night he fought Tommy Loughran in Miami as heavyweight champion of the world. It was a no-decision match and a bad one for the gang to make, but they had to do something because they were desperate for money at the time. If the Sharkey fight was crooked, it is probable that the entire end of Primo's purse had to be paid over for the fix.

The Loughran fight had to go on the level because no one had ever managed to tamper with Loughran, and neither he nor his manager was afraid of guns. And Tommy had another curious and valuable protection. He was a good Catholic, and many priests were his friends. The gunmen were a little shy of those padres, who might usually be found in twos and threes at Tommy's home or his training camps. But the mob figured that with a hundred-pound advantage in weight Carnera could take care of Loughran, who was little more than a light heavyweight and never was a hard hitter. During the fight Carnera hit Loughran more than a dozen of the same uppercuts that had stretched Sharkey twitching on the canvas, and never even reddened Tommy's face. Loughran was a cream-puff puncher and yet he staggered Carnera several times with right hands and was himself never in any kind of danger from a punch. He merely got tired from having Carnera leaning on him for half an hour. If nothing else, that fight beneath the Miami moon exposed how incompetent Carnera was as a bruiser, and how utterly false were the stories about his invincibility, besides casting fresh suspicion upon his knockout of Sharkey. We had all seen Loughran put on the floor by a 175-pounder. If a man weighing around 280 pounds, as Primo did for that fight, hit him flush on the jaw and couldn't drop him, and yet had knocked out one of the cleverest heavyweights in the business, it wasn't hard to arrive at a conclusion. It was obvious that he was a phony and the first stiff-punching heavyweight who was leveling would knock him out.

Max Baer did it the very next summer. The following summer Joe Louis did it again, and then an almost unknown Negro heavyweight by the name of Leroy Haynes accomplished the feat for the third time. And that was the beginning of the end of Primo.

His lucrative campaigns and the winning of the heavyweight championship had enriched everyone connected with him except poor Primo, who saw very little of the money he earned. There were too many silent partners and "boys" who had little pieces of him. Monsieur See had long since been dispensed with and shipped back to France for his health; he had served his purpose. But it was an evil day for Carnera when they chased Leon back to Paris, for Leon never would have permitted anyone to belt Carnera on his vulnerable chin. As suggested, the little Frenchman had a love for the big fellow whom he had taught and trained and watched over so carefully. The Duffy crowd had no love for anything. Fighters' chins were made to be smacked and they might just as well get used to taking the punches there.

It seemed as though their power was beginning to lose some of its effectiveness, exhausted perhaps by its own virus and viciousness, shortly after they had made Carnera champion. Primo escaped to Italy with his title and nothing else and later returned here for the disastrous fight with Loughran under the guidance of a little Italian banker by the name of Luigi Soresi, who appeared to be genuinely trying to get and keep for poor Carnera some of the money he was making.

The by-products of the Miami affair were typical and pathetic. Duffy and company were living over a Miami night club in style and spending money like water—Primo's money. Carnera was relegated to a cheap cottage back of the town with a trainer. No one really looked after him. No one cared particularly whether he trained or not. He came into the ring against Loughran twenty pounds overweight. Shortly after that, Duffy was clapped into the jug for a spell for some boyish pranks with his income tax, and from the cooler he wrote pleading letters at the time that Carnera was preparing to defend his title against Baer, maintaining that he was needed to guide, advise, and teach Primo, to prime him for the first serious defense of his title, and that he should be given furlough from quod to attend to this matter. Carnera vigorously denied that he needed him. He was only too delighted to have Duffy held in durance vile. Of course what was really killing Uncle Will was that he was where for the first time he couldn't get his fingers on a nice big slice of the sugar that big, stupid Wop would make for boxing Baer.

It is difficult to bag or fix a heavyweight championship prizefight, though it has been done. But in the post-war sports renaissance there was so much money at stake in a heavyweight championship fight that it took more cash than most could produce to purchase either champion or challenger. It stood to reason that if the champion figured to make a million dollars or more out of his title he wasn't going to sell out for any less. Too, the power of the gangs was weakening. Repeal dealt them a terrible blow and took away their chief source of revenue. Three or four years before, Carnera's title would have been safe because his handlers would not have accepted any challenger for the title unless he agreed to preserve the state of the champion's health throughout the encounter. And there were always ways and means of keeping a challenger from double-crossing.

But Duffy was in the sneezer, as the boys sometimes quaintly called the jailhouse, Carnera was broke and needed money. He could only get it by fighting Baer. And the Baer fight could not be fixed. Baer's reputation was good; at least, he had not been caught out in any shady fights. He was a powerful hitter and it was apparent that now at last the rest of us were going to be made privy to what it was that happened when Carnera was struck forcefully on the chin. We didn't have to wait long. He was knocked down three times in the first round, and lost his championship in the eleventh round on a technical knockout when he was helpless, having been knocked down a total of thirteen times during the ten and a half rounds.

Not, however, until he fought and was knocked out by Joe Louis was it apparent what a dreadful thing had been done to this great hulk of a man. Strange to feel pity and sympathy excited for one so gross and enormous and strong. But the out sizes of the world are not the happy men, and their bulk is often of little use or help to them. If anything, it is a handicap when up against the speed and timing and balance of a normal man. Carnera's great strength was practically useless to him in the ring. The hardest blow he could strike was little more than a push. True, if he caught you in a corner he could club you insensible, but no smart fighter is caught in corners, and the big man was never fast enough anyway to catch anyone but out-and-out tramps.

When he fought Joe Louis he was defensively but little better than he was the first time I saw him, which, as it happened, was not in Madison Square Garden, but in the smoky, stuffy, subterranean Salle Wagram, a little fight club in Paris where I happened to be one evening when Jeff Dickson was promoting a fight between Primo Carnera, who had then been fighting a little less than a year, and one Moise Bouquillon, a light heavyweight who weighed 174 pounds. Monsieur See was experimenting a little with his giant. It was obvious that Bouquillon was going to be unable to hurt him very much, but what I noted that evening and never forgot was that the giant was likewise unable to hurt the little Frenchman. Curiously, that fight was almost an exact duplicate of the one that Carnera as champion later fought with Loughran. Walter (Good-Time Charley) Friedman was there too. Many years later he told me quite frankly: "Boy, was that a lousy break for us that you come walking into that Salle Wagram that night and see that the big guy can't punch! Just that night you hadda be there. Leon wanted to see if he could go ten rounds without falling down. And you hadda be there. We coulda got away with a lot more if you don't walk in there and write stories about how he can't punch."

Joe Louis slugged Carnera into bleating submission, cruelly and brutally. Handsome Uncle Will Duffy was back in his corner again, jawing angrily at him when he was led trembling and quivering back to his chair after the referee had saved him again, one side of his mouth smashed in, dazed and dripping blood. The very first right-hand punch Louis hit him broke Carnera's mouth and hurt him dreadfully.

Here, then, was the complete sell. He had nothing. His title was gone, his money squandered by the gang. And the one thing he thought he had, an unbeatable skill in defense and an irresistible crushing power in attack that no man living could withstand, never existed. It was a fable as legendary as the great giants of mythology that he resembled. The carrion birds that had fed upon this poor, big, dumb man had picked him clean. They had left him nothing, not even his pride and his self-respect, and that probably was the cruelest thing of all.

In his last fight, the one with Haynes, he was again severely beaten about the head. One of his legs refused to function. The fight was stopped. While he lay in the hospital in New York for treatment, as I have said, he lay alone.

I often wonder what that hulk of a man thinks today as he looks back over the manner in which he was swindled, tricked and cheated at every turn, as he recalls the great sums of money that he earned, all of it gone beyond recall. The world has no place for him, not even as a freak in a circus, from whence he emerged and where he might happily have spent his life and become prosperous. Because as a giant, a terror and a horror, he stands exposed as a poor, unwilling fraud who was no mankiller at all, but a rather helpless, sad creature who, when slugged by a 185-pound mortal, either toppled stricken to the floor or staggered about or bled or had to be saved from annihilation by a third man who obligingly stepped between him and his tormentors.

He was born far, far too late. He belonged to the twelfth or thirteenth century, when he would have been a man-at-arms and a famous fellow with mace and halberd, pike or bill. At least he would have fought nobly and to the limit of his great strength, properly armed, because Carnera was a courageous fellow to the limit of his endurance, game and a willing fighter when aroused. In those days he would have won honor afield and would have got himself decently killed, or, surviving, would have been retired by his feudal lord to round out his days and talk over the old brave fights.

Today there is nothing left for this man but reflection upon his humiliations. He was just a big sucker whom the wise guys took and trimmed. What an epitaph for one who came from the ancient and noble race of giants.

All this took place in our country, Anno Domini 1930–1935.

Bob Considine

If journalism is the first draft of history, then in the glory days of news-papers, the wire-service reporter provided the first pass at the first draft. Few on the sports beat were ever faster at getting stories out to the nation's waiting papers than Bob Considine, the racehorse of the Hearst syndicate's International News Service. Though Considine (1906–1975) was far from a memorable wordsmith, he was much more than just a deadline sprinter. He was, at various times, a baseball writer for *The Washington Post*, sports editor and columnist for the *Washington Herald*, sports and political columnist for two New York dailies, the *American* and the *Daily Mirror*, and a radio com-mentator. Somehow he also managed to be a World War II correspondent, a screenwriter, and author or editor of more than twenty books, among them *Thirty Seconds Over Tokyo* (editing Doolittle Raid pilot Ted W. Lawson; 1943) and *The Babe Ruth Story* (1948). Like any good columnist, Considine had his critics, many of whom decried his anti-union and pro–Korean War stances. But when he covered Joe Louis's rematch with Max Schmeling in 1938, nary a word of complaint was uttered about the jingoism that permeated his rat-a-tat-tat prose.

Louis Knocks Out Schmeling

L ISTEN to this, buddy, for it comes from a guy whose palms are still wet, whose throat is still dry, and whose jaw is still agape from the utter shock of watching Joe Louis knock out Max Schmeling.

It was a shocking thing, that knockout—short, sharp, merciless, complete. Louis was like this:

He was a big lean copper spring, tightened and retightened through weeks of training until he was one pregnant package of coiled venom.

Schmeling hit that spring. He hit it with a whistling right-hand punch in the first minute of the fight—and the spring, tormented with tension, suddenly burst with one brazen spang of activity. Hard brown arms, propelling two unerring fists, blurred beneath the hot white candelabra of the ring lights. And Schmeling was in the path of them, a man caught and mangled in the whirring claws of a mad and feverish machine.

The mob, the biggest and most prosperous ever to see a fight in a ball yard, knew that there was the end before the thing had really started. It knew, so it stood up and howled one long shriek. People who had paid as much as $100 for their chairs didn't use them—except perhaps to stand on, the better to let the sight burn forever in their memories.

There were four steps to Schmeling's knockout. A few seconds after he landed his only punch of the fight, Louis caught him with a lethal little left hook that drove him into the ropes so that his right arm was hooked over the top strand, like a drunk hanging to a fence. Louis swarmed over him and hit with everything he had—until Referee Donovan pushed him away and counted one.

Schmeling staggered away from the ropes, dazed and sick. He looked drunkenly toward his corner, and before he had turned his head back Louis was on him again, first with a left and then that awe-provoking right that made a crunching sound when it hit the German's jaw. Max fell down, hurt and giddy, for a count of three.

He clawed his way up as if the night air were as thick as black water, and Louis—his nostrils like the mouth of a double-barreled shotgun—took a quiet lead and let him have both barrels.

Max fell almost lightly, bereft of his senses, his fingers touching the canvas like a comical stew-bum doing his morning exercises, knees bent and the tongue lolling in his head.

He got up long enough to be knocked down again, this time with his dark unshaven face pushed in the sharp gravel of the resin.

Louis jumped away lightly, a bright and pleased look in his eyes, and as he did the white towel of surrender which Louis' handlers had refused to use two years ago tonight came sailing into the ring in a soggy mess. It was thrown by Max Machon, oblivious to the fact that fights cannot end this way in New York.

The referee snatched it off the floor and flung it backwards. It hit the ropes and hung there, limp as Schmeling. Donovan counted up to five over Max, sensed the futility of it all, and stopped the fight.

The big crowd began to rustle restlessly toward the exits, many only now accepting Louis as champion of the world. There were no eyes for Schmeling, sprawled on his stool in his corner.

He got up eventually, his dirty gray-and-black robe over his shoulders, and wormed through the happy little crowd that hovered around Louis. And he put his arm around the Negro and smiled. They both smiled and could afford to—for Louis had made around $200,000 a minute and Schmeling $100,000 a minute.

But once he crawled down in the belly of the big stadium, Schmeling realized the implications of his defeat. He, who won the title on a partly phony foul, and beat Louis two years ago with the aid of a crushing punch after the bell had sounded, now said Louis had fouled him. That would read better in Germany, whence earlier in the day had come a cable from Hitler, calling on him to win.

It was low, sneaking trick, but a rather typical last word from Schmeling.

Richard Wright

As the Pittsburgh *Courier*, an important African American publication of the 1930s, noted of the rise of Joe Louis, the Brown Bomber "lifted an entire race out of the slough of inferiority, and gave them a sense of self-importance." The community's pleasure in that vicarious identification had been badly shaken by Louis's 1936 defeat at the hands of Max Schmeling, the German who knocked him out in the twelfth round of their first fight at Yankee Stadium. At the time still an emerging writer, Richard Wright (1908–1960) had been born in Mississippi and had spent his boyhood in the Deep South before moving to Chicago, where he had joined the Communist Party in 1933. After internal party squabbles shut down *Left Front*, the magazine he had edited in Chicago, Wright decamped for New York in 1937, the year the twenty-three-year-old Louis knocked out "Cinderella Man" James J. Braddock to become heavyweight champion of the world; the publication of *Uncle Tom's Children*, the first of what would be ten novels and nine books of non-fiction, came in 1938—the same year Louis defended his title in a rematch before seventy thousand spectators at Yankee Stadium. Wright's account of that bout and the unrestrained outburst of joy unleashed on the streets of Harlem by Louis's first-round knockout was written for *New Masses*. That publication could be counted on to carefully toe the party line, and whether they represented his own thoughts or were inserted at the whim of *New Masses*' editors, Wright's attempts to ascribe a political motive to the celebration sometimes seem heavy-handed. It seems doubtful, for instance, that swastika-bearing effigies were dragged through the streets of Harlem in any significant profusion that night. While not unmindful of the Nazis' racial policies, the overwhelming majority of African Americans were simply celebrating the triumph of one of their own—a victory in which Louis had avenged his only career defeat. As future NAACP leader Roy Wilkins would note, the more prevalent view among black Americans was that "it sounded pretty foolish to be against park benches marked JUDE in Berlin, but to be *for* park benches marked COLORED in Tallahassee, Florida."

While "High Tide in Harlem" was one of three Joe Louis articles that marked the author's first association with the iconic champion, it was hardly his last. Wright's reputation was secured with the 1940 publication of *Native Son*. The following year, the *New Amsterdam Star-News* published "Joe Louis Blues," a Wright poem written in the folk idiom, which was subsequently set to a traditional twelve-bar blues tune by Count Basie and recorded (under the supervision of John Hammond) by Paul Robeson, with Basie's band providing the accompaniment. Released as "King Joe, Parts 1 and 2," the 78 r.p.m. recording sold forty thousand copies within two months of its release. *New Masses* pronounced it "swell to dance to."

High Tide in Harlem:
Joe Louis as a Symbol of Freedom

THE colossal bowl of seventy thousand hazy faces, an oval-shaped tableau compounded of criss-crossed beams of light and shadow, waited almost in silence for the gong to sound that would start the Louis–Schmeling million-dollar fight. The gaze of the seventy thousand eyes was centered on the "squared circle," a single diadem-like spot of canvas lit to blinding whiteness under the intense glare of overhead floodlights. So dwarfed was the ring by the mammoth stadium that it seemed that each man and woman was straining forward to peer at a colorful puppet show.

The Louis–Schmeling fight for the heavyweight championship of the world at Yankee Stadium was one of the greatest dramas of make-believe ever witnessed in America, a drama which manipulated the common symbols and impulses in the minds and bodies of millions of people so effectively as to put to shame our professional playwrights, our O'Neills, our Lawsons, and our Caldwells. Promoter Mike Jacobs, prompted purely by commercial motives, has accidentally won the rare right, whether he wants to claim it or not, of wearing the purple robes customarily reserved for Euripides and Sophocles.

Each of the seventy thousand who had so eagerly jammed his way into the bowl's steel tiers under the open sky had come already emotionally conditioned as to the values that would triumph if *his* puppet won. Attached to each puppet, a white puppet and a black puppet, was a configuration of social images whose intensity and clarity had been heightened through weeks of skillful and constant agitation; social images whose emotional appeal could evoke attitudes tantamount to two distinct ways of life in the world today. Whichever puppet went down the Greek route to defeat that night would leave the path clear for the imperious sway of the balked impulses of one side or the other. The puppet emerging victorious would be the symbol of a fond wish gratified, would feed the starved faith of men caught in the mesh of circumstances.

Joe Louis, the black puppet who wore black trunks, was the betting favorite; but that was no indication as to how much actual sentiment there was for him among the seventy thousand spectators, for men like to bet on winners. And, too, just how much sentiment there was for Max Schmeling, the white puppet who wore purple trunks, no one, perhaps, will ever know; for now that the violent drama is ended the backers of the loser do not want to parade their disappointment for the scorn of others. But the two puppets were dissimilar enough in "race, creed, and previous condition of servitude" as to make their partisans wax militantly hopeful.

But out beyond the walls of the stadium were twelve million Negroes to whom the black puppet symbolized the living refutation of the hatred spewed forth daily over radios, in newspapers, in movies, and in books about their lives. Day by day, since their alleged emancipation, they have watched a picture of themselves being painted as lazy, stupid, and diseased. In helpless horror they have suffered the attacks and exploitation which followed in the wake of their being branded as "inferiors." True, hundreds of thousands of these Negroes would have preferred that that refutation could have been made in some form other than pugilism; but so effectively and completely have they been isolated and restricted in vocation that they rarely have had the opportunity to participate in the meaningful processes of America's national life. Jim Crowed in the army and navy, barred from many trades and professions, excluded from commerce and finance, relegated to menial positions in government, segregated residentially, denied the right of franchise for the most part; in short, forced to live a separate and impoverished life, they were glad for even the meager acceptance of their humanity implied in the championship of Joe Louis.

Visits to Joe Louis' training camp revealed throngs of Negroes standing around in a state of deep awe, waiting for just one glimpse of their champion. They were good, simple-hearted people, longing deeply for something of their own to be loyal to. When Joe appeared, a hush fell upon them and they stared. They took Joe into their hearts because he was a public idol and was respectfully enshrined in the public's imagination in a way they knew they would never be.

But because Joe's a Negro, even though he has to his credit a most enviable list of victories, there have been constant warnings issued by the Bilbos and Ellenders from south of the Mason-Dixon Line as to the wisdom of allowing a Negro to defeat a white man in public. The reactionary argument ran that such spectacles tended to create in Negroes too much pride and made them "intractable."

Naturally, Max Schmeling's victory over Louis two years ago was greeted with elation in reactionary quarters. A close study of Louis' stance, which revealed that he could be hit, together with a foul blow delivered after the bell, enabled the German boxer to win. Louis' defeat came as a shock to the boxing world and provided material for countless conversations and speculations. It was taken for granted that the second-rate Schmeling's defeat of the then reigning champion, the aging Braddock, was but a matter of time. But due to squabbles among promoters, Louis, not Schmeling, fought Braddock for the championship and won the title by a knockout in a thrilling bout in Chicago. Immediately the Nazi press, in America and in Germany, launched a campaign of slurs against Louis, dubbing him the "so-called champion," and declaring that Schmeling's prior victory over Louis was proof of "Negro inferiority." Schmeling boasted to the press that it would be easy for him to defeat the Negro again because (1) Negroes never forgot beatings, (2) his mere "white" presence would be enough to throw fear into Louis' heart, and (3) he would enter the ring with a "psychological edge" over the Negro. An open friend of Hitler and an avowed supporter of the Nazis, Schmeling caught the fancy of many reactionary Americans, plus the leaders of Nazi Germany, fascist Italy, Japan, and even certain circles in England. To bolster the aims of the forces of fascism, Schmeling's victory was interpreted to mean the ability of the "Aryan race to out-think inferior races." The logical implication of such a line of reasoning was that all Negroes, colonial people, and small nations were inherently backward, physically cowardly, a drag upon the rest of civilization, and should be conquered and subjected for the benefit of mankind.

But when faced with this specious proposition, the common people instinctively revolted. They knew that the majority of all prizefighters came from the so-called "backward people," that is, the working class; their capacity to fight stemming from an early life of toil in steel and iron foundries, coal mine, factories, and fields. Consequently, in his fight against Schmeling, Louis carried the good wishes of even the poor whites of the Deep South, something unparalleled in the history of America.

The appearance of the white puppet sent the crowd into a frenzy. The black puppet's ovation seemed incidental. The ring was cleared and the fight was on. The entire seventy thousand rose as one man. At the beginning of the fight there was a wild shriek which gradually died as the seconds flew. What was happening was so stunning that even cheering was out of place. The black puppet, contrary to all Nazi racial laws, was punching the white puppet so rapidly that the eye could not follow the blows. It was not really a fight, it was an act of revenge, of dominance, of complete mastery. The black puppet glided from his corner and simply wiped his feet on the white puppet's face. The black puppet was contemptuous, swift; his victory was complete, unquestionable, decisive; his blows must have jarred the marrow not only in the white puppet's but in Hitler's own bones.

In Harlem, that area of a few square blocks in upper Manhattan where a quarter of a million Negroes are forced to live through an elaborate connivance among landlords, merchants, and politicians, a hundred thousand black people surged out of taprooms, flats, restaurants, and filled the streets and sidewalks, like the Mississippi River overflowing in flood-time. With their faces to the night sky, they filled their lungs with air and let out a scream of joy that it seemed would never end, and a scream that seemed to come from untold reserves of strength. They wanted to make a noise comparable to the happiness bubbling in their hearts, but they were poor and had nothing. So they went to the garbage pails and got tin cans; they went to their kitchens and got tin pots, pans, washboards, wooden boxes, and took possession of the streets. They shouted, sang, laughed, yelled, blew paper horns, clasped hands, and formed weaving snake-lines, whistled, sounded sirens, and honked auto horns. From the windows of the tall, dreary tenements torn scraps of newspaper floated down. With the reiteration that evoked a hypnotic atmosphere, they chanted with eyes half-closed, heads lilting in unison, legs and shoulders moving and touching:

"Ain't you glad? Ain't you glad?"

Knowing full well the political effect of Louis' victory on the popular mind the world over, thousands yelled:

"Heil Louis!"

It was Harlem's mocking taunt to fascist Hitler's boast of the superiority of "Aryans" over other races. And they ridiculed the Nazi salute of the outstretched palm by throwing up their own dark ones to show how little they feared and thought of the humbug of fascist ritual.

With no less than a hundred thousand participating, it was the largest and most spontaneous political demonstration ever seen in Harlem and marked the highest tide of popular political enthusiasm ever witnessed among American Negroes.

Negro voices called fraternally to Jewish-looking faces in passing autos:

"I bet all the Jews are happy tonight!"

Men, women, and children gathered in thick knots and did the Big Apple, the Lindy Hop, the Truck—Harlem's gesture of defiance to the high cost of food, high rent, and misery. These ghetto-dwellers, under the stress of the joy of one of their own kind having wiped out the stain of defeat and having thrown the lie of "inferiority" into the teeth of the fascist, threw off restraint and fear. Each time a downtown auto slowed, it became covered with Joe Louis rooters, and the autos looked like clusters of black ripe grapes. A bus stopped and at once became filled with laughing throngs who "forgot" to pay their fares; children clambered up its tall sides and crawled over the hoods and fenders.

It was the celebration of Louis' victory over Carnera, Baer, Pastor, Farr, and Braddock all rolled into one. Ethiopian and American flags fluttered. Effigies of Schmeling chalked with the swastika were dragged through the streets.

Then, nobody knows from where and nobody bothered to ask, there appeared on the surface of the sea of people white placards hurling slogans of defiance at fascist pretensions and calling upon native lovers of democracy to be true to democratic ideals. *Oust Hitler's Spies and Agents; Pass the Anti-Lynching Bill; Down with Hitler and Mussolini; Alabama Produced Joe Louis; Free the Scottsboro Boys; Democracies Must Fight Fascism Everywhere.*

Carry the dream on for yourself; lift it out of the trifling guise of a prizefight celebration and supply the social and economic details and you have the secret dynamics of proletarian aspiration. The eyes of these people were bold that night. Their fear of property, of the armed police fell away. There was in their chant a hunger deeper than that for bread as they marched along. In their joy they were feeling an impulse which only the oppressed can feel to the full. They wanted to fling the heavy burden out of their hearts and embrace the world. They wanted to feel that their expanding feelings were not limited; that the earth was theirs as much as anybody else's; that they did not have to live by proscription in one corner of it; that they could go where they wanted to and do what they wanted to, eat and live where they wanted to, like others. They wanted to own things in common and do things in common. They wanted a holiday.

W. C. Heinz

They called themselves the New Journalists while drunk on self-congratulation. They were applying the techniques of fiction—scenes, character, dialogue—to the writing of fact, and to hear them talk in the '60s and '70s, you would have thought no one had done it before. But W. C. Heinz (1915–2008) had—as a World War II correspondent, New York newspaper sports columnist, and freelance writer for every magazine from *Sport* to *Cosmopolitan*. He also wrote the novel *The Professional* (1958), which stands among the best ever about boxing, *best* being an adjective that gets attached to a lot of Bill Heinz's work.

It's the same with *greatest*, as in Jimmy Breslin's assessment of "Brownsville Bum," published in *True* in 1951, as "the greatest magazine sports story I've ever read, bar none." Heinz wrote the story even though he never met its subject, a hell-raising middleweight named Al (Bummy) Davis, and only saw him fight once. "If the piece proves anything," Heinz said, "it is that if you are fortunate enough to find the right people who are perceptive enough and sensitive enough, you can still come to know a man."

Brownsville Bum

I^(T'S) a funny thing about people. People will hate a guy all his life for what he is, but the minute he dies for it they make him out a hero and they go around saying that maybe he wasn't such a bad guy after all because he sure was willing to go the distance for whatever he believed or whatever he was.

That's the way it was with Bummy Davis. The night Bummy fought Fritzie Zivic in the Garden and Zivic started giving him the business and Bummy hit Zivic low maybe 30 times and kicked the referee, they wanted to hang him for it. The night those four guys came into Dudy's bar and tried the same thing, only with rods, Bummy went nuts again. He flattened the first one and then they shot him, and when everybody read about it, and how Bummy fought guns with only his left hook and died lying in the rain in front of the place, they all said he was really something, and you sure had to give him credit at that.

"So you're Al Davis?" one of the hoods said. "Why you punch-drunk bum."

What did they expect Bummy to do? What did they expect him to do the night Zivic gave him the thumb and the laces and walked around the referee and bolted Bummy? Bummy could hook too good ever to learn how to hold himself in, if you want the truth of it.

That was really the trouble with Bummy. Bummy blew school too early, and he didn't know enough words. A lot of guys who fought Zivic used to take it or maybe beef to the referee, but Bummy didn't know how to do that. A lot of guys looking at four guns would have taken the talk and been thinking about getting the number off the car when it pulled away, but all Bummy ever had was his hook.

Bummy came out of Brownsville. In the sports pages they are always referring to Brownsville as the fistic incubator of Brooklyn, because they probably mean that a lot of fighters come out of there. Murder, Inc., came out of there, too, and if you don't believe it ask Bill O'Dwyer. If it wasn't for Brownsville maybe Bill O'Dwyer wouldn't have become the mayor of New York.

The peculiar thing about Brownsville is that it doesn't look so tough. There are trees around there and some vacant lots, and the houses don't look as bad as they do over on Second Avenue or Ninth Avenue or up in Harlem. Don't tell Charley Beecher, though, that you don't think it's so tough.

"What's the matter you sold the place?" Froike said to Charley the other day. "It ain't the same, now you sold it."

Charley Beecher used to run the poolroom with the gym behind it on the corner of Georgia and Livonia where Bummy used to train. It was a good little gym with a little dressing room and a shower, and Charley was a pretty good featherweight in the twenties, and his brother Willie, who was even a better fighter, fought Abe Attell and Johnny Dundee and Jack Britton and Leach Cross and Knockout Brown.

"For 17 years I was in business," Charley said. "Seventeen times they stuck me up."

He looked at Froike, and then he pointed with his two hands at his mouth and his ears and his eyes.

"I had guns here and here and here," he said. "All I ever saw was guns."

The worst part was that Charley knew all the guys. A week after they'd heist him they'd be back for a little contribution, maybe a C note. They'd be getting up bail for one of the boys, and they just wanted Charley to know there were no hard feelings about the heist, and that as long as he kept his dues up they'd still consider him friendly to the club. That's how tough Brownsville was.

Bummy had two brothers, and they were a big help. They were a lot older than Bummy, and the one they called Little Gangy and the other they called Duff. Right now Gangy is doing 20 to 40, just to give you an idea, and Bummy took a lot of raps for them, too, because there were some people who couldn't get back at Gangy and Duff so they took it out on the kid.

When Bummy was about seven his father used to run a candy and cigar store and did a little speaking on the side. In other words, he always had a bottle in the place, and he had Bummy hanging around in case anybody should say cop. When the signal would go up Bummy would run behind the counter and grab the bottle, and he was so small nobody could see him over the counter and he'd go out the back.

One day Bummy was going it down the street with the bottle under his coat and some real smart guy stuck out his foot. Bummy tripped and the bottle broke, and Bummy looked at the bottle and the whiskey running on the sidewalk and at the guy and his eyes got big and he started to scream. The guy just laughed and Bummy was lying right on the sidewalk in the whiskey and broken glass, hitting his head on the sidewalk and banging his fists down and screaming. A crowd came around and they watched Bummy, with the guy laughing at him, and they shook their heads and they said this youngest Davidoff kid must be crazy at that.

Davidoff was his straight name. Abraham Davidoff. In Yiddish they made Abraham into Ahvron and then Ahvron they sometimes make Bommy. All his family called him Bommy, so you can see they didn't mean it as a knock. The one who changed it to Bummy was Johnny Attell.

Johnny Attell used to run the fights at the Ridgewood Grove, a fight club in Brooklyn where some good fighters like Sid Terris and

Ruby Goldstein and Tony Canzoneri learned to fight, and Johnny and a nice guy named Lew Burton managed Bummy. When Bummy turned pro and Johnny made up the show card for the fight with Frankie Reese he put the name on it as Al (Bummy) Davis, and when Bummy saw it he went right up to John's office.

"What are you doing that for?" he hollered at Johnny. "I don't want to be called Bummy."

"Take it easy," Johnny said. "You want to make money fighting, don't you? People like to come to fights to see guys they think are tough."

They sure liked to come to see Bummy all right. They sure liked to come to see him get his brains knocked out.

The first time Johnny Attell ever heard of Bummy was one day when Johnny was coming out of the Grove and Froike stopped him. Froike used to run the gym at Beecher's and handle kids in the amateurs, and he was standing there talking to Johnny under the Myrtle Avenue El.

"Also I got a real good ticket seller for you," he said to Johnny after a while.

"I could use one," Johnny said.

"Only I have to have a special for him," Froike said. "No eliminations."

"What's his name?" Johnny said.

"Giovanni Pasconi," Froike said.

"Bring him around," Johnny said.

The next week Johnny put the kid in with a tough colored boy named Johnny Williams. The kid got the hell punched out of him, but he sold $200 worth of tickets.

"He didn't do too bad," Johnny said to Froike after the fight. "I'll put him back next week."

"Only this time get him an easier opponent," Froike said.

"You get him your own opponent," Johnny said. "As long as he can sell that many tickets I don't care who he fights."

The next week Johnny put him back and he licked the guy. After the fight Johnny was walking out and he saw the kid and Froike with about 20 people around them, all of them talking Yiddish.

"Come here, Froike," Johnny said.

"What's the matter?" Froike said.

"What is this guy," Johnny said, "a Wop or a Jew?"

"He's a Jew," Froike said. "His right name's Davidoff. He's only 15, so we borrowed Pasconi's card."

"He can sure sell tickets," Johnny said.

Bummy could sell anything. That's the way Bummy learned to fight, selling. He used to sell off a pushcart on Blake Avenue. He used to sell berries in the spring and tomatoes and watermelons in the summer and apples in the fall and potatoes and onions and beans in the winter, and there are a lot of pushcarts on Blake Avenue and Bummy used to have to fight to hold his spot.

"I was the best tomato salesman in the world," Bummy was bragging once.

It was right after he knocked out Bob Montgomery in the Garden. He stiffened him in 63 seconds and he was getting $15,000, and when the sports writers came into his dressing room all he wanted to talk about was how good he could sell tomatoes.

"You go over to Jersey and get them yourself," he was telling the sports writers. "Then you don't have to pay the middle guy. You don't put them in boxes, because when you put them in boxes it looks like you're getting ready to lam. When you only got a few around it looks like you can't get rid of them so what you gotta do is pile them all up and holler: 'I gotta get rid of these. I'm gonna give 'em away!'"

The sports writers couldn't get over that. There was a lot they couldn't get over about Bummy.

When Johnny turned Bummy pro he wasn't impressed by his fighting, only his following. Every time Bummy fought for Johnny in the Grove he'd bring a couple of hundred guys with him and they'd holler for Bummy. Everybody else would holler for the other guy, because now they knew Bummy was Jewish and the Grove is in a German section of Ridgewood, and this was when Hitler was starting to go good and there was even one of those German beer halls right in the place where the waiters walked around in those short leather pants and wearing fancy vests and funny hats.

The fight that started Bummy was the Friedkin fight. Bummy was just beginning to bang guys out at the Grove and Friedkin was already a hot fighter at the Broadway Arena and they lived only blocks apart. Friedkin was a nice kid, about three years older than Bummy, kind of a studious guy they called Schoolboy Friedkin, and there was nothing between him and Bummy except that they were both coming up and the neighborhood made the match.

Like one day Bummy was standing in the candy store and a couple of guys told him Friedkin was saying he could stiffen Bummy in two heats. Then they went to Friedkin and said Bummy said Friedkin was afraid to fight. At first this didn't take, but they kept it up and one day Bummy was standing with a dame on the corner of Blake and Alabama and Friedkin came along.

"So why don't you two fight?" the dame said.

"Sure, I'll fight," Bummy said, spreading his feet.

"Right here?" Friedkin said. "Right now?"

"Sure," Bummy said.

"I'll fight whenever my manager makes the match," Friedkin said, and he walked away.

Bummy couldn't understand that, because he liked to fight just to fight. He got right in the subway and went over to see Lew Burston in Lew's office on Broadway.

"Never mind making that Friedkin match," he said to Lew.

"Why not?" Lew said.

"Because when I leave here," Bummy said, "I'm going right around to Friedkin's house and I'm gonna wait for him to come out and we're gonna find out right away if I can lick him or he can lick me."

"Are you crazy?" Lew said.

By the time Johnny Attell made the fight outdoors for Dexter Park there was really a fire under it. They had show cards advertising it on the pushcarts on Blake Avenue and Friedkin's old man and Bummy's old man got into an argument on the street, and everybody was talking about it and betting it big. Then it was rained out five nights and Johnny sold the fight to Mike Jacobs and Mike put it into Madison Square Garden.

When Bummy started working for the fight Lew Burston came over to Beecher's to train him. When Bummy got into his ring clothes they chased everybody out of the gym, and Lew told Bummy to hit the big bag. Bummy walked up to the bag and spread his feet and pulled back his left to start his hook and Lew stopped him.

"Throw that hook away," Lew said.

"Why?" Bummy said. "What's wrong with it?"

"Nothing's wrong with it," Lew said, "only for this fight you'll have to lose that hook."

Before that Bummy was nothing but a hooker, but for weeks Lew kept him banging the big bag with rights. Then the night of the fight after Bummy was all taped and ready, Lew took him into the shower off the dressing room and he talked to Bummy.

"Now remember one thing," he said to Bummy. "I can tell you exactly how that other corner is thinking. They've got that other guy eating and sleeping with your hook for weeks. I want you to go out there and I don't want you to throw one right hand until I tell you. If you throw one right before I say so I'll walk right out on you. Do you understand?"

Bummy understood all right, he was like a kid with a new toy. He was a kid with a secret that only Bummy and Lew knew, and he went out there and did like Lew told him. Friedkin came out with his right glued along the side of his head, and for three rounds Bummy just hooked and hooked and Friedkin blocked, and a lot of people thought Friedkin was winning the fight.

"All right," Lew said, after the third round. "Now this time go right out and feint with the left, but throw the right and put everything on it."

"Don't worry," Bummy said.

Bummy walked out and they moved around for almost a minute and then Bummy feinted his hook. When he did Friedkin moved over and Bummy threw the right and Friedkin's head went back and down he went with his legs in the air in his own corner. That was all the fighting there was that night.

Now Bummy was the biggest thing in Brownsville. Al Buck and Hype Igoe and Ed Van Every and Lester Bromberg were writing about him in the New York papers, saying he was the best hooker since Charley White and could also hit with his right, and he had dough for the first time in his life.

He got $14,000 for the Friedkin fight. When he walked down the street the kids followed him, and he bought them leather jackets and baseball gloves and sodas, just to show you what money meant and how he was already looking back at his own life.

When Bummy was a kid nobody bought him anything and he

belonged to a gang called the Cowboys. They used to pull small jobs, and the cops could never find them until one night. One night the cops broke into the flat where the kids used to live with some dames, and they got them all except Bummy who was with his mother that night.

Sure, Bummy was what most people call tough, but if he felt sorry for you and figured you needed him he couldn't do enough. That was the way Bummy met Barbara and fell in love.

Bummy was 19 then and one day he and Shorty were driving around and Shorty said he wanted to go to Kings County Hospital and visit a friend of his who was sick, and there was this girl about 16 years old. They sat around for a while and Shorty did all the talking and then the next time they went to see the girl Shorty was carrying some flowers and he gave them to her.

"From him," Shorty said, meaning Bummy.

When the girl left the hospital Shorty and Bummy drove her home, and then every day for a couple of weeks they used to take her for a ride and to stop off for sodas. One day the three of them were riding together in the front seat and Bummy wasn't saying anything.

"Say, Bobby," Shorty said all of a sudden, "would you like to get married?"

The girl didn't know what to say. She just looked at Shorty.

"Not to me," Shorty said. "To him."

That was the way Bummy got married. That was Bummy's big romance.

After the Friedkin fight Bummy won about three fights quick, and then they made him with Mickey Farber in the St. Nick's. Farber was out of the East Side and had a good record, and one day when Bummy finished his training at Beecher's he was sitting in the locker room soaking his left hand in a pail of ice and talking with Charley.

That was an interesting thing about Bummy's left hand. He used to bang so hard with it that after every fight and after every day he boxed in the gym it used to swell up.

"I think I'll quit fighting," Bummy said to Charley.

"You think you'll quit?" Charley said. "You're just starting to make dough."

"They're making me out a tough guy," Bummy said. "All the news-papers make me a tough guy and I don't like it and I think I'll quit."

"Forget it," Charley said.

When Charley walked out Murder, Inc., walked in. They were all there—Happy and Buggsy and Abie and Harry and the Dasher—and they were looking at Bummy soaking his hand in the ice.

"You hurt your hand?" Buggsy said.

"No," Bummy said. "It's all right."

They walked out again, and they must have gone with a bundle on Farber because the day after Bummy licked Farber he was standing under the El in front of the gym and the mob drove up. They stopped the car right in front of him and they piled out.

"What are you, some wise guy?" Buggsy said.

"What's wrong with you?" Bummy said.

"What's all this you gave us about you had a bad hand?" Buggsy said.

"I didn't say I had a bad hand," Bummy said.

"You did," Buggsy said.

"Listen," Bummy said, spreading his feet the way he used to do it, "if you guys want a fight let's start it."

Buggsy looked at the others and they looked at him. Then they all got in the car and drove off, and if you could have been there and seen that you would have gone for Bummy for it.

That was the bad part about Bummy's rap. Not enough people knew that part of Bummy until it was too late. The people who go to fights don't just go to see some guy win, but they go to see some guy get licked, too. All they knew about Bummy was some of the things they read, and he was the guy they always went to see get licked.

Even the mob that followed Bummy when he was a big name didn't mean anything to him, because he could see through that. He could see they were always grabbing at him for what they could get, and that was the thing he never got over about the time he was train-ing in Billy West's place up in Woodstock, New York.

Bummy went up there after he came out of the Army, just to take off weight, and there are a lot of artists around there. Artists are dif-ferent people, because they don't care what anybody says about a guy and they either like him or they don't like him for what they think he is. They all liked him up there, and Billy used to say that Bummy could have been Mayor of Woodstock.

Billy had a dog that Bummy never forgot, either. Bummy used to run on the roads in the mornings and Billy's dog used to run with him. Every morning they'd go out together and one day another dog came out of a yard and went for Bummy and Billy's dog turned and went after the other dog and chased it off.

"Gee, this dog really likes me," Bummy said, when he got back to the house, and he said it like he couldn't believe it. "He's really my friend."

The fight that really started everybody hating Bummy, though, was the Canzoneri fight in the Garden. It was a bad match and never should have been made, but they made it and all Bummy did was fight it.

Canzoneri was over the hill, but he had been the featherweight champion and the lightweight champion and he had fought the best of his time and they loved him. When Bummy knocked him out it was the only time Tony was knocked out in 180 fights, and so they booed Bummy for it and they waited for him to get licked.

They didn't have to wait too long. After he knocked out Tippy Larkin in five they matched him with Lou Ambers. Just after he started training for Ambers he was in the candy store one day when an argument started between Bummy and a guy named Mersky. Nobody is going to say who started the argument but somebody called Bummy a lousy fighter and it wasn't Bummy. Somebody flipped a piece of hard candy in Bummy's face, too, and that wasn't Bummy either, and after Bummy got done bouncing Mersky up and down Mersky went to the hospital and had some pictures taken and called the cops.

The first Johnny Attell heard about it was the night after it happened. He was walking down Broadway and he met a dick he knew.

"That's too bad about your fighter," the cop said.

"What's the matter with him?" Johnny said.

"What's the matter with him?" the cop said. "There's an eight-state alarm out for him. The newspapers are full of it. He damn near killed a guy in a candy store."

The cops couldn't find Bummy but Johnny found him. He dug up

Gangy, and Gangy drove him around awhile to shake off any cops, and finally Gangy stopped the car in front of an old wooden house and they got out and went in and there was Bummy.

Bummy was sitting in a pair of pajama pants, and that was all he had on. There were four or five other guys there, and they were playing cards.

"Are you crazy?" Johnny said.

"Why?" Bummy said, playing his cards, but looking up.

"If the cops find you here they'll kill you," Johnny said. "You better come with me."

After Johnny talked awhile Bummy got dressed and he went with Johnny. Johnny took him back to New York and got him a haircut and a shave and he called Mike Jacobs. Jacobs told Johnny to take Bummy down to Police Headquarters, and when Johnny did that Sol Strauss, Mike's lawyer, showed up and he got an adjournment in night court for Bummy until after the Ambers fight.

The night Bummy fought Ambers there was Mersky right at ringside. He had on dark glasses and the photographers were all taking his picture and when Ambers beat the hell out of Bummy the crowd loved it.

The crowd, more than Ambers, hurt Bummy that night. He didn't like the licking Ambers gave him, but the hardest part was listening to the crowd and the way they enjoyed it and the things they shouted at him when he came down out of the ring.

"I quit," he said to Johnny in the dressing room. "You know what you can do with fighting?"

Johnny didn't believe him. Johnny was making matches for Jacobs in the Garden then and he matched Bummy with Tony Marteliano, but Bummy wouldn't train.

Only Johnny and Gangy knew this, and one day Johnny came out to Bummy's house and talked with Bummy. When that didn't do any good Lew Burston came out and he talked for four hours, and when he finished Bummy said the same thing.

"I don't want to be a fighter." Bummy said. "I like to fight. I'll fight Marteliano on the street right now, just for fun, but when I'm a fighter everybody picks on me. I want them to leave me alone. All I wanted was a home for my family and I got that and now I just want to hang around my mob on the street."

Johnny still didn't believe it. They put out the show cards, advertising the fight, and one day Bummy saw one of the cards in the window of a bar and he phoned Johnny in Jacobs' office.

"What are you advertising the fight for?" he said, and he was mad. "I told you I'm not gonna fight."

Before Johnny could say anything Jacobs took the phone. Johnny hadn't told him Bummy didn't want to fight.

"How are you, kid?" Jacobs said. "This is Mike."

"Listen, you toothless ———," Bummy said. "What are you advertising me for? I'm not gonna fight."

He hung up. Mike put the phone back and turned around and when he did Bummy was suspended and Johnny was out of the Garden and back in the Ridgewood Grove.

When Bummy heard what had happened to Johnny he went over to the Grove to see him. All the time Johnny was in the Garden Bummy was a little suspicious of him, like he was a capitalist, but now he was different.

"I came over to tell you something," he said to Johnny. "I'm gonna fight."

"Forget it," Johnny said. "You can't fight."

"Who says I can't fight?" Bummy said.

"The New York Boxing Commission," Johnny said. "You're suspended."

"Let's fight out of town," Bummy said. "We'll fight where I'm not suspended."

Johnny did it better. He took Bummy back to Mike and Bummy apologized and Bummy fought Marteliano. For nine rounds they were even, and with ten seconds to go in the last round Bummy landed the hook. Marteliano went down and the referee counted nine and the bell rang and it was another big one for Bummy and he was going again.

It was Johnny's idea to get Marteliano back, but Bummy saw Fritzie Zivic lick Henry Armstrong for the welterweight title and he wanted Zivic. If you knew the two guys you knew this was a bad match for Bummy, because he just didn't know how to fight like Zivic.

There were a lot of people, you see, who called Bummy a dirty fighter, but the Zivic fight made them wrong. The Zivic fight proved that Bummy didn't know how to do it.

When he came out of the first clinch Bummy's eyes were red and he was rubbing them and the crowd started to boo Zivic. In the second clinch it was the same thing, and at the end of the round Bummy was roaring.

"He's trying to blind me," he kept saying in the corner. "He's trying to blind me."

When it starred again in the second round Bummy blew. He pushed Zivic off and he dropped his hands and that crazy look came on that wide face of his and they could hear him in the crowd.

"All right, you ———," he said, "if you want to fight dirty, okay."

He walked right into Zivic and he started belting low. There was no trying to hide anything, and the crowd started to roar and before it was over people were on their chairs throwing things and the cops were in the ring and Bummy was fined $2,500 and suspended for life.

They meant it to be for life—which wouldn't have been very long at that, when you figure Bummy lived to be all of 26—but it didn't work out that way. About three weeks after the fight Bummy walked into Johnny's office with Shorty and Mousie, and they sat around for a time and Johnny could see Bummy was lost.

"You know what you ought to do?" Johnny said. "You ought to join the Army for a while until this blows over."

This was in December of 1940, before we got into the war. For a while Bummy sat there thinking, not saying anything.

"Could my buddies go with me?" he said.

"Sure," Johnny said.

So Johnny called up the recruiting officer and Bummy and Shorty and Mousie showed up and there were photographers there and it was a big show. Everybody was for it, and Ed Van Every wrote a story in *The Sun* in which he said this was a great move because the Army would teach Bummy discipline and get him in good physical shape.

That was a laugh. The first thing the Army did was split Bummy and Shorty and Mousie up and send them to different camps.

They sent Bummy to Camp Hulen, Texas, and their idea of discipline was to have Bummy cleaning latrines with a toothbrush.

"You got me into this," Bummy used to write Johnny. "I'm going crazy, so before I slug one of these officers you better get me out."

Johnny didn't get him out, but he got Mike Jacobs to get Bummy a leave to fight Zivic in the Polo Grounds for Army Emergency Relief. Bummy used to fight best at about 147 pounds, and when he came back from Texas he weighed close to 200.

"You look sharp in that uniform, Al," Zivic said to him when they signed for the bout.

"I'm glad you like it," Bummy said. "You put me in it."

You can imagine how Bummy was looking to get back at Zivic, but he couldn't do it. He hadn't fought for eight months, and Zivic was a real good fighter and he put lumps all over Bummy and in the tenth round the referee stopped it. They had to find Bummy to take him back to camp. They found him with his wife and they shipped him back, but then the Japs bombed Pearl Harbor and the Army decided it had enough trouble without Bummy and they turned him loose.

Bummy fought some of his best fights after that. He couldn't get his license back in New York but he fought in places like Holyoke and Bridgeport and Washington and Philadelphia and Elizabeth, New Jersey, and Boston. He didn't like it in those places, but he had to live, and so no matter where he fought he would always drive back to Brownsville after the fight and sometimes it would be four o'clock in the morning before he and Johnny would get in.

It's something when you think about Bummy and Brownsville, when you think of the money he made, almost a quarter of a million dollars, and the things he had thrown at him and the elegant places he could have gone. It was like what Lew Burston said, though, when he said the Supreme was Bummy's Opera, and the Supreme is a movie house on Livonia Avenue.

You have to remember, too, that Brownsville is only a subway ride from Broadway, but Bummy had never seen a real Broadway show until Chicky Bogad sent Bummy and Barbara to see *Hellzapoppin* the night before the second Farber fight.

"How long has this been going on?" Bummy said when they came out.

"How long has what been going on?" Chicky said.

"People like that on a stage," Bummy said.

"People on a stage?" Chicky said. "For years and years. For long before they had movies."

"Is that right? I'll have to see more of that," Bummy said, but he never did.

All of those fights Bummy had out of town were murders, too, because Bummy wasn't hard to hit, but the people liked to see him get hit and when the Republicans got back in power in New York, Fritzie Zivic put in a word for Bummy, saying he guessed he had egged the kid on, and Bummy got his license back. That's when they matched him with Montgomery.

"What you have to do in this one," they kept telling Bummy, "is walk right out, throw your right, and miss with it. Montgomery will grab your right arm, and that will turn you around southpaw and then you hit him with the hook."

They knew that was the only chance Bummy had, because if Montgomery got by the first round he figured to move around Bummy and cut him up. They drilled Bummy on it over and over, and they kept talking about it in the dressing room that night.

"Now what are you going to do?" Johnny Attell said to Bummy.

"I'm gonna walk right out and miss with my right," Bummy said. "He'll grab my arm and that'll turn me around southpaw and I'll throw my hook."

"Okay," Johnny said. "I guess you know it."

Bummy sat down then on one of the benches. He had his gloves on and his robe over him and he was ready to go when there was a knock on the door.

"Don't come out yet, Davis," one of the commission guys said through the door. "They're selling some War Bonds first."

When Bummy heard that he looked up from where he was sitting and you could see he was sweating, and then he keeled right over on the floor on his face. Johnny and Freddie Brown rushed over and picked him up and they stretched him on the rubbing table and Freddie brought him to, and now they weren't worried about whether Bummy would do what they told him. All they were worried about was whether they could get him in the ring.

They got him in the ring and Burston had him repeat what he was supposed to do. When the bell rang he walked right out and threw his right and missed around the head. Montgomery grabbed the arm and turned Bummy around, and when he did Bummy threw the hook and Montgomery went down. When he got up Bummy hit him again and that's all there was to it.

Montgomery was 10 to 1 over Bummy that night and they couldn't believe it. Bummy got $15,000 for that fight and he had borrowed $1,500 from Jacobs and the next day when Mike paid him off he told Bummy to forget the grand and a half.

"Take it out," Bummy said, throwing the dough on the desk. "You know damn well if he kayoed me like you thought he would you were gonna take it out."

Bummy thought he'd never be broke again. He got $34,000 the night Beau Jack beat him and $15,000 when Armstrong stopped him. Then somebody sold him the idea of buying that bar and grill and somebody else sold him a couple of nice horses and even after Dudy bought the bar and grill from him he was broke.

He should have been in training for Morris Reif the night he was shot. Johnny wanted him to fight Reif, just for the dough and to go as far as he could, but Bummy said that a lot of his friends would bet him and he didn't think he could beat Reif, so instead he was sitting in the back of Dudy's drinking beer and singing.

Bummy used to think he could sing like a Jewish cantor. He couldn't sing, but he was trying that night, sitting with some other guys and a cop who was off duty, when he looked through that lattice work at the bar and he saw the four guys with the guns.

"What the hell is this?" he said.

He got up and walked out and you know what happened. When Bummy stiffened the first guy one of the others fired and the bullet went into Bummy's neck. Then the three picked up the guy Bummy hit and they ran for the car. One of the guys with Bummy stuffed his handkerchief in the collar of Bummy's shirt to stop the blood, and Bummy got up and ran for the car. When he did they opened up from the car, and Bummy went flat on his face in the mud.

When the car started to pull away the cop who had been in the back ran out and fired. He hit one guy in the spine, and that guy died in Texas, and he hit another in the shoulder. The guy with the slug in his shoulder walked around with it for weeks, afraid to go to a doctor, and then one night a cop in plain clothes heard a couple of guys talking in a bar.

"You know that jerk is still walking around with the bullet in his shoulder?" the one said. "What bullet?" the second one said.

"The Bummy Davis bullet," the first said.

The cop followed them out, and when they split up he followed the first guy and got it out of him. Then the cops picked up the guy with the bullet and he sang. They picked up the other two in Kansas City and they're doing 20 to life. They were just punks, and they called themselves the Cowboys, the same as Bummy's old gang did.

It was a big funeral Bummy had. Johnny and Lew Burston paid for it. The papers had made Bummy a hero, and the newsreels took pictures outside the funeral parlor and at the cemetery. It looked like everybody in Brownsville was there.

Red Smith

Walter Wellesley Smith (1905–1982), better known as Red, set the standard for elegant prose in a daily sports column. He apprenticed on newspapers in Philadelphia, St. Louis, and Milwaukee before Stanley Woodward, the legendary editor he called "Coach," ushered him into the big time at the *New York Herald Tribune* in 1945. That bastion of great writing was where Smith published the following post-mortem on Joe Louis's 1951 fight with Rocky Marciano. When the *Trib* folded in 1966, Smith moved to *The New York Times*. He won a Pulitzer Prize there in 1976 for essays that revealed a viewpoint that had somehow become younger and more open-minded, yet he retained his old whimsy and affection for baseball, fishing, horseracing, and prize-fighting. Even when he was mugged in the chaos that erupted after the third Muhammad Ali–Ken Norton fight at Yankee Stadium, Smith made of the experience what he could. He was on the small side—"no bigger than a growler of beer," as he once wrote of someone else—and the young man who stole his wallet was both larger and more garishly dressed. The lad's purple pants and lime green shirt inspired a line that was vintage Red Smith: "I wonder what he's going to do with my Brooks Brothers charge card."

Night for Joe Louis

JOE LOUIS lay on his stomach on a rubbing table with his right ear pillowed on a folded towel, his left hand in a bucket of ice on the floor. A handler massaged his left ear with ice. Joe still wore his old dressing gown of blue and red—for the first time, one was aware of how the colors had faded—and a raincoat had been spread on top of that.

This was an hour before midnight of October 26, 1951. It was the evening of a day that dawned July 4, 1934, when Joe Louis became a professional fistfighter and knocked out Jack Kracken in Chicago for a fifty-dollar purse. The night was a long time on the way, but it had to come.

Ordinarily, small space is reserved here for sentimentality about professional fighters. For seventeen years, three months, and twenty-two days Louis fought for money. He collected millions. Now the punch that was launched seventeen years ago had landed. A young man, Rocky Marciano, had knocked the old man out. The story was ended. That was all except—

Well, except that this time he was lying down in his dressing room in the catacombs of Madison Square Garden. Memory retains scores of pictures of Joe in his dressing room, sitting up, relaxed, answering questions in his slow, thoughtful way. This time only, he was down.

His face was squashed against the padding of the rubbing table, muffling his words. Newspapermen had to kneel on the floor like supplicants in a tight little semicircle and bring their heads close to his lips to hear him. They heard him say that Marciano was a good puncher, that the best man had won, that he wouldn't know until Monday whether this had been his last fight.

He said he never lost consciousness when Marciano knocked him through the ropes and Ruby Goldstein, the referee, stopped the fight. He said that if he'd fallen in midring he might have got up inside ten seconds, but he doubted that he could have got back through the ropes in time.

They asked whether Marciano punched harder than Max Schmeling did fifteen years ago, on the only other night when Louis was stopped.

"This kid," Joe said, "knocked me out with what? Two punches. Schmeling knocked me out with—musta been a hundred punches. But," Joe said, "I was twenty-two years old. You can take more then than later on."

"Did age count tonight, Joe?"

Joe's eyes got sleepy. "Ugh," he said, and bobbed his head.

The fight mob was filling the room. "How did you feel tonight?" Ezzard Charles was asked. Joe Louis was the hero of Charles' boyhood. Ezzard never wanted to fight Joe, but finally he did and won. Then and thereafter Louis became just another opponent who sometimes disparaged Charles as a champion.

"Uh," Charles said, hesitating. "Good fight."

"You didn't feel sorry, Ezzard?"

"No," he said, with a kind of apologetic smile that explained this was just a prize fight in which one man knocked out an opponent.

"How did you feel?" Ray Arcel was asked. For years and years Arcel trained opponents for Joe and tried to help them whip him, and in a decade and a half he dug tons of inert meat out of the resin.

"I felt very bad," Ray said.

It wasn't necessary to ask how Marciano felt. He is young and strong and undefeated. He is rather clumsy and probably always will be, because he has had the finest of teachers, Charley Goldman, and Charley hasn't been able to teach him skill. But he can punch. He can take a punch. It is difficult to see how he can be stopped this side of the heavyweight championship.

It is easy to say, and it will be said, that it wouldn't have been like this with the Louis of ten years ago. It isn't a surpassingly bright thing to say, though, because this isn't ten years ago. The Joe Louis of October 25, 1951, couldn't whip Rocky Marciano, and that's the only Joe Louis there was in the Garden. That one was going to lose on points in a dreary fight that would have left everything at loose ends. It would have been a clear victory for Marciano, but not conclusive. Joe might not have been convinced.

Then Rocky hit Joe a left hook and knocked him down. Then Rocky hit him another hook and knocked him out. A right to the neck knocked him out of the ring. And out of the fight business. The last wasn't necessary, but it was neat. It wrapped the package, neat and tidy.

An old man's dream ended. A young man's vision of the future opened wide. Young men have visions, old men have dreams. But the place for old men to dream is beside the fire.

John Lardner

If you trace the careers of Dan Jenkins, Jim Murray, and Rick Reilly, the reigning funny men in contemporary American sportswriting, you will find a common source of inspiration: John Lardner (1913–1960). With his column in *Newsweek*, Lardner evoked laughter that didn't stop with his premature death, a month before his forty-eighth birthday. He was the son of Ring Lardner, baseball writer and legendary humorist, but he made his own way. He broke into print at *The New Yorker* at nineteen with a piece on the theater, and ultimately became a nearsighted but fearless World War II correspondent in both Europe and the Pacific. When he came home, Lardner augmented his 750-word *Newsweek* epistles with long, impeccably reported stories for magazines like *True* and *Sport*. Time and again he turned to boxing, deconstructing such seminal figures as Doc Kearns and Battling Siki. His best-remembered story, however, is his 1954 piece about Stanley Ketchel (1886–1910), a wild-haired middleweight who could be tamed only one way. It begins with what Red Smith called "the greatest novel ever written in one sentence."

Down Great Purple Valleys

S TANLEY KETCHEL was twenty-four years old when he was fatally shot in the back by the common-law husband of the lady who was cooking his breakfast.

That was in 1910. Up to 1907 the world at large had never heard of Ketchel. In the three years between his first fame and his murder, he made an impression on the public mind such as few men before or after him have made. When he died, he was already a folk hero and a legend. At once, his friends, followers and biographers began to speak of his squalid end, not as a shooting or a killing, but as an assassination—as though Ketchel were Lincoln. The thought is blasphemous, maybe, but not entirely cockeyed. The crude, brawling, low-living, wild-eyed, sentimental, dissipated, almost illiterate hobo, who broke every Commandment at his disposal, had this in common with a handful of Presidents, generals, athletes and soul-savers, as well as with fabled characters like Paul Bunyan and Johnny Appleseed: he was the stuff of myth. He entered mythology at a younger age than most of the others, and he still holds stoutly to his place there.

There's a story by Ernest Hemingway, "The Light of the World," in which a couple of boys on the road sit listening to a pair of seedy harlots as they trade lies about how they loved the late Steve Ketchel in person. This is the mythology of the hustler—the shiniest lie the girls can manage, the invocation of the top name in the folklore of sporting life. Ketchel is also an article of barroom faith. Francis Albertanti, a boxing press agent, likes to tell about the fight fan who was spitting beer and adulation at Mickey Walker one night in a saloon soon after Mickey had won a big fight.

"Kid," said the fan to Walker, "you're the greatest middleweight that ever came down the road. The greatest. And don't let anybody tell you different."

"What about Ketchel?" said Albertanti in the background, stirring up trouble.

"Ketchel?" screamed the barfly, galvanized by the name. He grabbed Walker's coat. "Listen, bum!" he said to Walker, "You couldn't lick one side of Steve Ketchel on the best day you ever saw!"

Thousands of stories have been told about Ketchel. As befits a figure of myth, they are half truth—at best—and half lies. He was lied about in his lifetime by those who knew him best, including himself. Ketchel had a lurid pulp-fiction writer's mind. He loved the clichés of melodrama. His own story of his life, as he told it to Nat Fleischer, his official biographer, is full of naïve trimmings about bullies twice his size whom he licked as a boy, about people who saved him from certain death in his youth and whom he later visited in a limousine to repay a hundredfold. These tall tales weren't necessary. The truth was strong enough. Ketchel was champion of the world, perhaps the best fist fighter of his weight in history, a genuine wild man in private life, a legitimate all-around meteor, who needed no faking of his passport to legend. But he couldn't resist stringing his saga with tinsel. And it's something more than coincidence that his three closest friends toward the end of his life were three of the greatest Munchausens in America: Willus Britt, a fight manager; Wilson Mizner, a wit and literary con man; and Hype Igoe, a romantic journalist. They are all dead now. In their time, they juiced up Ketchel's imagination, and he juiced up theirs.

Mizner, who managed Ketchel for a short time, would tell of a day when he went looking for the fighter and found him in bed, smoking opium, with a blonde and a brunette. Well, the story is possible. It has often been said that Ketchel smoked hop, and he knew brunettes by the carload, and blondes by the platoon. But it's more likely that Mizner manufactured the tale to hang one of his own lines on: "What did I do?" he would say. "What could I do? I told them to move over."

Ketchel had the same effect on Willus Britt's fictional impulse. When Britt, Mizner's predecessor as manager, brought Ketchel east for the first time from California, where he won fame, he couldn't help gilding the lily. Willus put him in chaps and spurs and billed him as a cowboy. Ketchel was never a cowboy, though he would have loved to have been one. He was a semi-retired hobo (even after he had money, he sometimes rode the rods from choice) and an ex-bouncer of lushes in a bagnio.

"He had the soul of a bouncer," says Dumb Dan Morgan, one of the few surviving boxing men who knew him well, "but a bouncer who enjoyed the work."

One of Bill Mizner's best bons mots was the one he uttered when he heard of Ketchel's death: "Tell 'em to start counting ten, and he'll get up." Ketchel would have lapped it up. He would have liked even better such things as Igoe used to write after Ketchel's murder—". . . the assassin's bullet that sent Steve down into great purple valley." The great purple valley was to Ketchel's taste. It would have made him weep. He wept when he saw a painting, on a wall of a room in a whorehouse, of little sheep lost in a storm. He wept late at night in Joey Adams' nook on Forty-third Street just off Broadway when song writers and singers like Harry Tierney and Violinsky played ballads on the piano. "Mother" songs tore Ketchel's heart out. He had a voice like a crow's, but he used to dream of building a big house someday in Belmont, Michigan, near his home town of Grand Rapids. In it there would be a music room where he would gather with hundreds of old friends and sing all night.

The record of his life is soaked in fable and sentiment. The bare facts are these:

Ketchel was born Stanislaus Kiecal on September 14, 1886. His father was a native of Russia, of Polish stock. His mother, Polish-American, was fourteen when Ketchel was born. His friends called him Steve. He won the world's middleweight championship in California at the age of twenty-one. He lost it to Billy Papke by a knockout and won it back by a knockout. He was champion when he died by the gun. He stood five feet nine. He had a strong, clean-cut Polish face. His hair was blondish and his eyes were blue-gray.

When you come to the statement made by many who knew him that they were "devil's eyes," you border the land of fancy in which Ketchel and his admirers lived. But there was a true fiendishness in the way he fought. Like Jack Dempsey, he always gave the impression of wanting to kill his man. Philadelphia Jack O'Brien, a rhetoric-lover whom he twice knocked unconscious, called Ketchel "an example of tumultuous ferocity." He could hit powerfully with each hand, and he had the stamina to fight at full speed through twenty- and thirty-round fights. He knocked down Jack Johnson, the finest heavyweight of his time, perhaps of any time, who outweighed him by thirty to forty pounds. He had a savagery of temperament to match his strength. From a combination of ham and hot temper, and to make things tougher on the world around him, he carried a Colt .44—Hype Igoe always spoke of it dramatically as the "blue gun"—which was at his side when he slept and in his lap when he sat down to eat. At his training camp at the Woodlawn Inn near Woodlawn Cemetery in the Bronx, New York, Ketchel once fired the gun through his bedroom door and shot his faithful trainer Pete (Pete the Goat) Stone in the leg when Pete came to wake him up for work. Ketchel then leaped into his big red Lozier car and drove Stone to the hospital for treatment.

"He sobbed all the way," said Igoe, "driving with one hand and propping up Pete's head with the other."

The great moments of Ketchel's life were divided among three cities: San Francisco, New York, and Butte, Montana. Each city was at its romantic best when Ketchel came upon it.

Ketchel was a kid off the road, looking for jobs or handouts, when he hit Butte in 1902 at the age of sixteen. He had run away from Grand Rapids by freight when he was fourteen. In Chicago, as Ketchel used to tell it, a kindly saloonkeeper named Socker Flanagan (whose name and function came straight out of Horatio Alger) saw him lick the usual Algeresque bully twice his size and gave him a job. It was Flanagan, according to Ketchel, who taught him to wear boxing gloves and who gave him the name of Ketchel. After a time the tough Polish boy moved west. He worked as a field hand in North Dakota. He went over the Canadian line to Winnipeg, and from there he described a great westering arc, through mining camps, sawmills, and machine shops, riding the rods of the Canadian National and the Canadian Pacific through rugged north-country settlements like Revelstoke, Kamloops and Arrowhead, in British Columbia, till he fetched up on the West Coast at Victoria. He had a .22 rifle, he used to recall, that he carried like a hunter as he walked the roads. In Victoria, he sold the .22 for boat fare down across the straits and Puget Sound to Seattle. In Seattle he jumped a Northern Pacific freight to Montana. A railway dick threw him off the train in Silver Bow, and he walked the remaining few miles of cinders into Butte.

Butte was a bona fide dime-novel town in 1902. It was made for Ketchel. Built on what they called "the richest hill in the world," it mined half the country's copper. The town looked sooty and grim by day, but it was red and beautiful by night, a patch of fire and light in the Continental Divide. As the biggest city on the northwest line between Minneapolis and Spokane, it had saloons, theaters, hotels, honky-tonks, and fight clubs by the score. Name actors and name boxers played the town. When Ketchel struck the state, artillery was as common as collar buttons.

Ketch caught on as a bellhop at a hotel and place of amusement named the Copper Queen. One day, he licked the bouncer—and became bouncer. As Dan Morgan says, he enjoyed the work; so much so that he expanded it, fighting all comers for twenty dollars a week for the operator of the Casino Theater, when he was not bulldogging drunks at the Copper Queen. If Butte was made for Ketchel, so was the fight game. He used to say that he had 250 fights around this time that do not show in the record book. In 1903 he was already a welterweight, well grown and well muscled.

All hands, including Ketchel, agree that his first fight of record, with Jack (Kid) Tracy, May 2, 1903, was a "gimmick" fight, a sample of a larcenous tradition older than the Marquis of Queensberry. The gimmick was a sandbag. Tracy's manager, Texas Joe Halliday, who offered ten dollars to anyone who could go ten rounds with his boy, would stand behind a thin curtain at the rear of the stages on which

Tracy fought. When Tracy maneuvered the victim against the curtain, Texas Joe would sandbag him. Ketchel, tipped off, reversed the maneuver. He backed Tracy against the curtain, and he and the manager hit the Kid at the same time. The book says, KO, 1 round.

The book also says that Ketchel lost a fight to Maurice Thompson in 1904. This calls for an explanation, and, as always, the Ketchel legend has one ready. A true folk hero does not get beat, unless, as sometimes happened to Hercules, Samson, and Ketchel, he is jobbed. At the start of the Thompson fight a section of balcony seats broke down. Ketchel turned, laughing, to watch—and Thompson rabbit-punched him so hard from behind that Ketch never fully recovered. In the main, the young tiger from Michigan needed no excuses. He fought like a demon. He piled one knockout on top of another. He would ride the freights as far as northern California, to towns like Redding and Marysville, carrying his trunks and gloves in a bundle, and win fights there. In 1907, after he knocked out George Brown, a fighter with a good Coast reputation, in Sacramento, he decided to stay in California. It was the right move. In later years, when Ketchel had become mythological, hundreds of storytellers "remembered" his Butte adventures, but in 1907 no one had yet thought to mention them. In California the climate was golden, romantic, and right for fame. And overnight Ketchel became famous.

When minstrels sing of Ketch's fights with Joe Thomas, they like to call Thomas a veteran, a seasoned, wise old hand, a man fighting a boy. That fact is, Thomas was two weeks older than Ketchel. But he had reputation and experience. When Ketchel fought him a twenty-round draw in Marysville—and then on Labor Day, 1907, knocked him out in thirty-two rounds in the San Francisco suburb of Colma—Ketchel burst into glory as suddenly as a rocket.

Now there was nothing left between him and the middleweight title but Jack Twin Sullivan. The Sullivans from Boston, Jack and Mike, were big on the Coast. Jack had as good a claim to the championship (vacated by Tommy Ryan the year before) as any middleweight in the world. But he told Ketchel, "You have to lick my brother Mike first." Ketchel knocked out Mike Twin Sullivan, a welter, in one round, as he had fully expected to do. Before the fight he saw one of

Mike's handlers carrying a pail of oranges and asked what they were for. "Mike likes an orange between rounds," said the handler.

"He should have saved the money," said Ketchel.

Mike Twin needed no fruit; Jack Twin was tougher. Jack speared Ketchel with many a good left before Ketchel, after a long body campaign, went up to the head and knocked his man cold in the twentieth round. On that day, May 9, 1908, the Michigan freight-stiff became the recognized world champion.

His two historic fights with Bill Papke came in the same year. Papke, the Illinois Thunderbolt from Spring Valley, Illinois, was a rugged counterpuncher with pale, pompadoured hair and great hitting power. Earlier in 1908 Ketchel had won a decision from him in Milwaukee. The first of their two big ones took place in Vernon, on the fringe of Los Angeles, on September 7. Jim Jeffries, the retired undefeated heavyweight champion—Ketchel's only rival as a national idol—was the referee. The legend-makers do not have to look far to find an excuse for what happened to Ketchel in this one. It happened at the start, and in plain sight. In those days it was customary for fighters to shake hands—not just touch gloves—when the first round began. Ketchel held out his hand. Papke hit him a left on the jaw and a stunning right between the eyes. Ketchel's eyes were shut almost tight from then on; his brain was dazed throughout the twelve rounds it took Papke to beat him down and win the championship.

Friends of Ketchel used to say that to work himself into the murderous mood he wanted for every fight he would tell himself stories about his opponents: "The sonofabitch insulted my mother. I'll kill the sonofabitch!" No self-whipping was needed for the return bout with Papke. The fight took place in San Francisco on November 26, eleven weeks after Papke's treacherous *coup d'état* in Los Angeles. It lasted longer than it might have—eleven rounds; but this, they tell you, was the result of pure sadism on Ketchel's part. Time after time Ketchel battered the Thunderbolt to the edge of coma; time after time he let him go, for the sake of doing it over again. It was wonderful to the crowd that Papke came out of it alive. At that, he survived Ketchel by twenty-six years, though he died just as abruptly. In 1936, Billy killed himself and his wife at Newport Beach, California.

It was around this time that Willus Britt brought his imagination to bear on Ketchel—that is, he moved in. Willus was a man who lived by piecework. An ex-Yukon pirate, he was San Francisco's leading fight manager and sport, wearing the brightest clothes in town and smoking the biggest cigars. He once had a piece of San Francisco itself—a block of flats that was knocked out by the 1906 earthquake. When Willus sued the city for damages, the city said the quake was an act of God. Willus pointed out that churches had been destroyed. Was that an act of God? The city said it didn't know, and would Willus please shut the door on the way out?

Britt won Ketchel over during some tour of San Francisco night life by his shining haberdashery and his easy access to champagne and showgirls. In this parlay, champagne ran second with Ketchel. He did drink, some, and the chances are that he smoked a little opium. But he didn't need either—he was one of those people who are born with half a load on. "His genes were drunk" is the way one barroom biologist puts it. His chief weaknesses were women, bright clothes, sad music, guns, fast cars, and candy.

Once, in 1909, after Britt had taken him in high style (Pullman, not freight) from the Coast to New York, Ketchel was seen driving on Fifth Avenue in an open carriage, wearing a red kimono and eating peanuts and candy, some of which he tossed to bystanders along the way. The kimono, gift of a lady friend, was a historical part of Ketchel's equipment. A present-day manager remembers riding up to Woodlawn Inn, Ketch's New York "training" quarters, with Britt one day, in Willus's big car with locomotive sound effects. As they approached the Inn, the guest saw a figure in red negligee emerge from the cemetery near by.

"What's that?" he asked, startled.

"That's Steve," said Britt, chewing his cigar defiantly.

Britt looked up Wilson Mizner as soon as he and Ketchel reached New York. Mizner, a fellow Californian and Yukon gold-rusher, was supposed to know "the New York angles"; Britt signed him on as an unsalaried assistant manager. Free of charge, Mizner taught Ketchel the theory of evolution one evening (or so the legend developed by Mizner runs). Much later the same night Mizner and Britt found Ketchel at home, studying a bowl of goldfish and cursing softly.

"What's the matter?" said Mizner.

"I've been watching these —— fish for nine hours," snarled Ketchel, "and they haven't changed a bit."

Mizner, a part-time playwright at this time and a full-time deadbeat and Broadway nightwatchman, was a focus of New York life in 1909–10, the gay, brash, sentimental life of sad ballads and corny melodrama, of late hours and high spending, in which Ketchel passed the last years of his life. Living at the old Bartholdi Hotel at Broadway and 23rd Street, playing the cabarets, brothels and gambling joints, Ketchel was gayer and wilder than ever before. He still fought. He had to, for he, Britt, and Mizner (unsalaried or not) were a costly team to support. Physically the champion was going downhill in a handcar, but he had the old savagery in the ring. His 1909 fight with Philadelphia Jack O'Brien ended in a riddle. O'Brien, a master, stabbed Ketchel foolish for seven rounds. In the eighth, O'Brien began to tire. In the ninth, Ketchel knocked him down for nine. In the tenth and last round, with seven seconds to go, Ketchel knocked O'Brien unconscious. Jack's head landed in a square flat box of sawdust just outside the ropes near his own corner, which he and his handlers used for a spittoon.

"Get up, old man !" yelled Major A. J. Drexel Biddle, Jack's society rooter from Philadelphia. "Get up, and the fight is yours!"

But Jack, in the sawdust, was dead to the world. The bout ended before he could be counted out. By New York boxing law at the time, it was a no-decision fight. O'Brien had clearly won it on points; just as clearly, Ketchel had knocked him out. Connoisseurs are still arguing the issue today. Win or lose, it was a big one for Ketchel, for O'Brien was a man with a great record, who had fought and beaten heavyweights. The next goal was obvious. Jack Johnson, the colored genius, held the heavyweight championship which Jim Jeffries had resigned. To hear the managers, promoters, and race patriots of the time tell it, the white race was in jeopardy—Johnson had to be beaten. Ketchel had no more than a normal share of the race patriotism of that era; but he was hungry, as always, for blood and cash, and he thought he could beat the big fellow. Britt signed him for the heavyweight title match late in the summer of 1909, the place to be Sunny Jim Coffroth's arena in Colma, California, the date, October 16.

"At the pace he's living, I can whip him," Ketch told a newspaperman one day. He himself had crawled in, pale and shaky, at 5 A.M. the previous morning. Johnson—on whom, at thirty-one, years of devotion to booze and women had had no noticeable effect whatever—called around to visit Ketchel in New York one afternoon in his own big car. He was wearing his twenty-pound driving coat, and he offered to split a bottle of grape with the challenger.

"I wish I'd asked him to bet that coat on the fight," said Ketchel afterward. "I could use it to scare the crows on my farm."

Ketchel was still dreaming of the farm, the big house in Belmont, Michigan, where he would live with his family and friends when he retired. He had a little less than one year of dreams left to him. One of these almost came true—or so the legend-makers tell you—in the bright sunshine of Colma on October 16. Actually, legends about the Ketchel–Johnson fight must compete with facts, for the motion pictures of the fight—very good ones they are, too—are still accessible to anyone who wants to see them. But tales of all kinds continue to flourish. It's said that there was a two-way agreement to go easy for ten rounds, to make the films more saleable. It's also said, by Johnson (in print) and his friends, that the whole bout was meant to be in the nature of an exhibition, with no damage done, and that Ketchel tried a double cross. It's also said, by the Ketchel faction, that it was a shooting match all the way and that Steve almost beat the big man fairly and squarely. Ketchel fans say Ketchel weighed 160; neutrals say 170; the official announcement said 180¼. Officially, Johnson weighed 205½; Ketchel's fans say 210 or 220.

There's no way of checking the tonnage today. About the fight, the films show this: Johnson, almost never using his right hand, carried his man for eleven rounds. "Carried" is almost literally the right word, for Johnson several times propped up the smaller fighter to keep him from falling. Once or twice he wrestled or threw him across the ring. Jack did not go "easy"; he did ruthless, if restrained, work with his left. One side of Ketchel's face looked as dark as hamburger after a few rounds. But in the twelfth round all parties threw the book away, and what followed was pure melodrama.

Ketchel walked out for the twelfth looking frail and desperate, his long hair horse-tailed by sweat, his long, dark trunks clinging to his legs. Pitiful or not to look at, he had murder in his mind. He feinted with his left, and drove a short right to Johnson's head. No one had ever hit Li'l Artha squarely with a right before, though the best artists had tried. Ketchel had the power of a heavyweight; and Johnson went down. Then, pivoting on his left arm on the canvas, he rolled himself across the ring and onto his knees. In the film you can almost see thoughts racing through his brain—and they are not going any faster than referee Jack Welch's count. Perhaps it was the speed of this toll that made up his mind. Johnson, a cocky fellow, always figured he had the whole world, not just one boxer, to beat, and he was always prepared to take care of himself. He scrambled to his feet at what Welch said was eight seconds. Ketchel, savage and dedicated, came at him. The big guy drove his right to Steve's mouth, and it was over.

No fighter has ever looked more wholly out than Ketchel did, flat on his back in the middle of the ring—though once, just before the count reached ten, he gave a lunge, like a troubled dreamer, that brought his shoulders off the floor. This spasmodic effort to rise while unconscious is enough to make the Ketchel legend real, without trimmings. It was an hour before Ketchel recovered his senses. Two of his teeth impaled his lip, and a couple more, knocked off at the gum, were caught in Johnson's glove.

Ketchel recuperated from the Johnson fight at Hot Springs, Arkansas. Sightseers saw him leading the grand ball there one night, dressed like the aurora borealis, with a queen of the spa on his arm. A few months later he was back in New York, touching matches to what was left of the candle. He kept on fighting, for his blonde-champagne-and-candy fund. They tell you that Mizner (Britt had died soon after the Johnson bout) once or twice paid money to see that Steve got home free in a fight—like the one with the mighty Sam Langford in April 1910, which came out "No decision—6." Dan Morgan says a "safety-first" deal was cooked up for Ketchel's second-to-last fight, a New York bout with a tough old hand named Willie Lewis. Dan's partner, and Willie's manager, was Dan McKetrick. On the night before the fight the two Daniels went to mass; and Morgan heard McKetrick breathe a prayer for victory (which startled him) and saw him drop a quarter in the contribution box. In the fight, Willie threw a dangerous punch at Ketchel, and Ketchel, alerted to treachery, stiffened Willie.

"You're the first man," said Morgan to McKetrick afterward, "that ever tried to buy a title with a two-bit piece."

"Tut, tut," said McKetrick. "Let us go see Ketchel, and maybe adopt him. If you can't beat 'em, join 'em."

McKetrick's hijacker's eye had been caught the night before by the sight of Mizner, nonchalant and dapper, sitting in a ringside seat drawing up plans for a new apartment for himself and Ketchel, instead of working in his fighter's corner. Maybe Ketch could be pried loose from that kind of management. Morgan and McKetrick called on Ketchel at the Bartholdi Hotel. They offered to take him off Mizner's hands. Ketchel, who respected Mizner's culture but not his ring wisdom, was receptive. The two flesh-shoppers went to see Mizner, to break the news to him.

"Why, boys, you can have the thug with pleasure," said Mizner. "But did he remember to tell you that I owe him three thousand dollars? How can I pay him unless I manage him?"

They saw his point. Mizner would need money from Ketchel to settle with Ketchel. Ketchel saw it, too, when they reported back to him. He turned white and paced the floor like a panther at the thought of being caged in this left-handed way. But he stayed under Mizner management.

Hype Igoe was Ketchel's closest crony in the final months that followed. To Hype, the supreme myth-maker, whatever Steve did was bigger than life. He used to tell and write of Ketchel's hand being swollen after a fight "to FIVE TIMES normal size!" He wrote of a visit Ketchel made, incognito, to a boxing booth at a carnival one time, when he called himself Kid Glutz and "knocked out SIX HEAVY-WEIGHTS IN A ROW!" He told a story about a palooka who sobbed in Ketchel's arms in the clinches in a fight one night. "What's the matter, kid?" asked Ketchel. Between sobs and short jolts to the body, his opponent explained that he was being paid ten dollars a round, and feared he would not last long enough to make the sixty dollars he needed to buy a pawnshop violin for his musical child. Ketchel carried him six rounds, and they went to the pawnshop together, in tears, with the money. The next time Hype wrote it, the fiddle cost two hundred dollars, Ketchel made up the difference out of his pocket, and he and the musician's father bailed out the Stradivarius, got drunk on champagne, and went home singing together.

There was a grimmer, wilder side of Ketchel's mind that affected the faithful little sports writer deeply. Ketchel used to tell Hype—he told many people—that he was sure he would die young. The prediction made a special impression on Igoe on nights when the two went driving together in the Lozier, with Ketchel at the wheel. As the car whipped around curves on two tires and Igoe yelped with fear, Ketchel would say, "It's got to happen, Hype. I'll die before I'm thirty. And I'll die in a fast car." Luckily for Hype and other friends, it happened in a different way when it happened, and Ketchel took nobody with him. The world was shocked by the Michigan Tiger's death, but on second thought found it natural that he should pass into the great purple valley by violence. To Igoe's mind it was the "blue gun" that Steve romantically took with him everywhere that was responsible.

Ketchel had knocked out a heavyweight, Jim Smith, in what proved to be the last fight of his life, in June 1910. Though he could fight, he was in bad shape, like a fine engine abused and over-driven. To get back his health he went to live on a ranch in Conway, Missouri, in the Ozarks, not far from Springfield. His host, Colonel R. P. Dickerson, was an old friend who had taken a fatherly interest in Ketchel for two or three years. Ketchel ate some of his meals at the ranch's cookhouse—he took an unfatherly interest in Goldie, the cook. Goldie was not much to look at. She was plain and dumpy. But because she was the only woman on the premises, Ketchel ignored this, as well as the fact that Walter Dipley, a new hand on the ranch, was thought to be her husband.

On the morning of October 16, as Ketchel sat at the breakfast table, Dipley shot him in the back with a .38 revolver. Ketchel was hit in the lung. He lived for only a few hours afterward.

Igoe used to say that it was because Ketchel had his own .44 in his lap, as always at meals, that he was shot from behind, and that he was shot at all. There was evidence later, after Dipley had been found by a posse with Ketchel's wallet in his possession, that husband and wife had played a badger game with money as the motive. Goldie, it turned out, was a wife in name only. Dipley, whose right name was Hurtz, had a police record. They were both sent to jail; Dipley, sentenced to life, did not get out on parole till twenty-four years later.

Ketchel's grave is in the Polish Cemetery in Grand Rapids. Visitors will find a monument over it, built by Colonel Dickerson—a slab of marble twelve and a half feet high, topped by a cross and showing these words:

STANLEY KETCHEL

BORN SEPT. 14, 1886

DIED OCT. 16, 1910

A Good Son and Faithful Friend

Legend has built an even more durable monument to Ketchel. Of the one in stone, a neighbor with a few drinks in him once said, "Steve could have put his hand through that slab with one punch."

Frank Graham

Frank Graham and Red Smith, the ultimate in friendly rivals, were known as 1 and 1A as together they looked for stories in dugouts before baseball games and traveled to the training camps of their era's best prizefighters. While Smith was the quintessential sports-page stylist for the *New York Herald Tribune*, Graham (1893–1965) abandoned the Olympian approach of his predecessors and graced the *New York Journal-American* with flesh-and-blood portraits of the games people play. Though he had only one eye and didn't take notes during interviews, he was a pioneer in capturing the vernacular of the heroes and heroines he engaged in conversation. But he could shift gears the way any self-respecting newspaperman can when he had to. Witness his impressionistic column on the Rocky Marciano–Ezzard Charles brawl on September 17, 1954, written with a dateline bearing down on him, a study in grace under pressure. When there was no time to find out what the fighters had to say, Graham said it all himself.

As It Was in the Long Ago

THIS must have been the way men fought on barges that, long ago, rode Benecia Bay or Long Island Sound or any of the waters that kept the landlocked police from interfering with a night's sport. They used but little of the space within the ropes, throwing smashing punches, bleeding from face cuts, yet never taking a backward step except under the driving force of a blow. Fighting with all they had to offer in blood and breath, oblivious to all about them as they hammered at each other, the sole idea in the mind of each being the destruction of the other.

This was last night in the Yankee Stadium, and these were Rocky Marciano and Ezzard Charles and this was prize-fighting the way it was meant to be. No fancy adornments pleasing to the minds of those who, not liking the sound of the word prize-fight, prate of boxing. They were Marciano and Charles . . . but they could have been

Corbett and Choynski or any of the other heroes of the old blood-letting days.

It was, men said of it who have seen fights these fifty years and more, one of the greatest they'd ever seen. When it was over Marciano still was the heavyweight champion of the world but there was blood all over his face. Charles's face was that of a gargoyle, beaten lopsided and lumped, and bleeding, too, and their bodies were raw from the punching.

Marciano had retained the title, but he hadn't been able to knock Charles out, or even to knock him down. Charles had failed, as it seems all men must fail who, having held the title once and lost it, try to take it back. But this was Charles's greatest fight and one for which he always will be remembered.

IN THE SIXTH ROUND . . . AND THE NINTH

The critical round was the sixth. Charles was ahead until then, as he figured to be. But in the sixth Rocky hurt him for the first time, slugged him and hurt him and bewildered him. Had him ready for the stretch . . . and lost him. Rocky was bleeding from cuts over and alongside his right eye and he was driving hard, trying to finish Charles, but he couldn't and Charles rallied as the round ended and hurt Rocky, too.

But that was the round. Ezzard was trapped now and although he fought as hard as he could to get out of the trap, he couldn't make it. For the space of a minute or so in the seventh round, it seemed he might take command again, but at the end of the round, Rocky still was the stronger, still the one throwing the jarring punches, still the boss of the ring.

After the ninth round, the fight plainly was Marciano's. He had Charles then as he'd had him in the sixth round and, again, Charles escaped. But it was just an escape for Ezzard, and no more than that, and he was sealed off from the victory he so much wanted and for which he strove so gallantly.

From there on he could hope only to survive. To be on his feet at the end of the fifteenth round. He didn't fight that way, though. He fought to win. He kept the action in the center of the ring and hit Rocky with many a punch. But by now there was no force behind his punches and Rocky took them and plunged in, or moved in with an awkward weave-and-bob, and when Charles tried to tie him up in close, as he did in the earlier rounds, he shook Charles off and rocked him and, in the press rows, they were wondering what held Ezzard up.

By the opening of the fifteenth round even those who had picked Marciano to win by a knockout were hoping that Charles would last the distance, and so he did, badly beaten, not seeming to know at times what he was doing, fighting, perhaps by instinct, he fended off the drive of the champion. Hit and hurt again and again though he was, it was not until the waning moments of the fight that he was herded to the ropes and there took a beating which, if time had allowed, would have sent him sprawling on the canvas.

THIS WAS AN EAGER AND DESPERATE MAN

It may be that Marciano never will have so hard a fight again. This, once more, was the Charles who had beaten Joe Louis and stopped Gus Lesnevich and others along the way. This was not the uncertain, the cautious Charles, who had lost fights he could have won with just a little determination.

This was an eager, desperate man, who had come to the ring so sure he was going to win; who gave everything he had to stave off defeat that, from the beginning, was inevitable. No man other than Marciano could have beaten Charles last night. Unfortunately for him, Marciano was the one who, round after round, was coming out of the opposite corner.

A. J. Liebling

A. J. Liebling (1904–1963) was as short as he was stout, and it is said that his feet, which didn't quite touch the floor when he sat at his desk at *The New Yorker*, jiggled merrily every time he wrote a good line. If that was the case, his feet must have been a study in constant motion, for Liebling was a fount of not just good lines but great ones. They enlivened his timeless essays about Manhattan characters, World War II, Louisiana politician Earl Long, food, Chicago, the press and, perhaps most memorably, boxing. Of the sweet science, he said it "is joined onto the past like a man's arm to his shoulder." Abbott Joseph Liebling—Joe to his friends—was introduced to the sport by an uncle, and became a scholar by soaking up the wisdom of the wizened cornermen he called his "explainers." No boxing writer is more revered than Liebling, as Stan Isaacs, the *Newsday* sports columnist, proved when he invited Vic Ziegel, then of the *New York Post*, to meet him in an Eighth Avenue saloon. Ziegel walked in, saw that it was a dump, and said, "Stan, why here?" Said Isaacs: "Joe liked it."

Both the following essays, first published in *The New Yorker* in 1952 and 1955, respectively, are drawn from Liebling's matchless boxing collection *The Sweet Science* (1956).

Kearns by a Knockout

THE division of boxers into weight classes is based on the premise that if two men are equally talented practitioners of the Sweet Science, then the heavier man has a decided advantage. This is true, of course, only if both men are trained down hard, since a pound of beer is of no use in a boxing match. If the difference amounts to no more than a couple of pounds, it can be offset by a number of other factors, including luck, but when it goes up to five or six or seven, it takes a lot of beating. The span between the top limit of one weight class and the next represents the margin that history has proved is almost impossible to overcome. Between middleweight and light heavyweight, for example, that gap is fifteen pounds. A middleweight champion may weigh, at the most, a hundred and sixty, and a light heavy a hundred and seventy-five. But some champions are more skillful than others, and every now and then one comes along who feels he can beat the title-holder in the class above him. That was what made it interesting to anticipate the match between Sugar Ray Robinson, the middleweight champion, and Joey Maxim, the champion of the light heavyweights, in June, 1952. As soon as I heard the match had been arranged, I resolved to attend it. I had seen Robinson in four fights, not including television, and knew that he was a very good fighter. I had heard that Maxim, whom I had never seen, was merely pretty good. But there was that fifteen pounds. It was the smaller man who appealed to the public's imagination, and to mine. Goliath would not have been a popular champion even if he had flattened David in the first round. Robinson is such a combination of skill and grace that I had a feeling he could do the trick. For exactly the same reason, the London fancy, back in 1821, made Tom Hickman, the Gas-Light Man, who weighed a hundred and sixty-five, a strong favorite over Bill Neat, at a hundred and eighty-nine. The Gas-Light Man, according to Egan, was "a host within himself—his fist possessing the knocking-down force of the forge-hammer—his brow contemptuously smiling at defeat—*to surrender* not within the range of his ideas, even to the extremity of perspective—and VICTORY, proud victory, only operating as a beacon to all his achievements." Neat was a mere plugger, but he "turned out the Gas."

One man who did not share the public's sentimental regard for Robinson was an old-time prizefighter, saloon-keeper, and manufacturer of fire extinguishers named Jack Kearns. This was not surprising, because Kearns, who in more glorious eras managed Jack Dempsey, the Manassa Mauler, and Mickey Walker, the Toy Bulldog, now happens to be the manager of Maxim. Not even Kearns hinted that Maxim was a great champion, but he said he had a kind nature. "All he lacks is the killer instinct," Jack maintained. "But he takes a good punch. When he's knocked down he always gets up." He once told a group of fight writers, "Maxim is as good a fighter as Dempsey, except he can't hit." Since that was all Dempsey could do, Kearns wasn't handing his new man much.

Kearns is as rutilant a personality as Maxim apparently isn't, and from many of the newspaper stories that appeared in the weeks leading up to the fight one would have thought that Kearns, not Maxim, was signed to fight Robinson. This was an impression Kearns seemed to share when I met him six days before the date set for the fight, in the large, well-refrigerated Broadway restaurant operated by his former associate Dempsey. The old champion and his manager quarreled spectacularly back in the twenties, but are now friendly. "This is my big chance," Kearns said, buying me a drink and ordering a cup of coffee for himself. He was one of the big speakeasy spenders but says he has been on the wagon for eight years. "Up to now, I had to stuff myself up and fight heavyweights," he said. "Me, the only white guy with a title. But now I got somebody I can bull around." By this he meant, I gathered, that, in order to obtain what he considered sufficiently remunerative employment in the past for Maxim, he had had to overfeed the poor fellow and spread the rumor that he had grown into a full-sized heavyweight. Then, after fattening him to a hundred and eighty, he had exposed him to the assault of more genuine giants, who had nearly killed him. But now, he implied, Maxim had an opponent he could shove around and control in the clinches. I said I hoped it would be a good fight to watch, and he said, "I got to be good. I can't afford to lay back. I got to keep moving him, moving him." As he said this, he picked off imaginary punches—Robinson's hooks, no doubt—with both hands and shoved straight out into space, to show how he would put on the pressure.

Most managers say "we" will lick So-and-So when they mean their man will try to, but Kearns does not allow his fighter even a share in the pronoun. He is a manager of the old school. His old-school tie, on the day I met him, was Columbia blue covered with sharps and flats in black, green, and cerise. The weaver of his shirt had imprisoned in it the texture as well as the color of pistachio ice cream. It was a wonder children hadn't eaten it off his back in the street, with the weather the way it was outside. He was wearing a pale-gray suit and skew-bald shoes, and his eyes, of a confiding baby blue, were so bright that they seemed a part of the ensemble. He has a long, narrow, pink face that widens only at the cheekbones and at the mouth, which is fronted with wide, friendly-looking incisors, habitually exposed in an ingenuous smile. The big ears folded back against the sides of his head are not cauliflowered. They are evidence that in his boxing days he was never a catcher. Kearns is slim and active, and could pass for a spry fifty-five if the record books didn't show that he was knocked out by a welterweight champion named Honey Mellody in 1901, when he must have been at least full-grown.

In the course of his boxing career, which was not otherwise distinguished, Kearns had the fortune to meet the two fighters who in my opinion had the best ring names of all time—Honey Mellody and Mysterious Billy Smith. Smith was also a welterweight champion. "He was always doing something mysterious," Kearns says. "Like he would step on your foot, and when you looked down, he would bite you in the ear. If I had a fighter like that now, I could lick heavyweights. But we are living in a bad period all around. The writers are always crabbing about the fighters we got now, but look at the writers you got now themselves. All they think about is home to wife and children, instead of laying around saloons soaking up information."

He told me in Dempsey's that he played nine holes of golf every day to keep his legs in shape. Since Kearns was obviously in such good condition, I saw no point in taking the three-hour ride to Grossinger's, in the Catskill Mountains, to see Maxim train.

I did go out to look at Robinson next day, however. He was training at Pompton Lakes, New Jersey, which is only an hour's drive from town. I got a free ride in one of the limousines chartered by the International Boxing Club, which was promoting the fight. There were four newspapermen with me, including a fellow named Frank Butler, from the *News of the World*, of London, who had seen both Robinson and Maxim fight in England and said Maxim could bash a bit when he liked. "He took all Freddie Mills' front teeth out with one uppercut," he said. "I rather think he'll do Robinson."

Any effect Mr. Butler's prediction might have had on me was dissipated by the atmosphere of the camp. When we arrived, a crowd had already gathered around George Gainford, Robinson's immense, impressive manager, on the lawn between the sleeping quarters and the press building. It was a mass interview. The topic of discussion was what Robinson was going to do with *two* championships after he whipped Maxim. Since Robinson would indubitably weigh under a hundred and seventy-five pounds for the fight, the light heavyweight title would be his if he won. But since Maxim would certainly weigh more than a hundred and sixty, he could not take the middleweight championship, no matter what he did to Robinson. The chairman of the New York State Athletic Commission, someone said to Gainford, had announced that if Robinson won the heavier championship, he would have to abandon the lighter one. It sounded to me like the kind of hypothetical problem harried publicity men so often cook up as fight day approaches. But Gainford, a vast ebon man, broad between the eyes, played it straight. "The Commission do not make a champion," he intoned. "Neither may the Supreme Court name him. The people of the world name him; that is democracy. And if Robinson emerge victorious, he will be champion in both classes until somebody defeat him."

"How about the welterweight championship?" somebody asked. Robinson was the welterweight champion (one hundred and forty-seven pounds) until he entered the middleweight class. He was never beaten at that weight.

"I do not want to make that weight," Gainford said majestically, using the first person singular as if he were Jack Kearns. He must weigh two hundred and forty.

While Gainford propounded, the fighter and three campmates were sitting around a table, unperturbed by the jostling visitors. They were playing hearts, and all shouting simultaneously that they were being cheated. Robinson put an end to the game by standing up and saying he had better get ready for his workout. He was wearing a green-and-white straw cap and a red-and-white Basque shirt and cinnamon slacks, and he looked as relaxed and confident as a large Siamese tomcat. Sam Taub, the I.B.C. press agent at the camp, led him into the press shack to be interviewed by "just the bona-fide newspapermen," and he sprawled gracefully on a narrow typewriter shelf, one leg straight out and the other dangling. Robinson is about six feet in length, very tall for a middleweight, and on casual inspection he seems more like a loose-limbed dancer than a boxer. A long, thin neck, the customary complement of long arms and legs, is a disadvantage to a boxer, because a man with his head attached that way doesn't take a good punch. The great layer of muscle on the back of Robinson's neck is the outward indication of his persistence. It is the kind that can be developed only by endless years of exercise—the sort of exercise no shiftless man will stick with.

"Have you ever fought a man that heavy?" a newspaperman asked him.

"Never a *champion* that heavy," Robinson said, smiling.

"Do you think you can hurt him?" the man asked.

"I can hurt anybody," the boxer said. "Can I hurt him enough is the question. I'll be hitting *at* him, all right."

"Have you a plan for the battle?" another fellow asked.

"If you have a plan, the other fellow is liable to do just the opposite," Robinson said.

"How are your legs?" somebody else asked.

"I hope they all right," Robinson said. "This would sure be a bad time for them to go wrong."

The interview broke up and the fighter went along to get into his ring togs. He worked four easy rounds with two partners, who didn't seem to want to irritate him. They sparred outdoors, in a ring on a kind of bandstand under the trees. Around the ring were bleachers, occupied by a couple of hundred spectators—Harlem people and visiting prizefighters and a busload of boys brought out from the city by the Police Athletic League. "We had three hundred paid admissions at a buck here last Sunday," Taub told me. "Sugar gave a dinner for sixty-five. 'My friends and relatives,' he said. They ate fifty-five chickens."

The newspapermen agreed that tepid sparring was all right, since Sugar Ray was as sharp as a tack already, and this was almost the end of his training. The thing about Robinson that gets you is the way he moves, even when shadowboxing. He finished off with a good long session of jumping rope, which he enjoys. Most fighters jump rope as children do, but infinitely faster. Robinson just swings a length of rope in his right fist and jumps in time to a fast tune whistled by his trainer. He jumps high in the air, and twists his joined knees at the top of every bound. When he jumps in double time to "I'm Just Wild About Harry," it's really something to see.

On the way back to town we all said he had never looked better.

The fight itself, as you have probably read, was memorable, but chiefly for meteorological reasons. It was postponed from the night of Monday, June twenty-third to that of Wednesday, June twenty-fifth, because of rain. Wednesday was the hottest June twenty-fifth in the history of the New York City Weather Bureau. I rode the subway up to the Yankee Stadium, where the fight was to be held, and the men slumped in the seats and hanging to the straps weren't talking excitedly or making jokes, as fight fans generally do. They were just gasping gently, like fish that had been caught two hours earlier. Most of those who had been wearing neckties had removed them, but rings of red and green remained around collars and throats to show the color of the ties that had been there. Shirts stuck to the folds of bellies, and even the floor was wet with sweat.

My seat was in a mezzanine box on the first-base line, and I felt a mountain climber's exhaustion by the time I had ascended the three gentle inclines that lead to the top of the grandstand, from which I had to descend to my seat. A fellow in a party behind me, trying to cheer his companions, said, "And you can tell your grandsons about this fight and how hot it was." The preliminaries were on when I arrived, and two wretched forms were hacking away at each other under the lights that beat down on the ring. I could see the high shine on the wringing-wet bodies, and imagined that each man must be praying to be knocked out as speedily as possible. They were too inept; the bout went the full distance of six rounds, and then both men collapsed in their corners, indifferent to the decision. A miasma of cigarette smoke hung over the "ringside" seats on the baseball diamond, producing something of the effect you get when you fly over a cloud bank. There was no breeze to dispel it, and the American flags on the four posts at the corners of the ring drooped straight down. It was a hundred and four degrees Fahrenheit in there, we were to learn from the newspapers next morning.

I missed the next two preliminaries because I was up at the top of the stand, waiting in line for a can of beer. The venders who usually swarm all over the place, obstructing your vision at crucial moments in a fight, had disappeared, on the one night when their presence would have been welcome. So the customers had to queue up—a death march to get to a bar tended by exactly two men. Meanwhile, the fights were invisible, but once one was locked in the line, the thought of giving up one's place unslaked became intolerable. Our line inched along toward a kind of Storm Trooper with a head like a pink egg. Rivulets of sweat poured from the watershed of his cranium, and his face appeared behind a spray, like a bronze Triton's in a fountain. At every third customer, he would stop the line and threaten to pack up and call it a day. We would look at him beseechingly, too thirsty even to protest, and after enjoying our humiliation for a while he would consent to sell more beer.

By the time I got back to my seat, Robinson and Maxim were in the ring and the announcer was proceeding with the usual tiresome introductions of somebodies who were going to fight somebody elses somewhere. Each boy, after being introduced, would walk over and touch the gloved right paw of each principal. The last one in was old Jersey Joe Walcott, the heavyweight champion, and the crowd evidenced torpid good will. I could see the vast Gainford in Robinson's corner, over toward third base, and, with the aid of binoculars, could discern that his face still wore the portentous, noncommittal expression of a turbaned bishop in a store-front church. Kearns had his back to me, but I could tell him by his ears. He was clad in a white T shirt with "Joey Maxim" in dark letters on the back, and he seemed brisker than anybody else in the ring. Maxim had his back to me, too. When he stood up, I could see how much thicker and broader through the chest he was than Robinson. His skin was a reddish bronze; Sugar Ray's was mocha chocolate.

Fighting middleweights, Robinson had always had a superiority over his foes in height and reach, together with equality in weight. Against Maxim he had equality in height and reach but the weight was all against him. His was announced as a hundred fifty-seven and a half and Maxim's as a hundred and seventy-three. The first ten rounds of the fight weren't much to watch. Maxim would keep walking in and poking a straight left at Robinson's face. Robinson would either take or slip it, according to his fortune, belt Maxim a couple of punches, and grab his arms. Then they would contend, with varying success, in close. Some of the fans would cry that Robinson wasn't hurting Maxim at all in these interludes, others that Maxim wasn't hurting Robinson at all. There seemed to be some correlation between their eyesight and where they had placed their money. Because of the nature of the combat, most of the work fell upon the referee, Ruby

Goldstein, a former welterweight then in his forties, who had to pull the men apart. In consequence, he was the first of the three to collapse; he had to leave the ring after the tenth round. I have never seen this happen in a prizefight before. Old-time photographs show referees on their feet at the end of twenty-five-round fights, and wearing waistcoats and stiff collars. It is a bad period all around.

Robinson had been hitting Maxim much more frequently than Maxim had been hitting him, but neither man seemed hurt, and both were slowing down from a pace that had never been brisk. Now the relief referee, Ray Miller, a snub-nosed little man with reddish hair, entered the ring, bringing with him more bounce than either of the contestants possessed. He must have been sitting on dry ice. Miller, also an old fighter, enjoined the fighters to get going. The crowd had begun clapping and stamping, midway in the fight, to manifest its boredom. Miller broke clinches so expeditiously in the eleventh and twelfth that the pace increased slightly, to the neighborhood of a fast creep. Up to then, it had been even worse than the first ten rounds of the previous year's fight between Sugar Ray and Randy Turpin, the milling cove. But that fight had ended in one wildly exciting round that made the fancy forget how dull the prelude had been.

This fight was to produce excitement, too, but of a fantastically different kind. In the eleventh round, Robinson hit Maxim precisely the same kind of looping right to the jaw that had started Turpin on the way out. The blow knocked the light heavy clear across the ring, but he didn't fall, and Robinson's legs, those miracles, apparently couldn't move Ray fast enough to take advantage of the situation. It may have been as good a punch as the one of the year before, but it landed on a man fifteen pounds heavier. Maxim shook his head and went right on fighting, in his somnambulistic way. Now all Sugar Ray had to do was finish the fight on his feet and he would win on points. But when he came out for the thirteenth, he walked as if he had the gout in both feet and dreaded putting them down. When he punched, which was infrequently, he was as late, and as wild, as an amateur, and when he wasn't punching, his arms hung at his sides. He had, quite simply, collapsed from exhaustion, like a marathon runner on a hot day. Maxim—at first, apparently, unable to believe his good fortune—began, after a period of ratiocination, to hit after him. He landed one or two fairly good shots, I thought from where I sat. Kearns must have been yelling to Maxim.

And then Robinson, the almost flawless boxer, the epitome of ring grace, swung, wildly and from far back of his shoulder, like a child, missed his man completely, and fell hard on his face. When he got up, Maxim backed him against the ropes and hit him a couple of times. The round ended, and Robinson's seconds half dragged, half carried him to his corner. He couldn't get off the stool at the end of the one-minute interval, and Maxim was declared the winner by a knockout in the fourteenth, because the bell had rung for the beginning of that round.

Sugar Ray, according to the press, was pretty well cut up over his defeat, and in his dressing room, after enough water had been sloshed on him to bring him to, he raved that divine intervention had prevented his victory. This refusal to accept the event is also an old story in the ring, but in the words of John Bee, a rival of Egan, it is "a species of feeling which soon wears out, and dies away, like weak astonishment at a nine days' wonder." On the day after the fight many of the sports writers took the line that Robinson had been beaten by the heat alone, and some of them even sentimentally averred that he had been making one of the most brilliant fights of his life right up to the moment when his legs gave out. They tried to reconcile this with their assertions that Maxim was a hopelessly bad fighter and had made a miserable showing until his unbelievable stroke of luck. It would have required no brilliance on anyone's part to outpoint the Maxim they described. But Goliath never would have been popular anyway.

The heat was the same for both men. This much is sure, though: Whenever a man weighing a hundred and fifty-seven has to pull and haul against a man weighing a hundred and seventy-three, he has to handle sixteen pounds more than his own weight. The other fellow has to handle sixteen pounds less than his. And when you multiply this by the number of seconds the men struggle during thirty-nine minutes of a bout like this, you get a pretty good idea of why they weigh prizefighters. The multiplication is more than arithmetical, of course; a man who boxes four rounds is more than four times as tired as if he had boxed one. I had no idea, from watching the fight, whether Maxim was pacing himself slowly, like Conn McCreary, the jockey who likes to come from behind, or whether he just couldn't get going any faster, like even Arcaro when his horse won't run. But I talked to Kearns a couple of days after the fight, and he left no doubt in my mind about what he wanted me to believe had happened. The nine holes of golf a day, he said, had kept him personally in such condition that he could exercise all the natural alacrity of his perceptions during the conflict. "The heat talk is an alibi and an excuse," he said. "Robinson was nailed good in the belly in the tenth round, and again in the twelfth, and he got a left hook and a right to the head at the end of the thirteenth, when he was on the ropes. If the bell hadn't a rang, he'd be dead. I didn't move Maxim until the twelfth round. I didn't have to. I knew I could win in any round when I got ready. The only reason I shoved Maxim in at all was because I wanted to win with a one-punch knockout. Robinson escaped by luck."

I paused to commit this to memory, and then asked Dr. Kearns, who seemed in high good humor, to what he attributed his victory. "Oh, I don't know," he said modestly. "Anybody who was around those old-time fights we used to have in the hot sun on the Fourth of July knew you had to rate any athalete according to what the heat was. Robinson figured he had any one of fifteen rounds in which to win in. He was going to try for a knockout in every round he fought. But I just told Maxim, 'Just keep this fellow moving, moving. Then he'll have to clinch and hang on.' After that, it just depended how quick I decided to move Maxim. It was up to me to pick the round. Next time I'll knock him out quicker."

"And who do you want next?" I inquired.

"I'd like that Walcott or Marciano," Dr. Kearns replied bravely. "I'll fight anybody in the world."

Since then Robinson has come back, at least as far as being middleweight champion again. After the Maxim fight he retired, and a fellow named Bobo Olson won the title after an elimination tournament among the inept left-overs. Robinson returned to the ring and stopped Mr. Olson in two rounds at Chicago, which was nice going, and the Cadillacs are back at his door. One fight-writer, reporting the victory, said Olson was a "burned-out hollow shell," which is like merging Pelion and Ossa, or Ford and General Motors, in the cliché business. He must have meant the shell of a broiled lobster after a shore dinner.

Maxim lost his title to a great man, who will be introduced in a later chapter of this book, named Archie Moore, but Dr. Kearns did not say after the bout, "Moore licked me." He said, "Moore licked Maxim."

Ahab and Nemesis

B ACK in 1922, the late Heywood Broun, who is not remembered primarily as a boxing writer, wrote a durable account of a combat between the late Benny Leonard and the late Rocky Kansas for the lightweight championship of the world. Leonard was the greatest practitioner of the era, Kansas just a rough, optimistic fellow. In the early rounds Kansas messed Leonard about, and Broun was profoundly disturbed. A radical in politics, he was a conservative in the arts, and Kansas made him think of Gertrude Stein, *les Six*, and non-representational painting, all novelties that irritated him.

"With the opening gong, Rocky Kansas tore into Leonard," he wrote. "He was gauche and inaccurate, but terribly persistent." The classic verities prevailed, however. After a few rounds, during which Broun continued to yearn for a return to a culture with fixed values, he was enabled to record: "The young child of nature who was challenging for the championship dropped his guard, and Leonard hooked a powerful and entirely orthodox blow to the conventional point of the jaw. Down went Rocky Kansas. His past life flashed before him during the nine seconds in which he remained on the floor, and he wished that he had been more faithful as a child in heeding the advice of his boxing teacher. After all, the old masters did know something. There is still a kick in style, and tradition carries a nasty wallop."

I have often thought of Broun's words in the years since Rocky Marciano, the reigning heavyweight champion, scaled the fistic summits, as they say in *Journal-Americanese*, by beating Jersey Joe Walcott. The current Rocky is gauche and inaccurate, but besides being persistent he is a dreadfully severe hitter with either hand. The predominative nature of this asset has been well stated by Pierce Egan, the Edward Gibbon and Sir Thomas Malory of the old London prize ring, who was less preoccupied than Broun with ultimate implications. Writing in 1821 of a milling cove named Bill Neat, the Bristol Butcher, Egan said, "He possesses a requisite above all the art that *teaching* can achieve for any boxer; namely, *one hit* from his right hand, given in proper distance, can gain a victory; but three of them are positively enough to dispose of a giant." This is true not only of Marciano's right hand but of his left hand, too—provided he doesn't miss the giant entirely. Egan doubted the advisability of changing Neat's style, and he would have approved of Marciano's. The champion has an apparently unlimited absorptive capacity for percussion (Egan would have called him an "insatiable glutton") and inexhaustible energy ("a prime bottom fighter"). "Shifting," or moving to the side, and "milling in retreat," or moving back, are innovations of the late eighteenth century that Rocky's advisers have carefully kept from his knowledge, lest they spoil his natural prehistoric style. Egan excused these tactics only in boxers of feeble constitution.

Archie Moore, the light-heavyweight champion of the world, who hibernates in San Diego, California, and estivates in Toledo, Ohio, is a Brounian rather than an Eganite in his thinking about style, but he naturally has to do more than think about it. Since the rise of Marciano, Moore, a cerebral and hyper-experienced light-colored pugilist who has been active since 1936, has suffered the pangs of a supreme exponent of *bel canto* who sees himself crowded out of the opera house by a guy who can only shout. As a sequel to a favorable review I wrote of one of his infrequent New York appearances, when his fee was restricted to a measly five figures, I received a sad little note signed "The most unappreciated fighter in the world, Archie Moore." A fellow who has as much style as Moore tends to overestimate the intellect—he develops the kind of Faustian mind that will throw itself against the problem of perpetual motion, or of how to pick horses first, second, third, *and* fourth in every race. Archie's note made it plain to me that he was honing his harpoon for the White Whale.

When I read newspaper items about Moore's decisioning a large, playful porpoise of a Cuban heavyweight named Nino Valdes and scoop-netting a minnow like Bobo Olson, the middleweight champion, for practice, I thought of him as a lonely Ahab, rehearsing to buck Herman Melville, Pierce Egan, and the betting odds. I did not think that he could bring it off, but I wanted to be there when he tried. What would *Moby Dick* be if Ahab had succeeded? Just another fish story. The thing that is eternally diverting is the struggle of man against history—or what Albert Camus, who used to be an amateur middleweight, has called the Myth of Sisyphus. (Camus would have been a great man to cover the fight, but none of the syndicates thought of it.) When I heard that the boys had been made for September 20, 1955, at the Yankee Stadium, I shortened my stay abroad in order not to miss the Encounter of the Two Heroes, as Egan would have styled the rendezvous.

In London on the night of September thirteenth, a week before the date set for the Encounter, I tried to get my eye in for fight-watching by attending a bout at the White City greyhound track between Valdes, who had been imported for the occasion, and the British Empire heavyweight champion, Don Cockell, a fat man whose gift for public suffering has enlisted the sympathy of a sentimental people. Since Valdes had gone fifteen rounds with Moore in Las Vegas the previous May, and Cockell had excruciated for nine rounds before being knocked out by Marciano in San Francisco in the same month, the bout offered a dim opportunity for establishing what racing people call a "line" between Moore and Marciano. I didn't get much of an optical workout, because Valdes disposed of Cockell in three rounds. It was evident that Moore and Marciano had not been fighting the same class of people this season.

This was the only fight I ever attended in a steady rainstorm. It had begun in the middle of the afternoon, and, while there was a canopy over the ring, the spectators were as wet as speckled trout. "The weather, it is well known, has no terrors to the admirers of Pugilism of Life," Egan once wrote, and on his old stamping ground this still holds true. As I took my seat in a rock pool that had collected in the hollow of my chair, a South African giant named Ewart Potgieter, whose weight had been announced as twenty-two stone ten, was ignoring the doctrine of Apartheid by leaning on a Jamaican colored man who weighed a mere sixteen stone, and by the time I had transposed these statistics to three hundred and eighteen pounds and two hundred and twenty-four pounds, respectively, the exhausted

Jamaican had acquiesced in resegregation and retired. The giant had not struck a blow, properly speaking, but had shoved downward a number of times, like a man trying to close an overfilled trunk.

The main bout proved an even less grueling contest. Valdes, eager to get out of the chill, struck Cockell more vindictively than is his wont, and after a few gestures invocative of commiseration the fat man settled in one corner of the ring as heavily as suet pudding upon the unaccustomed gastric system. He had received what Egan would have called a "ribber" and a "nobber," and when he arose it was seen that the latter had raised a cut on his forehead. At the end of the third round, his manager withdrew him from competition. It was not an inspiring occasion, but after the armistice eight or nine shivering Cubans appeared in the runway behind the press section and jumped up and down to register emotion and restore circulation. "*Ahora Marciano!*" they yelled. "Now for Marciano!" Instead of being grateful for the distraction, the other spectators took a poor view of it. "Sit down, you chaps!" one of them cried. "We want to see the next do!" They were still parked out there in the rain when I tottered into the Shepherd's Bush underground station and collapsed, sneezing, on a train that eventually disgorged me at Oxford Circus, with just enough time left to buy a revivifying draught before eleven o'clock, when the pubs closed. How the mugs I left behind cured themselves I never knew. They had to do it on Bovril.

Because I had engagements that kept me in England until a few days before the Encounter, I had no opportunity to visit the training camps of the rival American Heroes. I knew all the members of both factions, however, and I could imagine what they were thinking. In the plane on the way home, I tried to envision the rival patterns of ratiocination. I could be sure that Marciano, a kind, quiet, imperturbable fellow, would plan to go after Moore and make him fight continuously until he tired enough to become an accessible target. After that he would expect concussion to accentuate exhaustion and exhaustion to facilitate concussion, until Moore came away from his consciousness, like everybody else Rocky had ever fought. He would try to remember to minimize damage to himself in the beginning, while there was still snap in Moore's arms, because Moore is a sharp puncher. (Like Bill Neat of old, Marciano hits at his opponent's arms when he cannot hit past them. "In one instance, the arm of Oliver [a Neat adversary] received so paralyzing a shock in stopping the blow that it appeared almost useless," Egan once wrote.) Charlie Goldman would have instructed Marciano in some rudimentary maneuver to throw Moore's first shots off, I felt sure, but after a few minutes Rocky would forget it, or Archie would figure it out. But there would always be Freddie Brown, the "cut man," in the champion's corner to repair superficial damage. One reason Goldman is a great teacher is that he doesn't try to teach a boxer more than he can learn. What he had taught Rocky in the four years since I had first seen him fight was to shorten the arc of most of his blows without losing power thereby, and always to follow one hard blow with another—"for insurance"— delivered with the other hand, instead of recoiling to watch the victim fall. The champion had also gained confidence and presence of mind; he has a good fighting head, which is not the same thing as being a good mechanical practitioner. "A *boxer* requires a *nob* as well as a *statesman* does a HEAD, coolness and calculation being essential to *second* his efforts," Egan wrote, and the old historiographer was never more correct. Rocky was thirty-one, not in the first flush of youth for a boxer, but Moore was only a few days short of thirty-nine, so age promised to be in the champion's favor if he kept pressing.

Moore's strategic problem, I reflected on the plane, offered more choices and, as a corollary, infinitely more chances for error. It was possible, but not probable, that jabbing and defensive skill would carry him through fifteen rounds, even on those old legs, but I knew that the mere notion of such a *gambade* would revolt Moore. He is not what Egan would have called a shy fighter. Besides, would Ahab have been content merely to go the distance with the White Whale? I felt sure that Archie planned to knock the champion out, so that he could sign his next batch of letters "The most appreciated and deeply opulent fighter in the world." I surmised that this project would prove a mistake, like Mr. Churchill's attempt to take Gallipoli in 1915, but it would be the kind of mistake that would look good in his memoirs. The basis of what I rightly anticipated would prove a miscalculation went back to Archie's academic background. As a young fighter of conventional tutelage, he must have heard his preceptors say hundreds of times, "They will all go if you hit them right." If a fighter did not believe that, he would be in the position of a Euclidian without faith in the hundred-and-eighty-degree triangle. Moore's strategy, therefore, would be based on working Marciano into a position where he could hit him right. He would not go in and slug with him, because that would be wasteful, distasteful, and injudicious, but he might try to cut him up, in an effort to slow him down so he could hit him right, or else try to hit him right and then cut him up. The puzzle he reserved for me—and Marciano—was the tactic by which he would attempt to attain his strategic objective. In the formation of his views, I believed, Moore would be handicapped, rather than aided, by his active, skeptical mind. One of the odd things about Marciano is that he isn't terribly big. It is hard for a man like Moore, just under six feet tall and weighing about a hundred and eighty pounds, to imagine that a man approximately the same size can be immeasurably stronger than he is. This is particularly true when, like the light-heavyweight champion, he has spent his whole professional life contending with boxers—some of them considerably bigger—whose strength has proved so near his own that he could move their arms and bodies by cunning pressures. The old classicist would consequently refuse to believe what he was up against.

The light-heavyweight limit is a hundred and seventy-five pounds, and Moore can get down to that when he must, in order to defend his title, but in a heavyweight match each Hero is allowed to weigh whatever he pleases. I was back in time to attend the weighing-in ceremonies, held in the lobby of Madison Square Garden at noon on the day set for the Encounter, and learned that Moore weighed 188 and Marciano 188 ¼—a lack of disparity that figured to encourage the rationalist's illusions. I also learned that, in contrast to Jack Solomons, the London promoter who held the Valdes–Cockell match in the rain, the I.B.C., which was promoting the Encounter, had decided to postpone it for twenty-four hours, although the weather was clear. The decision was based on apprehension of Hurricane Ione, which, although apparently veering away from New York, might come around again like a lazy left hook and drop in on the point of the Stadium's jaw late in the evening. Nothing like that happened, but the postponement brought the town's theaters and bars another evening of good business from the out-of-town fight trade, such as they always get on the eve of a memorable Encounter.

("Not a bed could be had at any of the villages at an early hour on the preceding evening; and Uxbridge was crowded beyond all former precedent," Egan wrote of the night before Neat beat Oliver.) There was no doubt that the fight had caught the public imagination, ever sensitive to a meeting between Hubris and Nemesis, as the boys on the quarterlies would say, and the bookies were laying 18–5 on Nemesis, according to the boys on the dailies, who always seem to hear. (A friend of mine up from Maryland with a whim and a five-dollar bill couldn't get ten against it in ordinary barroom money anywhere, although he wanted Ahab.)

The enormous—by recent precedent—advance sale of tickets had so elated the I.B.C. that it had decided to replace the usual card of bad preliminary fights with some not worth watching at all, so there was less distraction than usual as we awaited the appearance of the Heroes on the fateful evening. The press seats had been so closely juxtaposed that I could fit in only sidewise between two colleagues—the extra compression having been caused by the injection of a prewar number of movie stars and politicos. The tight quarters were an advantage, in a way, since they facilitated my conversation with Peter Wilson, an English prize-ring correspondent, who happened to be in the row behind me. I had last seen Mr. Wilson at White City the week before, at a time when the water level had already reached his shredded-Latakia mustache. I had feared that he had drowned at ringside, but when I saw him at the Stadium, he assured me that by buttoning the collar of his mackintosh tightly over his nostrils he had been able to make the garment serve as a diving lung, and so survive. Like all British fight writers when they are relieved of the duty of watching British fighters, he was in a holiday mood, and we chatted happily. There is something about the approach of a good fight that renders the spirit insensitive to annoyance; it is only when the amateur of the Sweet Science has some doubts as to how good the main bout will turn out to be that he is avid for the satisfaction to be had from the preliminaries. This is because after the evening is over, he may have only a good supporting fight to remember. There were no such doubts—even in the minds of the mugs who had paid for their seats—on the evening of September twenty-first.

At about ten-thirty the champion and his faction entered the ring. It is not customary for the champion to come in first, but Marciano has never been a stickler for protocol. He is a humble, kindly fellow, who even now will approach an acquaintance on the street and say bashfully, "Remember me? I'm Rocky Marciano." The champion doesn't mind waiting five or ten minutes to give anybody a punch in the nose. In any case, once launched from his dressing room under the grandstand, he could not have arrested his progress to the ring, because he had about forty policemen pushing behind him, and three more clearing a path in front of him. Marciano, tucked in behind the third cop like a football ball-carrier behind his interference, had to run or be trampled to death. Wrapped in a heavy blue bathrobe and with a blue monk's cowl pulled over his head, he climbed the steps to the ring with the cumbrous agility of a medieval executioner ascending the scaffold. Under the hood he seemed to be trying to look serious. He has an intellectual appreciation of the anxieties of a champion, but he has a hard time forgetting how strong he is; while he remembers that, he can't worry as much as he knows a champion should. His attendants—quick, battered little Goldman; Al Weill, the stout, excitable manager, always stricken just before the bell with the suspicion that he may have made a bad match; Al Columbo—are all as familiar to the crowd as he is.

Ahab's party arrived in the ring a minute or so later, and Charlie Johnston, his manager—a calm sparrow hawk of a man, as old and wise in the game as Weill—went over to watch Goldman put on the champion's gloves. Freddie Brown went to Moore's corner to watch *his* gloves being put on. Moore wore a splendid black silk robe with a gold lamé collar and belt. He sports a full mustache above an imperial, and his hair, sleeked down under pomade when he opens operations, invariably rises during the contest, as it gets water sloshed on it between rounds and the lacquer washes off, until it is standing up like the top of a shaving brush. Seated in his corner in the shadow of his personal trainer, a brown man called Cheerful Norman, who weighs two hundred and thirty-five pounds, Moore looked like an old Japanese print I have of a "Shogun Engaged in Strategic Contemplation in the Midst of War." The third member of his group was Bertie Briscoe, a rough, chipper little trainer, whose more usual charge is Sandy Saddler, the featherweight champion—also a Johnston fighter. Mr. Moore's features in repose rather resemble those of Orson Welles, and he was reposing with intensity.

The procession of other fighters and former fighters to be introduced was longer than usual. The full galaxy was on hand, including Jack Dempsey, Gene Tunney, and Joe Louis, the *têtes de cuvée* of former-champion society; ordinary former heavyweight champions, like Max Baer and Jim Braddock, slipped through the ropes practically unnoticed. After all the celebrities had been in and out of the ring, an odd dwarf, advertising something or other—possibly himself—was lifted into the ring by an accomplice and ran across it before he could be shooed out. The referee, a large, craggy, oldish man named Harry Kessler, who, unlike some of his better-known colleagues, is not an ex-fighter, called the men to the center of the ring. This was his moment; he had the microphone. "Now Archie and Rocky, I want a nice, clean fight," he said, and I heard a peal of silvery laughter behind me from Mr. Wilson, who had seen both of them fight before. "Protect yourself at all times," Mr. Kessler cautioned them unnecessarily. When the principals shook hands, I could see Mr. Moore's eyebrows rising like storm clouds over the Sea of Azov. His whiskers bristled and his eyes glowed like dark coals as he scrunched his eyebrows down again and enveloped the Whale with the Look, which was intended to dominate his will power. Mr. Wilson and I were sitting behind Marciano's corner, and as the champion came back to it I observed his expression, to determine what effect the Look had had upon him. More than ever, he resembled a Great Dane who has heard the word "bone."

A moment later the bell rang and the Heroes came out for the first round. Marciano, training in the sun for weeks, had tanned to a slightly deeper tint than Moore's old ivory, and Moore, at 188, looked, if anything, bigger and more muscular than Marciano; much of the champion's weight is in his legs, and his shoulders slope. Marciano advanced, but Moore didn't go far away. As usual, he stood up nicely, his arms close to his body and his feet not too far apart, ready to go anywhere but not without a reason—the picture of a powerful, decisive intellect unfettered by preconceptions. Marciano, pulling his left arm back from the shoulder, flung a left hook. He missed, but not by enough to discourage him, and then walked in and hooked again. All through the round he threw those hooks, and some of them grazed Moore's whiskers; one even hit him on the side of the head. Moore didn't try much offensively; he held a couple of times when Marciano worked in close.

Marciano came back to his corner as he always does, unimpassioned. He hadn't expected to catch Moore with those left hooks anyway, I imagine; all he had wanted was to move him around. Moore went to his corner inscrutable. They came out for the second, and Marciano went after him in brisker fashion. In the first round he had been throwing the left hook, missing with it, and then throwing a right and missing with that, too. In the second he tried a variation—throwing a right and then pulling a shoulder back to throw the left. It appeared for a moment to have Moore confused, as a matador might be confused by a bull who walked in on his hind legs. Marciano landed a couple of those awkward hooks, but not squarely. He backed Moore over toward the side of the ring farthest from me, and then Moore knocked him down.

Some of the reporters, describing the blow in the morning papers, called it a "sneak punch," which is journalese for one the reporter didn't see but technically means a lead thrown before the other man has warmed up or while he is musing about the gate receipts. This had been no lead, and although I certainly hadn't seen Moore throw the punch, I knew that it had landed inside the arc of Marciano's left hook. ("Marciano missed with the right, trun the left, and Moore stepped inside it," my private eye, Whitey Bimstein, said next day, confirming my diagnosis, and the film of the fight bore both of us out.) So Ahab had his harpoon in the Whale. He had hit him right if ever I saw a boxer hit right, with a classic brevity and conciseness. Marciano stayed down for two seconds. I do not know what took place in Mr. Moore's breast when he saw him get up. He may have felt, for the moment, like Don Giovanni when the Commendatore's statue grabbed at him—startled because he thought he had killed the guy already—or like Ahab when he saw the Whale take down Fedallah, harpoons and all. Anyway, he hesitated a couple of seconds, and that was reasonable. A man who took nine to come up after a punch like that would be doing well, and the correct tactic would be to go straight in and finish him. But a fellow who came up on two was so strong he would bear investigation.

After that, Moore did go in, but not in a crazy way. He hit Marciano some good, hard, classic shots, and inevitably Marciano, a trader, hit him a few devastating swipes, which slowed him. When the round ended, the edge of Moore's speed was gone, and he knew that he would have to set a new and completely different trap, with diminished resources. After being knocked down, Marciano had stopped throwing that patterned right-and-left combination; he has a good nob. "He never trun it again in the fight," Whitey said next day, but I differ. He threw it in the fifth, and again Moore hit him a peach of a right inside it, but the steam was gone; this time Ahab couldn't even stagger him. Anyway, there was Moore at the end of the second, dragging his shattered faith in the unities and humanities back to his corner. He had hit a guy right, and the guy hadn't gone. But there is no geezer in Moore, any more than there was in the master of the Pequod.

Both came out for the third very gay, as Egan would have said. Marciano had been hit and cut, so he felt acclimated, and Moore was so mad at himself for not having knocked Marciano out that he almost displayed animosity toward him. He may have thought that perhaps he had not hit Marciano *just* right; the true artist is always prone to self-reproach. He would try again. A minute's attention from his squires had raised his spirits and slaked down his hair. At this point, Marciano set about him. He waddled in, hurling his fists with a sublime disregard of probabilities, content to hit an elbow, a biceps, a shoulder, the top of a head—the last supposed to be the least profitable target in the business, since, as every beginner learns, "the head is the hardest part of the human body," and a boxer will only break his hands on it. Many boxers make the systematic presentation of the cranium part of their defensive scheme. The crowd, basically anti-intellectual, screamed encouragement. There was Moore, riding punches, picking them off, slipping them, rolling with them, ducking them, coming gracefully out of his defensive efforts with sharp, patterned blows—and just about holding this parody even on points. His face, emerging at instants from under the storm of arms—his own and Rocky's—looked like that of a swimming walrus. When the round ended, I could see that he was thinking deeply. Marciano came back to his corner at a kind of suppressed dogtrot. He didn't have a worry in the world.

It was in the fourth, though, that I think Sisyphus began to get the idea he couldn't roll back the Rock. Marciano pushed him against the ropes and swung at him for what seemed a full minute without ever landing a punch that a boxer with Moore's background would consider a credit to his workmanship. He kept them coming so fast, though, that Moore tired just getting out of their way. One newspaper account I saw said that at this point Moore "swayed uncertainly," but his motions were about as uncertain as Margot Fonteyn's, or Artur Rubinstein's. He is the most premeditated and best-synchronized swayer in his profession. After the bell rang for the end of the round, the champion hit him a right for good measure—he usually manages to have something on the way all the time—and then pulled back to disclaim any uncouth intention. Moore, no man to be conned, hit him a corker of a punch in return, when he wasn't expecting it. It was a gesture of moral reprobation and also a punch that would give any normal man something to think about between rounds. It was a good thing Moore couldn't see Marciano's face as he came back to his corner, though, because the champion was laughing.

The fifth was a successful round for Moore, and I had him ahead on points that far in the fight. But it took no expert to know where the strength lay. There was even a moment in the round when Moore set himself against the ropes and encouraged Marciano to swing at him, in the hope the champion would swing himself tired. It was a confession that he himself was too tired to do much hitting.

In the sixth Marciano knocked Moore down twice—once, early in the round, for four seconds, and once, late in the round, for eight seconds, with Moore getting up just before the bell rang. In the seventh, after that near approach to obliteration, the embattled intellect put up its finest stand. Marciano piled out of his corner to finish Moore, and the stylist made him miss so often that it looked, for a fleeting moment, as if the champion were indeed punching himself arm-weary. In fact, Moore began to beat him to the punch. It was Moore's round, certainly, but an old-timer I talked to later averred that one of the body blows Marciano landed in that round was the hardest of the fight.

It was the eighth that ended the competitive phase of the fight. They fought all the way, and in the last third of the round the champion simply overflowed Archie. He knocked him down with a right six seconds before the bell, and I don't think Moore could have got up by ten if the round had lasted that long. The fight by then reminded me of something that Sam Langford, one of the most profound thinkers—and, according to all accounts, one of the greatest doers—of the prize ring, once said to me: "Whatever that other man wants to do, don't let him do it." Merely by moving in all the time and punching continually, Marciano achieves the same strategic effect that Langford gained by finesse. It is impossible to think, or to impose your thought, if you have to keep on avoiding punches.

Moore's "game," as old Egan would have called his courage, was beyond reproach. He came out proudly for the ninth, and stood and fought back with all he had, but Marciano slugged him down, and he was counted out with his left arm hooked over the middle rope as he tried to rise. It was a crushing defeat for the higher faculties and a lesson in intellectual humility, but he had made a hell of a fight.

The fight was no sooner over than hundreds of unsavory young yokels with New England accents began a kind of mountain-goat immigration from the bleachers to ringside. They leaped from chair to chair and, after they reached the press section, from typewriter shelf to typewriter shelf and, I hope, from movie star to movie star. "Rocky!" they yelled. "Brockton!" Two of them, as dismal a pair of civic ambassadors as I have seen since I worked on the Providence *Journal & Evening Bulletin*, stood on Wilson's typewriter and yelled "Providence!" After the fighters and the hick delinquents had gone away, I made my way out to Jerome Avenue, where the crowd milled, impenetrable, under the "El" structure.

If you are not in a great hurry to get home (and why should you be at eleven-thirty or twelve on a fight night?), the best plan is to walk up to the station north of the stadium and have a beer in a saloon, or a cup of tea in the 167th Street Cafeteria, and wait until the whole mess clears away. By that time you may even get a taxi. After this particular fight I chose the cafeteria, being in a contemplative rather than a convivial mood. The place is of a genre you would expect to find nearer Carnegie Hall, with blond woodwork and modern functional furniture imported from Italy—an appropriate background for the evaluation of an aesthetic experience. I got my tea and a smoked-salmon sandwich on a soft onion roll at the counter and made my way to a table, where I found myself between two young policemen who were talking about why Walt Disney has never attempted a screen version of Kafka's "Metamorphosis." As I did not feel qualified to join in that one, I got out my copy of the official program of the fights and began to read the high-class feature articles as I munched my sandwich.

One reminded me that I had seen the first boxing show ever held in Yankee Stadium—on May 12, 1923. I had forgotten that it *was* the first show, and even that 1923 was the year the Stadium opened. In my true youth the Yankees used to share the Polo Grounds with the Giants, and I had forgotten that, too, because I never cared much about baseball, although, come to think of it, I used to see the Yankees play occasionally in the nineteen-'teens, and should have remem-bered. I remembered the boxing show itself very well, though. It hap-pened during the spring of my second suspension from college, and I paid five dollars for a high-grandstand seat. The program merely said that it had been "an all-star heavyweight bill promoted by Tex Rick-ard for the Hearst Milk Fund," but I found that I could still remember every man and every bout on the card. One of the main events was between old Jess Willard, the former heavyweight champion of the world, who had lost the title to Jack Dempsey in 1919, and a young heavyweight named Floyd Johnson. Willard had been coaxed from retirement to make a comeback because there was such a dearth of heavyweight material that Rickard thought he could still get by, but as I remember the old fellow, he couldn't fight a lick. He had a fair left jab and a right uppercut that a fellow had to walk into to get hurt by, and he was big and soft. Johnson was a mauler worse than Rex Layne, and the old man knocked him out. The other main event, *ex aequo*, had Luis Angel Firpo opposing a fellow named Jack McAuliffe II, from Detroit, who had had only fifteen fights and had never beaten anybody, and had a glass jaw. The two winners, of whose identity there was infinitesimal preliminary doubt, were to fight each other for the right to meet the great Jack Dempsey. Firpo was so crude that Marciano would be a Fancy Dan in comparison. He could hit with only one hand—his right—he hadn't the faintest idea of what to do in close, and he never cared much for the business anyway. He knocked McAuliffe out, of course, and then, in a later "elimination" bout, stopped poor old Willard. He subsequently became a legend by going one and a half sensational rounds with Dempsey, in a time that is now represented to us as the golden age of American pugilism.

I reflected with satisfaction that old Ahab Moore could have whipped all four principals on that card within fifteen rounds, and that while Dempsey may have been a great champion, he had less to beat than Marciano. I felt the satisfaction because it proved that the world isn't going backward, if you can just stay young enough to remember what it was really like when you were really young.

Jimmy Cannon

Lonely and haunted personally, brilliant though erratic professionally, Jimmy Cannon (1910–1973) reveled in the perks of being the ultimate New York sports columnist. He dated fancy dames, hung out at Toots Shor's and the Stork Club, and enjoyed the ego massage of hearing Hemingway praise his work. Ultimately, however, he was a solo act, a high-school dropout from Greenwich Village who wrote with the rhythm of the streets as he battled Red Smith for supremacy in the city.

Cannon's syndicated column made him a big hitter in the *Post* and then the *Journal-American*, and his best work was about boxing. He scorned the flesh peddlers who made it what he called "the red-light district of sports," but he embraced fighters, cornermen, and all of the fight racket's other honest toilers. Even when he railed against Muhammad Ali, there was no forgetting his enduring line about Joe Louis: "He was a credit to his race—the human race." Cannon liked fighters with heart, moxie, and class whether they were champions (like Archie Moore, praised here in this 1955 paean to the fighter), hard-luck cases, or blue-collar dreamers. He wrote about the lot of them the only way he could: to be remembered for all time.

Archie

SOMEONE should write a song about Archie Moore who in the Polo Grounds knocked out Bobo Olson in three rounds. I don't mean big composers such as Harold Arlen or Duke Ellington. It should be a song that comes out of the backrooms of sloughed saloons on night-drowned streets in morning-worried parts of bad towns.

The guy who writes this one must be a piano player who can be dignified when he picks a quarter out of the marsh of a sawdust floor. They're dead, most of those piano players, their mouths full of dust instead of songs. But I'll bet Archie could dig one up in any town he ever made.

What Archie Moore is should be told in music because this is a guy who understands the truth of jazz. It must be a small song, played with a curfew-cheating stealth and sung in those butt-strangled voices the old guys had. There shouldn't be any parts for fiddles or horns because the kind of music I mean doesn't live in halls or theaters. It's the personal music those old men talked, more than crooned, when they were entertaining themselves to fight the loneliness.

It would have to be a hell of a song at that to grab Archie Moore. There must be in it the embarrassment of decent people ducking into pawn shops. It has to have that because Moore didn't get out of hock until last night when he scored his biggest pay night. It would have to catch sounds a man hears lying in a flea bag bed on a summer night in a slum.

Traveling second class and getting pushed around and borrowing would be in that song. It would define how a man of great skills suffers in obscurity in places like Tasmania because Archie Moore stiffened Frank Lindsay in that burg back in '40. The pug's fear of age would be in and knowing what you have is turning rotten with the years.

It isn't the blues I mean or boogie-woogie or bop. It's the kind of lament Tommy Lyman still sings in the basements of big cities. Anyplace the hustlers hung out, in any town, you used to get music like that. It belonged to them. They were songs about guys mad with booze or going crazy over a wrong broad or getting trimmed with shaved dice. Always, the guys in the song were broke. This was for those who had been betrayed or taken, mauled by junk or doing time on a wrong rap. The music's dead with the dead men and a lot of them had to be buried in the city bone yard on the cuff. If one of them's alive, Archie would know where to find him.

There he was last night, Archie Moore, the light-heavyweight champion of the world, who has fought in the Garden only once. The trash of the fight racket got there and pulled down scores. But Archie was boxing Joe Delaney in a joint called Adelaide in Australia. This was a nice one last night. It was no trouble at all for Archie.

There was all that guff about Olson being too quick, too agile, too young for Archie. So Archie let his 'stach grow and that horn player's beard up under his lip and put on his gold-lined, cream-colored silk bath-robe and walked down into the ring. He was like a master of cer-emonies standing in his corner, using both his mitts to shake hands with the pugs who were introduced. This was the easiest one they ever gave him. Generally, Archie looked stunted and flabby when you compared him to the guy he was fighting.

Middleweights don't con Archie even when they're champions. So Olson took the first round. Anyway, I gave it to him. But Archie had him measured and they should put that in the song, too. The night was clammily hot and Archie's a chubby guy even when he makes 175 and drains off the fat. Poor old Archie, they said. This kid will come in such a rush he'll make him back up.

But there was Olson backing up in the first round. Sure, he jabbed and he put a few combinations together. I saw that right Olson hit Archie with. But did you notice what happened when Archie took the shot with his right? The middleweight shuddered. He was gleaming with sweat and pale. He moved into the haven of a clinch.

It was very plain in the second. All Archie needed was one. He would get the range and let it go. So he stalled around, sneaking behind his crossed arms. He jabbed and blocked punches. Olson slipped some blows but Archie was in no hurry. Couple of times Olson nailed him but a hook told him that he was in there with the pawn shop champion who was trying to get out of hock.

The third only lasted a minute and nineteen seconds and that includes the ten Ruby Goldstein, the referee, counted. The right hand lead started Olson and then a right set him up. Then it was a left hook and Olson was down and numb. The second in Archie's corner began to unwrap the gold-lined robe. Olson was crawling across the ring. And then it was over.

But it isn't in this piece. It can't be. I don't know what Moore endured since '36, including the operation that put the welted scar on his belly. They tried to lose him and shut him out. They ran out on him and kept him poor. They forced him to fight in remote places. But now he's here. Marciano's got to be next. And that should be in the song.

James Baldwin

There was a literary logjam of epic proportions at ringside in Chicago for the 1962 heavyweight title fight between Floyd Patterson and Sonny Liston, created by the legendary press agent Harold Conrad, who had assembled four novelists who claimed to know something about boxing—Norman Mailer, Nelson Algren, Budd Schulberg, and England's Gerald Kersh—and one novelist who didn't, James Baldwin. Conrad said of Baldwin (1924-1987), who covered the fight for *Nugget* magazine, "He doesn't know a left hook from a kick in the ass," but Baldwin had the intellectual chops to offer a perceptive (and, at the time, unique) deconstruction of the surly ex-con Liston. Baldwin did his reporting in an atmosphere made tense by the presence of Mailer, who had just published a scathing review of Baldwin's novel *Another Country* (1962). To keep the peace, Conrad tried to leave an empty seat between the feuding authors on the night of the fight, but it was quickly appropriated by yet another member of the celebrity press corps—novelist and screenwriter Ben Hecht, who was covering Patterson–Liston for the *Hackensack Record*.

The Fight: Patterson vs. Liston

WE, the writers—a word I am using in its most primitive sense— arrived in Chicago about ten days before the baffling, bruising, an unbelievable two minutes and six seconds at Comiskey Park. We will get to all that later. I know nothing whatever about the Sweet Science or the Cruel Profession or the Poor Boy's Game. But I know a lot about pride, the poor boy's pride, since that's my story and will, in some way, probably, be my end.

There was something vastly unreal about the entire bit, as though we had all come to Chicago to make various movies and then spent all our time visiting the other fellow's set—on which no cameras were rolling. Dispatches went out every day, typewriters clattered, phones rang; each day, carloads of journalists invaded the Patterson or Liston camps, hung around until Patterson or Liston appeared; asked lame, inane questions, always the same questions, went away again, back to those telephones and typewriters; and informed a waiting, anxious world, or at least a waiting, anxious editor, what Patterson and Liston had said or done that day. It was insane and desperate, since neither of them ever really *did* anything. There wasn't anything for them *to* do, except train for the fight. But there aren't many ways to describe a fighter in training—it's muscle and sweat and grace, it's the same thing over and over—and since neither Patterson nor Liston were doing much boxing there couldn't be any interesting thumbnail sketches of their sparring partners. The "feud" between Patterson and Liston was as limp and tasteless as British roast lamb. Patterson is really far too much of a gentleman to descend to feuding with anyone, and I simply never believed, especially after talking with Liston, that he had the remotest grudge against Patterson. So there we were, hanging around, twiddling our thumbs, drinking Scotch, and telling stories, and trying to make copy out of nothing. And waiting, of course, for the Big Event, which would justify the monumental amounts of time, money, and energy which were being expended in Chicago.

Neither Patterson nor Liston have the *color*, or the instinct for drama which is possessed to such a superlative degree by the marvelous Archie Moore, and the perhaps less marvelous, but certainly vocal, and rather charming Cassius Clay. In the matter of color, a word which I am not now using in its racial sense, the Press Room far outdid the training camps. There were not only the sports writers, who had come, as I say, from all over the world: there were also the boxing greats, scrubbed and sharp and easygoing, Rocky Marciano, Barney Ross, Ezzard Charles, and the King, Joe Louis, and Ingemar Johansson, who arrived just a little before the fight and did not impress me as being easygoing at all. Archie Moore's word for him is "desperate," and he did not say this with any affection. There were the ruined boxers, stopped by an unlucky glove too early in their careers, who seemed to be treated with the tense and embarrassed affection reserved for faintly unsavory relatives, who were being used, some of them, as sparring partners. There were the managers and trainers, who, in public anyway, and with the exception of Cus D'Amato, seemed to have taken, many years ago, the vow of silence. There were people whose functions were mysterious indeed, certainly

unnamed, possibly unnamable, and, one felt, probably, if undefin-
ably, criminal. There were hangers-ons and protégés, a singer somewhere around, whom I didn't meet, owned by Patterson, and another
singer owned by someone else—who couldn't sing, everyone agreed,
but who didn't have to, being so loaded with personality—and there
were some improbable-looking women, turned out, it would seem,
by a machine shop, who didn't seem, really, to walk or talk, but rather
to gleam, click, and glide, with an almost soundless meshing of gears.
There were some pretty incredible girls, too, at the parties, impeccably blank and beautiful and rather incredibly vulnerable. There were
the parties and the post mortems and the gossip and speculations and
recollections and the liquor and the anecdotes, and dawn coming up
to find you leaving somebody else's house or somebody else's room
or the Playboy Club; and Jimmy Cannon, Red Smith, Milton Gross,
Sandy Grady, and A. J. Liebling; and Norman Mailer, Gerald Kersh,
Budd Schulberg, and Ben Hecht—who arrived, however, only for the
fight and must have been left with a great deal of time on his hands—
and Gay Talese (of the *Times*), and myself. Hanging around in
Chicago, hanging on the lightest word, or action, of Floyd Patterson
and Sonny Liston.

I am not an *aficionado* of the ring, and haven't been since Joe
Louis lost his crown—*he* was the last great fighter for me—and so I
can't really make comparisons with previous events of this kind.
But neither, it soon struck me, could anybody else. Patterson was, in
effect, the *moral* favorite—people *wanted* him to win, either because
they liked him, though many people didn't, or because they felt that
his victory would be salutary for boxing and that Liston's victory
would be a disaster. But no one could be said to be enthusiastic about
either man's record in the ring. The general feeling seemed to be that
Patterson had never been tested, that he was the champion, in effect,
by default; though, on the other hand, everyone attempted to avoid
the conclusion that boxing had fallen on evil days and that Patterson
had fought no worthy fighters because there were none. The desire
to avoid speculating too deeply on the present state and the probable future of boxing was responsible, I think, for some very odd and
stammering talk about Patterson's personality. (This led Red Smith to
declare that he didn't feel that sports writers had any business trying
to be psychiatrists, and that he was just going to write down who hit

whom, how hard, and where, and the hell with why.) And there was very sharp disapproval of the way he has handled his career, since he has taken over most of D'Amato's functions as a manager, and is clearly under no one's orders but his own. "In the old days," someone complained, "the manager told the fighter what to do, and he did it. You didn't have to futz around with the guy's *temperament*, for Christ's sake." Never before had any of the sports writers been compelled to deal directly with the fighter instead of with his manager, and all of them seemed baffled by this necessity and many were resentful. I don't know how they got along with D'Amato when he was running the entire show—D'Amato can certainly not be described as either simple or direct—but at least the figure of D'Amato was familiar and operated to protect them from the oddly compelling and touching figure of Floyd Patterson, who is quite probably the least likely fighter in the history of the sport. And I think that part of the resentment he arouses is due to the fact that he brings to what is thought of—quite erroneously—as a simple activity a terrible note of complexity. This is his personal style, a style which strongly suggests that most un-American of attributes, privacy, the will to privacy; and my own guess is that he is still relentlessly, painfully shy—he lives gallantly with his scars, but not all of them have healed—and while he has found a way to master this, he has found no way to hide it; as, for example, another miraculously tough and tender man, Miles Davis, has managed to do. Miles's disguise would certainly never fool anybody with sense, but it keeps a lot of people away, and that's the point. But Patterson, tough and proud and beautiful, is also terribly vulnerable, and looks it.

I met him, luckily for me, with Gay Talese, whom he admires and trusts, I say luckily because I'm not a very aggressive journalist, don't know enough about boxing to know which questions to ask, and am simply not able to ask a man questions about his private life. If Gay had not been there, I am not certain how I would ever have worked up my courage to say anything to Floyd Patterson—especially after having sat through, or suffered, the first, for me, of many press conferences. I only sat through two with Patterson, silently, and in the back—he, poor man, had to go through it every day, sometimes twice a day. And if I don't know enough about boxing to know which questions to ask, I must say that the boxing experts are not one whit more imaginative, though they were, I thought, sometimes rather more insolent. It was a curious insolence, though, veiled, tentative, uncertain—they couldn't be sure that Floyd wouldn't give them as good as he got. And this led, again, to that curious resentment I mentioned earlier, for they were forced, perpetually, to speculate about the man instead of the boxer. It doesn't appear to have occurred yet to many members of the press that one of the reasons their relations with Floyd are so frequently strained is that he has no reason, on any level, to trust them, and no reason to believe that they would be capable of hearing what he had to say, even if he could say it. Life's far from being as simple as most sports writers would like to have it. The world of sports, in fact, is far from being as simple as the sports pages often make it sound.

Gay and I drove out, ahead of all the other journalists, in a Hertz car, and got to the camp at Elgin while Floyd was still lying down. The camp was very quiet, bucolic, really, when we arrived; set in the middle of small, rolling hills; four or five buildings, a tethered goat—the camp mascot; a small green tent containing a Spartan cot; lots of cars. "They're very car-conscious here," someone said of Floyd's small staff of trainers and helpers. "Most of them have two cars." We ran into some of them standing around and talking on the grounds, and Buster Watson, a close friend of Floyd's, stocky, dark, and able, led us into the Press Room. Floyd's camp was actually Marycrest Farm, the twin of a Chicago settlement house, which works, on a smaller scale but in somewhat the same way, with disturbed and deprived children, as does Floyd's New York alma mater, the Wiltwyck School for Boys. It is a Catholic institution—Patterson is a converted Catholic—and the interior walls of the building in which the press conferences took place were decorated with vivid mosaics, executed by the children in colored beans, of various biblical events. There was an extraordinarily effective crooked cross, executed in charred wood, hanging high on one of the walls. There were two doors to the building in which the two press agents worked, one saying *Caritas*, the other saying *Veritas*. It seemed an incongruous setting for the life being lived there, and the event being prepared, but Ted Carroll, the Negro press agent, a tall man with white hair and a knowledgeable, weary, gentle face, told me that the camp was like the man. "The man lives a secluded life. He's like this place—peaceful and far away." It was not all that peaceful, of course, except naturally; it was otherwise menaced and inundated by hordes of human beings, from small boys, who wanted to be boxers, to old men who remembered Jack Dempsey as a kid. The signs on the road, pointing the way to Floyd Patterson's training camp, were perpetually carried away by souvenir hunters. ("At first," Ted Carroll said, "we were worried that maybe they were carrying them away for another reason—you know, the usual hassle—but no, they just want to put them in the rumpus room.") We walked about with Ted Carroll for a while and he pointed out to us the house, white, with green shutters, somewhat removed from the camp and on a hill, in which Floyd Patterson lived. He was resting now, and the press conference had been called for three o'clock, which was nearly three hours away. But he would be working out before the conference. Gay and I left Ted and wandered close to the house. I looked at the ring, which had been set up on another hill near the house, and examined the tent. Gay knocked lightly on Floyd's door. There was no answer, but Gay said that the radio was on. We sat down in the sun, near the ring, and speculated on Floyd's training habits, which kept him away from his family for such long periods of time.

Presently, here he came across the grass loping, rather, head down, with a small, tight smile on his lips. This smile seems always to be there when he is facing people and disappears only when he begins to be comfortable. Then he can laugh, as I never heard him laugh at a press conference, and the face which he watches so carefully in public is then, as it were, permitted to be its boyish and rather surprisingly zestful self. He greeted Gay, and took sharp, covert notice of me, seeming to decide that if I were with Gay, I was probably all right. We followed him into the gym, in which a large sign faced us, saying *So we being many are one body in Christ.* He went through his workout, methodically, rigorously, pausing every now and again to disagree with his trainer, Dan Florio, about the time—he insisted that Dan's stopwatch was unreliable—or to tell Buster that there weren't enough towels, to ask that the windows be closed. "You threw a good right hand that time," Dan Florio said; and, later, "Keep the right hand *up. Up!*" "We got a floor scale that's no good," Floyd said, cheerfully. "Sometimes I weigh two hundred, sometimes I weigh 'eighty-eight." And we watched him jump rope, which he must do according to some music in his head, very beautiful and gleaming and far away, like a boy saint helplessly dancing and seen through the steaming windows of a storefront church.

We followed him into the house when the workout was over, and sat in the kitchen and drank tea; he drank chocolate. Gay knew that I was somewhat tense as to how to make contact with Patterson—my own feeling was that he had a tough enough row to hoe, and that everybody should just leave him alone; how would *I* like it if I were forced to answer inane questions every day concerning the progress of my work?—and told Patterson about some of the things I'd written. But Patterson hadn't heard of me, or read anything of mine. Gay's explanation, though, caused him to look directly at me, and he said, "I've seen you someplace before. I don't know where, but I know I've seen you." I hadn't seen him before, except once, with Liston, in the Commissioner's office, when there had been a spirited fight concerning the construction of Liston's boxing gloves, which were "just about as flat as the back of my hand," according to a sports writer, "just like wearing no gloves at all." I felt certain, considering the number of people and the tension in that room, that he could not have seen me *then*—but we do know some of the same people, and have walked very often on the same streets. Gay suggested that he had seen me on TV. I had hoped that the contact would have turned out to be more personal, like a mutual friend or some activity connected with the Wiltwyck School, but Floyd now remembered the subject of the TV debate he had seen—the race problem, of course—and his face lit up. "I *knew* I'd seen you somewhere!" he said, triumphantly, and looked at me for a moment with the same brotherly pride I felt—and feel—in him.

By now he was, with good grace but a certain tense resignation, preparing himself for the press conference. I gather that there are many people who enjoy meeting the press—and most of them, in fact, were presently in Chicago—but Floyd Patterson is not one of them. I think he hates being put on exhibition, he doesn't believe it is real; while he is terribly conscious of the responsibility imposed on him by the title which he held, he is also afflicted with enough imagination to be baffled by his position. And he is far from having acquired the stony and ruthless perception which will allow him to stand at once within and without his fearful notoriety. Anyway, we trailed over to the building in which the press waited, and Floyd's small, tight, shy smile was back.

But he has learned, though it must have cost him a great deal, how to handle himself. He was asked about his weight, his food, his measurements, his morale. He had been in training for nearly six months ("Is that necessary?" "I just like to do it that way"), had boxed, at this point, about 162 rounds. This was compared to his condition at the time of the first fight with Ingemar Johansson. "Do you believe that you were overtrained for that fight?" "Anything I say now would sound like an excuse." But, later, "I was careless—not overconfident, but careless." He had allowed himself to be surprised by Ingemar's aggressiveness. "Did you and D'Amato fight over your decision to fight Liston?" The weary smile played at the corner of Floyd's mouth, and though he was looking directly at his interlocutors, his eyes were veiled. "No." Long pause. "Cus knows that I do what I want to do—ultimately, he accepted it." Was he surprised by Liston's hostility? No. Perhaps it had made him a bit more determined. Had he anything against Liston personally? "No. I'm the champion and I want to remain the champion." Had he and D'Amato ever disagreed before? "Not in relation to my opponents." Had he heard it said that, as a fighter, he lacked viciousness? "Whoever said that should see the fights I've won without being vicious." And why was he fighting Liston? "Well," said Patterson, "it was my decision to take the fight. You gentlemen disagreed, but you were the ones who placed him in the Number One position, so I felt that it was only right. Liston's criminal record is behind him, not before him." "Do you feel that you've been accepted as a champion?" Floyd smiled more tightly than ever and turned toward the questioner. "No," he said. Then, "Well, I have to be accepted as the champion—but maybe not a good one." "Why do you say," someone else asked, "that the opportunity to become a great champion will never arise?" "Because," said Floyd, patiently, "you gentlemen will never let it arise." Someone asked him about his experiences when boxing in Europe—what kind of reception had he enjoyed? Much greater and much warmer than here, he finally admitted, but added, with a weary and humorous caution, "I don't want to say anything derogatory about the United States. I am satisfied." The press seemed rather to flinch from the purport of this grim and vivid little joke, and switched to the subject of Liston again. Who was most in awe of whom? Floyd had no idea, he said, but, "Liston's confidence is on the surface. Mine is within."

And so it seemed to be indeed, as, later, Gay and I walked with him through the flat, midwestern landscape. It was not exactly that he was less tense—I think that he is probably always tense, and it is that, and not his glass chin, or a lack of stamina, which is his real liability as a fighter—but he was tense in a more private, more bearable way. The fight was very much on his mind, of course, and we talked of the strange battle about the boxing gloves, and the Commissioner's impenetrable and apparent bias toward Liston, though the difference in the construction of the gloves, and the possible meaning of this difference, was clear to everyone. The gloves had been made by two different firms, which was not the usual procedure, and, though they were the same standard eight-ounce weight, Floyd's gloves were the familiar, puffy shape, with most of the weight of the padding over the fist, and Liston's were extraordinarily slender, with most of the weight of the padding over the wrist. But we didn't talk only of the fight, and I can't now remember all the things we *did* talk about. I mainly remember Floyd's voice, going cheerfully on and on, and the way his face kept changing, and the way he laughed; I remember the glimpse I got of him then, a man more complex than he was yet equipped to know, a hero for many children who were still trapped where he had been, who might not have survived without the ring, and who yet, oddly, did not really seem to belong there. I dismissed my dim speculations, that afternoon, as sentimental inaccuracies, rooted in my lack of knowledge of the boxing world, and corrupted with a guilty chauvinism. But now I wonder. He told us that his wife was coming in for the fight, against his will "in order," he said, indescribably, "to *console* me if—" and he made, at last, a gesture with his hand, downward.

Liston's camp was very different, an abandoned racetrack in, or called, Aurora Downs, with wire gates and a uniformed cop, who lets you in, or doesn't. I had simply given up the press conference bit, since they didn't teach me much, and I couldn't ask those questions. Gay Talese couldn't help me with Liston, and this left me floundering on my own until Sandy Grady called up Liston's manager, Jack Nilon, and arranged for me to see Liston for a few minutes alone the next day. Liston's camp was far more outspoken concerning Liston's attitude toward the press than Patterson's. Liston didn't like most of the press and most of them didn't like him. But I didn't, myself, see any reason why he *should* like them, or pretend to—they had certainly never been very nice to him, and I was sure that he saw in them merely some more ignorant, uncaring white people, who, no matter how fine we cut it, had helped to cause him so much grief. And this impression was confirmed by reports from people who *did* get along with him—Wendell Phillips and Bob Teague, who are both Negroes, but rather rare and salty types, and Sandy Grady, who is not a Negro, but is certainly rare, and very probably salty. I got the impression from them that Liston was perfectly willing to take people as they were, if they would do the same for him. Again, I was not particularly appalled by his criminal background, believing, rightly or wrongly, that I probably knew more about the motives and even the necessity of this career than most of the white press could. The only relevance Liston's—presumably previous—associations should have been allowed to have, it seemed to me, concerned the possible effect of these on the future of boxing. Well, while the air was thick with rumor and gospel on this subject, I really cannot go into it without risking, at the very least, being sued for libel; and so, one of the most fascinating aspects of the Chicago story will have to be left in the dark. But the Sweet Science is not, in any case, really so low on shady types as to be forced to depend on Liston. The question is to what extent Liston is prepared to cooperate with whatever powers of darkness there are in boxing; and the extent of his cooperation, we must suppose, must depend, at least partly, on the extent of his awareness. So that there is nothing unique about the position in which he now finds himself and nothing unique about the speculation which now surrounds him.

I got to his camp at about two o'clock one afternoon. Time was running out, the fight was not more than three days away, and the atmosphere in the camp was, at once, listless and electric. Nilon looked as though he had not slept and would not sleep for days, and everyone else rather gave the impression that they wished they could—except for three handsome Negro ladies, related, I supposed, to Mrs. Liston, who sat, rather self-consciously, on the porch of the largest building on the grounds. They may have felt as I did, that training camps are like a theater before the curtain goes up, and if you don't have any function in it, you're probably in the way.

Liston, as we all know, is an enormous man, but surprisingly trim. I had already seen him work out, skipping rope to a record of "Night Train," and, while he wasn't nearly, for me, as moving as Patterson skipping rope in silence, it was still a wonderful sight to see. The press has really maligned Liston very cruelly, I think. He is far from stupid; is not, in fact, stupid at all. And, while there is a great deal of violence in him, I sensed no cruelty at all. On the contrary, he reminded me of big, black men I have known who acquired the reputation of being tough in order to conceal the fact that they weren't hard. Anyone who cared to could turn them into taffy.

Anyway, I liked him, liked him very much. He sat opposite me at the table, sideways, head down, waiting for the blow: for Liston knows, as only the inarticulately suffering can, just how inarticulate he is. But let me clarify that: I say suffering because it seems to me that he has suffered a great deal. It is in his face, in the silence of that face, and in the curiously distant light in the eyes—a light which rarely signals because there have been so few answering signals. And when I say inarticulate, I really do not mean to suggest that he does not know how to talk. He is inarticulate in the way we all are when more has happened to us than we know how to express; and inarticulate in a particularly Negro way—he has a long tale to tell which no one wants to hear. I said, "I can't ask you any questions because everything's been asked. Perhaps I'm only here, really, to say that I wish you well." And this was true, even though I wanted Patterson to win. Anyway, I'm glad I said it because he looked at me then, really for the first time, and he talked to me for a little while.

And what had hurt him most, somewhat to my surprise, was not the general press reaction to him, but the Negro reaction. "Colored people," he said, with great sorrow, "say they don't want their children to look up to me. Well, they ain't teaching their children to look up to Martin Luther King, either." There was a pause. "I wouldn't be no bad example if I was up there. I could tell a lot of those children what they need to know—because—I passed that way. I could make them *listen*." And he spoke a little of what he would like to do for young Negro boys and girls, trapped in those circumstances which so nearly defeated himself and Floyd, and from which neither can yet be said to have recovered. "I tell you one thing, though," he said, "if I was up there, I wouldn't bite my tongue." I could certainly believe that. And we discussed the segregation issue, and the role, in it, of those prominent Negroes who find him so distasteful. "I would never," he said, "go against my brother—we got to learn to stop fighting among our own." He lapsed into silence again. "They said they didn't want me to have the title. They didn't say that about Johansson." "They" were the Negroes. "*They* ought to know why I got some of the bum raps I got." But he was not suggesting that they were *all* bum raps. His wife came over, a very pretty woman, seemed to gather in a glance how things were going, and sat down. We talked for a little while of matters entirely unrelated to the fight, and then it was time for his workout, and I left. I felt terribly ambivalent, as many Negroes do these days, since we are all trying to decide, in one way or another, which attitude, in our terrible American dilemma, is the most effective: the disciplined sweetness of Floyd, or the outspoken intransigence of Liston. *If I was up there, I wouldn't bite my tongue.* And Liston is a man aching for respect and responsibility. Sometimes we grow into our responsibilities and sometimes, of course, we fail them.

I left for the fight full of a weird and violent depression, which I traced partly to fatigue—it had been a pretty grueling time—partly to the fact that I had bet more money than I should have—on Patterson — and partly to the fact that *I* had had a pretty definitive fight with someone with whom I had hoped to be friends. And I was depressed about Liston's bulk and force and his twenty-five-pound weight advantage. I was afraid that Patterson might lose, and I really didn't want to see that. And it wasn't that I didn't like Liston. I just felt closer to Floyd.

I was sitting between Norman Mailer and Ben Hecht. Hecht felt about the same way that I did, and we agreed that if Patterson didn't get "stopped," as Hecht put it, "by a baseball bat," in the very beginning—if he could carry Liston for five or six rounds—he might very well hold the title. We didn't pay an awful lot of attention to the preliminaries—or I didn't; Hecht did; I watched the ball park fill with people and listened to the vendors and the jokes and the speculations: and watched the clock.

From my notes: Liston entered the ring to an almost complete silence. Someone called his name, he looked over, smiled, and winked. Floyd entered, and got a hand. But he looked terribly small next to Liston, and my depression deepened.

My notes again: Archie Moore entered the ring, wearing an opera cape. Cassius Clay, in black tie, and as insolent as ever. Mickey Allen sang "The Star-Spangled Banner." When Liston was introduced, some people boo'd—they cheered for Floyd, and I think I know how this made Liston feel. It promised, really, to be one of the worst fights in history.

Well, I was wrong, it was scarcely a fight at all, and I can't but wonder who on earth will come to see the rematch, if there is one. Floyd seemed all right to me at first. He had planned for a long fight, and seemed to be feeling out his man. But Liston got him with a few bad body blows, and a few bad blows to the head. And no one agrees with me on this, but, at one moment, when Floyd lunged for Liston's belly—looking, it must be said, like an amateur, wildly flailing—it seemed to me that some unbearable tension in him broke, that he lost his head. And, in fact, I nearly screamed, "Keep your head, baby!" but it was really too late. Liston got him with a left, and Floyd went down. I could not believe it. I couldn't hear the count and though Hecht said, "It's over," and picked up his coat, and left, I remained standing, staring at the ring, and only conceded that the fight was really over when two other boxers entered the ring. Then I wandered out of the ball park, almost in tears. I met an old colored man at one of the exits, who said to me, cheerfully, "I've been robbed," and we talked about it for a while. We started walking through the crowds and A. J. Liebling, behind us, tapped me on the shoulder and we went off to a bar, to mourn the very possible death of boxing, and to have a drink, with love, for Floyd.

Gay Talese

Gay Talese (b. 1932) became the point man for the New Journalism after he wrote a story for *Esquire* in 1962 about Joe Louis's grudging journey to middle age. Talese opened his piece with a scene that felt like something out of a movie and unwound with the pacing and elements of fiction. Overnight, other writers began trying the same approach, with varying success. Talese remained the reigning master of narrative nonfiction as he moved on to write significant books about *The New York Times* (where he worked as a reporter for twelve years), the Mafia, his Italian American roots, and sex in America. Never forgotten, however, was the importance of his meticulously observed magazine profiles of such cultural icons as Frank Sinatra and Joe DiMaggio. Though Floyd Patterson, the subject of a 1964 *Esquire* profile collected in Talese's book *The Overreachers* (1965), didn't capture the national imagination the way they did, he was nevertheless a subject of fascination and speculation because of the anguish he suffered as king of the world's heavyweights. When Patterson began talking, Talese seized the moment to examine the kind of insecurities athletes rarely admit to.

―――――――――

Floyd Patterson

A t *the foot of a mountain in upstate New York, about sixty miles from Manhattan, there is an abandoned country clubhouse with a dusty dance floor, upturned barstools, and an untuned piano; and the only sounds heard around the place at night come from the big white house behind it—the clanging sounds of garbage cans being toppled by raccoons, skunks, and stray cats making their nocturnal raids down from the mountain.*

The white house seems deserted, too; but occasionally, when the animals become too clamorous, a light will flash on, a window will open, and a Coke bottle will come flying through the darkness and smash against the cans. But mostly the animals are undisturbed until daybreak, when the rear door of the white house swings open and a broad-shouldered Negro appears in gray sweat clothes with a white towel around his neck.

He runs down the steps, quickly passes the garbage cans and proceeds at a trot down the dirt road beyond the country club toward the highway. Sometimes he stops along the road and throws a flurry of punches at imaginary foes, each jab punctuated by hard gasps of his breathing—"hegh-hegh-hegh-hegh"—and then, reaching the highway, he turns and soon disappears up the mountain.

At this time of morning farm trucks are on the road, and the drivers wave at the runner. And later in the morning other motorists see him, and a few stop suddenly at the curb and ask: "Say, aren't you Floyd Patterson?"

"No," says Floyd Patterson. "I'm his brother, Raymond."

The motorists move on, but recently a man on foot, a disheveled man who seemed to have spent the night outdoors, staggered behind the runner along the road and yelled, "Hey, Floyd Patterson!"

"No, I'm his brother, Raymond."

"Don't tell *me* you're not Floyd Patterson. I know what Floyd Patterson looks like."

"Okay," Patterson said, shrugging, "if you want me to be Floyd Patterson, I'll be Floyd Patterson."

"So let me have your autograph," said the man, handing him a rumpled piece of paper and a pencil.

He signed it—"Raymond Patterson."

One hour later Floyd Patterson was jogging his way back down the dirt path toward the white house, the towel over his head absorbing the sweat from his brow. He lives alone in a two-room apartment in the rear of the house, and has remained there in almost complete seclusion since getting knocked out a second time by Sonny Liston.

In the smaller room is a large bed he makes up himself, several record albums he rarely plays, a telephone that seldom rings. The larger room has a kitchen on one side and on the other, adjacent to a sofa, is a fireplace from which are hung boxing trunks and T-shirts to dry, and a photograph of him when he was the champion, and also a television set. The set is usually on except when Patterson is sleeping, or when he is sparring across the road inside the clubhouse (the ring is rigged over what was once the dance floor), or when, in a rare moment of painful honesty, he reveals to a visitor what it is like to be the loser.

"Oh, I would give up anything to just be able to work with Liston, to box with him somewhere where nobody would see us, and to see if I could get past three minutes with him," Patterson was saying, wiping his face with the towel, pacing slowly around the room near the sofa. "I *know* I can do better. . . . Oh, I'm not talking about a rematch. Who would pay a nickel for another Patterson–Liston match? I know *I* wouldn't. . . . But all I want to do is get past the first round."

Then he said, "You have no idea how it is in the first round. You're out there with all those people around you, and those cameras, and the whole world looking in, and all that movement, that excitement, and 'The Star-Spangled Banner,' and the whole nation hoping you'll win, including President Kennedy. And do you know what this all does? It blinds you, just blinds you. And then the bell rings, and you go at Liston and he's coming at you, and you're not even aware that there's a referee in the ring with you.

". . . Then you can't remember much of the rest, because you don't want to. . . . All you recall is, all of a sudden, you're getting up, and the referee is saying, 'You all right?' and you say, 'Of *course* I'm all right,' and he says, 'What's your name?' and you say, 'Patterson.'

"And then, suddenly, with all this screaming around you, you're down again, and know you have to get up, but you're extremely groggy, and the referee is pushing you back, and your trainer is in there with a towel, and people are all standing up, and your eyes focus directly at no one person—you're sort of floating.

"It's not a *bad* feeling when you're knocked out," he said. "It's a *good* feeling, actually. It's not painful, just a sharp grogginess. You don't see angels or stars; you're on a pleasant cloud. After Liston hit me in Nevada, I felt, for about four or five seconds, that everybody in the arena was actually in the ring with me, circled around me like a family, and you feel warmth toward all the people in the arena after you're knocked out. You feel lovable to all the people. And you want to reach out and kiss everybody—men and women—and after the Liston fight somebody told me I actually blew a kiss to the crowd from the ring. I don't remember that. But I guess it's true because that's the way you feel during the four or five seconds after a knockout. . . .

"But then," Patterson went on, still pacing, "this good feeling leaves you. You realize where you are, and what you're doing there, and what has just happened to you. And what follows is a hurt, a confused hurt—not a physical hurt—it's a hurt combined with anger; it's a what-will-people-think hurt; it's an ashamed-of-my-own-ability hurt . . . and all you want then is a hatch door in the middle of the ring—a hatch door that will open and let you fall through and land in your dressing room instead of having to get out of the ring and face those people. The worst thing about losing is having to walk out of the ring and face those people. . . ."

Then Patterson walked over to the stove and put on the kettle for tea. He remained silent for a few moments. Through the walls could be heard the footsteps and voices of the sparring partners and the trainer, who live in the front of the house. Soon they would be in the country club getting things ready should Patterson wish to spar.

Patterson wants to continue as a prizefighter but his wife, whom he rarely sees any more, and most of his friends think he should quit. They point out that he does not need the money. Even he admits that from investments alone on his $8,000,000 gross earnings he should have an annual income of about $35,000 for the next twenty-five years. But Patterson, who is only twenty-eight years old and barely scratched, cannot believe that he is finished. He cannot help but think that it was something more than Liston that destroyed him—a strange, psychological force was also involved—and unless he can fully understand what it was, and learn to deal with it in the boxing ring, he may never be able to live peacefully anywhere but under this mountain. Nor will he ever be able to discard the false whiskers and mustache that, ever since Johansson beat him in 1959, he has carried with him in a small attaché case into each fight so he can slip out of the stadium unrecognized should he lose.

"I often wonder what other fighters feel, and what goes through their minds when they lose," Patterson said, placing the cups of tea on the table. "I've wanted so much to talk to another fighter about all this, to compare thoughts, to see if he feels some of the same things I've felt. But who can you talk to? Most fighters don't talk much anyway. And I can't even look another fighter in the eye at a weigh-in, for some reason.

"At the Liston weigh-in, the sportswriters noticed this, and said it showed I was afraid. But that's not it. I can never look *any* fighter in the eye because . . . well, because we're going to fight, which isn't a nice thing, and because . . . well, once I actually did look a fighter in the eye. It was a long, long time ago. I must have been in the amateurs then. . . . And when I looked at this fighter, I saw he had such a nice face. . . . And then he looked at *me* . . . and *smiled* at me . . . and *I* smiled back! . . . It was strange, very strange. When a guy can look at another guy and smile like that, I don't think they have any business fighting.

"I don't remember what happened in that fight, and I don't remember what the guy's name was. I only remember that, ever since, I have never looked another fighter in the eye. . . ."

The telephone rang in the bedroom. Patterson got up to answer it. It was his wife, Sandra. So he excused himself, shutting the bedroom door behind him.

Sandra Patterson and their four children live in a $100,000 home in an upper-middle-class white neighborhood in Scarsdale, New York. Floyd Patterson feels uncomfortable in this home surrounded by a manicured lawn and stuffed with soft furniture, and, since losing his title to Liston, he has preferred living full time at his camp, which his children have come to know as "Daddy's house." The children, the eldest of whom is a six-year-old daughter named Jeannie, do not know exactly what their father does for a living. But Jeannie, who watched the last Liston–Patterson fight on closed-circuit television, accepted the explanation that her father performs in a kind of game where the men take turns pushing one another down; he had his turn pushing them down, and now it is their turn.

The bedroom door opened again, and Floyd Patterson, shaking his head, was very angry and nervous.

"I'm not going to work out today," he said. "I'm going to fly down to Scarsdale. Those boys are picking on Jeannie again. She's the only Negro in this school, and the older kids give her a rough time, and some of the older boys tease her and lift up her dress all the time. Yesterday she went home crying, and so today I'm going down there and plan to wait outside the school for those boys to come out, and . . ."

"How old are they?" he was asked.

"Teenagers," he said. "Old enough for a left hook."

Patterson telephoned his pilot friend, Ted Hanson, who stays at the camp and does public relations work for him, and has helped teach Patterson to fly. Five minutes later Hanson, a lean white man with a crewcut and glasses, was knocking on the door; and ten minutes later both were in the car that Patterson was driving almost recklessly over the narrow, winding country roads toward the airport, about six miles from the camp.

"Sandra is afraid I'll cause trouble; she's worried about what I'll do to those boys; she doesn't want trouble!" Patterson snapped, swerving around a hill and giving his car more gas. "She's just not firm enough! She's afraid. . . . She was afraid to tell me about that grocery man who's been making passes at her. It took her a long time before she told me about that dishwasher repairman who comes over and calls her '*baby.*' They all know I'm away so much. And that dishwasher repairman's been to my home about four, five times this month already. That machine breaks down every week. I guess he fixes it so it breaks down every week. Last time, I laid a trap. I waited forty-five minutes for him to come, but then he didn't show up. I was going to grab him and say, 'How would you like it if I called *your* wife "*baby*"? You'd feel like punching me in the nose, wouldn't you? Well, that's what I'm going to do—if you ever call her "*baby*" again. You call her Mrs. Patterson; or Sandra, if you know her. But you don't know her, so call her Mrs. Patterson.' . . . And then I told Sandra that these men, this type of white man, he just wants to have some fun with colored women. He'll never marry a colored woman, just wants to have some fun. . . ."

Now he was driving into the airport's parking lot. Directly ahead, roped to the grass air strip, was the single-engine, green Cessna that Patterson bought and learned to fly in Denver before the second Liston fight. Flying was a thing Patterson had always feared—a fear shared by, maybe inherited from, his manager, Cus D'Amato, who still will not fly.

D'Amato, who began training Patterson when the fighter was fourteen years old and exerted a tremendous influence over his psyche, is a strange but fascinating man of fifty-six who is addicted to spartanism and self-denial and is possessed by suspicion and fear: he avoids subways because he fears someone might push him onto the tracks; never has married because he believes a wife might be duped by his enemies; never reveals his home address because he suspects snipers.

"I must keep my enemies confused," D'Amato once explained. "When they are confused, then I can do a job for my fighters. What I do not want in life, however, is a sense of security; the moment a person knows security, his senses are dulled—and he begins to die. I also do not want many pleasures in life; I believe the more pleasures you get out of living, the more fear you have of dying."

Until a few years ago, D'Amato did most of Patterson's talking, and ran things like an Italian *padrone*. But later Patterson, the maturing son, rebelled against the Father Image. After losing to Sonny Liston the first time—a fight D'Amato had urged Patterson to resist —Patterson took flying lessons. And before the second Liston fight Patterson had conquered his fear of height, was master at the controls, was filled with renewed confidence—and knew, too, that even if he lost he at least possessed a vehicle that could get him out of town, fast.

But it didn't. After the flight, the little Cessna, weighed down by too much luggage, became overheated ninety miles outside of Las Vegas. Patterson and his pilot companion, having no choice but to turn back, radioed the airfield and arranged for the rental of a larger plane. When they landed, the Vegas air terminal was filled with people leaving town after the fight. Patterson hid in the shadows behind a hangar. His beard was packed in the trunk. But nobody saw him.

Later the pilot flew Patterson's Cessna back to New York alone. And Patterson flew in the larger, rented plane. He was accompanied on this flight by Ted Hanson, a friendly forty-two-year-old, thrice-divorced Californian, who once was a crop duster, a bartender, and a cabaret hoofer; later he became a pilot instructor in Las Vegas, and it was there that he met Patterson. The two became good friends. And, when Patterson asked Hanson to help fly the rented plane back to New York, Hanson did not hesitate, even though he had a slight hangover that night—partly due to being depressed by Liston's victory, partly to being slugged in a bar by a drunk after objecting to some unflattering things the drunk had said about the fight.

Once in the airplane, however, Ted Hanson became very alert. He had to be because, after the plane had cruised awhile at ten thousand feet, Floyd Patterson's mind seemed to wander back to the ring, and the plane would drift off course, and Hanson would say, "Floyd,

Floyd, how's about getting back on course?" and then Patterson's head would snap up and his eyes would flash toward the dials. And everything would be all right for a while. But then he was back in the arena, reliving the fight, hardly believing that it had really happened. . . .

". . . And I kept thinking, as I flew out of Vegas that night, of all those months of training before the fight, all the roadwork, all the sparring, all the months away from Sandra . . . thinking of the time in camp when I wanted to stay up until 11:15 P.M. to watch a certain movie on the Late Show, but I didn't because I had roadwork the next morning. . . .

"And I was thinking about how good I'd felt before the fight, as I lay on the table in the dressing room. . . . I remember thinking, 'You're in excellent physical condition, you're in good mental condition—but are you vicious?' But you tell yourself, 'Viciousness is not important now, don't think about it now; a championship fight's at stake, and that's important enough and, who knows? maybe you'll get vicious once the bell rings.'

"And so you lay there trying to get a little sleep . . . but you're only in a twilight zone, half-asleep, and you're interrupted every once in a while by voices out in the hall, some guy's yelling, 'Hey, Jack,' or 'Hey, Al,' or, 'Hey, get those four-rounders into the ring.' And when you hear that you think, 'They're not ready for you yet.' So you lay there . . . and wonder, 'Where will I be tomorrow?' 'Where will I be three hours from now?' . . . Oh, you think all kinds of thoughts, some thoughts completely unrelated to the fight . . . you wonder whether you ever paid your mother-in-law back for all those stamps she bought a year ago . . . and you remember that time at 2 A.M. when Sandra tripped on the steps while bringing a bottle up to the baby . . . and then you get mad and ask: 'WHAT AM I THINKING ABOUT THESE THINGS FOR?' . . . and you try to sleep . . . but then the door opens and somebody says to somebody else, 'Hey, is somebody gonna go to Liston's dressing room to watch 'em bandage up?'

"And so then you know it's about time to get ready. . . . You open your eyes. You get off the table. You glove up, you loosen up. Then Liston's trainer walks in. He looks at you, he smiles. He feels the bandages and later he says, 'Good luck, Floyd,' and you think, 'He didn't have to say that; he must be a nice guy.'

"And then you go out, and it's the long walk, always a long walk, and you think, 'What am I gonna be when I come back this way?' Then you climb into the ring. You notice Billy Eckstine at ringside leaning over to talk to somebody, and you see the reporters—some you like, some you don't like—and then it's 'The Star-Spangled Banner,' and the cameras are rolling, and the bell rings. . . .

"How could the same thing happen twice? How? That's all I kept thinking after the knockout. . . . Was I fooling these people all these years? . . . Was I ever the champion? . . . And then they lead you out of the ring . . . and up the aisle you go, past those people, and all you want is to get to your dressing room, fast . . . but the trouble was in Las Vegas they made a wrong turn along the aisle, and when we got to the end, there was no dressing room there . . . and we had to walk all the way back down the aisle, past the same people, and they must have been thinking, 'Patterson's not only knocked out, but he can't even find his dressing room.' . . .

"In the dressing room I had a headache. Liston didn't hurt me physically—a few days later I only felt a twitching nerve in my teeth—it was nothing like some fights I've had: like that Dick Wagner fight in '54 when he beat my body so bad I was urinating blood for days. . . . After the Liston fight, I just went into the bathroom, shut the door behind me, and looked at myself in the mirror. I just looked at myself, and asked, 'What happened?' and then they started pounding on the door, and saying, 'C'm'on out, Floyd, c'm'on out; the press is here, Cus is here, c'm'on out, Floyd.' . . .

"And so I went out, and they asked questions, but what can you say? . . . What you're thinking about is all those months of training, all the conditioning, all the depriving; and you think, 'I didn't have to run that extra mile, didn't have to spar that day, I could have stayed up that night in camp and watched the Late Show. . . . I could have fought this fight tonight in no condition.' . . ."

"Floyd, Floyd," Hanson had said, "let's get back on course. . . ."

Again Patterson would snap out of his reverie, and refocus on the Omnirange, and get his flying under control. After landing in New Mexico, and then in Ohio, Floyd Patterson and Ted Hanson brought the little plane into the New York air strip near the fight camp. The green Cessna that had been flown back by the other pilot was already there, roped to the grass at precisely the same spot it was on this day five months later, on this day when Floyd Patterson was planning to fly it toward perhaps another fight—a fight with some schoolboys in Scarsdale who had been lifting up his six-year-old daughter's dress.

Patterson and Ted Hanson untied the plane, and Patterson got a rag and wiped from the windshield the splotches of insects. Then he walked around behind the plane, inspected the tail, checked under the fuselage, then peered down between the wing and the flaps to make sure all the screws were tight. He seemed suspicious of something. D'Amato would have been pleased.

"If a guy wants to get rid of you," Patterson explained, "all he has to do is remove these little screws here. Then, when you try to come in for a landing, the flaps fall off, and you crash."

Then Patterson got into the cockpit and started the engine. A few moments later, with Hanson beside him, Patterson was racing the little plane over the grassy field, then soaring over the weeds, then flying high above the gentle hills and trees. It was a nice take-off.

Since it was only a forty-minute flight to the Westchester airport, where Sandra Patterson would be waiting with a car, Floyd Patterson did all the flying. The trip was uneventful until, suddenly behind a cloud, he flew into heavy smoke that hovered above a forest fire. His visibility gone, he was forced to the instruments. And at this precise moment a fly that had been buzzing in the back of the cockpit flew up front and landed on the instrument panel in front of Patterson. He glared at the fly, watched it crawl slowly up the windshield, then shot a quick smash with his palm against the glass. He missed. The fly buzzed safely past Patterson's ear, bounced off the back of the cockpit, circled around.

"This smoke won't keep up," Hanson assured. "You can level off."

Patterson leveled off.

He flew easily for a few moments. Then the fly buzzed to the front again, zigzagging before Patterson's face, then landed and proceeded to crawl across the panel. Patterson watched it, squinted. Then he slammed down at it with a quick right hand. Missed.

Ten minutes later, his nerves still on edge, Patterson began the descent. He picked up the radio microphone—"Westchester tower . . . Cessna 2729 uniform . . . three miles northwest . . . land in one-six on final. . . ." And then, after an easy landing, he climbed quickly out of the cockpit and strode toward his wife's station wagon outside the terminal.

But along the way a small man smoking a cigar turned toward Patterson, waved at him, and said, "Say, excuse me, but aren't you . . . aren't you . . . Sonny Liston?"

Patterson stopped. He glared at the man, bewildered. He wasn't sure whether it was a joke or an insult, and he really did not know what to do.

"Aren't you Sonny Liston?" the man repeated, quite serious.

"No," Patterson said, quickly passing by the man, "I'm his brother."

When he reached Mrs. Patterson's car, he asked, "How much time till school lets out?"

"About fifteen minutes," she said, starting up the engine. Then she said, "Oh, Floyd, I just should have told Sister, I shouldn't have . . ."

"*You* tell Sister; *I'll* tell the boys. . . ."

Mrs. Patterson drove as quickly as she could into Scarsdale, with Patterson shaking his head and telling Ted Hanson in the back, "Really can't understand these school kids. This is a religious school, and they want $20,000 for a glass window—and yet, some of them carry these racial prejudices, and it's mostly the Jews who are shoulder-to-shoulder with us, and . . ."

"Oh, Floyd," cried his wife, "Floyd, *I* have to get along here. *You're* not here, *you* don't live here, *I* . . ."

She arrived at the school just as the bell began to ring.

It was a modern building at the top of a hill, and on the lawn was the statue of a saint and, behind it, a large white cross.

"There's Jeannie," said Mrs. Patterson.

"Hurry, call her over here," Patterson said.

"Jeannie! Come over here, honey."

The little girl, wearing a blue school uniform and cap, and clasping books in front of her, came running down the path toward the station wagon.

"Jeannie," Floyd Patterson said, rolling down his window, "point out the boys who lifted your dress."

Jeannie turned and watched as several students came down the path; then she pointed to a tall, thin curly-haired boy walking with four other boys, all about twelve to fourteen years of age.

"Hey," Patterson called to him, "can I see you for a minute?"

All five boys came to the side of the car. They looked Patterson directly in the eye. They seemed not at all intimidated by him.

"You the one that's been lifting up my daughter's dress?" Patterson asked the boy who had been singled out.

"Nope," the boy said, casually.

"Nope?" Patterson said, caught off guard by the reply.

"Wasn't him, Mister," said another boy. "Probably was his little brother, Dennis."

Patterson looked at Jeannie. But she was speechless, uncertain. The five boys remained there, waiting for Patterson to do something.

"Well, er, where's Dennis?" Patterson asked.

"Hey, Dennis!" one of the boys yelled. "Dennis come over here."

Dennis walked toward them. He resembled his older brother; he had freckles on his small, upturned nose, had blue eyes, dark curly hair and, as he approached the station wagon, he seemed equally unintimidated by Patterson.

"You been lifting up my daughter's dress?"

"Nope," said Dennis.

"Nope!" Patterson repeated, frustrated.

"Nope, I wasn't lifting it," Dennis said. "I was just touching it a little . . ."

The other boys stood around the car looking down at Patterson, and other students crowded behind them, and nearby Patterson saw several white parents standing next to their parked cars; he became self-conscious, began to tap nervously with his fingers against the dashboard. He could not raise his voice without creating an unpleasant scene, yet could not retreat gracefully; so his voice went soft, and he said, finally, "Look, Dennis, I want you to stop it. I won't tell your mother—that might get you in trouble—but don't do it again, okay?"

"Okay."

The boys calmly turned and walked, in a group, up the street.

Sandra Patterson said nothing. Jeannie opened the door, sat in the front seat next to her father, and took out a small blue piece of paper that a nun had given her and handed it across to Mrs. Patterson. But Floyd Patterson snatched it. He read it. Then he paused, put the paper down, and quietly announced, dragging out the words, *"She didn't do her religion."*

Patterson now wanted to get out of Scarsdale. He wanted to return to camp.

After stopping at the Patterson home in Scarsdale and picking up Floyd Patterson, Jr., who is three, Mrs. Patterson drove them all back to the airport. Jeannie and Floyd, Jr., were seated in the back of the plane, and then Mrs. Patterson drove the station wagon alone up to camp, planning to return to Scarsdale that evening with the children.

It was 4 P.M. when Floyd Patterson got back to the camp, and the shadows were falling on the country club, and on the tennis court routed by weeds, and on the big white house in front of which not a single automobile was parked. All was deserted and quiet; it was a loser's camp.

The children ran to play inside the country club; Patterson walked slowly toward his apartment to dress for the workout.

"What could I do with those schoolboys?" he asked. "What can you do to kids of that age?"

It still seemed to bother him—the effrontery of the boys, the realization that he had somehow failed, the probability that, had those same boys heckled someone in Liston's family, the school yard would have been littered with limbs.

While Patterson and Liston both are products of the slum, and while both began as thieves, Patterson had been tamed in a special school with help from a gentle spinster; later he became a Catholic convert, and learned not to hate. Still later he bought a dictionary, adding to his vocabulary such words as "vicissitude" and "enigma." And when he regained his championship from Johansson, he became the great black hope of the Urban League.

He proved that it is not only possible to rise out of a Negro slum and succeed as a sportsman, but also to develop into an intelligent, sensitive, law-abiding citizen. In proving this, however, and in taking pride in it, Patterson seemed to lose part of himself. He lost part of his hunger, his anger—and as he walked up the steps into his apartment, he was saying, "I became the good guy. . . . After Liston won the title, I kept hoping that he would change into a good guy, too. That would have relieved me of the responsibility, and maybe I could have been more of the bad guy. But he didn't. . . . It's okay to be the good guy when you're winning. But when you're losing, it is no good being the good guy. . . ."

Patterson took off his shirt and trousers and, moving some books on the bureau to one side, put down his watch, his cufflinks and a clip of bills.

"Do you do much reading?" he was asked.

"No," he said. "In fact, you know I've never finished reading a book in my whole life? I don't know why. I just feel that no writer today has anything for me; I mean, none of them has felt any more deeply than I have, and I have nothing to learn from them. Although Baldwin to me seems different from the rest. What's Baldwin doing these days?"

"He's writing a play. Anthony Quinn is supposed to have a part in it."

"Quinn?" Patterson asked.

"Yes."

"Quinn doesn't like me."

"Why?"

"I read or heard it somewhere; Quinn had been quoted as saying that my fight was disgraceful against Liston, and Quinn said something to the effect that he could have done better. People often say that—*they* could have done better! Well, I think that if *they* had to fight, *they* couldn't even go through the experience of waiting for the fight to begin. They'd be up the whole night before, and would be drinking, or taking drugs. They'd probably get a heart attack. I'm sure that if I was in the ring with Anthony Quinn I could wear him out without even touching him. I would do nothing but pressure him, I'd stalk him, I'd stand close to him. I wouldn't touch him, but I'd wear him out and he'd collapse. But Anthony Quinn's an old man, isn't he?"

"In his forties."

"Well, anyway," Patterson said, "getting back to Baldwin, he seems like a wonderful guy. I've seen him on television and, before the Liston fight in Chicago, he came by my camp. You meet Baldwin on the street and you say, 'Who's this poor slob?'—he seems just like another guy; and this is the same impression *I* give people when they don't know me. But I think Baldwin and me, we have much in common, and someday I'd just like to sit somewhere for a long time and talk to him. . . ."

Patterson, his trunks and sweat pants on, bent over to tie his shoelaces, and then, from a bureau drawer, took out a T-shirt across which was printed *The Deauville*. He has several T-shirts bearing the same name. He takes good care of them. They are souvenirs from the high point of his life. They are from the Deauville Hotel in Miami Beach, which is where he trained for the third Ingemar Johansson match in March of 1961.

Never was Floyd Patterson more popular, more admired than during that winter. He had visited President Kennedy; he had been given a $25,000 jeweled crown by his manager; his greatness was conceded by sportswriters—and nobody had any idea that Patterson, secretly, was in possession of a false mustache and dark glasses that he intended to wear out of Miami Beach should he lose the third fight to Johansson.

It was after being knocked out by Johansson in their first fight that Patterson, deep in depression, hiding in humiliation for months in a remote Connecticut lodge, decided he could not face the public again if he lost. So he bought false whiskers and a mustache, and planned to wear them out of his dressing room after a defeat. He had also planned, in leaving his dressing room, to linger momentarily within the crowd and perhaps complain out loud about the fight. Then he would slip undiscovered through the night and into a waiting automobile.

Although there proved to be no need to bring the disguise into the second or third Johansson fights, or into a subsequent bout in Toronto against an obscure heavyweight named Tom McNeeley, Patterson brought it anyway; and, after the first Liston fight, he not only wore it during his forty-eight-hour automobile ride from Chicago to New York, but he also wore it while in an airliner bound for Spain.

"As I got onto this plane, you'd never have recognized me," he said. "I had on this beard, mustache, glasses, and hat—and I also limped, to make myself look older. I was alone. I didn't care what plane I boarded; I just looked up and saw this sign at the terminal reading 'Madrid,' and so I got on that flight after buying a ticket.

"When I got to Madrid I registered at a hotel under the name 'Aaron Watson.' I stayed in Madrid about four or five days. In the daytime I wandered around to the poorer sections of the city, limping, looking at the people, and the people stared back at me and must have thought I was crazy because I was moving so slow and looked the way I did. I ate food in my hotel room. Although once I went to a restaurant and ordered soup. I hate soup. But I thought it was what old people would order. So I ate it. And, after a week of this, I began to actually think I was somebody else. I began to believe it. . . . And it is nice, every once in a while, being somebody else. . . ."

Patterson would not elaborate on how he managed to register under a name that did not correspond to his passport; he merely explained, "With money, you can do anything."

Now, walking slowly around the room, his black silk robe over his sweat clothes, Patterson said, "You must wonder what makes a man do things like this. Well, I wonder too. And the answer is, I don't know . . . but I think that within me, within every human being, there is a certain weakness. It is a weakness that exposes itself more when you're alone. And I have figured out that part of the reason I do the things I do, and cannot seem to conquer that one word—*myself*—is because . . . is because . . . I am a coward. . . ."

He stopped. He stood very still in the middle of the room, thinking about what he had just said, probably wondering whether he should have said it.

"I am a coward," he then repeated, softly. "My fighting has little to do with that fact, too. I mean you can be a fighter—and a *winning* fighter—and still be a coward. I was probably a coward on the night I won the championship back from Ingemar. And I remember another night, long ago, back when I was in the amateurs, fighting this big, tremendous man named Julius Griffin. I was only 153 pounds. I was petrified. It was all I could do to cross the ring. And then he came at me, and moved close to me . . . and from then on I don't know anything, I have no idea what happened. Only thing I know is, I saw him on the floor. And later somebody said, 'Man, I never saw anything like it. You just jumped up in the air, and threw thirty different punches.' . . ."

"When did you first think you were a coward?" he was asked.

"It was after the first Ingemar fight."

"How does one see this cowardice you speak of?"

"You see it when a fighter loses. Ingemar, for instance, is not a coward. When he lost the third fight in Miami, he was at a party later at the Fontainebleau. Had I lost, I couldn't have gone to that party. And I don't see how he did. . . ."

"Have you no hate left?"

"I have hated only one fighter," Patterson said. "And that was

Ingemar in the second fight. I had been hating him for a whole year before that—not because he beat me in the first fight, but because of what he did after. It was all that boasting in public, and his showing off his right-hand punch on television, his thundering right, his 'toonder and lightning.' And I'd be home watching him on television, and *hating* him. It is a miserable feeling, hate. When a man hates, he can't have any peace of mind. And for one solid year I hated him because, after he took everything away from me, deprived me of everything I was, he *rubbed it in*. On the night of the second fight, in the dressing room, I couldn't wait until I got into the ring. When he was a little late getting into the ring, I thought, 'He's holding me up; he's trying to unsettle me—well, I'll get him!'"

"Why couldn't you hate Liston in the second match?"

Patterson thought for a moment, then said, "Look, if Sonny Liston walked into this room now and slapped me in the face, then you'd see a fight. You'd see the fight of your life because, then, a principle would be involved. I'd forget he was a human being. I'd forget I was a human being. And I'd fight accordingly."

"Could it be, Floyd, that you made a mistake in becoming a prizefighter?"

"What do you mean?"

"Well, you say you're a coward; you say you have little capacity for hate; and you seemed to lose your nerve against those schoolboys in Scarsdale this afternoon. Don't you think you might have been better suited for some other kind of work? Perhaps a social worker, or . . ."

"Are you asking why I continue to fight?"

"Yes."

"Well," he said, not irritated by the question, "first of all, I love boxing. Boxing has been good to me. And I might just as well ask you the question: 'Why do you write?' Or, 'Do you retire from writing every time you write a bad story?' . . . And as to whether I should have become a fighter in the first place, well, let's see how I can explain it. . . . Look, let's say you're a man who has been in an empty room for days and days without food . . . and then they take you out of that room and put you into another room where there's food hanging all over the place . . . and the first thing you reach for, you eat. When you're hungry, you're not choosy, and so I chose the thing that was closest to me. That was boxing. One day I just wandered into a gymnasium and boxed a boy. And I beat him. Then I boxed another boy. I beat him, too. Then I kept boxing. And winning. And I said, 'Here, finally, is something I can do!'

"Now I wasn't a sadist," he quickly added. "But I liked beating people because it was the only thing I could do. And whether boxing was a sport or not, I wanted to make it a sport because it was a thing I could succeed at. And what were the requirements? Sacrifice. That's all. To anybody who comes from Bedford-Stuyvesant in Brooklyn, sacrifice comes easy. And so I kept fighting, and one day I became heavyweight champion, and I got to know people like you. And you wonder how I can sacrifice, how I can deprive myself so much. You just don't realize where I've come from. You don't understand where I was when it began for me.

"In those days, when I was about eight years old, everything I got I stole. I stole to survive, and I did survive, but I seemed to hate myself. Even when I was younger, my mother told me I used to point to a photograph of myself hanging in the bedroom and would say, 'I don't like that boy!' One day my mother found three large X's scratched with a nail or something over that photograph of me. I don't remember doing it. But I do remember feeling like a parasite at home. I remember how awful I used to feel at night when my father, a longshoreman, would come home so tired that, as my mother fixed food for him, he would fall asleep at the table because he was that tired. I would always take his shoes off and clean his feet. That was my job. And I felt so bad because here I was, not going to school, doing nothing, just watching my father come home; and on Friday nights it was even worse. He would come home with his pay, and he'd put every nickel of it on the table so my mother could buy food for all the children. I never wanted to be around to see that. I'd run and hide. And then I decided to leave home and start stealing—and I did. And I would never come home unless I brought something that I had stolen. Once I remember I broke into a dress store and stole a whole mound of dresses, at 2 A.M., and here I was, this little kid, carrying all those dresses over the wall, thinking they were all the same size, my mother's size, and thinking the cops would never notice me walking down the street with all those dresses piled over my head. They did, of course. . . . I went to the Youth House. . . ."

*

Floyd Patterson's children, who had been playing outside all this time around the country club, now became restless and began to call him, and Jeannie started to pound on his door. So Patterson picked up his leather bag, which contained his gloves, his mouthpiece, and adhesive tape, and walked with the children across the path toward the club.

He flicked on the light switches behind the stage near the piano. Beams of amber streaked through the dimly-lit room and flashed onto the ring. Then he walked to one side of the room, outside the ring. He took off his robe, shuffled his feet in the rosin, skipped rope, and then began to shadowbox in front of a spit-stained mirror, throwing out quick combinations of lefts, rights, lefts, rights, each jab followed by a *"hegh-hegh-hegh-hegh."* Then, his gloves on, he moved to the punching bag in the far corner, and soon the room reverberated to his rhythmic beat against the bobbling bag—rat-tat-tat-*tetteta*, rat-tat-tat-*tetteta*, rat-tat-tat-*tetteta*, rat-tat-tat-*tetteta*!

The children, sitting on pink leather chairs, moved from the bar to the fringe of the ring, watched him in awe, sometimes flinching at the force of his pounding against the leather bag.

And this is how they would probably remember him years from now: a dark, solitary, glistening figure punching in the corner of a forlorn spot at the bottom of a mountain where people once came to have fun—until the country club became unfashionable, the paint began to peel, and Negroes were allowed in.

As Floyd Patterson continued to bang away with lefts and rights, his gloves a brown blur against the bag, his daughter slipped quietly off her chair and wandered past the ring into the other room. There, on the other side of the bar and beyond a dozen round tables, was the stage. She climbed onto the stage and stood behind a microphone, long dead, and cried out, imitating a ring announcer, "LADIEEEES AND GENTLEMEN . . . tonight we present . . ."

She looked around, puzzled. Then, seeing that her little brother had followed her, she waved him up to the stage and began again: "LADIEES AND GENTLEMEN . . . tonight we present . . . FLOYDIE PATTERSON . . ."

Suddenly, the pounding against the bag in the other room stopped. There was silence for a moment. Then Jeannie, still behind the microphone and looking down at her brother, said, "Floydie, come up here!"

"No," he said.

"Oh, come up here!"

"NO," he cried.

Then Floyd Patterson's voice, from the other room, called: "Cut it out. . . . I'll take you for a walk in a minute."

He resumed punching—rat-tat-tat-*tetteta*—and they returned to his side. But Jeannie interrupted, asking, "Daddy, how come you sweating?"

"Water fell on me," he said, still pounding.

"Daddy," asked Floyd, Jr., "how come you spit water on the floor before?"

"To get it out of my mouth."

He was about to move over to the heavier punching bag—but just then the sound of Mrs. Patterson's station wagon could be heard moving up the road.

Soon she was in Patterson's apartment cleaning up a bit, patting the pillows, washing the teacups that had been left in the sink. One hour later the family was having dinner together. They were together for two more hours; then, at 10 P.M., Mrs. Patterson washed and dried all the dishes, and put the garbage out in the can—where it would remain until the raccoons and skunks got to it.

And then, after helping the children with their coats and walking out to the station wagon and kissing her husband good-bye, Mrs. Patterson began the drive down the dirt road toward the highway. Patterson waved once, and stood for a moment watching the tail lights go, and then he turned and walked slowly back toward the house.

Barney Nagler

Elfin and bespectacled, dapper and soft-spoken, Barney Nagler (1912–1990) looked as if he should have been teaching a Shakespeare seminar rather than rooting around in boxing's dark corners. But he was as fearless as he was unassuming, and when justice and fair play were threatened—it has been known to happen in the sweet science—he could turn into a barracuda, as evinced in the column he began writing for New York's *Morning Telegraph* in 1950 and, after that publication went out of business, for the *Daily Racing Form*. Nagler's greatest show of journalistic courage, however, was his two-fisted book attacking corruption, *James Norris and the Decline of Boxing* (1964). It shined an unwavering light on the mobsters Frankie Carbo and Blinky Palermo as they arranged a devious transfer of the world's welterweight championship in a series of events so complex that the fighters involved may not have known what was happening—but Barney Nagler did.

---

from

James Norris and the Decline of Boxing

CARMEN BASILIO, the son of an onion farmer in Chittenango, New York, near Syracuse, took up boxing in high school. By 1948, he was fighting as a professional in upstate New York rings. He was an aggressive little fellow possessed of a deep sense of decency and determination. He was soft-spoken and articulate, and a vigorous and sharp competitor in the ring.

When Arcel's Saturday night bouts were being televised, Basilio was one of his star performers. The bustling welterweight twice fought Billy Graham in Syracuse in bouts promoted by Norman Rothschild, an upstart in the promotorial business who was not yet ensnared in Norris's orbit. Suddenly, Basilio's vital services were no longer available to Arcel.

Basilio's managers were John DeJohn, a handsome, olive-skinned, dark-haired native of Syracuse, and Joe Netro, an obese resident of Ithaca, New York. One afternoon during the summer of 1953, DeJohn was invited to take lunch with Carbo in the Warwick Hotel in New York City. He was flattered by the invitation and accepted. When he arrived at the Raleigh Room in the hotel, he found two others lunching with Carbo. One was Wallman, the other was Angel Lopez, owner of the Chateau Madrid night club in New York and the manager of Kid Gavilan, the welterweight champion.

Lopez' presence, in terms of developments, was anomalous. Later he would testify before the New York State Athletic Commission that he had received $50,000 as his share in Arcel's Saturday night promotions, but on this occasion he was being used as a tool in Carbo's plot to "steal" Basilio away from Arcel and present him on a platter to Norris's International Boxing Club.

Carbo's method was simple. He offered Basilio, through DeJohn, an opportunity to fight Gavilan for the world welterweight championship in Syracuse on Friday night, September 18, 1953. DeJohn demurred. He did not want the match because he believed Basilio was not ready to cope with a fighter of Gavilan's ability.

"You'll make a lot of money," Carbo insisted.

"What do you mean, I'll make a lot of money?" DeJohn demanded.

"Well, look, if you are going to fight for the championship, you are going to get 20 per cent, and the champion gets 40 per cent, and they will draw a lot of money, which means that you will earn more money than you ever earned."

Carbo took a pencil and began writing numbers on the tablecloth in an attempt to prove that Basilio would earn a considerable sum by fighting Gavilan.

"If you win the championship," Carbo continued, "you are going to make a lot more money with him."

"It looks all right to me," DeJohn said.

When word of the match was brought to Basilio, he did not believe it. In all honesty, he knew he was not one of the IBC's boys. A year before, he had fought Chuck Davey, one of Jim Norris's darlings, in the Chicago Stadium. He had opened cuts on Davey's left cheek and over his right eye. When the fight was over, the decision went to Davey. Basilio rushed to his dressing room and proceeded to assail verbally the officials, his opponent, and the International Boxing Club.

"It was a lousy house decision," Basilio insisted, "and if it had been somewhere else they'd have stopped it. It's nice to be on the 'right' side—the IBC's side."

But now, unexpectedly he had himself became one of Norris's "house" fighters. In the ring with Gavilan, he won many more friends; he knocked Gavilan down in the second round. This was an astounding achievement, because Gavilan had been floored only once before in his career. It was a close fight and when it was over, one of the judges voted for Basilio. The referee and the other judge cast their ballots for Gavilan. Basilio had lost officially, but he was certainly the leading challenger for Gavilan's championship.

In the ordinary course of sportsmanship, Basilio should have been given a return bout with Gavilan immediately, but Carbo had many allies to satisfy. Gavilan's next bout was against Bratton, Wallman's fighter. He beat Bratton mercilessly and moved on to make still another of Carbo's clients, Blinky Palermo himself, happy.

Palermo's fighter was Johnny Saxton, a bug-eyed kid out of Harlem. Even then Saxton was a nervous lad who was psychically unfit for the ring; in the years ahead he would break down mentally and turn to burglary and petty thievery to keep alive.

Gavilan met Saxton in Philadelphia on October 20, 1954. The bout was a travesty. Neither fighter landed a vital blow. Saxton was inept, indifferent, and a failure. Gavilan was only slightly better. The fight was malodorous, but the decision was even worse. The decision went to Saxton.

The entire country had seen the bout on television. The outcry was widespread. Dan Parker, writing in the New York *Mirror*, said:

> Jack Kearns told some friends before the fight to send in all they had on Saxton who, he said, couldn't lose. In New York many fans who tried to put money on Saxton were told that they could bet only on Gavilan. After the fight (?), Palermo said there would be no return match for Gavilan. And before and after it, Goombar Carbo lavishly entertained fight mobsters from all over America at a hotel suite. He had good reason to celebrate.

A few days after Saxton's unwarranted coronation, Carbo ran a party at the St. Moritz Hotel in New York. Gavilan was present. He walked up to Carbo and in Cuban-accented English, said, "Mr. Blinky Palermo told me that they do whatever you want. That's what he told me. And if that what you told him, for what they do to me I want my return match."

"Right," Carbo said.

Gavilan was never given a chance to regain the championship. There were mob obligations elsewhere.

In Boston, Tony DeMarco was managed by Anthony ("Rip") Valenti, a friend of Carbo's. He got first crack at Saxton and, as expected, knocked out Saxton. In Syracuse, DeJohn and Netro were determined to get Basilio another opportunity to fight for the world's welterweight championship. In pursuit of the match, they hit upon an upstate link to Carbo—Gabe Genovese, a barber by profession who, years before, had shared with Carbo in the management of Babe Risko, a world middleweight champion.

Genovese established a rate of exchange. He would exert his influence on Carbo and, in return, would be cut in on Basilio's purses. During 1955 he received $5,000 from DeJohn and Netro. Basilio was matched to meet DeMarco for the welterweight title in Syracuse's War Memorial Auditorium on June 10, 1955. Basilio won on a knockout in twelve rounds. Five months later he repeated the knockout in the Boston Garden.

Carbo still had to take care of Palermo, his colleague. Saxton had been sidetracked in the process of Carbo's maneuvering, and now Palermo was insisting that Carbo prove his affection by getting Saxton back into the picture. Norris went right along with the program. He signed Basilio to defend his title against Saxton in the Chicago Stadium, March 14, 1956. The bout went the full fifteen rounds, and Saxton somehow received the decision, although Basilio was the obvious winner.

Dismayed, Basilio returned to New York. He went before the New York State Athletic Commission and asked Julius Helfand, who had succeeded Christenberry as chairman, to permit Saxton to fight in New York. Helfand had been adamant in this regard. He had turned down Palermo's application for a license and Palermo, in rebuttal, had insisted that Saxton would never box in New York State.

"Let Saxton sign his own contract," Basilio pleaded. "New York is the only place I can get a fair shake."

Helfand granted Basilio's request. Rothschild, the Syracuse promoter, was determined to promote, as Norris's partner, the return bout between Basilio and Saxton in Syracuse. Like all others in boxing, he knew that Carbo was the boss, although Norris had the monopoly. He, too, appealed to Genovese.

"It'll cost $10,000," Genovese said.

"It's a deal," Rothschild said.

Basilio knocked out Saxton in nine rounds on September 12, 1956, in a bout promoted by Rothschild in Syracuse. Carbo laughed. His man Genovese had delivered on both sides of the street, from Basilio and Rothschild. It was a pattern that was to be repeated again and again, and it eventually would result in bitter consequences for Genovese, Palermo, and Carbo.

Murray Kempton

Elegant and unpredictable, Murray Kempton (1917–1997) was a classicist by training, a liberal newspaper columnist by conscience, and a bicycle rider in a three-piece suit because he never bothered to get a driver's license. He pedaled through Manhattan's streets right up to the end of his days, leaving people who recognized him to wonder whether he was off to cast a withering eye on Bill Clinton or give his unexpected blessing to some prison-bound mobster. In a career spent primarily at the pre–Rupert Murdoch *New York Post* and *Newsday*, Kempton focused on politics, labor, and race, with a little jazz, baseball, and boxing mixed in to soothe his soul. He won a Pulitzer Prize and National Book Award, wrote for *Esquire* and *The New York Review of Books*, and produced two stellar works of nonfiction, *Part of Our Time* (1955) and *The Briar Patch* (1973). His essays and columns were collected in *America Comes of Middle Age* (1963) and *Rebellions, Perversities, and Main Events* (1994). Even when his subject was sports, however, Kempton didn't check his IQ or his honor at the door. His appraisal of Sonny Liston in the following 1964 piece from *The New Republic* shows that the man on the bike was nobody's pushover.

The Champ and the Chump

JUST before the bell for the seventh round, Cassius Clay got up to go about his job. Suddenly, he thrust his arms straight up in the air in the signal with which boxers are accustomed to treat victory and you laughed at his arrogance. No man could have seen Clay that morning at the weigh-in and believed that he could stay on his feet three minutes that night. He had come in pounding the cane Malcolm X had given him for spiritual support, chanting "I am the greatest, I am the champ, he is a chump." Ray Robinson, that picture of grace who is Clay's ideal as a fighter, pushed him against the wall and tried to calm him, and this hysterical child turned and shouted at him, "I am a great *performer*, I am a great *performer*."

Suddenly almost everyone in the room hated Cassius Clay. Sonny Liston just looked at him. Liston used to be a hoodlum; now he was our cop; he was the big Negro we pay to keep sassy Negroes in line and he was just waiting until his boss told him it was time to throw this kid out.

British journalists who were present remembered with comfort how helpful beaters like Liston had been to Sanders of the River; Northern Italian journalists were comforted to see on Liston's face the look that *mafiosi* use to control peasants in Sicily; promoters and fight managers saw in Clay one of their animals utterly out of control and were glad to know that soon he would be not just back in line but out of the business. There were two Catholic priests in attendance whose vocation it is to teach Sonny Liston the values of organized Christianity, and one said to the other: "Do you see Sonny's face? You *know* what he's going to do to this fellow."

The great legends of boxing are of managers like Jack Hurley, who had taken incompetent fighters and just by shouting their merits, against all reason built them up for one big payday at which they disgraced themselves and were never heard from again. Clay had created himself the way Hurley created his paper tigers. His most conspicuous public appearance in the week before he was to fight had been a press conference with the Beatles. They were all very much alike—sweet and gay. He was an amateur Olympic champion who had fought twenty professional fights, some of them unimpressive; and he had clowned and blustered about how great he was until he earned his chance from a Liston who, if he could not respect him as an opponent, could recognize him as a propagandist skilled enough to fool the public. A reporter had asked Liston if he thought the seven to one odds against Clay were too long, and he answered: "I don't know. I'm not a bookmaker. I'm a fighter." But there was no hope Clay could win; there was barely the hope that he could go like a gentleman. Even Norman Mailer settled in this case for organized society. Suppose Clay won the heavyweight championship, he asked; it would mean that every loudmouth on a street corner could swagger and be believed. But if he lay down the first time Liston hit him, he would be a joke and a shame all his life. He carried, by every evidence unfit, the dignity of every adolescent with him. To an adult a million dollars may be worth the endurance of being clubbed by Sonny Liston; but nothing could pay an adolescent for just being picked up by the bouncer and thrown out.

On the night, Clay was late getting to the dressing room and he came to stand in back of the arena to watch his younger brother fight one of the preliminaries. He spoke no word and seemed to look, if those blank eyes could be said to look, not at the fighters but at the lights above them. There was a sudden horrid notion that just before the main event, when the distinguished visitors were announced, Cassius Clay in his dinner jacket might bounce into the ring, shout one more time that he was the greatest, and go down the steps and out of the arena and out of the sight of man forever. Bystanders yelled insults at him; his handlers pushed him toward his dressing room, stiff, his steps hesitant. One had thought him hysterical in the morning; now one thought him catatonic.

He came into the ring long before Liston and danced with the mechanical melancholy of a marathon dancer; it was hard to believe that he had slept in forty-eight hours. Liston came in; they met in the ring center with Clay looking over the head of that brooding presence; then Clay went back and put in his mouthpiece clumsily like an amateur and shadowboxed like a man before a mirror and turned around, still catatonic, and the bell rang and Cassius Clay went forward to meet the toughest man alive.

He fought the first round as though without plan, running and slipping and sneaking punches, like someone killing time in a poolroom. But it was his rhythm and not Liston's; second by slow second, he was taking away the big bouncer's dignity. Once Liston had him close to the ropes—where fighters kill boxers—and Clay, very slowly, slipped sideways from a left hook and under the right and away, just grazing the ropes all in one motion, and cut Liston in the eye. For the first time there was the suspicion that he might know something about the trade.

Clay was a little ahead when they stopped it. Liston had seemed about to fall on him once; Clay was caught in a corner early in the fifth and worked over with the kind of sullen viciousness one cannot imagine a fighter sustaining more than four or five times in one night. He seemed to be hurt and walked back, being stalked, and offering only a left hand listlessly and unimpressively extended in Liston's face. We thought that he was done and asking for mercy, and then that he was tapping Liston to ask him to quiet down a moment and give the greatest a chance to speak, and then we saw that Clay's legs were as close together as they had been before the round started and that he was unhurt and Liston just wasn't coming to him. It ended there, of course, although we did not know it.

"I told ye'," Cassius Clay cried to all of us who had laughed at him. "I told ye'. I just played with him. I whipped him so bad and wasn't that good. And look at me: I'm still pretty."

An hour later he came out dressed; a friend stopped him and the heavyweight champion of the world smiled and said he would be available in the morning. His eyes were wise and canny, like Ray Robinson's.

George Plimpton

He had his nose bloodied by Archie Moore, was tackled by Alex Karras, pitched to Willie Mays, lost at golf to Sam Snead and at tennis to Pancho Gonzales, but nobody had more fun than George Plimpton (1927–2003). He carved out a niche as the foremost practitioner of participatory journalism, a "professional amateur" whose unique balance of insight and self-deprecating humor made him beloved by his subjects and readers alike. Plimpton, who made numerous cameo appearances in Hollywood films, was more familiar to the younger generation as a pitchman in television commercials that bordered on self-parody, but he was widely admired in literary circles as a co-founder of *The Paris Review* and by his peers as a first-rate journalist capable of the splendid reportage on display in this 1964 *Harper's* piece. Plimpton's upper-crust accent registered on Ali in a very special way. Never great at recalling names, the champ simply referred to Plimpton as "Kennedy."

Miami Notebook: Cassius Clay and Malcolm X

I.

THE press was incensed at Cassius Clay's behavior before the Liston fight. You could feel it. They wanted straight answers, and they weren't getting them. Usually, particularly with fighters, the direct question of extreme simplicity—which is of great moment to the sportswriters—will get a reply in kind. "Champ," asks the sportswriter, "how did you sleep last night and what did you have for breakfast?" When the champ considers the matter and says he slept real fine and had six eggs and four glasses of milk, the sportswriter puts down, "*gd sleep 6 eggs 4 gl milk*," on his pad, and a little while later the statistic goes out over Western Union.

But with Clay, such a question simply served to unleash an act, an entertainment which included poetry, the brandishing of arms and canes, a chorus thrown in—not a dull show by any standard, even if you've seen it a few times before. The press felt that the act—it was constantly referred to as an "act"—was born of terror or lunacy. What *should* have appealed, Cassius surely being the most colorful, if bizarre, heavyweight since, well, John L. Sullivan or Jack Johnson, none of this seemed to work at all. The press's attitude was largely that of the lip-curling disdain the Cambridge police have toward the antics of students heeling for the *Harvard Lampoon.*

One of the troubles, I think—it occurred to me as I watched Clay at his last press conference on February 24 before the fight—is that his appearance does not suit his manner. His great good looks are wrong for the excessive things he shouts. Archie Moore used the same sort of routine as Clay to get himself a shot at both the light-heavyweight and heavyweight championships—self-promotion, gags, bizarre suits, a penchant for public speaking—but his character was suited to it, his face with a touch of slyness in it, and always humor. So the press was always very much in his support, and they had much to do with Moore's climb from obscurity. At his training camp outside San Diego—the Salt Mines it is called, where Cassius himself did a tour at the start of his career—Moore has built a staircase in the rocks, sixty or seventy steps, each with a reporter's name painted in red to symbolize the assistance the press gave him. Clay's face, on the other hand, does not show humor. He has a fine grin, but his features are curiously deadpan when the self-esteem begins, which, of course, desperately needs humor as a softening effect. Clay himself bridled at the resentment he caused. It must have puzzled him to be cast as the villain in a fight with Liston, who on the surface at least, had absolutely no flair or panache except as a symbol of destructiveness.

Clay made a short, final address to the newspapermen. "This is your last chance," he said. "It's your last chance to get on the bandwagon. I'm keeping a list of all you people. After the fight is done, we're going to have a roll call up there in the ring. And when I see so-and-so said this fight was a mismatch, why I'm going to have a little ceremony and some *eating* is going on—eating of words." His manner was that of the admonishing schoolteacher. The press sat in their rows at the Miami Auditorium staring balefully at him. It seemed incredible that a smile or two wouldn't show up on a writer's face. It was so wonderfully preposterous. But I didn't see any.

2.

In the corridors around the press headquarters in the Miami Auditorium, one was almost sure to run into King Levinsky, a second-rate heavyweight in his prime (he was one of Joe Louis's bums of the month) who fought too long, so that it had affected him, and he is now an ambulatory tie-salesman. He would appear carrying his ties, which are labeled with a pair of boxing gloves and his name, in a cardboard box, and he'd get rid of them in jig time. His sales technique was formidable: he would single out a prospect, move down the corridor for him fast, and sweeping an arm around the fellow's neck pull him in close . . . to within range of a hoarse and somewhat wetly delivered whisper to the ear: "From the King? You buy a tie from the King?" The victim, his head in the crook of the fighter's massive arm, would mumble and nod weakly, and fish for his bankroll. Almost everyone had a Levinsky tie, though you didn't see too many people wearing them. When the King appeared around a corner, the press would scatter, some into a row of phone booths set along the corridor. "Levinsky!" they'd say and move off quickly and officiously. Levinsky would peer around and often he'd pick someone *in* a phone booth, set his cardboard box down, and shake the booth gently. You'd see him watching the fellow inside, and then the door would open and the fellow would come out and buy his tie. They only cost a dollar.

Sometimes Levinsky, if he knew he'd already sold you a couple of ties, would get you in the crook of his arm and he'd recount things he thought you ought to know about his career. "Joe Louis finished me," he'd say. "In one round that man turned me from a fighter to a guy selling ties." He said this without rancor, as if Louis had introduced him to a chosen calling. "I got rapport now," he'd say—this odd phrase—and then he'd let you go. Clay came down the corridors after the weigh-in and Levinsky bounded after him. "He's gonna take you, kid," he hollered. "Liston's gonna take you, make you a guy selling ties . . . partners with me, kid, you kin be *partners* with me." Clay and his entourage were moving at a lively clip, canes on high, shouting that they were ready to "rumble," and it was doubtful the chilling offer got through.

At the late afternoon press parties in the bar of the Roney Plaza, the promoters had another fighter at hand—the antithesis of

Levinsky—a personable Negro heavyweight, Marty Marshall, the only man to beat Liston. The promoters brought him down from Detroit, his hometown, to impress the writers that Liston wasn't invincible, hoping that this notion would appear in their columns and help promote a gate lagging badly since the fight was universally considered a mismatch. Marshall met Liston three times, winning the first, then losing twice, though decking Liston in the second, always baffling him with an unpredictable attack. Liston blamed his one loss on making the mistake of dropping his jaw to laugh at Marshall's maneuvers, and *bam*, getting it broken with a sudden punch.

Marshall didn't strike one as a comic figure. He is a tall, graceful man, conservatively dressed, a pleasant face with small, round, delicate ears, and a quick smile. Greeting him was a complex matter, because he was attended for a while by someone who introduced him by saying, "Shake the hand that broke Sonny Liston's jaw!" Since Marshall is an honest man and it was a left hook that did the business, his *left* would come out, and one had to consider whether to take it with one's own left or with the right, before getting down to the questions. There was almost always a circle around him in the bar. The press couldn't get enough of what it was to be in the ring with Liston. Marshall didn't belittle the experience (after all, he'd been beaten twice), and indeed some of the things he said made one come away with even more respect for the champion.

"When I knocked him down with that hook in the second fight, he got up angry," said Marshall. "He hit me three shots you shouldn't've thrown at a bull. The first didn't knock me down, but it hurt so much I went down anyway."

"Geezus," said one of the reporters.

"Does he say anything—I mean when he's angry—can you see it?"

"No," said Marshall. "He's silent. He just comes for you."

"Gee*zus*," said the reporter again.

We all stood around, looking admiringly at Marshall, jiggling the ice in our glasses.

One of the writers cleared his throat. "I heard a story about the champion this morning," he said. "He does his roadwork, you know, out at the Normandy Golf Course, and there was this greenskeeper working out there, very early, pruning the grass at the edge of a water hazard, the mist coming off the grass, very quiet, spooky, you know, and he hears this noise behind him and there's Liston there, about ten feet away, looking out of his hood at him, and this guy gives a big scream and pitches forward into the water."

"Yeah," said Marshall. He was smiling. "I can see that."

3.

Each fighter had his spiritual adviser, his *guru* at hand. In Liston's camp was Father Murphy, less a religious adviser than a confidant and friend of the champion. In Clay's camp was Malcolm X, who was then one of the high officials of the Black Muslim sect, indeed its most prominient spokesman, though he has since defected to form his own black nationalist political movememt. For months he had been silent. Elijah Muhammad, the supreme leader, the Messenger of Allah, had muzzled him since November for making intemperate remarks after the assassination of President Kennedy. But he had been rumored to be in Miami, and speculation was strong that he was there to bring Cassius Clay into the Muslim fold.

I was riding in a car just after the weigh-in with Archie Robinson, who is Clay's business manager and closest friend—a slightly built young man, not much older than Clay, one would guess, very polite and soft-spoken—and he asked me if I'd like to meet Malcolm X. I said yes, and we drove across Biscayne Bay to the Negro-clientele Hampton House Motel in Miami proper—a small-town hotel compared to the Babylon towers across the bay, with a small swimming pool, a luncheonette, a pitch-dark bar where you had to grope to find a chair, with a dance floor and a band which came on later, and most of the rooms in balconied barrackslike structures out back. It was crowded and very lively with people in town not only for the fight but also for an invitation golf tournament.

I waited at a side table in the luncheonette. Malcolm X came in after a while, moving by the tables very slowly. Elijah Muhammad's ministers—Malcolm X was one of them—are said to emulate him even to the speed of his walk, which is considerable. But the luncheonette was not set up for a swift entrance. The tables were close together, and Malcolm X came by them carefully—a tall, erect man in his thirties, a lean, intelligent face with a long pronounced jaw, a wide mouth set in it which seems caught in a perpetual smile. He was carrying one of the Cassius Clay camp's souvenir canes, and with his horn-rimmed glasses, his slow stately walk, and with Robinson half a step behind him, guiding him, I thought for a second that he'd gone blind. He sat down, unwrapped a package of white peppermints which he picked at steadily, and began talking. Robinson sat with us for a while, but he had things to attend to.

I took notes from time to time, scratching them down on the paper tablecloth, then in a notebook. Malcolm X did not seem to mind. He said he was going to be unmuzzled in March, which was only five days away. He himself wrote on the tablecloth once in a while—putting down a word he wanted to emphasize. He had an automatic pen-and-pencil set in his shirt pocket—the clasps initialed FOI on one (Fruit of Islam, which is the military organization within the Muslim temple) and ISLAM on the other. He wore a red ring with a small crescent.

Malcolm X's voice is gentle, and he often smiles broadly, but not with humor, so that the caustic nature of what he is saying is not belied. His manner is distant and grave, and he asks, mocking slightly, "Sir?" when a question is not heard or understood, leaning forward and cocking his head. His answers are always skilled, with a lively and effective use of image, and yet as the phrases came I kept thinking of Cassius Clay and *his* litany—the fighter's is more limited, and a different sort of thing, but neither of them ever *stumbles* over words, or ideas, or appears balked by a question, so that one rarely has the sense of the brain actually working but rather that it is engaged in rote, simply a recording apparatus playing back to an impulse. Thus he is truly intractable—Malcolm X—absolutely dedicated, self-assured, self-principled, with that great energy . . . the true revolutionary. He does not doubt.

When give-and-take of argument is possible, when what Malcolm X says can be doubted, his assurance and position as an extremist give him an advantage in debate. He appreciates that this is so, and it amuses him. "The extremist," he said, "will always ruin the liberals in debate—because the liberals have something too nebulous to sell, or too impossible to sell—like the Brooklyn Bridge. That's why a white segregationalist—what's his name, Kilpatrick—will destroy Farmer, and why William Buckley makes a fool of Norman Mailer, and why Martin Luther King would lose a debate with me. Why King? Because integration is ridiculous, a dream. I am not interested in dreams, but in the nightmare. Martin Luther King, the rest of them, they are thinking about dreams. But then really King and I have nothing to debate about. We are both indicting. I would say to him: 'You indict and give them hope. I'll indict and give them no hope.'"

I asked him about the remarks that had caused him his muzzling by Elijah Muhammad. His remarks about the assassination had been taken out of context, he said, though it would be the sheerest hypocrisy to suggest that Kennedy was a friend to the Negro. Kennedy was a politician (he wrote down the word on the paper tablecloth with his FOI pencil and circled it)—a "cold-blooded politician" who transformed last year's civil rights march on Washington into a "crawl" by endorsing the march, joining it, though it was supposed to be a protest against the country's leaders . . . a politician's trick which tamped out the fuse though the powder keg was there. Friend of the Negro? There never had been a politician who was the Negro's friend. Power corrupts. Lincoln? A crooked, deceitful hypocrite, claiming championship to the cause of the Negro who, one hundred years later, finds himself singing "We Shall Overcome." The Supreme Court? Its decision is nothing but an act of hypocrisy . . . nine Supreme Court justices expert in legal phraseology tangling the words of their decision in such a way that lawyers can dilly-dally over it for years—which of course they will continue to do. . . .

I scribbled these phrases, and others, on the paper tablecloth, mildly surprised to see the Muslim maxims in my own handwriting. We talked about practicality, which is the weakest area of the Muslim plans, granted the fires of resentment are justifiably banked. Malcolm X was not particularly concerned. What may be illogical or impractical in the long run is dismissed as not being pertinent to the *moment*—which is what the Negro must concern himself with. He could sense my frustration at this. It is not easy to dismiss what is practical. He had a peppermint and smiled.

I changed the subject and asked him what he did for exercise.

"I take walks," he said. "Long walks. We believe in exercise, physical fitness, but as for commercial sport, that's a racket. Commercial sport is the pleasure of the idle rich. The vice of gambling stems from it." He wrote down the word "Promoter" on the tablecloth with his FOI pencil and circled it. "The Negro never comes out ahead—never *one* in the history of the sport."

"Clay perhaps."

"Perhaps." He liked talking about Clay. "I'm interested in him as a human being," he said. He tapped his head. "Not many people know the quality of the mind he's got in there. He fools them. One forgets that though a clown never imitates a wise man, the wise man can imitate the clown. He is sensitive, very humble, yet shrewd—with as much untapped mental energy as he has physical power. He should be a diplomat. He has that instinct of seeing a tricky situation shaping up—my own presence in Miami, for example—and resolving how to sidestep it. He knows how to handle people, to get them functioning. He gains strength from being around people. He can't stand being alone. The more people around, the better—just as it takes water to prime a country well. If the crowds are big in there tonight in the Miami Auditorium, he's likely to beat Liston. But they won't be. The Jews have heard he's a Muslim and they won't show up."

"Perhaps they'll show up to see him taken," I said.

"Sir?" he said, with that slight cock of the head.

"Perhaps . . ."

"When Cassius said, 'I am a man of race,'" Malcolm X went on, "it pleased the Negroes. He couldn't eliminate the color factor. But the press and the white people saw it another way. They saw him, suddenly, as a threat. Which is why he has become the villain—why he is booed, the outcast." He seemed pleased with this.

Wasn't it possible, I asked, that the braggart, the loudmouth was being booed, not necessarily the Black Muslim? After all, Clay had been heartily booed during the Doug Jones fight in Madison Square Garden, and that was before his affiliation with the Muslims was known.

"You, *you* can't tell," replied Malcolm X. "But a Negro can feel things in sounds. The booing at the Doug Jones fight was good-natured—I was there—but the booing is now different . . . defiant . . . inflamed by the columnists, all of them, critical of Cassius for being a Muslim."

"And as a fighter?"

"He has tremendous self-confidence," said Malcolm X. "I've never heard him mention fear. Anything you're afraid of can whip you. Fear magnifies what you're afraid of. One thing about our religion is that it removes fear. Christianity is based on fear."

I remarked that the Muslim religion, since it has its taboos and promises and threats, is also based on fear—one remembers that British soldiers extracted secrets from terrified Muslim captives by threatening to sew them up for a while in a pig's skin.

Malcolm X acknowledged that the Muslims had to adapt Islam to their purposes. "We are in a cage," he said. "What must be taught to the lion in a cage is quite different from what one teaches the lion in the jungle. The Muhammadan abroad believes in a heaven and a hell, a hereafter. Here we believe that heaven and hell are on this earth, and that we are in the hell and must strive to escape it. If we can adapt Islam to this purpose, we should. For people fighting for their freedom there is no such thing as a bad device."

He snorted about peaceful methods. "The methods of Gandhi?" Another snort. "The Indians are hypocrites. Look at Goa. Besides, they are the most helpless people on earth. They succeeded in removing the British only because they outnumbered them, out*weighed* them—a big dark elephant sitting on a white elephant. In this country the situation is different. The white elephant is huge. But we will catch him. We will catch him when he is asleep. The mice will run up his trunk when he is asleep.

"Where? They will come out of the alley. The revolution always comes from the alley—from the man with nothing to lose. Never the bourgeois. The poor Negro bourgeois, with his golf clubs, his golfing hat"—he waved at the people in the lunchroom—"he's so much more frustrated than the Negro in the alley; he gets the doors slapped shut in his face every day. But the explosion won't come from him. Not from the pickets, either, or the nonviolent groups—these masochists . . . they *want* to be beaten—but it will come from the people *watching*—spectators for the moment. They're different. You don't know. It is dangerous to suggest that the Negro is nonviolent.

"There *must* be retribution. It is proclaimed. If retribution came to the Pharaoh for his enslavement of six hundred thousand, it will come to the white American who enslaved twenty million and robbed their minds."

"And retribution, that is in the Koran?"

"Sir?"

"The Koran . . . ?"

He said, "Chapter 22, verse 102."

I put the numbers down, thinking to catch him out; I looked later. The verse reads: *"The day when the trumpet is blown. On that day we assemble the guilty white-eyed (with terror)."*

"These are the things you are teaching Cassius?"

"He will make up his own mind."

He popped a peppermint in his mouth. We talked a little longer, somewhat aimlessly. He had an appointment with someone, he finally said, and he stood up. The noise of conversation dropped noticeably in the luncheonette as he stood up and walked out, erect and moving slowly, holding his gaudy souvenir cane out in front of him as he threaded his way between the tables; the people in the golfing hats watched him go.

4.

I went out into the lobby of the hotel, just standing around there feeling low. A phrase from Kafka, or rather the *idea* of some phrases from *The Trial*, came to me. I looked them up the other day: "But I'm not guilty, said K. It's a mistake. Besides, how can a man be guilty? We're all men. True, said the priest: but that's how the guilty talk."

The lobby was crowded. I didn't feel comfortable. I went out to the street and stood *there*, watching the traffic. The cars came by going at sixty, none of them taxis. I went back to the lobby. The armchairs, not more than four or five, were occupied. I wouldn't have sat down anyway.

Then a fine thing happened. I was talking into the desk telephone, trying to find Archie Robinson, and a Negro, a big fellow, came up and said softly, "Hello, man, how's it?"—smiling somewhat tentatively, as if he wasn't quite sure of himself. I thought he was talking to someone else, but when I glanced up again, his eyes were still fixed on me. "We looked for you in New York when we came through," he said.

I recognized him, the great defensive back on the Detroit Lions, Night Train Lane, a good friend. "Train!" I shouted. I could sense people turn. It crossed my mind that Malcolm X might be one of them. "Hey!" I said. *"Hey!"* Lane looked a little startled. He hadn't remembered me as someone who indulged in such effusive greetings. But he asked me to come back to his room where he had friends, most of them from the golf tournament, dropping in for drinks and beans. I said that would be fine.

We went on back. Everyone we passed seemed to know him. "Hey man," they'd call, and he'd grin at them—a strong presence, an uncomplicated confidence, absolutely trusting himself. He had the room next to mine at the Detroit Lions' training camp (I was out there, an amateur among the pros, trying to play quarterback and write a book about it) and it was always full of teammates, laughing and carrying on. A record player, set on the floor, was always going in his room—Dinah Washington records. He had married her earlier in the year, her ninth or tenth husband, I think. The volume was always up, and if you came up from the practice field late, her voice would come at you across the school grounds. She had died later that year.

His room was small and full of people. I sat quietly. Train offered me some beans, but I wasn't hungry. He said, "What's wrong with you, man?"

"I'm fine," I said.

"Hey!" someone called across the room. "Was that you in the lunchroom? What you doin' talking to that guy X?"

"Well, I was listening to him," I said.

"They were telling around," this man said, "that X had a vision—he seen Cassius win in a *vision*."

Someone else said that in a fight they'd rather be supported by a Liston left jab than a Malcolm X vision. A big fine hoot of laughter went up, and Night Train said it was the damnedest co-in-ci-dence but a *horse* named Cassius had won one of the early races at Hialeah that afternoon—perhaps *that* was Malcolm X's vision.

They talked about him this way, easily, matter-of-factly. They could take him or leave him, which for a while I'd forgotten. Malcolm X had said about them: "They all know I'm here in the motel. They come and look at me through the door to see if I got horns . . . and you can see them turning things over in their minds."

5.

The day after he beat Liston, Cassius turned up at a news conference at the Miami Beach Auditorium. The rumor was that he had gone to Chicago for the Muslim celebrations there, and the press was surprised when he appeared—and even more so at his behavior, which was subdued. Since a microphone system had gone out, his voice was almost inaudible. Cries went up which one never expected to hear in Clay's presence: "What's that, Clay? Speak up, Cassius!"

Archie Robinson took me aside and told me that he and Clay had dropped in on the celebrations at the Hampton House Motel after the fight, but it had been too noisy, so they'd gone home. It was quieter there, and they had been up until four A.M. discussing Cassius's "new image."

I remarked that this was a rare kind of evening to spend after winning the heavyweight championship. I'd met a younger singer named Dee Some-thing-or-other who had been waiting for Clay outside his dressing room after the fight. She had some idea she was going to help Cassius celebrate. She was very pretty. She had a singing engagement at a nightclub called the Sir John. Her mother was with her. She was very anxious, and once in a while when someone would squeeze in or out of the dressing room she'd call out: "Tell Cassius that Dee . . ." The girl was calm. "I call him Marcellus," she said. "A beautiful name. I can say it over and over."

The newspapermen waiting to get into the dressing room looked admiringly at her. "Clay's little fox," they called her, using Clay's generic name for girls—"foxes"—which is half affectionate and half suspicious; he feels that girls can be "sly" and "sneaky" and are to be watched warily. When the new champion finally emerged from his dressing room in a heavy press of entourage, photographers, and newspapermen, he seemed subdued and preoccupied. He didn't glance at Dee, who was on her toes, waving shyly in his direction. "Marcellus," she called. The crowd, packed in tight around him, moved down the corridor, and photobulbs flashing. The mother looked quite put out.

6.

The living accommodations for Liston and Clay were as different as their fighting styles. Liston had a big place on the beach, a sixteen-room house next to the Yankees' owner, Dan Topping, reportedly very plush, wall-to-wall carpeting, and each room set up like a golf-club lounge—a television set going interminably, perhaps someone in front of it, perhaps not, and then invariably a card game.

Clay's place was on the mainland, in North Miami, in a low-rent district—a small plain tater-white house with louvered windows, a front door with steps leading up to a little porch with room for one chair, a front yard with more chairs set around and shaded by a big ficus tree with leaves dusty from the traffic on Fifth Street. His entire entourage stayed there, living dormitory-style, two or three to a room. Outside the yard was almost worn bare. There wasn't a neighborhood child on his way home from school who didn't pass by to see if anything was up. Films were shown there in the evening, outside, the children sitting quietly until the film started. Then the questions and the exclamations would come, Clay explaining things, and you could hardly hear the soundtrack. Only one film kept them quiet. That was the favorite film shown two or three times, *The Invasion of the Body Snatchers* . . . watched wide-eyed in the comforting sounds of the projector and the traffic going by occasionally on Fifth Street. When the big moths would show up in the light beam, almost as big as white towels they seemed, a yelp or two would go up, particularly if a body was being snatched at the time, and the children would sway for one another.

The children were waiting for Clay when he drove up from his press conference the day after the fight. So was Malcolm X, a camera slung from his neck; his souvenir cane was propped against the ficus tree. The children came for the car, shouting, and packing in around so that the doors had to be opened gingerly. Clay got out, towering above them as he walked slowly for a chair in the front yard. The litany started almost as soon as he sat down, the children around him twelve deep, Malcolm X at the periphery, grinning as he snapped pictures.

"Who's the king of kings?"

"*Cassius Clay!*"

"Who shook up the world?"

"*Cassius Clay!*"

"Who's the ugly bear?"

"*Sonny Liston!*"

"Who's the prettiest?"

"*Cassius Clay!*"

Sometimes a girl, a bright girl, just for a change would reply "*me*," pointing a finger at herself when everyone else was shouting "*Cassius*

Clay," or she might shout "*Ray Charles*," and the giggling would start around her, and others would join in until Clay, with a big grin, would have to hold up a hand to reorganize the claque and get things straightened out. Neither he nor the children tired of the litany. They kept at it for an hour at a time. Malcolm X left after a while. There were variations, but it was essentially the same, and it never seemed to lack for enthusiasm. The noise carried for blocks.

We went inside while this was going on. The main room, with an alcove for cooking, had sofas along the wall. The artifacts of the psychological campaign against Liston were set around—signs which read "settin' traps for the Big Bear," which had been brandished outside his training headquarters, and a valentine, as tall as a man, complete with cherubs, which had been offered Liston and which he had refused. It stood in a corner, next to an easel. Newspapers were flung around—there had been some celebrating the night before—and someone's shoes were in the middle of the room. Souvenir canes were propped up by the side of the stove in the cooking alcove. It was fraternity-house clutter.

I was standing next to Howard Bingham, Clay's "official" photographer. "It was fun, wasn't it?" I asked.

"Oh, my," he said. "We have the *best* time here."

He had joined up with Clay after the George Logan fight in California, about Clay's age, younger perhaps, and shy. He stutters a bit, and he told me that he didn't take their kidding lying down. He said: "I walk around the house and sc . . . sc . . . scare people, jump out at them. Or they d . . . doze off on the c . . . couch, and I sneak around and tickle them on the nose, y'know, with a piece of string. Why I was agitating C . . . C . . . Cassius for half an hour once when he was dozing off. And I give the hot f . . . f . . . feet around here, a lot of that. We had a high time."

I asked what Cassius's winning the championship meant for him.

"Well, of course, that must make me the greatest ph . . . ph . . . photographer in the world." He couldn't keep a straight face. "Oh please," he said. His shoulders shook. "Well, I'll tell you. I'm going to get me a mo . . . mo . . . mohair wardrobe, that's one thing."

At the kitchen table Archie Robinson was sorting telegrams, stacked up in the hundreds. He showed me some of them—as impersonal as an injunction, from the long sycophantic messages from people they had to scratch around to remember, to the tart challenges from fighters looking to take Clay's title away from him. Clay wasn't bothering with them. He was going strong outside—his voice rising above the babble of children's voices: "Who shook up the world?"

"Cassius Clay!"

I wandered back to his room. It was just large enough for a bed, the mattress bare when I looked there, an armchair, with clothes including his Bear Huntin' jacket thrown across it, and a plain teak-colored bureau which had a large-size bottle of Dickinson's witch hazel standing on it. A tiny oil painting of a New England harbor scene was on one wall, with a few newspaper articles taped next to it, illustrated, describing Clay at his most flamboyant. A training schedule was taped to the mirror over the bureau. It called for "all" to rise at five A.M. The bedclothes were in a corner. One corner of the mattress was covered with Cassius Clay's signature in a light-blue ink, flowery with the C's tall and graceful, along with such graffiti as: "Cassius Clay Is Next Champ"; "Champion of the World"; "Liston Is Finished"; "The Next Champ: Cassius Clay" . . .

Outside, it had all come true. His voice and the answers were unceasing. "You," he was calling to the children, "you all are look- ing . . . at . . . the . . . champion . . . of . . . the . . . whole . . . wide . . . world."

Larry Merchant

Larry Merchant (b. 1931) enhances HBO's boxing shows as a blunt truth-seeker, a voice of reason, and a man who knows when only laughter will suffice. More than half a century ago, however, Merchant was a leader in the revolution that swept the sports sections of American newspapers. He became sports editor and columnist of the *Philadelphia Daily News* at age twenty-six and quickly set about replacing the old fallbacks of cliché and hero worship with fearlessness, social consciousness, and whimsy. In 1966 Merchant moved on to the *New York Post* (where this 1968 column on the passionate fandom of composer David Amram first appeared) and let others worry about editing while he cemented his stature as one of the nation's foremost sports columnists. Before shifting to television full-time, he wrote three books, *And Every Day You Take Another Bite* (1971), *The National Football Lottery* (1973), and *Ringside Seat at the Circus* (1976). Of course, not all his subjects appreciated his refusal to adore them unconditionally. Joe Namath, forever besieged by Merchant, said, "I'm tired of being written about by $100-a-week creeps." To which Merchant replied, "I am not a $100-a-week creep. I'm a $200-a-week creep."

Beethoven to Boxing

BOLTON LANDING—Somewhere between the Spectrum in Philadelphia and the Lake George Opera Festival in Glens Falls, a man got out of his car, squatted on his hands "to let the blood rush to my head and wake me up," jogged six laps around a gas pump and drove off into the night.

David Amram, composer, jazz musician, author, fight fan, was traveling the route between a Gypsy Joe Harris and, say, Shakespeare. It is a journey he often takes, although he doesn't always go 550 miles to do it, as he did the other day, making the round trip from the site of the premiere of his opera, "Twelfth Night," to see a couple of middle-weights addle each other's intellect.

Sometimes David Amram merely walks to the National Maritime Union from his Greenwich Village garret for the Friday night club fights. And then there was the time in May when a piece of his was played at Carnegie Hall. Upon its completion he raced up to the Garden to watch Bob Foster beat Dick Tiger for the light-heavyweight championship, and when that was over, happily in four rounds, he raced back for the end of the concert.

A former gym teacher-boxing instructor, David Amram, age 37, recently completed an autobiography ("Vibration," to be published by MacMillan in September), the score for the movie of "The Subject Was Roses," and his opera. Racing to catch the preliminaries of Gypsy Joe Harris vs. Emile Griffith—he is always racing somewhere, always out of breath, as if he had just gone 15 rounds with Willie Pep—he enthused breathlessly, as he enthuses before every card, "It's going to be fantastic."

For him it actually is. He has been a super fight fan since he saw 12 year-old Puggy King box in junior high school in Washington, D.C. "I love the science, the psychology, and the drama," he said. "And when a cat gets in the ring he's in there alone. Nobody can help him—no musicians, no accountants, lawyers, agents, or friends." He always makes the preliminaries "because I've known so many good musicians who went undiscovered."

And of course he views the action and the spectacle with a very singular eye.

Unlike many professional skeptics, for example, he saw nothing clownish in the antics of Gypsy Joe Harris. "It's a style of survival," Amram said. "You can see he was the little kid on the street who had to improvise to survive. You can hear him saying to some tough guy, 'Now wait a minute,' and soon he disappears. It's like a jazz musician without a lip. He has to develop a style within his limitations. Sometimes, with hard work, they become better than natural musicians, like a pianist with small hands who practices a great deal and develops his technique by having more energy than anyone else, or like Demosthenes, who could hardly speak, so he went to the ocean with pebbles in his mouth and practiced until he became a great orator. Beethoven wasn't a natural either, like Mozart, who woke up in the morning and wrote beautiful music. Beethoven had to struggle and slave."

Harris is exciting to watch, not because of his showmanship, although that's fun and gets the public on his side and can confuse opponents. He's exciting because he has tremendous reflexes and defensive ability—and because he constantly is skirting the edge of disaster by leaving himself exposed and coming within a fraction of an inch of being creamed. It's like a French horn player playing jazz, always in danger of missing notes, but when you perfect your technique you sail through it so easily that nobody knows how hard it is. The people who root for Harris live lives that skirt the edge of disaster. They understand him.

Griffith is like a musician who doesn't have the feeling for improvisation, so he studies scientifically and plays out of his fund of knowledge. He applies himself, practices, stays in condition. He's a pro.

Amram has mixed feelings but unrestrained appreciation for Muhammad Ali as an athlete. "He's an artist who happens to be in boxing," he said, "but I don't like the way he humiliated Patterson and Terrell. To be a true artist you must be human too. He's a genius as a boxer, though, a fantastic improvisor. He reminds me of Dizzy Gillespie in the '40s, when he was technically and musically so far ahead of everyone that few people understood him, but he had such good humor and showmanship that he was enjoyed and appreciated anyway.

"One thing I don't enjoy are brawlers. They remind me of musicians who can't play well, so they play loud."

Through his varied career as a French hornist and pianist, Amram has met many fighters—Johnny Bratton, Sandy Saddler, Ezzard Charles, Archie Moore. Yesterday he showed that he may have learned something about the manly art from them. Amram appeared on a panel at the Saratoga Center for the Performing Arts with composer Aaron Copland, Ravi Shankar, the sitar virtuoso, and a pompous critic. A philosophical sparring session with the critic ended with the audience bursting into applause for an Amram counterpunch. "He had me on the ropes," said David Amram, "and I knocked him out."

Joe Flaherty

His was an all-too-short career, much of it spent writing about his favorite blood sports, boxing and politics, but its most remarkable aspect may have been the improbable sequence of events at its fairytale inception. At age thirty, Joe Flaherty (c. 1936–1983) was still a laborer on the New York waterfront whose unpaid (and often un-bylined) stories occasionally appeared in his Brooklyn community weekly. When the weekly deemed his account of a rowdy police gathering too hot to handle, a friend surreptitiously sent it to *The Village Voice*. Impressed, the *Voice*'s editors hired Flaherty to write a follow-up story, an assignment that ended when the fledgling reporter came to blows with one of his subjects. Flaherty's next piece incensed Pete Hamill, largely because it painted an unflattering picture of a middleweight named Joe Shaw, in whom Hamill, Norman Mailer, and George Plimpton had acquired an interest. *The New York Times Magazine* then asked Flaherty to write an expanded follow-up about the feuding Brooklynites, thus launching a career that would produce bylines in magazines from the *Saturday Review* to *Playboy*, the journalism collection *Chez Joey* (1974), the novels *Fogarty & Co.* (1973) and *Tin Wife* (1983), and *Managing Mailer* (1970), an account of his experience as campaign manager for Norman Mailer's 1969 mayoral run. As Flaherty put it: "A lesson for young journalists: in your early rounds forget the body and go for the head."

Flaherty's obituary for Sonny Liston ran in *The Village Voice* on January 14, 1971.

Amen to Sonny

WILL no one say amen? After reading and listening to the New York press, it seems that Charles "Sonny" Liston's soul will be politely consigned to damnation.

Milton Gross of the *Post*, the Eleanor Roosevelt of the sports pages, said in last Wednesday's column that he'd decided not to call his boy Floyd Patterson with the news of Sonny's death till the following day, knowing that Floyd would say: "Gee, that's terrible. I'm sorry."

Then Miltie hypothetically buried Floyd (in St. Peter's Basilica, one presumes) and commented: "I know Liston wouldn't have said the same." So much for a séance in a wet afternoon daily.

Another Patterson acolyte of old, Howard Cosell, appeared on ABC's six o'clock news and, in his best Battle of Britain tones, told us that it would be "unethical and unprincipled" for him to praise Sonny, concluding that there would be "no requiem for this heavyweight." This, of course, is the same Cosell who "ethically" gloated over Pete Rozelle's muscling Joe Namath during the Bachelors III affair. Sonny would have understood—he always understood the smart money.

And on the late ABC news Jim Bouton, the icky iconoclast whose reporting is so giggly that—in the words of Dorothy Parker—it makes you want to "fwow up," dismissed Liston with a cute anecdote, proceeding to interview ex-footballer-author Dave Meggyesy (*Out of Their League*) about the comparisons between racism in football and everyday American life and the similarities between football and the military-industrial complex, blah, blah. . . . The interview led one to believe that the only thing out of Meggyesy's league is the English language.

But what about Floyd himself? The *Daily News* told us that Patterson, upon being informed of Liston's death, exclaimed: "No, no! I had told them I would fight Liston again." Such humanity! It would crack the vaults of heaven. Poor Sonny done went and died before Floyd could cure his psyche. The eternal truth is that even in his present condition Liston would be 8 to 5 over Patterson.

Well, the reader may justifiably say that the back of the hand is the only tribute a blackguard deserves. After all, the man was busted twenty times. He was a union goon, ran with the mob, cracked heads with the same niftiness a short-order cook prepares "two over light." True, so very true. But transgressions always are forgiven in boxing if the sinner prostrates himself in front of his better sinners—namely, promoters, managers, and boxing commissioners. But like Ali after him, Sonny was a psychic breakthrough in the sport and in the American (both black and white) mind. He was a blatant mother in a fucker's game.

He arrived at a time when hopes of integration were high in the air, and Patterson and Ralph Bunche were everybody's prototypical black men. I can't recall anyone I know (with the exception of the Philadelphia-based writer Jack McKinney) who publicly wanted Liston to beat Patterson for the heavyweight championship. In Patterson's corner were clustered Jimmy Baldwin, Norman Mailer, Pete Hamill, and the NAACP (which didn't even want Patterson to give Liston the fight, because of what Liston would do to the "Negro image"). As Ali murdered the myth of the sixties, so Liston was the pall-bearer of the fifties' liberalism. He embodied what they didn't want to recognize—that our streets spawn a sea of Sonnys. Like the song, "Night Train," to which he jumped rope, he was that underground fear we wouldn't face—the menacing black man who invaded the subway of our souls at four in the morning. In short, Sonny was a badass nigger.

But Liston was only a minor-leaguer in evil compared to the sport at which he toiled, a crude crusher in the domain of charlatans. He wasn't allowed a license in New York State, and indeed, he wasn't even allowed to be introduced in the Garden ring before fights. This, while such erstwhile solid citizens as Rocky Graziano (who evaded the military before it became fashionable) and Jake LaMotta (a self-confessed dumper) were wildly applauded. Of course, this is the same New York that denied Ali a license for being unpatriotic until a $10,000,000 gate appeared on the horizon and transformed him from a traitor to a pugilistic Patton. Ah, what the green can do for the old red, white, and blue!

Promoters are blessed with more positions than either Nixon or the *Kama Sutra*. I remember when I was working on a piece about the late Frankie DePaula, an Italian fighter who used to fill the Garden as if it were a church on Palm Sunday. DePaula came under indictment for grand theft, and I called the Garden for his home phone number, only to be told: "It's a funny thing, Joe. We never had that guy's phone number." This was the same DePaula who had worked his way to a light heavyweight shot in the Garden by looking over the titanic likes of "Irish" Jimmy McDermott, a one-handed clover. But then again, one must forgive promoters. Their fantasies always are unfulfilled. Imagine if they were able to get St. Patrick vs. Mother Cabrini for fifteen rounds.

Now Sonny was a dishonorable man, as I've said. He understood his trade admirably. Asked to say a kind word about his opponents before a fight, he usually responded: "I'd like to run him over with a truck." No dainty doggerel that to entice the Dylan left and the older lib-labs. In fact, Sonny went so far as to say he'd like to leave his wheel marks on the executive board of the NAACP. No charisma.

One must know how to jerk and jolt the Liberal Establishment at the same time. Night trains have no subtle shift in gears; shifty road-sters are more the liberal style. It takes an Ali to tune their senses. Who could convince them he was a legitimate critic of the Vietnam war but a cat so sly he was contented to flunk the selective service test for years until the qualifications were lowered and he became eligible? So, like the unseated Saul, he then became a minister. One has to reread sports columns twice these days to decipher if they are about Ali or William Sloane Coffin. Will no one say amen?

Was Sonny Satan? Not really, but he'd make a helluva under-study. I first met him a couple of years ago in the Main Street Gym in Los Angeles, where he was starting his comeback. He sat in a small cubicle, naked and sweating after a workout. He just stared at me, not speaking while I waited to be assigned a furnace in his kingdom. In a booming castrato voice I finally asked: "Is thirty-six really your age?" Slowly, he looked up, and I looked down, hoping the Divine Edi-tor would cancel that question. He boomed: "My mammy says I'm thirty-six. Are you calling my mammy a fuckin' liar?" After some neat verbal footwork, I convinced him Mother Liston would make George Washington out to be an old forked-tonguer, and, by God, he smiled. A big, wide-open grin that was as honest as his snarl. He talked of how he was the son of a sharecropper who had had twenty-five chil-dren and "whupped me every day." Hold your faint hearts still, you socially aware, that was not Sonny's bag. In the next sentence spiced with his salacious grin, he paid his papa his due: "Twenty-five kids. My daddy was a champion at what he did, too." As his wife, Geral-dine, said: "That man has mother wit." Sure enough.

It was a wit matured and gnarled in gutters, in prisons. The low-down logic of every hustler who knows the cosmic truth that a bullet from a gun on the end of a pimp's silk suit travels faster and deadlier than the best left hook ever honed in a gym. But mother wit he did have, and his repertoire wasn't limited.

He could deliver a classic geographical put-down to a judge in the City of Brotherly Love when confronted with a speeding rap:

"I'd rather be a lamppost in Denver than mayor of Philadelphia." He outcrazied the Crazies by announcing he was thinking of becoming a Catholic priest. Now that would have been a test of Pope John's liberalism.

He had a built-in shit detector second only to Papa's. When he'd beaten Chuck Wepner bloody for eight rounds in Jersey City, someone asked him if Wepner wasn't one of the gamest men he'd ever seen, and Liston replied: "His manager is gamer." A better line about boxing has never been uttered.

I spent five days with Liston in Los Angeles, some of them spectacular, some sour. You always could sense his mood from the way he used the word "shit." On bad days he grunted "Shith"; on his good days he strung the word out on a clothesline till it stretched to "Shee-ee-it." He would not talk about his losses to Ali, except to mumble: "I was overtrained for the second bout." On Ali's impending imprisonment he became a savvy Satan: "He like to say how pretty he is. They like pretty people in prison." A low-bred mother wit.

The final day I spent with Liston, we met a hippie when we were leaving the gym. He presented Sonny with a "fight song" that he wanted him to give to Sammy Davis, Jr., to sing on television. The song was a simpleminded rhyme, extolling Sonny's ferocity, and he got a kick out of it. The hippie then told him he'd like to make Liston a pair of sandals like those he was wearing. Liston put his huge, flat foot up against the hippie's and went into a Bunyanesque fable to the effect that there wasn't enough leather in the West to cover the great man's foot. The hippie loved the instant legend. As we left, the kid gave him a tin triangle with the words "Jesus, Mary, Joseph" pin-scratched on each angle. The boy said it was "to keep the champ safe."

As we drove away from the gym in his Cadillac, Liston turned the triangle over and over between his thumb and forefinger, extolling the madness of hippies. "Those cats are right," he said. "They don't worry about a fuckin' thing in the world."

We passed a campaign headquarters for Robert Kennedy (then still alive), and Liston exploded: "Tell me, with six million dollars, why the fuck do these people want to be President? All that money, and they want worries. That hippie is smarter. Their old man made all that money smuggling scotch, and they want to become President to tell the people to keep sober. Shit, six million dollars." I asked him what he'd do if he had $6,000,000, and the storm subsided as the country boy leaned his head back and in philosophical reverie replied: "I'd buy me the finest pussy in the United States of America." And, concluding his American Dream, Charles "Sonny" Liston with a flip of his thumb sent Jesus, Mary, and Joseph in flight formation into the middle of Wilshire Boulevard.

Was he the bastard everyone says he was? To many, yes. To others, such as Claude Brown, he was the only man alive who could have quelled the Watts riots. I'm not pleading for his life-style—a bastard, maybe, or, perhaps more fair, he did bastardly deeds. But he should be judged in context. He was better than the sport he practiced and the men who rule it. In fact, he was one of boxing's most legitimate sons. When greed, hypocrisy, and corruption complete their *ménage á trois*, a Sonny Liston will always be plucked from the breach.

And he was a lot better than the hucksters for sport who now so cavalierly dismiss his life. One could go into a social tract on that life, but Sonny would only stretch a "Shee-ee-it" over the analysis. He was what he was. A villain perhaps, but also once the king of the heavyweights, and it is only fitting that one should find his epitaph in a play populated by an aging king and a bastard:

> This is the excellent foppery of the world, that, when we are sick in fortune—often the surfeit of our own behaviour,—we make guilty of our disasters the sun, the moon, and the stars: as if we were villains by necessity; fools by heavenly compulsion; knaves, thieves, and treachers, by spherical predominance; drunkards, liars, and adulterers, by an enforced obedience of planetary influence; and all that we are evil in, by a divine thrusting on—an admirable evasion of whoremaster man, to lay his goatish disposition on the charge of a star! My father compounded with my mother under the dragon's tail; and my nativity was under Ursa major; so that it follows, I am rough and lecherous. Tut, I should have been that I am, had the maidenliest star in the firmament twinkled on my bastardizing. . . ."

Amen.

Dick Schaap

The last best look America got at Dick Schaap (1931–2001) was when he was reining in the runaway egos on ESPN's *The Sports Reporters* while miraculously keeping the conversation going. He was the perfect host, unflappable, amiable and whip-smart, but that was just one facet of a career in which he touched every journalistic base imaginable: sports editor of *Newsweek*, city editor and star columnist of the *New York Herald Tribune*, correspondent for nightly newscasts on NBC and ABC, co-author, with the Green Bay Packers' Jerry Kramer, of the bestselling *Instant Replay* (1968), and editor of *Sport* magazine (where the following mid-career evaluation of Muhammad Ali was published in 1971). In one sixteen-month stretch, Schaap wrote nine books, an outpouring he attributed to the demands of alimony. He was, however, more than just a writer to subjects as disparate as Robert F. Kennedy, Lenny Bruce, Joe Namath, and Muhammad Ali. He was their friend. And the friends of Dick Schaap knew where he could be found on Monday nights—at Rao's, the Italian restaurant in East Harlem where reservations are famously hard to come by. But there was always a table for him.

Muhammad Ali Then and Now

IN some ways, it seems so long ago: John F. Kennedy was a handsome young Senator, starting to campaign for the presidency of the United States.

In some ways, it seems like yesterday: Richard M. Nixon was starting to campaign for the presidency of the United States.

It was August, 1960, when I first met Cassius Marcellus Clay, when he was 18 years old and brash and wide-eyed and naive and shrewd, and now more than a decade has elapsed, and John F. Kennedy is dead, and Richard M. Nixon is president, and those two facts, as well as anything, sum up how much everything has changed, how much everything remains the same.

It is ridiculous, of course, to link presidents and prize fighters, yet somehow, in this case, it seems strangely logical. When I think back to the late summer of 1960, my most persistent memories are of the two men who wanted to be president and of the boy who wanted to be heavyweight champion of the world.

And he was a boy—a bubbling boy without a serious thought in his head, without a problem that he didn't feel his fists or his wit would eventually solve.

He is so different now. He is so much the same.

We met a few days before he flew from New York to Rome to compete in the 1960 Olympic Games. I was sports editor of *Newsweek* then, and I was hanging around a Manhattan hotel where the American Olympic team had assembled, picking up anecdotes and background material I could use for my long-distance coverage of the Games. I spent a little time with Bob Boozer, who was on the basketball team, and with Bo Roberson, a broad jumper who later played football for the Oakland Raiders, and with Ira Davis, a hop-step-and-jump specialist who'd played on the same high school basketball team with Wilt Chamberlain and Johnny Sample. And then I heard about Cassius Clay.

He was a light-heavyweight fresh out of high school in Louisville, Kentucky, and he had lost only one amateur bout in two years, a decision to a southpaw named Amos Johnson. He was supposed to be one of the two best pro prospects on the boxing team, he and Wilbert McClure, a light-middleweight, a college student from Toledo, Ohio. I offered to show the two of them, and a couple of other American boxers, around New York, to take them up to Harlem and introduce them to Sugar Ray Robinson. Cassius leaped at the invitation, the chance to meet his idol, the man whose skills and flamboyance he dreamed of matching. Sugar Ray meant big money and fancy cars and flashy women, and if anyone had told Cassius Clay then he would someday deliberately choose a course of action that scorned those values, the boy would have laughed and laughed and laughed.

I wasn't just being hospitable, offering to show the boxers around. I figured I could maybe get lucky and pick up a story. I did. And more.

On the ride uptown, Cassius monopolized the conversation. I forget his exact words, but I remember the message: I'm great, I'm beautiful, I'm going to Rome and I'm gonna whip all those cats and then I'm coming back and turning pro and becoming the champion of the world. I'd never heard an athlete like him; he had no doubts, no fears, no second thoughts, not an ounce of false humility. "Don't mind him," said McClure, amiably. "That's just the way he is."

He was, even then, an original, so outrageously bold he was funny. We all laughed at him, and he didn't mind the laughter, but rode with it, using it to feed his ego, to nourish his self-image.

But there was one moment when he wasn't laughing, he wasn't bubbling. When we reached Sugar Ray's bar on Seventh Avenue near 124th Street, Robinson hadn't shown up yet, and Cassius wandered outside to inspect the sidewalks. At the corner of 125th Street, a black man perched on a soapbox was preaching to a small crowd. He was advocating something that sounds remarkably mild today—his message, as I recall, was simply buy black, black goods from black merchants, but Cassius seemed stunned. He couldn't believe that a black man would stand up in public and argue against white America. He shook his head in wonderment. "How can he talk like that?" Cassius said. "Ain't he gonna get in trouble?"

A few minutes later, as a purple Lincoln Continental pulled up in front of the bar, Cassius literally jumped out of his seat. "Here he comes," he shouted. "Here comes the great man Robinson."

I introduced the two of them, and Sugar Ray, in his bored, superior way, autographed a picture of himself, presented it to Cassius, wished the kid luck in the Olympics, smiled and drifted away, handsome and lithe and sparkling.

Cassius clutched the precious picture. "That Sugar Ray, he's something," he said. "Someday *I'm* gonna own two Cadillacs—and a Ford for just getting around in."

I didn't get to Rome for the Olympics, but the reports from the *Newsweek* bureau filtered back to me: Cassius Clay was the unofficial mayor of the Olympic Village, the most friendly and familiar figure among thousands of athletes. He strolled from one national area to the next, spreading greetings and snapping pictures with his box camera. He took hundreds of photographs—of Russians, Chinese, Italians, Ethiopians, of everyone who came within camera range. Reporters from Europe and Asia and Africa tried to provoke him into discussions of racial problems in the United States, but this was eight years before John Carlos and Tommie Smith. Cassius just smiled and danced and flicked a few jabs at the air and said, as if he were George Foreman waving a tiny flag, "Oh, we got problems, man, but we're working 'em out. It's still the bestest country in the world."

He was an innocent, an unsophisticated good-will ambassador, filled with kind words for everyone. Shortly before he won the Olympic light-heavyweight title, he met a visitor to Rome, Floyd Patterson, the only man to win, lose and regain the heavyweight championship of the world, and Cassius commemorated Patterson's visit with one of his earliest poems:

"You can talk about Sweden,
  You can talk about Rome,
  But Rockville Centre's
  Floyd Patterson's home.
  A lot of people said
  That Floyd couldn't fight,
  But they should've seen him
  On that comeback night . . ."

There was no way Cassius could have conceived that, five years later, in his most savage performance, he would taunt and torture and brutalize Floyd Patterson.

The day Cassius returned from Rome, I met him at New York's Idlewild Airport—it's now called JFK; can you imagine what the odds were against both the fighter and the airport changing their names within five years?—and we set off on a victory tour of the town, a tour that ranged from midtown to Greenwich Village to Harlem.

Cassius was an imposing sight, and not only for his developing light-heavyweight's build, 180 pounds spread like silk over a 6-foot-2 frame. He was wearing his blue American Olympic blazer, with USA embroidered upon it, and dangling around his neck was his gold Olympic medal, with *PUGILATO* engraved in it. For 48 hours, ever since some Olympic dignitary had draped the medal on him, Cassius had kept it on, awake and asleep.

"First time in my life I ever slept on my back," he said. "Had to, or that medal would have cut my chest."

We started off in Times Square, and almost immediately a pass-erby did a double-take and said, "Say, aren't you Cassius Clay?"

Cassius's eyes opened wide. "Yeah, man," he said. "That's me. How'd you know who I is?"

"I saw you on TV," the man said. "Saw you beat that Pole in the final. Everybody knows who you are."

"Really?" said Cassius, fingering his gold medal. "You really know who I is? That's wonderful."

Dozens of strangers spotted him on Broadway and recognized him, and Cassius filled with delight, spontaneous and natural, thriving on the recognition. "I guess everybody do know who I is," he conceded.

At a penny arcade, Cassius had a bogus newspaper headline printed: CASSIUS SIGNS FOR PATTERSON FIGHT. "Back home," he said, "they'll think it's real. They won't know the difference."

He took three copies of the paper, jammed them into his pocket, and we moved on, to Jack Dempsey's restaurant. "The champ around?" he asked a waiter.

"No, Mr. Dempsey's out of town," the waiter said.

Cassius turned and stared at a glass case, filled with cheesecakes. "What are them?" he asked the waiter.

"Cheesecakes."

"Do you have to eat the whole thing," Cassius said, "or can you just get a little piece?"

Cassius got a little piece of cheesecake, a glass of milk and a roast beef sandwich. When the check arrived and I reached for it, he asked to see it. He looked and handed it back; the three items came to something like two and a half dollars. "Man," he said. "That's too much money. We coulda gone next door"—there was a Nedick's hot dog stand down the block—"and had a lot more to eat for a whole lot less money."

From Dempsey's, we went to Birdland, a jazz spot that died in the 1960s, and as we stood at the bar—with Cassius holding a Coke "and put a drop of whisky in it"—someone recognized him. "You're Cassius Clay, aren't you?" the man said.

"You know who I is, too?" said Cassius.

Later, in a cab heading toward Greenwich Village, Cassius confessed, at great length, that he certainly must be famous. "Why," he said, leaning forward and tapping the cab driver on the shoulder, "I bet even you know that I'm Cassius Clay, the great fighter."

"Sure, Mac," said the cabbie, and Cassius accepted that as positive identification.

In Greenwich Village, in front of a coffeehouse, he turned to a young man who had a goatee and long hair and asked, "Man, where do all them beatniks hang out?"

In Harlem, after a stroll along Seventh Avenue, Cassius paused in a tavern, and some girl there knew who he was, too. She came over to him and twirled his gold medal in her fingers and said that she wouldn't mind if Cassius took her home. We took her home, the three of us in a cab. We stopped in front of her home, a dark building on a dark Harlem street, and Cassius went to walk her to her door. "Take your time," I said. "I'm in no hurry. I'll wait with the cab."

He was back in 30 seconds.

"That was quick," I said.

"Man," he said, "I'm in training. I can't fool around with no girls."

Finally, deep into the morning, we wound up at Cassius's hotel room, a suite in the Waldorf Towers, courtesy of a Louisville business-man who hoped someday to manage the fighter. We were roughly halfway between the suites of Douglas MacArthur and Herbert Hoover, and Cassius knew who one of them was.

For an hour, Cassius showed me pictures he had taken in Rome, and then he gave me a bedroom and said goodnight. "Cassius," I said, "you're gonna have to explain to my wife tomorrow why I didn't get home tonight."

"You mean," said Cassius, "your wife knows who I is, too?"

A few months later, after he turned professional, I traveled to Louisville to spend a few days with Cassius and write a story about him. In those days, we couldn't go together to the downtown restau-rants in Louisville, so we ate each night at the same place, a small restaurant in the black section of town. Every night, Cassius ordered the same main course, a two-pound sirloin, which intrigued me because nothing larger than a one-pound sirloin was listed on the menu.

"How'd you know they served two-pound steaks?" I asked him the third or fourth night.

"Man," he said, "when I found out you were coming down here, I went in and told them to order some."

In the few months since Jack Dempsey's, Cassius had discovered the magic of expense accounts.

But he was still as ebullient, as unaffected, as cocky and as winning as he had been as an amateur. He was as quick with a needle as he was with his fists. One afternoon, we were driving down one of the main streets of Louisville, and I stopped for a traffic light. There was a pretty white girl standing on the corner. I looked at her, turned to Cassius and said, "Hey, that's pretty nice."

Cassius whipped around. "You crazy, man?" he said. "You can get electrocuted for that! A Jew looking at a white girl in Kentucky!"

In 1961, his first year as a professional, while he was building a string of victories against unknowns, Cassius came to New York for a visit with his mother, his father and his younger brother, Rudolph. Rudy was the Clay the Louisville schoolteachers favored: he was quiet, polite, obedient. Later, as Rahaman Ali, he became the more militant, the more openly bitter, of the brothers.

I took the Clays to dinner at Leone's, an Italian restaurant that caters to sports people and mostly to tourists. To titillate the tourists, Leone's puts out on the dinner table a huge bowl filled with fruit. Cassius took one look at the bowl of fruit, asked his mother for the large pocketbook she was carrying and began throwing the fruit into the pocketbook. "Don't want to waste any of this," he said.

The first course was prosciutto and melon, and Cassius recoiled. "Ham!" he said. "We don't eat ham. We don't eat any pork things." I knew he wasn't kosher, and I assumed he was stating a personal preference. Of course, Muslims don't eat pork, and perhaps his Muslim training had already begun. I still suspect, however, that he simply didn't like pork.

After dinner, we went out in a used Cadillac Cassius had purchased with part of the bonus he received for turning pro (sponsored by nine Louisville and one New York businessmen, all white), and Cassius asked me to drive around town. On Second Avenue, in the area that later became known as the East Village, I pulled into a gas station. It was a snowy night, and after the attendant, a husky black man, had filled the gas tank, he started to clean off the front window. "Tell him it's good enough, and we'll go," I said to Cassius.

"Hey, man," Cassius said. "It's good enough, and we'll go."

The big black man glowered at Cassius. "Who's doing this?" he said. "You or me?"

Cassius slouched down. "You the boss, man," he said. "You the boss."

The attendant took his time wiping off the front windshield and the back. "Hey, Cash," I said, "I thought you told me you were the greatest fighter in the world. How come you're afraid of that guy?"

"You kidding?" said Clay. "He looks like Sonny Liston, man."

During the middle 1960s, when Cassius soared to the top of the heavyweight division, I drifted away from sports for a while, covering instead politics and murders and riots and lesser diversions. I didn't get to see any of his title fights, except in theaters, and, of course, I didn't see him. But our paths crossed early in 1964; by then, as city editor of the *New York Herald Tribune*, I was very much interested in the emerging Black Muslim movement. At first, I didn't know that Cassius was, too.

Through a contact within the Muslim organization, I learned that Cassius, while training in Miami for his first title fight with Sonny Liston, had flown to New York with Malcolm X and had addressed a Muslim rally in Harlem. As far as anyone knew, that was his first commitment to the Muslims, although he had earlier attended a Muslim meeting with Bill White and Curt Flood, the baseball players (all three attended out of curiosity), and he had been seen in the company of Malcolm X (but so had Martin Luther King).

When the *Herald Tribune* decided to break the story of Clay's official connection with the Muslims, I tried to reach him by telephone half a dozen times for him to confirm or deny or withhold comment on the story. I left messages explaining why I was calling, and I never heard from him. The story broke, and I heard from mutual acquaintances that Cassius was angry.

The first time I saw him after that—by then, he had adopted the name Muhammad Ali—he was cool, but the next time, in St. Louis, where he was addressing a Muslim group, he was as friendly as he had ever been. He quoted Allah, he paid tribute to the Honorable Elijah Muhammad yet he still answered to the nickname, "Cash." He even insulted me a few times, a sure sign that he was no longer angry.

He had been stripped of his heavyweight title, and he was fighting through the courts his conviction for refusing induction into the armed forces. I could see him changing, but it was never the words he mouthed that signified the change. His logic was often upside-down, his reasoning faulty, and yet, despite that, he had acquired a new dignity. The words didn't make any difference; the actions did. He had taken a dangerously costly step because of something he believed in. I might not share his belief or fathom the way he arrived at that belief, but still I had to respect the way he followed through on his beliefs, the way he refused to cry about what he was losing.

Yet it was during this period, when I sympathized with his stand, when I found that some segments of the sportswriting world were exhibiting more venom, more stupidity and more inaccuracies than I had thought even they were capable of, that Muhammad took the only step of his career I deeply resent. He turned his back on Malcolm X.

I don't know the reasoning. I don't know why he chose Elijah Muhammad over Malcolm X in the dispute between the leader of the Muslims and his most prominent disciple. I can't, therefore, say flatly that he made the wrong choice, even though I believe he made the wrong choice. Malcolm was a gifted man, an articulate and compassionate man. But I can say that Muhammad showed, for the one time in his life, a totally brutal personal—away from the ring—side. It is brutal to turn on a friend without one word of explanation, without one word of regret, with only blind obedience to the whims of a leader. I have tried, since then, to bring up the subject of Malcolm X with Muhammad Ali several times, and, always, he has tuned out. His expressive face has turned blank. His enthusiasm has turned to dullness. Maybe he is embarrassed. He should be.

During Muhammad's 43 months away from the ring, I bumped into him occasionally and found him still to be the only professional fighter who was, personally, both likable and exciting. (Floyd Patterson and Jose Torres, for example, are likable, but not often personally exciting; Ingemar Johansson was exciting.) At one point, David Merrick, the theatrical producer, professed an interest in sponsoring a legal battle to get Muhammad back his New York State boxing license; Merrick wanted to promote an Ali fight in New York for a worthy cause, which was not, in this case, David Merrick.

I arranged a meeting between the two, and Muhammad swept

into Merrick's office and stopped, stunned by the decor, the entire room done in red-and-black. "Man," said Muhammad, "you got to be part black to have a place like this. You sure you ain't black?"

It was the only time I ever saw David Merrick attempt to be charming.

The legal fight never materialized, not through Merrick, and Muhammad continued his road tour, speaking on college campuses, appearing in a short-lived Broadway play, serving as a drama critic, reviewing "The Great White Hope" for *Life*. One night, I accompanied him to a taping of the *Merv Griffin Show*—he was a regular on the talk-show circuit—and during the show, outlining his Muslim philosophy, he spoke of his belief in whites sticking with whites and blacks with blacks.

Afterward, as we emerged from the studio, he was engulfed by admirers, calling him "Champ" and pleading for his autograph. He stopped and signed and signed and signed, still soaking as happily in recognition as he had almost a decade earlier, and finally—because he was late for an appointment—I grabbed one arm and my wife grabbed the other and we tried to shepherd him away. He took about five steps and then looked at my wife and said, "Didn't you hear what I said about whites with whites and blacks with blacks?"

She dropped his arm and Muhammad laughed and danced away, like a man relishing a role.

In the fall of 1969, when the New York Mets finished their championship baseball season in Chicago, Muhammad and I and Tom Seaver had dinner one night at a quiet restaurant called the Red Carpet, a place that demanded a tie of every patron except the dethroned heavyweight champion.

The conversation was loud and animated, dominated by Muhammad as always, and about halfway through the meal, pausing for breath, he turned to Seaver and said, "Hey, you a nice fella. You a sportswriter?"

When we left the restaurant, we climbed into Muhammad's car, an Eldorado coupe, pink with white upholstery, with two telephones. Two telephones in a coupe! "C'mon, man," he said to Seaver. "Use the phone. Where's your wife? In New York? Well, call her up and say hello."

Seaver hesitated, and Muhammad said, "I'll place the call. What's your number?"

Seaver gave Muhammad the phone number, and Muhammad reached the mobile operator and placed the call, and when Nancy Seaver picked up the phone, she heard a deep voice boom. "This is the baddest cat in the world, and I'm with your husband and five hookers."

Nancy Seaver laughed. Her husband had told her he was having dinner with the champ.

Later, we returned to my hotel room, and after a few questions about his physical condition, Muhammad took off his suit jacket and his shirt and began shadow-boxing in front of a full-length mirror. For 15 straight minutes, he shadow-boxed, letting out "whoosh, whoosh," the punches whistling, a dazzling display of footwork and stamina and sheer unbelievable speed, all the time telling Seaver his life story, his religious beliefs and his future plans.

"I never saw anything like that in my life," said Seaver afterward.

Neither had anyone else.

A few weeks later, in the fall of 1969, Muhammad appeared as a guest on a sports-talk show, a show in which I served each week as sub-host and willing straight man for Joe Namath. For each show, we had one sports guest and one non-sports guest, and that week Muhammad was joined by George Segal, the actor.

After the interview with Muhammad, Joe and I began chatting with Segal, and the subject of nudity came up. Segal had just finished filming a nude or semi-nude scene with Barbra Streisand in "The Owl and the Pussycat." As the conversation about nudity began Muhammad visibly stiffened. "What's the matter?" Joe said. "How you feel about that, Muhammad?"

Muhammad's reaction was immediate. He was affronted and insulted. He was a minister, and he did not know that the show was going to deal with such blasphemy, and he was about to walk off the stage rather than join in, or even tolerate, such talk.

"Aw, c'mon," Joe said.

Muhammad sat uncomfortably through the remainder of the show, punctuating his distaste with winces and grimaces. It made for a very exciting show, and when it was over, Joe and I both sort of apologized to Muhammad for embarrassing him. "I gotta act like that," Muhammad explained. "You know, the FBI might be listening, or the CIA, or somebody like that."

He is now 29 years old. He has been a professional fighter for a full decade and he has fought 31 times, and he has never been beaten.

On March 8, he faces Joe Frazier, who has also never been beaten, who is younger, who is considerably more single-minded. Logic is on Frazier's side. Reason is on Frazier's side.

But logic and reason have never been Muhammad Ali's strong suits. They were never Cassius Clay's either. His game always will be emotion and charm and vitality and showmanship.

Eight weeks before the night of the Frazier fight, the telephone rang in my bedroom late one night. I picked it up. "Hello," I said.

"The champion of the world," said the caller. "I'm back from the dead."

I hope so. The man-child should be the heavyweight champion of the world. It is the only role he was born to play.

Norman Mailer

Wherever he went, Norman Mailer (1923–2007) always assumed he was the most important man on the premises. It wasn't a surprising opinion, considering that his first novel, *The Naked and the Dead* (1948), made him a bestselling author at twenty-five and that he later won Pulitzer prizes for two works of nonfiction, *The Armies of the Night* (1968) and *The Executioner's Song* (1979). The Brooklyn-born, Harvard-educated Mailer ultimately turned his authorial focus on John F. Kennedy, Marilyn Monroe, Adolf Hitler, Pablo Picasso, Lee Harvey Oswald, and God. As if that weren't enough, he also ran for mayor of New York in 1969—with Jimmy Breslin as his running mate and Joe Flaherty as his campaign manager.

Perhaps it was inevitable that Mailer would write about Muhammad Ali, the one person whose ego was as colossal as his. The result was *The Fight* (1975), his book-length deconstruction of Ali's 1974 "Rumble in the Jungle" with George Foreman in Kinshasa, Zaire. To write it, Mailer employed a hybrid of reporting and imagination that he called "narrative non-fiction." Not surprisingly, the end product shimmered with dazzling prose. But it was hard to find a kind word for Mailer among the veteran fight people and boxing writers who were in Zaire. Both the publicist Bobby Goodman and Ferdie Pacheco, Ali's physician and cornerman, accused Mailer of putting himself in scenes he was never part of. Most likely, he got his inside information from George Plimpton, who sat next to him at ringside and seems to have gotten around more than Mailer did.

Far more damning was the criticism of the way Mailer described Ali's trainer, Angelo Dundee, loosening the ring ropes with a wrench before the fight. Mailer, reporting as fact what he didn't see or bother to confirm, got it all wrong. What Dundee did, and he will tell you so, was *tighten* the ropes, and he did it the day before the fight, when Mailer wasn't around. Not that Dundee knew how Ali would employ the ropes in defeating Foreman. That was strictly Ali's improvisational wizardry at work, and Mailer paints an incomparable picture of it. Somehow, when he arrived at the most important part of the story, the genius in him managed to conquer the gremlin.

---

from

The Fight

RIGHT-HAND LEADS

G EORGE would. George was certainly going to hit him in the belly. What a battle was to follow. If the five-minute warning had just been given, it passed in a rush. There was a bathroom off the dressing room and to it Ali retired with his manager, the son of Elijah Muhammad, Herbert Muhammad, a round-faced benign-looking man whose features offered a complete lack of purchase—Herbert Muhammad gave the impression nobody would know how to take advantage of him too quickly. He was now dressed in a priestly white robe which ran from his shoulders to his feet, a costume appropriate to his function as a Moslem minister, for they had gone into the next room to pray and their voices could be heard reciting verses of the Koran—doubtless such Arabic was from the Koran. In the big room, now empty of Ali, everybody looked at everyone and there was nothing to say.

Ferdie Pacheco returned from Foreman's dressing room. "Everything's okay," he stated. "Let's roll." In a minute Ali came out of the bathroom with the son of Elijah Muhammad. While he shadowboxed, his manager continued to pray.

"How are things with Foreman?" someone asked Pacheco, and he shrugged. "Foreman's not talking," he said. "They got him covered with towels."

Now the word came down the line from the stadium outside. "Ali in the ring, Ali in the ring."

Solemnly, Bundini handed Ali the white African robe which the fighter had selected. Then everybody in the dressing room was on their way, a long file of twenty men who pushed and were hustled through a platoon of soldiers standing outside the door and then in a gang's rush in a full company of other soldiers were racing through the gray cement-brick corridors with their long-gone echoes of rifle shots and death. They emerged into open air, into the surrealistic bliss and green air of stadium grass under electric lights, and a cheer of no vast volume went up at the sight of Ali, but then the crowd had been waiting through an empty hour with no semifinal to watch, just an empty ring, and hours gone by before that with dancers to watch, more dancers, then more tribal dancers, a long count of the minutes from midnight to four. The nation of Zaïre had been awaiting this event for three months, now they were here, some sixty thousand, in a great oval of seats far from that ring in the center of the soccer field. They must be disappointed. Watching the fighters would prove kin to sitting in a room in a housing project studying people through a window in another housing project on the other side of a twelve-lane freeway. The fighters would work under a big corrugated tin shed roof with girders to protect the ring and the twenty-five hundred ringside seats from tropical downpour, which might come at any minute on this night so advanced already into the rainy season. Heavy rains were overdue by two weeks and more. Light rain had come almost every afternoon and dark portentous skies hung overhead. In America that would speak of quick summer storms, but the clouds in Africa were patient as the people and a black whirling smoky sky could shift overhead for days before more than a drop would fall.

Something of the weight of this oncoming rain was in the air. The early night had been full of oppression, and it was hot for so early in the morning, eighty degrees and a little more. Thoughts, however, of the oncoming fight left Norman closer to feeling chill. He was sitting next to Plimpton in the second row from the ring, a seat worth traveling thousands of miles to obtain (although counting two round trips, the figure might yet be twenty-five thousand miles—a barrel of jet lag for the soul). In front of them was a row of wire service reporters and photographers leaning on the apron of the ring; inside the ropes was Ali checking the resin against his shoes, and offering flashes of his shuffle to the study of the crowd, whirling away once in a while to throw a kaleidoscope-dozen of punches at the air in two seconds no more—one-Mississippi, two-Mississippi—twelve punches had gone by. Screams from the crowd at the blur of the gloves. He was all alone in the ring, the Challenger on call for the Champion, the Prince waiting for the Pretender, and unlike other fighters who wilt in the long minutes before the titleholder will appear, Ali seemed to be taking royal pleasure in his undisputed possession of the space. He looked unafraid and almost on the edge of happiness, as if the discipline of having carried himself through the two thousand nights of sleeping without his title after it had been taken from him without ever losing a contest—a frustration for a fighter doubtless equal in impact to writing *A Farewell to Arms* and then not being able to publish it— must have been a biblical seven years of trial through which he had come with the crucial part of his honor, his talent, and his desire for greatness still intact, and light came off him at this instant. His body had a shine like the flanks of a thoroughbred. He looked fully ready to fight the strongest meanest man to come along in Heavyweight circles in many years, maybe the worst big man of all, and while the Prince stood alone in his ring, and waited out the minutes for the Champion to arrive and had his thoughts, whatever they were, and his private communion with Allah, however that might feel, while he stood and while he shuffled and while he shadowboxed the air, the Lord Privy Seal, Angelo Dundee from Miami, went methodically from ring post to ring post and there in full view of ringside and the stadium just as methodically loosened each of the four turnbuckles on each post which held the tension of each of the four ropes, and did it with a spoke and a wrench he must have put in his little carrying bag back at Nsele and transported on the bus and carried from the dressing room to this ring. And when the ropes were slack to his taste, loose enough for his fighter to lean way back, he left the ring and returned to the corner. Nobody had paid any particular attention to him.

Foreman was still in his dressing room. Later Plimpton learned a detail from his old friend Archie Moore. "Just before going out to the ring, Foreman joined hands with his boxing trust—Dick Sadler, Sandy Saddler, and Archie—in a sort of prayer ritual they had practiced (for every fight) since Foreman became Champion in Jamaica," Plimpton wrote. "Now they were holding hands again in Zaire, and Archie Moore, who had his head bowed, found himself thinking that he should pray for Muhammad Ali's safety. Here's what he said: 'I was praying, and in great sincerity, that George wouldn't *kill* Ali. I really felt that was a possibility.'" So did others.

Foreman arrived in the ring. He was wearing red velvet trunks with a white stripe and a blue waistband. The colors of the American flag girded his middle and his shoes were white. He looked solemn, even sheepish, like a big boy who as Archie said "truly doesn't know his own strength." The letters GF stood out in embossed white cloth from the red velvet of his trunks. GF—Great Fighter.

The Referee, Zack Clayton, Black and much respected in his profession, had been waiting. George had time to reach his corner, shuffle his feet, huddle with the trust, get the soles of his shoes in resin, and the fighters were meeting in the center of the ring to get instructions. It was the time for each man to extort a measure of fear from the other. Liston had done it to all his opponents until he met Ali who, then Cassius Clay at the age of twenty-two, glared back at him with all the imperative of his high-destiny guts. Foreman, in turn, had done it to Frazier and then to Norton. A big look, heavy as death, oppressive as the closing of the door of one's tomb.

To Foreman, Ali now said (as everybody was later informed), "You have heard of me since you were young. You've been following me since you were a little boy. Now, you must meet me, your master!"— words the press could not hear at the time, but Ali's mouth was moving, his head was twelve inches from Foreman's, his eyes were on the other. Foreman blinked, Foreman looked surprised as if he had been impressed just a little more than he expected. He tapped Ali's glove in a move equal to saying, "That's *your* round. Now *we* start."

The fighters went back to their corners. Ali pressed his elbows to his side, closed his eyes and offered a prayer. Foreman turned his back. In the thirty seconds before the fight began, he grasped the ropes in his corner and bent over from the waist so that his big and powerful buttocks were presented to Ali. He flexed in this position so long it took on a kind of derision as though to declare: "My farts to you." He was still in such a pose when the bell rang.

The bell! Through a long unheard sigh of collective release, Ali charged across the ring. He looked as big and determined as Foreman, so he held himself, as if *he* possessed the true threat. They collided without meeting, their bodies still five feet apart. Each veered backward like similar magnetic poles repelling one another forcibly. Then Ali came forward again, Foreman came forward, they circled, they feinted, they moved in an electric ring, and Ali threw the first punch, a tentative left. It came up short. Then he drove a lightning-strong right straight as a pole into the stunned center of Foreman's head, the unmistakable thwomp of a high-powered punch. A cry went up. Whatever else happened, Foreman had been hit. No opponent had cracked George this hard in years and no sparring partner had dared to.

Foreman charged in rage. Ali compounded the insult. He grabbed the Champion around the neck and pushed his head down, wrestled it down crudely and decisively to show Foreman he was considerably rougher than anybody warned, and relations had commenced. They circled again. They feinted. They started in on one another and drew back. It was as if each held a gun. If one fired and missed, the other was certain to hit. If you threw a punch, and your opponent was ready, your own head would take his punch. What a shock. It is like seizing a high-voltage line. Suddenly you are on the floor.

Ali was not dancing. Rather he was bouncing from side to side looking for an opportunity to attack. So was Foreman. Maybe fifteen seconds went by. Suddenly Ali hit him again. It was again a right hand. Again it was hard. The sound of a bat thunking into a watermelon was heard around the ring. Once more Foreman charged after the blow, and once more Ali took him around the neck with his right arm, then stuck his left glove in Foreman's right armpit. Foreman could not start to swing. It was a nimble part of the advanced course for tying up a fighter. The referee broke the clinch. Again they moved through invisible reaches of attraction and repulsion, darting forward, sliding to the side, cocking their heads, each trying to strike an itch to panic in the other, two big men fast as pumas, charged as tigers—unseen sparks came off their moves. Ali hit him again, straight left, then a straight right. Foreman responded like a bull. He roared forward. A dangerous bull. His gloves were out like horns. No room for Ali to dance to the side, stick him and move, hit him and move. Ali went back, feinted, went back again, was on the ropes. Foreman had cut him off. The fight was thirty seconds old, and Foreman had driven him to the ropes. Ali had not even tried to get around those outstretched gloves so ready to cuff him, rough him, break his grace, no, retreating, Ali collected his toll. He hit Foreman with another left and another right.

Still a wail went up from the crowd. They saw Ali on the ropes. Who had talked of anything but how long Ali could keep away? Now he was trapped, so soon. Yet Foreman was off his aim. Ali's last left and right had checked him. Foreman's punches were not ready and Ali parried, Ali blocked. They clinched. The referee broke it. Ali was off the ropes with ease.

To celebrate, he hit Foreman another straight right. Up and down the press rows, one exclamation was leaping, "He's hitting him with *rights.*" Ali had not punched with such authority in seven years. Champions do not hit other champions with right-hand leads. Not in the first round. It is the most difficult and dangerous punch. Difficult to deliver and dangerous to oneself. In nearly all positions, the right hand has longer to travel, a foot more at least than the left. Boxers deal with inches and half-inches. In the time it takes a right hand to travel that extra space, alarms are ringing in the opponent, counterattacks are beginning. He will duck under the right and take off your head with a left. So good fighters do not often lead with their right against another good fighter. Not in the first round. They wait. They keep the right hand. It is one's authority, and ready to punish a left which comes too slowly. One throws one's right over a jab; one can block the left hook with a right forearm and chop back a right in return. Classic maxims of boxing. All fight writers know them. Off these principles they take their interpretation. They are good engineers at Indianapolis but Ali is on his way to the moon. Right-hand leads! My God!

In the next minute, Ali proceeded to hit Foreman with a combination rare as plutonium: a straight right hand followed by a long left hook. Spring-zing! went those punches, bolt to the head, bolt to the head; each time Foreman would rush forward in murderous rage and be caught by the neck and turned. His menace became more impressive each time he was struck. If the punches maddened him, they did not weaken him. Another fighter would be staggering by now. Foreman merely looked more destructive. His hands lost no speed, his hands looked as fast as Ali's (except when he got hit) and his face was developing a murderous appetite. He had not been treated so disrespectfully in years. Lost was genial George of the press conferences. His life was clear. He was going to dismember Ali. As he kept getting hit and grabbed, hit and grabbed, a new fear came over the rows at ringside. Foreman was awesome. Ali had now hit him about fifteen good punches to the head and not been caught once in return. What would happen when Foreman finally hit Ali? No Heavyweight could keep up the speed of these moves, not for fourteen more rounds.

But then the first was not even over. In the last minute, Foreman forced Ali to the ropes, was in on him, broke loose, and smashed a right uppercut through Ali's gloves, then another. The second went like a spear through the top of Ali's skull. His eyes flew up in consternation, and he grabbed Foreman's right arm with his left, squeezed it, clung to it. Foreman, his arm being held, was still in a mood to throw the good right again, and did. Four heavy half-smothered rights, concussive as blows to the heavy bag, went up to the head, then two down to the body, whaling on Ali even as he was held, and it was apparent these punches hurt. Ali came off the ropes in the most determined embrace of his life, both gloves locked around the back of Foreman's neck. The whites of Ali's eyes showed the glaze of a combat soldier who has just seen a dismembered arm go flying across the sky after an explosion. What kind of monster was he encountering?

Foreman threw a wild left. Then a left, a right, a left, a left and a right. Some to the head, some to the body, some got blocked, some missed, one collided with Ali's floating ribs, brutal punches, jarring and imprecise as a collision at slow speed in a truck.

With everybody screaming, Ali now hit Foreman with a right. Foreman hit him back with a left and a right. Now they each landed blows. Everybody was shaking their head at the bell. What a round!

Now the press rows began to ring with comment on those right-hand leads. How does Ali dare? A magnificent round. Norman has few vanities left, but thinks he knows something about boxing. He is ready to serve as engineer on Ali's trip to the moon. For Ali is one artist who does not box by right counter to left hook. He fights the entirety of the other person. He lives in fields of concentration where he can detect the smallest flicker of lack of concentration. Foreman has shown himself a lack of quiver flat to the possibility of a right. Who before this had dared after all to hit Foreman with a right? Of late his opponents were afraid to flick him with a jab. Fast were Foreman's hands, but held a flat spot of complacency before the right. He was not ready for a man to come into the ring unafraid of him. That offered its beauty. But frightening. Ali cannot fight every round like this. Such a pace will kill him in five. Indeed he could be worried as he sits in the corner. It has been his round, but what a force to Foreman's punches. It is true. Foreman hits harder than other fighters. And takes a very good punch. Ali looks thoughtful.

There is a sound box in the vicinity, some small loudspeaker hooked into the closed circuit, and on it Norman can hear David Frost, Jim Brown, and Joe Frazier talking between rounds, an agreeable sense of detachment thereby offered for they are on the other side of the press rows. Listening to them offers the comfort of a man watching a snowstorm from his fireplace. Jim Brown may have said last night that Ali had no chance, but Brown is one athlete who will report what he sees. "Great round for Muhammad Ali," he comments. "He did a fantastic job, although I don't think he can keep up this pace."

Sullenly, Joe Frazier disagrees. "Round was even . . . very close."

David Frost: "You wouldn't call that round for Ali?"

Joe is not there to root Ali home, not after Ali called him ignorant. "It was very close. Ali had two or three good shots to the face while George been landing body shots."

Foreman sits on his stool listening to Sadler. His face is bemused as if he has learned more than he is accustomed to in the last few minutes and the sensation is half agreeable. He has certainly learned that Ali can hit. Already his face shows lumps and welts. Ali is also a better wrestler than any fighter he has faced. Better able to agitate him. He sits back to rest the sore heat of his lungs after the boil of his fury in the last round. He brings himself to smile at someone at ringside. The smile is forced. Across the ring, Ali spits into the bowl held out for him and looks wide awake. His eyes are as alive as a ghetto adolescent walking down a strange turf. Just before the bell, he stands up in his corner and leads a cheer. Ali's arm pumps the air to inspire the crowd, and he makes a point of glowering at Foreman. Abruptly, right after the bell, his mood takes a change.

As Foreman comes out Ali goes back to the ropes, no, lets himself be driven to the corner, the worst place a fighter can be, worst place by all established comprehension of boxing. In the corner you cannot slip to the side, cannot go backward. You must fight your way out. With the screech that comes up from a crowd when one car tries to pass another in a race, Foreman was in to move on Ali, and Ali fought the good rat fight of the corner, his gloves thrown with frantic speed at Foreman's gloves. It became something like a slapping contest—of the variety two tall kids might show when trying to hit the other in the face. It is far from orthodox practice, where you dart out of a corner, duck out of a corner, or blast out. Since Ali kept landing, however, and Foreman did not, George retreated in confusion as if reverting to memories of fights when he was ten years old and scared—yes, Ali must have made some psychological choice and it was well chosen. He got out of the corner and held Foreman once again by the head in a grip so well applied that Foreman had the pensive expression of a steer being dogged to the ground by a cowboy.

Once the referee separated them, Ali began to back up across the ring. Foreman was after him throwing fast punches. "Show him," George's corner must have instructed, "that your gloves are as fast as his." Suddenly Foreman hit Ali with a straight hard right. Ali held on to Foreman to travel through the shock. After the fight he would say that some of Foreman's punches went right down to his toes, and this must have been one of them. When the fighters were separated, Foreman chased Ali to the ropes, and Ali pulled out a new trick, his full inch and a half of reach. He held his arms in Foreman's face to keep him off. The round was almost a minute gone before Ali got in his first good punch, another right. But Foreman charged him and pushed him, driving down on Ali's gloves with his own gloves, stalking him back and back again, knocking Ali's gloves away when he didn't like the character of their moves. Foreman was beginning to dictate how the fight should be. If a bully, he was a master bully. He did not react to the dictation of others, liked his own dictation. The force he sought in serenity had locked him on a unilinear road; it was working now. Ali kept retreating and Foreman caught him again. Hard! Once more, Ali was holding on with both hands, back of the neck, back of the bicep, half writhing and half riding with the somewhat stifled punches Foreman kept throwing. Foreman had begun to dominate the action to the point where Ali's best course seemed to be obliged to take what was left of each punch after the attempt to smother it. He kept trying to wrestle Foreman to a stop.

But then Ali must have come to a first assessment of assets and weaknesses, for he made—somewhere in the unremarked middle of the round—he must have made a decision on how to shape the rest of the fight. He did not seem able to hurt Foreman critically with those right-hand leads. Nor was he stronger than Foreman except when wrestling on his neck, and certainly he could not afford any more of those episodes where he held onto Foreman even as George was hitting him. It was costly in points, painful, and won nothing. On the other hand, it was too soon to dance. Too rapid would be the drain on his stamina. So the time had come to see if he could outbox Foreman while lying on the ropes. It had been his option from the beginning and it was the most dangerous option he had. For so long as Foreman had strength, the ropes would prove about as safe as riding a unicycle on a parapet. Still what is genius but balance on the edge of the impossible? Ali introduced his grand theme. He lay back on the ropes in the middle of the second round, and from that position he would work for the rest of the fight, reclining at an angle of ten and twenty degrees from the vertical and sometimes even further, a cramped near-tortured angle from which to box.

Of course Ali had been preparing for just this hour over the last ten years. For ten years he had been practicing to fight powerful sluggers who beat on your belly while you lay on the ropes. So he took up his station with confidence, shoulders parallel to the edge of the ring. In this posture his right would have no more impact than a straight left but he could find himself in position to cover his head with both gloves, and his belly with his elbows, he could rock and sway, lean so far back Foreman must fall on him. Should Foreman pause from the fatigue of throwing punches, Ali could bounce off the ropes and sting him, jolt him, make him look clumsy, mock him, rouse his anger, which might yet wear Foreman out more than anything else. In this position, Ali could even hurt him. A jab hurts if you run into it, and Foreman is always coming in. Still, Ali is in the position of a man bowing and ducking in a doorway while another man comes at him with two clubs. Foreman comes on with his two clubs. In the first exchange he hits Ali about six times while Ali is returning only one blow. Yet the punches to Ali's head seem not to bother him; he is swallowing the impact with his entire body. He is like a spring on the ropes. Blows seem to pass through him as if he is indeed a leaf spring built to take shock. None of his spirit is congested in his joints. Encouraged by the recognition that he can live with these blows, he begins to taunt Foreman. "Can you hit?" he calls out. "You can't hit. You push!" Since his head has been in range of Foreman's gloves, Foreman lunges at him. Back goes Ali's head like the carnival boy ducking baseballs. Wham to you, goes Ali, catapulting back. Bing and sting! Now Foreman is missing and Ali is hitting.

It is becoming a way to fight and even a way to live, but for Ali's corner it is a terror to watch. In the last thirty seconds of this second round, Ali hits out with straight rights from the ropes fast as jabs. Foreman's head must feel like a rivet under a riveting gun. With just a few seconds left, Foreman throws his biggest punch of the night, an express train of a left hook which leaves a spasm for the night in its passing. It has been a little too slow. Ali lets it go by in the languid unhurried fashion of Archie Moore watching a roundhouse miss his chin by a quarter of an inch. In the void of the effort, Foreman is so off-balance that Ali could throw him through the ropes. "Nothing," says Ali through his mouthpiece. "You have no aim." The bell rings and Foreman looks depressed. There has been premature desperation in that left. Ali shakes his head in derision. Of course that is one of Ali's basic tricks. All through his first fight with Frazier he kept signaling to the crowd that Joe failed to impress him. All the while Ali was finding himself in more trouble.

THE MAN IN THE RIGGING

IT seems like eight rounds have passed yet we only finished two. Is it because we are trying to watch with the fighters' sense of time? Before fatigue brings boxers to the boiler rooms of the damned, they live at a height of consciousness and with a sense of detail they encounter nowhere else. In no other place is their intelligence so full, nor their sense of time able to contain so much of itself as in the long internal effort of the ring. Thirty minutes go by like three hours. Let us undertake the chance, then, that our description of the fight may be longer to read than the fight itself. We can assure ourselves: It was even longer for the fighters.

Contemplate them as they sit in their corners between the second and third rounds. The outcome of the fight is not yet determined. Not for either. Ali has an enormous problem equal to his enormous confidence. Everybody has wondered whether Ali can get through the first few rounds and take Foreman's punch. Now the problem has been refined: Can he dismantle Foreman's strength before he uses up his own wit?

Foreman has another problem; he may not be as aware of it as his corner. There is no fear in his mind that he will fail to win the fight. He does not think about that any more than a lion supposes it will be unable to destroy a cheetah; no, it is just a question of catching Ali, a maddening frustration. Still the insult to his rage has to worry his corner. They can hardly tell him not to be angry. It is Foreman's rage after all which has led him to knock out so many fighters. To cut it off is to leave him cowlike. Nonetheless he must contain his anger until he catches Ali. Otherwise he is going to wear himself out.

So Sadler works on him, rubs his breasts and belly, Sadler sends his fingers into all the places where rage has congested, into the meat of the pectorals and the muscle plating beneath Foreman's chest, Sadler's touch has all the wisdom of thirty-five years of Black fingers elucidating comforts for Black flesh, sensual are his fingers as he plucks and shapes and shakes and balms, his silver bracelet shining on his Black wrist. When Sadler feels the fighter is soothed, he begins to speak, and Foreman takes on the expression of a man whose head is working slowly. He has too much to think about. He spits into the bowl held before him and nods respectfully. He looks as if he is listening to his dentist.

In Ali's corner, Dundee, with the quiet concern of a sommelier, is bringing the mouth of the adhesive-taped water bottle to Ali's lips, and does it with a forefinger under the neck so the bottle will not pour too much as he tips it up. Ali rinses and spits with his eyes off on the serious calculation of a man weighing grim but necessary alternatives.

Joe Frazier: "George is pounding that body with shots. He's hurting the body. Ali shouldn't stay on that rope. . . . If he don't move or cut George, George will walk him down. He need to move. He don't need to stay on that rope. For what reason's he on the *rope*?" Frazier sounds offended. Even the sound of the word worries him. Joe Frazier would consider himself *gone* if he had to work there. Rope is an ugly and miserable kuntu.

Jim Brown replies: "Ali is punishing George Foreman even *though* he's on the rope. He's getting some tremendous blows in and"—the wisdom of the professional football player—"at some point that can tell."

The bell. Once more Ali comes out of the corner with a big and threatening face as if this round for certain he will bring the attack to Foreman and once again sees something wrong in the idea, profoundly wrong, shifts his plan instantly, backs up and begins to play the ropes. On comes Foreman. The fight has taken its formal pattern. Ali will go by choice to the ropes and Foreman will chase him. Now in each round Ali will work for thirty or forty seconds or for so much even as a minute with his back no more than a foot or two from the top rope, and he is on the rope as often as not. When the strength of the mood, or the logic of the clinch suggests that the virtue of one set of ropes has been used up, he will back off across the ring to use another set. He will spend on an average one-quarter of each round on each of the four sides of the ring. He might just as well be drawing conscious strength from the burial gods of the North, the West, the East and the South. Never has a major fight been so locked into one pattern of movement. It appears designed by a choreographer who knows nothing about the workings of legs and is endlessly inventive about arms. The fight goes on in exactly this fashion round after round, and yet it is hardly boring, for Ali appears in constant danger, and is, and is not. He is turning the pockets of the boxing world inside out. He is demonstrating that what for other fighters is a weakness can be for him a strength. Foreman has been trained to cut instinctively from side to side in such a way as to spoil Ali's ability to circle, Foreman has learned how to force retreat to the ropes. But Ali makes no effort to get away. He does not circle, neither does he reverse his circle. Instead he backs up. Foreman's outstretched arms become a liability. Unable to cuff at a dancing target, he must probe forward. As he does, Ali keeps popping him with straight lefts and rights fast as karate strokes. But then Ali's wife has a black belt in karate.

Sooner or later, however, Foreman is always on him, leaning on him, banging him, belting away with all the fury George knows how to bring to the heavy bag. Ali uses the ropes to absorb the bludgeoning. Standing on one's feet, it is painful to absorb a heavy body punch even when blocked with one's arms. The torso, the legs and the spine take the shock. One has to absorb the brunt of the punch. Leaning on the ropes, however, Ali can pass it along; the ropes will receive the strain. If he cannot catch Foreman's punches with his gloves, or deflect them, or bend Foreman's shoulder to spoil his move, or lean away with his head, slip to the side, or loom up to hug Foreman's head, if finally there is nothing to do but take the punch, then Ali tightens his body and conducts the shock out along the ropes, so that Foreman must feel as if he is beating on a tree trunk which is oscillating against ropes. Foreman's power seems to travel right down the line and rattle the ring posts. It fortifies Ali's sense of relaxation—he has always the last resort of composing himself for the punch. When, occasionally, a blow does hurt, he sticks Foreman back, mean and salty, using his left and right as jabs. Since his shoulders are against the ropes, he jabs as often with his right as his left. With his timing it is a great jab. He has a gift for hitting Foreman as Foreman comes in. That doubles or triples the force. Besides he is using so many right jabs Foreman must start to wonder whether he is fighting a south-paw. Then comes the left jab again. A converted southpaw? It has something of the shift of locus which comes from making love to a brunette when she is wearing a blond wig. Of course, Ali has red wigs too. At the end of the round, Ali hits Foreman with some of the hard-est punches of the fight. A right, a left, and a right startle Foreman in their combination. He may not have seen such a combination since his last street fight. Ali gives a look of contempt and they wrestle for a few seconds until the bell. For the few extra seconds it takes Foreman to go to his corner, his legs have the look of a bedridden man who has started on a tour of his room for the first time in a week. He has almost stumbled on the way to his stool.

In the aisle, Rachman Ali began to jeer at Henry Clark. "Your man's a chump," Rachman said. "Ali's going to get him." Clark had to look worried. It was hardly his night. First his own fight had been postponed, then called off, now he was watching George from a crate in the aisle. Since he had a big bet on George, this last round offered its woes.

In the corner Sadler was massaging Foreman's right shoulder and George was gagging a bit, the inside of his lips showing a shocking frothy white like the mouth of an overgalloped horse.

Nonetheless, he looked lively as he came out for the bell. He came right across the middle of the ring to show Ali a new kind of feint, a long pawing movement of his hands accompanied by short moves of his head. It was to a different rhythm as if to say, "I haven't begun to show what I know."

He looked jaunty, but he was holding his right hand down by the waist. Fatigue must have lent carelessness to what he did, for Ali immediately answered with an insulting stiff right, an accelerating hook and another right so heavy to Foreman's head that he grabbed for a clinch, first time in the fight. There, holding on to Ali while ver-tigo collided with nausea, and bile scalded his breath, he must have been delivered into a new awareness, for George immediately started to look better. He began to get to Ali on the ropes and hit him occasionally, and for the first time in a while was not getting hit as much himself. He was even beginning to jam a number of Ali's rhythms. Up to now, whenever Ali took a punch, he was certain to come off the ropes and hit Foreman back. A couple of times in this round, however, even as Ali started his move, George would jam his forearm into Ali's neck, or wrestle him to a standstill.

All the while Ali was talking. "Come on, George, show me something," he would say. "Can't you fight harder? That ain't hard. I thought you was the Champion, I thought you had punches," and Foreman working like a bricklayer running up a pyramid to set his bricks would snort and lance his arms in sudden unexpected directions and try to catch Ali bouncing on the rope, Ali who was becoming more confirmed every minute in the sinecure of the rope, but at the end of the round, Foreman caught him with the best punch he had thrown in many a minute, landing just before the bell, and as he turned to leave Ali, he said clearly, "How's that?"

It must have encouraged him, for in the fifth round he tried to knock Ali out. Even as Ali was becoming more confident on the ropes, Foreman grew convinced he could break Ali's defense. Confidence on both sides makes for war. The round would go down in history as one of the great rounds in Heavyweight boxing; indeed it was so good it forged its own frame as they battled. One could see it outlined forever in lights: *The Great Fifth Round of the Ali–Foreman fight!*

Like much of greatness, the beginnings were unremarked. Foreman ended the fourth round well, but expectation was circling ringside that a monumental upset could be shaping. Even Joe Frazier was admitting that George was "not being calm." It took John Daly to blurt out cheerfully to David Frost, "Ali is winning all the way for me and I think he's going to take it within another four rounds!"

Foreman didn't think so. There had been that sniff of victory in the fourth, the good punch which landed—"How's that?" He came out in the fifth with the conviction that if force had not prevailed against Ali up to now, more force was the answer, considerably more force than Ali had ever seen. If Foreman's face was battered to lumps and his legs were moving like wheels with a piece chipped out of the rim, if his arms were beginning to sear in the lava of exhaustion and his breath come roaring to his lungs like the blast from a bed of fire, still he was a prodigy of strength, he was *the* prodigy, he could live through states of torture and hurl his cannonade when others could not lift their arms, he had been trained for endurance even more than execution and back in Pendleton when first working for this fight had once boxed fifteen rounds with half a dozen sparring partners coming on in two-round shifts while Foreman was permitted only thirty seconds of rest between each round. He could go, he could go and go, he was tireless in the arms, yes, could knock down a forest, take it down all by himself, and he set out now to chop Ali down.

They sparred inconclusively for the first half-minute. Then the barrage began. With Ali braced on the ropes, as far back on the ropes as a deep-sea fisherman is braced back in his chair when setting the hook on a big strike, so Ali got ready and Foreman came on to blast him out. A shelling reminiscent of artillery battles in World War I began. Neither man moved more than a few feet in the next minute and a half. Across that embattled short space Foreman threw punches in barrages of four and six and eight and nine, heavy maniacal slamming punches, heavy as the boom of oaken doors, bombs to the body, bolts to the head, punching until he could not breathe, backing off to breathe again and come in again, bomb again, blast again, drive and steam and slam the torso in front of him, wreck him in the arms, break through those arms, get to his ribs, dig him out, dig him out, put the dynamite in the earth, lift him, punch him, punch him up to heaven, take him out, stagger him—great earthmover he must have sobbed to himself, kill this mad and bouncing goat.

And Ali, gloves to his head, elbows to his ribs, stood and swayed and was rattled and banged and shaken like a grasshopper at the top of a reed when the wind whips, and the ropes shook and swung like sheets in a storm, and Foreman would lunge with his right at Ali's chin and Ali go flying back out of reach by a half-inch, and half out of the ring, and back in to push at Foreman's elbow and hug his own ribs and sway, and sway just further, and lean back and come forward from the ropes and slide off a punch and fall back into the ropes with all the calm of a man swinging in the rigging. All the while, he used his eyes. They looked like stars, and he feinted Foreman out with his eyes, flashing white eyeballs of panic he did not feel which pulled Foreman through into the trick of lurching after him on a wrong move, Ali darting his expression in one direction while cocking his head in another, then staring at Foreman expression to expression, holding him in the eye, soul to soul, muntu to muntu, hugging his head, peeking through gloves, jamming his armpit, then taunting him on the edge of the ropes, then flying back as Foreman dove forward, tantalizing him, maddening him, looking for all the world as cool as if he were sparring in his bathrobe, now banishing Foreman's head with the turn of a matador sending away a bull after five fine passes were made, and once when he seemed to hesitate just a little too long, teasing Foreman just a little too long, something stirred in George like that across-the-arena knowledge of a bull when it is ready at last to gore the matador rather than the cloth, and like a member of a cuadrilla, somebody in Ali's corner screamed, "Careful! Careful! Careful!" and Ali flew back and just in time for as he bounced on the ropes Foreman threw six of his most powerful left hooks in a row and then a right, it was the center of his fight and the heart of his best charge, a left to the belly, a left to the head, a left to the belly, a left to the head, a left to the belly, another to the belly and Ali blocked them all, elbow for the belly, glove for the head, and the ropes flew like snakes. Ali was ready for the lefts. He was not prepared for the right that followed. Foreman hit him a powerful punch. The ring-bolts screamed. Ali shouted, "Didn't hurt a bit." Was it the best punch he took all night? He had to ride through ten more after that. Foreman kept flashing his muscles up out of that cup of desperation boiling in all determination, punches that came toward the end of what may have been as many as forty or fifty in a minute, any one strong enough to send water from the spine to the knees. Something may have finally begun to go from Foreman's n'golo, some departure of the essence of absolute rage, and Ali reaching over the barrage would give a prod now and again to Foreman's neck like a housewife sticking a toothpick in a cake to see if it is ready. The punches got weaker and weaker, and Ali finally came off the ropes and in the last thirty seconds of the round threw his own punches, twenty at least. Almost all hit. Some of the hardest punches of the night were driven in. Four rights, a left hook and a right came in one stupendous combination. One punch turned Foreman's head through ninety degrees, a right cross of glove and forearm that slammed into the side of the jaw; double contact had to be felt; once from the glove, then from the bare arm, stunning and jarring. Walls must begin to crack inside the brain. Foreman staggered and lurched and glared at Ali and got hit again, zing-bing! two more. When it was all over, Ali caught Foreman by the neck like a big brother chastising an enormous and stupid kid brother, and looked out to someone in the audience, some enemy or was it some spiteful friend who said Foreman would win, for Ali, holding George around the neck, now stuck out one long white-coated tongue. On the other side of the ropes, Bundini was beaming at the bell.

"I really don't believe it," said Jim Brown. "I really don't believe it. I thought he was hurt. I thought his body was hurt. He came back. He hit Foreman with everything. And he winked at *me*." Did he wink or stick out his tongue?

In the aisle, Rachman was screaming at Henry Clark. "Your fighter's a chump. He's an amateur. My brother is killing him. My brother is showing him up!"

THE EXECUTIONER'S SONG

So began the third act of the fight. Not often was there a better end to a second act than Foreman's failure to destroy Ali on the ropes. But the last scenes would present another problem. How was the final curtain to be found? For if Foreman was exhausted, Ali was weary. He had hit Foreman harder than he had ever hit anyone. He had hit him often. Foreman's head must by now be equal to a piece of vulcanized rubber. Conceivably you could beat on him all night and nothing more would happen. There is a threshold to the knock-out. When it comes close but is not crossed, then a man can stagger around the ring forever. He has received his terrible message and he is still standing. No more of the same woe can destroy him. He is like the victim in a dreadful marriage which no one knows how to end. So Ali was obliged to produce still one more surprise. If not, the unhappiest threat would present itself as he and Foreman stumbled through the remaining rounds. There is agony to elucidate even a small sense of the aesthetic out of boxing. Wanton waste for an artist like Ali to lose then the perfection of this fight by wandering down a monotonous half hour to a dreary unanimous decision.

A fine ending to the fight would live in legend, but a dull victory, anticlimactic by the end, could leave him in half a legend—overblown in reputation by his friends and contested by his enemies—precisely that state which afflicted most heroes. Ali was fighting to prove other points. So he said. So Ali had to dispose of Foreman in the next few rounds and do it well, a formidable problem. He was like a torero after a great faena who must still face the drear potential of a protracted inept and disappointing kill. Since no pleasure is greater among athletes than to overtake the style of their opponent, Ali would look to steal Foreman's last pride. George was an executioner. Ali would do it better. But how do you execute the executioner?

The problem was revealed in all its sluggish intricacies over the next three rounds. Foreman came out for the sixth looking like an alley cat with chewed-up brows. Lumps and swellings were all over his face, his skin equal to tar that has baked in the sun. When the bell rang, however, he looked dangerous again, no longer a cat, but a bull. He lowered his head and charged across the ring. He was a total demonstration of the power of one idea even when the idea no longer works. And was immediately seized and strangled around the neck by Ali for a few valuable and pacifying seconds until Zack Clayton broke them. Afterward, Foreman moved in to throw more punches. His power, however, seemed gone. The punches were slow and tentative. They did not reach Ali. Foreman was growing glove-shy. His fastest moves were now in a nervous defense that kept knocking Ali's punches away from his own face.

At this point Ali proceeded to bring out the classic left jab everyone had been expecting for the first round. In the next half-minute, he struck Foreman's head with ten head-ringing jabs thrown with all the speed of a good fencer's thrust, and Foreman took them in apathy to compound the existing near-apathy of his hopes. Each time his head snapped back, some communciation between his mind and his nerves must have been reduced. A surgical attack.

Yet something in Foreman's response decided Ali to give it up. Perhaps no more than his own sense of moderation. It might look absurd if he kept jabbing Foreman forever. Besides, Ali needed rest. The next two minutes turned into the slowest two minutes of the fight. Foreman kept pushing Ali to the ropes out of habit, a dogged forward motion that enabled George to rest in his fashion, the only way he still knew, which was to lean on the opponent. Ali was by now so delighted with the advantages of the ropes that he fell back on them like a man returning home in quiet triumph, yes, settled in with the weary pleasure of a working man getting back into bed after a long day to be treated to a little of God's joy by his hardworking wife. He was almost tender with Foreman's laboring advance, holding him softly and kindly by the neck. Then he stung him with right and left karate shots from the shoulder. Foreman was now so arm-weary he could begin a punch only by lurching forward until his momentum encouraged a movement of the arm. He looked like a drunk, or rather a somnambulist, in a dance marathon. It would be wise to get him through the kill without ever waking him up. While it ought to be a simple matter to knock him down, there might not be enough violence left in the spirit of this ring to knock him out. So the shock of finding himself on the floor could prove a stimulant. His ego might reappear: once on the floor, he was a champion in dramatic danger of losing his title—that is an unmeasurable source of energy. Ali was now taking in the reactions of Foreman's head the way a bullfighter lines up a bull before going in over the horns for the kill. He bent to his left and, still crouched, passed his body to the right under Foreman's fists, all the while studying George's head and neck and shoulders. Since Foreman charged the move, a fair conclusion was that the bull still had an access of strength too great for the kill.

Nonetheless, Foreman's punches were hardly more than pats. They were sufficiently weak for any man in reasonable shape to absorb them. Still, Foreman came on. Sobbing for breath, leaning, almost limping, in a pat-a-pat of feeble cuffs, he was all but lying over Ali on the ropes. Yet what a problem in the strength of his stubbornness itself. Endless powers of determination had been built out of one season of silence passing into another. The bell rang the end of the sixth. Both men gave an involuntary smile of relief.

Foreman looked ready to float as he came to his corner. Sandy Saddler could not bring himself to look at him. The sorrow in Foreman's corner was now heavier than in Ali's dressing room before the fight.

In his corner Ali looked thoughtful, and stood up abstractedly before the bell and abstractedly led a cheer in the stadium, his arm to the sky.

The cheer stirred Foreman to action. He was out of his corner and in the middle of the ring before the bell rang. Ali opened his eyes wide and stared at him in mock wonder, then in disdain as if to say, "Now you've done it. Now you're asking for it." He came out of his corner too, and the referee was pushing both men apart as the bell rang.

Still it was a slow round, almost as slow as the sixth. Foreman had no speed, and in return Ali boxed no faster than he had to, but kept shifting more rapidly than before from one set of ropes to another. Foreman was proving too sluggish to work with. Once, in the middle of the round, Foreman staggered past Ali, and for the first time in the fight was literally nearer the ropes. It was a startling realization. Not since the first five seconds of the fight had Ali crossed the center of the ring while moving forward. For seven rounds his retreating body had been between Foreman and the ropes except for the intervals when he traveled backward from one set of ropes to another. This time, seeing Foreman on the ropes instead, Ali backed up immediately and Foreman slogged after him like an infantryman looking at the ground. Foreman's best move by now might be to stand in the center of the ring and invite Ali to come to him. If Ali refused, he would lose the luster of his performance, and if he did come forward it would be George's turn to look for weaknesses. While Foreman waited for Ali, he could rest. Yet George must have had some unspoken fear of disaster if he shifted methods. So he would drive, thank you very much, into the grave he would determine for himself. Of course, he was not wholly without hope. He still worked with the idea that one punch could catch Ali. And with less than a minute left, he managed to drive a left hook into Ali's belly, a blow that indeed made Ali gasp. Then Foreman racked him with a right uppercut strong enough for Ali to hold on in a clinch, no, Foreman was not going to give up. Now he leaned on Ali with one extended arm and tried to whale him with the other. He looked like he was beating a rug. Foreman had begun to show the clumsiness of a street fighter at the end of a long rumble. He was reverting. It happened to all but the most cultivated fighters toward the exhausted end of a long and terrible fight. Slowly they descended from the elegance of their best style down to the knee in the groin and the overhead punch (with a rock in the fist) of forgotten street fights.

Ali, half as tired at least, was not wasting himself. He was still graceful in every move. By the end of the round he was holding Foreman's head tenderly once more in his glove. Foreman was becoming reminiscent of the computer Hal in *2001* as his units were removed one by one, malfunctions were showing and spastic lapses. All the while something of the old panache of Sadler, Saddler, and Moore inserted over those thousands of hours of training still showed in occasional moves and gestures. The weakest slaps of his gloves, however, had begun to look like entreaties. Still his arms threw punches. By the end of the seventh he could hardly stand: yet he must have thrown seventy more punches. So few were able to land. Ali had restricted himself to twenty-five—half at least must have gone to target. Foreman was fighting as slowly as a worn-out fighter in the Golden Gloves, slow as a man walking up a hill of pillows, slow as he would have looked if their first round had been rerun in slow motion, that was no slower than Foreman was fighting now, and thus exposed as in a film, he was reminiscent of the slow and curving motions of a linebacker coiling around a runner with his hands and arms in the slow-motion replay—the boxing had shifted from speed and impact to an intimacy of movement. Delicately Ali would cradle Foreman's head with his left before he smashed it with his right. Foreman looked ready to fall over from exhaustion. His face had the soft scrubbed look of a child who has just had a dirty face washed, but then they both had that gentle look boxers get when they are very tired and have fought each other very hard.

Back in the corner, Moore's hands were massaging Foreman's shoulders. Sandy Saddler was working on his legs. Dick Sadler was talking to him.

Jim Brown was saying, "This man, Muhammad Ali, is *unreal*." When Jim used the word, it was a compliment. Whatever was real, Jim Brown could dominate. And Frazier added his humor, "I would say right now my man is not in the lead. I got a feeling George is not going to make it."

On the aisle, Rachman was still calling out to Henry Clark. "Henry, admit it, your man is through, he's a chump, he's a street fighter. Henry, admit it. Maybe I'm not a fighter, I know I'm not as good as you, but admit it, admit it, Muhammad has whipped George."

Except he hadn't. Not yet. Two rounds had gone by. The two dullest rounds of the fight. The night was hot. Now the air would become more tropical with every round. In his corner, Ali looked to be in pain as he breathed. Was it his kidneys or his ribs? Dundee was talking to him and Ali was shaking his head in disagreement. In contrast to Foreman, his expression was keen. His eyes looked as quick as the eyes, indeed, of a squirrel. The bell rang for the eighth round.

Working slowly, deliberately, backing up still one more time, he hit Foreman carefully, spacing the punches, taking aim, six good punches, lefts and rights. It was as if he had a reserve of good punches, a numbered amount like a soldier in a siege who counts his bullets, and so each punch had to carry a predetermined portion of the work.

Foreman's legs were now hitched into an ungainly prance like a horse high-stepping along a road full of rocks. Stung for the hundredth time with a cruel blow, his response was to hurl back a left hook that proved so wild he almost catapulted through the ropes. Then for an instant, his back and neck were open to Ali, who cocked a punch but did not throw it, as though to demonstrate for an instant to the world that he did not want to flaw this fight with any blow reminiscent of the thuds Foreman had sent to the back of the head of Norton and Roman and Frazier. So Ali posed with that punch, then moved away. Now for the second time in the fight he had found Foreman between himself and the ropes and had done nothing.

Well, George came off the ropes and pursued Ali like a man chasing a cat. The wild punch seemed to have refreshed him by its promise that some of his power was back. If his biggest punches were missing, at least they were big. Once again he might be his own prodigy of strength. Now there were flurries on the ropes which had an echo of the great bombardment in the fifth round. And still Ali taunted him, still the dialogue went on. "Fight hard," said Ali, "I thought you had some punches. You're a weak man. You're all used up." After a while, Foreman's punches were whistling less than his breath. For the eighteenth time Ali's corner was screaming, "Get off the ropes. Knock him out. Take him home!" Foreman had used up the store of force he transported from the seventh to the eighth. He pawed at Ali like an infant six feet tall waving its uncoordinated battle arm.

With twenty seconds left to the round, Ali attacked. By his own measure, by that measure of twenty years of boxing, with the knowledge of all he had learned of what could and could not be done at any instant in the ring, he chose this as the occasion and lying on the ropes, he hit Foreman with a right and left, then came off the ropes to hit him with a left and a right. Into this last right hand he put his glove and his forearm again, a head-stupefying punch that sent Foreman reeling forward. As he went by, Ali hit him on the side of the jaw with a right, and darted away from the ropes in such a way as to put Foreman next to them. For the first time in the entire fight he had cut off the ring on Foreman. Now Ali struck him a combination of punches fast as the punches of the first round, but harder and more consecutive, three capital rights in a row struck Foreman, then a left, and for an instant on Foreman's face appeared the knowledge that he was in danger and must start to look to his last protection. His opponent was attacking, and there were no ropes behind the opponent. What a dislocation: the axes of his existence were reversed! He was the man on the ropes! Then a big projectile exactly the size of a fist in a glove drove into the middle of Foreman's mind, the best punch of the startled night, the blow Ali saved for a career. Foreman's arms flew out to the side like a man with a parachute jumping out of a plane, and in this doubled-over position he tried to wander out to the center of the ring. All the while his eyes were on Ali and he looked up with no anger as if Ali, indeed, was the man he knew best in the world and would see him on his dying day. Vertigo took George Foreman and revolved him. Still bowing from the waist in this uncomprehending position, eyes on Muhammad Ali all the way, he started to tumble and topple and fall even as he did not wish to go down. His mind was held with magnets high as his championship and his body was seeking the ground. He went over like a six-foot sixty-year-old butler who has just heard tragic news, yes, fell over all of a long collapsing two seconds, down came the Champion in sections and Ali revolved with him in a close circle, hand primed to hit him one more time, and never the need, a wholly intimate escort to the floor.

The referee took Ali to a corner. He stood there, he seemed lost in thought. Now he raced his feet in a quick but restrained shuffle as if to apologize for never asking his legs to dance, and looked on while Foreman tried to rouse himself.

Like a drunk hoping to get out of bed to go to work, Foreman rolled over, Foreman started the slow head-agonizing lift of all that foundered bulk God somehow gave him and whether he heard the count or no, was on his feet a fraction after the count of ten and whipped, for when Zack Clayton guided him with a hand at his back, he walked in docile steps to his corner and did not resist. Moore received him. Sadler received him. Later, one learned the conversation.

"Feel all right?"

"Yeah," said Foreman.

"Well, don't worry. It's history now."

"Yeah."

"You're all right," said Sadler, "the rest will take care of itself."

In the ring Ali was seized by Rachman, by Gene Kilroy, by Bundini, by a host of Black friends old, new and very new, who charged up the aisles, leaped on the apron, sprang through the ropes and jumped near to touch him. Norman said to Plimpton in a tone of wonder like a dim parent who realizes suddenly his child is indeed and indubitably married, "My God, he's Champion again!" as if one had trained oneself for years not to expect news so good as that.

In the ring Ali fainted.

It occurred suddenly and without warning and almost no one saw it. Angelo Dundee circling the ropes to shout happy words at reporters was unaware of what had happened. So were all the smiling faces. It was only the eight or ten men immediately around him who knew. Those eight or ten mouths which had just been open in celebration now turned to grimaces of horror. Bundini went from laughing to weeping in five seconds.

Why Ali fainted, nobody might ever know. Whether it was a warning against excessive pride in years to come—one private bolt from Allah—or whether the weakness of sudden exhaustion, who could know? Maybe it was even the spasm of a reflex he must have refined unconsciously for months—the ability to recover in seconds from total oblivion. Had he been obliged to try it out at least once on this night? He was in any case too much of a champion to allow an episode to arise, and was back on his feet before ten seconds were up. His handlers having been lifted, chastened, terrified and uplifted again, looked at him with faces of triumph and knockdown, the upturned mask of comedy and the howling mouth of tragedy next to each other in that instant in the African ring.

David Frost was crying out: "Muhammad Ali has done it. The great man has done it. This is the most joyous scene ever seen in the history of boxing. This is an incredible scene. The place is going wild. Muhammad Ali has won." And because the announcer before him had picked the count up late and was two seconds behind the referee and so counting eight when Clayton said ten, it looked on all the closed circuit screens of the world as if Foreman had gotten up before the count was done, and confusion was everywhere. How could it be other? The media would always sprout the seed of confusion. "Muhammad Ali has won. By a knockdown," said Frost in good faith. "By a knockdown."

Back in America everybody was already yelling that the fight was fixed. Yes. So was *The Night Watch* and *Portrait of the Artist as a Young Man.*

Robert Lipsyte

As a precocious nineteen-year-old Columbia graduate, Robert Lipsyte (b. 1938) planned to head to California, where he would write novels and screenplays and loll on the beach, but financial necessity forced him to take a job as a *New York Times* copyboy. Next thing he knew, he was a baseball writer covering spring training when, to his surprise, he was assigned the heavyweight championship fight between Sonny Liston and Cassius Clay. "Because most people thought Liston would knock the kid out in the first round, the editors didn't want to send the *real* boxing reporter," Lipsyte said. He was soon swept up in the transformation of American sportswriting in the '60s, a witty, tough-minded columnist who dealt with social issues as boldly as he did action in the ring and on the playing field. He relinquished his column to write a boxing-themed novel, *The Contender* (1967), and several books of young-adult fiction before returning to the *Times* as the hip *éminence grise* of its sports page. His moving profile of Nigerian middleweight Dick Tiger ran in *The Atlantic* in September 1975. Lipsyte currently hosts a PBS series for aging baby boomers, and has just completed a memoir called—what else?—*An Accidental Sportswriter* (2010).

Pride of the Tiger

THE first time I saw Dick Tiger he was waiting for me in front of the old Madison Square Garden, a homburg perched on top of his head. The homburg was much too small, and I thought he looked comical. It was years before I learned that he always bought his hats a size too small, so he could share them with his brothers back home in Nigeria.

I introduced myself to Tiger and he shook my hand gravely. Then he turned and began moving down Eighth Avenue on the balls of his feet, like a big black cat. His manager and I followed.

"Nigerian fighters are very good, very tough," said his manager. "They're closer to the jungle."

Over his shoulder, Tiger said, "There is no jungle in Nigeria."

"It's just an expression, Dick, just a figure of speech," said the manager. "I mean they're hungry fighters."

Tiger stopped. "Hungry fighters." He winked at me. "We eat hoo-mon bee-inks. Medium rare."

We walked a mile and a half to the gym where he was training because Tiger would not consider a cab, even if I paid. It was said around town that Tiger had the terminal cheaps. I followed him into a dressing room and watched him shed the comedy of his clothes. As the homburg, the brown sports jacket, the blue tie and white shirt disappeared into a rusty metal locker, Tiger seemed to grow larger. The blue tribal tattoos across his chest and back rippled over knotty muscle. He seemed suddenly savage, dangerous.

But there was only gentleness in his eyes, and humor twitched at the corners of his wide mouth. I watched him tape his hands slowly and with great care, first winding the dirty gray bandages around and around, then placing the sponge across the knuckles, then wrapping on the adhesive. I asked him why he didn't have his manager or trainer perform this daily chore, now that he was middleweight champion of the world.

"I am a travelin' man, and I got to do things myself, a fighter should know these things," he said. "This is my business. I don't want to spoil myself for someday when there is no one around to help me."

He was thirty-four years old at the time, and had been champion for less than a year. He was training in New York, where facilities and sparring partners were the best, for the second defense of that championship, to be held in Ibadan, Nigeria. Tiger was taking this fight very seriously. It would be Nigeria's first world title fight, and his own real homecoming. "It is very important I win," he said. "For pride. They receive me different, people, when I am champion."

This was June, 1963, and I had interviewed few fighters. I watched Tiger work out for two hours, methodically, intensely, oblivious of sound and movement around him. Great silver globules of sweat formed, swelled, exploded on his forehead, and he never wiped them away. He weighed about 160 pounds then, and his 5'8" body was unusually hard and fit. His calisthenics were so violent that they seemed beyond human tolerance; I was sure his eyes would pop out of his head as he twisted his neck, that his muscles and veins would burst through his skin.

We talked again after he was finished. His voice was softer now, his body more relaxed. He had been born in Amaigbo, a remote eastern Nigerian town in the rain forests of the Benin River delta, a town that appeared on few maps. He was raised on a farm and educated in English and Ibo at an Anglican mission school. At nineteen he went to the city of Aba to work in his brother's grocery store. At a local boys' club he learned to box.

He had been christened Richard Ihetu, Ibo for "what I want," but assumed the ring name Dick Tiger for his early pro fights against the likes of Easy Dynamite and Super Human Power. He kept the name when a British promoter brought him to England to fight on the Blackpool–Liverpool circuit. He was lonely and chilled in the dank foreign gyms, and he lost his first four fights. Letters from his family in Nigeria were beseeching him to give up the foolishness and return to his father's farm or his brother's grocery store. Tiger gave himself one more chance. In his fifth fight, he knocked out a Liverpool boy in ninety seconds, and Richard Ihetu, farmer and clerk, disappeared forever.

He first came to America in 1959, and lived with his pregnant wife in third-rate Manhattan hotels, cooking meals on a hot plate and running in Central Park. He slowly gained a reputation among boxing promoters as an honest workman. He was always in top condition, he always gave his best. He would never be spectacular, he did not have a great deal of boxing finesse or personal "color," but he was dependable and tough. His wife gave birth to twins, then to a third child in 1960. Tiger sent her back to Nigeria and began commuting between New York and Aba. Now he lived in fourth-rate hotels, walked whenever possible, window-shopped for entertainment, sent every penny home. After he won the title in 1962, he was able to send more money home, but he did not improve the quality of his living conditions or his clothing. I asked him if he was saving his money for something special.

"This will not always be my business. I want money," he said, rubbing his fingers together. "Six hundred thousand to start a big business. Now all I have is a house and a Peugeot, that is all."

We left the gym together and took the subway uptown. We made small talk on the ride, and he told me the only tiger he had ever seen was in a cage in the Liverpool zoo. My stop came first. I got off the train, and looked back at him through the window. In his clothes again, he was just a chunky man in a too-small homburg, hanging from an overhead strap, jostled by a rush-hour crowd.

I went back to the office and wrote a tidy Sunday feature story, my specialty. A month later, I read that he had won his bout in Ibadan. I was glad of that; something about Tiger had touched me.

In December of that year, 1963, he defended his title against Joey Giardello in Atlantic City. It was my first championship fight, and my notes were unusually voluminous, including the first stanza of the Nigerian anthem, which was played before the fight began.

> "Nigeria, we hail thee,
>
> Our own dear native land.
>
> Though tribe and tongue may differ
>
> In brotherhood we stand."

Tiger lost the fifteen-round fight by a decision. I knew he would be very upset. He had become a national hero in Nigeria: he had been awarded a medal, Member of the British Empire, in Lagos, and he was amassing property in Aba. In a few days he would be returning home a loser.

But the next morning he smiled at me and said amiably, "Look at my face. I don't look like I was in a fight last night. I did a bit of dancing last night with Giardello, and I am a fighter, not a dancer. I thought I did enough to win, as he kept running away."

He shrugged and sighed. "These days you get a title by running away."

We shook hands gravely and said good-bye. I would have liked to tell him that I was sorry he had lost, but the words stuck in my throat. It seemed somehow unprofessional, and Tiger was a professional.

Giardello promised Tiger a rematch within six months, but it was two years before they met again. Giardello enjoyed his championship hugely and did nothing to endanger it, like fighting someone who might take it away. Tiger, meanwhile, waited patiently and rarely fought: his reputation as a head-down, hands-up, straight-ahead slugger who plodded into his opponent and beat away scared off anyone who didn't need to fight him for a payday or a shot at the title.

By the time they met again I was a regular boxing writer, veteran of the Clay–Liston spectacles, a seasoned observer who almost knew A. J. Liebling's *The Sweet Science* by heart. I even kept my own score-card, which usually conflicted with the judges'. I was also a great deal more appreciative of Dick Tiger, now that I had interviewed many other boxers and watched them train and fight. Of all athletes, box-ers are generally the friendliest and the most dedicated, and Tiger had the most heart and soul of them all.

I liked Joey Giardello, but I was secretly rooting for Tiger to win back his title the night of the rematch in Madison Square Garden. Tiger was shorter and lighter and older than Giardello, but from the opening bell, when a Nigerian *etulago* set a thumping drumbeat, Tiger doggedly followed Giardello around the ring, pressing and batter-ing and slugging. Giardello stayed on his feet as a point of pride. At the start of the fifteenth and last round, with the decision certain for Tiger, Giardello leaned forward and whispered, "Nice fight."

Tiger did not hold the title very long this time, either. He was over thirty-six years old, and the strain of keeping his weight below the 160-pound middleweight limit sapped his strength. Emile Griffith, the welterweight champion, who could no longer keep his weight below 147 pounds, moved up in class and beat him. So, logically, Tiger decided to move up in class, too. In the winter of 1966 he beat the brilliant but erratic Jose Torres and became light heavyweight champion. The morning after that fight I visited his shabby hotel room. He greeted me with the same amiable, win-or-lose smile.

"The people all said that Tiger is finished, that he looks a hundred years old, and now they come around to pat my head and tell me I'm a good boy." He shrugged. "That's life."

His investments in Nigeria were doing well, he told me, although he was concerned by the mounting violence and political instabil-ity. Many thousands of his fellow Ibo tribesmen had been slaugh-tered in pogroms in northern Nigeria. The Ibo, who were Christians, were civil servants and small businessmen in the Moslem north. Ibo were fleeing back to their native lands in eastern Nigeria. Tiger's holdings were in Aba, in the eastern region, where he lived in a large, air-conditioned home, owned several buildings, operated several businesses and shops, and had a chauffeur for his Mercedes-Benz limousine. He was still optimistic about the future of his six children and the many nieces and nephews that he took pride and joy in supporting.

Tiger fought Torres again the following spring, as usual giving away height and weight and age, and he beat him again. This time, when the decision was announced, fights broke out in the balcony and bottles of wine and rum smashed on the Garden floor and sprayed the crowd with shards of glass. There was blood and there were a number of injuries. I wrote most of my story crouched under the Garden ring, with my typewriter on my knees. The incident was discussed and written about for several days, and then dismissed as one of those cultural-ethnic-economic-sporting inevitabilities. Garden officials blamed "a few nuts or hoodlums" who wanted to read about themselves in the papers. Torres said he was proud of his fellow Puerto Ricans for showing their "support" of him, and Lipsyte analyzed the random violence as an expression of the class struggle. The boxing commissioner declared: "A hundred years ago Charles Dickens went to a fight with William Makepeace Thackeray and wrote about a riot in London."

It was an ironic send-off for Tiger, who flew back home into the Nigerian civil war.

The next time I saw him, in March of 1968, the smile was gone. His mouth was twisted, his voice high and tense. His square hands plucked at his baggy gray suit pants.

"I used to be a happy man, but now I have seen something I have never seen before. I read about killing and war, but I had never seen such things. Now, I have seen massacres."

He bounded from the straight-backed hotel chair and began fishing in his bureau drawers, through pamphlets and books and newspaper clippings. "Ah, here," he said, almost reverentially opening tissue paper. "This is Aba." He spread the photographs on the bed.

"The hospital. There were eight patients and a doctor when the planes came and threw bombs around. Hired pilots. The Nigerians can't fly planes. They are a thousand years behind civilization, that is why they are doing everything wrong.

"The open market, look at that. In that corner, that is a hand. A little girl's hand. What does she know of war? This woman burned. These men dead, not even soldiers. This is a woman, too. No, it is not rags, it was a woman."

He carefully repacked the photographs, and sat down again. "The Nigerian radio says Dick Tiger of Nigeria will defend his light heavyweight championship against Bob Foster in Madison Square Garden on May 24. Dick Tiger of Nigeria. They still claim me and they would kill me, they want to kill us all. I am a Biafran. And we just want to live."

I asked him about his family, which now included seven children. He said he had moved them back to Amaigbo while he tended his businesses in Aba. "I do not worry so much anymore. The children have learned to take cover quickly when they hear the planes. It is the fighter planes we worry about. The bombs fall slowly. If you see them you can run away. But you never see the bullets."

Foster knocked him cold in the fourth round of the fight. Tiger went straight down, his head smacked the canvas sickeningly. He twitched on his back like a turtle on its shell. He had to be helped up. In his dressing room he managed a smile at the crowd, which included various countrymen, boxing buffs, and Giardello. "Since I been winning I never had my fans stay in my dressing room so long. Now, I'm a loser and everybody's here. I guess I am a good man."

He left the United States without his light heavyweight title, but with enough currency to buy a planeload of tinned meat and powdered milk in Lisbon and fly it into Biafra.

In the summer of 1968 there were reports of 6000 Ibos a day dying of malnutrition and disease and wounds. Occasionally we would hear that Tiger was dead, too. And sometimes we would hear that he was hiding out in Brooklyn.

He reappeared in September to fight an upcoming young light heavyweight, Frankie DePaula.

I visited him in training. I was completing my first year as a columnist, and I had tried to stay away from boxing, to break the identification and establish my credentials in other sports. But Tiger had become a touchstone for me; I think I derived some symbolic nourishment from watching him tape his own hands. The honest, independent workman, a man of dignity and courage.

"If I had been a flashy fellow," he told me, "with fancy clothes and many women and big cars and nightclubs every night, I would have trouble. But I have never been a flashy fellow; I eat what is there to eat, I just dress, you know . . ."

"And still you have nothing now."

"This is true. I saved all my money and brought it home. I had apartment buildings in Lagos and Port Harcourt and Aba, and a movie and factories and shops and now, with the shelling, I guess it is all gone. Everything I have saved. But I am not sorry. If I had been a flashy fellow when I had lots of money, what would I do with myself now?"

He was training in the evening because he could no longer afford professional sparring partners; he sparred against dockers coming off work. He spent his days at the Biafra Mission, reading cables and dispatches. He disputed reports in American newspapers that the Nigerians were in complete control of almost all the cities.

"In every city they are still fighting," he said. "The Biafran fights to the end; the Nigerian will kill him anyway. The plan is to kill every Biafran over two years old. Then all the children will pray to the sun and moon instead of God, and never know who their fathers were. That is why we fight to survive."

We walked out of the dressing room to the training ring. In the hallway, a schoolboy caught his own reflection in the mirror of a vending machine, and jabbed at it.

Tiger smiled. "When I was young, if I ever saw my shadow I had to fight it, I always boxed at mirrors. No more. I am just one old man."

He was thirty-nine, and he looked even older in his fight with DePaula. Tiger won, but in the late rounds he seemed to be melting like a candle.

He took his money and disappeared again.

I didn't see him for more than a year: my second year as a columnist, and probably the most interesting. The Mexico City Olympics. The Jets Super Bowl. The Aqueduct Boycott. The Mets World Series. The start of the Knicks' first championship season.

The rehabilitation of Muhammad Ali began: liberals discovered that his antiwar stand was compatible with theirs, even if his racial views were not, and sprang to defend his constitutional rights. Together they would prove that the American legal system worked perfectly for anyone with the money and the power to go all the way.

I began to wish I had more time to think and read and talk to people, to stop writing so much and with such assurance. Columnists have to write with assurance because they are paid to raise The Truth. As that second year slipped into a third year, as the column became progressively easier to write, as my work brought me greater access to people I wanted to talk with, I found I was less and less sure of what I knew absolutely. Was I growing wiser, losing my nerve, taking myself too seriously, getting bored? Was I over the hill, choking in the clutch, hearing footsteps, getting fat?

In November of 1969, Tiger sluggishly won a dreary decision over a light heavyweight no one had heard of before, or would hear of again. A victory that had meaning only when translated into milk and salt and meat. On December 5 we sat down at a table in a publicity office of the Garden to discuss a matter that had suddenly become very urgent to Tiger. The medal he had received in Lagos in 1963 had grown too heavy in his mind to keep. When he read that John Lennon had returned his M.B.E. award for reasons that included Britain's involvement in the Nigerian civil war, Tiger decided to mail back his medal, too. But he needed help with the accompanying letter. Garden officials had not wanted to become involved in his protest, and had called Dave Anderson, then covering boxing for the New York *Times*. Dave called me. I had misgivings. I had always been contemptuous of sportswriters who acted as go-betweens for professional clubs and city governments, for high school athletes and college recruiters, for out-of-work coaches and potential employers. They were no longer honest journalists, I thought, they could no longer be trusted by their readers. They were supposed to cover stories, not make them happen.

But I had known and written about Tiger for more than six years; he had always been cooperative and friendly. I would be his amanuensis, no more: not a single idea or even word of mine would slip into the letter; it would make a good column for my readers, my kind of column, a famous athlete taking a principled stand on a headline issue that transcended sports. I didn't think, This is a very important cause, life, freedom, justice. I should be involved and make a worthwhile contribution as a human being. In those days I thought being an honest journalist was enough.

We wrote the letter and addressed it to the British Ambassador, Washington, D.C.

> "I am hereby returning the M.B.E. because every time I look at it I think of millions of men, women and children who died and are still dying in Biafra because of the arms and ammunition the British Government is sending to Nigeria and its continued moral support of this genocidal war against the people of Biafra."

He signed it "Dick Tiger Ihetu."

We walked across Eighth Avenue in the brilliant, chilly afternoon, and up the post office steps. Tiger said, "If they ask me how much it's worth, what should I say?"

I shrugged. "We should try to pawn it and find out."

"I'll say a million dollars." Tiger laughed for the first time. "I'll say fifty or a hundred, just so it gets there."

The clerk behind the registry wicket hefted the package and shook his head. "No good, you got Scotch tape on it. Go around the corner, they'll give you some brown paper."

Another line. He stood very quietly, a small black hat perched on his head, his body muffled in a fur-lined coat. I would always remember him for being overdressed and patient. He was always cold, and he was always willing to wait, for a bout, for a return bout, for a shot at a title. He was forty then, picking up fights wherever he could, waiting for one more big payday. If there had been no war, he would be retired in Aba, a rich man. He had been financially wiped out, but he said he could not complain, many others had lost all their property, and many, many others had lost their families and their lives.

A clerk finally handed him a long strip of gummed brown paper and a wet sponge in a glass dish. Tiger took it to a writing desk and began to tear the brown paper into small strips, his thick fingers careful and precise, the fingers of a man who taped his own hands.

When he finished the package he proudly held it up for me. "Now I know there is something else I can do."

We waited for the registry clerk silently. "Okay," he said, nodding at the package, then flipping it. "What's in it?"

"A medal," said Tiger softly.

"What's it worth?"

"I don't know. Fifty, hundred dollars?"

"No value," said the clerk, to himself. He weighed it, registered it, asked Tiger if he wanted it to go airmail. Tiger said, "Yes."

"One sixty."

Tiger gave him two dollar bills, and counted his change. He adjusted his scarf as he walked out into the bright street, and smiled, and shook my hand gravely and could only say, "Well . . . ," and shrug, and start down the steps. I never saw him again.

In the summer of 1971, after working briefly as a guard in the Metropolitan Museum of Art, Dick Tiger returned to his native land. He was penniless, and brought nothing home except the cancer in his liver. He died that December, in Aba, at the age of forty-two.

Mark Kram

Mark Kram (1933–2002) so feared flying that he nearly scared his editors at *Sports Illustrated* into sending someone else to cover the 1975 "Thrilla in Manila" showdown between Muhammad Ali and Joe Frazier. He found the courage to board the plane crossing the Pacific by gulping down all the tranquilizers he could lay hands on. Even then, Ali, ever the prankster, raised the hair on the back of Kram's neck by shaking his seat and warning him in a sepulchral voice that they were doomed to crash.

The image of a terrified Kram hardly squares with the muscular, evocative prose that defined his magazine work. His special touch could be found on stories about everything from baseball to ballet dancers, but it was boxing that moved him most profoundly. It inspired his tales of one-eyed fighters, wayward champions, and Depression-era hobos who bred their sons for the ring. Most of all, boxing gave him the third and final battle between Ali and Frazier. In the brutality that consumed them, Kram found not just courage but nobility, humanity, even compassion. And from that raw material, he wove the fight story of all fight stories.

"Lawdy, Lawdy, He's Great"

IT was only a moment, sliding past the eyes like the sudden shifting of light and shadow, but long years from now it will remain a pure and moving glimpse of hard reality, and if Muhammad Ali could have turned his eyes upon himself, what first and final truth would he have seen? He had been led up the winding, red-carpeted staircase by Imelda Marcos, the First Lady of the Philippines, as the guest of honor at the Malacañang Palace. Soft music drifted in from the terrace as the beautiful Imelda guided the massive and still heavyweight champion of the world to the long buffet ornamented by huge candelabra. The two whispered, and then she stopped and filled his plate, and as he waited the candles threw an eerie light across the face of a man who only a few hours before had survived the ultimate inquisition of himself and his art.

The maddest of existentialists, one of the great surrealists of our time, the king of all he sees, Ali had never before appeared so vulnerable and fragile, so pitiably unmajestic, so far from the universe he claims as his alone. He could barely hold his fork, and he lifted the food slowly up to his bottom lip, which had been scraped pink. The skin on his face was dull and blotched, his eyes drained of that familiar childlike wonder. His right eye was a deep purple, beginning to close, a dark blind being drawn against a harsh light. He chewed his food painfully, and then he suddenly moved away from the candles as if he had become aware of the mask he was wearing, as if an inner voice were laughing at him. He shrugged, and the moment was gone.

A couple of miles away, in the bedroom of a villa, the man who has always demanded answers of Ali, has trailed the champion like a timber wolf, lay in semi-darkness. Only his heavy breathing disturbed the quiet as an old friend walked to within two feet of him. "Who is it?" asked Joe Frazier, lifting himself to look around. "Who is it? I can't see! I can't see! Turn the lights on!" Another light was turned on, but Frazier still could not see. The scene cannot be forgotten; this good and gallant man lying there, embodying the remains of a will never before seen in a ring, a will that had carried him so far —and now surely too far. His eyes were only slits, his face looked as if it had been painted by Goya. "Man, I hit him with punches that'd bring down the walls of a city," said Frazier. "Lawdy, Lawdy, he's a great champion." Then he put his head back down on the pillow, and soon there was only the heavy breathing of a deep sleep slapping like big waves against the silence.

Time may well erode that long morning of drama in Manila, but for anyone who was there those faces will return again and again to evoke what it was like when two of the greatest heavyweights of any era met for a third time, and left millions limp around the world. Muhammad Ali caught the way it was: "It was like death. Closest thing to dyin' that I know of."

Ali's version of death began about 10:45 A.M. on Oct. 1 in Manila. Up to then his attitude had been almost frivolous. He would simply not accept Joe Frazier as a man or as a fighter, despite the bitter lesson Frazier had given him in their first savage meeting. Esthetics govern all of Ali's actions and conclusions; the way a man looks, the way he moves is what interests Ali. By Ali's standards, Frazier was not pretty as a man and without semblance of style as a fighter. Frazier was an affront to beauty, to Ali's own beauty as well as to his precious concept of how a good fighter should move. Ali did not hate Frazier, but he viewed him with the contempt of a man who cannot bear anything short of physical and professional perfection.

Right up until the bell rang for Round One, Ali was dead certain that Frazier was through, was convinced that he was no more than a shell, that too many punches to the head had left Frazier only one more solid shot removed from a tin cup and some pencils. "What kind of man can take all those punches to the head?" he asked himself over and over. He could never come up with an answer. Eventually he dismissed Frazier as the embodiment of animal stupidity. Before the bell Ali was subdued in his corner, often looking down to his manager, Herbert Muhammad, and conversing aimlessly. Once, seeing a bottle of mineral water in front of Herbert, he said, "Watcha got there, Herbert? Gin! You don't need any of that. Just another day's work. I'm gonna put a whuppin' on this nigger's head."

Across the ring Joe Frazier was wearing trunks that seemed to have been cut from a farmer's overalls. He was darkly tense, bobbing up and down as if trying to start a cold motor inside himself. Hatred had never been a part of him, but words like "gorilla," "ugly," "ignorant"—all the cruelty of Ali's endless vilifications—had finally bitten deeply into his soul. He was there not seeking victory alone; he wanted to take Ali's heart out and then crush it slowly in his hands. One thought of the moment days before, when Ali and Frazier with their handlers between them were walking out of the Malacañang Palace, and Frazier said to Ali, leaning over and measuring each word, "I'm gonna whup your half-breed ass."

By packed and malodorous Jeepneys, by small and tinny taxis, by limousine and by worn-out bikes, 28,000 had made their way into the Philippine Coliseum. The morning sun beat down, and the South China Sea brought not a whisper of wind. The streets of the city emptied as the bout came on public television. At ringside, even though the arena was air-conditioned, the heat wrapped around the body like a heavy wet rope. By now, President Ferdinand Marcos, a small brown derringer of a man, and Imelda, beautiful and cool as if she were relaxed on a palace balcony taking tea, had been seated.

True to his plan, arrogant and contemptuous of an opponent's worth as never before, Ali opened the fight flat-footed in the center of the ring, his hands whipping out and back like the pistons of an enormous and magnificent engine. Much broader than he has ever been, the look of swift destruction defined by his every move, Ali seemed indestructible. Once, so long ago, he had been a splendidly plumed bird who wrote on the wind a singular kind of poetry of the body, but now he was down to earth, brought down by the changing shape of his body, by a sense of his own vulnerability, and by the years of excess. Dancing was for a ballroom; the ugly hunt was on. Head up and unprotected, Frazier stayed in the mouth of the cannon, and the big gun roared again and again.

Frazier's legs buckled two or three times in that first round, and in the second he took more lashing as Ali loaded on him all the meanness that he could find in himself. "He won't call you Clay no more," Bundini Brown, the spirit man, cried hoarsely from the corner. To Bundini, the fight would be a question of where fear first registered, but there was no fear in Frazier. In the third round Frazier was shaken twice, and looked as if he might go at any second as his head jerked up toward the hot lights and the sweat flew off his face. Ali hit Frazier at will, and when he chose to do otherwise he stuck his long left arm in Frazier's face. Ali would not be holding in this bout as he had in the second. The referee, a brisk workman, was not going to tolerate clinching. If he needed to buy time, Ali would have to use his long left to disturb Frazier's balance.

A hint of shift came in the fourth. Frazier seemed to be picking up the beat, his threshing-blade punches started to come into range as he snorted and rolled closer. "Stay mean with him, champ!" Ali's corner screamed. Ali still had his man in his sights, and whipped at his head furiously. But at the end of the round, sensing a change and annoyed, he glared at Frazier and said, "You dumb chump, you!" Ali fought the whole fifth round in his own corner. Frazier worked his body, the whack of his gloves on Ali's kidneys sounding like heavy thunder. "Get out of the goddamn corner," shouted Angelo Dundee, Ali's trainer. "Stop playin'," squawked Herbert Muhammad, wringing his hands and wiping the mineral water nervously from his mouth. Did they know what was ahead?

Came the sixth, and here it was, that one special moment that you always look for when Joe Frazier is in a fight. Most of his fights have shown this: you can go so far into that desolate and dark place where the heart of Frazier pounds, you can waste his perimeters, you can see his head hanging in the public square, may even believe that you have him, but then suddenly you learn that you have not. Once more the pattern emerged as Frazier loosed all of the fury, all that has made him a brilliant heavyweight. He was in close now, fighting off Ali's chest, the place where he has to be. His old calling card—that sudden evil, his left hook—was working the head of Ali. Two hooks ripped with slaughterhouse finality at Ali's jaw, causing Imelda Marcos to look down at her feet, and the President to wince as if a knife had been stuck in his back. Ali's legs seemed to search for the floor. He was in serious trouble, and he knew that he was in no-man's-land.

Whatever else might one day be said about Muhammad Ali, it should never be said that he is without courage, that he cannot take a punch. He took those shots by Frazier, and then came out for the seventh, saying to him, "Old Joe Frazier, why I thought you were washed up." Joe replied, "Somebody told you all wrong, pretty boy."

Frazier's assault continued. By the end of the tenth round it was an even fight. Ali sat on his stool like a man ready to be staked out in the sun. His head was bowed, and when he raised it his eyes rolled from the agony of exhaustion. "Force yourself, champ!" his corner cried. "Go down to the well once more!" begged Bundini, tears streaming down his face. "The world needs ya, champ!" In the eleventh, Ali got trapped in Frazier's corner, and blow after blow bit at his melting face, and flecks of spittle flew from his mouth. "Lawd have mercy!" Bundini shrieked.

The world held its breath. But then Ali dug deep down into whatever it is that he is about, and even his severest critics would have to admit that the man-boy had become finally a man. He began to catch Frazier with long right hands, and blood trickled from Frazier's mouth. Now, Frazier's face began to lose definition; like lost islands reemerging from the sea, massive bumps rose suddenly around each eye, especially the left. His punches seemed to be losing their strength. "My God," wailed Angelo Dundee. "Look at 'im. He ain't got no power, champ!" Ali threw the last ounces of resolve left in his body in the thirteenth and fourteenth. He sent Frazier's bloody mouthpiece flying into the press row in the thirteenth, and nearly floored him with a right in the center of the ring. Frazier was now no longer coiled. He was up high, his hands down, and as the bell for the fourteenth round sounded, Dundee pushed Ali out saying, "He's all yours!" And he was, as Ali raked him with nine straight right hands. Frazier was not picking up the punches, and as he returned to his corner at the round's end the Filipino referee guided his great hulk part of the way.

"Joe," said his manager, Eddie Futch, "I'm going to stop it."

"No, no, Eddie, ya can't do that to me," Frazier pleaded, his thick tongue barely getting the words out. He started to rise.

"You couldn't see in the last two rounds," said Futch. "What makes ya think ya gonna see in the fifteenth?"

"I want him, boss," said Frazier.

"Sit down, son," said Futch, pressing his hand on Frazier's shoulder. "It's all over. No one will ever forget what you did here today."

And so it will be, for once more had Frazier taken the child of the gods to hell and back. After the fight Futch said: "Ali fought a smart fight. He conserved his energy, turning it off when he had to. He can afford to do it because of his style. It was mainly a question of anatomy, that is all that separates these two men. Ali is now too big, and when you add those long arms, well . . . Joe has to use constant pressure, and that takes its toll on a man's body and soul." Dundee said: "My guy sucked it up and called on everything he had. We'll never see another one like him." Ali took a long time before coming down to be interviewed by the press, and then he could only say, "I'm tired of bein' the whole game. Let other guys do the fightin'. You might never see Ali in the ring again."

In his suite the next morning he talked quietly. "I heard somethin' once," he said. "When somebody asked a marathon runner what goes through his mind in the last mile or two, he said that you ask yourself why am I doin' this. You get so tired. It takes so much out of you mentally. It changes you. It makes you go a little insane. I was thinkin' that at the end. Why am I doin' this? What am I doin' here in against this beast of a man? It's so painful. I must be crazy. I always bring out the best in the men I fight, but Joe Frazier, I'll tell the world right now, brings out the best in me. I'm gonna tell ya, that's one helluva man, and God bless him."

John Schulian

John Schulian (b. 1945) launched his sportswriting career with a freelance story for *Sports Illustrated* about a Baltimore fight promoter with a gym above a strip joint. A year later, in 1975, *The Washington Post* hired him to cover pro football, and two years after that, he was at the *Chicago Daily News*, hailed as one of the country's leading sports columnists. When the *News* folded in 1978, Schulian took his column to the city's *Sun-Times* and set out on an improbable career path. He turned down an offer from *The New York Times* to succeed Red Smith; published a well-regarded collection of his boxing writing, *Writers' Fighters and Other Sweet Scientists* (1983); and left the *Sun-Times* after a dust-up with an editor imported by new owner Rupert Murdoch. In 1986, Schulian startled friends and colleagues by jumping from the *Philadelphia Daily News* to Hollywood. He broke into television with a script for *L. A. Law* and worked on *Miami Vice*, *Wiseguy*, and *Midnight Caller* before co-creating *Xena: Warrior Princess*. Through it all, he wrote regularly for *GQ* and *SI* and maintained his affection for boxing. In his debut script for *Miami Vice*, Schulian made Randall "Tex" Cobb, the roguish former heavyweight contender, the first of many characters he has killed in the name of drama. "Nowhere to Run" was Schulian's *Sun-Times* column for April 1, 1979.

Nowhere to Run

IT was a glorious place, the Del Prado Hotel was. If you listen closely, you can still hear the echoes of the young lovers and swaggering big leaguers who used to make its lobby so fresh, so vibrant. But to open your eyes in there is to see the other side of midnight. The furniture is cheap and frayed, and the old folks arrayed on it live with a fear dramatized by a sign taped to the front desk: SORRY, NO MONEY ON PREMISES—PLEASE PAY RENT BY CHECK OR MONEY ORDER. Yes, that is what has become of Hyde Park's leading hostelry, and the change is a hurting thing for everybody except the lost soul dozing in the corner, the one the fight crowd used to call Honey Boy.

He lives in a world that skirts reality, a world filled with panhandling buddies and visions of old movies, a world where no one can hurt him. Late at night, when he is alone in the lobby, alone with his jumbled thoughts, he will rise from the couch where he sleeps and slowly walk toward the full-length mirror. He will raise his fists and bend at the knees and, suddenly, he will be Johnny Bratton, welterweight champion, once again. Never mind that his hair is more gray than black or that he is an easy fifty pounds over his fighting prime. You can't take the past away from him.

He bobs and weaves, jabs, recalculates the old combinations—all in slow motion. How sad and yet how perfect for the setting. It is as if you aren't allowed in the front door of the woebegone Del Prado unless you, too, represent faded elegance.

Johnny Bratton showed up one evening last winter, in the middle of his one-way trip to nowhere. A chill ran through the lobby, for its elderly white denizens did not know how to deal with a black drifter who was caked with street grime and whose long silences were punctuated by bursts of unexpected laughter. There was no predicting that he would soon be running errands for new friends, receiving invitations to breakfast, or whistling at Patricia Bock, the hotel's salty manager, and getting away with it. Indeed, Patricia Bock had to be grabbed by the arm and shaken before she would stop looking down her nose at this uninvited guest.

"Don't you know who that is?" asked the man who runs the variety shop.

"No," she said.

"That's Johnny Bratton."

"So?"

"Do you remember Joe Louis?"

"Oh, he was my idol."

"Well, that man there was as famous as Joe Louis."

The point would have been exaggerated anywhere other than the South Side. But on the turf where Johnny Bratton discovered that he could be somebody, however briefly, it was the stone truth. So he found a roof to cover his head during the blizzard of '79 and, no matter how ragged he was, the Del Prado boasted its first celebrity since American League teams declared the neighborhood unsafe for their precious athletes. "The hotel doesn't look like the Astor anymore," Patricia Bock says now, "so why should anyone care?"

Johnny Bratton wasn't supposed to have to rely on charity, though. In the late forties and the early fifties, when he was fighting in Chicago Stadium and on TV, when it was all you could do to escape reading about him getting ready for a fight or winding down from one, he thought he had gone over the wall from hard times. He was a taxi driver's son, a Du Sable High School dropout, but he wore zoot suits and gold cuff links and cruised the city in a Cadillac bearing the name "Honey Boy" and a Jaguar bearing the name "Johnny B." And the marvel of it was, the soft life didn't make him a pushover in the ring.

"I could do it all," he says, "but I had to do it under my conditions. You understand? My conditions."

He had a style that would have become a man trying to sneak into the house past his sleeping wife. It was capable of turning crowds venomous even when he was beating Charlie Fusari for the old National Boxing Association's welterweight title in 1951. Still, there was something about Johnny Bratton that endured longer than the memory of his caution. Perhaps it can best be described as courage.

He came to the fore when boxing moved at a relentless pace. A victory meant the loser got another fight, and if the loser won that one, there had to be a rubber match. Just look at Johnny Bratton's record. He fought the brutal Ike Williams three times. He battled Holly Mims twice within twenty-one days, with a lesser bout sandwiched in between. And nobody who witnessed his last chance to regain the championship, when Kid Gavilan carved him up for fifteen rounds, ever will forget his absolute refusal to retreat or surrender. Afterwards, he lay on his dressing room table unable to speak.

The problems Johnny Bratton had always were supposed to be physical—an impacted tooth that led to a fractured jaw or tiny hands that crumbled like potato chips. But what got him in the end was his mind.

He was not punchy.

He was mad.

"It started getting worse after my last fight," he says. "I got beat by Del Flanagan. The referee patted me on my back and told me I was through. I was twenty-six or twenty-seven. A couple years later, I went to the state hospital at Manteno. I had a private room. Do you think they were giving private rooms to psychopaths in 1954? I wasn't no psychopath. I even had my picture in the paper. Do you remember that? They had a picture of me looking out the window. I was in my room."

There were other rooms in other hospitals and, finally, Johnny Bratton was allowed to step back onto the streets seventeen years ago. He has walked them ever since, refusing to settle at a halfway house or with an older brother. There is always a letter from Hitler or a covered wagon surrounded by Indians to distract him, to let him know he must keep moving. "You don't understand, do you?" he says, and looks for a bus that will carry him to safety. If he is lucky, it will pass a movie theater and he can hop off and take refuge there. Movies give him something to cling to, something he can't seem to find anywhere else.

"The fella next to you kinda looks like Paul Muni, don't he?" Johnny Bratton says. "I seen Paul Muni in a lot of pictures. Him and Errol Flynn. I don't think Errol Flynn ever made a bad picture. But he got in trouble, right? Him and all his women. Me, what I think you got to do is live a good reputation, like James Cagney. Yessir, the Yankee Doodle Dandy hisself."

On Rush Street, that mecca of clip joints and cut-rate love, they say they have never seen anyone who knew as much about movies as Johnny Bratton. Sooner or later, he makes it up there every day to win his daily bread—and drink—with his vast knowledge. And if that fails, there is always out-and-out panhandling. "He can put the arm on you pretty good," says one old fight guy. "I figure it's good for a sawbuck if he sees me." To be sure, Johnny Bratton is always looking, always moving. He pauses only to gaze at his reflection in the windows of a disco.

What he sees is a slightly stooped figure cloaked in a dirty overcoat; rising up out of the coat's collar is a face on which scar tissue and a goatee fight for prominence. What he sees is what the conventioneers and the swinging singles don't always want to see. The pattern is never altered: a handout here, a turndown there, and don't scare any well-dressed women. He can get by that way, Johnny Bratton can. He won't get rich, but another day will be done and he will have bus fare back to Hyde Park, back to the Del Prado.

The septuagenarians who live there worry about him on those nights when he doesn't show up, and he seems to sense it, even enjoy it. But just as he is getting comfortable, perhaps for the first time in a long time, some hotshot outfit is pumping $4.5 million into the Del Prado to gussy it up again. When the old furniture goes, Johnny Bratton will have to go, too. You can say time is running out on him if you like, but of course that really started long, long ago.

Vic Ziegel

Amid New York's carnivorous tabloids and yammering sports talk shows, Vic Ziegel (1931–2010) was a beacon of sanity, that rare sports columnist who never forgot that the by-product of games is supposed to be fun. He could listen to a certain loquacious boxing promoter and find the inspiration for the acronym to end all acronyms: DKTUHTWNBFCRMB (Don King Telling Us How Tyson Will Next Be Fighting in the Coliseum in Rome, My Brother). Even more impressive, Ziegel could find the humor in his own battles with deadlines: "If you miss once, nothing happens. If you miss too many times, they make you sports editor." And they did, at the *New York Daily News*, in 1985. He spent five years on the job before he returned to writing a column and making readers laugh. It was an art he had perfected while covering baseball and boxing for the *New York Post*, and throughout his fifty-year career, he practiced it at greater length in magazines like *New York*, *Rolling Stone*, *Esquire*, and *Sport*. As the following 1980 *Inside Sports* story proves, even Roberto Duran's maximum-security stare was no match for Ziegel's wit.

Roberto Duran's New York State of Mind

RALPH and Steve, chinchillas, live in window cages in New York's fur district, just down the street from Gleason's Gym. Steve is wrapped around a stick, training for the day he'll occupy the same position on mademoiselle's shoulder. Ralph is asleep, unaware of the excitement a few doors away.

Standing in front of Gleason's a quartet of three-piece suits, talking about a jump in the Dow, is crowding a kid whose T-shirt sleeves are rolled to display a snake-and-knife tattoo. The front of the line is about 20 people away, all waiting for a glimpse of Roberto Duran, the fighter with the burning eyes, the former lightweight champion challenging Sugar Ray Leonard's welterweight title.

Don Turner, a local trainer, is standing inside the front door at Gleason's, helping out today because of the size of the crowd and because he can extend an open palm and say, "One dollar." Something about the tone of his voice, and the size of his palm, has produced the admission price every time. So far.

"One dollar."

"Why I got to pay?" The visitor is staring at Turner's shoulder.

"Everybody pay today. Duran sparring."

"I just want to use the phone."

"Okay." Turner points to the wall. "Phone's over there. Just gimme a dollar."

Turner passes the bill to Sammy Morgan, a heavyset man sitting behind a high counter. Sammy doesn't like to say how many dollar bills he's holding. Maybe 100, maybe 125. He will say how many paid on the same day a week earlier, when Duran wasn't there. "We got three," Sammy says.

Duran spars in the ring at the far end of the gym, almost directly under a narrow balcony. Most of his audience is pressed against the railing. Others stand on the stairs leading to the balcony. There's a crush inside the empty ring near the door, some perched on the ropes for a better view. "Off the ropes," is another thing Turner says. He has more success with "one dollar."

Latecomers fill the aisle between the rings and the wall. When Duran finishes sparring he jumps rope. His fans push back to give him room, but every few seconds the jump rope slaps against somebody's shirt and drops. Duran glares. "Fa chrissake," yells co-trainer Ray Arcel, "get away from him." Impossible. Packed so tight, the spectators can barely move. Duran folds the rope. The workout is over.

"He likes New York, he likes to train here," says co-trainer Freddy Brown, "but how can he?" Arcel, 81, and Brown, 71, are the wise old heads who have honed Duran's skills for the past eight years. Arcel, when he's not screaming, sounds like the chairman of a college English department. Brown is a white-haired man with a nose that resembles a low flush in clubs. His sentence structure is equally dazzling.

"These people don't let him train," Brown says. "They bother him too much. They don't let him work. Not that they don't want to let him work. But they want him. They're right on top of him. They want to hug him, they want to pat him on the back, they want to shake his hand, they want autographs, they want pictures, they want this, they want that. It interferes. He likes it but it stops him from working. He gets into mischief. That's why we cut his workouts in New York."

Soon, they'll be hiking to Grossinger's, the Catskill Mountains resort that's two hours from the city. Grossinger's and Gleason's: The only thing they have in common are the chinchillas. "Sure, the mountains are better than here," Brown insists. "Anything's better than here. But the best place was in Panama. Where the army trained. There was nobody there. Nobody. I had to sleep in a bunk. Duran too. Everybody, the sparring partners, we slept in bunks. The food wasn't too good, but ya ate it like the army eats it. They don't give ya nothing good, the army. Duran don't care. If it's good steak or bad steak, he'll eat it. Food, to him, is nothing. He don't ask for this, he don't ask for that. The reason his weight goes up now and then is that he cheats. At night, he'll go someplace, grab a soda, this and that, and come back the next day and he's heavier. We have it out. So the next day he won't do it. And the following day he won't do it. Then he cheats again. In Panama, with the army guys, he got on line in the morning and ate eggs, whatever the army got. Nobody bothered him. He got plenty of work, plenty of rest."

It's just before the move to Grossinger's, and it isn't the best of times. For one thing, Duran doesn't have any clean socks.

"The socks are in my car," Luis Henriquez says. Henriquez, an honorary vice-consul of Panama based in New York, represents Carlos Eleta, Duran's millionaire manager. He makes calls from a desk in promoter Don King's office. ("My connection to the third world nations," King says of Henriquez. Exactly how another boxing promoter, now among the missing, once described King.) Very soon, Henriquez says, he's planning to become an independent, representing fight managers, finding the best deals. I first met Henriquez when Duran won the lightweight title from Ken Buchanan in 1972. He had a question then: "Tell me something about your country. How is it possible that you can kill a man here, plead temporary insanity and they let you off? But write one bad check, goddamn, and they send you to jail."

Henriquez is driving his brown and tan Rolls-Royce to Duran's hotel. His conversation is still concerned with money; his, Duran's. "He owns an apartment building in a middle-class neighborhood in Panama City. With the money from this fight he wants to buy a building in a better neighborhood. Money's what this game is all about. Too many guys had it and lost it. *Stupid*. This fight is important because it can put him, financially, where he ought to be. Right now, he don't have as much as he should. He's good-natured. He gives too much away. He sees what I got, this car, my clothes, and it used to make him angry. Carlos Eleta finally told him, 'Never mind what Luis does with his money, he's working for you.' He believes that now. We're buddy-buddy. Those socks I got in my trunk, they called me up and said he needed them. Okay, no trouble, I'm bringing them."

He glances at his watch. He's late. "We're going to go through a few red lights. Don't worry . . . I got a diplomatic license." I'm not worried. Somehow, I've always known that my last ride would not be the delivery of a half dozen pair of athletic socks to Roberto Duran.

Duran is sharing a suite at the Mayflower with his 18-year-old brother, Armando, and an uncle, Socrates Garcia. Duran has the bedroom and the two others use the sofa bed in the sitting room. When Henriquez arrives, the three family members are sitting up in Duran's bed, watching a Spanish-language channel. Domino tiles are scattered on an end table. A pair of athletic socks is draped across a lampshade, drying. Henriquez presents his gifts, removing them from the bag with a magician's flourish. The fighter isn't amused. Henriquez introduces me. The look on Duran's face says he is happier to see the socks.

Almost nine years ago, when Duran made his first appearance in New York, I covered his fight against a journeyman named Benny Huertas. Duran blazed out of his corner and finished Huertas in about a minute. He was awesome. But I couldn't help noticing that he neglected to shower after the fight. "Duran hardly worked up a sweat," I wrote, "and a good thing too, because he didn't bother to shower." Duran, I found out later, hated the line. "I reminded him," Henriquez is saying now, "that you were the guy who put in the paper he don't shower. He remembers you."

And I remember a Duran who destroyed opponents with animal ferocity, the quicker the better. Seventy-one fights, 55 knockouts, 24 in two rounds or less. His one loss, to Esteban DeJesus eight years ago, was avenged twice in title bouts, another pair of knockouts. He made a dozen defenses of his lightweight title. Eleven knockouts. One of them sent Ray Lampkin to a Panamanian hospital. "If I trained," Duran said, "I would kill him." One sweet man.

Suddenly, when he took on the 147-pound division in 1978, the knockouts were harder to come by. Duran seems to have lost that ability to overwhelm an opponent. He fought three times last year, winning each bout only after the scorecards were tallied. His followers point to his last two fights, knockout victories, to make the argument that Duran is still a hard guy. But he was fighting passport pictures—Josef Nsubuga, from Uganda, and Wellington Wheatley, the Ecuadorian.

Does it bother him that he isn't putting away the best people? "No," Duran says. "Why should it? Let them think what they want. What can I do if the other man runs?" The truth is, lightweights run even better than heavier fellows. Running was never a wonderful strategy against Duran.

"He hasn't been as awesome as a welterweight because these fellas he's fighting now take a better punch than lightweights," Freddy Brown concedes. "He's going up to bigger men. It's like a light-heavyweight, say Bob Foster, when he fought Frazier and them other guys. His punches didn't mean nothing. With the light-heavies he was a killer. But when he went into the heavyweights they took his punches like he was nothing. And *he* got knocked out."

That can't happen here, the trainer says. "Moving up hasn't cost Duran his punching power. When he hits ya, he hurts ya. I don't care who it is. Take Palomino. Who ever knocks him down? *He* knocks Palomino down. He's like a Marciano." Ah, Marciano. Brown worked with Rocky Marciano in all his title fights. "He'd go along and hit ya, and nothing would happen and all of a sudden he'd hit ya that good one and that was it. Duran's the same way. To me, Marciano was one of the best one-punch fighters we ever had. Duran's got that same thing."

Duran, who turns 29 the week he begins punching at Leonard, June 20 in Montreal, is beginning his 14th year as a professional, a long time to keep the pilot light operating behind those glowing eyes. When he began ballooning to 170 pounds between title defenses, the shift to the welterweight class was inevitable. As champion, he trained hard to lop off the weight; not so hard the last few years.

He explained his failure to score a knockout against Carlos Palomino by saying the weather in New York bothered him. But that fight was held in late June. So, was Duran saying the weather was unseasonably cold? It doesn't seem likely. And if he meant it was too hot, what's the point of growing up in sweltering Panama City? (Translation: He didn't train.)

Last September he went 10 rounds, and was cut, against a stranger named Zeferino Gonzalez. Duran says he was sick for three weeks before the fight and Brown wanted him to pull out and the only reason he fought was that he had already spent the three weeks in Las Vegas. Huh? (Translation: See above.)

"When he was on top as a lightweight, he didn't know who he was fighting," Arcel says. "He didn't know their names, didn't know anything about them. He didn't care. And it didn't matter. Our job is to get him where he was when he beat Buchanan. If he gets that way, mentally, *and* he's in shape . . ."

When Duran began his training in New York—"We're getting him in the cycle, we're moving him around, we're shaking his ass a little," Arcel says—he was at 159 pounds. Not bad for step one. Mentally? Well, the day he had the close call with the clean socks, he told Henriquez he had a cold and a slight fever. But he went to the gym and beat off the usual crowd. One of his sparring partners was Kevin Rooney, a young pro with four fights. For two rounds, Rooney stayed with Duran, trading, catching, coming back. At the end of two, Brown sent Rooney away and called for another sparring partner. Mentally, this was for Duran's benefit. Rooney, for his part, was asking for more. Later, when Rooney was punching the speed bag, he talked about Duran. "He's great," Rooney said. "And when he gets in shape . . ."

This was another of those afternoons that proved Duran couldn't train at Gleason's and jump rope at the same time.

With the fight still two months away, the Duran camp seems determined to show some early jitters. Arcel explodes when he discovers that three Yankees—Reggie Jackson, Luis Tiant, Ed Figueroa—will be visiting the gym for the urgent business of publicity photos. "I been in thousands of fight camps," Arcel fumes, loud enough to be heard at Pompton Lakes, "and I handled thousands of fighters. But I never heard of anything like this. Who cares if the ballplayers are supposed to be here? We don't need them. Screw the ballplayers."

Then it's Duran's turn. After he is told that today he is to buy a suit for the press conference later in the week, Duran remembers he has a cold; that his one-dollar admirers are getting on his nerves *and* his toes. Maybe it bothers him that young Kevin Rooney didn't understand he was in with *manos de piedra*, the hands of stone. Who knows? Could be, he doesn't like to buy suits. In any case, he isn't going shopping.

Two hours later, to prove how seriously all this should be taken, Duran is back in his hotel room, smiling, admiring a beige suit. ("We call it copper or light rust," the salesman says. Henriquez had persuaded the salesman to come to the hotel for this one-suit shopping spree. Along with a tailor. And four other suits for Duran's appraisal.) Duran decided on the beige silk number in approximately the same time he needed to dispatch Benny Huertas. "How much?" I asked. "Four seventy-five," the salesman answers. "A special price?" The salesman gives me a strange look.

The press conference decided the winner of the fight. We have Ray Arcel's word on that. After the interviews—Leonard talks mostly about money, Duran only about winning—the Panamanian and his trainer become separated. They meet again in the corridor. Arcel embraces his fighter, keeping his hands tight on Duran's shoulder, wrinkling the silk, and puts his hawk nose close to Duran's face. "You won the title right there," Arcel says firmly. "The other guy was full of crap. He's scared. As soon as he goes back to his room he's going to go in the bathroom."

Duran nods, laughing. He runs off a couple of sentences in Spanish and Henriquez, standing at his side, holds out both his palms. Much joyous slapping. "What he said," Henriquez says, struggling with his laughter, "he says, where he comes from, in the ghetto, they got a saying: those that blink, blow. Leonard, he was blinking."

The good mood continues through lunch. "We all invited," Henriquez says, explaining the pig's head, with stuffed olives for eyes, sitting at the center of Duran's table. A sign identifies the monstrosity as "Sugar Ray Lener." Mentally, Duran is having a splendid time. "Steak," he tells the waiter. "Well done, *bien, bien.*" Arcel whispers, "He loves steak. This is a kid who had to steal to live, who fought to eat. Now, he can't eat enough."

Does Duran remember his first steak? He smiles and tells the story to Henriquez, who plays it back. "He was an amateur and his manager took him to eat in a restaurant. First time in a real restaurant. The manager wanted a drink and Roberto, he told him to walk over and get it. It was a big restaurant, see, and the manager needed to take a long walk. He tricked the manager. Instead of eating one steak, he ordered two. By the time the manager got back to the table, the steaks were gone. They didn't last three minutes."

When this steak arrives, Freddy Brown intercepts Duran's plate and dumps the french fries. Duran takes the usual three minutes. The waiter is offering dessert. "No dessert," Brown says. Duran mimes a helpless shrug, points to the pig. The welterweight champion will pay for this prison diet.

Duran wants his translator to make sure I understand one thing: "This fight, this chance to win a second title, is the greatest thing to happen to me. I was dying to fight Leonard. Or Benitez. Or Cuevas. Any welterweight champ. I can't believe I'm getting this chance so quick. I'm so happy. . . . I just can't express that happiness in words. Maybe if you ask me . . ."

But there is nothing left to ask. Nothing he hadn't covered in that last intense speech. Instead, he's offered dessert. Mentally. "Tell me about the one knockout that's not on your record. The horse."

Duran smiles. "There was a fair in his neighborhood," Henriquez translates, "and he was in love with a fine girl but he didn't have any money. They promised him that if he knocked the horse down they would give him two bottles of whiskey and $10."

"Did he knock the horse down with one punch?"

"*Si.* One punch."

"How old was he?"

"Fifteen years old."

"How old was the horse?"

"He say, ask the horse."

Leonard Gardner

Leonard Gardner's *Fat City* (1969) stands tall among the greatest boxing novels, a blue-collar masterpiece that captures the dreams and desperation on the bottom rung of the California fight circuit. Gardner (b. 1933) never wrote another novel, but *Fat City*'s impact is still being felt long after its publication in 1969. It is a touchstone for novelists like Denis Johnson, was taught in writing classes at Yale, and paved the way for Gardner to become a writer-producer on the Emmy-winning television series *NYPD Blue*. Gardner's introduction to show business came when the legendary director John Huston adapted *Fat City* for the big screen in 1972, starring Stacy Keach and a young Jeff Bridges. The movie proved as memorable in its way as the book, largely because Huston left the screenplay in the author's hands. Afterward, Gardner returned to writing fiction, in short form, while making occasional forays into journalism. He wrote boxing pieces for *Esquire* and *Sport*, but his most lasting work is this *Inside Sports* dissection of the first Roberto Duran–Sugar Ray Leonard fight in 1980.

Sweeter than Sugar

As a child I had no doubt that Joe Louis was a greater man than Franklin D. Roosevelt, and in the tales I heard of great heroes, Corbett, Jeffries, Gans, Ketchel and Dempsey ranked right along with Perseus and Daniel Boone. I put myself to sleep reciting the order of champions, and to the end of my father's life the subject of boxing kept the two of us from ever reaching that lonely gulf where child and parent no longer have anything of passionate interest to say to one another. My father's last words to me, in fact, an hour or two before his death, were, "Do you think Big Train Liston can win the title again?"—a confusion of two heavyweights, Amos Lincoln and Sonny Liston, that was as definite an indication of his failing powers as any medical test could have provided. In his mid-seventies he had a speed bag in the attic he could still punch into a rhythmic blur, and in his early eighties he had his last fight, on State Street in Santa Barbara, with a panhandler who put his hand in my father's pocket. "I gave him the Fitzsimmons shift," my father said. His hands were badly bruised.

The shift was the arcane maneuver with which Bob Fitzsimmons had conquered Jim Corbett in 1897 and won the heavyweight championship, and which had apparently become lost to the body of modern boxing technique. In my childhood we practiced it with the gloves on in the backyard, and my father, no longer a young man, executed it with confusing speed. He would feint at my head with his left, feint with his right, shoot his right foot in front of his left foot and let go a left hook he would pull up short at my solar plexus, re-enacting a turning point in history.

The idea was to put the same weight of the body behind the left as you got behind the right, through a sudden shift to southpaw. Sometimes the punch wasn't pulled quite short enough, and I got a sense of how Corbett was undone by the gangly, bald-headed Fitz, who my father swore weighed only 157 pounds. It was a peculiar series of moves, that shift, and a little alarming when the whole works came swirling at you. But nobody I saw at that time used it, and I don't recall having seen a version of it until Roberto Duran came on the scene and tore through a decade of lightweights.

I first saw Duran in 1972, on television, when he won the lightweight title from Ken Buchanan with an electrifying attack. It was unfortunate that the bout ended after the 13th round, with Buchanan on the floor from a low blow. Buchanan was ruled unable to continue, and so Duran became champion.

It was a sour ending to the bout, but Buchanan had been overwhelmed from the opening bell and there was no doubt of Duran's superiority. He had fought as if possessed. Over the years Duran acquired finesse, but without losing any of that unrelenting aggressiveness that gave his fights such excitement. In his final defense of his lightweight title he showed fine ring skills, knocking out Esteban DeJesus in 12 rounds. Duran then retired as undisputed lightweight champion, in an era so overpopulated with WBA and WBC champions that the concept of a true world champion is eroding.

Duran had epitomized the old-fashioned hungry fighter, but with wealth he ate too well and his appetite cost him his title. He had to move up to the welterweights, and now he was getting a shot at a media hero and new champion, Sugar Ray Leonard. Leonard was a 9-to-5 favorite. The consensus, when the bout was announced, was that a lightweight's frame couldn't stay in there with a welterweight's frame, especially if the welterweight had the fastest hands in the business and could punch.

Before leaving for Montreal I called a friend who for many years had contributed to the cultural stature of the city of Stockton, California, by matching the right Mexican with the right Filipino. We talked over the old argument that a good big man beats a good little man.

"What about Fitzsimmons?" he said.

In the restaurant of the Hotel Bonaventure, I was eating an early supper when Duran appeared. With him were his Panamanian bodyguards, some Panamanian friends, and one of his two elderly trainers, Freddie Brown, who is 73 and was smoking a cigar and looking disgusted. They were accompanied by a terrific din of Latin music out of Duran's tape deck, which was the size of a small suitcase. Trumpet blasts, voices, thumps, clacks, strums, ringings and high-pitched whistles poured from the box at a volume close to that favored by campaign cars cruising neighborhoods before election day.

Duran put his tape deck on the table, sprawled in a chair, and began loudly beating time on the table. He was bearded, wore a T-shirt in praise of Panama, jeans, a white cap and a pair of rainbow suspenders. His black eyes gazed vacantly, his head and shoulders rocked, and he appeared a captive of his own restless energy. He let out a few sharp cries, then took up a knife and spoon, beating them together even as the waitress took the orders. When he spoke his voice filled the room.

At the table next to mine a couple was speaking with raised voices.

"Why do they let people like that in here? Why don't they throw him out?"

"They must be some of Duran's crowd," the man said.

"That *is* Duran," I told him.

"Is *that* Duran? Is that really Duran?" he called back. "Then I've just decided who I'm pulling for. The other guy."

When Duran's steak arrived, Brown intercepted it and with a look of scorn dumped the french-fried potatoes onto his own plate.

Duran cut the steak into large chunks which he held up on his fork and gnawed hastily. Within a very few minutes he had finished his meal and was walking out with his bodyguards and his music.

Out in the lobby, Duran was signing autographs with careful block printing, while Brown stood gazing into space, chewing his cigar. Slightly stooped, he wore red-and-gray checkered trousers high over a small paunch, and a multicolored sport coat with a zigzag pattern. Brown had worked with Marciano and many other champions, acquiring a degree of immortality as the cut man who closed the rip in Rocky's nose in his second bout with Ezzard Charles. Brown's own nose had been hammered flat. I had heard that 50 years ago he had considered plastic surgery, but then had decided to hell with it.

"Roberto sure looks up for this one," I said.

Brown kept gazing and chewing. "He hasn't been in this good a shape since the second DeJesus fight six years ago."

"Is that why he didn't work out today? Are you afraid of overtraining him?"

"Overtrain?" he said, staring at me with utter exasperation. "How can you get overtrained? You're either in shape or you're not. What does overtrained mean? I never heard of such a thing. You got to work hard. If you don't you're not in shape to fight. This is the most talked about fight of all time." He relit his cigar. "Let me tell you something," he said. "There's a lot of tension in this fight. But it favors experience. Duran's been through all this before. But the tension's getting to Leonard. He's worried. Leonard didn't want this fight. The commission made him take it. He wanted to fight Cuevas."

This was a source of confidence for the Duran camp, which included Don King. King was co-promoting the bout with his rival, Bob Arum, whom he has been known to call The Snake. Arum's headquarters were across the street in Le Regence Hyatt and he always managed to appear without King at press conferences, where he predicted record-breaking sums from the closed-circuit telecast. King had been trying to make the match for some time. Leonard had been ordered by the WBC to defend against Duran, the number one contender, or risk being stripped of his title. Negotiations began, instead, between Leonard and Pipino Cuevas, who holds the WBA version of the title. But Duran is such a national hero in Panama that the president himself is his friend, and so officials in the government of

Panama, specifically Colonel Ruben Paredes, a commander of the Panamanian national guard, interceded with the WBA, whose president, Rodrigo Sanchez, is Panamanian.

The result was that negotiations broke down between Cuevas and Leonard, who was then forced to sign with Duran. Arum claimed Leonard would gross $8 to $10 million. As the bout drew near he was calling it "the dream fight of the century." And Don King declared himself "ecstatic with delight."

"Dundee didn't want this fight," Brown said. "They did everything they could to avoid this fight."

Angelo Dundee, Leonard's manager, gave me his line on Duran in the bar at the top of the Hyatt. A singer was singing as he spoke. "Duran's a heel-to-toe guy," he said. "He takes two steps to get to you. So the idea is don't give him the two steps. Don't move too far away. The more distance you give Duran, the more effective he is. What you don't do against aggression is run from it, because then he picks up momentum. My guy won't run from him.

"Duran waves at you with his hand. He gives you movement of his body, slipping from side to side. He won't come straight in. He'll try to feint you. He misses you with an overhand right. He turns southpaw, comes back with a left hook to the body. My guy's going to be moving side to side. And he's going to go to the body. Nobody ever hit Duran in his weak spot." Dundee poked his fingers under his ribs. "He doesn't do his homework on the table. He's soft. Leonard's the puncher in this fight. I think Leonard's going to knock him out in 10 or 11 rounds. Because Duran hasn't destroyed anybody as a welterweight. The reason being that he's hitting on bigger guys and the bigger guys are able to absorb it more than the little guys. He was devastating as a lightweight, but he never was one of those one-punch knocker-outers. He was a grinder. Ray's going to nail him. Ray's going to stop him in his tracks with the jab. Leonard's got so much talent they haven't seen it yet."

Dundee, who has the manner and appearance of a gentle professor, didn't like the singer's moves. He pointed out her whole repertoire of mechanical gestures. He liked her songs well enough to sing a few lines himself, but he particularly disliked the way she kept handling her hair. As we rode down to the lobby, Dundee went into a reflective mood often observed in elevators. "I got the greatest respect for Duran," he said. "I've known him for years. I talk Spanish with him and I know what kind of a guy he is. He's a sweetheart and he's a great fighter. I don't take anything away from him. He's great at what he does, but he's a heel-toe guy."

Both Duran and Leonard worked out at a hockey arena converted to a gym. Leonard boxed brilliantly, hitting on the move, slipping punches and countering with combinations that seemed to flow from him effortlessly. Once he knocked down a sparring partner so picturesquely that the young man, from Leonard's hometown boxing club, got up with what seemed a smile of aesthetic appreciation. At intervals, while Leonard skipped rope, a trainer would mop his sweat from the floor with a towel. Sweating in the dressing room, he talked with newsmen, some of his statements sounding rehearsed, with an eye toward boosting the gate. At the close of the session he took up a newspaper and looked it over while an aide knelt and removed his boxing shoes.

Duran held few press conferences, and his dressing room was filled with noisy friends from Panama. He was indeed a heel-toe man, but he got around the ring quickly, occasionally sending a sparring partner reeling from a right hand thrown with an authority and form that stirred memories of great righthand punchers of the past. He tugged and hauled, bulled his man into the ropes, and swung viciously to the body. He clowned, beating the speed bag with his head, skipping rope like a drunk, then leaping high, then hopping while in a squat, whirling the rope flamboyantly. And all through the workout, in the ring and on the bag and rope, he emitted strange shrill cries. They were not snorts and grunts many boxers make when punching. They were oohs and aahs, wailed in a sharp, high-pitched staccato, like cries of birds, and seemed to strike an emphasis, set a rhythm or express exuberance. He was an appealing eccentric.

Three days before the fight Duran shadowboxed two 10-minute rounds, and energy poured from him. Joyously he prowled the ring, swaying and bobbing. He squatted, leaped high, and turned. He punched the ropes, the corner pads, circled the ring and, like a child or a cat, tapped the hands of the men grasping the ropes. Brown leaned on the top strand, trying to smile as punches shot past his face. Weaving and punching, emitting his cries and shrieks, exchanging insults with his friends in the bleachers, Duran seemed possessed by the wild joy of his own vitality. After nine weeks of training, the nearness of the fight seemed to fill him with happiness. He ducked through the ropes, and just as he was about to jump to the floor, his 81-year-old co-trainer, Ray Arcel, stepped quickly over and reached up and lifted him down from the ring.

"He gets so excited he doesn't know what he's doing," said Arcel. "I had a fighter jump out of the ring once and he hurt his leg and couldn't fight."

I remembered Arcel from my childhood, when he handled a long procession of Louis' victims.

Back in the lobby of the Hotel Bonaventure I found Arcel relaxing in a chair. His eyes are dark and impenetrable, his mouth set, his prominent nose well-shaped despite fights in New York streets and rings that preceded his career as a trainer. He wore a dark tie, a striped shirt, and a navy blue sport coat, and had the stern, dignified appearance of a retired judge. He had trained Ross, Braddock, Zale and more than a dozen other champions, and had been in Charles' corner the night he sliced up Marciano's nose. But Benny Leonard was the gem of all his fighters. He had worked with Leonard in 1931 and 1932 when the stock market crash forced the great lightweight champion out of retirement.

I asked his opinion of the new Leonard.

"We'll find out what this guy has to offer in the first round," Arcel said. "Leonard's a master craftsman. I don't underestimate him, but I'm going to find out early how much stamina he has. I want to see if he can take a body beating and stand up for the first six or seven rounds. He looks good but who's he fought? Duran was in against good opposition in the lightweights. Guys like Buchanan and Lampkin and DeJesus were good boxers. That guy Bizzarro was like a deer. But could they keep it up for 15 rounds?

"The only reason Duran was ineffective as a welterweight was because he wasn't in condition. The fights meant nothing to him, except Palomino. He could still be a lightweight. He won't listen. A fighter's got to have some kind of self-control. He can't just eat every kind of crap. He's like a kid. He didn't have to be a welterweight but now that he is, he's still good enough to beat everybody. He's strong enough to handle the bigger men."

"Mickey Walker did it," I said. "He even beat heavyweights."

"Mickey Walker was a drunk," said Arcel. "Jack Kearns made a drunk out of him. Tunney was a terrible drunk, too, after he retired. Disgusting. Liquor is a terrible thing. Did you know it was Benny Leonard who taught Tunney how to beat Greb? I was right there in the gym and I saw what he showed him. Leonard was a great student of boxing. He could do it all."

"I've wondered about the no-decision bouts in those days," I said. "You take a look at Benny Leonard's record and he's got a lot of knockouts in the important bouts but a lot of the no-decision bouts went the limit. Did they go all out in those no-decision bouts or did they have an understanding to go easy?"

In an instant Arcel came out of his chair and was facing me, his eyes combative.

"The fighter never lived that Benny Leonard would have to ask to go easy on him!"

"I didn't mean it that way," I said. "I meant did *he* go easy on *them*?"

"He *had* to go easy! He couldn't get anybody to fight him if he didn't agree to carry them."

In the men's room of the Hotel Bonaventure, sports pages with the daily fight news in English and French were tacked on a bulletin board above the urinals. Panamanians crowded the lobby. When Duran passed through they went along with him and sometimes Arcel had to shove them away. "If you love this guy so much, leave him alone!" he yelled.

Arcel and Brown were upset. Carlos Padilla had been named referee by Jose Sulaiman, president of the WBC, who was staying across the street in Leonard's hotel. Padilla had been the referee who stopped Wilfred Benitez with six seconds to go when he lost the championship to Sugar Ray Leonard. More recently, he had worked the first Antuofermo–Minter middleweight title bout.

"He breaks you before you get in there," complained Arcel. "Remember what he did to Antuofermo? He prevented a man from defending his title successfully. Then what recourse do you have? You lose a fight, then two days later it's all forgotten. I want a referee in there that'll let my fighter fight, that's all."

To a tremendous roar, Duran came up the steps and through the ropes. As he moved restlessly around the ring he appeared loose and confident and charged with a predatory intensity. The rain that had fallen during the preliminaries had stopped now, but many of the ringside spectators still sat encased in the black plastic rubbish bags distributed by the Olympic Stadium staff.

Although the ring was under a canopy, wet spots showed along the apron of the blue canvas. Holding the ropes, Duran worked his feet in the resin box and Brown and Arcel had a moment to speak to Padilla before the roar came up again and Leonard approached the ring, surrounded by a large entourage of friends and his cornermen— Dundee and the two trainers who have been with him since his first amateur fights, Dave Jacobs and Janks Morton.

The instructions took place without delay. The seconds ducked out through the ropes and the fighters stood facing one another across the ring. When the two came out at the bell, Duran looked short by comparison, with short, powerful legs and the thick neck that helps a fighter absorb the force of blows to the head. As he advanced on Leonard, feinting with his head and shoulders, his disadvantage in reach was evident. Yet he stepped in almost immediately to hit Leonard solidly to the head with his right and left. Standing flat-footed, both men landed hard jabs. Then Duran attacked with a rush, driving Leonard to the ropes, where he hit him some terrible blows to the body and established what was to be the pattern of the fight.

Leonard fought back and when he had punching room, drove in his jab. But Duran was fighting with the fierceness of a man whose whole being willed one thing. He swarmed over Leonard with startling violence. When his right missed he banged in with his head and he kept Leonard on the ropes with the fury of his attack. When Leonard covered up, arms tied against his body and gloves shielding his face, Duran beat on his arms as in a frenzy to take something out of him, some resilience or sense of control, and in that first round he took some of his strength, too. He landed a hook to the liver that might've put another fighter on the canvas in a knot of pain.

Through the first five rounds Duran overpowered him. With quick and unpredictable moves he hit hard at long range. In close, he grabbed and mauled, chopping hooks to Leonard's ribs and head, grappling and hitting, while Leonard covered and fought back in flurries. But Leonard was taking heavy punishment. His jab, so quick and accurate in other bouts, seemed to have deserted him. Often, at long range, he stood flat-footed as Duran stalked him, and he hesitated until Duran led and was swarming over him again, and then he would open up and trade with him, but this was Duran's kind of fight and he excelled at it.

Arcel and Brown had no more worries about Padilla. He stood back and let the battle rage in the clinches. Sometimes, instead of separating the two, Padilla would simply slap away a grasping hand, allowing the infighting to go on. When he did push them apart, Leonard would move toward him, putting him in the line of Duran's charge and gaining a moment of respite. Duran came in without fear of Leonard's power, and took what he had to take, but his feints were deceptive and he was ducking and slipping and rolling with punches. He had moves Leonard was unable to solve. Again and again Leonard's back was against the ropes. He seemed unable to slip and sidestep as he had against the 27 professionals he had fought previously. Duran, with the experience of 71 bouts, was showing him the roughest secrets of the trade.

Leonard proved to have extraordinary durability and gameness in those rounds. There were times when I doubted he could survive them. In the middle rounds Leonard began to come back. He fought head to head with Duran, slamming him with hard combinations that had no apparent effect. Duran kept coming. Between rounds, Dundee, his face grave, was shouting at Leonard to move and box, but Leonard went on slugging as if unable to move.

It became a contest of fighting heart, and resulted in exchange after fierce exchange, a slugfest between two men with great speed and punching skills. Leonard was hurt on the ropes in the 11th, a round of bitter trading, and in the 13th his knees were buckled by a left hook. Still he fought back, taking lefts and rights on the jaw and coming back with hard, quick flurries in a round of almost constant exchanges. With disregard of danger, their bodies steaming in the misty, humid air, both fighters traded punches in the fastest and most stubbornly fought round of the fight. Drawing on the depths of his stamina, Leonard finished strong enough to win the last two rounds. In the final seconds, Duran dropped his arms and stuck out his chin in a taunt that may have come from frustration over the unyielding toughness he had encountered in Leonard.

The fight was Duran's, although the judges made it close. One scored 10 rounds even. With that kind of judging, there seemed the possibility of a draw, but the voting, after a correction in addition, was unanimous: 145–144, 148–147, 146–144. Duran had taken the title, but both men had fought with such fire that the fight would rank with the great ones.

The ring filled with excited fans and security guards. Several fights broke out and it appeared Duran was scuffling with somebody, too. His interpreter, Luis Henriquez, was squared off with Wilfred Benitez, the former champion, who was asked by Howard Cosell to comment on the fight, and had abandoned his post to yell insults at Duran. A security guard picked him up and was about to throw him over the ropes into the press section when I convinced him that Wilfred was a valuable commodity.

Afterward, in the press room, a jubilant Duran, his chest bare, was asked what had made the difference for him, and he placed his hand over his heart.

His heart indeed had been indomitable. However, there was enough controversy in the press room to insure that the lawyers and promoters would be talking about a rematch. Dundee was displeased with the refereeing. He called the fight a wrestling match. There were debates over why Leonard had slugged and not boxed. The opinion was offered that he had chosen the wrong strategy. But I believed what I had seen—a good man giving his best while outfought. By pressuring him, crowding him and hurting him, Duran had taken away Leonard's advantages.

At three o'clock that morning, Arcel was leaving the hotel with Carlos Eleta, Duran's manager, and other friends to look for an all-night restaurant, and I walked along with them. We talked about the fight, and I asked Arcel if he was satisfied with the refereeing.

"Yes, I thought Padilla did a good job," he said. "Freddie and I had a talk with him. I told him the whole world was watching. This was the fight everybody wanted to see, and he should let the fighters fight."

Someone asked if Duran was the greatest fighter he had ever trained. For a while Arcel didn't answer, as if unwilling to compromise his devotion to the legendary Benny Leonard, whom he considered the greatest he had ever seen. But then the past seemed to give up its hold on him. He was tired, and he told me that Benny Leonard was all used up by the time he had worked with him. At last, Arcel said, "Yes," and a moment later added, "Duran is the best fighter in the world."

Budd Schulberg

He was the only man to be both the winner of an Academy Award (for *On the Waterfront* in 1954) and an inductee into the International Boxing Hall of Fame (Class of 2002), but those seemingly disparate honors only hint at the broad scope of this remarkable writer. Budd Schulberg (1914–2009) was born the son of a studio mogul (Paramount chief B. P. Schulberg) in the age of silent film (Hollywood's first talkie, *The Jazz Singer*, was released in 1927, the year of his bar mitzvah) who endured well into the Twitter Age. Imbued with an enduring devotion to boxing at an early age, Schulberg sparred with Young Stribling in a deckside ring on the *Ile de France* on a 1929 Atlantic crossing, and was subsequently the American boxer's guest at his London fight against the ungainly Italian giant Primo Carnera. Having thus been exposed to the future heavyweight champion's ineptitude a good half-dozen years before most Americans wised up to the scam, Schulberg would later use Carnera's mob-manipulated career as the basis for his 1947 novel *The Harder They Fall*, widely considered among the finest boxing novels ever written; the 1956 movie version starred Humphrey Bogart in his final film role.

His 1981 autobiography *Moving Pictures* (which includes the reminiscence of Benny Leonard excerpted in this volume) was accurately subtitled "Memories of a Hollywood Prince," but the scathing portrayal of Tinseltown in his best-selling 1941 first novel *What Makes Sammy Run* turned the Prince into a Hollywood Pariah. He had already written several screenplays, including *Winter Carnival*, a 1939 collaboration with F. Scott Fitzgerald that got both men fired after a wild, drunken weekend in New Hampshire, later depicted in his 1950 novel *The Disenchanted*. As a naval officer attached to the OSS, Lt. Schulberg personally arrested the pro-Nazi filmmaker Leni Riefenstahl in his role for the prosecution in the Nuremburg Trials. After his discharge he returned to fiction, publishing scores of short stories, including "Your Arkansas Traveler," later the vehicle for his 1957 screenplay *A Face in the Crowd*. Boxing, though, remained his passion. Schulberg was *Sports Illustrated*'s first boxing correspondent, and his knowledgeable fistic coverage for mainstream and boxing magazines, as well as in newspapers (the bittersweet take on Muhammad Ali's penultimate fight in 1980 included here was written as a column for the *New York Post*), subsequently collected in his *Sparring With Hemingway* (1995) and *Ringside* (2007). He also authored a 1972 book on Ali's first fight with Joe Frazier, *Loser and Still Champion*.

Perhaps in acknowledgement of the role his father had played in nurturing his own love affair with the sweet science, he passed along the favor: thirteen-year-old Benn Schulberg accompanied his father to Madison Square Garden for the Riddick Bowe–Michael Dokes fight in 1993, and for the next sixteen years (Budd covered his last fight, between Miguel Cotto and Joshua Clottey at Madison Square Garden, in June 2009) Budd and Benn Schulberg were an inseparable 1 and 1A entry at ringsides from New York to Las Vegas. Although at age ninety-five Schulberg communicated by e-mail, owned a cell phone, and regularly contributed to a number of boxing websites, he could still be baffled by technology. "A car we had rented in Vegas had a GPS, so I'd punched in the address of our destination when we left the hotel," recalled Benn, who has carried on the family legacy as a boxing writer and film producer in his own right. "We'd probably been driving for twenty minutes when my Dad turned to me with an exasperated look and said 'Who *is* this woman? And how does she know where we're *going*?'"

The Fight (The King Is Dead)

HERE in Las Vegas, this glittering, easy-come, easy-go capital of the Western world, where the losers outnumber the winners a thousand-to-one, Muhammad Ali joined the silent majority at last.

True, your average loser doesn't walk away with eight million spondulicks (which he will share with his partners Herbert Muhammad, the Internal Revenue Service, and an entourage that will be out Monday looking for new ways to live in the manner to which they have become accustomed through the providential Mr. Ali). But losing is *losing* and, even with his record jackpot, the most theatrical and controversial of all heavyweight champions has bowed out uncharacteristically—not with a bang but a whisper.

After last night's pathetic performance—no jab, no legs, more dope than rope—the song is ended, but no member of Ali's believers would like to think that the memory of the Holmes fiasco will linger on. The ghetto children, who took heart from the float-and-sting of their black butterfly, and their white counterparts would like to remember the razzle and the dazzle that befuddled Liston and the heart and mind that conquered Frazier and Foreman. Not a single note of that honey melody was to be heard in Ali's round-after-round catching as a sharp, serious, credible new champion, Larry Holmes, pitched his shutout against the battered ghost.

There are two kinds of champions, commission-appointed and popularly acclaimed. Last night, even for the last of the diehards, Larry Holmes became the heavyweight champion of the world. Now this writer knows how Jack London felt when he picked Jim Jeffries over Jack Johnson and how the sentimentalists wept when they hung with Joe Louis against Rocky Marciano. This corner had voted against the logic and with the myth. But the moment comes when reality prevails against dreams, romance, and dancing old-fashioned two-steps with the past. It is as painful as it is healthy to admit, "The king is dead . . ."

Before I began writing this requiem, Joe Louis was wheeled down the aisle to ringside. The bell for Round 1 of Holmes–Ali was yet to ring. Here are my notes, verbatim: "Joe Louis wheeled in—mouth hangs open—eyes staring—what is he seeing? He holds his head in his hands. An attendant wipes spittle from his mouth. His head sags. He sees nothing. The crowd cheers as Ali comes down the aisle. Louis doesn't see him. Doesn't hear the cheers."

Our Joe Louis, the greatest before "The Greatest," destroyer of Billy Conn and Maxie Baer and Max Schmeling, slumped beside me in his wheelchair. After the early rounds of the fight last night that Louis was attending without seeing, a fight in which Larry Holmes established immediate dominance and exposed Muhammad as an old man, we found ourselves calling on the Lord of this cruel sport to spare us the sight of a wheelchair for Ali.

If the live gate was a record 6 million, with another 45 million in theaters around the world, the paying customers, many of whom felt they were rope-a-doped, were cheated of the most furious exchange of the evening.

From where I sat near Ali's corner—by coincidence in almost the same relationship to his corner I enjoyed in his victory over Liston in Miami sixteen years ago—it looked as if Angelo Dundee wanted to stop the fight when he saw that Ali was no longer able to defend himself. Another round or two and this prideful warrior might have been as damaged as his ex-doctor Ferdie Pacheco thinks he already is. The faithful Bundini Brown backed Ali's wish to go on with the ordeal. Bodyguard Pat Patterson tried to separate Angelo and Bundini. Then Patterson looked down at Herbert Muhammad, sitting directly in front of me. Herbert had not been able to watch the fight for at least the previous two rounds. Herbert gave Patterson a little hand signal and then buried his head in his hands.

The Holmes–Ali fight was over and so was Bundini–Dundee.

In the silence of the crowd, subdued by the disappointing spectacle, Sylvester Stallone, a rocky-eyed optimist, found something glorious in the effort Ali made and in the glory that had come to Larry Holmes. While I pretended to agree with him, because he spoke dramatic logic, my heart still belonged to the old music. That music had stopped now. Holmes and Stallone were dancing to a different bongo. And while we look before and after, and pine for what is not, is it not time to welcome new champions who pay their dues?

from

Moving Pictures

WHEN my father was organizing Preferred Pictures in New York and getting ready to set up shop at the Mayer–Schulberg Studio in Los Angeles, he was a passionate fight fan. An habitué of the old Garden on Madison Square, his favorite fighter was the Jewish lightweight Benjamin Leiner who fought under the *nom-de-boxe* of Benny Leonard. On the eve of my seventh birthday, my hero was neither the new cowboy star Tom Mix nor the acrobatic Doug Fairbanks. I didn't hoard and trade face cards of the current baseball stars like the other kids on Riverside Drive. Babe Ruth could hit 54 homers that year (when no one else had ever hit more than 16 in the history of the League) and I really didn't care. The legendary Ty Cobb could break a batting record almost every time he came up to the plate, but no chill came to my skin at the mention of his name. That sensation was reserved for Benny Leonard.

He was doing with his fists what the Adolph Zukors and William

Foxes, and soon the L. B. Mayers and the B. P. Schulbergs, were doing in their studios and their theaters, proving the advantage of brain over brawn, fighting the united efforts of the *goyische* establishment to keep them in their ghettos.

Jewish boys on their way to *shul* on the Sabbath had tasted the fists and felt the shoeleather of the righteous Irish and Italian children who crowded them, shouted "You killed our Christ!", and avenged their gentle Savior with blows and kicks. But sometimes the little yid surprised his racist foes by fighting back, like Adolph Zukor, or Abe Attell, who won the featherweight championship of the world at the turn of the century, or Abe Goldstein, who beat up a small army of Irish contenders on his way to the bantamweight title. But our super-hero was Benny Leonard. "The Great Benny Leonard." That's how he was always referred to in our household. There was The Great Houdini. The Great Caruso. *And* The Great Benny Leonard.

My father gave me a scrapbook, with a picture of Benny in fighting stance on the cover, and I recognized his face and could spell out his name even before I was able to read. In 1920 he was only 24 years old, just four years younger than my hero-worshipping old man, but he had been undefeated lightweight champion of the world ever since he knocked out the former champion, Freddie Welsh, in the Garden.

B.P. knew Benny Leonard personally. All the up-and-coming young Jews in New York knew Benny Leonard personally. They would take time off from their lunch hour or their afternoon activities to watch him train. They bet hundreds and often thousands of dollars on him in stirring contests against Rocky Kansas, Ever Hammer, Willie Ritchie, Johnny Dundee, Pal Moran, Joe Welling. . . . He was only five foot six, and his best fighting weight was a few pounds over 130, but he was one of those picture-book fighters who come along once or twice in a generation, a master boxer with a knockout punch, a poised technician who came into the ring with his hair plastered down and combed back with a part in the middle, in the approved style of the day, and whose boast was that no matter whom he fought, "I never even get my hair mussed!" After his hand was raised in victory, he would run his hand back over his sleek black hair, and my father, and Al Kaufman, and Al Lichtman, and the rest of the triumphant Jewish rooting section would roar in delight, as Ali's fans were to raise the decibel level at the sight of the Ali Shuffle. To shake the hand of Benny

Leonard was to touch greatness and to share in his invincibility. To see him climb into the ring sporting the six-pointed Jewish star on his fighting trunks was to anticipate sweet revenge for all the bloody noses, split lips, and mocking laughter at pale little Jewish boys who had run the neighborhood gauntlet.

One of my father's friends practically cornered the market on the early motion-picture insurance business. But all through his life he would be singled out as the incredible amateur boxer who had sparred with Benny Leonard and had actually knocked Great Benny down! Every time Artie Stebbins came to our house, my father prefaced his arrival by describing that monumental event. Artie Stebbins had a slightly flattened nose and looked like a fighter and it was whispered that he would have gone on to a brilliant professional career except for an unfortunate accident in which his opponent had died in the ring. No matter how modestly he dismissed the legendary knockdown of Benny Leonard—"I think Benny slipped . . ." or "I just happened to tag him right"—that knockdown remained with him as a badge of honor. My father would say with a note of awe, "He might have been another Benny Leonard!"

But when I was going on seven, there was only one Benny Leonard; my scrapbook fattened on his victories. In those days fighters fought three or four fights in a single month. Benny had been an undernourished 15-year-old when he first climbed into the professional ring, getting himself knocked out by one Mickey Finnegan in two rounds. He was knocked out again by the veteran Joe Shugrue when he was only sixteen. But from the time he reached the seasoned age of eighteen, he had gone on to win more than a hundred and fifty fights, in an era in which the lightweight division was known for its class. The Great Benny Leonard had gone to the post twenty-six times in 1919 alone, and almost every one of his opponents was a name to the cognoscenti. As for me, I had only one ambition, to become a world champion like The Great Benny Leonard. Or rather, two ambitions, for the second was to see him in action.

I had asked my father if he could take me to the Joe Welling fight, but he thought I was a little young to stay up so late. Instead he had promised to tell me all about it when he came home. That night, I waited for Father to bring news of the victory. In what round had our Star of the Ghetto vanquished the dangerous Joe Welling? How

I wished I were in Madison Square Garden! Old enough to smoke big cigars and go to the fights like my father!

I have no idea what time Daddy got home that night. Probably three or four in the morning. Where had he gone with his pals after the fight? The Screen Club? The Astor? Jack and Charlie's? A dozen other speakeasies? The apartment of a friendly or ambitious young extra girl who hoped to become a Preferred feature player? When my father finally gave me the blow-by-blow next evening, he admitted that our hero had underestimated Welling's appetite for punishment. Ben and the rest of the young Jewish fancy had bet that Welling would fall in ten, as Leonard had predicted. But Welling was nobody's pushover, and he had even fought the referree who finally stopped the fight. B.P. was out five hundred smackers. He and his pals had gone back to the dressing room to see the triumphant Benny, and the fistic Star of David, still proud of his hair-comb, apologized for leading his rooters astray. B.P. told Benny about my scrapbook, and The Great B.L. promised to autograph it for me. Then the boys went out on the town to celebrate Jewish Power.

When father told me about the Joe Welling fight and helped me paste the clippings into my bulging scrapbook, I begged him to take me with him to the next Great Benny Leonard fight. "When you're a little older," he promised.

In the early weeks of 1921, he brought me the news. Great Benny had just signed to defend his title against Richie Mitchell in Madison Square Garden! Now Richie Mitchell was no ordinary contender. He was a better boxer than Joe Welling, and a harder puncher. He was three inches taller than Benny Leonard, in the prime of his youth, strength, and ability at 25, and he had more than held his own against all the good ones and some of the great ones: Wolgast, Kilbane, Tendler, Dundee, Charley White, Joe Rivers. . . . Only once in his impressive nine-year career had Richie Mitchell been knocked out. Benny had turned the trick back when I was three years old. My old man had taken the train to Milwaukee to see it, and had come back flushed with victory and victory's rewards.

Now it was time for the rematch, and Richie Mitchell had come to New York confident of reversing the only loss on his record. The day of the fight I boasted to my classmates, "I'm g-g-going to M-M-Madison Square Garden tonight t-to s-see The G-G-Great

B-B-Benny Leonard!" Even if they had been able to understand me, I don't think the other kids would have known what I was talking about. When it came to boxing they were illiterates. They simply had no idea that the rematch between Benny Leonard and Number One Contender Richie Mitchell was an event more earthshaking than the election of a new President, the arrival of Prohibition, or the publication of the first novel by Scott Fitzgerald.

Finally, the moment arrived. Mother had dressed me warmly for this mid-January adventure. I was wearing long white stockings and a blue velvet suit with fur-lined coat and hat. All that was lacking was one of my father's big Cuban cigars. But it didn't matter. I would smoke it vicariously as I sat snugly beside him in the front ringside seats near our idol's corner that B.P. always got from Leonard.

"Well, Buddy," my father said as we got out of the cab near the crowded entrance to the Garden, "I kept my promise. Your mother thought you were still too young, but I wanted you to see The Great Benny Leonard in his prime, because it's something you'll remember the rest of your life."

There were thousands and thousands of big people, a lot of them wearing derbies, a lot of them puffing on big cigars, a lot of them red-faced from winter wind and the forbidden but ever-plentiful alcohol, bellying and elbowing their way toward the ticket-takers.

As we reached the turnstile, my father urged me ahead of him and held out a pair of tickets. A giant of a guard in uniform glanced at my father, then looked in vain for the holder of the other ticket. When he saw where Father was pointing, his voice came down to me in a terrible pronouncement, like God's: "What are ya, nuts or somethin'? You can't take that little kid in here! Ya gotta be sixteen years old!"

My father argued. He bargained and bribed. But in a city known for its Tammany Hall corruption, we had come upon that rare bird, an honest guardian of the law.

By this time Father was telling me to, for Christ's sake, stop crying! He was frantic. The preliminaries had already started, and in those days before television and radio, there were no extra bouts standing by to hold the audience until the pre-announced time for the star bout. If there were early knockouts in the prelims, B.P. ran the risk of missing The Great Benny. And we were all the way down on Madison Square at East 26th Street, miles away from home on Riverside Drive near 100th Street. If traffic was heavy he might miss the event of a lifetime. But there was nothing for it but to hail a cab, tell the driver to speed across town and up the West Side, wait for him to dispose of his sobbing and expendable baggage, and race back to the Garden. Delivered to my mother, awash with tears, I stammered out my tale of injustice. I would have to wait ten long years to be admitted to the Garden and by that time our champion would be retired from the ring. Now I would never see him, I cried, never in my whole life!

Mother tried everything in her extensive repertoire of child psychology to console me. But it was too late. For me life simply had come to an end at the entrance to the turnstile of Madison Square Garden.

To ease the tragedy, I was allowed to wait up until Father came home. And this time, sensitive to the crisis, he did not linger with his cronies over highballs at a friendly speakeasy. He came directly from the Garden, his fine white skin flushed with the excitement of what had happened.

B.P. had given the taxi driver an extra five-spot to disregard the speed limits and get him back to the Garden on a magic carpet. As he rushed through the turnstile and looked for the aisle to his seat, he heard a roar from the crowd that was like the howl of a jungle full of wild beasts. Everybody was standing up and screaming, blocking his view. A frantic glance at the second clock told him it was the middle of Round Three. When he got closer to his seat and was able to see the ring, the spectacle that presented itself was the Unbelievable. There on the canvas was our champion. And not only was his hair mussed, his eyes were dimmed as he tried to shake his head back to consciousness. The count went on, "Six . . . seven . . . eight . . ." Thousands of young Jews like my father were shouting, "Get up! Get up, Benny! Get up!" And another multitude of anti-Semitic rooters for Mitchell, "You got 'im, Richie! You got that little mockie sonuvabitch!" But just before the count of ten Leonard managed to stagger to his feet.

No, I wasn't there, but my father had caught the lightning in a bottle and had brought it home for me. I sat there watching the fight as clearly as if home television had been installed thirty years ahead of time. Our Benny was on his feet but the quick brain that usually directed the series of rapid jabs and classic right crosses was full of cobwebs. Billy Mitchell was leaning through the ropes and cupping his old fighter's hands to urge his son to "Move in, move in, Richie, finish 'im!" And Richie was trying, oh how he was trying, only a split second from being Lightweight Champion of the World, one more left hook, one more punishing right hand. . . . But Benny covered up, rolled with the punches, slipped a haymaker by an instinctive fraction of an inch, and managed to survive until the bell brought Leonard's handlers into the ring with smelling salts, ice, and the other traditional restoratives.

In the next round Richie Mitchell sprang from his corner full of fight, running across the ring to keep the pressure on Leonard and land his bruising combinations while he still held the upper hand. Everybody in the Garden was on his feet. Everybody was screaming. There had never been such a fight in all of Father's ringside nights, all the way back to 1912 when he had first started going to the fights with Adolph Zukor and the Famous Players crowd. Benny was retreating, boxing cautiously, gradually beginning to focus on Mitchell's combative eyes. "On his bicycle," they called it, dodging and running and slipping off the ropes, using all the defensive tactics he had learned in his street fights on the Lower East Side and in those one hundred and fifty battles inside the ropes. And as he retreated he was talking to Mitchell—shades of Ali half a century later!—"Is that the best you can do? I thought you hit harder than that. Look, I'll put my hands down, what do you wanna bet you can't hit me? Come on, if you think you've got me hurt, why don't you fight? You look awful slow to me, Richie, looks like you're getting tired. . . ."

That round had been more of a debate than a boxing match, with Benny winning the verbal battle and Richie swinging wildly and futilely as he tried to chop Benny down. At the end of the round the ferocious Richie Mitchell did look tired and a little discouraged. The drumfire of backtalk from Leonard had disconcerted him. He had let Benny get his goat, exactly what the champion wanted. Some remorseless clock in his head was telling him that he was blowing the chance of a lifetime. In the next round, Benny was The Great Benny again. His head clearing, his body weathering the storm, he was ready to take charge. Back on his toes, he was beginning to move around the slower Mitchell, keeping him off balance with jabs and rocking his head back with that straight right hand. Near the end of the round Mitchell went to his knees.

How many times Father refought Round Six for me over the years. Benny Leonard's hair was combed straight back again. There was no more talking to distract his opponent. Benny was all business. Lefts and rights found Mitchell's now-unprotected face. Both eyes were cut and blood dripped from his nose. Caught in a buzz saw of fast hard punches that seemed to tear his face apart, the brave Irish brawler went down. But took his count and rose again to face more of the same. Now it was not boxing but slaughterhouse seven and the more humane among the crowd, including the Benny Leonard fans who had bet a bundle it would be over in eight, were imploring the referee to "Stop it! Stop it!" For Mitchell was down again, and he seemed to be looking directly into his own corner, but there was so much blood running down into his eyes that he was unseeing.

"I was watching his father, Billy Mitchell," my father told me. "I could see the whole thing being fought out in Billy Mitchell's face. He was holding a bloody towel, the towel with which he had just wiped the face of his son. His own blood was on that towel. His son Richie got up again. God almighty, he was game. He would look at Benny as if to say 'You're going to have to kill me to stop me.' And Benny, he told us this a lot of times, he loved to win but he doesn't like to punish them once he knows he has them licked. He was hoping the referee would stop the fight. But the ref waved him on. Maybe he was betting on Mitchell. Maybe he figured anyone with the punch of a Richie Mitchell deserved that one extra round to see if he could land a lucky or a desperate blow. Now it seemed as if the entire Garden was chanting together, 'Stop it! Stop it! For God's sake, *stop it!*' And then as the slaughter went on, as The Great Benny Leonard went on ripping Richie Mitchell's face to bloody shreds, finally Billy Mitchell, that tough Mick, couldn't stand it any longer. He raised the bloody towel and tossed it over the top rope into the ring. And then, while Richie's kid brother Pinky and another handler climbed into the ring to revive their battered contender, Pop Mitchell lowered his head into his arms on the apron of the ring and cried like a baby."

Ralph Wiley

When Ralph Wiley (1952–2004) hired on at the *Oakland Tribune* in 1975, he discovered that his newly earned college degree qualified him to fetch coffee and sandwiches for the publisher. In a few short years, however, he rose to San Francisco Giants beat writer, then to featured sports columnist, which gave him the showcase to coin the term "Billyball" and, more importantly, to pave the way for the new wave of African American sports writers. At age thirty, Wiley moved to *Sports Illustrated*, where he spent a decade before jumping to ESPN and a panoply of assignments that included appearing regularly on *The Sports Reporters*, writing for *ESPN: The Magazine*, and serving as the original Page 2 columnist on ESPN.com. In addition to his sports-themed books *Serenity: A Boxing Memoir* (1989) and the posthumous collection *Classic Wiley* (2005), he co-authored books with Spike Lee, Dexter Scott King, and Eric Davis, and published three collections of social commentary, *Why Black People Tend To Shout* (1991), *What Black People Should Do Now* (1993), and *Dark Witness* (1996). His account of the tragic 1982 Mancini–Kim fight and its aftermath was first published in *Sports Illustrated*.

Then All the Joy Turned to Sorrow

R AY "BOOM BOOM" MANCINI held his swollen left hand in front of him like a jewel while shading his battered brow with his right. The bright lights were harsh and unwelcome. There were questions in Mancini's heart about what had just happened in the ring, though he didn't yet know the full horror of what had occurred. Was the WBA lightweight title he had just defended successfully against South Korea's Duk Koo Kim worth this? Was anything? "Why do I do it?" Mancini asked himself. "Why do I do this? I'm the one who has to wake up tomorrow and look at myself." He fingered the purple, misshapen area around his left eye. "A badge of honor," he said in a morbid tone. Minutes earlier, a less reflective Mancini had scored a technical knockout of Kim nineteen seconds into the fourteenth round, and Kim had been carried from the outdoor ring at Caesars Palace in Las Vegas on a stretcher. This was to have been an epilogue to the Aaron Pryor–Alexis Arguello WBA junior welterweight title fight the night before. Tragically, it became a nightmare.

The twenty-three-year-old Kim, who rained an incredible number of blows on Mancini and in return was pounded by even more, was injured by two right hands his head could not bear. Kim was taking just four breaths per minute when he was transported from the ring to an ambulance that was destined for Desert Springs Hospital.

Kim then underwent two-and-a-half hours of brain surgery, performed by Dr. Lonnie Hammargren, a local neurosurgeon, who removed a 100-cc. blood clot from the right side of Kim's brain. The clot, Dr. Hammargren said, was the result of a broken blood vessel and "due, in all probability, to one tremendous punch to the head." Had the punch been part of the thirty-nine-blow bombardment Mancini had delivered in the opening fifty seconds of the thirteenth round? Was it the first of the final two rights in the fourteenth? Or the second? Or could the damage have been done not by Mancini's fists but by Kim's head hitting the canvas after the final blow? Could Kim's brain have been damaged before the fight? "The hemorrhage was quite fresh," the neurosurgeon said on Saturday night. "The trauma was caused by one punch."

Dr. Hammargren had previously performed two similar operations, one on a Japanese kick boxer, the other on another fighter. "Both men wound up normal, but this outcome will be much worse. Mr. Kim had a right subdural hematoma," said Dr. Hammargren two hours after the surgery was completed. "He's very critical, with terminal brain damage. There is severe brain swelling. The pressure will go up and up, and that will be it. He'll die. His pupils have been fixed since he arrived. We have him on the respirator now. His body responds slightly to painful stimulus, and that is the only real sign of life we've had. They tell me he fought like a lion in the thirteenth round. Well, nobody could fight like that with a blood clot on his brain."

As *SI* went to press Monday evening, Kim, who had almost no remaining brain function, was being maintained by a life-support system.

Kim had indeed fought like a lion. Through the thirty-nine minutes of the previous rounds and those final nineteen seconds, the crowd of 6,500 at Caesars was sated with action, as was a CBS television audience. And everyone, especially co-promoter Bob Arum, seemed pleased when the fight was over. But later, at the hospital, Arum was somber. "Suspend boxing for a few months," he suggested, and he called for headgear for boxers and more heavily padded gloves. "Get a blue-chip medical panel to investigate this thing first, and then suspend boxing," Arum said. "It is the height of irresponsibility to allow this to happen, and the old excuses are not working."

Back at Caesars, Mancini learned of the severity of Kim's injuries and left his suite in the company of his parents and father Tim O'Neill, the family priest, to seek refuge elsewhere.

Before the fight, Kim's training methods, which included hammering a tire with a sledgehammer 200 times daily and ingesting large amounts of ginseng and garlic, and his style had not impressed the boxing cognoscenti. His anonymity seemed to diminish his 17–1–1, eight-KO record and his No. 1 ranking by the WBA. But he was to become a haunting foe for Mancini, who now finds, eerily, that he may fight Kim forever, and in doing so, fight himself.

Mancini is five-foot-six, the same as Kim. Mancini fought low. Kim fought lower. Mancini is righthanded, Kim lefthanded. There was a quarter-inch difference in reach, a half-pound in weight, little difference in power, and absolutely none in approach. "It was murderous," said Mancini's manager, Dave Wolf, immediately after the bout, unaware at the time that the comment would soon take on a macabre ring. "It was like Ray was fighting a mirror. I hope the people who said Kim was nothing are impressed now."

Mancini was left with several impressions by the 14th round. In the third, an infrequent Kim right lead—or perhaps it was a clash of heads—ripped open Mancini's left ear. Blood spouted, and only ice and pressure by cornerman Paul Percifield kept the wound closed. In that same round, one of Mancini's left hooks caught Kim's head too high and at a bad angle. The hand, badly bruised by the blow, began to swell, eventually to twice normal size. In the eighth, Mancini's left eye began to puff and color.

Kim's left hooks and slashing rights had exacted a toll, but Kim had been punished, too, though he showed it less. When the fighters began the fourteenth, the mirror's image was still there. Mancini broke the pattern by stepping to the right as Kim's left whistled by. Mancini hooked his own wounded left ineffectually, but now Kim was off-center, exhausted, and facing Mancini's corner. Mancini drove off his right foot and delivered the first of the final pair of rights on the point of the Korean's chin.

A glancing left hook followed, then a crushing right which sent Kim to the canvas. Kim landed heavily on his back and head, rolled over in slow motion, grabbed a middle strand of the ropes and stared blankly at the timekeeper. Kim's eyes dilated while the outdoor stadium rocked in celebration. "He was desperate, and I was hoping. My left hand was killing me," Mancini said. "But I felt that first right all the way up my arm." Twice Kim failed to regain his footing, but somehow he beat the count. Referee Richard Green looked at Kim's unfocused eyes and buckling legs and stopped the fight. "He was not there, and I wasn't going to let him go any further," said Green, who has officiated half a dozen world title fights, including Larry Holmes–Muhammad Ali. Green was absolved of any blame for failing to stop the fight sooner by the attending ringside physician, Dr. Donald Romeo, who worked to revive Kim. Kim's cornermen had offered no protest when the fight ended. "He just wouldn't go down," one of them said. "He had great pride."

Perhaps Kim's pride had been too great. Wolf returned from the hospital eight hours after the fight, at 11 P.M., sobered. "Pol Tiglao [Kim's American representative and translator and agent for a number of Oriental fighters] told me that a couple of days before the fight, Kim had written 'Kill or Be Killed' in Korean on a lampshade in his room," Wolf said. "He was a warrior going to war. Apparently he viewed this as a death match." Wolf then discounted Arum's suggestions. "I don't know what a blue-ribbon panel could do," he said. "It was not a case of defective equipment, or a fighter being allowed to go too far, or any impropriety. It was one or two unfortunate punches. And those rights at the end were not nearly the best punches Ray had thrown during the fight."

The youngest of five children born to rice and ginseng farmers, Kim came from Kang Won-Do province in Korea, 100 kilometers east of Seoul. "He was the strongest of the family's three sons," said H. R. Lee, a Korean journalist with the *Hankook Ilbo*, who traveled to Las

Vegas with Kim's small entourage and a larger group of Korean partisans. "He was not injured before the fight. He was in the best condition of his life."

Kim had been a shoeshine boy, tour guide, and baker's assistant before starting an amateur boxing career in 1976. His only hobby, according to Lee, was "music listening," but Tiglao said he also enjoyed reading. After a 29–4 amateur record, he turned professional in 1978, working with 100 other fighters in Seoul's Tong-a Gymnasium. He was the best of the lot and won the Orient and Pacific Boxing Federation lightweight title last February. He received $20,000 to fight Mancini.

Mancini studied film of Kim and other southpaw fighters for weeks. "We figured he'd come out kamikaze," Mancini said. "After looking at the film, I didn't care what anyone said," Mancini's trainer, Murphy Griffith, declared. "I had Ray train as if it was the fight of his life."

So it was. Mancini started the first round with a booming left hook to the jaw, but Kim answered with two of his own, and the barrages from both sides continued for the first nine rounds, the only variation being target. When Mancini went to the liver or rib cage, Kim answered. Mancini hooked with the hooker and found the tactic somewhat lacking. Kim seemed to land the harder punches. At the end of the ninth, a left rocked Mancini back on his heels, and Kim extended his arms upward in exultation. "He was getting lower than me," Mancini said. "I was supposed to be off him, but a lot of times when a guy is sitting in front of you like that, you want to move in and shoot. But he was getting his punches off first." Said Griffith, "Ray had to adjust. We didn't know Kim would be that tough. He was skillful, smart. Ray couldn't get below him, where he likes to be. But Ray's physical conditioning determined the fight. By the 13th round, the guy was looking for the hook. I told Ray to go with the right."

In fact, that decision had been made some ten rounds earlier, when Mancini hurt his hand. "Every time I hit him in the head, it killed me," Mancini said shortly after the battle, unaware of the terrible irony. The constant pounding from Mancini began to tell on Kim in the tenth, when Green took a point from Kim for hitting-and-holding. Green was berated by Mancini's corner throughout the fight about that tactic, borderline low blows, hitting after the bell, and Kim's headfirst rushes. "He wasn't dirty," insisted Mancini, who appeared to win every round from the tenth on. "Rough and tough, not dirty. We both hit heads. We both hit low. He was just the worst type of guy to fight." Said Wolf, "Already I can look back and see that [Green] did an excellent job."

By the eleventh, though his left eye was purple and hideously swollen, Mancini had taken control of the fight. He fired a left hook that buckled Kim's knees, and now he began to land three punches to Kim's one. At one point Kim went to one knee, but Green correctly ruled it a push. Mancini ended the twelfth scoring from a distance. He gave himself a clap and made an exaggerated nod at the end of the round. In the thirteenth, Mancini swarmed over Kim, starting the unanswered thirty-nine-punch sequence with a straight right hand. The right side of Kim's jaw ballooned and appeared to be broken, but he weathered that storm and even managed to punch out a weak combination. Then came the fourteenth, the sidestep, and Mancini's initial right, apparently unseen by Kim. He reeled back, defenseless, and the second right landed point blank on his jaw.

"Let all these guys who are screaming for a piece of Ray settle with Kim first. A temporary champion would have lost to Kim today," Wolf said at the conclusion of the bout. Later, after spending four hours at the hospital and being told that Kim didn't have long to live, Wolf said, "Ray is taking this hard, and his parents are pretty shook up also. I haven't given a single thought to how this may affect Ray as a fighter, and maybe that sounds silly, but that's the last concern right now. How it affects him as a person is what concerns me. I do think he's a very strong kid and sometime in the future he will be able to look at this, in the context of great pain, and see that once he stepped into that ring with Kim there was nothing he could have done."

On Sunday morning, one hour before attending a mass conducted by Father O'Neill at the Tropicana Hotel, Mancini issued a statement on CBS, which had televised the fight. Dark glasses covering his closed left eye, his damaged hand resting on the arm of the couch in his suite, Mancini said, "I'm very saddened. I'm sorry it had to happen, and it hurts me bad that I was part of it. I hope they realize I didn't intentionally hurt him. I don't blame myself, but I can't alienate myself.

"I'm a Christian, and I've been praying that I'll get some answers to questions that have been popping through my mind," Mancini said softly. "I have to rely on my faith to get me through this. It could easily have been me, and who is to say that it won't be me next time? I'm not saying I'll retire, but right now I'm not thinking of future fights. I have to see what happens to Mr. Kim. I need time to heal."

His was to be one of the last of Mancini's modest purses—his career earnings were pushed over $1 million by a $250,000 guarantee against forty-five percent of the gross revenue from this fight. Howard Davis was a likely springtime opponent. And then, of course, there was Pryor. Arguello, the only man to beat Mancini, is still the WBC lightweight champion. "I had always pictured myself coming back and doing that to Alexis," Mancini had said while viewing Pryor's destruction of Arguello Friday night. "We'd be interested in Pryor," Wolf said at the time.

Emile Griffith fought 80 times after Benny "Kid" Paret died following their fight on March 24, 1962. Griffith was 24 at the time of the Paret bout, a career fighter comfortably lost in his craft. Is Mancini, still impressionable at 21 and a young man for whom "money is no god," different? "They are both sensitive individuals," said Gil Clancy, CBS boxing analyst and former manager of Griffith, who happens to be the nephew of Mancini's trainer. "It took something out of Emile Griffith," said Clancy. "Griffith got hate mail, but he got encouragement, too. Ray will have to deal with the same things." Murphy Griffith said, "For a while it was doubtful that Emile would ever come back. He was a sensitive man. But time heals. He had to realize that what happened wasn't his will. People say it affected him until the end of his career. I think it did. Man, you don't forget. Some can handle it, some can't. How it will happen in Ray's case, only time will tell. He's got a good head, but a human is a human."

Former heavyweight champion Max Baer never approached a fight with the same intensity following the death of Frankie Campbell soon after their fight in San Francisco on Aug. 24, 1930. Jimmy Doyle died 17 hours after fighting Sugar Ray Robinson for the welterweight crown in Cleveland on June 24, 1947. At a subsequent hearing

Robinson was asked whether he knew he had Doyle in serious trouble. "They pay me to get them in trouble," said Robinson.

Mancini's box-office appeal had had nearly everyone who could make the weight calling him to try to get a fight. Despite his 24-1, nineteen-KO record, Mancini inspired confidence in contenders. Their pre-Las Vegas feelings can be summed up in the words of Hector Camacho, an undefeated junior lightweight from New York's Spanish Harlem. "You can't play Mancini cheap, he's the man right now," Camacho had said the night before the Mancini–Kim fight. "He's strong, he'll beat on you, but when the time comes he won't knock me out. He's the guy that will make me. He will make me. He's good, but he don't have that, you know, that greatness."

"Look, I know people either think I'm a bum or a superstar," Mancini had said. "I don't care what they think. I know where I am. Somewhere in between." Later, just before he'd heard the news of Kim's condition, Mancini decided something. "This badge of honor," he said, studying his face in the mirror. "Well, ugly as it is, I'm proud of it." Then the nightmare came. Now there are only questions with no simple answers.

Pat Putnam

Pat Putnam's matriculation at the sports department of the *Miami Herald* preceded the arrival in Miami Beach of a young boxer named Cassius Clay at the Fifth Street Gym. Putnam's superb coverage of the early career of the man who became Muhammad Ali did not escape the notice of the editors of *Sports Illustrated*, who poached him away to New York in 1968. In his twenty-seven-year tenure as a senior writer for *SI*, Putnam (1930–2005) filed more than five hundred stories from forty-eight states and more than thirty foreign countries, but his most frequent dateline was Las Vegas, where he held court at the Galleria Bar at Caesars by day and from his favorite stool at the Flame Steakhouse by night. He established a routine that served him well for nearly four decades on the boxing beat: in the hours immediately following a major bout, Putnam usually visited both winner and loser in their hotel suites for a private audience (his stature as the nation's most visible fight scribe was such that even the haughtiest of champions was happy to comply with this arrangement) before returning to his own quarters to go a caffeine-fueled fifteen rounds with the typewriter. (More often than not his copy had to be filed before dawn the following morning.) An envious colleague once rated Putnam "the best boxing writer since Liebling," and this account of the 1985 Hagler–Hearns conflagration, the most explosive three-round fight in boxing history, does nothing to diminish that characterization.

Eight Minutes of Fury

THERE was a strong wind blowing through Las Vegas Monday night, but it could not sweep away the smell of raw violence as Marvelous Marvin Hagler and Thomas Hearns hammered at each other with a fury that spent itself only after Hearns had been saved by the protecting arms of referee Richard Steele. The fight in a ring set up on the tennis courts at Caesars Palace lasted only a second longer than eight minutes, but for those who saw it, the memory of its non-stop savagery will remain forever.

Hagler's undisputed middleweight championship was at stake, and for the first time since he won it from Alan Minter in 1980, people had been questioning his ability to retain it. In the weeks leading up to the fight, Hagler fumed as the odds tilted back and forth before settling on the champion by the narrowest of margins. Hagler's pride was sorely stung, and a deep burning anger wrote his battle plan.

It was a simple strategy, one that could have been designed by Attila: Keep the swords swinging until there are no more heads to roll, give no quarter, take no prisoners. There would be only one pace, all-out: only one direction, forward.

It was a gamble, for Hagler would be exposing his 30-year-old body to the cannons that had knocked out 34 of the 41 men his 26-year-old challenger had faced and had earned Hearns the nickname Hit Man. "But he ain't never hit Marvin Hagler," the champion sneered. "I've taken the best shots of the biggest hitters in the middleweight division, and I've never been off my feet [Hagler considers his knockdown by Juan Roldan a slip]. And this guy isn't even a middleweight. Hit Man, my ass."

Hearns, as the challenger, came into the ring first—tall and strikingly muscular at 159¾ pounds—wearing a red robe with yellow trim. He jumped up and down to limber up his leg muscles, and then he strolled around the ring smiling. Hagler followed, in a royal-blue robe over trunks of the same color. Most champions keep challengers waiting alone in the ring as long as possible, but Hagler had warmed up well in his dressing room and he wanted to make his appearance while the sweat was still oiling his body. Entering the ring he fixed Hearns with a scowl that never wavered, not even during Doc Severinsen's trumpet version of the National Anthem.

When the bell rang, the war was immediately on. "I think Marvin may come out so fired up that we'll just have Tommy stick and move," Emanuel Steward, the challenger's manager, had said. "Hagler will be so juiced up, after seven or eight rounds it'll rob his strength. Then we'll go for the late knockout."

But Steward underestimated just how juiced up the champ would be. Hagler never gave Hearns a chance to do anything but fight for his life. The 5'9½" champion swept over his 6'2" opponent like a 159¼-pound tidal wave. There were no knockdowns in the first round, but only because both men were superbly conditioned and courageous athletes. Surely each hit the other with plenty of blows powerful enough to drop lesser mortals. In all, 165 punches (by computer count) were thrown by both fighters: 82 by Hagler, 83 by the challenger.

Startled by the intensity of Hagler's assault, Hearns replied in kind. He's normally a sharpshooter from the outside, but only 22 of his 83 punches were jabs. Hagler, attacking Hearns's slender middle with his first volley, threw none. "I started slugging because I had to," Hearns admitted later. "Marvin started running in, and I had to protect myself."

It was a sensational opening round. Both fighters were rocked during the violent toe-to-toe exchanges, and midway through the round the champion's forehead over his right eye was ripped open either by a Hearns right hand or elbow. With Hagler not bothering with defense, Hearns went for the quick kill. His gloves became a red blur as he rained punch after punch on the champion's head—and it would prove his undoing.

"He fought 12 rounds in one," Steward said later.

Returning to his corner, Hearns wore the drained expression of a man who had already fought for 36 minutes.

"What are you doing?" Steward screamed. "You've got to stick and move. Jab. Don't fight with him."

In the champ's corner, Dr. Donald Romeo, the chief physician of the Nevada State Athletic Commission, was examining the cut on Hagler's forehead. Another abrasion had begun to form under the eye. Satisfied that the cut on the forehead was harmless, Romeo returned to his seat.

"Don't change," Hagler's trainer, Goody Petronelli, told the champion. "Just keep your hands up a little higher. Don't worry about the cut. Just keep charging and keep the pressure up."

"O.K.," said Hagler. "I won't worry about the cut. If you go to war, you're going to get wounded."

Hagler's pace in the second round was only slightly less relentless. "When I see blood," said the champion, "I become a bull." He came out ready to gore whatever was in his path, and although Hearns rocked him midway through the round with a strong right cross, Hagler never for an instant eased the pressure. "All that right hand did," said Hagler, "was make me even madder."

A veteran of 64 professional fights (all but two of them victories), Hagler could sense the strength seeping away from Hearns's body. As he went back to his corner after the second round, the champion knew the fight was just about over.

"This cut isn't bad, but it's bleeding a lot," said Petronelli, as he worked on Hagler's forehead. "Let's not take any chances. Take him out this round."

"He's ready to go," said Hagler, spitting a mouthful of water into a pail. "He's not going to hurt me with that right hand. I took his best, and now I'm going to knock him out."

As in the first two rounds, Hagler came out at full fury. Forcing himself up on his toes, Hearns tried to hold him off with jabs, but had little left. Hagler waded through the challenger's jabs, pressing forward, always punching. Hearns was not backing down, but he was backing up. One of Hearns's jabs widened the cut on Hagler's forehead, and as blood came roaring down the champion's face, Steele signaled time-out and stepped in. He led Hagler back to his corner to be reexamined by Romeo.

"Can you see all right?" the physician asked over the screams of 15,088 outraged fans.

"No problem," said Hagler. "I ain't missing him, am I?"

Romeo again motioned to Steele that the fight could continue.

Deciding that he didn't want the outcome determined by anyone but himself, Hagler moved in, first firing a short left and then a smashing right to the side of Hearns's head. Dazed, the challenger floundered backward across the ring.

The pursuing Hagler unloaded a right and a left, and then leaped in with an overhand right that thundered against Hearns's head. On instinct alone, the challenger tried to clinch, but then he went down.

As Steele picked up the count, Hearns lay on his back, arms outstretched, eyes open but unseeing. With great will, Hearns rolled over and brought himself to his feet at the count of nine. But Steele, after studying the challenger's glazed eyes, wisely signaled a cease-fire. The time was 2:01 of the third round.

With blood still streaming down his face and onto his chest, Hagler leaped into the air at least $5.7 million richer. It was his 11th title defense, leaving him on track in his drive to surpass Carlos Monzon's middleweight record of 14.

Hearns had to be carried back to his corner, and it was several mintues before he could stand on his own two feet. Later, Hearns, who is still WBC junior middleweight champ and who stands to bank at least $5.4 million from the fight, went into Hagler's dressing room. "We made a lot of money, but we gave them a good show," Hearns said. "Tell you what. You move up and fight the light heavies, and I'll take care of the middleweights."

Hagler laughed. "You move up," he said.

After receiving four stitches for the cut in his forehead, Hagler went to a party in the Augustus Room at Caesars. He spoke briefly to the celebrators. Then, with his wife, Bertha, he watched a video of the fight. After seeing the knockout for the fourth time, Hagler smiled and applauded. He looked at his watch. It was midnight. "Let's go," he said to Bertha. His work was done.

Pete Hamill

Although he has earned acclaim as a novelist and screenwriter, Pete Hamill (b. 1935) is regarded as the quintessential New York newspaperman. A columnist for both the *Post* and the *Daily News*, the onetime high school dropout eventually became editor-in-chief of both papers, and his journalism has appeared in *The New York Times, Newsday*, and *The Village Voice*. This piece, written in November 1985 for the latter on the occasion of Cus D'Amato's death, echoes his introduction to journalism. Following service in the U.S. Navy, Hamill studied art on the GI Bill, and in 1958 was working as the art director of *Atlantis*, a Greek-language weekly. In the midst of laying out one edition, he suggested to editor Jimmy Vlasto that running a few stories in English might improve circulation, and the editor challenged him to try his own hand at writing one. Hamill chose to profile a promising Puerto Rican middleweight who trained under D'Amato at the nearby Gramercy Gym. Hamill was paid $25 for what was his first published story, and the occasion boded well for both subject and author. By the time José Torres won the world light-heavyweight title seven years later, his lifelong friend Hamill had become the lead columnist for the *Post*.

Up the Stairs with Cus D'Amato

IN those days, you had to pass a small candy stand to get to the door of the Gramercy Gym on East 14th Street. The door was heavy, with painted zinc nailed across its face and a misspelled sign saying "Gramacy Gym," and when you opened the door, you saw a long badly lit stairway climbing into darkness. There was another door on the landing, and a lot of tough New York kids would reach that landing and find themselves unable to open the second door. They'd go back down the stairs, try to look cool as they bought a soda at the candy stand, then hurry home. Many others opened the second door. And when they did, they entered the tough, hard, disciplined school of a man named Cus D'Amato.

"First thing I want to know about a kid," Cus said to me once, on some lost night in the '50s, "is whether he can open that door. Then when he walks in, I look at him, try to see what he's seeing. Most of them stand at the door. They see guys skipping rope, shadowboxing, hitting the bags. Most of all, they see guys in the ring. Fighting. And then they have to decide. Do they want this, or not? If they want it, they stay, they ask someone what they should do. Most of them are shy, for some reason. Almost all fighters. They whisper. You tell them to come back, and you'll see what can be done. They have to spend at least one night dealing with fear. If they come back the second time, then maybe you have a fighter."

I wasn't a fighter, but I came up those stairs almost every day in the late '50s and early '60s, and in some important ways I learned as much from Cus D'Amato as the fighters did. I was living then on 9th Street and Second Avenue, working nights at the *Post*, and I'd wake up around three in the afternoon and walk to 14th Street and hang out with the fighters. My friend José Torres was then the hottest young middleweight in the city and one of Cus D'Amato's fighters. He had lost by one point to Laszlo Papp in the finals of the '56 Olympics in Melbourne, and when he came to New York from Puerto Rico he placed his career in the hands of Cus.

"I didn't know anything about New York," he said. "I didn't know very much about boxing. Most of all, I didn't know anything about life. So I learned about everything then from Cus."

Cus, who died last week at seventy-seven after a long struggle with pneumonia, was one of the best teachers I ever met. He was a tough, intelligent man who was almost Victorian in his beliefs in work and self-denial and fierce concentration. For years he'd lived alone in the office of the gym, accompanied only by a huge boxer dog named Champ; there were books on the shelves (he loved the Civil War and essays on strategy and tactics and almost never read novels, although he admired W. C. Heinz's *The Professional*) and a gun somewhere and a small black-and-white TV set and a pay phone on the wall. After Floyd Patterson became champion in 1956, Cus took an apartment over a coffee shop on 53rd Street and Broadway and bought some elegantly tailored clothes and a homburg; but, talking to him, I always sensed that his idea of paradise was that room and the cot in the office of the Gramercy Gym.

"You can't want too many things," he said to me one wintry evening, after the fighters had gone, the speed bags were stilled, and we stood at the large gym windows while snow fell into 14th Street. "The beginning of corruption is wanting things. You want a car or a fancy house or a piano, and the next thing you know, you're doing things you didn't want to do, just to get the *things*. I guess maybe that's why I never got married. It wasn't that I didn't like women. They're nice. It's nice. It's that women want *things*, and if I want the woman, then I have to want the things she wants. Hey, I don't want a new refrigerator, or a big TV, or a new couch. . . ."

Cus wanted his fighters to be champions, to have money and glory, but he truly didn't seem to want much for himself. Once a bum made his way to the Gramercy from the White Rose bar across the street; Cus gave him a dollar, the next day five bums showed up, and the day after that, almost forty. The fighters laughed, as Cus dispensed singles, and then Cus said, "That's it, that's all. You want to come back here, bring trunks!" He was a sucker for old fighters. Once when Cus had the shorts (he had to declare bankruptcy in 1971) Ezzard Charles came around to see him; the great light-heavyweight and former heavyweight champion was a broken man, confined to a wheelchair; he needed a thousand, and Cus borrowed the money, gave it to the old champion, and never heard from Charles again. When Patterson won the championship by knocking out Archie Moore on November 30, 1956, Cus used his share of the purse to make Floyd an elaborate $35,000 jewel-encrusted crown; a few years later, Patterson wouldn't even talk to Cus. Cus once quoted Gene Fowler to me: "Money is something to throw off the back of trains."

He loved style in fighters and in writers, too. His favorite sports writers were Jimmy Cannon, Dick Young, and Dan Parker, all of whom took shots at him in print from time to time ("I don't mind, they gotta job to do and I'm not perfect"), but he also said that the sports writer who moved him most consistently was the elegant Frank Graham of the *Journal-American*. Later, when Torres became friends with Norman Mailer, Cus started to read his work, as if inspecting it for signs of moral decay. "The guy is really good, isn't he? He's like a Robinson, he can box, he can punch. . . ."

He cherished great fighters—Ray Robinson, Joe Louis, Muhammad Ali, Sandy Saddler, Willie Pep, Tommy Loughran—but sometimes, late at night, sitting over coffee, he'd talk about the fighter that didn't exist: the perfect fighter, the masterpiece. "The ideal fighter has heart, skill, movement, intelligence, creativity. You can have everything, but if you can't make it up while you're in there, you can't be great. A lot of guys have the mechanics and no heart; lots of guys have heart, no mechanics; the thing that puts it together, it's mysterious, it's like making a work of art, you bring everything to it, you make it up when you're doing it."

Toward the end, he thought perhaps that he had the perfect heavyweight at last in young Michael Tyson, who has now knocked out all nine of his professional opponents, six in the first round. "He's strong, he's brave, he's in condition, and most of all, he's got that other thing, the mysterious thing," Cus said, the last time I saw him. "I have no doubt he'll be a champion. But more than that, he might be a great fighter."

There were a lot of good fighters at the Gramercy in the late '50s: Joe Shaw, a fierce-punching 140-pounder; light-heavyweight Jim Boyd, who'd won the gold medal in Melbourne; two more light-heavyweights named Sylvester Banks and Paul Wright; a wonderful southpaw featherweight named Floyd Smith; and some fine amateurs ranging from bantamweight Georgie Colon to light-heavyweight Simon Ramos. But as Cus became more involved managing Patterson and Torres, the day-to-day training was left to Joe Fariello (now educating Mark Breland). Cus was away at camp with Patterson; he was up at Stillman's with Torres to find experienced professionals for sparring partners. And during the same period, Cus was waging his wars with both the International Boxing Club and Madison Square Garden. Some people thought he grew increasingly paranoid.

"If this goes down instead of up," he said to me one day as we stepped in the elevator in a midtown office building, "we're in trouble."

He laughed, but Cus meant it, too. The Mob was all over boxing when Cus brought his first good fighters out of the Gramercy Gym. The hoodlums cut into fighters, arranged tank jobs, fixed judges. Frankie Carbo was called the underworld's commissioner of boxing, a vicious punk who lived off other men's sweat and controlled a number of managers. Carbo was friendly, sort of, with Jim Norris, a rich bum with a hoodlum complex who ran the IBC out of the old Garden on Eighth Avenue and 50th Street. There's no room here to relate the details of Cus D'Amato's sustained contest with Norris, Carbo, and the Garden. Certainly he was on the moral high ground, but the terrible thing was that his personal crusade also hurt his fighters.

We'll never know how good Patterson and Torres might have become if they'd been fighting more often, battling those fighters who were controlled by the IBC and the Garden. Certainly Torres would have made more money. I remember one main event he had to take in Boston when he was still a hot fighter in New York. The total purse came to $28.35. Joe Fariello said, "Joe, you take the $20, I'll take the $8, and we'll send the 35¢ to Cus." Patterson did get rich, and Torres did become champion years later than he should have, and in the wrong division (he was one of the greatest middleweights I ever saw, but had to settle for the light-heavyweight championship in 1965). But the competitive fire of Shaw withered from lack of action; the others drifted away.

"It breaks my heart sometimes, thinking about those kids not fighting," he said to me once. "But I don't see any other way."

That was the problem. From 1959 on, Cus never worked a corner for any of his fighters; he didn't even hold a manager's license, as a result of the botched promotion of the 1959 Patterson–Johansson fight, when it appeared (but was never proved) that Cus helped bring Fat Tony Salerno in as a money man. The fighters did their best, and for some fights Cus would come to camp, work with them, talk strategy and tactics. But Patterson broke with him, and Torres was forced to go with another manager (Cain Young) to get his chance at a title. Around the time Torres retired, Cus moved upstate, far from the gyms of the city. "I like it up there," he said once. "I like the clear skies, the lake, where I go fishing. It's beautiful. Beautiful." Did he miss the gym on 14th Street? "Yeah," he said. "Sometimes. . . ."

The last time I saw him was almost exactly a year ago, on the 57th floor of the World Trade Center. We were there to watch Torres be sworn in as chairman of the New York State Athletic Commission, the first professional fighter and the first Puerto Rican ever to hold the job. "I'm so proud of José, I can't explain it," Cus said. We talked about Tyson and other things. And then I asked him if he'd ever gone back to the Gramercy Gym since he sold it in the '70s. "No," he said, and looked up at José, who was standing with Mario Cuomo at the front of the room. "No, I don't like to look back."

And so I did the looking back, sitting in the packed, brightly lit conference room, remembering Cus talking to me when I was 20 about the uses of fear, the meaning of courage, the need to concentrate energy and purpose in all things, and how I'd tried and failed so often to follow his lessons. I'd modeled a character on Cus in one of my novels, and he'd liked the book but objected when he saw the TV movie; on the screen, John Cassavetes stood on a ring apron talking to a fighter and smoking a cigarette. "What manager would *do* that? What kind of *example* would he be showing to a kid?" I remembered that conversation, and after José was sworn in, I turned to Cus and said, "Listen, Cus, I want to thank you for everything." He squinted suspiciously at me. "What do you mean?" he said, and I said, "For letting me climb the stairs."

He nodded, turned away, and said, "You goddamned writers."

I'm sorry I never got to explain.

Pete Dexter

One night in 1981, when he was a city columnist for the *Philadelphia Daily News*, Pete Dexter (b. 1943) walked into a bar that he might not have made it out of alive if a heavyweight fighter named Randall "Tex" Cobb hadn't been there to save him. Dexter had written about a drug death in the neighborhood and the bar's denizens didn't appreciate it. They showed up to greet him bearing weapons. "Pete," said Cobb, "I hope that's the softball team." It wasn't.

When Dexter recovered from the near-fatal beating he received, he had no more taste for alcohol and a lot more time to write. He has since produced seven novels, most notably *Paris Trout* (1988), which won the National Book Award and established him as one of his generation's premier fiction writers. His latest novel, *Spooner* (2009), is as tender and comedic as the others are dark and haunting, but a streak of humanity runs through them all, just as it does in the following essay, first published in 1985 and collected in Dexter's *Paper Trails* (2007). There is something profoundly ethical, even noble, about the father and son at the heart of it. If anybody could find such men in boxing, it was Dexter.

---

from

Paper Trails

THE first day the fighter came into the gym he went two rounds with a weight lifter from New Jersey who was just learning to keep his hands up—and he tried to hurt him.

I didn't know if it was something between them or if the fighter just had a mean streak. Some of them do. Whatever it was, the fighter went after him, turning his weight into his punches, missing some, but dropping enough right hands in so that at the end of the two rounds the whole left side of the weight lifter—without ever having been hit perfect—was blotted pink. It's an honest gym, and what happened wasn't particularly violent, but it was out of place.

I was sitting by the windows with Mickey Rosati at the time, and his son, little Mick.

The two of them are with each other all day. They work together in their garage downstairs, they run together, they box each other two or three times a week. The kid is a world-class amateur. They know each other inside out—moves and moods—and I've never heard a hard word between them. You get the feeling sometimes that they're the same person, spaced about thirty years apart.

Up in the ring, the weight lifter was getting packed into the corner like one shirt too many in a hamper. "What's that about?" I said.

Mickey shook his head. "They're both from Jersey," he said. "Maybe they got on each other's nerves."

The weight lifter had a brother named Dennis. He was fourteen years older—closing in on forty—and two or three times a week the two of them came over the bridge from New Jersey to work out.

The gym sits on a narrow street in South Philadelphia where people park on the sidewalks and sneakers hang from the telephone wires. Inside, it's honest and clean; at least, for a gym it's clean. We are not speaking here of Nautilus-center clean, but people have been known to hit the bucket when they spit, and when Mickey's hawk—which is another story—used the ring for a bathroom one afternoon, the spot was scoured with Lysol before anybody fought again. That might not sound like much, but in most gyms, hawk shit will petrify before anybody cleans it up.

The weight lifter liked to box when he could; Dennis wasn't as serious. He slapped at the heavy bags or shadow-boxed, and once in a while he mentioned that he ought to be getting paid for his entertainment value, which was probably true. If it came into his head, Dennis said it.

During the month or two Dennis and his brother had been coming up, Mickey had spent some time in the ring with the brother, getting him used to the feel of soft punches, showing him how to relax.

At the start, the brother had gone home depressed. Dennis reported it while Mickey was doing sit-ups on an elevated board, his teeth biting a cold cigar. "My brother's got guys terrified of him in Jersey," Dennis said. "He can't believe somebody as old as you could do that to him. All weekend long he's messed up."

Mickey lay back on the board and closed his eyes. "Suddenly," he said, the cigar moving in his teeth, "I don't feel like doing sit-ups no more."

As a step in the mending, Dennis and his brother decided Mickey probably wasn't human; at least they had no idea he could be beaten or hurt. They called him the Punching Machine.

You could see how they might think that. Mickey Rosati is fifty-one years old and left-handed, and he can still fight. But he is fifty-one years old. His shoulders hurt him after he works out, he gets poison ivy just looking at the woods, and the speed he had when he won twenty-two straight fights back in the fifties isn't there like it was. On brains and shape, he would still beat most of the four- and six-round fighters at his weight in the world, but he pays more to stay that way than anybody who isn't around him could know.

The fighter from Jersey was back two weeks later. He came in with Dennis. Mickey was sitting in a chair, holding a cold cigar in his teeth, trying not to scratch his arms. He was just back from the Pocono Mountains, poison-ivyed half to death. He'd gone there for squirrels. Mickey has been hunting since he was seven years old—ever since he went after stray cats in the alleys of South Philadelphia with a baseball bat. As he gets older, though, he gets gentler, and cares less about the shooting and more about just being outside. This weekend, as a matter of fact, he'd left his gun in the cabin.

"This same path, I must've walked it a hundred times," he said. "But this time, I was just walking along, and you know, there's apples in all those trees. Millions of them. I been through there a hundred times, and I never saw the apples before . . ."

Dennis bent over him then. "Hey, Mick, I told this guy you'd give him two or three rounds," he said.

Mickey looked at Dennis, then at the fighter, putting together what was doing. "All right," he said. Mickey will always give you the benefit of the doubt; he will always give you his time.

The fighter dressed and wrapped his hands and then got laced into a pair of black gloves. He loosened up five or ten minutes, then fit his mouthpiece over his teeth and climbed into the ring.

Mickey slipped his unwrapped hands into an old pair of pull-on gloves and got in with him. He doesn't use a mouthpiece or headgear. He was giving away twenty-five pounds, and twenty-five years. "Three rounds?" he said.

The fighter said, "I don't know if I'm even in shape to finish one." Mickey has been around gyms all his life and knew better than that.

The bell rang and the fighter came straight at him, throwing right hands and hooks, trying to hurt him. Little Mickey sat down a yard from the ropes and watched.

Mickey took the punches on his arms and gloves and shoulders, moving in and out, relaxed. A minute into the round, he threw a long, slow right hook at the fighter's head, which the fighter blocked, and a short left under his ribs. Which he never saw.

The punch stopped the fighter cold. For two or three seconds he couldn't breathe, he couldn't move his hands. In those seconds, Mickey could have ended it and gone back to his chair and let him go. And when the fighter could breathe again, he began to find Mickey with some of the right hands.

The gym was quiet, except for the sounds of the ring itself. Mickey and the fighter seemed even for a round and a half, but somewhere in it the fighter got stronger. He used his elbows and shoulders; Mickey gave ground and landed some hooks to the side, but his punches didn't have much on them.

Between rounds Mickey walked in circles, breathing through his teeth, looking at the floor. I thought about being fifty-one years old, working all day pulling transmissions and engines, and then coming upstairs with bad shoulders and poison ivy and having to fight life and death with some kid who didn't even know who you were.

The third round started, and the fighter, if anything, was throwing harder now. Mickey let the punches hit his arms and sides and glance off his head, moving in the direction they pushed him. One of them scraped some skin off his eyebrow.

The fighter followed him, forgetting what had happened to him in the first round, forgetting that Mickey hadn't hurt him when he was helpless. And then I heard little Mickey say, "He's got him now." I looked down at him to see how he knew that, and by the time I looked back up, Mickey was hitting the fighter with twelve clean punches in a row.

For the last minute and a half of the fight, Mickey hit him with everything he threw. When the fighter tried to come back at him, it opened him up for something else.

At the end, he had stopped fighting and was leaning against the ropes covering up. Mickey patted the fighter on the head, climbed out of the ring, and worked two hard rounds on the heavy bag, jumped rope, and then put a cigar between his teeth and did sit-ups, looking happier all the time.

I said to his son, "He shouldn't have to do that."

Little Mickey said, "Yeah, but you know my father. He liked the challenge, having to do it . . ."

I looked around the gym—a clean, honest room with enough windows so you could feel the street—and as nice as it was, that's what it was for. Having to do it. Not every day or every week, but if you're going to box, then once in a while it's going to happen.

And Mickey doesn't own the place by accident. Now and then you've got to let the dog out of the house to run.

Driving home from the gym that night, I told him I wouldn't have patted the fighter on the head, no matter how grateful I was that he tried to kill me.

Mickey said, "Yeah, I should have bit him." His mood was getting better and better. He looked down at his arms, though, touched his neck where the poison ivy was. "Five days," he said, "before it goes away. I lie in bed at night, thinking about scratching it or not."

"That long?"

"The doctor said they got some kind of shot, it gives you the worse case you ever got, and then you don't get it anymore. You can't take the shot when you already got poison ivy, though. You got to be cured, and then they can give it to you, and then they can cure you. Probably."

He shook his head. "There's nothing you can do about poison ivy," he said, "but stay out of the way."

He dabbed at the scrape over his eye. "And what good is that?"

Thomas Hauser

Thomas Hauser's breakthrough into boxing came with *The Black Lights* (1986), his stunning tour de force that unmasked the inner workings of the sport. A lawyer by training, Hauser (b. 1946) had written the bestselling *The Execution of Charles Horman* (1978; later released as *Missing*) and a dozen other books when he was granted permission to work as an embedded journalist in the training camp of WBC junior welterweight champion Billy Costello as the fighter prepared for a title defense. When the promoter attempted to pull off a last-minute bait-and-switch, Hauser had a ringside seat for the extraordinary events described in this account, which *The New York Times* called "a tense showdown between Don King and Mike Jones that is more gripping than anything in the ring." *The Black Lights* turned out to be the beginning of an enduring affinity for boxing. Hauser has since written several books about the sport, including *Muhammad Ali: His Life and Times* (1991), widely considered the definitive biography of its subject.

---

from

The Black Lights

THE room looked as though it had been furnished by Hollywood central casting. Red carpet, plush leather sofas, a formica desk and glass-topped conference table with two huge American flags standing in the background. The wall opposite the door was primarily windows. An adjacent wall bore sixty plaques awarded to King by various civic and boxing organizations. Opposite that was a fully mirrored wall. Three color televisions stood on a wall unit to one side of the door. A fully stocked bar was on the other. The ceiling was also mirrored. Only one autographed photograph graced the walls—a picture of two men with the inscription, "To Don King, Best wishes, Hugh Hefner." Behind the desk, at floor level so they weren't visible from most parts of the room, six television screens attached to closed-circuit cameras monitored the rest of the townhouse.

Don King was seated at the desk, dressed in brown slacks, a white shirt with faint brown stripes, and a brown silk tie. His face looked tired. Rumor had it that the promoter was suffering from diabetes and high blood pressure. And perhaps more troubling, he was the target of an ongoing investigation by the Organized Crime Task Force of the United States Attorney's Office for the Southern District of New York. In public King joked about the situation. "Investigation is my middle name," he said. "My plight is to be investigated from the day I was born until the day I die." But in private King was far less flippant about the matter. Indeed, in a recent civil lawsuit he had refused to answer questions other than his name and address, and had taken the Fifth Amendment 364 times.*

As Mike and Clancy entered, Don King looked up from his desk. "What a life," he muttered. "Once I was poor and hungry. Now I got money to spend and no time to eat." Then, he gestured toward Mike. "Gil, I just can't believe this guy. Nine months ago Mike Jones was chasing me all over the country, begging to fight Bruce Curry for twenty-five thousand dollars. Now I'm chasing him, begging him to take a hundred and fifty thousand."

"I know how you feel," Mike said, "but I have to go by my instincts. Billy just isn't prepared for Mamby."

"Hell, Mamby ain't prepared for Costello. If your man turns this fight down, people be talking about him the same way they talk about Gerry Cooney. Costello will never live it down. They'll say he don't fight nobody."

"Styles make fights."

"Yeah, Mike, I know. But the way you work, you always find problems with styles. This opponent's too fat. This one's too slow. This one's too tall. This one's too wiry. Hell, when you say the words 'world champion' that means you fight everybody. If your man don't fight this thirty-seven-year-old opponent, he should retire."

*On December 13, 1984, six weeks after his October 29 meeting with Mike Jones and Gil Clancy, King and an aide were indicted by a federal grand jury on twenty-three counts of income tax evasion, filing false and fraudulent income tax returns, and conspiracy with regard to the concealment of over $1 million in unreported income. [*King was acquitted but the aide was convicted of the tax-fraud charges—ed.*]

Don King was warming up. His words were coming incredibly fast, yet each one was rich and resonant, enunciated with the ring of a carnival barker.

"Mike," Clancy interrupted. "You're depriving Billy of his right to become a great fighter. And you're depriving him of a pretty good payday too."

"But he'll still be champion."

"A diminished champion."

"Mike," King said, picking up the assault. "I hate to see you make this mistake. I got too much respect and admiration for you. Up until now, Billy Costello has been a worthy champion, but if you turn this fight down he'll no longer be worthy. A coward dies a thousand deaths; a brave man dies but once."

Don King was known for pulling out all the stops to get what he wanted. In 1977 George Foreman had retired from boxing to preach the Gospel for a small church in Texas. With the heavyweight ranks growing thin, one day Foreman received a breathless telephone call from Don King.

"George, I just had this vision."

"What did you see, Don?"

"It was like a dream, George. It looked like Mr. Hayward Moore [a friend of Foreman's who had just died]. He was leading you and me together, and you were back in boxing, entering the ring with a cross on your robe and trunks."

"Don," Foreman had answered. "You don't put the cross on your robe. You put it on your heart."

Now Don King was putting the pressure on Mike. Clancy's loyalty was to CBS. King, obviously, was concerned with his own interests. Mike's job was to protect Billy. At six o'clock he excused himself and telephoned Victor at Gleason's Gym. Once again Victor said "no" to Mamby. When Mike returned, King was on the telephone. "Just a minute," the promoter said. "Here he is." Then he handed the receiver to Mike.

The voice at the other end belonged to Jose Sulaiman.

"Mike, I do not understand why you will not fight Saoul Mamby. For the good of boxing, I urge you to accept this fight."

The screws were being tightened.

"Jose, I just don't think it's the right fight for my fighter."

Don King picked up on another receiver. "Jose, this man is hurting boxing. And I love boxing."

Mike wouldn't budge. Finally King changed the subject for a moment, telling Sulaiman that he had received the tape of an interview aired recently on CNN in which he'd effusively praised the WBC president. Sulaiman expressed interest in hearing the tape, and King called his stepson Carl into the room, instructing him to hold the telephone receiver to a television set while the entire interview was played. Partway through the tape, which lasted thirty minutes, another King aide came into the room with a tape of Mamby's 1983 loss to Ronnie Shields. Again Mike retired to the second-floor video room. Mamby looked less impressive than on the earlier tape. His legs seemed weak. After three rounds, Mike picked up the telephone, and called Victor.

"Victor, come over to 32 East 69th Street. I want you to look at a tape with me."

Victor replied that he was in the middle of training Gerry Cooney, and would need at least an hour to get there. Mike told King and Clancy that he was going across the street to the Westbury Hotel for a drink. When he returned, Victor still hadn't arrived. Meanwhile King's staff had unearthed a tape of Mamby's most recent fight, against Kevin Austin the preceding July. Mike watched it. Mamby's legs looked strong again.

Victor arrived at 6:45 P.M., and Mike took him out onto the street where they could talk without fear of eavesdropping devices.

"How did Billy look today in the gym?"

"Very good. He boxed four rounds with Bruce Williams, and won all of them."

"Billy could be the first person ever to knock out Mamby."

"Mike, I don't like the style for Billy; not on short notice. To fight Mamby there's too many things Billy has got to do different."

"The pressure is on. CBS, Don King, the WBC—they're all pressing."

"But none of them care about Billy."

At seven o'clock, King and Clancy went across the street for a beer at a bar called Confetti's. When they returned, Mike and Victor were on the second floor watching a tape of Shields versus Mamby. Clancy telephoned CBS for a status report. The network had decided if necessary to substitute Mark Holmes versus Odell Hadley, and broadcast it with Garza–Meza from Las Vegas.

At seven-thirty Mike reentered Don King's office. Everybody was tired.

There was an ugly edge to King's voice. "Are you ready to fight?"

"I've watched the tapes," Mike answered. "I've consulted again with Victor. We don't want this fight. Billy signed to fight Leroy Haley, not Saoul Mamby. We want to fight. We'll fight all the big names—Pryor, Mancini, Hatcher, Oliva—but not Mamby. That's it."

"Who do you think you are, motherfucker?"

"Pardon?"

"Who do you think you are, motherfucker? You can pull that shit with Gerry Cooney because he's big and he's white, but not with Billy Costello, man. Not with Costello."

"Look, Don—"

"You're a liar, man. You know that." King's voice was rising. "Nine months ago you was begging me for a shot at Curry. You was crawling and begging and you said, 'Give us a chance at Curry and we'll fight anybody after that.' Well, you're a fucking chickenshit coward, and your fighter is too."

"Don, there's a lot of brave managers out there who don't do what's best for their fighters."

A Shakespearean rage was building. "Fuck you, man. Fuck you. You don't care shit about your fighter. You're just playing ego games, sucking the blood out of your fighter's heart. You're gonna be a fat rich white boy living out on Long Island, and your fighter will be hungry. If you think Billy Costello is fighting for me again after this, man, give it up."

"Don, if that's the way you feel, release us from the options, and we'll find someone else to promote Billy."

In one motion, Don King picked the telephone off his desk and slammed it down. Papers flew. The receiver spun off and twisted wildly, dangling in midair.

"You ain't worried about your fighter looking bad," King shrieked. "You're worried about losing. You're a coward, man, and your fighter is too; a chickenshit coward."

"Billy Costello's not afraid of anybody."

"Fuck you, man. Fuck you. Get out of my office. Don't want to see you again. But I'll get you, motherfucker. It's just a matter of time, that's all. It's just a matter of time."

The weather outside was unseasonably warm for the end of September. Mike walked the twelve blocks to the Park Lane Hotel, and took the elevator to 3814. Billy was dressed in a plaid shirt and jeans. The room looked out over southern Manhattan.

For several minutes Mike recounted what had happened. "Maybe I was wrong," he said at the finish. "I don't know. I did what I thought was best for you."

Billy sat silently, the emotions of the moment written on his face.

"Are you disappointed?"

"Yeah, but you're the manager. You make the deals. All I do is fight."

"You're still champ."

"It don't feel like it."

The two men talked for another twenty minutes. Then Mike rose to leave.

"Hey, Mike," Billy said softly. "You know something. It's all bullshit."

That night shortly before midnight, the telephone rang in Room 3814 of the Park Lane Hotel. Billy Costello reached across the bed, past the ornate headboard covered with silk damask, and picked up the receiver.

"Billy, this is Mike. I'd like you to do a favor for me."

"What is it?"

"This Saturday I want you to go up to Kingston and kick Saoul Mamby's ass."

Bill Barich

In the nearly half-century since A. J. Liebling made his last appearance at ringside, one writer after another has been nominated as the great man's spiritual heir. Bill Barich (b. 1943) can lay claim to actual lineal succession. As Barich recalled in his foreword to Liebling's posthumous boxing collection *A Neutral Corner*, the *New Yorker*'s legendary editor, William Shawn, "had a severe distaste for boxing, and after [Liebling's] death all coverage of boxing vanished from the magazine for over three decades." In 1985 Shawn did green-light Barich's proposed story on the Ray "Boom-Boom" Mancini–Livingston Bramble fight in Reno, which the editor envisioned as a cautionary tale that would incorporate an American Medical Association study on the cumulative effect of concussive blows. "My story was then assigned to a science editor, who had very little interest in boxing," Barich said, "and of course in the end Shawn never could bring himself to run it." Barich eventually found a home for his orphaned story, "Never Say Never," at the *Missouri Review* in 1986 and, better yet, wrote many of the boxing stories that appeared in the post-Shawn *New Yorker*.

Never Say Never: Ray Mancini's Last Fight

O N a cold winter morning in Youngstown, Ohio, Ray (Boom Boom) Mancini, who had once been the lightweight champion of the World Boxing Association, said goodbye to his mother and father and left home for Nevada to begin training for the most important fight of his career. His final training camp was at the El Dorado Hotel, in downtown Reno, and when he arrived there he found large cardboard cutouts of himself propped against slot machines in the casino. There were banners that said "Welcome, Boom Boom!" and "The El Dorado Welcomes Ray Mancini!," and several gamblers in polyester gathered around to wish him luck. Mancini was used to such treatment. In boxing circles, he had always been a big star, and he knew how to smile and make small talk, and also how to accept a handshake without doing any damage to the instruments that had helped him to earn almost six million dollars in purse money.

Mancini had an executive suite of rooms in the El Dorado, closed off from public view. Like most veteran boxers, he despised the discipline and routine of getting into shape, so he was glad to be meeting a boxer for whom he had a genuine dislike—Livingstone Bramble, a complex and worldly-wise Rastafarian from the Virgin Islands. Bramble had taken Mancini's title away in Buffalo, New York, in June of 1984. Mancini had not been himself that night. He'd felt sick and out of sorts, as if he were coming down with the flu. He thought that Bramble had proved to be an unworthy champion. This had less to do with Bramble's talent than with his comportment. He had insulted the Mancini family and had done stupid things, like messing around with voodoo and boxing with a chicken. These antics had grated against Mancini's own love of the fight game, his respect for its rituals and institutions, and had increased his desire for revenge.

He did his roadwork in the high desert country, running along paths that skirted the base of snowcapped mountains. He skipped rope, tossed around a medicine ball, and kept tabs on his weight. Almost every afternoon, he sparred with his sparring partners in a full-sized ring at the El Dorado. He was a compactly built man, thickly muscled. He had a broken nose and a scarred face, but he still dreamed of becoming an actor someday. Among his friends he counted Playboy bunnies and movie stars. He knew Mickey Rourke and Sly Stallone. He knew Frankie Avalon well, and Avalon had told him that whenever you do a film you leave a chunk of your life behind. That made sense to Mancini. He was twenty-three years old, and his brief and sometimes tragic time in the ring was drawing to a close.

Mancini started his career as a pro by fighting in and around Youngstown. He told local reporters that he was dedicating himself to winning a lightweight title in honor of his father, Lenny, the original Boom Boom, who had been a contender himself until he was wounded on a French battlefield during the Second World War. This made for good copy, and Mancini soon picked up a canny, ambitious manager, David Wolf, a former sportswriter who knew the value of a property. With Wolf guiding him, steering him away from potentially dangerous opponents, Mancini followed a cautious path to the top, and in May, 1982, after a vicious loss to Alexis Arguello, he beat a shopworn fighter, Arturo Frias, to become the W.B.A. champ.

Mancini was still handsome and relatively unmarked when he knocked out Frias, and his good-natured personality had made him very popular with fans. He was white, Italian, and eminently marketable. The television networks loved him because he had crossover appeal and attracted both men and women. Mancini had never been a stylish boxer; there was little art to his hooks or jabs. He had won twenty-three of his twenty-four pro bouts simply by giving better than he got, by being more courageous and intense than his opponents. The only drawback to his flailing approach was that it had cost him dearly. In swarming over other fighters, he'd left himself open to blows, and he'd been hit more often, and with better shots, than less aggressive men.

He had his first title defense in November, 1983, against the South Korean boxer Duk Koo Kim, in a match that CBS televised. There were more qualified fighters around, but Mancini was kept clear of them. Duk Koo Kim was a mystery man. Though the W.B.A. ranked him first in the lightweight division, he had never fought in the United States, and he spoke no English. Apparently, he saw himself as a warrior going into battle, defending the flag of his nation. On a lampshade in his motel room he scrawled "Kill or be killed." In the ring, he turned out to be a fierce but unskilled brawler, and he lasted through thirteen brutal rounds before Mancini dropped him. Duk Koo Kim did not get up again, nor did he ever regain consciousness. He died of a cerebral hemorrhage in a Las Vegas hospital, and his mother donated his vital organs to science. A month later, she killed herself by drinking poison.

In boxing, there is an ample history of accidental death, but Mancini is a sensitive man, and the fight left him devastated. A devout Catholic, he spent months consulting his family and his parish priest before deciding to go on. He acquitted himself fairly well in four subsequent bouts, including a promotion held in Italy, but then he came up against Livingstone Bramble, who—unlike Mancini—had risen through the ranks without a management team to help him. Mancini was a heavy favorite to win the fight, but Bramble surprised him. He is a wicked counterpuncher, and he sliced through Mancini's attack and took him apart. Mancini bled so badly from cuts around his eyes that the bout had to be stopped in the fourteenth round. He spent the night in a Buffalo hospital, under observation. He had lacerations in both eyelids. One took eight stitches to close; the other took six.

Mancini had received such a beating that boxing insiders were concerned about his health. Bob Arum, a promoter who had worked with him, stated publicly that Ray should retire, and some other people agreed. Mancini was rich and famous, and since he had achieved his goal, he seemed to have no real reason to go on. He just wasn't giving as good as he got anymore. The Home Box Office network had done a computer analysis of the Bramble fight which showed that Mancini had thrown an amazing fourteen hundred and eight punches—more than a hundred per round. But he had landed only three hundred and thirty-eight, or twenty-four per cent. Bramble had landed fifty-three per cent of his punches. In spite of such evidence, Mancini pushed for a rematch. The truth was that he didn't like being a loser. Already his market value had begun to decline. A publishing company had shelved his autobiography, and a magazine had cancelled its plans for a feature.

The idea of a rematch was fine with Bramble and his manager, Lou Duva. Mancini still had drawing power, and he would insure that the fight would be sold to television. (Without the money and legitimacy that television grants, boxing would not survive as a major sport.) Bramble, on his own, held no interest for the networks. He had no fans, except among reggae lovers and people from the islands, and advertisers would find it hard to be enthusiastic about a worshipper of Haile Selassie who wore his hair in dreadlocks and spoke of himself as one of the world's oppressed. Also, Bramble's boxing style was too subtle for the medium. He was a defensive fighter, calculating and intelligent, and he seldom got into trouble. In order to appreciate him, a viewer had to understand boxing as a sport, not spectacle. On the other hand, Mancini worked in broad strokes. Action was his metier, and his walloping delivery was perfect for an audience that was used to watching car crashes and cops chasing junkies through the streets of Miami.

Once Mancini had announced his intention, he had to be accommodated in certain ways. According to a W.B.A. rule, a rematch cannot be sanctioned unless each boxer has fought somebody else in the interim—this prevents a boxer from taking a dive in exchange for a guaranteed rematch. Bramble had fought Edwin Curet; the rule was waived for Mancini. In the W.B.A. rankings, Mancini was only third, so Tyrone Crawley, the No. 1 contender, had to be paid off to step aside. Crawley got a hundred and fifty thousand dollars and a contract to fight the winner. To resolve questions about Mancini's condition, Dave Wolf mailed around a packet of letters from private physicians which described the positive results of many tests. In the summer of 1984, Mancini had a CAT scan, and Dr. Jeffrey Schwartz, a Manhattan orthopedic surgeon who was his chief medical adviser, found no subtle changes or irregularities in his brain tissue.

But Dr. Schwartz was concerned about the delicate skin around Mancini's eyes. The skin was so tender that Mancini suffered subcutaneous cuts whenever he did any sparring; then, by the time an actual fight rolled around, the cuts were primed to burst to the surface, as they had done in Buffalo. Dr. Schwartz advised Mancini to wear a protective mask while he was training, but Mancini was reluctant to do so, fearing that his fans and the media would see it as a sign of weakness.

A W.B.A. site-selection committee chose Reno for the fight. More and more championships are being held in Nevada, because casino owners are willing to contribute toward the site-selection fees that the W.B.A. demands. Reno city fathers estimated that five million dollars in ancillary profits would spill over to local businesses, much of it in gambling action. After some negotiations, Dan Duva, Lou Duva's son, signed on to promote the rematch through his company, Main Events. He shopped around the live-broadcast rights and sold them to HBO for more than a million dollars. CBS bought the right to show a videotape no sooner than a week after the fight. That put the promotion into the black, and Duva paid each fighter about three-quarters of a million dollars. It was unusual for a challenger to get as much as a champ, but boxing is a sport in which almost no point of reference is absolute.

A big-money fight always energizes a gambling town, so Reno was happy to play host to Ray Mancini. His fans began to fly in a few days before the bout and took advantage of package deals at various casinos. There were hometown boys from Ohio, high rollers in spring pastels, blond women in clingy, off-brand jeans; and almost every day they convened at the El Dorado to watch their boy sweat. Both Mancini and his trainer, a fierce-looking man named Murphy Griffith, whose shaved head most often reposed inside a New York Yankees cap, felt that he'd overtrained for the first match with Bramble, losing his edge in the gym, and they were monitoring his progress closely, trying to get him to peak at the right moment. The fans were banking on this, betting heavily on Mancini even though he was a three-to-one underdog, and they offered enthusiastic support.

"Boom Boom!" they shouted. Or, more pointedly, "Whip the freak!"

The last press conference before the fight took place on a balmy afternoon in mid-February, 1985. Mancini arrived a few minutes before Bramble. Dressed casually, with his longish black hair combed back in an airy pompadour, he strolled in with some other young man of approximately the same size. They looked like members of a boxing club, clean-cut kids from the suburbs. The press-kit photos of Mancini all dated from the Frias bout, so it was disconcerting to see how much his face had changed since then. He wasn't unmarked anymore. His nose was broader, more splayed, and the skin was stretched tight over his cheekbones, as if it had no give left in it. Around his eyes, the flesh was pearly and shone under the lights. Only his charm was still intact. He was warm, open, and modest, and around him there gathered a palpable glow. When he smiled, his eyes flashed in their abused sockets, and the joy he took in his trade was manifest. He was glad to be a boxer, willing to accept the grueling dictates of the game, and the press respected him for that and acted as if he, not Bramble, were the champ.

"You going to retire after this one, Ray?" somebody asked.

"I don't make predictions," Mancini said.

Livingstone Bramble entered the room and sat at the other end of the table, playing a street tough to hype the fight. He understood the age-old ring drama of white against black, good against evil, and he handled the villain's role with finesse. In his sunglasses and his Bramble brim, a flat, multicolored pancake of a hat, he brooded on cue and pretended to cast a juju spell on his opponent. He gave Mancini a ceramic skull made in Taiwan, and then, from a little sack, he brought out a voodoo doll and stuck pins in it. "Your eyes jumping around yet, Ray?" he asked. "I told you I'd do anything to win." Bramble seemed to have no sense that he had crossed over an invisible border into the land of bad taste. Nobody knew what to make of him, not even his manager. He had a capacity for reinventing himself, baffling the white folks with his jive.

Bramble had been invited to train at the M-G-M Grand Hotel, a monolith out in the desert that had once burned up in a fire, dealing many gamblers the ultimate bad hand, and he was driving the security force crazy. He walked through the casino at all hours with a pet boa constrictor draped around his neck, enjoying the fact that he was pulling off a stunt that no other black dude was ever likely to duplicate. The M-G-M lion, caged on a lower level of the hotel, caught a whiff of the snake one night and reverted to jungle genotype, roaring and snorting, but that was no skin off Bramble's back. He knew that his championship was provisional, and he took a carpe diem attitude toward it, enjoying himself while he could.

Bramble seemed relaxed around the Grand, but he had some secret worries. As an amateur, he'd never won a rematch, and he thought he might be the one who was cursed. He was angry at Dave Wolf, because Wolf kept insinuating that Bramble and his entourage (sunglasses, Bramble brims, black satin warm-up jackets) were using drugs. Lou Duva was also steamed about the accusation, and he had charged in return that Mancini's corner was much more likely to use an illegal substance—Monsole's solution, a banned medication that quickly closes cuts. (If Monsole's dribbles into a fighter's eye, it can blind him.) In a pact forged at a W.B.A. rules meeting, Duva and Wolf had agreed that their fighters would submit to a urinalysis after their match.

In addition, Bramble was upset about the treatment he'd been getting from the press. He was tired of hearing how wonderful Mancini was, how Mancini embodied all the traditional (and wonderful) American virtues. All Rastafarians know themselves to be eternal underdogs laboring under the weight of Babylon culture, and one night, as Bramble stood outside the Grand, waiting for an attendant to find his car—it was lost in the parking lot—so he could go out to a vegetarian dinner, he spoke of his dissatisfaction.

"It's always the same, man," he said. "Everybody telling you what to do. You know what I'm getting for this fight? Seven hundred fifty

thousand. Mancini, he's probably getting more. You call that justice?" Bramble sighed and shook his head. "Boxing, it ain't never
going to change."

After the press conference Bramble vanished from sight, gone off to
some special chamber to replenish his juices, but Mancini continued
to put on a show at the El Dorado. The crowd attending his final performance was larger than ever, and they howled when he bopped in
to a Hall & Oates tune blaring from a ghetto-blaster. He took off his
robe, climbed into the ring, and did some calisthenics, moving at top
speed. He was in superb condition. His legs were solid from the roadwork he'd done, and he was trim and flat through the middle. The
fight was fast approaching, so he didn't spar—he had to protect his
hands—but he laced on gloves anyway and threw punches at a pair of
padded mitts that Murphy Griffith held up as targets. His hooks were
powerful, coming from a low center of gravity, but his jabs lacked
snap, and bystanders wondered aloud if they'd have any effect on
Bramble, whose head was reputed to be as hard as a coconut.

While Mancini danced around the ring, Fabulous Ford Jennings,
one of his sparring partners, watched from a distance and wearily
unwrapped tape from his hands. He was a lean, brown-skinned man,
rather tall for a lightweight. He had run through his own set of calisthenics, doing situps and pushups and working a punching bag.
This was the fourth time Jennings had trained with a champ, and the
trappings of stardom no longer thrilled him. Sick of living in a room
above a casino, he spoke wistfully of Fort Worth, his hometown,
where he had turned pro at the age of eighteen.

"I'll tell you, I don't ever want to see another slot machine or craps
table," he said, letting the tape fall away from his fingers in thick rib-
bons. "You know what I'd rather see? Cows, pastures, and cracked old
streets. I'd like to see some nature. That's what I'd rather see."

Jennings claimed to have started boxing when he was seven and
maintained that in his twenty pro bouts he had been hit—really hit—
just once. If you asked him where, he'd point to a scar over an eye and
state proudly that he hadn't needed any stitches—all he'd needed
was a damn butterfly bandage to close the wound. He bragged that
Mancini hadn't been able to touch him, but sparring partners invariably believe that they can outbox their employers. Maybe Jennings

was just building his confidence. He hadn't had a fight in over ten months, and he was eager for action. He blamed "manager problems," as boxers often do, and said he'd even written to the Texas State Athletic Commission about his plight. He had a new manager now, and felt that he was back on track.

In the evening, after a shower and a change of clothes, Jennings stationed himself at an upstairs bar in the El Dorado, wearing copious gold chains around his neck and making himself available to any feminine fringe benefits that might pass his way. His roommate, Raymond Reyes, another sparring partner, sat with him. Reyes was an intelligent young Puerto Rican from Manhattan, and he'd fought very little. He spoke in complex sentences and wanted to present himself as a well-rounded person, because he figured that would increase his chances of going on TV. Nobody cared to interview a fighter who couldn't talk, Reyes maintained.

Three times, Raymond Reyes had been in the Golden Gloves at Madison Square Garden. Intimidated by the perfect V-shaped torsos of the men he'd fought, he'd lost each bout, but he thought he was older and wiser now, a professional. The man he most admired was Hector (Macho) Camacho, a lightweight contender who'd had manager problems and problems with marijuana. In Camacho he saw a neat blend of flash and bravado. Reyes considered himself an aware person, somebody who understood the risks in boxing. He had seen punch-drunk fighters around the gym, and he planned to retire when he was twenty-eight or twenty-nine, before his own brain turned to mush. He was having a good time in Reno, maybe the time of his life, and he wanted to let his dream stretch out for just as long as he could.

In the literature of boxing, the punch-drunk fighter is a stock character. His speech is slurred; he walks with a stagger or on his heels; his memory is impaired; and his perceptual motor ability is diminished. In medical terms, the syndrome is known as dementia pugilistica. Scientists in Great Britain began to investigate it more than thirty years ago and soon amassed incontrovertible evidence that most former boxers were afflicted to some degree. This prompted the editors of The·Lancet, the principal British journal of medicine, to state, in 1959, that the medical case against boxing was so strong that they were compelled to work toward its abolition. Boxing is still quite popular throughout the United Kingdom.

In the United States, there was little research into the physical effects of boxing until recently, when the Journal of the American Medical Association started publishing editorials and papers that constituted an all-out assault on the sport. Dr. George Lundberg, the Journal's editor, contended that boxing is as medically unsound as cigarette smoking, or driving while drunk. Its sole purpose was for one man to inflict injury on another, and on that basis alone, he said, it should be banned. The editorials caused a controversy, and Lundberg received angry letters from pro-boxing colleagues, who accused him of trying to deprive boxers of their rights in a free society. None of the correspondents took issue with the scientific data; it was as convincing as it had been abroad.

Of the research papers published in the Journal to date, the most troubling is "Brain Damage in Modern Boxers." In it, a team of New York doctors give an account of how they found unequivocal signs of cerebral dysfunction in eighty-seven per cent of the pro boxers they studied. The doctors' sample was admittedly small, being made up of eighteen volunteers—thirteen former pros, two active pros, and three active Golden Glovers. The former pros were between twenty-five and sixty years old. They hadn't retired for medical, neurological, or psychological reasons, and they had no known history of drug or alcohol abuse. They'd had, on the average, a total of eighty-three amateur and pro bouts each. The average number of pro bouts was twenty-nine. Only one of the pros was a slugger, like Ray Mancini. The others were artful boxers, who practiced self-defense.

The subjects took a battery of neurological tests, including an EEG and a CAT scan. The three Golden Glovers (who had fought about as much as Raymond Reyes) had no measurable brain damage, although there were indications of subtle brain injury. Thirteen of the fifteen pros had abnormal results. They suffered from a variety of complaints, such as disorientation, confusion, temporary amnesia, and Parkinsonian disturbance. The doctors noted that the subjects were successful boxers, not bums. Among them were two world champs, two national Golden Gloves champs, a Pan American Games champ, and three ranking contenders. These were men who could take a punch. In their four hundred and sixteen bouts, they'd been knocked out just sixteen times.

The paper was not definitive, but it had many serious implications for the sport. Brain damage was not the result of a single hard knock-out punch, as some boxers believed; rather, it appeared to be related to the amount of time a fighter spent in the ring and to the amount of punishment he received. Nor was brain damage confined to pro-fessionals; it showed up among amateurs. One of the active pros had fought just once for money, but he already had a cavum septum pellucidum—a cave, or tear, in the membrane that separates the lobes of the brain. He'd had thirty-four amateur bouts and countless hours of sparring. Furthermore, brain damage seemed to be a widespread condition among fighters. Its early stages were often undetectable, except through the use of sophisticated, expensive technology, such as a CAT scan. Worse still, the condition was degenerative, and symp-toms often did not materialize for years.

"The cumulative effect of multiple subconcussive blows is a likely etiology," the doctors concluded. In response to their work, the A.M.A. adopted a resolution that states, in part, "Despite some posi-tive aspects of the sport, the American public is best served by strong A.M.A. opposition to boxing at all levels."

The Lawlor Events Center, on the campus of the University of Nevada, was filled almost to capacity for the Reno Rematch. Dan Duva put the crowd at about twelve thousand people and the gate at about eight hundred thousand dollars. The ringside seats at Lawlor went for two hundred dollars apiece, and in them were W.B.A. officials, local politi-cians, media types, lounge comedians, showgirls, aspiring showgirls, and showgirls who'd fallen on rough times and were turning tricks. A few cowboys from the range wandered around, half-blasted, done in by many reloads of whiskey at a bar near the arena that featured dead, stuffed animals—big-horn sheep, a water buffalo—in glass cases, just like a museum.

There were six bouts on the undercard at Lawlor. They were part of the netherworld of boxing, in which certain chosen fighters are "built up" for the big time. In such bouts, young boxers who have potential and whose looks, style, or race might make them attractive to the TV networks take turns defeating journeymen—tomato cans, they're called. The journeymen have no union to represent them as other professional athletes do, so they don't work for a fixed rate of pay. They have no medical benefits or pension plan. Their job is to travel from state to state and get knocked out, usually as quickly as possible. They take the same risks that champions do, but they take them for peanuts.

Dave Wolf handled two of the young boxers on the undercard. In order to sign Mancini, Dan Duva had agreed to sign them as well, and to find them opponents and put their pictures in the fight program. Wolf had the right to approve the opponents, as every manager does, and he considered himself an excellent judge of what was appropriate. In his six and a half years as a manager, his charges had lost only seven times.

For Louis Espinosa, a junior lightweight, Wolf approved Juan (El Tigre) Romero, who had lost about a third of his pro bouts. Espinosa worked Romero over, hitting him so hard and so often that when Romero went down, in the fifth, he waved a bright red glove and shouted, "*No mas! No mas!*" For Donny Poole, a Canadian welterweight, Wolf approved Chino Bermudez, a tall, slightly flabby man in his thirties whose eyes had an Oriental cast. Bermudez came from either Los Angeles or Tijuana, and he'd had seventy-four recorded pro bouts. In his youth, he'd been a winner, but now he lost consistently. He had arrived in Reno not long before the fight, and when he stepped onto a scale at the weigh-in, dressed in the clothes of a fieldhand, he proved to be ten pounds overweight. He had looked unlikely then, but in the ring he looked downright implausible. Every now and then, he did something well, drawing on memory, but Poole hit him almost at will. Bermudez went down in the second, swooning, and went down twice more in the third before the fight was stopped.

Dan Duva would say later that he couldn't do much about the caliber of such bouts. Managers just wouldn't let a hot prospect go against somebody who might beat him, not unless the money was right. As for Dave Wolf, he didn't think that the fights had been mismatches. In his opinion, Romero was a decent boxer, and Bermudez, a wily veteran, had actually taught some things to Donny Poole. Besides, there were budgetary considerations involved. Romero was part of an inexpensive package deal out of Phoenix, which also included Tony Cisneros, another knockout victim. Jerry Lewis (twelve wins, thirteen losses) wasn't part of the package. Vince Dunfee knocked him out, and Lewis went home to California and got word that his license to fight in that state would not be renewed. Chino Bermudez got a similar notification, and headed for Mexico.

Ray Mancini, wearing a red silk robe, paraded into the arena throwing punches and kisses. The crowd, mostly white, rose as a body and cheered when he slipped through the ropes. Moments later, Livingstone Bramble made his entrance, to Bob Marley's "Buffalo Soldier," a reggae song about black men who'd been conscripted into the Union Army and forced to kill Indians. "I'm just a buffalo soldier, fighting for survival," Marley sang, and Bramble, in black trunks adorned with a yellow skull-and-crossbones, danced in the ring, eyes closed, while in a front row, his supporters from the Virgin Islands held aloft his infant son. Bramble's dreadlocks were slick with Vaseline, and so were his nose and cheeks. The fans booed him, but Bramble had expected as much. "In America," he'd once said, "if you're different they say you're strange."

The fight started briskly. Mancini came out smoking and carried the fight to Bramble. Bramble's height advantage and superior reach— he had several inches on the challenger—made things difficult, but Mancini compensated, as always, with courage and daring. He stood toe-to-toe with the bigger man and took three punches in order to land one. Bramble scored points throughout these exchanges, refusing to brawl. Instead, he waited patiently and looked for openings. When he threw a jab, he threw it with authority, in a clockwork way, often aiming for the eyes. Mancini was honed as sharp as he could be, but his scar tissue and the subcutaneous cuts he'd got in training soon betrayed him. In the second round, Bramble sliced a cut into his right eyelid; the skin around his left eye began to swell and turn red. Then, in the fifth, Bramble opened an inch-long gash near the left lid, so that blood flowed down Mancini's cheek, as if he'd been slashed with a razor.

Somehow, Mancini kept himself together. He had a fine sixth round, wiping the blood away with his gloves and slowing Bramble with a series of efficient hooks to the body, but Bramble took charge again in the seventh, working the eyes, jabbing at them, widening the cuts. When Mancini returned to his corner at the bell, he complained to his cornermen. "I can't see," he said. His cut man, Paul Percifield, closed the wounds as best he could, but Bramble opened them again in the eighth, and the referee called in the ringside physician, Dr. Charles Filippini, and sought a medical opinion as to whether or not Mancini should continue.

Dr. Filippini is in general practice in Reno. The Nevada State Athletic Commission paid him a pittance for his work, and he looked on it as he might on community service. He had presided at many fights, including four championships, but he'd stopped only one of them. He was aware that he was in a difficult position. There were millions of dollars riding on Mancini, and his fans were desperate for him to finish, since he appeared to be behind on points. Also, Dr. Filippini knew that most boxing people mistrust physicians, and he wasn't sure how Mancini's corner would react to his presence. At other fights, he had been blocked from examining injured men, elbowed aside by irate trainers. "They just want us around to pick up the pieces," he would remark later.

Dr. Filippini had given pre-fight physicals to all the boxers on the card, but the exams were cursory, and he wished he could do more. He had read the A.M.A. research, and it gave him cause for concern. He thought that every boxer should have a CAT scan at the start of his career and then after every bout so he could at least be informed of any change in his brain tissue. But a CAT scan is expensive, and Dr. Filippini didn't know where the money was going to come from, except perhaps from the TV networks. He leaned over the ropes, pried open Mancini's closed eye with his fingers, and peered into the bloody socket, determining that Mancini's eyelids weren't split and that his retinas were not detached. In essence, the cuts were a soft-tissue trauma. They might look awful, and impair Mancini's vision to some degree, but they would do him no permanent harm.

So Mancini fought on. But the bout was not the same anymore— it did not seem clean or fair. Now a man with a handicap was pitted against a boxer in his prime. Mancini's talent and bravery were not at issue. His body had just let him down. As he circled the ring, flicking his gloves against his eyes to wipe away the blood, he was reminiscent of many other champs in the final stages of their careers. There was something very moving and very sad about his pursuit of

Bramble, something that went to the root of boxing's problems. It was a sport that did not know where to draw the line. The line, such as it was, kept shifting, subject to crude economies—to the demands of networks, boxing organizations, promoters, and the other vested interests in control. On this point the record was clear: only rarely did a fighter get out of the game before it was too late.

Because Mancini had a touch of greatness, he landed punches, even good punches, but the blood still flowed. It spotted his chest and speckled his shoulders and back. Bramble was distressed by what he saw. If the eyes had been his, he would have quit and come back another day. Most boxers do not like to inflict unnecessary punishment, but Bramble had no choice. He had hammered Mancini last time out, and yet he had been behind on the judges' scorecards. So Bramble worked the eyes. In all, he would hit Mancini six hundred and seventy-four times. Two hundred and fifty-five of those punches would strike Mancini in the face.

The image of a wounded fighter extending himself beyond reasonable limits has always been integral to the mythology of boxing. Maybe there was a period in history when a fan could have watched in innocence as Mancini got hit, admiring his competitive spirit, but that period had passed. The scientific evidence was in, and it told the truth about what was happening. When Mancini was hit on the jaw, or on the side of his head, his soft brain swirled and glided within his skull, imperilling blood vessels and nerve endings. His future as a person with charm and charisma—his future as a human being—was at risk.

Mercifully, the fight ended. Among most reporters who had kept score, Bramble was an easy winner, ahead by three or four points, although a few dissenters gave the match to Mancini. The judges, too, scored in favor of Bramble, but only by a point on each card. The HBO computer analysis showed that Mancini had connected with just twenty-eight per cent of his punches; Bramble had connected with fifty-five percent. Once again, Mancini had been beaten decisively, but he was ecstatic to have survived. When he met the press after the bout, he delivered a non-stop monolog fueled by a mixture of oxygen and adrenaline. He wore a maroon towel over his head, like a burnoose. His left eye was purple and almost shut. "I hope I've been good for boxing," he said. "I tried."

Somebody asked him if he were hurting.

"I'm not going to lie and say I'm not," said Mancini. "But to what extent?"

Lenny Mancini—broken nose, shock of white hair—sat next to his son, and a reporter asked him if he wanted Ray to keep fighting. "If it was up to me, I'd say forget about it," Lenny said.

"He always says that," Ray said. "I'm his baby."

Another reporter asked Mancini if he planned to retire. He said he had to think about it. "To thine own self be true," he said. "You guys didn't know I knew Shakespeare, did you?"

He laughed and invited everybody to a big party at the El Dorado. Then, he went off to a hospital, where twenty-seven stitches were taken in his eyelids and around his eyes. By midnight, he was back in his suite, eating a dish of chocolate ice cream.

In the morning, at the M-G-M Grand, Bramble, still casual in jeans and Bramble brim, referred to himself as the lightweight champion of the universe. When somebody asked him why he hadn't used his right hand very much during the fight, he said it was because the glove on it had not come from the belly part of the cow.

"Are you going to honor your contract with Tyrone Crawley?" a reporter asked.

Bramble was going to leave that up to his manager. The chump he really wanted to fight was Hector Camacho, who had been at ringside in a gold lamé suit and a pair of rhinestone-studded sunglasses. W.B.A. rankings aside, Camacho was worth a significant piece of cake.

"With Crawley, you get a guy who's a stinking fighter," Lou Duva said. He has a face like Broderick Crawford. "I don't like a Crawley fight. There's nothing good about him stylewise. It would just stink out the joint." He meant that Crawley had a style that was similar to Bramble's and might give Bramble trouble. He also meant that Crawley had no marquee value and might not sell to television.

Shortly after this, the full weight of Babylon came thrashing down on Bramble. The post-fight urinalysis revealed a banned substance in his urine—ephedrine, a crystalline alkaloid commonly used for relief of hay fever, asthma, and nasal congestion. Taken in large doses or injected intramuscularly, it elevates blood pressure and works as a stimulant. At first, Bramble was puzzled by how it had gotten into his system. He was a vegetarian, a true health freak, and he avoided chemicals of all description. But everyday he did swallow a capsule of Chi Power, a supposedly Chinese herbal concoction that he bought at natural foods stores. Chi Power contained Ma Huang, or Ephedra sinica. The Nevada State Athletic Commission, uninterested in Orientalia, fined Bramble fifteen thousand dollars.

Then his big payday with Hector Camacho dispersed into the ozone. The Crawley fight was scheduled instead, but Bramble broke a hand in training, and NBC cancelled its contract. For a time, the fight languished in limbo. When it was rescheduled, Crawley injured himself, and NBC again cancelled its contract. More months dragged by, and Bramble, a king without a kingdom, became so depressed that he told one of his handlers that he was thinking about moving to Montana and buying himself a cattle ranch. (In February, 1986, Bramble finally fought and defeated Crawley in an impressive performance. He had fired Lou Duva as his manager, and Duva was suing him for part of his purse. Of the five bouts broadcast on TV that weekend, Bramble's received the highest rating.)

In the weeks following the fight, Ray Mancini took it easy. For the first time in five years, he let his body rest. When CBS broadcast its videotape, he appeared on camera live, without Bramble, and offered through puffy lips a revised version of recent events. Now he claimed that he'd won the fight convincingly, and that Bramble's drug use ought to cost him the title. In New York, Dr. Schwartz examined Mancini again and told him that his cuts would be fully healed in a few months. Mancini flew to Florida and played some golf.

For a while, he couldn't make up his mind about retirement. Every few days, he would phone Dave Wolf and ask if any new fight offers had come in. Wolf was getting plenty of them, all for big bucks. Mancini was still white and still popular. Would he be able to turn down a million dollars to go up about five pounds and fight a leading junior welterweight? Mancini himself didn't know for sure. How many

Americans could refuse a million bucks for taking a beating? And it wasn't really the punishment that Mancini was concerned about—he had no idea if he could go through another training camp. He was tired of paying dues, and he had other options. Cosmo wanted him for a photo session on bachelor hunks, and the William Morris Agency had signed him to a contract.

Mancini decided to move to Los Angeles. He bought a house there and put in time around the swimming pool. His movie star friends understood what he was going through and how a million-dollar deal rumbles around in your head. One day, he started working out in a gym at Mickey Rourke's house. He took it slowly, testing himself, but he just couldn't do it anymore. He'd had it with sacrifice and pain, so he called a press conference and said that he was hanging up his gloves to pursue a career as an actor. Probably he would never be a great thespian, but he thought he had it in him to do Rambo-type roles. He believed that he could make a go of it in Hollywood, but he would not rule out the possibility that maybe, in the future, if the circumstances were right, he might return to the ring.

"One thing I've learned," Mancini said. "Never say never."

George Kimball

George Kimball (b. 1943), bearded and garrulous, looking like nothing so much as a character out of *The Canterbury Tales*, took the long way to ringside. An Army brat, he lived all over the world as a child, lost an eye, attended the Iowa Writers Workshop, published his novel *Only Skin Deep* (1968) at age twenty-four, edited the literary journals *Grist* and *Ploughshares*, and ran unsuccessfully for sheriff of Douglas County, Kansas, promising to legalize marijuana. In the 1970s, he began writing sports for Boston's counterculture weekly, the *Phoenix*; a decade later the *Boston Herald* hired him to write a sports column that for twenty-five years bristled with keen insight, rollicking prose, and a contrary streak as wide as the Big Dig (as is evident from the following take on the controversial 1987 Leonard–Hagler match). When Roberto Duran was pilloried for telling Sugar Ray Leonard *"No mas,"* Kimball argued that it was the ultimate macho protest against Leonard's cutie-pie tactics. There is even a boxing theme in Kimball's retirement, as he writes about the sport among other American subjects for *The Irish Times* (his columns are collected in *American at Large*, 2008) and *TheSweetScience. com* and is the author of *Four Kings: Leonard, Hagler, Hearns, Duran, and the Last Great Era of Boxing* (2008). And when he married his wife Marge in 2004, George Foreman officiated the ceremony.

Leonard–Hagler:
The Fight and Its Aftermath

For an event that continues to weigh so heavily on the national consciousness (survey the contents of any saloon in America and you're more likely to find a consensus about the Vietnam War than over who really won history's biggest prizefight on 6 April 1987), it seems odd that the more vivid vestigial images took place outside the ring.

More than any one punch thrown over the course of forty-eight minutes, for instance, there is the recollection of the round-card girl

347

during one of the preliminary fights—this one between Lupe Aquino and Davey Moore—climbing under the ring ropes only to have her left breast flop fully out of her skimpy dress top. The spontaneous ovation greeting that exposure was overshadowed a round later by the chorus of boos with which the Caesars Palace crowd pelted the ring when one of her colleagues climbed into the ring and her boobs did not fall out.

A spirited exchange between promoter Bob Arum and his arch-rival Don King that took place shortly after the final bell is also indelibly etched in memory, more so than any single minute of fighting that took place in the preceding twelve rounds. This one took place right in front of me at ringside: King, correctly anticipating that Ray Charles Leonard was about to be named the winner, thereby casting the middleweight title on to the open market for the first time in a decade, began to climb into the ring to join the celebration. Arum, the smaller by far and apparently unmindful of King's track record in *mano a mano* fights (King's enthusiasm in winning one of these bought him a stretch for manslaughter) leapt on to his back, initiating a wrestling match in which he ripped one of the pockets from King's expensive jacket. This one was ultimately quelled in Arum's favour by a large Caesars security guard, who escorted King from the ring as the latter addressed him as 'a lousy black motherfucker.'

And, much later that evening, as Marvin Hagler slowly made his way through the deserted and litter-strewn lot beside the Caesars tennis courts that had served as a makeshift stadium, there was the image of Hagler coming across two vendors loading a truck with unconsumed Budweiser. The Hollywood glitterati and Vegas high-rollers had long since departed in celebratory swarms in the direction of the casino tables when Hagler stopped and asked 'Hey, how 'bout a six-pack?'

One of the concessionaires looked up and recognised him. 'You're the champ, Marvin,' he grinned and handed over two cases of beer. Hagler took them back to his room. No one would be surprised if he drank them all that night.

But the fight itself? Sure, you remember the southpaw champion opening up with an orthodox, right-handed attack, and stubbornly pursuing this course of action long after its ineffectiveness had become apparent. You remember the final round and Leonard calling to his corner 'How much time?', and when he was told 'One minute!' Ray raised his glove in celebratory triumph as he danced away, secure in the knowledge that at least on this night Marvin Hagler wasn't going to get him. And a snarling, huffing Hagler, realising the same thing, mockingly hoisted his own glove aloft as he vainly chased Leonard through the final seconds.

You think you remember Goody Petronelli in the corner, repeatedly dispatching advice to Hagler: 'Rough him up inside!' But it dawns on you later that you couldn't possibly have heard that at ringside; Hagler's corner was clear across the ring, so the memory is a faulty one, inspired instead from the countless viewings of the fight on videotape. The image is no less valid, though: the tone of the voice clearly implies 'Keep roughing him up inside,' although Leonard did not have a mark on him.

That night at ringside it was similarly difficult to discern what Leonard retrospectively labelled the turning-point of the fight. When Hagler finally turned nasty in the fifth round he might have turned the tide himself: in his round-by-round for the Associated Press, Fast Eddie Schuyler summarised the concluding moments: 'Hagler got in a left to the head, then a hook to the body. Hagler landed a short left to the face. Leonard landed a left to the face. Hagler got in a good left to the head in Leonard's corner. Hagler got a good right and left to the head with 30 seconds left. They were fighting the range. Hagler had Leonard against the ropes. Hagler landed a right at the bell.' My own equally cryptic version of the round's conclusion did note that as the bell sounded ending that round Leonard woozily eyed Hagler and then stumbled—no, staggered—back to his stool.

It was months later that Ray Leonard recapitulated the moment. 'I was definitely in trouble. I thought I was gone. But then I looked Marvin in the eye and I realised, "He doesn't even know I'm hurt. He doesn't know it!" I knew then I had him.'

The odd part of this is that Leonard had won the first four rounds on the score cards of two judges (as well as my own), yet it was the first round he decisively lost that he continues to regard as pivotal. My own hastily composed description of what happened that night read: 'Any delusions that the corner had been turned were quickly laid to rest the next round. As Hagler pressed the attack, Leonard was a veritable will o' the wisp, dancing about as Hagler's mighty blows flew harmlessly all around him, pausing long enough to land an effective flurry of his own just before the bell.

'Although Hagler came back to win the next three rounds—win them everywhere, in any case, but on the score card of Mexican judge Jo Jo Guerra, who wound up scoring the bout a lopsided 118–110 in Leonard's favour—he was clearly in for a fight; just when Leonard was looking shaky at the end of the ninth, he rallied and stood toe to toe with Hagler as the bell rang. There would be more of these confrontations in the fight's final stages. Leonard was landing more punches, but seemingly getting the worse of the exchanges. (As Hagler moved in for one bit of infighting, Leonard's trainer Angelo Dundee was shouting "Watch that bald-headed sucker's head!" to referee Richard Steele.)'

If the evening's events for the most part remain a blur, the nebulous spectre of Leonard playing the master toreador to Hagler's raging bull continue to dominate. Pick almost any round and it is the same: Ray landing more punches, albeit ones of dubious usefulness, Hagler missing but eliciting more pain when he did manage to land.

The debate rages over who won the fight. Two judges, Lou Filippo and Dave Moretti, saw it 115–113, but had different winners. Guerra, who will probably never score a major fight again, gave Leonard all but two rounds. Having covered all of Hagler's title fights dating back to that rainy night in London when he won the championship from Alan Minter, I went into this bout plainly disposed towards the champion, but scored the fight 116–114 (six-four-two) in Leonard's favour. A subsequent viewing of the tape caused me to alter one of the even rounds, and I scored it seven-four-one, Leonard, the second time around.

Clearly, there is room for philosophical argument on both sides: Leonard's punches never did any real damage, other than to pile up points, while Hagler's were clearly more lethal—when they managed to connect. In terms of 'Clean Punches' the fight was no better than a wash. 'Aggression?' Hagler was obviously the aggressor for most of the night; but the operative word in this category is supposed to be effective aggression. And it seemed to me that Leonard's mastery of another category of supposedly equal importance, 'Defence,' was at least sufficient to offset any supposed edge Hagler might have built up here.

With the first three criteria more or less a push, then, it seemed and seems to me that in the fourth—'Ring Generalship'—there was a clearcut dominance on the part of Leonard. It was Leonard who dictated the terms under which this battle was waged. It was Ray who was able to lead Marvin around by the nose, forcing him to fight Leonard's fight rather than his own. Leonard did what he wanted to do and denied Hagler what he wanted to do for the better part of the evening.

There are persuasive arguments to be made in the other direction, none more eloquent than the case Hugh McIlvanney, the Boxing Bard of Scotland, made in a *Sports Illustrated* retrospective a few weeks later. But not even Marvin Hagler was arguing that he had dominated the fight. At least not that night he wasn't. Even after claiming that the fight had been 'stolen' from him, Hagler privately offered that he thought the fight should have been a split decision, only in his favour.

'A split decision should go to the champion,' he complained. 'I've never seen a split decision go to the other guy . . . He should have had to beat me more decisively. He never knocked me down. It was the same as the first Antuofermo fight [which, with Hagler the challenger, ended in a draw]. It's the second tie in my life. That's Las Vegas—a gambling town. I've done a lot for boxing and I wish they didn't take it away like that.' As Hagler headed off in search of the six-pack that would grow to eight of them before he reached his room, his wife Bertha murmured 'He was afraid this was going to happen. And I know he's mad right now. Mad and hurt.'

Gracious in defeat, Leonard proclaimed in the ring that Hagler 'is still a champion to me.' Hagler would later take this to claim that Leonard believed he had lost the fight. The name-calling had only just begun.

'He called me a sissy,' reported Leonard.

'He fought like a girl,' claimed Marvin.

Although each fighter had insisted for months beforehand that this fight would be his last, the controversy seemed to cry out for a rematch. In his post-fight commentary, Hagler had even suggested that the decision had been a means of forcing one: 'I believe the boxing world wants me back, and the only way they can keep me here is with a rematch,' he complained somewhat illogically.

But despite a year of talking, a rematch seems further away than ever. The seeds of discontent that were sown that night had already begun to sprout the next morning. 'I'm not taking anything away from Ray Leonard,' said Pat Petronelli the next morning, 'but this guy Jo Jo Guerra is a disgrace. He ought to be put in jail. Ask Leonard if he thought Marvin Hagler only won two rounds.'

The perfect irony of this response was that Guerra had not been included on the initially proposed slate of ringside officials for the big fight. The original panel—comprised of Moretti, Filippo, and Great Britain's Harry Gibbs, along with that of referee Steele—had been submitted to representatives of both fighters beforehand by the WBC. The Petronellis had objected to Gibbs.

Despite 'philosophical' differences they would later voice, the reason for the prejudice was plain and simple: Gibbs was an English-man. And the memory of the night seven years earlier when Hagler had stopped Alan Minter in London's Wembley Arena to capture the middleweight title, only to be driven from the ring by a fusillade of beer cans at the moment he should have been awarded the cham-pionship belt, was one that had never left them. For Pat and Goody Petronelli, if not for Marvin Hagler himself, it was reason enough to hate a whole country.

So they hemmed and hawed for a while about the supposed incli-nation of British fight officials to penalise infighting and then made their peremptory challenge to Gibbs. Then, at the pre-fight rules meeting, they went one further. 'We want a Mexican judge,' they demanded. So they got one. Harry Gibbs flew home to England and didn't even watch the fight. Two weeks later he got the chance to see it on British television tape-delay. He scored the fight for Hagler.

The complaints about Guerra's scoring hardly precipitated the bitter post-fight breach, though. Even Angelo Dundee was able to shrug the next day and admit that 'unfortunately, one of the judges wasn't with us last night.' But then, just ten days later, a Boston tele-vision sportscaster went on the air with an uncorroborated rumour that an investigation was underway in Nevada following reports that an unidentified gambler who had bet a massive amount on Leonard had improperly influenced one of the judges to swing the fight to the challenger.

As it turned out, an investigation was not underway, but following the widespread circulation of John Dennis's story, Nevada

officials were forced to initiate one. In order to avoid potential conflict of interest charges, Nevada commissioner Duane Ford turned the
matter over to a special investigator representing the state attorney
general's department.

It did not require the services of Sherlock Holmes to discern that
the gambler in question was sometime fight manager Billy Baxter,
and that the judge whose ethics had been called into question was
not Guerra, but Moretti. After an investigation lasting several months
both men were completely exonerated.

Neither Leonard nor his handlers ever accused the Hagler camp
of complicity in the bogus 'fix' story, but it scarcely helped to smooth
things over. Dennis had in the past been close to Hagler and the
Petronellis, who were not above using him as a conduit when they
wanted to leak a story—and the mere fact that they took no steps to
refute or deny it only exacerbated matters. Others suspected that the
'fix' story might have been initiated by Arum himself since, had sufficient evidence been found to warrant the mandating of a rematch,
Arum would have got that fight, too. The promoter vociferously
denied any role in the proceedings.

'What gets me,' complained Leonard's attorney and manager
Mike Trainer, 'is that Ray never uttered a peep after he lost the first
fight to Duran, one that in our minds was equally disputable. All this
bellyaching, all this complaining, all these excuses, it's made Ray very
disappointed in Marvin. He hasn't been a very good sport about the
whole thing.'

Indeed, even as Hagler continued to grouse about a rematch,
another Leonard confidant suggested that had Hagler come out of
the ring and simply said, 'Well, I thought I won, but I guess the judges
saw it differently. Let's do it again,' Ray might have said, 'Sure.' As
it was, everything Hagler and his people did over the next several
months only soured Ray on the idea of fighting again. Or at least
fighting Marvin again. But this whole sour grapes attitude they've
had since the moment they stepped out of the ring is not going to
have its desired effect, I can tell you that. 'If they really wanted to
fight Ray again, the last things they should have been doing is running around telling people they got robbed and the fight was fixed
and all that bullshit like that.'

At a packed press conference in Washington six weeks later,

Leonard announced his retirement. 'Why should we believe you this time?' he was asked. 'You're retired now, but will you ever fight again?'

'No,' he insisted, just before adding with a twinkle, 'but you guys know me!'

By late June Hagler was back in the news, this time as the recipient of a court order obtained by his wife Bertha, who had charged him with, among other things, assault. Newspapers—particularly those in London, where I happened to be at the time—were quick to label him a wife-beater. Only later did it develop that the 'assault' in question consisted of Marvin throwing rocks at his wife's car, his way of expressing his disapproval over the fact that she had returned to the family home at something like three in the morning.

It was a painful episode for Marvin Hagler who valued his relationship with his children above all else. Suddenly he found himself visiting them only at the pleasure of the court. Taking up a reclusive residency in downtown Boston, he only rarely ventured out. His only public sightings became late-night visits to the discos and nightclubs of Boston, while his attorneys attempted to smooth things out with his wife, who had by now retained Marvin Mitchelson.

There was certainly no indication that he ever intended to fight again, although Arum, with the likely connivance of the Petronellis, managed to tease Thomas Hearns and his manager Emanuel Steward.

Hagler emerged from his shell in order to serve as television commentator for the broadcasts of the very fights that divided up his old domain—or at least the two of them that Arum was promoting. He was in Italy with ESPN to watch Sumbu Kalambay outpoint Iran Barkley for the WBA version of the middleweight title last October. In the same country five years earlier Kalambay had played a supporting role in one of Hagler's defences, struggling to beat Marvin's then sparring partner Buster Drayton on the undercard of Hagler's second knockout of Fulgencio Obelmejias in San Remo.

From there Hagler flew straight to Vegas to watch Hearns annex the WBC crown by knocking out Juan Roldan. Hagler had to sit at ringside and deliver the closed-circuit commentary on a 'title' fight whose participants consisted of two men he himself had already knocked out. Leonard was also present.

Much later that night the two chanced to land in the men's room of a Las Vegas meat-market-cum-disco called Botany's at precisely the same moment. Leonard made one last stab at offering the olive branch.

'Some fight, huh?' he chirped to Hagler as he sidled up alongside him at the urinal. In response he got an icy stare of silence.

As Hagler started away Leonard accosted him. 'Hey, I'm not here to make friends,' spat Leonard. The two have not spoken since.

Months later, very possibly as his resentment grew, Leonard's interest began to revive. In January he allowed that he 'wouldn't consider fighting again unless Marvin sat down and talked with me first,' which seemed to open the door.

'I wish I could tell you I can read him all the time, but I can't,' admitted Trainer. 'Sometimes I don't know what he's thinking. Sometimes I'm not sure he does himself. But I do know that he's wanted to sit down with Marvin one-on-one for a long time. I'm sure that every time he sits down to watch a big fight, the juices start flowing and he gets to thinking about fighting again. But if you get him to sit down for a beer a few hours later when he's thinking about the commitment that entails, I'm not sure he's ready to do that.'

With no response from Hagler, Leonard turned up the volume a few weeks later. In an interview with a Washington television station he said, 'If Marvin wants to fight me he has to come to me and talk about it first.' The week after that, while guesting on the syndicated *Oprah Winfrey Show*, he took off the gloves for real: 'Hagler never gave me credit,' groused Leonard. 'I beat him fair and square. He made allegations that some of the officials in Nevada were corrupt and what have you. I think it's unprofessional, and I want to beat him up.'

This managed to wake Marvin up, even though Hagler seemed uneager to agree to a rematch with no title at stake. 'Let him go get another belt first,' the former champion huffed in response. 'If he really wanted to fight again, why did he give up the title?'

Leonard's latest stance is that 'all Marvin has to do is call me up.'

'If I ever do call him,' says Hagler, 'it'll be collect.'

Which is where the rift stands today. It seems tragic in several respects. Hagler is left surrounded by shattered dreams, while Leonard seems genuinely wounded by the dissolution of what he had once considered a warm friendship—even though Hagler insists 'we were never really friends.' Maybe so, but they were and are both friends of mine, to the extent that before they fought I had publicly gone on record urging each of them to retire—Ray out of consideration for his eyesight, and Marvin after the John Mugabi fight had unmasked the very erosion of skills that Leonard would exploit a year later. And if I didn't think they should fight the first time, I can hardly countenance a rematch; even if it were something both wanted.

Meanwhile, the alternative seems to be listening to them call each other names for a few more years. I don't much look forward to that either.

Gerald Early

Gerald Early (b. 1952), acclaimed as an essayist, poet, and cultural critic, is the Merle King Professor of Modern Letters at Washington University in St. Louis. He is a nationally recognized authority on subjects as various as baseball, boxing, jazz, and twentieth-century American history. He has been a regular contributor to NPR's "Fresh Air," was the editor of *The Muhammad Ali Reader* (1998), and served as a consultant to Ken Burns's documentaries *Baseball* (1994), *Jazz* (2001), and *Unforgivable Blackness: The Rise and Fall of Jack Johnson* (2005). Twice a Grammy nominee (for best album notes), he was the curator for the Missouri History Museum's 2001 exhibition on Miles Davis; his 1994 collection *The Culture of Bruising: Essays on Prizefighting, Literature, and Modern American Culture* earned him the National Book Critics Circle Award. As the following essay from his 1989 collection *Tuxedo Junction* shows, Early's engagement with the sweet science can be traced to his youth in Philadelphia, a city famous for producing top middleweights and practitioners of a certain punch. As Randall "Tex" Cobb, a heavyweight who lives there, once observed, "Even the winos throw left hooks."

Ringworld

I. YESTERDAY

When there is a touch of true symbolism,
it is not of the nature of a ruin or
a remains embedded in the present structure,
it is rather an archaic reminiscence.
—D. H. Lawrence, *Apocalypse*

JEFF CHANDLER, former World Boxing Association bantamweight champion, received, at the end of 1984, the sort of bad news that men in his profession are apt to expect if not to accept. Nineteen eighty-four had not been a good year for him; indeed, it had true Orwellian overtones or, at least, must have reminded him of those blues lyrics that said, "If it wasn't for bad luck, I wouldn't have no luck at all." He lost his title in the summer by being thoroughly thrashed before a national television audience by Richard Sandoval. The loss was particularly galling for two reasons: first, he was so completely outgunned and overmatched by Sandoval that one would not have expected him to win the title again in a rematch; and, second, he had just been referred to as "possibly one of the greatest bantamweights in history" in a cover story on him that appeared in the July 1983 issue of *The Ring*. But in this case injury was added to insult when he required eye surgery this fall for the removal of a cataract and was told by his doctor that he could promptly forget all ideas about avenging his defeat and regaining his title, because, as a result of the surgery, he could never even wipe his eye very hard again, much less fight in a ring. He joins a growing list of professional boxers who, in recent years, either have had to quit because of eye injuries or were unsuccessful in attempting comebacks after eye surgery: Sugar Ray Seales, Sugar Ray Leonard, Earnie Shavers, Harold Weston, and Hilmer Kenty among others. Stories of fighters being beaten to death in the ring give the general public the impression that brain damage and death are the most common and feared injuries for fighters. Actually, relatively few fighters die in the ring, and few are incapacitated mentally as a result of fighting or, at least, no more mentally incompetent than before they entered the ring. Most *do* suffer some eye damage; there are more than a few ex-pugs running around with poor vision or no vision at all because of fists or wayward thumbs thrown their way during fighting days.

In connection with this business about fighters with poor vision, there is a very interesting story about a half-blind fighter who had a half-decent career, better than half decent, really, since he fought for a title, an opportunity few fighters ever procure. (Of course, stories like this abound in prizefighting, a sport that is extremely self-conscious of its own mythology, nearly as much as baseball.) Gypsy Joe Harris, flamboyant welterweight and middleweight of the sixties, fought for many years although he was entirely blind in one eye. He memorized the eye chart in the doctor's office of the Pennsylvania State Athletic Commission, so, ironically, his blind eye was certified as having perfect vision. Harris was good enough, with his one eye, to become a leading contender and even to make the cover of *Sports Illustrated*. I remember as a boy once watching Harris play pool in a pool hall in North Philadelphia. He was well-known for doing his most strenuous training in the pool halls and taverns and cabarets of North Philadelphia. *That*, more than the blind eye, proved to be his undoing when he fought for the championship. A group of us South Philadelphia boys risked life and limb by leaving our neighborhood to go to a North Philadelphia gym to watch Harris train for a fight. We had all decided on an effective and simple course of action should we run into any of the brutally tough North Philly gangs: "haul ass" like Olympic sprinters and pray that we could dodge bullets faster than the enemy could fire them at us. Gang warfare was no longer an engagement involving chains and rocks; knives, pistols, and rifles were the rule. And every gang in the city wanted to make its reputation by "copping a few homicides." When we arrived at the gym, we were told that Harris was in the pool hall down the street. We were, of course, instantly and indelibly impressed when we met him. Probably the ambience of the pool hall, with the radio blaring and all the old and young black men standing around, made a deeper imprint on us than if we had seen him sweating through a workout in the gym. He was dressed in a fancy-cut suit of sharkskin, I think, which was a popular style in those days, wore several expensive rings, had a grandly expensive car parked in front of the place, and a very lovely woman sitting behind him as he ran balls with an amazing proficiency and an affected nonchalance. (This remembrance is admittedly at variance with what I knew of Harris at the time and what I read about him many years later. He was noted for never being dressed up, for having a fairly plain girlfriend, for being a man of simple, working-class taste. Yet this is how I remember seeing him and I cannot help but wonder if I have collapsed the memory with that of another fighter or perhaps another famous black entertainer. Harris was a pool fanatic; that much I recall correctly.) His bald head, which the public found so menacing, was covered by a slight film of sweat. He did not look like a boxer but rather like a street-smart hustler. Harris regaled the crowd for a time with a bit of bombastic rhetoric about what he would do to his opponent, which could be reductively but safely captured by the words: "I'm gonna kick the motherfucker's ass." I have never heard any good fighter speak about his opponent in any other way. Shortly after, Harris left with the very beautiful woman on his arm.

One of the old-timers, cigarette dangling, hard-conked hair, who remained in the hall after many others had cleared out following Harris's departure began to shoot some pool using Harris's cuestick. He started muttering to himself about how he knew Ezzard Charles in Chicago back during the days when "that boy was a good fighter. Yeah, that boy got himself all messed with the leeches and the bitches. Gypsy Joe's shit is gettin' ragged just like Charles's. If he don't watch out, he might wind up like Charles, needin' to pass water and without a pot to piss in." None of us boys knew how Ezzard Charles, great heavyweight contender of the fifties who had glorious encounters with Joe Louis, Jersey Joe Walcott, and Rocky Marciano, wound up, and we surely did not care. We knew only that, whatever Charles's past, we certainly liked Harris's present immensely. Among the boys who were there was a very, very young Jeff Chandler. Perhaps he was more impressed than any of us.

I do not know what happened to Gypsy Joe Harris, but I do remember that a year or two after his retirement a Philadelphia sports columnist wrote a story telling how Harris needed a job. A few years after that I heard that he had been working in a meat-packing place for a time but had been laid off. He was, I was told, less than slick.

There was a black street gang in South Philadelphia known as the Fifth and South Streets gang, which could never be found on the intersection of Fifth Street and South Street. In fact, while growing up, I do not recall *anything* being on the corner of Fifth and South Streets; even the Jewish merchants who operated cheap clothing stores in that area for years had boarded up their shops and escaped to the middle-class nirvana of Mount Airy. That corner seemed to be not only lonely and blighted, not simply sucked and drained, but fully charged with a profound cosmic desertion. Perhaps this was exacerbated by the fact that a mere two blocks away at Sixth and Lombard stood the oldest black church in America—the grand Mother Bethel A.M.E. Church founded by Richard Allen in 1794. There seemed to be a haunting, almost Manichaeistic contrast between the two locations: the mighty monument of the black urban past and the ghostly emptiness of the black urban present in strange and uneasy proximity.

The boys of the Fifth and South Streets gang could be found some six blocks away on the corner of Fifth and Carpenter, in the glass-strewn main parking lot of the Southwark Plaza projects. I can remember when those projects were built and opened and when the use of the word "plaza" did not sound quite like a shabby stab at something parodically grandiose. The buildings, when they were new, were nice, livable quarters, better than what most of the people in the neighborhood had been accustomed to living in. Times change, as Bob Dylan once noted, and buildings of this sort deteriorate rapidly when occupied by people of this sort. Nowadays, I suppose the animals in the Philadelphia Zoo live in more comfort and less fear than the folk in these highrise projects.

The Fifth and South Streets gang was a very inept outfit, spending most of its time running away from the bigger and stronger gangs in the area: the Thirteenth and Fitzwater Streets gang, Seventh Street gang, and Twenty-third and Tasker Streets gang. Part of the source of the ineptitude was the very small size of the gang; also, internal dissension splintered the gang into at least three separate entities. Third, and most important, was the gang's sheer inability to do what a street gang is organized to do: terrorize those who are outside the fold. I think that during all the years that street gangs were a potent crime force in Philadelphia, the Fifth and South Streets gang may have killed one or two boys, a horrible and horrifying achievement, yet quite insignificant compared to what many other gangs were able to do in this regard. But these boys were no different from the boys in the other gangs. In this ragtag outfit, the boys drank cheap red wine, sniffed glue in brown paper bags, blowing them in and out like a bellows, played basketball endlessly, read comic books, played pinball, and spent the time when they were absolutely bored fighting each other. It struck me even as a child, watching the corner boys from the position of outsider, that they seemed both utterly bored and inexcusably lazy, a most volatile combination.

Two boys whom I remember very well from this gang are TM and LS, partly because I had the dubious distinction of having fistfights with both of them while in elementary school and losing to both of them rather badly, and partly because as young adults they made the front page of every newspaper in the city. LS and another man, both junkies, murdered and robbed two elderly Jews one morning as they were walking down the steps of their synagogue. The booty amounted to ten dollars, which I think came to a ratio of about ten cents for every year of their sentences. TM was a fugitive on a bench warrant; in other words, he failed to appear in court for an outstanding charge while out on bail. The police trapped him in his girlfriend's apartment in the Southwark Plaza projects. In the shootout that ensued, TM killed one policeman but was, quite miraculously, taken alive. He was given a life sentence plus fifty years. In the fourth grade, these two boys were among my best friends; by the seventh grade, they were two of the most vicious boys in the neighborhood; by the eighth grade, they were no longer going to school and were sniffing several bags of glue a day; by the ninth grade, they were heroin addicts and were robbing passersby at knife point. Despite these other activities, they continued to fight with their gang on all occasions upon which they were called. This is an old story that everyone knows; that is, everyone knows the tiresome plot without really comprehending the symbolism. The tale of the city's poor boys is a tough, hermeneutically inscrutable text, after all.

It is out of this cauldron of violence and inertia, depravity and bravado, distorted masculinity and strange fellowship that emerged Jeff Chandler and, indeed, nearly every other good fighter from South Philadelphia currently working his trade. Chandler fought for the Fifth and South Streets gang; Frank (the Animal) Fletcher, a fading middleweight contender, fought with the Seventh Street gang; Matthew Saad Muhammad, known in his youth as Matthew Franklin, and light-heavyweight champion of the world in the late seventies and early eighties, fought for the Thirteenth and Fitzwater Streets gang; and Tyrone Everett, the amazingly talented lightweight who was killed by his girlfriend several years ago, fought for the Twenty-third and Tasker Streets gang.

It is the easiest thing in the world to say that professional boxing ought to be banned because it is savage, corrupt, and a dangerous health threat to the men who participate in it. Yet this moralistic rage of the righteous misses a few major points: First, to ban boxing would not prevent the creation of boxers since *that* process, *that* world would remain intact. And what are we to do with these men who know how to do nothing but fight? I suppose we can continue to lock them in our jails and in our ghettos, out of our sight and untouched by our regard. That, in the end, is precisely what those who wish to ban boxing really want to do: not to safeguard the lives of the men who must do this work but simply to sweep one excessively distasteful and inexplicable sin of bourgeois culture under the rug. Second, those who wish to ban boxing know that they will simply condemn those men to surer deaths by not legally recognizing the sport. Boxing banned will simply become what it was in eighteenth- and nineteenth-century England, a very popular underground, *totally* unregulated sport. Finally, I think it is fitting to have professional boxing in America as a moral eyesore: the sport and symbol of human waste in a culture that worships its ability to squander. And, after all, these men are selling their ability to the highest bidder, getting whatever the market will bear. Professional boxing is capitalism's psychotic vision. Or, as Jeff Chandler said when he quit being an amateur, after his third fight, "If I have to do this for a living, I'd rather get paid, any day!"

II. TODAY

Strength and violence are lonely gods. . . .
—Albert Camus, "The Minotaur, or Stopping in Oran"

Can you do the jerk?
Then watch me work.
Can you do the fly?
Then watch me try.
Bring it up. . . .
—James Brown, "Bring it Up"

One of the ultimate observations of the ultimate absurdity of the way of things in this world is not that most people are not very good at what they do. In this case we might all imagine doing something, *anything* well enough to achieve a reassuring uncritical and uncriticizable anonymity, the counterpane of slouching invisibility. Rather it is that most people not only are not very good at what they do but are not very interesting or interested in the doing. It is bad enough when our courage and imagination fail in the moment of truth; then we become nothing more than limping lumps of mediocrity. We experience far worse when our standards and ideals and expectations rise up to meet us more than halfway in our slide.

At any local boxing show, such as the one I attended during Christmas while I was in Dallas, rather fancifully entitled "Boxarama"— which, of course, brings to mind some fanciful device of Hollywood during the early 1960s called Cinerama—one expects to see more than a few fighters who would bring no disgrace upon themselves if they quietly retired from the ring and sought another line of work. The true boxing fan shows up at such cards as this in hopes that the wizardry of a Muhammad Ali or Ray Leonard, the intensity of a Roberto Duran, or the technical skill of a Marvelous Marvin Hagler might be seen in some inchoate form in a young man at an early stage in his career. There is a sheer delightful excitement that is matched by few experiences in this life when one sees potential greatness in a performer. Inevitably, at most local boxing matches, these hopes are dashed rather rudely and the true boxing fan settles back in his chair in a state of relaxed, even cozy boredom, enjoying with a certain relishing and cultivated indifference the sublime differential between what is not there and what is.

A few years ago one would not have expected to find much local boxing in Dallas or in the state of Texas for that matter, except possibly in the areas where Mexicans are dominant, they being traditional lovers and practitioners of the sport. There was not much support for boxing in this state, where football was and still is the provincial obsession. Boxing, just as recently as the middle seventies, was seen by Texans as a sport of the East Coast or West Coast, where thugs and immigrants grew in bunches. One had to go to a city like, say, Philadelphia to see local prizefights, a city where, as heavyweight Randall Cobb once described it, "even the winos know how to jab." Some changes have occurred in Texas in the last six to eight years: First, several boxers from the Lone Star State have achieved national reputations. There are the Curry brothers from Houston; Donald is the current World Boxing Association welterweight champ and Bruce is the former world junior welterweight champ. There is "Rockin'" Robin Blake, current lightweight contender from Levelland; former lightweight champion Ruben Munoz from Dallas; the brilliant, strong, but dangerously psychotic Tony Ayala, middleweight from San Antonio, now in jail serving time for robbing and raping a schoolteacher; and former bantamweight champ Gaby Canizales from Laredo. Texas has produced more than a few good fighters in recent days to live up to its past reputation as the state that produced the Galveston Giant, Jack Johnson, the first black heavyweight champ. Also, with the huge influx of northerners and easterners and Mexicans into Texas in the last ten years, an audience has been created for the sport. A sizable swath of the population in the state no longer makes the "hook 'em, Horns" sign as a form of greeting.

The fights took place on a very warm and very rainy evening at a place called the Conquistador Ballroom in the Marriott Market Center, a location better suited for a political fund-raising dinner than an evening of boxing. A fair-sized crowd of 300 or so patrons appeared, including a fair number of women. These women were not simply those who were accompanying boyfriends or husbands, or women who seemed to be groupies, although they were well represented, but rather a good many women who were fight fans—who came out to cheer their favorites as lustily as did the men. Often, women are not taken seriously as true lovers of the sport: they are seen as the adornment on the arm of some man (e.g., the gangster's moll, the politician's mistress), usually wearing a mink coat and fancy jewelry. Or they are symbolically cast as the round girl—the obligatory buxom, scantily clad young woman who walks across the ring after each round during each fight with a card announcing the number of the upcoming round—who becomes the prize in the game itself. In the world of boxing, because fighters are not permitted to have sex during their six weeks of training—"Fucking makes a fighter weak," one trainer once told me—women become, ironically, both the totem and the taboo. Is boxing the psychological quest for the primeval male and his primeval past when the relationship between men and women was imagined to be so much simpler because it was so much clearer? Is boxing the last sport where a man can be an unambiguous hero because the virtues needed for success in this endeavor—the daring, endurance, and heart of the adventurer—are so traditionally and exclusively perceived as male?

Being an outsider and completely unfamiliar with the hometown favorites, I watched the fights with more disinterested curiosity than ardent passion. It is an odd sense of displacement that one has when one cannot root for the local heroes, an essential act of participation for the fan at fights such as these. The crowd, of course, always informed me when the fighters were announced just who the prince of the moment was. I was never in the dark for very long about that. Many of the fighters apparently were from Houston and Tyler but were well received in Dallas nonetheless. The Houston fighters also brought along a sizable contingent of supporters who sat across from me and shouted advice and encouagement to their "homeboys" with an almost evangelical fervor:

"Work the left, Reggie; work the left. Everything off the jab."

"OK, man, beautiful. All night long. Just work the jab all night long."

"Throw that right over the top, Ford. Throw the wild right."

"You's hurting the boy. Go on in. He ain't got nothing."

"Hey, come on, Ray. It ain't nothing but something to do. It ain't nothing but a little work."

"Hurt 'im in the body, man. The boy ain't got no body. Just bust that sucker's ribs."

There were eight fights on the card—originally, it was a ten-fight card, but two were canceled because the fighters did not show up—including two ten-round main events. Of the sixteen fighters only two—Kenneth and Anthony Releford, brothers and both welterweights—displayed enough talent to have any real hope of ever entertaining the possibility of fighting for a title. They each fought a particularly peace-loving, dreadful Mexican fighter who, like a worker with his eyes constantly on the time clock, seemed more interested in collecting a check than in winning the fight. Kenneth stopped his opponent with a powerful right cross in the third round; Anthony stopped his with a barrage of blows in the second. For the amount of resistance that they put up, the Mexican fighters might have done the crowd a favor and called it a day in the first round. They did provide the one service of sticking around long enough so that the Releford brothers could show the crowd a small sampling of their wares. I hope those men will get a chance to fight boxers in the top ten of their division before the end of the year; they are nearly ready for that.

The last fight of the evening was the most interesting because it struck me as the most dismal and distressing. It was a contest between two heavyweights—the big boys are always saved as the highlight of any boxing card—a bald-headed, heavy-muscled Trinidadian named John "Young Duran" Williams and a white fighter from Tyler named Mickey "Rapid Fire" Prior. Williams, whose nickname of "Young Duran" was the mystery of the evening since he did not resemble the renowned champion from Panama in physical appearance or in fighting style, nearly dwarfed Prior in both height and weight. Indeed, despite the fact that both men were heavyweights and weighed over 200 pounds, the fight resembled more an encounter between a heavyweight and a middleweight.

Prior lived up to his nickname and started out very fast, landing a barrage of punches to the head and body of Williams, who simply stood in the corner and absorbed a fearful beating. It would have been a favor to the humanity of the fans, even if they were not aware of it, for the fight to have ended in the first round. Unfortunately, Williams survived the round despite nearly buckling to the canvas twice. From the second round through the tenth and final round, the fight became a very perverse joke. Williams began to land very ponderous rights to the head of Prior, who continued his relentless attack, constantly pinning Williams in the corner and pummeling him furiously. But it became very apparent to me, despite the crowd's vociferous cries of approval for all the "heavy action," that neither of these men knew the first thing about boxing. Round after round, as the crowd screamed with delight, these two men simply bashed each other. In one round it would appear that Williams was finished, but in the next Prior would seem out on his feet. By the sixth round, the drubbing that each man had so primitively absorbed became apparent to the eye of the observer. Prior's mouth was pouring blood like a faucet, so much blood that Williams's white trunks were now a solid pink. Williams, on the other hand, had thick swellings all over his face. I sat in agitated boredom. It was a terrible, terrible fight. There was nothing to cheer in this blood-letting, and ironically, despite all the punches that were being thrown, this fight, because both men were so incompetent, was the most tedious event of the evening. I thought it would never end. The Mexicans earlier on the card had the right idea: it was better to go through the motions of the work and get the check than to get beat up for the benefit and entertainment of, well, of us, the audience. We did not merit witnessing two human beings putting out so much in such an undignified yet strangely poignant way in return for so little. When the fight ended, the audience was on its feet cheering these two hapless, thoroughly whipped, completely fatigued young men. When the fight was declared a draw, usually an unpopular decision with most fight crowds, the patrons cheered again. I suppose the crowd did not see the decision in the same way I did: a draw, it seemed, simply announced that instead of having one winner, which the fighters and the fans always demand, there were two losers. The decision seemed an elaborate con; both men were severely beaten and both now had nothing to show for it. Alas, it never fails to happen to me these days that I am always discomforted by watching some prizefight, that before it is all over I am asking myself why these men are doing this and why I am here. And I must face the ugly fact about myself that I am here because I like boxing more than I dislike it, and I suppose those men are in the ring because they like it, too, and, more important, like me, need to like it. Boxing seems to teach the same lesson to me in recent years, the same very unkind lesson to which I have not hardened myself: The world is either denigrating self-surrender and denial (the used-up Mexican fighters) or it is stupid, pointless affirmation (Williams versus Prior). And why not deny and surrender when the terms of affirmation offer nothing very much better? If the world has taken the best, why not let it take the rest, as Billie Holiday used to sing. And what are those like the Releford brothers but the illusions that allow us, as Samuel Beckett writes, to go on. Or as I heard an old black preacher once shout to his congregation: "When God's on fire, you can't stand the light; but when the devil's on fire, you love the warmth."

As I was leaving the ballroom I thought about the days when I was a boy and would go to the Uptown Theatre and see all the black R&B stars. My favorite was James Brown. And I used to love it when the M.C. would announce Brown's appearance by saying in a stuttering way: "Can your . . . I mean, can your . . . I wanna know, can your heart stand it?" I remembered the days of the corner boys fighting in vacant lots and playgrounds, saying to one another to bolster each other's courage on days of heavy weather: "Your heart gotta stand it. You gotta stand up to the shit and take it like a man."

I had forgotten my umbrella. I realized when I reached the exit door that it was still under my seat. I walked back for it in a hurry; my wife was waiting for me outside. Standing beside the ring, pouring sweat in tiny rivulets was John Williams, the Trinidadian, talking to a small collection of the faithful. He looked disgusted and in a very heavy accent he was telling those who would listen that he thought he had won the fight. He had some sympathetic ones heeding his words. "I had more heart," he said quietly. "I proved I got more heart than the other guy. I had more left at the end." I picked up my umbrella and stopped beside the fighter for about twenty seconds, then turned and departed abruptly. I did not want to hear it. I had heard it all before, long ago. I knew he had more left at the end. I knew *his* heart could stand it. But after all these years of watching fights, I was beginning to wonder how much *I* had left, how much *my* heart could stand it.

Richard Hoffer

For nineteen years, Richard Hoffer (b. 1949) brought a Lieblingesque intelligence, grace, and wry humor to the boxing pieces he wrote for *Sports Illustrated*. The first of them was the 1989 cover story "Still Hungry After All These Years," the tale of George Foreman as he transformed himself from brutish to avuncular while marching toward a showdown with Mike Tyson (which never happened). Hoffer was one of the stars of the *Los Angeles Times*'s sports department when he handed it in, but *SI* soon claimed him for its own. In those days, great boxing writing was more than a tradition at the magazine—it set the standard for writing about all sports. Hoffer, like Mark Kram, William Nack, George Plimpton, and A. J. Liebling before him, kept it that way. He went on to write a critically acclaimed book about Tyson's implosion, *A Savage Business*, in 1998. Ten years later he left the magazine to jump into the literary world with both feet. His departure and a decline in interest in boxing led to a tectonic shift in *SI*'s priorities. The magazine began covering the sport almost as an afterthought, as if Hoffer had turned off the lights on his way out the door.

Still Hungry After All These Years

IN 1965, when George Foreman left Houston, there was only the one Dairy Dream, and a man had to be purposeful indeed to gather about him a burger and fries. But by 1977, when Foreman returned in retirement, that great city had put folks on the moon, developed indoor baseball and constructed fast-food restaurants on every available corner. A man could simply mean to drive down the street for stamps and somehow there would be this bucket of Original Recipe on the seat next to him.

It was the dawning of a great era, a time when a hungry man, say a man newly released from a training regimen, could order from a menu at one intersection, move along for a few blocks until the sack was exhausted and then drive through a Wendy's or a McDonald's. And the great thing was, he never had to be embarrassed by his appetite. It wasn't like he was returning to that same Dairy Dream for a refill 20 minutes later. *Would you look who's back! Better take another steer to the kill room!* No, the great thing was that he could just keep driving down the street. And if it did get to the point where a man might be recognized by his gluttony, well, he could simply speak to that most non-judgmental of all kitchen service, the curbside clown.

And the variety was astonishing. Foreman, in fact, was pleased to see that his own particular boulevard of broken seams, Westheimer Road, in southwest Houston, was welcoming the fast-food fish franchises. Not since Wendy's introduced its double-meat burger had Foreman seen the industry make this kind of leap of innovation. It was quite a time. Try to picture a Rolls-Royce Corniche, a big round man in overalls at the wheel, gliding down Westheimer Road, two trips a night, the car nosing into drive-throughs: a Burger King or a Jack-in-the-Box or one of "the Kentucky fellas" or—brand new!—battered halibut.

So you understand how Foreman might have gotten out of fighting trim. But was this the worst of it? No, it was not. Foreman had forsaken boxing for the pulpit in 1977 and in time gathered his own flock under the banner of the Church of the Lord Jesus Christ. Such parishioners as he had often called on him for help with spiritual problems, but it was Foreman's observation that these problems were frequently solved somewhere between the stove and table, without much help from him.

"This is the truth," he says. "I'd walk through the door and smell the chicken, the biscuits, the gravy, and soon I was at the table. And it was: You want another of these ham hocks? Or: Can I give you another slice of cornbread? Then nobody could remember what the problem was and they'd say, Well, we're having this or that next week, and I'd be back for a couple of weeks. And I wouldn't lie to you but that's the way it was for about seven years."

So of course a man would grow large, what with his lay ministry and his high-caloric cruising of Westheimer. By his own reckoning, Foreman, a magnificently proportioned 220 pounds as the heavyweight champion of the world, had ballooned to "300-and-some-odd pounds," and the "odd" is generally believed to be in increments of

20. He was huge and, as entrepreneurs identified new foods to deep-fry, was getting bigger.

None of this was anybody's business but his tailor's until the day Foreman decided to make a comeback. Then he became what has been one of sport's more cherished icons, the boxer/buffoon. Fat, foolish and 40, and all that stands in his way is Mike Tyson, a nice little package of youth, conditioning and violence. Folks, the gag writers whispered among themselves, there will be comedy tonight.

There is an unnecessary cruelty in this, a meanness that Foreman is able to shrug off. About all he ever wanted to do was to get enough to eat. He remembers Saturday nights, waiting for his mother to come home from a restaurant where she worked. "She'd buy a gigantic hamburger, big and round, and bring it home," he says. "We're talk-ing about seven children. And she'd give everybody a little piece. And I'd sit there and nurse that little piece, kiss it a little bit, smell it and finally eat that little piece. There was nothing more I wanted in life than to be able to have enough food."

The gag writers allowed Foreman no special courtesy because of this leftover hunger. And so they gathered together two years ago when, after a 10-year layoff, he entered the ring for a bout with Steve Zouski. Foreman had apparently cut back to one trip a night up and down Westheimer and had gotten down to 267 pounds. But the gag writers were nonetheless delighted with the remaining flab that jig-gled before their eyes. Most of them couldn't help but point out that George Foreman, lovable as he had become in retirement, had finally bitten off more than he could chew.

The comeback has now gone 18 fights without a loss, all of them won by TKOs. It has been barnstorming more than anything else, with Foreman appearing in such venues as Sacramento; Orlando, Fla.; Springfield, Mo.; and Phoenix. The opponents have been roundly ridiculed while Foreman himself remains ridiculously round—253 at his last weigh-in.

Hardly anybody sees progress—some, in fact, see fraud—yet it is agreed that a Foreman–Tyson match is becoming inevitable. As in the old days, before casinos became the sites of choice, countries are expressing interest in sponsoring the fight. Boxing being what it is, Foreman is becoming an economic imperative.

Perhaps, also, there are people who remember that Foreman, every so often, stops to remake himself in one image or another. He has done turns as mugger, patriot, boxing champion and preacher. None of these remakes has involved much advance planning, but they seem to have been prompted by all kinds of corny happenstance—a television commercial, for one. But whenever Foreman does decide to turn his life upside down, he does it with conviction and with success. So, if he wants to be a 40-year-old heavyweight champion. . . .

Question: Why be a 40-year-old heavyweight champion? The boxer/ buffoon is sitting in the George Foreman Youth and Community Center, a stucco building near Houston Intercontinental Airport. The building is one of the few in the neighborhood that is not up on blocks. The humidity is daunting. Foreman has just finished three rounds of shadowboxing in the youth center's boxing ring, which, along with some weights on the side, is the center's principal apparatus. The sweat is pouring off him, and you wonder why he isn't a light heavyweight instead of, well, what he is.

Foreman has answered the question a dozen different ways. When he was practicing his measured savagery in the '70s—knocking down Joe Frazier six times in two rounds to win the title, in Kingston, Jamaica—he was hardly known for his comedy bits. He had instead adopted former stablemate Sonny Liston's approach to public comportment, which was to glare a lot and issue sweeping statements of doom. But now he has worked the comeback into a kind of lounge act.

He mentions the taxes on his ranch in Marshall, Texas; he mentions his girth; he mentions his wife; he mentions his many children. He also has a routine about middle age and how every man with salt and pepper in his beard will be able to look in the mirror after Foreman destroys Tyson and yell, "Yippi-i-ti-yee!" It's acceptable material. But seriously, folks.

"O.K. Biggest reason? Biggest reason was my brother Roy. He had a gym on the south side of town," Foreman explains. "I don't know why he got into boxing. Soul-searching, I guess, trying to help kids. Someone gave him a building and I even gave him a bag from my days. Told me he was helping children, getting them into an amateur tournament, something of that sort."

Foreman felt a vague distaste for boxing at this stage of the game, and he was dubious about Roy's efforts to help kids by teaching them to fight. After his last fight, a 12-round losing decision to Jimmy Young in Puerto Rico in 1977, Foreman had had a religious experience in the dressing room, and from then on he had put as much distance between himself and boxing as possible. He wore suits, and he shaved his head and face, so nobody would confuse this storefront preacher with that moving mountain of malevolence from the '70s.

"I figured I could never be involved again in boxing because what would my congregation say," he says. "Me, a preacher, helping kids learn to hit one another." Strange talk, of course, from someone who once roamed Houston's Fifth Ward as a one-man scourge. "But one day I stopped in from doing some business, and Roy was signing up kids for his boxing program and this lady came in to bring her boy. I guess for a certain age, the mothers had to sign for them. And this was a young mother, but you could tell she was upset. This boy, he was maybe 14 or 15 years old, and the mother, she gave me a look as if to say, George Foreman, you could really help this boy, maybe take him off the street, make a good boxer out of him, keep him out of trouble. And I looked back to her as if to say, If you really want to help this boy, bring him to church. You don't need athletics, you need church. You need someone to tell him about the Bible and what's right and wrong. I remember walking away, thinking that."

Some months later Foreman thought to ask his brother, Whatever became of that kid, anyway? Roy reported that the boy and an accomplice had held up a gas station in George's own proper suburb of Humble, and that the attendant shot the accomplice and the would-be boxer shot the attendant. Roy thought he was doing about eight years. "All these lives were devastated because I didn't have time or I was ashamed of what my congregation would think of me," he says. "That was 1983, when I stopped being able to sleep at night."

Foreman has made a fortune in boxing; he and Muhammad Ali pulled down $5 million apiece for their fight in Zaïre. He spent a fortune, of course. He had properties scattered throughout the West; he bought a lion and a tiger, and he got a prize bull just because he admired its musculature. He bought a German shepherd for $21,000. This in addition to the usual extravagances: enough cars to start his own dealership, and all appliances as soon they were invented. To this day, friends will mention a piece of electronics by saying, "The first VCR [microwave, camcorder, etc.] I ever saw was in George's house."

"But there was always a pocket that wouldn't go, the money for me and my family to live happily ever after on," says Foreman. So out of that pocket, a low-six-figure income, came funds for his youth center, which he operates with Roy, funds for scholarships, funds for whatever the kids needed.

"I had it going real good, but each month it was starting to eat into my principal a little more," Foreman says. He thought there was plenty of principal left until one day his attorney came down to the center, stood over by the basketball hoop, and said that Foreman would have to let this place go because he was a lot closer to becoming Joe Louis than Father Flanagan. "I almost cried. Well, I said, I'll just start supporting it more. And I took on speaking engagements, booked myself around the country, just preaching.

"So this guy near Georgia invited me out and told me he would pay me so much for three nights. He'd donate it to the center. Well, O.K. He told me he already had the money, but when I got there, he started collecting. He didn't have the money. He looked at the collection and said, 'Now look here. George Foreman is doing so much for these kids, they're your kids, help him with this program.' He counted it again and then said, "Wait a minute, you can do better than this.' Man, I never felt so hurt and embarrassed in my life. And I made a vow. I said, I'll never do this again. I know how to make money. I went back and put on my boxing trunks."

Why be a 40-year-old champion? The short answer is, So you can sleep nights.

This latest life change is the least of Foreman's remarkable transformations. He used to be one of those kids he now aims to help. Not the kind who might shoot up a gas station. That would have been a considerable upgrade for his character. He was quite a bit worse, even if unarmed.

Lester Hayes, the Los Angeles Raider defensive back and another famous athlete to survive life in the Fifth Ward—a gritty section of small frame cottages on the north side of Houston—was six years younger than Foreman but hardly removed from his reach. Hayes, like everybody else, was a member of a gang, one of about 12 in the neighborhood, each representing a specific interest. There were fighting gangs, of course, but there was also a dancing gang, whose members spent the day fast-stepping down the gravel streets. The great spectator fun came when a dancing gang accidentally shimmied into a fighting gang. Hayes's gang specialized "in doing mischievous things." Like? "Oh, pillaging the neighborhood 7-Eleven, things of that nature," Hayes says. But Foreman's Hester House gang—George was the lead enforcer in a gang named after a nearby athletic center—wreaked a more practical kind of mischief.

"First time I met George Foreman I was in the seventh grade, hanging around a neighborhood store," Hayes says. "Up walks George Foreman and he asks me to loan him a nickel. I was eating a greasy-spoon hamburger, too, so he asks me for a bite of that. He took the entire burger.

"The next time I saw George, the idea of a nickel was null and void. I loaned him a quarter. It seemed to me huge inflation was taking place. Of course, I would have gone home and found a quarter for him if I didn't have one on me. He was a very, very big kid and had a reputation for savage butt kickings. That was his forte. So by the early age of 12, I had met George Foreman twice and I found both occasions extremely taxing."

Foreman was "the neighborhood small-change collector," Hayes says. "Anybody on George's turf had to pay a silver coin toll, tax-free income, and then take a terrible beating. I will say this of George: He was a smart gangster in that he would tax you first and then kick your butt. But he wasn't a very nice thing."

Foreman and a small circle of friends used these coins to get a start on the day's serious mugging. They bought cheap wine and then, emboldened, found victims of more financial means than pips like Lester Hayes. When Foreman tells the story, it is not to marvel at his meanness but at his ignorance. "We didn't even know this was wrong," he says. "I remember once, two boys and myself, we robbed a guy. Threw him down. I could hold the guy because I was strong, and the sneaky fella would grab the money. And then we'd run until we couldn't hear the guy screaming anymore. And then we'd walk home as if we'd just earned some money on a job, counting it. We didn't even know we were criminals."

His ignorance astonishes him still. "I thought a hero was a guy with a big, long scar down his face, a guy who'd come back from prison, a guy maybe killed a man once. Can you imagine, my goal was to have a scar on my cheek? I tell you, I wore a Band-Aid across my cheek until the day I could get a real one."

By most accounts Foreman wouldn't have had to wait long for a scar of his own. His father was living apart from the family, and there was just so much a mother could enforce on this growing boy. School wasn't much of an influence; he hardly went. Sports meant nothing to him. And he was even outstripping his gang's small-change ambitions.

Yet he didn't feel resigned to this life. He was surprised to realize that, after a cousin caught him sneaking back into his bedroom after lunch on a school day. She told him. Go ahead, go on back to sleep. And he said, No, you got it wrong, I was on my way to school, really. She said, Don't lie, don't bother. Nobody in this family, nobody from around here is gonna become anything anyway, so go on back to sleep. Don't fight it. You know you're not gonna be nothing.

Foreman became furious. "I got my clothes back on and left. I'd show her. I didn't go to school, of course, but I wasn't going to sit there and let her tell me I wasn't going to be anything. I just didn't know anything to be."

Shortly thereafter, Foreman saw Jim Brown in a commercial on TV. Brown was a hero to Foreman. Saw him back over a goal line once, three defenders hanging on to him. Foreman walked like Brown, talked like him. Listened to him. There was Jim Brown on TV saying, Hey, why not be somebody, join the Job Corps. On the strength of that, Foreman packed himself off to Oregon. He didn't know exactly what he could be, but he could at least be it somewhere else.

What he was in the Job Corps was principally a thug in a new outfit. But Foreman was coming into contact with potential influences—like the Mr. America who showed up and delivered a cornball speech about being an American. Ninety-nine kids in a hundred would have hooted the guy right out of town. The guy did a few push-ups with the biggest kid in camp on his shoulders, things like that. He closed with this spiel about being an American. Don't worry what other kids call you, he said. You're an American. Nobody can take that from you. Cornball. But Foreman felt so disfranchised that the news he was an American—the idea that he belonged to anything—struck him with bulletin force and made him weep. "To you it doesn't mean any-thing," he says. "You got to understand, a person whose only heroes are bandits, guys with scars across their faces, and here's a person tell-ing you you're an American." It had never even occurred to him. Up to that point, Foreman didn't have any use for the national anthem. "It meant the end of the broadcast day."

What was it with Jim Brown, with this Mr. America, interfering in the life of George Foreman? They couldn't sleep nights?

All of George Foreman's famous fights were staged in exotic locales. He won the Olympic gold medal in Mexico City—no small feat in that he had had less than two years of training in the sport. But it became even bigger when Foreman walked around the ring waving an American flag. This was the season of black-gloved fists, remember.

When he beat Frazier for the title in '73, it was a tremendous upset. The match had been intended to kill time until Frazier and Muham-mad Ali could fight again. Foreman was high-quality stuff, but unpracticed and generally considered to have been set up with soft touches. This was to be a $375,000 payday for the young patriot, and then he would be sent on his way. But Foreman demolished Frazier, whose reputation for violence was then worldwide. The Fifth Ward survivors must have shrugged over that one: What did we tell you?

For a guy who waved the flag, Foreman hardly ever fought under it. He defended his title in Tokyo, in Caracas and then in Zaïre. Ah, Zaïre. The big brute completely neutralized by the cunning of Ali. What could the Fifth Ward survivors have made of that?

Then there was an exhibition in Toronto—five men in one night—his swan song in San Juan against Young, and the immediate spiritual revelation that followed. He also had a pretty big fight back in 1966 in Pleasanton, Calif., a fight not much reported and seen by only a dozen or so youth counselors. The Job Corps may have saved Lester Hayes's skin but it didn't guarantee everyone's safety. On this par-ticular day Foreman was administering a terrific butt kicking to some kid who probably wished Jim Brown had never been born.

Doc Broadus, a man who fancied berets and riding quirts, was a

Job Corps supervisor at the time. His special interest was developing boxers. He figures that's why the panicky counselors finally came to him that day, explaining that this great big guy, this 16-year-old, was endangering a fellow volunteer's life that minute. Ten counselors couldn't handle him.

So Broadus left his gym and walked out to see what was happening. Broadus was prepared to be more disgusted with the helpless staff—"all these educated counselors"—than with this great big guy. But the level of violence on which this great big guy was working truly impressed him. "He was stomping the kid, being very brutal about it," Broadus says. He remembers thinking that there was a state prison, Santa Rita, across the street, and what Foreman was doing qualified him for immediate admission there, no waiting.

Broadus walked into the middle of this, parted the terrified counselors who stood helplessly by and walked right up to Foreman. "Hey, big man," Broadus said. "Why don't you pick on somebody your own size."

You are tempted to look through George Foreman's life and ask, Why did these certain words, or this commercial, or that speech galvanize him? What was it about these small meddlings that kept turning his life around?

Well, Broadus's approach wouldn't make one think of Mr. Chips, but for Foreman, it would have to do. Foreman let his poor victim drop to the ground and turned to look at this strange man. Broadus remembers that look, and he remains surprised by it to this day. "It was a look, like asking for help. It was all over his face: Help me. Here he was, big and strong, everybody afraid of him, and he was giving me this look. It kind of tickled me. It was like he had been waiting all his life for this."

Broadus put his arm around Foreman and said, "C'mon, big fella, let's walk and talk."

Before you knew it, Foreman had become Olympic champion under Broadus's supervision, and then heavyweight champion of the world under Dick Sadler. He was rich and famous. Because somebody told him to pick on kids his own size? Because Mr. America told him he belonged somewhere? Because Jim Brown made a commercial? Sure.

*

There are probably all kinds of people who can help a kid who's a little down and out. But Foreman found he was newly adrift when he became rich and famous. Where are the role models for somebody who turns 25 and is offered $5 million paydays?

Take the idea of buying things. Foreman says the experience is highly overrated, and he gave it a pretty fair chance, too. As the money rolled in he bought, by his guess, 10 cars. A 32-foot mobile home. Quarter-million-dollar homes in Houston and Livermore, Calif. Exotic animals. He boned up on the breeding of German shepherds and finally bought that prize dog from Germany.

He was going by the book. "People said, You become champ, you'll need you a fleet of cars. So I got to be champ and that's all I looked for, a fleet of cars. Nobody told me about nothing else. Maybe a house with a pool, so I got that. It was the idea of having that scar again. About like that."

It wasn't as satisfying as it should have been. Foreman knew for sure something was wrong with this setup when Jim Brown, his old hero and now a Hollywood personality, came to his spread in Livermore to do a TV piece on him. Brown surveyed the layout and said, "One day I'm gonna have it together like you." Foreman was stunned. "What did I have together? A shack? Some rocks around a swimming pool, which I didn't even use? I had to pay people to come out, just to eat my potato chips. It was all frustrating, buying, buying, buying, and you still feel something is missing. But that day I realized fame was not going to give me anything if Jim Brown didn't already have it."

If it's no fun being 24 and champion of the world, try being 25 and former champion, which was what Foreman became rather quickly. Who teaches you how to handle *that*? Where was the Doc Broadus for a young millionaire with a newly reopened hole in his psyche?

You can hardly talk about Foreman without talking of his loss to Ali. Although Ali was thought to have been in it for little more than a quick payday, there were strange factors at work. The scene in Zaïre was one Foreman couldn't handle, not with Ali doing the staging. Nobody realized it, but Foreman was doomed.

Bill Caplan, his longtime p.r. man, says, "He was feeling bewitched. Ali was doing all these things with witch doctors, and George was feeling very uncomfortable." For some of the pre-fight campaign, he withdrew to government quarters and surrounded himself with Zaïrian secret police. He was entirely inaccessible. Caplan remembers seeing him in a hotel lobby—Foreman had moved out of the government quarters one morning when he looked up from his bed and saw a lizard hanging from the ceiling above him—and passing him a note requesting him for a press conference. Foreman wadded it up and dropped it on the floor.

It was a bad time. Nobody spoke. "The one area where we did have contact was ping-pong," Caplan says. This was the big sport in the Foreman camp. Archie Moore, Foreman's chief strategist then as now, used to walk around with a wicker basket, like Little Red Riding Hood, and make a great show of producing his paddles and getting a game going. It was Moore's belief that Foreman's psyche was better served by allowing him to win.

For some reason, Foreman preferred playing Caplan, even though the only way they communicated those days was by note. Caplan would see Foreman arrive with his secret police cadre, and a game would soon be on. "I beat him every day," Caplan says. "Archie would say, Let him win. No way." It was the p.r. man's only available dignity.

There were many curious things about the fight. Ali's rope-a-dope is the most talked about after all these years. Foreman would later complain of food doctored by "whoopee powder," of ropes loosened by "professional slickers," of sabotage in his own corner. He complained that Sadler, his manager, failed to get him up in time after Ali knocked him down in the eighth round. When he was counted out, the only person who seemed concerned was Caplan, who was first into the ring to console the fallen champ. Actually, he was the only one doing any consoling. Foreman's corner had disappeared in disgust.

Still, what do you make of this? The fight ended, and some 200 newsmen crowded into Foreman's sweltering dressing room. The sullen intimidator, the man who would be Sonny Liston, was lying on a table; the silence was as dramatic as it was uncomfortable. He finally sat up and said, "I have a statement to make." Pens and pads were poised. "I just want to say that tonight"—big pause—"I found a true friend in Bill Caplan."

Even with a true friend, though, it was several years before

Foreman learned to live with that defeat. He would wake up in a sweat, thinking about the fight. In fact, it wasn't until 1978 that he was able to let it go. He was talking to a reporter, and he found himself saying, "Man, he whipped me fair and square. He'd probably whip me again." And the weight of that loss seemed to slide off him.

By then he had suffered another remarkable defeat, the decision to Young, lost in the heat of San Juan in 1977. At first it didn't seem to amount to much. "He got the decision," Foreman remembers, "but only because it got so hot in there and I wanted to get out." Foreman was not at all disappointed in how things had gone.

But, as in Zaïre, the postfight minutes were confusing and surprising. Foreman was cooling off and saying to himself, Man, who cares about a boxing match? I still got everything. If I wanted to, I could retire now, go to the country. I could retire and die.

Now, where did the idea of dying come from? And then Foreman felt himself plunged "into a deep, dark nothing, like out in a sea, with nothing over your head or under your feet.

"Just nothing," Forman says, "nothing but nothing. A big dark lump of it. And a horrible smell came with it. A smell I haven't forgotten. A smell of sorrow. You multiply every sad thought you ever had, it wouldn't come close to this. And then I looked around and I was dead. That was it. I thought of everything I worked for. I hadn't said goodbye to my mother, my children. All the money I hid in safe-deposit boxes! You know how paper burns and when you touch it, it just crumbles. That was my life. I looked back and saw it crumble, like I'd fallen for a big joke.

"And then I said, I don't think this is death. I still believe in God. And I said that and I was back alive in the dressing room. And I could feel the blood flowing through my veins."

It was a wonderful sensation. Says Foreman, "For a moment, I felt I was somebody."

Gil Clancy, his trainer for that fight, says Foreman was suffering from heat prostration. Foreman smiles at the idea. Even as he was undergoing this experience, he knew nobody would believe him. "You know that feeling I was supposed to get from being champion?

What that scar was supposed to give me? I had that feeling in that room. They thought I was crazy, and I don't blame them."

From then on he has led the life of a preacher, appearing on Houston street corners and eventually in his own church, a small metal building a block from his youth center, where he conducts three meetings a week. With a good sermon, he says, he can sometimes get a little bit of that feeling. "To this day I've been searching, trying to get that feeling and keep it."

Except for expenses eating into his principal, the case of George Foreman would have ended there, with Foreman chasing that spiritual high. There certainly were no regrets about leaving boxing. "I hadn't balled my fist in 10 years," he says. He didn't have a TV for some time, so the passing parade of heavyweights went by largely unnoticed.

But, there were those expenses. Foreman is not the first aging heavyweight champ to return to the ring—nor the first fighter to donate his earnings to a youth center—and rarely has it been a good idea. The boxing establishment seems to have come down solidly against his comeback. NBC boxing commentator Ferdie Pacheco says he always thought that Foreman and Rocky Marciano were the only guys who ever got out of boxing on time. But to come back now? Quite simply, Pacheco says, "This is pathetic. It shouldn't be allowed. He's overage, inept. This whole thing is a fraudulent second career to build a money fight with Tyson."

Emanuel Steward, trainer of Thomas Hearns, among others, is similarly disgusted. On hand for the latest of Foreman's fights, a two-round TKO of Bert Cooper on June 1, he said, "A traveling road show. It just proves, you keep something out there long enough and the people will start to believe. Never in the history of boxing have there been so many handpicked bums."

Foreman has been choosy about his opponents—to a fault, some say. Bob Arum promoted some of his early fights but grew frustrated when Foreman began nixing possible opponents. Arum had a fight made for Foreman and Anders Ecklund. "But lo and behold," says Arum, "he said Ecklund was too tough. Hits too hard."

Arum got to like Foreman, actually; here was a fighter who would book economy for a flight to an ESPN fight and then upgrade with his own money. But after a while it became clear that Foreman was not going to stand for any competition on his way to a blockbuster fight. Arum dropped him.

Foreman defends his choice of opponents by saying he has had to start from the ground up, so of course he would have to take it easy. "I didn't come back and say, I want the Cadillac in the window," he says. Not right away. "Anyway, I heard this same stuff the first time I came up."

Yet men more pragmatic than Arum have come to accept a Foreman–Tyson fight as inevitable. Dan Duva, who promotes Evander Holyfield, came nosing around one of Foreman's fights. Would he be interested in Foreman as an opponent? "Sure." Because Foreman is for real? "I make no editorial comment about George Foreman's abilities," he said, laughing. "But this is the biggest fight out there."

There are other elements to the Foreman scenario. Rick Kulis, who distributes the pay-per-view on the West Coast for big fights, says, first, there are very few opponents left for Tyson. "And Foreman represents the old guard, when you had clear-cut champions. He also represents the link to, you could say, integrity, when a champion was a champion outside the ring as well. And he's one of about four fighters independent of Don King."

The people who will have to sell this fight will not overlook Foreman's evangelical calling, especially as it plays against Tyson's bad-boy image. A story line never hurts the promotion.

"I used to think that George would have to fight a Top 10 guy," says Kulis. "But it looks like George was right. He knew they'd eventually have to come back to him if he remained unhurt and undefeated. As it looks like there is no one out there to take on Tyson, the feeling becomes more and more. Why not George?"

Because of Foreman's style and size—he is 6'3" to Tyson's 5'11"—there are some who believe that he is the one man made to topple Tyson. Trainer Angelo Dundee says, "I give him a shot, because George Foreman is devastating against short guys. I'm open-minded. I can be showed."

Then, too, there is a school of thought that says Tyson's list of victims is no more impressive than Foreman's is.

"Tyson has fought and knocked a lot of guys out," Foreman says, "but they were prey. He's never seen anything like me. I'm not the best of fighters, by any means. I'm just the only one of my kind that's around—guys who throw punches. Sonny Liston. Cleveland Williams. Hooks that break your jaw. Joe Frazier. Predators."

Foreman has indeed been a thumping presence on this comeback, yet every critic eventually comes around to this: He has yet to stop anybody with a 10 count. All stoppages have been by referees. The worst was his last one, when Bert Cooper sat on his stool after two rounds and refused to come out. He said Foreman's punches were "buzzing" his brain.

Still, even these critics think that Foreman, though he can't win, will hang in there with Tyson. "In truth, I don't think Tyson could take Foreman out that quickly," says Arum. "Foreman will give you rounds, even if he has absolutely no chance."

Kulis agrees. "I cannot picture Mike Tyson running across the ring and knocking him down in 73 seconds." This is a fight that evidently has a grudging appeal. "I'd be eager to promote it," Kulis says.

Foreman is eager to have it, and with it the millions he can use to sustain the youth center and open others. Whereas he was once driven by a rage he couldn't understand, he is now fueled by compassion. Is this going to work? There is nothing about him that would seem to suit him for the desperate work he will have to do on fight night, not anymore. And never mind his age or size. Here is a man who used to train attack dogs, but who is now shopping for a "floppy kind of dog" more suitable for his kids. "I don't want no dog that will bite somebody," Foreman says. Is this the personality required to face down Mike Tyson?

But maybe there are other kinds of desperation. After all, who knows what a man goes through, a man who can cry at the spoilage of youth, at the waste, at the thought of all those kids with scars on their cheeks, kids who never heard Jim Brown, Mr. America, Doc Broadus, maybe George Foreman. Who knows what a man goes through, a man who can't sleep nights?

Mike Lupica

As the sun sets on the newspaper business as America has known it, there is every possibility that Mike Lupica (b. 1952) will take his place in history as the last great New York sports columnist. After capturing the city's attention as a precocious basketball writer for the *Post,* he moved to a column at the *Daily News* that he wrote as if he would settle for nothing less than to be mentioned in the same breath with Red Smith, Jimmy Cannon, and Larry Merchant. He was all of twenty-five. He has since done double duty as a regular on ESPN's *The Sports Reporters* and written a series of young-adult novels and biographies of Reggie Jackson and Bill Parcells. Where boxing is concerned, however, Lupica has been an infrequent visitor. Still, when he was moonlighting as *Esquire*'s sports columnist, he knew enough to tackle the oft-indicted, seldom-convicted Don King as the subject of this 1991 profile. Though at a severe disadvantage in height, weight, and hair, Lupica emerged triumphant.

———————

Donfire of the Vanities

THE brownstone on the Upper East Side of Manhattan is quiet for now, quiet the way a subway platform is before the train comes. You know the D is on the way, you can even feel the ground shake a bit, see some light way back in the tunnel. The train hasn't arrived yet. Don King has just left his office in another part of Manhattan.

On the table inside the front door there is a pile of books: *Hit Men, My Father Rudolf Hess, Winning Through Intimidation, Atlas Shrugged,* and the new novel by Sidney Sheldon. His dining area has a fax machine and a copy machine. On the desk in his study, he has the biggest bottle of extra-strength Tylenol you can buy. There is expensive sound equipment and a VCR, a Sergio Mendes tape, and a video-cassette of the movie *Ball of Fire,* probably one of Tyson's. There is a red-velvet crown and a glass jar filled with gumdrops and a smaller jar filled with hard candy.

An elderly maid steps from the kitchen. "He's comin'," she says.

"Somebody called a few minutes ago." She disappears up the stairs, and the Manhattan home of Don King is quiet again. No shouting, no prison-yard rap, none of the "nigger" talk he had given Spike Lee on that HBO documentary before the Mike Tyson–Alex Stewart fight. Maybe this home is more like a theme park than a subway station, a theme park before the gates open in the morning.

Behind King's desk, four black-and-white television screens monitor security. This is no surprise. The owner of this place has not only made several fortunes in his life, he has made enemies too. Before he got into boxing, he was the numbers king of Cleveland. He spent three years and eleven months in jail for manslaughter. Now, twenty years later, King is late for an interview because he has been busy making another kind of killing, closing out a $200 million deal with Showtime. He has taken Mike Tyson and Julio Cesar Chavez away from HBO. A few days earlier he told Spike Lee what a racist, oppressive society we live in. You're a nigger when you're born and a nigger when you die, he said. If you make a pile of money, you're just a rich nigger.

The front door opens now and the D train rumbles in. King is shouting at his longtime matchmaker and sideman, Al Braverman.

"Don't want any of them tellin' me about white folks, Al!" King shouts. "They gonna tell *me* about white folks?" He tries a laugh, but it comes out flat. "Shit," he says. "I've got a Ph.D. in Caucasianism."

Don King shouts for the next two hours. It is part prison-yard rap and it is part the rap of a Baptist preacher. It is angry, very angry, and funny, and brilliant, and completely ridiculous. He quotes Shakespeare and the Bible, and talks about Goebbels and Cosby and Oprah and Tyson and Evander Holyfield. Mostly he talks about Don King. He says he's been investigated by the IRS, the CIA, and Interpol.

"I beat all three!" King says. "Not even Spiro T. Agnew can say that!"

In 1972 he promoted an Ali exhibition for a black hospital in Cleveland. Ali fought four guys, two rounds each. Then King promoted the Ali–Foreman fight in Zaire. He was co-promoter for the "Thrilla in Manila."

"I watched the first Ali–Frazier fight in prison," he used to brag. "And I promoted the third one." In this brownstone now, fifteen years from Manila, after what seems like a million big boxing promotions, I say to King, "If this country is as racist as you say, they'd find a way to hold you back."

"They do," he says. "If I was white, I'd be on the cover of *Time*, *Newsweek*, *Life*, *Forbes*. I'd be on every magazine that was worth its salt; they'd have me there."

"If you were white, you'd probably be leveraged out like Trump is. You'd be one of those Murdoch guys."

"No, no, I would have been too good for that. You've got to understand, I'm dealing with these guys without a formal education. The difference is my capability and my diligence and my ability to persevere. I've never used my blackness as an excuse. I've never got no fighter based on being black. My performance is the only thing that's carried me through. You've been told the nigger is worthless, that he's shiftless, lethargic, and sloppy. He lies and steals. Stereotype image of black folks. So I got me a new appraiser. An appraiser that tells me America is a great country. If you have faith in God and you persevere, you will overcome. So now I've overcome. I've been blocked out of many deals because I'm black. But I don't let that bother me. I want to deal with what is real and pragmatic. Everybody wants to make money."

King gives answers like this to the most innocent of questions. In an age when sports figures have been conditioned to talk in perfect sound bites, he is the first rap opera.

"What would happen if a controversial white man said the things about blacks you said about whites?" I ask him. "Do you think that moves us along? Or do you think it polarizes people even more?"

"The system has to be changed. The prevailing attitude of subordinating, demeaning, degrading, humiliating, dehumanizing black people hasn't changed. I try to explain what Hitler did, and the best way I can explain it is in my own humble opinion. . . . The Jew was the nigger of Germany. I live for the day when all people are clothed in dignity. But to prove my point I have to symbolize it with something dramatic enough to get people's attention. The Jew was the nigger of Germany. Hitler did what the white American did over here in racism. He did it with propaganda."

*

Larry Holmes once said that Don King "looks black, lives white, and thinks green." Holmes is one of a number of boxers who say that Don King cheated them. Tim Witherspoon is another. You call go all the way to junior welterweights like Saoul Mamby.

In boxing, it is illegal to be both promoter and manager, a conflict of interest where a fighter can only lose. King's way around that is to make his son, Carl, the manager. Witherspoon says he signed two contracts with Carl King. The one filed with boxing commissions, he says, had Carl taking 33 percent commission. The other, the real one, had Carl taking 50 percent.

Both Kings deny any improprieties in their dealings with boxers. Of course, the father does it at full shout.

"Larry Holmes is the best testimony in the world for me," he says. "Here's a very nondescript, bland man, who just incidentally happens to be black. Very talented boxer. Nobody would fight against him. Don King's ingenuity brought him to the top and left him with $20 million."

"So why is he mad at you?"

"He's mad at me because he has an Oedipus complex."

"Larry Holmes is mad at you because he loves his mother?"

"No, no, Oedipus and his father. It's a parental thing. I've done more for Larry Holmes and the Holmes family than his father ever did. I've done more for Larry Holmes than he could do for himself. . . . I taught him how to read and write. I'm talking about sitting up at night, trying to help this human being elevate himself. Now we find him being one of my condemners."

Don King is the same father figure to Mike Tyson that he says he was to Holmes. Their relationship is very good for him. He thinks the current heavyweight champ, Evander Holyfield, is a fraud. He says he should be stripped of his title for fighting George Foreman before Tyson because Tyson is the number-one contender and, in most people's minds, still the heavyweight champion of the world.

"Evander Holyfield's a nigger. He's going to be a nigger till he dies," King says. "If he's rich he's going to be a rich nigger, if he's poor he's going to be a poor nigger. When he gets through running away from his commitment [to fight Tyson], he ain't going to have nowhere to go. Big business spits on the name of Holyfield. . . . The people who like him like him 'cause he's docile. Holyfield can be controlled. 'Run Johnny. Sing Johnny. Dance Johnny.'"

King predicts that Foreman will win the title from Holyfield in April, fight "bums" in Europe for a year or two, and retire without ever giving Tyson a shot at his title. I tell him that Tyson shouldn't have to wait years for another shot at the title.

"You're the most brilliant man I've run across," he says. "You touch my heart."

He is one of the most remarkable figures in the history of sports. And he could have become the important black voice he desperately wants to be. Up close with King, you see the brains, you see the charm, you see the passion. Ultimately, though, you have to see the hustler in him. The man is full of anger. It is more impressive than his whole range of thought, from Hitler to the Bible. King knows how smart he is. But he wants more. He wants respect. Unfortunately, he is trapped in this wild-haired character he created for himself. No one can see past it. King understands that, and it makes him mad.

"They try to vilify me," he says. "They try to make me the worst motherfucker that ever lived. Make everybody think I hate people. Try to make me a racist, but that's impossible because I've never used racism to get where I'm at. You go to my office, you'd think it's a white office, that I'm a token nigger."

King is at his best in his own courtroom, defense attorney and character witness and judge and jury all at once, asking and answering the questions, shouting down his accusers. But when all that is finished you have to ask yourself: Are they *all* lying? Holmes and Witherspoon and Tony Tubbs and Pinklon Thomas? Or is King a hypocrite, screaming about racism on one hand and preying on black fighters himself? He was supposed to be the impartial promoter of the Tyson–Douglas fight in Tokyō, but he tried to get the decision overturned in Tyson's favor as soon as the fight was over. It made him look like a fraud.

At 2:00 in the afternoon, I shut off the tape recorder and put it in my briefcase. King keeps shouting. I put on my sport jacket and then my overcoat. He does not acknowledge that I am leaving.

"They are trying to make the truth unbelievable and the untruth believable!" he shouts.

I stand there with my coat on and my briefcase in my hand and King shouts for another thirty minutes. There is something mesmerizing about it. I can understand how it happens, how a fighter like Witherspoon gets in the same room with him and signs his life away.

It is 2:40 in the afternoon when I get to the street. King is still shouting as I walk toward Third Avenue. I look back. A blond woman in running clothes is staring at him as if he were a spaceship.

Joyce Carol Oates

Of all the women who have been drawn moth-like to boxing, from wives to fighters, trainers, and promoters, there has never been one quite like Joyce Carol Oates (b. 1938). One of America's best and most prolific fiction writers, Oates was introduced to the sweet science as a child by her father and has written memorably and unsentimentally about it. "Boxing," she wrote in her book *On Boxing* (1987), "is for men, and is about men, and is men. A celebration of the lost art of masculinity all the more trenchant for being lost." Time and again, she has returned to the subject of Mike Tyson, the erstwhile heavyweight champion who had no more power over the fates than he did over himself. Perhaps her most incisive analysis of him is the following essay from 1992, which steps back from the tabloid glare of Tyson's rape trial and subsequent imprisonment and describes how boxing, celebrity, race, sex, and the justice system combined to cast a net over the lost boy of Bedford-Stuyvesant.

Rape and the Boxing Ring

MIKE TYSON'S conviction on rape charges in Indianapolis is a minor tragedy for the beleaguered sport of boxing, but a considerable triumph for women's rights. For once, though bookmakers were giving 5-1 odds that Tyson would be acquitted, and the mood of the country seems distinctly conservative, a jury resisted the outrageous defense that a rape victim is to be blamed for her own predicament. For once, a celebrity with enormous financial resources did not escape trial and a criminal conviction by settling with his accuser out of court.

That boxing and "women's rights" should be perceived as opposed is symbolically appropriate, since of all sports, boxing is the most aggressively masculine, the very soul of war in microcosm. Elemental and dramatically concise, it raises to an art the passions underlying direct human aggression; its fundamentally murderous intent is not obscured by the pursuit of balls or pucks, nor can the participants expect help from teammates. In a civilized humanitarian society, one would expect such a blood sport to have died out, yet boxing, sponsored by gambling casinos in Las Vegas and Atlantic City, and broadcast by cable television, flourishes: had the current heavyweight champion, Evander Holyfield, fought Mike Tyson in a title defense, Holyfield would have earned no less than $30 million. If Tyson were still champion, and still fighting, he would be earning more.

The paradox of boxing is that it so excessively rewards men for inflicting injury upon one another that, outside the ring, with less "art," would be punishable as aggravated assault, or manslaughter. Boxing belongs to that species of mysterious masculine activity for which anthropologists use such terms as "deep play": activity that is wholly without utilitarian value, in fact contrary to utilitarian value, so dangerous that no amount of money can justify it. Sports-car racing, stunt flying, mountain climbing, bullfighting, dueling—these activities, through history, have provided ways in which the individual can dramatically, if sometimes fatally, distinguish himself from the crowd, usually with the adulation and envy of the crowd, and traditionally, the love of women. Women—in essence, Woman—is the prize, usually self-proffered. To look upon organized sports as a continuum of Darwinian theory—in which the sports-star hero flaunts the superiority of his genes—is to see how displays of masculine aggression have their sexual component, as ingrained in human beings as any instinct for self-preservation and reproduction. In a capitalist society, the secret is to capitalize upon instinct.

Yet even within the very special world of sports, boxing is distinct. Is there any athlete, however celebrated in his own sport, who would not rather reign as the heavyweight champion of the world? If, in fantasy at least, he could be another Muhammad Ali, or Joe Louis, or indeed, Mike Tyson in his prime? Boxing celebrates the individual man in his maleness, not merely in his skill as an athlete—though boxing demands enormous skill, and its training is far more arduous than most men could endure for more than a day or two. All athletes can become addicted to their own adrenaline, but none more obviously than the boxer, who, like Sugar Ray Leonard, already a multimillionaire with numerous occupations outside the ring, will risk serious injury by coming back out of retirement; as Mike Tyson has said, "Outside of boxing, everything is so boring." What makes boxing repulsive to many observers is precisely what makes boxing so fascinating to participants.

This is because it is a highly organized ritual that violates taboo. It flouts such moral prescriptions as "Thou shalt not kill." It celebrates, not meekness, but flamboyant aggression. No one who has not seen live boxing matches (in contrast to the sanitized matches broadcast over television) can quite grasp its eerie fascination—the spectator's sense that he or she is a witness to madness, yet a madness sanctioned by tradition and custom, as finely honed by certain celebrated practitioners as an artist's performance at the highest level of genius, and, yet more disturbing, immensely gratifying to the audience. Boxing mimics our early ancestors' rite of bloody sacrifice and redemption; it excites desires most civilized men and women find abhorrent. For some observers, it is frankly obscene, like pornography; yet, unlike pornography, it is not fantasy but real, thus far more subversive.

The paradox for the boxer is that, in the ring, he experiences himself as a living conduit for the inchoate, demonic will of the crowd: the expression of their collective desire, which is to pound another human being into absolute submission. The more vicious the boxer, the greater the acclaim. And the financial reward—Tyson is reported to have earned $100 million. (He who at the age of 13 was plucked from a boys' school for juvenile delinquents in upstate New York.) Like the champion gladiators of Roman decadence, he will be both honored and despised, for, no matter his celebrity, and the gift of his talent, his energies spring from the violation of taboo and he himself is tainted by it.

Mike Tyson has said that he does not think of boxing as a sport. He sees himself as a fantasy gladiator who, by "destructing" opponents, enacts others' fantasies in his own being. That the majority of these others are well-to-do whites who would themselves crumple at a first blow, and would surely claim a pious humanitarianism, would not go unnoted by so wary and watchful a man. Cynicism is not an inevitable consequence of success, but it is difficult to retain one's boyish naiveté in the company of the sort of people, among them the notorious Don King, who have surrounded Tyson since 1988, when his co-manager, Jim Jacobs, died. As Floyd Patterson, an ex-heavyweight champion who has led an exemplary life, has said, "When you have millions of dollars, you have millions of friends."

It should not be charged against boxing that Mike Tyson *is* boxing in any way. Boxers tend to be fiercely individualistic, and Tyson is, at the least, an enigma. He began his career, under the tutelage of the legendary trainer Cus D'Amato, as a strategist, in the mode of such brilliant technicians as Henry Armstrong and Sugar Ray Robinson. He was always aware of a lineage with Jack Dempsey, arguably the most electrifying of all heavyweight champions, whose nonstop aggression revolutionized the sport and whose shaved haircut and malevolent scowl, and, indeed, penchant for dirty fighting, made a tremendous impression upon the young Tyson.

In recent years, however, Tyson seems to have styled himself at least partly on the model of Charles (Sonny) Liston, the "baddest of the bad" black heavyweights. Liston had numerous arrests to his credit and served time in prison (for assaulting a policeman); he had the air, not entirely contrived, of a sociopath; he was always friendly with racketeers, and died of a drug overdose that may in fact have been murder. (It is not coincidental that Don King, whom Tyson has much admired, and who Tyson has empowered to ruin his career, was convicted of manslaughter and served time in an Ohio prison.) Like Liston, Tyson has grown to take a cynical pleasure in publicly condoned sadism (his "revenge" bout with Tyrell Biggs, whom he carried for seven long rounds in order to inflict maximum damage) and in playing the outlaw; his contempt for women, escalating in recent years, is a part of that guise. The witty obscenity of a prefight taunt of Tyson's—"I'll make you into my girlfriend"—is the boast of the rapist.

Perhaps rape itself is a gesture, a violent repudiation of the female, in the assertion of maleness that would seem to require nothing beyond physical gratification of the crudest kind. The supreme macho gesture—like knocking out an opponent and standing over his fallen body, gloves raised in triumph.

In boxing circles it is said—this, with an affectionate sort of humor—that the heavyweight champion is the 300-pound gorilla who sits anywhere in the room he wants; and, presumably, takes any female he wants. Such a grandiose sense of entitlement, fueled by the insecurities and emotions of adolescence, can have disastrous consequences. Where once it was believed that Mike Tyson might mature into the greatest heavyweight of all time, breaking Rocky Marciano's record of 49 victories and no defeats, it was generally acknowledged that, since his defeat of Michael Spinks in 1988, he had allowed his boxing skills to deteriorate. Not simply his ignominious loss of his title to the mediocre James (Buster) Douglas in 1990, but subsequent lackluster victories against mediocre opponents made it clear that Tyson was no longer a serious, nor even very interesting, boxer.

The dazzling reflexes were dulled, the shrewd defensive skills drilled into him by D'Amato were largely abandboned: Tyson emerged suddenly as a conventional heavyweight like Gerry Cooney, who advances upon his opponent with the hope of knocking him out with a single punch—and does not always succeed. By 25, Tyson seemed already middle aged, burnt out. He would have no great fights after all. So, strangely, he seemed to invite his fate outside the ring, with sadomasochistic persistence, testing the limits of his celebrity's license to offend by ever-escalating acts of aggression and sexual effrontery.

The familiar sports adage is surely true, one's ultimate opponent is oneself.

It may be objected that these remarks center upon the rapist, and not his victim; that sympathy, pity, even in some quarters moral outrage flow to the criminal and not the person he has violated. In this case, ironically, the victim, Desiree Washington, though she will surely bear psychic scars through her life, has emerged as a victor, a heroine: a young woman whose traumatic experience has been, as so few traumas can be, the vehicle for a courageous and selfless stand against the sexual abuse of women and children in America. She seems to know that herself, telling *People* magazine, "It was the right thing to do." She was fortunate in drawing a jury who rejected classic defense ploys by blaming the victim and/or arguing consent. Our criminal-justice system being what it is, she was lucky. Tyson, who might have been acquitted elsewhere in the country, was unlucky.

Whom to blame for this most recent of sports disgraces in America? The culture that flings young athletes like Tyson up out of obscurity, makes millionaires of them and watches them self-destruct? Promoters like Don King and Bob Arum? Celebrity hunters like Robin Givens, Tyson's ex-wife, who seemed to have exploited him for his money and as a means of promoting her own acting career? The indulgence generally granted star athletes when they behave recklessly? When they abuse drugs and alcohol, and mistreat women?

I suggest that no one is to blame, finally, except the perpetrator himself. In Montieth Illingworth's cogently argued biography of Tyson, "Mike Tyson: Money, Myth and Betrayal," Tyson is quoted, after one or another public debacle: "People say 'Poor guy.' That insults me. I despise sympathy. So I screwed up. I made some mistakes. 'Poor guy,' like I'm some victim. There's nothing poor about me."

Jerry Izenberg

The roots of Jerry Izenberg's nearly sixty-year career as a sportswriter can be traced to Stanley Woodward, the fiercely principled giant who may have been the best newspaper sports editor ever. Woodward, bounced from the *New York Herald Tribune* after a dust-up with the publisher, was working at the *Newark Star-Ledger* the day he met Izenberg (b. 1930) in 1956, and when he returned to the *Trib* shortly afterward, he took the kid along and parked him at a desk next to Red Smith. By 1962 the *Trib* was ready to fire Woodward again, so he steered Izenberg back to Newark, where he remained until giving up his four-times-a-week column in 2008. His pieces combined Smith's love of language with Woodward's insistence on justice and integrity. He wrote about every sport, but none better than boxing, as this 1994 obituary for storied trainer Ray Arcel shows. There was as much room in his heart for fighters and trainers who made nary a dime as there was for champions. And it seemed as though he filed away every word he heard, because everywhere he went, he could be heard saying, "You got a minute? Let me tell you a story."

My Friend, My Teacher

RAY ARCEL died yesterday. When his wife Stephanie called to tell me, I tried to tell myself this was not the time to cry and the only reason I got away with it for a little while was the fact that I knew he never would have stood for it.

So after a while, I walked across the room and looked at two framed photographs and they seemed to speak volumes.

In the first, he is in the fighter's corner between rounds, in front of him and slightly to the left, and he is speaking softly into his ear in the way that only Ray Arcel could . . . taking the two of them to a place beyond the steamy arena . . . beyond the roar of 15,000 Panamanians . . . beyond the sweat and the pain which mark this business and into a private world of caring teacher and passionate student.

The fighter is Roberto Duran at a time when he weighed just 135 pounds and there isn't an ounce of fat on his body. Ray's right hand is placed gently against Duran's chest and the two heads are so close they are almost touching and you can almost hear Ray saying:

"Look, this fellow is dropping his left hand and all you have to do is . . ."

You stare at the frozen tableau and the mind's eye summons up the image of this man-child of the Panama streets, who came to Arcel as a know-it-all, one-handed puncher and emerged, after what followed within the cramped, aging classroom which was the old Gleason's Gym, as a champion for the ages.

It triggers up the electricity of the night they came into the old Garden to challenge a magnificent boxer from Scotland named Ken Buchanan for the lightweight championship. Duran was then 21 years old; Arcel, 72.

Buchanan had won 43 of 44 fights with a classic jab and a thorough command of the ring's geography, moving his opponents around with the efficiency of a chess master. There were bagpipers in the building that night to salute the champion. The jab would befuddle young Duran, the reasoning went. The challenger was overmatched.

But Ray Arcel knew they were wrong even before the bell rang.

He had taken a wild puncher and taught him how to box—box as no lightweight had for decades—without yielding an ounce of his punching power. Duran's English was non-existent back then. Arcel had no Spanish at all. But he was a teacher's teacher and he outlined the perfect fight.

And just before the bell for the round, when Arcel could sense that Buchanan was beginning to break, he shook his right fist in Duran's face, leaned over, much as he did in the framed photograph, and said softly but with no less passion:

"Go . . . go now . . . go . . . punch . . . punch . . . punch. . . you come back champion." Then he lifted him off the stool and shoved him forward into the ring.

And it happened just the way Ray said it would.

The pupil would become a fighter for all time. Older, heavier, stronger, he would whip Ray Leonard up in Montreal eight years later and then there would come the night of "no mas."

Ray Arcel was 80 years old the night Duran spit the bit and quit against Leonard in the Superdome. Afterward, back in the hotel room, he was pale and weak and depressed. It was 2 A.M.

Then, the telephone rang and whoever was on the other end was saying that the Louisiana Commission was going to hold a meeting right then back in the dome to suspend Duran. Arcel, visibly shaken, asked whether the fighter or his manager was going to be there. When the answer came back, "No," he said, "I'm coming over."

There was a long, ornate cement path leading from the hotel to the dome. A fine, cold drizzle was falling and the stones beneath our feet turned slippery as ice. He took my arm and as we walked he never said a word. Then we were inside and he told the commission:

"I don't know what happened tonight. But I know how Roberto Duran began in life and I know what he willed himself to become. I know the honor he has brought this business, which sometimes doesn't deserve it. I know his pride. And I know you cannot do this thing like this. He deserves better, and if you don't understand that and do this to him you will wake up tomorrow and you will be ashamed."

When he finished speaking, there was no doubt he had won his point. Then he turned and we walked very slowly out into the night, through the rain and back to the hotel lobby. And then he said:

"I don't know what happened tonight. I have never felt so hurt."

"So why did you go?" I asked him.

And he paused and looked at me, almost in bewilderment, before he said:

"Go? I had to go. He is my fighter and I am his trainer and, whatever happens down the road, it will stay that way until he gets on that airplane tomorrow. When a man says, 'Train me. I trust you,' then you owe him."

I have often thought about that. I remember a manager and another fighter and the fighter lay dying in the hospital, where he was taken after being knocked out, and when they asked the manager who they should call, he replied:

"I don't know. I don't even know where he lives."

In this cruel, often brutal, business, Ray Arcel was a giant of a man, who bled for every fighter he ever trained, who dared tell managers, "Do not take this fight because your fighter can't handle it," and who asked his fighters the same question after each day's work in the gym, four-rounders and champions alike (and he trained more champions than any other trainer who ever lived):

"What did you learn today?"

I look at that other picture and now he is 91 and he is standing with Stephanie in front of a Canastota, N.Y., fire engine on the day he was inducted into the Boxing Hall of Fame. They have matching Panama hats. Ray is wearing a sleeveless sweater and his only concession to the summer is that he has loosened his tie a notch. On his face is the mother of all smiles.

I look at the smile and, as articulate as he was, I still marvel at how much he could convey without saying a word. When he smiled, he lit up the entire room and your heart as well. And when he gave you "the look" . . . well, you responded.

"The look" was part Talmudic scholar on the one hand and the conscience you should have had on the other. It could freeze a fighter. It could do a fair number on a civilian, too. I remember the weekend he came down to visit and he got off the train and he looked at the weight I had gained. He looked at my waistline, and then he looked in my eyes.

I went out and took off 20 pounds that summer before I dared see him again and, when I did, his smile became a laugh and I would have gone out and taken off another 20 if he'd asked me. Whatever the issue, whatever the time, when I had a problem, a single conversation with him would set me straight. He never gave me an answer. He just reminded me how to figure it out.

There were three men in my life who were at once teachers and fathers and the guardian angels I never deserved.

And now all three are gone.

The first was my dad, who never complained and who was blue collar right down to the dye stains on his hands, which no solvent could ever completely erase, every night when he came home from work. He taught me everything I ever learned about laughter and obligations and how, no matter how heavily the second seemed to mitigate against the first, to never let it get in the way.

The second was Stanley Woodward, my sports editor at two

different papers, and whatever little I learned about this business and whatever little success I had, Stanley shoved me toward it.

And then there was Ray—who taught me about dignity and courage. The former just by being with him and the latter through his long battle against leukemia.

People say you have to learn how to win.

Maybe.

But he taught me something more important. He showed me how to live.

William Nack

Before William Nack (b. 1941) wrote a word about boxing, he had established himself as the premier horseracing writer of the last half-century. He combined a paleontologist's passion for detail with a poet's gift for language to become a star at *Sports Illustrated* for more than twenty years, and his acclaimed book *Secretariat: The Making of a Champion* (1975) burnished his reputation. Nack widened his focus to include baseball, basketball, even chess, but the most beguiling subjects he found were in the fight racket: Sonny Liston, Rocky Marciano, the Long Count, and perhaps the greatest test of his powers, Joe Frazier's undying hatred for Muhammad Ali. The hatred was born not of Frazier's two losses in three fights with Ali, but of the hurtful, unthinking words with which Ali bombarded Smokin' Joe. For Ali the trash talk was just show business, a way to hype a rivalry that stands among boxing's greatest. But for Frazier, it was a dagger to the heart. "'The Fight's Over, Joe'" (1996), captures the pain that wound up consuming him.

"The Fight's Over, Joe"

I T is always the punch a fighter does not see that hurts the most, and the little girl was so sweet and innocent-looking, standing shyly at her mother's side, that there was no way Joe Frazier could have seen it coming.

The former heavyweight champion of the world was sitting under a tent on the banks of the Delaware River in Philadelphia, at a place called Penn's Landing, where his touring autograph show had set up shop at an outdoor festival. With his son Marvis, Joe trains and manages fighters out of his Broad Street gym in Philly, but he also spends an inordinate amount of time signing his name in that long, sweeping script on photographs of himself and on merchandise from his portable store. On this languid September afternoon, under a sign that announced MEET YOUR PHILLY SPORTS HEROES, flanked by stacks of SMOKIN' JOE hats ($10) and T-shirts ($23), Frazier was signing everything put in front of him, gratis, schmoozing with parents as he posed for pictures with their children and hamming it up for the cameras. He was all grins and merriment for the scores of people who had waited in the sun for an audience.

At about 2:30 P.M., Frazier looked up and saw a petite and demure 10-year-old, Ginnysue Kowalick, her head slightly bowed, standing across the table. "My daughter doesn't know you too well, Joe," said the girl's mother, Marilyn Kowalick. "She has a question, but she's too shy to ask."

Frazier nodded. "O.K." he said.

"She wants to know if you ever beat Muhammad Ali," Marilyn said.

A scowl passed like a shadow down Frazier's face, and for a long moment he sat reeling in his chair, leaning back as his eyes rolled wildly from side to side, and he groaned, groping for words: "Aggh h. . . . Ohhh. . . . Agghh. . . ."

Alarmed at Frazier's reaction, Marilyn leaned forward and said, "I'm sorry."

At last reassembling his scattered faculties, Frazier looked at Ginnysue and said, "We locked up three times. He won two, and I won one. *But look at him now.* I think I won all three."

Two days earlier, at the Essex House in New York City, the object of Frazier's turbulent emotions sat folded on a couch in a suite of rooms overlooking Manhattan's Central Park. He lay back and fumbled with his third package of shortbread cookies. White crumbs speckled his black shirt—the remains of his day, the emblematic story of his life. Ali had just spent most of an afternoon signing a limited edition of large photographs that showed him, dressed in luminous white, holding the Olympic torch during the opening ceremonies of the 1996 Games in Atlanta. He was in New York for the screening of yet another documentary celebrating his life, this one a TNT production with the unlikely title, *Muhammad Ali: The Whole Story.*

Ali speaks in barely a whisper now, unless he has an audience, and then his voice rises raspingly, just enough to carry a room. Surrounded by a small group of fans and followers at the Essex House earlier that day, he could not resist the chance to perform. He raised his right fist in the air and said, "This is the piston that got to Liston!" He also asked the gathering, "Know what Lincoln said when he woke up from a two-day drunk?"

A dozen heads craned forward. Ali's eyes widened in shock. "I freed the *whoo*?" he blurted to the nearly all-white audience. High, nervous laughter filled the room.

"I saw Joe Frazier in Philly last week," a voice nearby said quietly.

Ali's eyes grew wide again. "Joe Fraysha?" he whispered.

He has known for years of Frazier's anger and bitterness toward him, but he knows nothing of the venom that coursed through Frazier's recent autobiography, *Smokin' Joe*. Of Ali, Frazier wrote, "Truth is, I'd like to rumble with that sucker again—beat him up piece by piece and mail him back to Jesus. . . . Now people ask me if I feel bad for him, now that things aren't going so well for him. Nope. I don't. Fact is, I don't give a damn. They want me to love him, but I'll open up the graveyard and bury his ass when the Lord chooses to take him."

Nor does Ali know what Frazier said after watching him, with his trembling arm, light the Olympic flame: "It would have been a good thing if he would have lit the torch and fallen in. If I had the chance, I would have pushed him in."

Nor does Ali know of Frazier's rambling diatribe against him at a July 30 press conference in Atlanta, where Frazier attacked the choice of Ali, the Olympic light heavyweight gold medalist in 1960 and a three-time heavyweight champion of the world, as the final bearer of the torch. He called Ali a "dodge drafter," implied that Ali was a racist ("He didn't like his white brothers," said Frazier) and suggested that he himself—also an Olympic champion, as a heavyweight, in 1964—would have made a better choice to light the flame: "Why not? I'm a good American. . . . A champion is more than making noise. I could have run up there. I'm in shape."

And while Frazier asserts at one turn that he sees "the hand of the Lord" in Ali's Parkinson's syndrome (a set of symptoms that include tremors and a masklike face), he also takes an eerily mean-spirited pride in the role he believes he played in causing Ali's condition. Indeed, the Parkinson's most likely traces to the repeated blows Ali took to the head as a boxer—traumas that ravaged the colony of dopamine-producing cells in his brain—and no man struck Ali's head harder and more repeatedly than Frazier.

"He's got Joe Frazier-itis," Frazier said of Ali one day recently, flexing his left arm. "He's got left-hook-itis."

Ali's wife, Lonnie, shields him from such loutish and hateful pronouncements. "I don't want him hearing negative things," Lonnie says. "It's trash."

Ali has been living rent free in Frazier's head for more than 25 years, ever since Ali—after being stripped of his heavyweight championship in 1967 for refusing induction into the U.S. Army, and then serving a 3½-year suspension from boxing—emerged from his banishment and immediately set about regaining his title, which by then was held by Smokin' Joe. At Ali's urgent pleading, Frazier backed him in his fight to regain his boxing license, but no sooner had that been accomplished than Ali began cruelly berating his benefactor, a man who had grown up mule-poor in Beaufort, South Carolina, the son of a struggling farmer and bootlegger. The young Frazier had migrated to Philly, taken up boxing and become the precursor of Rocky Balboa, training by tenderizing sides of beef in a kosher slaughterhouse with his sibilant left hook.

Over the next five years, from their first fight in New York City, on March 8, 1971, until their third and last in Manila on Oct. 1, 1975, Ali humiliated and enraged and ultimately isolated Frazier, casting him as a shuffling and mumbling Uncle Tom, an ugly and ignorant errand boy for white America. But the most lasting characterization of all was the one Ali coined on their way to the Philippines in '75, the one that came near the end of the singsong rhyme he would deliver with that mischievous smirk on his moon-bright face: "It will be a killa and a chilla and a thrilla when I get the gorilla in Manila!"

Of all the names joined forever in the annals of boxing—from Dempsey–Tunney to Louis–Schmeling, from Zale–Graziano to Leonard–Hearns—none are more fiercely bound by a hyphen than Ali–Frazier. Not Palmer–Nicklaus in golf nor Borg–McEnroe in tennis, as ardently competitive as these rivalries were, conjure up anything remotely close to the epic theater of Ali–Frazier. Their first fight, snagged in the most turbulent political currents of our time, is widely viewed as the greatest single sporting event of this half century. And the third fight—for its savagery, its shifting momentum and its climactic moment, in which the two men sat battered on their stools— is regarded, by consensus, as the most surpassing prizefight in history.

So here it is, 25 years after Ali–Frazier I, and Frazier is burning like the flame that Ali set off with his Olympic torch. Feeling that history has treated him unfairly, Frazier is haunted and overshadowed by his old tormentor, the very figure he did most to help create. Frazier was one of the greatest of all gladiators, but today he finds himself cast as just another player in the far larger drama of Ali's life. He is trapped and frozen in the Ali mystique, a dragonfly embedded in the amber of Ali's life and times.

For Ali is as near to a cultural saint as any man of our era. His appearance on the Atlanta stage was a window, thrown suddenly open, on the long journey he has taken through the lights and shadows of our unresolved past—America's past. As his left arm shook, he lit the flame and choked the breath of a nation. His life has become an extended public appearance: He swims among crowds wherever he goes, leading with the most recognizable chin on the planet. He tells old knock-knock jokes, receives visitors like a Middle East potentate and signs off on the next book about his life. And now and again, just for old times' sake, he leans over to whisper in Joe Frazier's ear.

As he did when his eyes widened in that suite at the Essex House. And then he gave the impish grin. "Joe Fraysha?" Ali said. "You seen the gorilla? From Manila?"

The geometry of the lives of Ali and Frazier is forever fixed in history. The line between them, once as curved and sweeping as a left hook and as long as a flicking jab, is today as irreducibly short as the one that joins their names. The two men left each other scarred in different ways. Ali's wounds are visible on the surface; you can see them on his face. Frazier's wounds lie deeper within; you can hear them in the pain in his voice.

There had never been a night like this one in New York City. By 10:30 P.M. on the evening of March 8, 1971, when the two fighters climbed into the ring at Madison Square Garden, Ali in red trunks and Frazier in green-and-gold brocade, there was a feral scent and crackle to the place. The Garden was a giant bell jar into which more than 20,000 people had drifted, having passed through police barricades that rimmed the surrounding streets. They came in orange and mint-green and purple velvet hot pants, in black leather knickers and mink and leopard capes, in cartridge belts and feathered chapeaux and pearl-gray fedoras. Some sported hats with nine-inch brims and leaned jauntily on diamond-studded walking sticks. Manhattan listed toward Babylon.

"I looked down from the ring, and it was a sea of glitter," recalls Eddie Futch, who was then Frazier's assistant trainer. "I have never seen any boxing event that had so many celebrities."

Angelo Dundee, Ali's trainer, was making his way through the tumult to the ring when he heard someone call his name: "Hey, Ange!" Dundee looked up. Frank Sinatra snapped his picture; the singer was working for *Life* magazine. Burt Lancaster was doing radio commentary. Ringside seats had sold for $150, but scalpers were getting $1,000. "Plumage, pimps and hustlers," says Bobby Goodman, the fight publicist. The fighters were each getting a record $2.5 million, an astronomical sum in those days, and the worldwide television audience was 300 million. The Garden ring was the wrist on which America was checking its pulse.

The boxer-dancer with the beautiful legs had arrived to do battle against the puncher-plodder with the thick thighs. Of course, the fans had come to see more than a classic clash of styles. The match was billed as the Fight of the Century, and the sporting world had been waiting for it for more than three years, ever since Frazier knocked out Buster Mathis in 11 rounds on March 4, 1968, to win the vacant New York heavyweight title and begin laying claim to being the toughest man on earth—the toughest, at least, with a passport. The previous year Ali had been stripped of his world championship and his freedom to travel abroad, and during his ensuing 43-month absence from the ring, Frazier buried his implacable hook into every heavyweight who stood in his way, finally winning the vacant world title on Feb. 16, 1970, by knocking out Jimmy Ellis in the fifth round.

During his exile Ali, who had to earn his money on the college lecture circuit, began to knock at Frazier's door, seeking help to get back his license to fight, saying that an Ali–Frazier match would make them both rich. "He'd come to the gym and call me on the telephone," says Frazier. "He just wanted to work with me for the publicity so he could get his license back. One time, after the Ellis fight, I drove him from Philadelphia to New York City in my car. Me and him. We talked about how much we were going to make out of our fight. We were laughin' and havin' fun. We were friends, we were great friends. I said, 'Why not? Come on, man, let's do it!' He was a brother. He called me Joe: 'Hey, Smokin' Joe!' In New York we were gonna put on this commotion."

For Ali, the most gifted carnival barker in the history of sports, the commotion was father to the promotion. So when Frazier stopped his car in midtown Manhattan and walked into a store to buy a pair of shoes, Ali leaped out, his eyes bulging, and cried, "It's Joe Frazier, ladies and gentlemen! Smokin' Joe! There he is! He's got my title! I want my title! He ain't the champ, he's the chump. I'm the people's champ!"

Frazier, a proud and soft-spoken rural Southerner, had never witnessed anything like this. It rattled him at first. Butch Lewis, a companion of Frazier's and later a promoter himself, explained to him what Ali was doing: "He's not disrespecting you. This is Ali! This is what will make the payday. *This is not personal.*"

Lewis says the men shared more than anyone knows. Frazier knew that Ali was in need of money. On at least two occasions, Lewis says, Frazier slipped Ali cash when he needed it, once giving him $2,000 to pay an overdue bill at the City Squire Motor Inn in New York City. But now Ali was dabbing curare on the tip of his rhetoric.

All through Ali's youth in Louisville and his early years as a champion, he had been a blend of his chesty, arrogant, yakety-yak father, Cassius Clay Sr., and his gentle, uncommonly sweet mother, Odessa. "Ali is softhearted and generous to a fault," says his former fight doctor, Ferdie Pacheco. "Essentially a sweet guy whose whole demeanor aims to amuse, to entertain and be liked." Yet there was a period in Ali's life, after he revealed that he had joined the separatist Black Muslims in 1964, when that side of his personality disappeared— "when he was not particularly pleasant to anyone," says Pacheco, recalling the two years before Ali's exile, when he fought Floyd Patterson and Ernie Terrell. "He was a hateful guy."

Neither Patterson nor Terrell would call him Ali—they used what he called his "slave name," Cassius Clay—and so in the ring he played with each of them as a cat would with a wounded mouse, keeping them alive to torture them. "What's my name?" he demanded of them as he landed his punches at will. Goodman, who was Terrell's publicist then, says, "He gave Ernie a merciless beating around the eyes. Ernie had double vision for a long time."

If Ali emerged from his exile years a softer man, as many contend, he had not forgotten how to sting and wound an opponent. "There was an awful mean streak in Ali," says Dave Wolf, then one of Frazier's confidants. "He did to Joe verbally what he did to Terrell physically."

The Ali who had laughed and bantered with Frazier, who had raised all that good-natured commotion in Manhattan, now appeared to be a man transformed—stripped of his disguise. "Joe Frazier is too ugly to be champ," Ali said. "Joe Frazier is too dumb to be champ. The heavyweight champion should be smart and pretty, like me. Ask Joe Frazier, 'How do you feel, champ?' He'll say, 'Duh, duh, duh.'" That played to the most insidious racial stereotype, the dumb and ugly black man, but Ali reached further: "Joe Frazier is an Uncle Tom." And further: "Ninety-eight percent of my people are for me. They identify with my struggle. . . . If I win, they win. I lose, they lose. Anybody black who thinks Frazier can whup me is an Uncle Tom."

In fact, because of Ali's work for racial justice and because of the sacrifices he made in his stand against the Vietnam War, the vast majority of blacks—as well as an increasing number of whites—saw his battles as theirs and were drawn to him as a force for social change. The most prominent voices of the 1960s, a decade torn by conflict and rebellion, had been silenced. Dr. Martin Luther King Jr. was dead. Bobby Kennedy was dead. Senator Eugene McCarthy had drifted like a blip off the screen. Ali alone remained alive in the ruins—the most commanding voice for and symbol of the decade's causes.

In the months leading up to the fight, he brought to bear all the horsepower of his eloquence. His demeaning of Frazier, Ali now says, had but one purpose: "To sell tickets." Of course, Frazier says there was no need to sell anything, because their purses were guaranteed, but this argument ignores the fact that Ali was always selling more than tickets. The consummate performer, he was selling himself. And there are those who say that Ali's rhetoric was merely a part of his act, the tappety-tap-tap of his everyday walking shtick. But whatever compelled him to violate all canons of fairness and decency in his portrayal of Frazier—whether it was meanness, bravado or a calculated plan to enrage and rattle his opponent—he succeeded in isolating Frazier from the black community.

And Frazier? He felt manipulated, humiliated, and betrayed. "He had me stunned," Frazier says. "This guy was a buddy. I remember looking at him and thinkin', What's wrong with this guy? Has he gone crazy? He called me an Uncle Tom. For a guy who did as much for him as I did, that was cruel. I grew up like the black man—he didn't. I cooked the liquor. I cut the wood. I worked the farm. I lived in the ghetto. Yes, I tommed; when he asked me to help him get a license, I tommed for him. For him! He betrayed my friendship. He called me stupid. He said I was so ugly that my mother ran and hid when she gave birth to me. I was shocked. I sat down and said to myself, I'm gonna kill him. O.K.? Simple as that. I'm gonna kill him!"

So by the time they climbed through the ropes that night in the Garden, the lure of the fight went far beyond the exquisitely contrasting ring styles of the two men. For many viewers Ali was still the mouth that poured, the renegade traitor and rabble-rouser whose uppity black ass needed dusting. For many others, of course, he symbolized all successful men of color who did not conform in a white man's world—and the hope that one, at least *one*, would overcome. Frazier had done nothing to earn the caricature of Uncle Tom, but Ali had lashed him to that stake as if to define their war in black and white. Frazier knew the scope of Ali's appeal. A Bible-raised man, he saw himself as David to Ali's Goliath.

"David had a slingshot," Frazier says. "I had a left hook."

For 14 rounds, almost a full hour in which the Garden never stopped rocking, Frazier pursued and pounded the former champion like a man simultaneously pushing a plow and chopping wood. Ali won the first two rounds, dancing and landing jabs and stinging rights, but by the third, under a remorseless body attack climaxed by a searing hook to the ribs, his feet had begun to flatten, and soon he was fighting toe-to-toe, his back pushed against the ropes.

It was a fight with two paces, fast and faster, and among its abiding images is that of Frazier, head down and body low, bobbing and weaving incessantly, taking lashing lefts and rights from Ali, then unloading that sweeping hook to the jaw, and Ali waving his head defiantly—*No, no, that didn't hurt*—and coming back, firing jabs and hooks and straight rights to Frazier's head. It was soon clear that this was not the Ali of old, the butterfly who had floated through his championship years, and that the long absence from the ring had stolen his legs and left him vulnerable. He had always been a technically unsound fighter: He threw punches going backward, fought with his arms too low and avoided sweeping punches by leaning back instead of ducking. He could get away with that when he had the speed and reflexes of his youth, but he no longer had them, and now Frazier was punishing him.

Frazier quickened the tempo in the third and fourth, whaling Ali with lefts and rights. Ali moved as he fired jabs and landed rights and shouted at Frazier, "Do you know I'm God?"

"God, you're in the wrong place tonight," Frazier shot back. "I'm takin' names and kickin' ass!"

The Garden crowd was on its feet. Frazier mimicked Ali in the fifth, dropping his hands and laughing as Ali struck him with a left and a right. Frazier's ferocious head and body attacks began to slow Ali down, but the former champion scored repeatedly as Frazier moved in, and by the start of the eighth the crowd was chanting, "Ali! Ali! Ali!" Looking inspired, Frazier bore in, crashing a hook on Ali's head and following it up with two rights. After Ali mockingly tapped him on the head, Frazier drove a fiery hook into the ex-champ's jaw, and after the bell that ended the round members of the crowd were chanting, "Joe! Joe! Joe!"

Starting the 11th Frazier was winning on two of the three cards, and it was here that he took possession of the fight. As Ali stood in a neutral corner, Frazier stepped inside and let fly a thunderous hook to the jaw that snapped Ali's neck and buckled his legs. Ali looked gone. A hard right sent him sagging on the ropes. Another wobbled him again. At the bell he was still on his feet, but he moved shakily back to his corner.

If Ali–Frazier I was the most memorable athletic event of our time, surely it was the 15th round that made it so. About twenty seconds after the opening bell, Frazier threw the most famous left hook in boxing history and raised the evening to the realm of myth. The punch began south of his brocade trunks, somewhere down in Beaufort, and rose in a whistling arc that ended on the right side of Ali's jaw, just above the point of the chin. Ali sprawled on his back, the tassels on his shoes flying in the air. "I looked up," Ali says today, "and I was on the floor."

Frazier turned and walked away. Earlier in the fight, after pounding Ali with hooks to the head, he had asked his cornermen, "What is keeping this guy up?" Now he asked it again as he turned and saw Ali climb slowly to his feet at the count of four. Frazier won a unanimous decision—"I kicked your ass!" he would yell at Ali as the final bell sounded—but among the enduring moments of that night was the one in which a battered Ali rose off that deck.

The two fighters sent each other to the hospital. Ali went briefly for a swollen right jaw, which made him appear to need a tooth extraction, and a lumpy-faced Frazier was in and out for two weeks for treatment of exhaustion, high blood pressure and kidney problems. The two men also left each other irreversibly diminished. They would never be the same fighters again.

Thirty-five months would pass before they would meet for Ali–Frazier II, on Jan. 28, 1974, at the Garden. But by then the context in which they fought had changed so dramatically that there is no comparing the two bouts. On Jan. 22, 1973, Frazier had lost his title when George Foreman hit him a few times with his wrecking-ball right and knocked him senseless in the second round in Kingston, Jamaica. So there was no championship at stake in Ali–Frazier II. By then, too, the social causes of the '60s were no longer issues of great ardency. But the Vietnam War had become such a national plague that Ali's popularity had climbed at roughly the same rate that the war's had declined.

The only thing that remained the same was Frazier's incandescent animus toward Ali, unappeased by his victory in '71. Five days before the second fight, sitting together before a national TV audience on ABC, they were discussing the first bout when Frazier referred to Ali's visit to the hospital. "I went to the hospital for 10 minutes," Ali shot back. "You went for a month."

"I was resting," Frazier said.

"That shows how dumb you are," Ali said. "People don't go to a hospital to rest. See how ignorant you are?"

Frazier had not had much formal schooling, and Ali had touched his hottest button. "I'm tired of you calling me ignorant all the time," snapped Frazier. "I'm not ignorant!" With that, he rose and towered over Ali, tightening his fists, his eyes afire. When Ali's brother, Rahaman, rushed to the stage, Frazier turned to him and said, "You in this too?" Here Ali jumped to his feet and grabbed Frazier in a bear hug. They rolled off the stage and onto the studio floor, and Goodman remembers Frazier holding one of Ali's feet and twisting it, like the head of a chicken, while Futch screamed, "Joe! Joe! Don't twist off his foot! There won't be a fight."

Ali was bug-eyed as Frazier left in a fury. "Did you see how wide Clay's eyes opened up?" Frazier said. "Now I really got him scared!"

Frazier got nothing. Ali won an easy 12-round decision, nearly knocking Frazier out in the second round and then clinching and smothering whatever attack Frazier tried to mount inside. Indeed, Ali put on a boxing clinic, fighting at his range instead of Frazier's, and many of Frazier's sweeping hooks appeared to lack the snap they'd had three years before. The Ali–Frazier rivalry might have ended right there, in fact, if Ali had not taken events into his hands so magnificently nine months later, on Oct. 30 in Kinshasa, Zaire, knocking out Foreman—the baddest man on the planet—in an upset that staggered the memory and fired the imagination.

Ali's victory in Africa eventually led to Ali–Frazier III, the final combat, in the Philippines. Here the two fighters got guaranteed purses, $4.5 million for Ali and $2 million for Frazier, plus a percentage of the gross. Once again Ali had become the largest draw in sports, and once again he went at Frazier with a vengeance, correcting his diction and carrying around, in his shirt pocket, a small rubber gorilla. At a press conference before the fight, Ali pulled out the doll in front of Frazier and began beating it, saying, "All night long, this is what you'll see. Come on, gorilla! We're in Manila! Come on, gorilla, this is a thrilla!" Black people cringed, but not a few whites laughed, and Frazier felt again the heat of his simmering anger.

No one knew what to expect when these two aging fighters came together that morning in Manila. Several major U.S. newspapers didn't bother sending a writer to cover the fight. But those who were there witnessed prizefighting in its grandest manner, the final epic in a running blood feud between two men, each fighting to own the heart of the other. The fight called upon all of their will and courage as they pitched from one ring post to another emitting fearful grunts and squeals.

By the end of the 10th round Ali looked like a half-drowned man who had just been pulled from Manila Bay. His aching body slumped, glistening with sweat. He had won the early rounds, snapping his whiplike jab on Frazier's face, but as in '71 Frazier had found his rolling rhythm after a few rounds, and by the fifth he had driven Ali into his corner and was thumping his body like a blacksmith. Ali's trainer was frantic. "Get outta the goddam corner!" screamed Dundee. It was too late. The fight had shifted from Ali to Frazier.

For the next five rounds it was as if Frazier had reached into the darkest bat cave of his psyche and freed all his pent-up rage. In the sixth he pressed and attacked, winging three savage hooks to Ali's head, the last of which sent his mouthpiece flying. For the first time in the fight, Ali sat down between rounds. Frazier resumed the attack in the seventh, at one point landing four straight shots to the body, at another point landing five. In the ninth, as Ali wilted, the fighting went deeper into the trenches, down where Frazier whistles while he works, and as he landed blow upon blow he could hear Ali howling in pain. In his corner after the 10th, Ali said to Pacheco, "This must be what dyin' is like."

Frazier owned the fight. He was sure to regain his title. And then came the 11th. Drew (Bundini) Brown, Ali's witch doctor, pleaded with him, "Go down to the well once more!" From wherever it is that such men draw the best and noblest of themselves, Ali emerged reborn. During the next four rounds he fought with a precision and fury that made a bloody Frazier weave and wobble. In the 12th Ali landed six consecutive punches to Frazier's head, and moments later he slammed home eight more. By the end of the round an archipelago of lumps had surfaced around the challenger's eyes and brow.

Futch could see Frazier's left eye closing. Before the 13th he told his boxer, "Move back and stand up a little, so you can see the target better." That was just what Ali needed, more room and a taller man to fire at. "Boy, did he take advantage of that," says Futch. Ali threw punches in flurries, so many blows that Frazier reeled helplessly. A right cross sent Frazier's white mouthpiece twirling four rows into the seats. Futch kept thinking, *Ali has to slow down. He cannot keep this pace. Not into the 14th round!* By then Frazier's face was a misshapen moonscape, both eyes closing, and in the 14th Ali fired barrages and raked a nearly blind Frazier with rights and lefts. Futch stared at Ali and thought, *Incredible!* When the bell tolled, it tolled for Joe.

"The fight's over, Joe," Futch told him before the beginning of the 15th.

Frazier jumped from his stool. He said, "Eddie—"

"Just sit down, Joe."

A benumbed and exhausted Ali, his lips scraped raw, lay on a cot in his locker room in Manila and summoned Marvis Frazier, Joe's 15-year-old son, to his side. "Tell your dad the things I said I really didn't mean," Ali said.

Marvis reported back to his father. "He should come to me, son," Joe told him. "He should say it to my face."

Back in the States, Ali called Lewis and asked him for Frazier's private number. Ali told Lewis that he wanted to apologize to Frazier for some of the things he had said. Lewis called Frazier, but, he says, Frazier told him, "Don't give it to him."

In the 21 years since then, Ali and Frazier have seen each other at numerous affairs, and Frazier has barely disguised the loathing he feels toward his old antagonist. In 1988, for the taping of a film called *Champions Forever*, five former heavyweight title holders—Ali, Frazier, Foreman, Larry Holmes and Ken Norton—gathered in Las Vegas. A crowd of people were at Johnny Tocco's Gym for a morning shoot when Frazier started in on Ali, who was already debilitated by Parkinson's. "Look at Ali," Frazier said. "Look what's happened to him. All your talkin', man. I'm faster than you are now. You're damaged goods."

"I'm faster than you are, Joe," Ali slurred. Pointing to a heavy bag, Ali suggested a contest: "Let's see who hits the bag the fastest."

Frazier grinned, not knowing he was back in the slaughterhouse. He stripped off his coat, strode to the bag and buried a dozen rapid-fire hooks in it, punctuating each rip with a loud grunt: "Huh! Huh! Huh!" Without removing his coat, Ali went to the bag, assumed the ready stance and mimicked one Frazier grunt: "Huh!" He had not thrown a punch. He turned slowly to Frazier and said, "Wanna see it again, Joe?" In the uproar of hilarity that ensued, only Frazier did not laugh. Ali had humiliated him again.

After the shoot, at a luncheon for the fighters, Frazier had too much to drink, and afterward, as people milled around the room and talked, he started walking toward Ali. Thomas Hauser, Ali's chronicler, watched the scene that unfolded over the next 20 minutes. Holmes quietly positioned himself between Ali and Frazier. "Joe was trying to get to Ali," Hauser says, "but wherever Joe went, left or right, Holmes would step between him and Ali. Physically shielding him. Joe was frustrated. After about 10 minutes of this, Foreman walked up to Larry and said, 'I'll take over.'" So for the next 10 minutes Frazier quietly tried to get around 290 pounds of assimilated Big Macs. At one point Frazier leaned into Foreman, but Foreman only leaned back. "Keep it cool, Joe," Foreman whispered. "Be calm."

Ali had no idea this was going on. "He was walking around like Mr. Magoo," says Hauser. "He was oblivious."

While Frazier's hostility toward Ali was well known to the fight crowd, it was not until his book came out last spring that he took his venom public. When Phil Berger, who wrote the book, began interviewing Frazier last fall and heard what he wanted to say about Ali, he warned Frazier of the damning impact it would have. "Ali's become like a saintly figure," Berger said.

Too bad, the fighter replied. "That's the way I feel."

With his book and his unseemly harangue against Ali at the Olympics, which had the strong whiff of envy, Frazier may have done himself irreparable damage among the legions who have admired him so steadfastly. What he wants from Ali is an apology for those long years of vilification—the apology he did not want to hear when Lewis called him on Ali's behalf after Manila.

Ali has expressed contrition more than once for the things he said. In Hauser's 1991 oral history *Muhammad Ali: His Life and Times*, Ali says, "I'm sorry Joe Frazier is mad at me. I'm sorry I hurt him. Joe Frazier is a good man. I couldn't have done what I did without him, and he couldn't have done what he did without me."

Wolf understands Frazier's rage, but he sees Ali today and does not see the man behind the cruel jibes of the past. "I'm not sure that part exists anymore," Wolf says. "Whether it is the Parkinson's or just maturing, that part of him is gone." So that leaves Frazier, imprisoned in the past, raging against a ghost.

Lewis, still a close friend of Frazier's, has pleaded with him to cut

Ali loose. At the real root of Frazier's discontent, says Lewis, is his sense that history has not dealt with him fairly—that his Olympic triumph and his heavyweight championship years have been forgotten, and that time has turned him into just another stitch in the embroidery of Ali's legend. "You have your place in history, and Ali has his," Lewis tells Frazier. "You can't reflect back in bitterness. Let it go."

Futch's gentle voice still rings the clearest. His words in Manila, after 14 savage rounds that left Frazier's eyes nearly as blind as his heart is now, still echo faint but true. "The fight's over, Joe. . . . The fight's over, Joe. . . . The fight's over, Joe."

Mark Kriegel

Mark Kriegel (b. 1963) had written his first novel, *Bless Me Father* (1995)—a barely fictionalized cautionary tale based on his observation of the relationship between mobster-turned-stoolie Sammy "The Bull" Gravano and his son, a reluctant pugilist—in his days as sports columnist for the *New York Post* and later for the *Daily News*, but until his abrupt and involuntary departure from the newspaper business in 2000 he had never seriously contemplated writing books for a living. Newly divorced and with a young daughter to support, he had little choice, and he plunged headlong into a process of painstaking research that landed him, in 2005, on *The New York Times* bestseller list with his widely-acclaimed *Namath* (2004). With *Pistol* (2007), an insightful exploration of the star-crossed basketball icon Pete Maravich, Kriegel once again explored the father-son relationship. Having already written what many consider the two best sports biographies published in the twenty-first century, Kriegel has returned to his boxing roots with a biography of Ray "Boom-Boom" Mancini currently underway. In this 1996 *Esquire* portrait of Oscar De La Hoya, Kriegel brought the inbred cynicism of a street-smart New York newspaperman to his deconstruction of the California boxer's carefully nurtured "Golden Boy" image—one that, until Kriegel arrived on the scene, had for the most part gone unchallenged by his colleagues.

The Great (Almost) White Hope

YOU need more than a map to make it from the barrio to Brentwood as Oscar De La Hoya has, arriving this summer morning at the Riviera Country Club for a celebrity golf outing. It's not that there aren't any homeboys in the house, just that most of them are parking cars or cutting grass or busing tables. The Spanish stucco clubhouse stands like a monument to all that's supposed to be good and gracious in southern-California society. And Oscar fits right in.

Over brunch in the ballroom, the twenty-three-year-old

champion—I have to keep reminding myself he's a *fighter*—is receiving a steady stream of well-wishers. Most of them are colonels and captains in the corporate culture—Peerless Faucet, Sherwin-Williams, Owens Corning—clean-shaven, backslapping gentlemen calling one another amigo.

The occasion is to benefit local Boy Scout chapters. The tournament chairman and his wife thank Oscar profusely. Like De La Hoya, most of the scouts are from East L. A. They're just not as blessed. Some live below the poverty line, explains the chairman's wife, and others are in wheelchairs. "It's a worthy cause," she says.

Oscar nods gravely. He knows the drill. He's "giving back to the Community"—the phrase you hear again and again—though it's never quite clear what community these people mean.

Now he's introduced to a woman who runs a "Hispanic advertising agency," as it's described for my benefit. "So nice of you," she gushes, a flutter in her lashes. "Young men need role models."

And grown men need autographs. Even here, the signature sharks and memorabilia mercenaries are never far behind, armed with their indelible markers, glossies, and spongy red Everlast gloves. *Can you sign, Oscar, please . . . and this one for my girl; she's a big fan.* Next, there's some guy doing a boxing movie. The stars are already attached, but what he'd *really* like is for Oscar to do a cameo.

De La Hoya indulges each request with equal earnestness. He's more of a sales rep than anybody in the room. He's selling an image. In an aside, he confesses, "Gotta go along with it. Gotta be the perfect person. Somebody's always watching."

So he gives them that shy smile, that teenager's voice still the slightest bit soprano. His manners are precious. And he's as pretty as he is polite. In his khakis and his baseball cap, Oscar De La Hoya could be one of those fresh-faced kids in ads for the Gap or Benetton. At another angle, he could be Speed Racer, the perversely perfect creation of Japanese animators. And still another take: In another time and place, in another movie, he'd have played the matador opposite Ava Gardner. Oscar De La Hoya looks like anything but what he is.

I saw him last at Caesars Palace in Las Vegas, where he won the 140-pound superlightweight championship by dispatching a deity of Mexican machismo named Julio César Chavez. There was so much blood in the ring, and every drop of it Chavez's, that a custodial worker was sent in with a mop before the walkout bout could begin. When I mention the mop, De La Hoya leans closer to shield himself from the glad-handers. His eyes have become animated. Suddenly, he's all there.

"A mop?" he asks. "Really, a mop? Wow."

De La Hoya opened a gash above Chavez's left eye a minute into the fight. It was like a razor cut, a red thread. But De La Hoya attacked the wound until it was the size of a baby's mouth. Then, in the fourth and final round, came a left hand thrown from an acute angle, something between a hook and an uppercut, a punch that seemed to explode Chavez's nose, making shrapnel of cartilage and tissue and blood.

"Oh, that felt good," says De La Hoya, now dreamy with delight. He's never had a sip of liquor, but blood, even the recollection of blood, gets him high. "I wish he had two noses," he says.

So it turns out our sugarcoated salesman has a sadist in his soul. But that's only the first in a collection of contradictions that define Oscar De La Hoya: He's the pretty boy of an ugly business; a child star spinning in a constellation of has-beens; Mexican by his blood, American in his inclinations; barrio by birth, country club by preference.

He lives in a condo in Whittier, the town that gave us Richard Nixon. But now he's talking of moving again. Maybe Bel Air. Maybe South Pasadena.

"I read it's even more exclusive than Beverly Hills."

And back in East L. A., he will again be called an aspiring white boy, charged with selling out and abandoning the Community. In fact, that's not the case. De La Hoya isn't nearly old enough to forget where he came from. If that's not enough, there's the food stamp he keeps in his wallet to remind him. Then there are the scholarships in his name. He even renovated the old Resurrection gym on Lorena Street. Now it's the Oscar De La Hoya Boxing Youth Center.

Yes, he's *giving back*. But that misses the point.

Here in the ballroom, as a busboy refills Oscar's water glass, something becomes clear: There's already an incalculable distance between De La Hoya and the barrio of his birth. He knows better than these mere businessmen that greed is good. This latest and greatest of

Golden Boys has an intimate, almost philosophical comprehension of Reverend Ike's old theorem—the best way to help the poor is not to be one of them. Still, that misses the point, too.

Oscar is a fighter. It is not the barrio he avoids but another place. Call it what it's been called before: Palookaville, that punchers' purgatory where broken boxers live in poverty and chagrin. They all seem to get there, one way or another, traveling the pug's path from Kid to Bum. In Palookaville, the Ali Shuffle is a palsied jig. Mando Ramos, of Palookaville by way of East L. A., would shoot up and shiver with junk. And Bobby Chacon, another erstwhile Golden Boy from the 'hood, collects cans and bottles for deposit.

Chacon was there, poor and punchy and picking up cans in the back of the Olympic Auditorium in L. A. as Chavez and De La Hoya kicked off their publicity tour all those months ago.

That's a role model.

"I learned from him," says De La Hoya. "I learned from them all."

Oscar De La Hoya may prove to be the greatest fighter of his time, even great enough to save his sorry-ass sport. He has time and talent on his side, but also instincts as old as his blood. His grandfather Vicente was an amateur featherweight in Durango, Mexico. His father, Joel, arrived in Los Angeles when he was sixteen and went on to a brief pro career. He was 9-3-1 as a lightweight before finding steadier, less perilous work in a warehouse of an air-conditioning manufacturer.

Joel De La Hoya would lace the gloves for Oscar's first fight at a local boys' club. Oscar was six. And though these earliest stories are apocryphal—did Oscar draw blood or just tears?—one detail is absolutely clear, that which he recalls again and again:

He got money for winning.

His first purses were dollar bills, bestowed by the men of the neighborhood. They kept passing him dead presidents, too, just as long as he kept winning. So he augmented his instinct, conditioning himself to smell money with blood. Where Oscar was going, there'd be a lot of both.

He trained at the Hollenbeck Youth Center on First Street and at Resurrection, an old church itself resurrected as a gym. De La Hoya provided a new take on an old character: the fighter as a child star.

In a way, he saw the barrio through a bubble. He walked the

streets, but the streets never walked on him. Strange for a boy from the 'hood, but stranger still for that boy to be a fighter. He has none of the macho mannerisms. Even in the ring, he has no bop. No wiggle. No funky step. No profane homeboy homilies for Oscar De La Hoya.

"I was taught to have manners," he sniffs.

De La Hoya's arrogance is beyond idiom. He had neither a street-fight ("never, not once," he says) nor a skateboard. But he had ambition in abundance. Oscar De La Hoya was fed aspirations the way other kids are fed Frosted Flakes. Everybody had high hopes—the father, the family, the neighborhood. Listen long enough to all the happy horseshit about the Community and role models and you'd believe that physicality combined with the vaguest virtue is enough to gentle the conditions in the slums.

"Ever since I was a little kid," he says, "I had to be some kind of example."

He'd never be one of the boyz. But there was always the sense that his success would be shared by all of East Los Angeles. Even the gang bangers knew enough not to mess with him. Everybody was rooting for Oscar. Do it for us, *ese*. Do it for us.

At the age of eleven, Oscar watched on TV as another East L. A. fighter did it *for us*. His name was Paul Gonzales, and he won a gold medal in the 1984 Olympics.

"I remember cheering for him on TV," says De La Hoya. "He was the hero for us—all of us."

But then, quite abruptly, De La Hoya suffered his first and final attack of rebellion. Perhaps he understood then what Gonzales admits only now, that "the pressure of representing my country was nothing compared to representing my neighborhood." Or perhaps, as De La Hoya says, "I was just tired. I just wanted to be in the street, playing football or baseball, whatever. I wanted, you know, a normal life." But something about normal life, that discrepancy between a child star's expectation and a real kid's reality, just didn't feel right.

"After a few months, I realized what I had to lose," he says. It wasn't a difficult decision, going back to the gym. "I didn't have that many friends, anyway."

Besides, what he had was more than an aptitude for hitting people. And none of the men watching from ringside understood quite so well as a woman. Cecilia De La Hoya, a seamstress and occasional singer, was the first to recognize a spooky duality in her boy.

"She used to say she didn't recognize me, her own son, when I went in the ring," he says. "She said she saw red in my eyes. She said she saw a beast. And she was right, always right. When I see blood, I want to see more."

He had the body to enable his bloodlust. The fighter you see today looks much like the fighter he's always been. Then, as now, he had cobra quickness, an unnaturally strong lead hand (he does everything lefty except fight), and the advantage of superior reach and leverage. He was always tall—he'd grow to almost five eleven—a stick figure except for the shoulders, those puncher's engines. He's built as if jets had been mounted on a biplane.

Joel De La Hoya, chief architect of his son's ambition, looked to Paul Gonzales as a blueprint. Gonzales recalls Oscar's father coming to the Resurrection, where a former vice cop named Al Stankie was wrapping his hands. Stankie had trained Gonzales for the '84 games. There was even supposed to be a Gonzales movie, *The Cop and the Kid*.

"Train my son, Oscar," said the elder De La Hoya. "Make him a gold medalist, too."

So for a time, the two Golden Boys shared a trainer. But while Gonzales's career was already in decline, De La Hoya was beginning an ascent unlike any the neighborhood had seen. For a while, he had a private tutor to help make up for all the school he missed while competing on the amateur circuit. But, really, how many kids with tutors could knock opponents unconscious—two of them in an afternoon? Oscar was 225 wins against 5 losses as an amateur, winning more championships, titles, and trophies than he could count.

"Now win the gold medal," Gonzales told him, "and you'll always have pussy."

You imagine that sheepish smile—embarrassed, perhaps, but never quite innocent—in response. There wasn't much time for girls. Oscar missed the prom at Garfield High to fight a Cuban at Fort Bragg, North Carolina. He vowed to throw himself a prom. After the Olympics. It was always after the Olympics.

In 1990, Cecilia De La Hoya watched the beast in her son win his weight class at the Goodwill Games in Seattle. Oscar had no idea she'd missed a week of radiation treatment to be there. It wasn't until they'd returned that she tried to explain about breast cancer, showing him the burns on her back left by the treatments.

She died on October 28 of that year. To honor her, Oscar vowed to win a gold medal at the Barcelona Olympics and present it at her grave. He did just that, against an unholy pressure. He was a role model, a soldier for God and country, for family and friends, for East L. A., and for the memory of his mother. He was nineteen. Oscar's Story, as some movie producers were now calling it, had acquired elements that were meaningful, maudlin, and, most of all, marketable.

Understand what made for such fame and fortune, what made a Latin boxer so mainstream. The most improbable blessing of all, that which made Oscar De La Hoya separate and singular, that which he got from his mother, is his face. Let's hear nothing of narcissism; pretty boy is the beast's best disguise. But also, the telltale sign of uncanny resilience.

Consider a fighter's years in the ring. Try to quantify the punishment and pain. Impossible. There's only the physical evidence, what precedes slurred speech and thick thoughts: blunted features, ridges of scar tissue, a wandering eye, cauliflower ear. There's a school of thought, much of it Mexican, that regards these various uglinesses as ennobling. There's an expectation that the fighter be willing to take a lot just to give a little.

"If I was scarred, if my nose was all busted up, they'd love me," De La Hoya says. "But I'm not going to apologize to the Mexican fans for not getting hit. I'm not going to apologize for being better than my opponents."

Don't mistake the fighter with heart for an eager masochist. And don't misunderstand his wounds—tattoos acquired on the road to Palookaville. De La Hoya even fired a trainer on account of ugliness. His name was Carlos Ortiz. He was once the lightweight champion of the world. But his face told Oscar of that place he did not want to go. "His nose had been broken, and he'd been cut up so many times," says De La Hoya. "I did not want to have that face."

He'd rather have the face that can make his fights feel like Menudo concerts, what with all the young girls in the crowd. His is the face boyfriends hate. And his is the face fighters wish to ruin, especially Mexican fighters.

Such good looks inspire not just envy but terror. As the punches accumulate—already seventeen years in the ring for Oscar—the still-pretty face can be construed in terms almost metaphysical. A pretty face means the mathematics of macho do not apply. And from one fighter to another, it also means this: I'll treat her real good when you're in Palookaville.

Trying to gauge the various distances—between Oscar and the Community, the barrio and the country club—I'm cruising with Paul Gonzales through the Flats, a stretch of low-slung khaki-colored projects, the concrete pueblos of East L. A. Deserted courtyards are dotted with metal crosses, clothesline posts that have the effect of a soldiers' cemetery. Kiddie gangstas in shades stand sentry, arms crossed. This week's cool is black high-top Converse, no laces. Driving Fourth Street now, domain of the Quatro Flats crew, its graffiti tags like hieroglyphics on an endless stretch of wall: Wicked and Whisper, Spooky and Smiley, Lilo and Cuko. Moving along, there's a "Stop the Violence" mural. Then the black Aztec eagle made popular by Cesar Chavez and the United Farm Workers.

Now look up: the billboard. There he goes, million-dollar smile. EL CAMPEÓN DE LA PROTECCIÓN EN GEL! Buy gel antiperspirant. Be like Oscar.

"Snake," says Gonzales, gesturing at the billboard. "Just 'cause he grew up in East L. A. don't mean he's from the 'hood."

After all these years, Gonzales is positioned for the counterpunch, the perfect spokesman to articulate these resentments against the Golden Boy. After all, Paul Gonzales was once a Golden Boy himself. But also, Kid Barrio.

He was eleven, riding in the backseat of a Chevy Impala, when the fragments of buckshot and glass embedded themselves in the back of his head. "Gang-banging?" he says. "I guess you could say I was." At thirteen, he was stabbed while beating down a grown man who'd called him a punk. That was right in front of his house, 129 Paseo Los

Alisos, Unit 56. That's Primera Flats, kid. No private home like where Oscar grew up.

Paul Gonzales won the gold at nineteen, same age as Oscar. Only he was not nearly so blessed. It was said of Gonzales that a lion's heart beat within a sparrow's body. Even as he accepted his medal, he had three broken bones in his right hand, dislocations of the elbow and shoulder, and a broken toe. That would be the story of his pro career as well. He'd grow only to bantamweight, and it seemed as if every time he hit somebody, he broke something else. Today, Gonzales tells kids at the Hollenbeck Youth Center to stay in school and stay off drugs. At thirty-one, he has long since retired, without a championship or big money, without any of what Kid Barrio once expected.

He began calling Oscar a "snake" after a 1993 *Los Angeles Times* piece in which his former protégé charged him with, of all things, forgetting where he came from. "He'd tell everybody he wasn't Mexican," Oscar told the paper. "He was cocky and rude. I'll never make a mistake like that."

Now Gonzales says, "I met him at the airport when he came back from Barcelona. I told him, 'Don't forget where you came from.' And look at him now. Thinks just 'cause he's got money, he can get pussy whenever he wants. Thinks his shit smells rosy."

Gonzales became another guy from East L. A. who found himself rooting for De La Hoya's opponents. Let's see: There was Rafael Ruelas, then 43–1, who had to sneak across the border from the mountain village of Yerba Buena, Mexico, at the age of seven before settling in the San Fernando Valley. Oscar called him "a good little fighter," then knocked him senseless in the second round.

"Oscar's people are picking them right," says Gonzales, unimpressed.

Then there was Genaro "Chicanito" Hernandez, from South-Central L. A. He was 32–0–1. Before the fight, Oscar returned to Garfield High School, his alma mater, where he donates money for scholarships. The kids threw eggs at him. It hurt, though not nearly as much as he would hurt his opponent. What De La Hoya did to Hernandez's nose was enough to make Chicanito quit.

"I thought Chicanito would win," Gonzales shrugs.

Then, of course, there was Julio César Chavez, 97–1–1, of Culiacán, the hardscrabble town known as Mexico's Medellín, for its reputation for drugs and violence. The publicity tour began with boos as Oscar was introduced to his hometown crowd at the Olympic Auditorium. But Oscar turned those boos into blood and money.

"Oscar beat a great fighter," says Gonzales. "But that great fighter was already on his way down."

Gonzales's envy is as palpable as his sweat during our sweltering tour of the barrio. He leans forward, an urgent look in his eyes, wanting me so much to understand. "Oscar got lucky, see. Serious luck. Am I ugly? My face ain't scarred and people like me. I play golf, I live in the suburbs, but I come around and help out the kids. There was supposed to be a movie, *The Cop and the Kid*. I don't know what happened. They're selling Oscar to white America. . . . I was sellable. My story was sellable."

He's giving himself up now, but in doing so he defines another distance, this one almost infinitesimal, but far enough to divide riches from regret. I feel for Gonzales but now admire De La Hoya even more. So close is Palookaville, even for the Golden Boys.

Oscar De La Hoya lives alone in a guarded, gated community. He's got a two-car garage and two bedrooms overlooking the pool. But I couldn't tell you the difference between Oscar's condo and the others. They all have that prefab look. Out front, there's a white Lamborghini and a black BMW, also a license plate mounted on the garage wall, ELA GOLD.

Inside, Oscar sits in a living room adorned with a framed poster of Marilyn Monroe, James Dean, and Humphrey Bogart drinking at a bar. He's watching *Entertainment Tonight* on a fifty-inch screen. The cast of *Friends* is holding out for more money. "How much are they asking for?" the champ wants to know.

Jennifer Aniston's father, himself an actor, explains that, show business being what it is, he wants his daughter to get all she can while she can. Besides, says Mr. Aniston, "I'd like to keep living in the manner to which I've grown accustomed."

Oscar nods at the screen, as if he knows from experience how this will play out.

Soon, the limousine arrives to take him to Television City to do *The Late Late Show with Tom Snyder*. "I feel blessed," he says. "Nothing has gone wrong. Even things that went wrong went right. I truly feel my mother is looking out for me."

He's said this before. It's part of his routine. But then he surprises me. He says he visits her grave before and after each fight. "That's how I know the round I'll knock them out," he says. "I'm just sitting there, talking to her, and it comes to me. I call out a round. I feel that's the round she wants me to end it. It's been like that for the last eight or nine fights. A number just pops into my head."

It's difficult to imagine Oscar, such a rational kid, so square with common sense, having a discourse with the dead. I ask if he had Chavez losing in the fourth.

"Actually, I had five," he says. "Before the fifth round."

"That's what she told you?"

He shrugs.

The freeway arcs over East Los Angeles, past King Taco. He once told me of meeting his ex-fiancée there. Her name was Veronica. She was a schoolteacher and a beauty queen. "Like someone you'd see on TV," Oscar once said.

I saw them nestling in a booth at Planet Hollywood after the Chavez fight. It seemed as if the whole neighborhood, certainly all those who had dogged him, was falling over one another to pay their respects to the new champ and his girl.

"She was a nice girl and everything," he says. "But I can't trust a bit. Not a girl. Can't trust a woman, not at all."

There's a distant look on his face as he stares out the window. The subject is closed. After a beat, he thinks to add, "Now I'm free like a bird. Girls, girls, girls."

He does his own monologue with Tom Snyder, wiping the sweat from his palms just before he goes on. He smiles the right smile, says the right things. Perfection is born of practice, and Oscar De La Hoya knows all the answers, even how to look like he gives a shit. I'm reminded of what he said, almost apologetically, in the country-club ballroom: "Gotta go along with it."

Snyder asks about the Chavez fight.

"I would have loved for it to continue," says De La Hoya. "Just one more round, another minute."

Sure, another minute and the beast would have won by hemorrhage.

Now let's open up the phone lines—North Bergen, New Jersey, you're on. Sounds like a girl up past her bedtime. "You look good to be a boxer," she coos.

Next caller, a teenybopper from Vancouver. "What do you look for in a girl?" she asks.

Oscar flashes the smile that sells deodorant. "Patience and understanding."

The next morning, De La Hoya attends a press conference to announce his upcoming fight with Miguel Angel Gonzalez, another Mexican champion, forty-one wins without a loss. And after Gonzalez, there's supposed to be a January rematch with Chavez. Then he's expected to come up to 147 pounds to fight a great if aging welterweight in Pernell Whitaker. Three fights, $25 million.

And a lot more where that came from.

As he suffers no deficiency in attitude or preparation, De La Hoya, now 22–0, figures to run the table. All that's unknown is his chin. But right now, he looks to be what Sugar Ray Leonard was more than a decade ago—the star bright enough to illuminate others, to clarify a new constellation.

"He can make $100 million in purses, easy," says his promoter, Bob Arum.

He can make twice that. The business of boxing is business. But what goes down behind closed doors is far colder than what goes on in the ring. Remember that fighters are typically owned in "pieces," as if investors can buy the piece of their choosing: heart or hands or balls. Remember that the next time a promoter runs over the body of his own broken boxer to crown the new Kid on whom he now has options. Or the next time you hear of rankings purchased in bribe money. Remember it when some sportscaster declares that Ali's mind is "sharp as ever." And in considering this Golden Boy, remember the generations of can't-miss kids now sipping methadone or collecting cans or nursing on that witch's tit called regret.

The great Julio César Chavez sucks on it, too. He supported a whole neighborhood back in Culiacán, his Community. But the whole time, he was borrowing against his next purse. Now he finally gets paid—the De La Hoya fight was twice his biggest payday—and what happens? The IRS takes $2.6 million in current and back taxes.

The sanctioning bodies get another $200,000. And Don King, the promoter who had him on allowance all those years, sues for the $1.35 million he says Chavez still owes. Soon after the fight, his wife files for divorce, and the Mexican treasury department wants him for tax fraud.

Not too long ago, he was the greatest fighter in the world. But no one would ask Julio César Chavez, who speaks only Spanish, to smile and sell deodorant. After all, he still stinks of the streets.

"It took him ninety-nine fights to realize what the business of boxing was all about," says De La Hoya.

And by then it was too late.

Chavez was already being escorted to Palookaville, by a pretty boy, no less.

Most fighters go entire careers, wrecking themselves in the process, without ever knowing what De La Hoya somehow knows in his blood. It's a blessing, a survival skill, but also a malignancy. In commerce, as in love, he's bound by suspicion, not sentiment.

"I can't trust anyone," he says. "Sometimes, I don't trust myself."

He'll cut you off and not look back. Al Stankie brought him through the amateur ranks. But before the Olympics, Al Stankie was busted for drunken driving, so he had to go.

Shelly Finkel, a manager especially esteemed by boxing standards, bankrolled De La Hoya's amateur career. Finkel spent more than $100,000 on the fighter and his family. "His father came to me, physically crying, and said, 'My wife is dying, would you help me?'" Finkel recalls. "So I paid for what was necessary. I paid for Oscar's mother's chemotherapy and her burial."

But just after the Olympics, Finkel learned that his services would no longer be needed. Team De La Hoya had a better deal.

The management duo of Steve Nelson and Robert Mittleman had offered a $1 million bonus in return for the standard one-third piece of the fighter. But the money went quickly. Joel De La Hoya bought a new house in Montebello, a suburb of East L. A. His old friend Robert Alcazar—the man who succeeded Stankie as trainer—took his cut. And Oscar bought the Lamborghini. His only reckless period— spending up to $10,000 a week—would last until he fired Nelson and Mittleman in December 1993.

Oscar said he hadn't received his payments on time. But in fact, he never much cared for Mittleman and Nelson. Their final offense was insisting on the palooka-faced trainer, Ortiz. The parties would reach an out-of-court settlement. But things haven't been quite the same between fighter and his father, who initially sided with the managers.

Today, De La Hoya listens to other grown-ups. There's Mike Hernandez, a respected Chevrolet dealer from East L. A. whom he calls "my adviser." And there's Alcazar's replacement as head trainer, Jesus Rivero, the "Professor," a venerable Mexican who insists that his student study the two Williams: Shakespeare and Pep. Oscar knows the bard even better than the boxer. He's obsessed with betrayal. "Trust?" he says. "I guess I trust my brother, Joel, my little sister, Ceci, my father."

"Your father?"

"What happened caused friction. . . . But we stuck together."

He doesn't want to talk about his father.

"Do you trust the Professor?"

"Can't say I do, can't say I don't," he says. "I trust him in the ring."

"Your adviser?"

"He's my adviser."

"Yes, but do you trust him?"

"It's tough to say, do you *trust* somebody."

No, he doesn't trust. And he plays along, using a press agent's patter to guard the interiors of his emotional life. He keeps his distance. But he keeps his dignity, too. And that's the most difficult thing for a fighter to do. I can't say what will become of Oscar De La Hoya, but I can swear what won't. He won't be caught grabbing ass at the bar. He won't make a "comeback" to satisfy various debts to the IRS or an ex-wife or his own unfulfilled promise. He won't go out drooling or shaking. He won't be sold off in pieces, either.

"I own 100 percent of Oscar De La Hoya." His eyes narrow, just a hint of that beast who smells blood with money. "What fighter can say that?"

"Do me a favor, amigo, get me a picture of Oscar and the boys."

So it begins, the Boy Scout benefit at the Riviera, known for years as "Hogan's Alley" but more recently as "O. J.'s old club." De La Hoya plays with a group from Owens Corning. The caddie is Flip Wilson's son. Oscar has been golfing just a year and a half, minus the months spent in training, and already shoots in the mid-eighties. But more than that is his natural ease in country-club society, so far from the culture of boxing. It's not just the hushed etiquette or the breeze rustling through the eucalyptus trees. Golf is a bloodless sport. And it's difficult to reconcile this kid lining up his putt with the sadist who felt some sort of ecstasy in making homeboy Hernandez "bleed like a fountain."

He sinks a twenty-footer.

"That," he says, "is what makes it all worth it."

The groundskeepers and maintenance men, also born to the barrio, shoot odd sidelong glances his way, not unlike the stare of that sentry back in Quatro Flats. But the look on the women preparing lunch is pure adoration. A blushing volunteer tracks him down on the fairway. She says they met back in '92. He doesn't remember but goes along with it anyway.

The De La Hoya autograph is requested without respite, those autograph hounds still sniffing around. The guys from Owens Corning have gloves and posters for him to sign, too. The club pro apologizes even as he hands Oscar a golf ball.

"I've signed smaller," says Oscar. "Try signing a G-string."

Was that a wink? I can't tell. Soon, he'll have his picture taken with the crippled Boy Scouts. Finally, when he comes in off the course, an old man rushes to give him a big hug. "Anytime you want to be my guest here, please let me know. Just stay the way you are, young man."

"Excuse me," says Oscar. "I have a previous appointment."

He gives a shrug but not her name. And for a mere moment, his sheepish smile gives way to a shit-eating grin. Then he gets in the tinted cockpit of his six-figure ride, the black BMW to indulge his secret solitary extravagance: speed. Pedal hits the metal as he heads down Sunset, past all those brown-faced kids selling maps to the stars, putting all the distance he can between himself and Palookaville.

David Remnick

One can safely say there has never been a boxing writer quite like David Remnick (b. 1958). Not only is he the author of biographies of both President Obama (*The Bridge*, 2010) and Muhammad Ali (*King of the World*, 1998), he won the Pulitzer Prize for his book about the collapse of the Soviet Empire, *Lenin's Tomb* (1993). In 1998, at the age of forty, Remnick was named editor of *The New Yorker*, a stunning achievement for someone who, when people in journalism first noticed him, was one of a succession of bright young men *The Washington Post* dispatched to cover big fights. Sometimes it was Thomas Boswell, the elegant baseball writer; sometimes John Ed Bradley, a former LSU football co-captain who would go on to write novels. And then there was Remnick, not long out of Princeton, with a shy smile and a genuine sense of reserve, sitting back and taking in everything about the sweet science that he could. As his unflinching 1997 assessment of Mike Tyson's ruined career proves, he learned his lessons well.

Kid Dynamite Blows Up: Mike Tyson

THE conventions of the ring demand that a fighter in training become a monk. For months at a time, he hardens his body on roadwork and beefsteak, and practices an enforced loneliness—even (tradition has it) sexual loneliness—the better to focus the mind on war. Mike Tyson's monastery in the Nevada desert is a mansion next door to Wayne Newton's mansion, and it could be said to lack the usual austerity. There is a chandelier worthy of Cap d'Antibes. There is a painting on silk of Diana Ross. There are books, magazines, a big television, leather couches. But the diversions are not what they could be. When Tyson is not preparing for fights, he keeps lions and tigers around as pets and wrestles with them. "Sometimes I go swimming with the tiger," he told a visitor. "But, personally, I'm a lion man. Lions are very obedient, like dogs." Tyson was keeping his pets elsewhere, though. He has estates in Ohio, in Connecticut, and off a

434

fairway on the Congressional Country Club, in Bethesda, Maryland. The big cats are most often in Ohio. The Nevada mansion is surrounded by life-size statues of warrior heroes whom Tyson has read about and come to revere: Genghis Khan, Toussaint-Louverture, Alexander the Great, Hannibal. "Hannibal was very courageous," Tyson said. "He rode elephants through Cartilage." In a week's time, Tyson himself would be going through cartilage, too.

After spending three years in an Indiana prison for raping a teenager named Desiree Washington, Tyson went back to fighting in 1995. He denied to the end that he had ever raped anyone, but he said he was a better man now. Tyson converted to Islam—indeed, the bumper sticker on his Bentley reads "I ♥ Allah"—and he told his visitors in jail that he had spent his time studying the Koran, Machiavelli, Voltaire, Dumas, the lives of Meyer Lansky and Bugsy Siegel, "and a lot of Communist literature." He ordered up icons for his shoulders, a diptych tattoo: Arthur Ashe on one side, Mao Zedong on the other. He declared himself ready to regain his place in boxing. He would reclaim not only his title but also his image of invincibility. Iron Mike. Kid Dynamite. Once more, he would be the fighter who had expressed only disappointment after a knockout of one Jesse Ferguson, saying, "I wanted to hit him one more time in the nose so that bone could go up into his brain."

But after easily dispatching a selection of unworthies who provided an extended warmup drill worth tens of millions of dollars, Tyson finally met a real fighter, if not a great one, named Evander Holyfield, who backed him down and beat him up. Holyfield took Tyson's title last November, in one of the cleverest displays of boxing guile since February 1964, when Muhammad Ali, then Cassius Clay, stunned another invincible—Tyson's fistic precursor, Sonny Liston. Liston, like Tyson, had grown up in an environment of crime and never left it; Liston had done time for armed robbery, he mugged people, he beat up a cop, he broke heads for the Mob. And, like Tyson, he was considered a killer in the ring, unbeatable. Against Clay, Liston had been favored so strongly that the lead boxing writer for *The New York Times* skipped the fight and left it to a rookie in the office, Robert Lipsyte. But Clay, with his magnificent speed, dodged Liston's plodding bombs and bloodied the big man's eye. Liston quit on his stool, claiming a sore shoulder. Against Holyfield, Tyson had been similarly unmasked. "He's like any bully," said Gil Clancy, one of the game's legendary trainers. "Once Tyson saw his own blood, he backed down." The referee stopped the beating in the eleventh round. When it was over, Tyson was in such a daze that he turned to one of his handlers and asked, "What round did I knock him out in?"

The rematch with Holyfield would be worth thirty million dollars to Tyson, thirty-five million to Holyfield. The fight's promoter, Don King, whose good word, of course, is all one ever needs, promised record receipts for the live gate and pay-per-view television: "A hundred and fifty million, maybe two hundred million. After all, we got three billion people in Red China alone!" Whatever. If Tyson won, he would regain not only his championship but also his place as "the baddest man on the planet." Holyfield would be remembered as a fighter who on a given night had risen above himself and then, in the rematch, fell to earth.

After coming out of jail, Tyson showed signs of domestic stability. In April, he married a doctor named Monica Turner. (Turner's first husband was sentenced to ten years in prison on a cocaine-dealing charge.) Tyson and Turner have one child; another is due this summer. Until now, marriage had been a miserable topic for Tyson. His first wife, the television star Robin Givens, was famously manipulative. She had been a Sarah Lawrence girl and, even in public, treated Tyson with an airy condescension. There were, in some cynical corners, suspicions that Givens had actually married for money. Tyson was not slow to express his annoyance. The former light-heavyweight champion José Torres once asked Tyson what the best blow he had ever thrown was. "Man, I'll never forget that punch," Tyson said. "It was when I fought with Robin in Steve's apartment. She really offended me and I went *bam*, and she flew backward, hitting every fucking wall in the apartment." The marriage ended in divorce.

Unlike Givens, Turner has, for the most part, stayed out of her husband's business affairs and out of camera range, and there have been no reports of fights, physical or otherwise. Turner mainly stayed away from Las Vegas. Tyson's most frequent visitors at his desert house were the members of his entourage, each in his own way a sterling influence: Don King, a former numbers runner from Cleveland who once stomped a man to death in a dispute over six hundred dollars and then became the greatest carnival barker since Barnum; Tyson's co-managers, Rory Holloway, an old friend, and John Horne, a failed standup comic from Albany who specializes in yelling at reporters; Tyson's trainer, Richie Giachetti, a street guy from Cleveland who worked with Larry Holmes; and a self-described "master motivator" named Steve (Crocodile) Fitch, who admits that "in another life" he spent five years in jail for manslaughter. ("But I didn't do it," he told me. "A complete setup.") Crocodile proved to be a prophetic character. During the week leading up to the fight, he could be seen in fatigues and wraparound shades, all the while screaming his suggestive war cries: "It's time for ultimate battle! Ultimate battle! Time to bite! Time to bite!"

Tyson avoided the press—especially the print media. Horne and Holloway had done a good job of convincing him that the papers were filled with nothing but lies, that the New York reporters on the boxing beat—Michael Katz, of the *Daily News*, Wallace Matthews, of the *Post*—were out to get them. Early in the morning, before the sun was high, Tyson ran along the empty desert roads. Then he sparred in the gym. His workouts were closed. For recreation, he watched one gangster movie after another, sometimes through the night. He is partial to James Cagney, Edward G. Robinson, and John Garfield. He can recite whole scenes of *Raging Bull*, *On the Waterfront*, and—his favorite—*The Harder They Fall*.

Tyson would have preferred to be alone—or, at least, alone with his entourage and his movies—but Don King knew that in order to rouse pay-per-view orders the goat had to be fed. Tyson would not allow interviews at his house, but five days before the fight he agreed to go out to King's place to meet with a group of writers. And so on an afternoon of long shadows and hundred-degree heat a couple of white vans pulled out of the driveway of the MGM Grand Hotel, away from the new family-friendly downtown, away from the Brooklyn Bridge and the black glass Pyramid of Cheops, away from the palace of the Caesars and the Folies Bergere, out of earshot, finally, of the unending music of the city, the air-conditioned hum and the mad electronic ringing of a thousand acres of slot machines and the slushy spill of silver coins pouring into curved silver trays. Don King does not live on the Strip. He lives out where it is quiet, at the outermost edge of the city, where the desert resumes.

In all honesty, no one would ride to the edge of the desert to talk with Evander Holyfield. No one much cared about Holyfield. He was likable enough. But he was dull copy. He hadn't raped anyone. He hadn't been to jail. He talked about Jesus Christ all the time and literally sang gospel music while hitting the heavy bag. He seemed like a good fellow, but what story did he offer? He talked in the polite clichés of doing my best, having faith in my abilities and in the will of God—but what did he mean? Heavyweight championship fights, from the days of John L. Sullivan onward, are stories, morality plays, and this story, regardless of its end, was all about Tyson. This was a war between middle-class aspiration and ghetto insolence, gospel and rap. Without Tyson there was no sense of danger, no interest, no hundred million dollars.

"People are full of shit. They want to see something dark," Tyson's former trainer Teddy Atlas told me. "People want to feel close to it and in on it, but, of course, only from the distance of their suburban homes. They want to have the benefit of comfort, security, safety, respect, and at the same time the privilege of watching something out of control—even promote it being out of control—as long as we can be secure that we're not accountable for it. With Tyson, the dark thing was always the anticipation that someone was going to get knocked out. The whole Kid Dynamite thing. But we wanted to believe that the monster was also a nice kid. We wanted to believe that Mike Tyson was an American story: the kid who grows up in the horrible ghetto and then converts that dark power into a good cause, into boxing. But then the story takes a turn. The dark side overwhelms him. He's cynical, he's out of control. And now the story is even better. It's like a double feature now, like you're getting *Heidi* and *Godzilla* at the same time."

King's minions wanted the reporters to understand that this was a special invitation—a very rare one, these days. The whole charade seemed absurd to the reporters who had been around boxing for a while. Until not so long ago, fighters before a big bout were available athletes, the least guarded of men. Like sultans, they often used to greet their visitors propped up on a few pillows in bed; reporters would sit perched at the edge of the bed or hard on the floor, notebooks out, ready to catch pearls. Archie Moore, the great light-heavyweight, could unburden himself of a monologue worthy of

Molly Bloom or the Duke of Gloucester. Boxers were free of the solemn self-importance of modern athletes in the team sports. They liked having people around. In the moments before fighting for the championship, Floyd Patterson napped in his dressing room, and a few writers were allowed to stay around, close enough to register the movement under the champion's eyelids, the timbre of his snore. Patterson would describe his dreams, the depths of his fear. He talked and talked, one of the great analysands of the prize ring.

Tyson used to be like that. When he was coming up as a fighter, and even as a young champion, he loved to talk to the press, tell his story. He was immensely aware of himself as the star of an ongoing Cagney movie. Some writers even saw a sweetness in him, the yearning for love and a home. Certainly it was a life beyond the imagination of the middle-class reporters who came calling. He was the kid from Amboy Street in Brooklyn's Brownsville, an especially vicious and hopeless delinquent. When he was six, his idea of a prank was to slit his big brother's arm with a razor while he slept. His father was nowhere in evidence, his mother was overwhelmed by poverty. Tyson idolized the pimps and the thieves in the neighborhood, and by the time he was ten he was mugging old ladies and shooting into crowds for kicks. As he told his story, he could sense the titillation in the writer, and more details would pour out: "I'd shoot real close to them, skin them or something, make them take off their pants and then go run in the streets." After he had racked up dozens of arrests and was sent off to reform school, Cus D'Amato, an old and eccentric trainer who had settled upstate, along the Hudson, took him in. D'Amato was a kindly paranoiac. When he was still working out of the Gramercy Gym, in Manhattan, he used to sleep in the back with nothing to keep him company but a shotgun and a dog. To his fighters, he was a kind of Father Divine, at once inspiring and full of righteous gas. He preached the value of terror, the way that all fighters faced fear and the good ones learned to harness it, to make it their friend. He was an ascetic. Money, he said, "was something to throw off the back of trains." Writers loved D'Amato, the way any writer would have loved, say, Moll Flanders had she been presented, whole, in real life, and available for quotation.

Tyson represented D'Amato's last hope—the chance, after Patterson and José Torres, to have a third world champion. As if to satisfy every convention of the boxing movie, D'Amato "adopted" Tyson, became his legal guardian, but he died a year before his "son" won the crown. On winning the title, Tyson wept. If only Cus had seen it, he said, if only Cus were here. It was over the top, even for Hollywood, but not for the conventions of the boxing story.

Tyson was also good copy partly because he was brutal and unabashed about being so. Unlike Ali, whose helium rants usually had more to do with camp comedy or the prophecies of Elijah Muhammad than with the violence of his profession, Tyson was blunt, clinical. He knew he had been trained to hurt other men, and he saw no good reason to deflect attention from that. He was in the beating business and he had never acquired the tact or the reflexes to say he didn't enjoy it. In his comically high voice, he spoke of throwing punches with "bad intentions to vital areas," of blows to the heart, to the kidneys, to the liver, and the pleasure he took in delivering them. He talked of his yearning to break an opponent's eardrum, to shatter his will, to make him "cry like a woman."

At the same time, Tyson was self-aware, almost academic in his regard for boxing. In a time when most baseball players hardly know the name Jackie Robinson, Tyson grew obsessed not just with all the obvious contemporaries and near contemporaries but also with Harry Greb and Kid Chocolate, with Willie Pep and Stanley Ketchel. The writers ate that up. With boxing under attack as crippling, as atavistic and cruel, his talk made them feel that their subject was important, somehow—not merely a skein of beatings in the parking lots of betting parlors but a matter of aesthetics and history. Tyson spent hundreds of hours watching old fights, and from those films he not only learned the details of his craft but also assumed certain traits of favored precursors. He cut his hair to resemble Jack Dempsey's. He took to wearing bulky button-up sweaters because he had seen such sweaters on some of the old fighters in the old newsreels. And so, while Tyson's story was not Ali's, while he lacked that level of wit, physical improvisation, and epic, his story was a good one, good enough for half a dozen biographies, good enough, certainly, to make him the best-paid athlete in history.

We drove out Flamingo Road, past the plastic-surgery parlors, past all the clip joints and software palaces that look as if they were built last week. We arrived at a "gated community," one of the high-security mansion neighborhoods that you see now in every city where there is sun and money and heightened fear of larceny. We rang the buzzer and the gates swung open. Don King's house is Spanish style, perhaps—a riot of white stucco. There were Range Rovers and BMWs parked outside and an enormous satellite dish parked on the roof. We walked up the front steps and were greeted by a portrait of Don King. The real thing was in the kitchen.

"Welcome! Welcome to my home!" he boomed. King invited us in for an early dinner. He had ordered out from Popeyes.

King is the evil genius of boxing, the latest in a long line. His electrified hair is merely a way to use "personality" to hide his substance. In his way, he is even more powerful than the so-called Octopus Inc., of the nineteen-fifties—James Norris's corrupt International Boxing Club. Tyson, like so many boxers, cannot bear King. He does not especially trust King. But he does business with King, because King is the singular presence in big-time boxing. They make a lot of money together, and so Tyson is as indulgent of King's conniving as King is of Tyson's tantrums. There is no profit in judgment.

In the kitchen, King was telling me that three billion people would watch the fight: The key was penetration, he said—that is, how many people would sign up for the fifty-dollar fee and order the fight on pay-per-view. "If we get ten percent of the universe, then we'll be fine," he added. He never quite explained what that meant. He knew I would not bother to ask. "Mike generates more capital than anyone in the history of the world. Why do they want to destroy him, the goose that laid the golden egg?"

After a long wait, Tyson showed up. He took his place on a white leather couch. As he waited for the first question, he assumed the expression of a man who has eaten a bad egg and is waiting to be sick. One by one the questions came, and Tyson answered them in a way designed to make the questioner feel like an idiot. Yes, he felt good. No, he wouldn't make the same mistakes again against Holyfield. Yes, he expected to win. But, no, it wouldn't change his life if he lost. "The way my deals are set up, I'm pretty much set." At times, he spoke as a man obsessed less with a fight than with the rational distribution of his mutual funds.

To be with Tyson even for just a couple of hours is to witness the power of a ghetto kid's fatalism. He has, his accountants claimed, all he could ever want. He will never—or should never—end up like Joe Louis, coked up on the casino floor, working as a greeter. And yet he is forever saying "My life is over" and "I am taking the blows for my children." He has a boundless sense of self-drama, of the dark future. Even here, surrounded by his co-managers Rory Holloway and John Horne, he said he had no friends, he trusted no one. And who could doubt him?

"We have to trust, but people by nature are not to be trusted," Tyson said. "That's just the way it is. I got a Machiavellian effect as far as that's concerned. I'm not a philosopher, I'm not Machiavelli in that respect, but you can't be a person always willing to do good in an environment where people are always willing to do bad. You know what I mean?

"I have no friends, man. When I got out of prison, all my old friends, they had to go. If you don't have a purpose in my life, man, you have to go. . . . Why would you want someone around in your life if they have no purpose? Just to have a pal or a buddy? I got a wife. My wife can be my pal and buddy. I'm not trying to be cold, but it's something I picked up. . . . If I'm gonna get screwed, I'm not gonna get screwed over by the people that screwed me before. I'm gonna get screwed by the *new* people.

"I've been taken advantage of all my life. I've been used, I've been dehumanized, I've been humiliated, and I've been betrayed. That's basically the outcome of my life, and I'm kind of bitter, kind of angry at certain people about it. . . . Everyone in boxing makes out well except for the fighter. He's the only one who suffers, basically. He's the only one who's on Skid Row. He's the only one who loses his mind. He sometimes goes insane, he sometimes goes on the bottle, because it's a highly intensive, pressure sport, and a lot of people lose it. There's so much you can take and then you break."

In an effort to lighten Tyson's mood, some of the writers started asking about a subject close to his heart: his new family. For a few moments, he was as fuzzy as a character in *thirtysomething*.

"That's all I have, my children," he said. "Wives are known to run off and fall in love with other people, because they are human, even die. But you have to take care of children. . . . The way I see it is that every fight I have is for their future. Every fight. Every fight is a different future for my children." Tyson said that he played games with his kids, ate ice cream with them. "They love *Barney*," he said. "I *hate Barney*.

"I have a stepdaughter and one day she was crying and she says, 'Mama, Jane don't want to play with me today.' And I burst out, 'She doesn't want to play with you? Then fuck her!' My wife didn't like that too much. But we're different people. She studied psychology and believes in working on a kid's mind. I believe in being strict—if you get out of line, you're getting hit! They're too young for that now, but I'm a strong believer in that. I think kids should learn discipline. If they get out of line, they should learn discipline. At what age? I don't know. Ten years old?

"See, I've been beaten all my life. My kids have parents, one's a doctor, a bright woman, and a father who's a . . . a father who's rich. I had an alcoholic and a pimp for parents. So they're gonna have a great life, if they don't turn out to be bad children. . . . I just don't want them out on the street, because these hustlers, they can be very exciting, people gravitate to them. I survived it, but they may not be lucky enough to survive. All my real friends are in prison or dead. The ones still out are so messed up on drugs they don't know their own name."

It was as if Tyson knew something that no one else knew—not his accountants, not his managers. He was convinced of his own wretched end. Nothing, save the well-being of his kids, would please him. Last summer, Tyson threw himself a million-dollar three-day-long thirtieth-birthday party at his estate in Farmington, Connecticut. There were magnums of Cristal, and cigars rolled specially for the occasion. Tyson handed out BMWs and Range Rovers to six of his flunkies. And yet he had an awful time. "I don't know half the people here," he said as he wandered his many acres. "This isn't what I wanted."

Horne and Holloway may know nothing about boxing, but they have been expert at feeding Tyson's sense of persecution. "Nobody's on our side," Tyson told us as his co-managers nodded like proud puppeteers. "The courts are against us, the corporations are against us, the news reporters are against us, the papers—your bosses—are against us. We have nobody on our side, and we're still fighting and we're still doing well. If we had you guys on our side, we'd be a phenomenon!"

From the back of the room, King yelled, "If you would just print the truth! You write what people throw out to you as a smoke screen!"

"The fact is, they call us monsters, that we're inhuman, they want people to be afraid of us," Tyson said. (In fact, Tyson has always cultivated that image. He once told his former friend José Torres, "I like to hurt women when I make love to them. I like to hear them scream with pain, to see them bleed. It gives me pleasure.")

"Who do you mean?" one of the reporters said. "Who's calling you monsters?"

"You. Not you individually, but reporters," Tyson said. "They write that we're monsters, that we're hideous, that we commit heinous crimes."

"Let's take the Newfield book, for example," said King, referring to Jack Newfield's scrupulous biography of him. "The Newfield book is all lies, and yet everyone uses it as the defining factor on me! Everything in there is a lie! So a guy who's a good writer knows how to *speculize* and *dramatize* those lies! You know what I mean?"

"They hope it leads to you being incarcerated," said Horne, who was standing at Tyson's shoulder.

"Look," Tyson said. "Don is still a fool to have you over to his house and talk to you. He had to beg me to come over here and talk to you, because of what you guys write about me. The people that know me, love me, they read this. It feels like shit.

"And this guy, knowing you guys ain't gonna give him no justice, he still, stupidly, has you guys in his house talking to you, knowing you'll write it was a good fight and then try to put his ass in jail. They're gonna write some madman tales, how he robbed this guy and killed this other guy. I don't know. I wasn't there when he killed the guy, but, shit, if a guy got killed he was probably doing something he wasn't supposed to be doing. You know what I mean? I'm a strong believer in that. Not in a drive-by shooting, but very few people get killed for no reason, from where I come from."

King was delighted by this moving show of support. "Just watch me prove that he attacked me," he said. "All I want is fair play! I'm still crazy enough to love America!"

We, the Americans, must have been moved to the core. There was a long silence. A European writer shyly turned to Tyson and said, "Mike, with all of that said, why don't you come out more and go on Larry King again, and go on David Letterman and set the record straight?"

Tyson's eyes narrowed. He flapped his hand in disgust. "Ah, fuck y'all. Fuck y'all," he said. "I don't have to suck your dick to justify me being a good guy. Listen, man, I'm a man! I don't go begging someone to love me."

"It's not begging," the European ventured. "It's—"

"Yes, it is!" Tyson said. "You see, O. J. Simpson, he's going around all the time trying to prove his innocence. By court of law, he's innocent. Maybe common sense tells you he's not, but in a court of law he's innocent. I'm not going to go around saying, 'Well, I've done this or this for this organization.' The hell with that, man."

Now Horne started egging Tyson on. "When the intention is to destroy you from the beginning, you can't get no level playing field to set the record straight," Horne said. "Let me say one thing. All of us live different lives. None of y'all have lived the lives that we have. We have different perceptions of things. . . . You guys go into back rooms, you conference about everything, you help each other out, to destroy somebody who is the only reason you are all out here. No other fighter takes you out of the country, no other fighter makes your jobs so interesting."

Finally, Tyson had the presence of mind to wave Horne off, to settle King down. All he really wanted us to know was that he was unknowable. He had probably given more interviews, in his time, than Dora ever gave to Freud, but it didn't matter. "Look," he said. "I'm harder on myself than the goddam reporters. But they don't know me well enough to write what I'm about, that I'm a monster, that I'm this or that. No one knows me. . . . I'd like to be written up like the old-timers. There's no doubt about it, I'm a wild man. I've had my share of the good times. But that's just part of the business, that's just who Mike is. I work hard, I live hard, I play hard, I die hard."

Like mediocre fiction, fights for the heavyweight championship of the world are invariably freighted with the solemnity of deeper meanings. It is not enough that one man shock another's brain and send him reeling. There must be politics, too—or, at least, great lumps of symbol, historical subplots, metaphysical frosting. In team sports—in football, baseball, basketball—there are individual stars, there are rivalries, but, finally, the athletics is the thing. A team athlete's talent is often the mastery of some peculiar and relatively recent invention: kicking a pig's bladder through a set of posts, swinging a stick of polished ash, tossing a ball through an iron hoop. Boxing is ancient, simple, lonely. There is hardly any artifice at all. Padded gloves and the gauze and tape underneath do little to protect the fighters; they merely prevent broken hands, and allow for more punching, more pain. Boxers go into the ring alone, nearly naked, and they succeed or fail on the basis of the most elementary criteria: their ability to give and receive pain, their will to endure their own fear. Since character —the will of a person stretched to extremes—is so obviously at the center of boxing, there is an undeniable urge to know the fighters, to derive some meaning from the conflict of those characters.

John L. Sullivan's triumphs were triumphs of the working class, the immigrant wave, "the people." Joe Louis fought the moral war over German fascism—fascism coming in the bruised and prostrate person of Max Schmeling. Most of all, the fights have come to be parables tinctured with the issues and conflicts of race. Indeed, some of the first boxing matches in America were held on plantations before the Civil War. White slave owners (the promoters) set up fights between their chattel. The slaves were often commanded to fight to the death. Was it such a great leap from there to the MGM Grand? "If [the heavyweights] become champions they begin to have inner lives like Hemingway or Dostoyevsky, Tolstoy or Faulkner, Joyce or Melville or Conrad or Lawrence or Proust," Norman Mailer wrote twenty-six years ago in *Life.*

> Dempsey was alone and Tunney could never explain himself and Sharkey could never believe himself nor Schmeling nor Braddock, and Carnera was sad and Baer an indecipherable clown; great heavyweights like Louis had the loneliness of the ages in their silence, and men like Marciano were mystified by a power which seemed to have been granted them. With the advent, however, of the great modern Black heavyweights, Patterson, Liston, then Clay and Frazier, perhaps the loneliness gave way to what it had been protecting itself against— a surrealistic situation unstable beyond belief. Being a Black heavyweight champion in the second half of the twentieth century (with Black revolutions opening all over the world) was now not unlike being Jack Johnson, Malcolm X, and Frank Costello all in one.

Black fighters found themselves fighting intricate wars over racial types, over shifting notions of masculinity, decency, and class. In 1962, with the endorsements of President Kennedy and the National Association for the Advancement of Colored People, Floyd Patterson fought in the name of the black middle class and white liberals against Liston, the gruff ex-con, who represented, as Amiri Baraka (then LeRoi Jones) put it, "the big black Negro in every white man's hallway, waiting to do him in." But Patterson was not physically equal to his preposterous moral task. Liston flattened him in the first round. So shamed was Patterson that he fled Comiskey Park disguised in a fake beard and mustache and drove all night back to New York. He had not merely been defeated. He had let down the race; he had not fulfilled his meaning, his role in the story.

It is hard to imagine today the sense of disappointment in Patterson's loss. A columnist for the *Los Angeles Times* wrote that having Liston as champion "is like finding a live bat on a string under your Christmas tree." Some papers felt free to refer to Liston as a "jungle beast," a "gorilla." Only Murray Kempton, writing in the *Post*, was able to find an arch note of optimism in Liston's ascent. "The Negro heavyweights, as Negroes tend to do, have usually given that sense of being men above their calling," Kempton wrote. "Floyd Patterson sounded like a Freedom Rider. We return to reality with Liston. We have at last a heavyweight champion on the moral level of the men who own him. This is the source of horror which Liston has aroused; he is boxing's perfect symbol. He tells us the truth about it. The heavyweight championship is, after all, a fairly squalid office."

Liston tried desperately to please. He promised to be a good champion, to emulate Joe Louis. He explained that he had been one of twenty-five children in rural Arkansas, that he was illiterate, abused by a violent father. He apologized for his "terrible mistakes." But the country seemed not to accept the apologies; it was hard for whites and blacks alike to countenance a man who, when asked why he would not join in the civil rights marches in the South, had answered, "I ain't got no dog-proof ass." People only laughed when Liston started associating with priests. After Cassius Clay beat Liston in Miami— and then, as Muhammad Ali, beat him again—his story took a tragic course. Liston retired to Las Vegas, where he fought a little, hung out with gangsters like Ash Resnick, and in 1971 died with a needle in his arm. The funeral procession went down the Strip. For a few minutes, people came out of the casinos, squinting in the sun and saying farewell to Liston. The Ink Spots sang "Sunny."

For a long time, especially since coming home from prison, Tyson has seen himself in Liston. Watching films of Liston working out to the old James Brown rendition of "Night Train," he said, was "orgasmic."

"Sonny Liston, I identify with him the most," he said. "That may sound morbid and grim, but I pretty much identify with that life. He wanted people to respect him or love him, but it never happened. You can't make people respect and love you by craving it. You've got to *demand* it.

"People may not have liked him because of his background, but the people who got to know him as an intimate person have a totally different opinion. He had a wife. I'm sure she didn't think he was a piece of garbage. . . . Everyone respected Sonny Liston's ability. The point is respecting him as a man. No one can second-guess my ability, either. But I'm going to be respected. I demand that. You have no choice. You couldn't be in my presence if you didn't."

A few weeks before the fight, I went up to Michigan to see Liston's conqueror. Muhammad Ali lives on a manicured farm in a small town near the Indiana border called Berrien Springs. It was obvious to everyone who saw him tremble as he ignited the Olympic torch in Atlanta that Parkinson's disease has all but silenced Ali and placed a grim mask on what had been the century's most sparkling face. But out of the way of television cameras, which make him nervous and even more rigid than usual, Ali can show delight. He is especially delighted to watch himself when his body was fluid and his voice the most widely recognized in the world. We spent the better part of an afternoon watching videotapes of his fights, the early fights with Liston and then the first bout against Patterson. Ali leaned back and smiled as he watched himself, in black and white, dissect Liston, duck his blows, and sting him with jabs until Liston looked very slow and very sad.

"Ah, Sonny," Ali said. "The big ugly bear!"

Now Liston was quitting. He sat slumped on his stool. Now Ali's younger self was standing at the ropes, hysterical in his triumph, shouting down at the reporters who had dismissed him as a loud-mouth and a fake, "Eat your words! Eat your words! I am the greatest!"

"They all thought I'd lose," Ali said. "Thought he'd tear me up."

After a while, I asked Ali about Tyson and whether he compared to Liston.

"Liston was faster than Tyson, but came straight ahead," he said. His voice was whispery, almost all breath.

"Could Tyson have beaten you?" I asked.

"Don't make me laugh," Ali said, and he was laughing. "Tyson don't have it. He don't *have* it." For a second, I wondered what "it" was, but then The Greatest made it clear. He pointed to his head.

About a week later, I took the ferry to Staten Island to visit Teddy Atlas, who had trained Tyson when he was learning to fight in Cus D'Amato's gym. Atlas is one of boxing's most appealing characters, the son of a doctor who used to treat patients in the ghetto for a couple of dollars. He was rebellious, a street kid who learned to box. A knife fight on Rikers Island left him with a scar on his face that runs from his hairline to his jawline. When Atlas was barely twenty, D'Amato taught him how to train fighters and then entrusted him with Tyson. Atlas taught Tyson the catechism according to D'Amato, the peekaboo style of holding the gloves up near the face, the need to overcome the fear inside. During one amateur fight, Tyson told Atlas between rounds that his hand was broken and he couldn't go on, but Atlas knew it was just fear, the fear of disgrace, and he pushed Tyson back out into the ring and to a victory.

Atlas, however, grew disillusioned as he saw D'Amato indulge Tyson in one ugly incident after another. Tyson harassed girls in school, beat other kids up, threatened teachers, and D'Amato nearly always found a way to make it good with the school, with the police. He would have his champion, one way or another. He was not raising a son, after all. He was raising a fighter. But in 1982, when Tyson molested Atlas's adolescent sister-in-law, Atlas lost it. He held a gun to Tyson's head and threatened him. D'Amato never punished Tyson. He did, however, get rid of Atlas.

Tyson's co-manager John Horne had told me that "the only difference between Mike Tyson and Michael Jordan is Mr. and Mrs.

Jordan." But Atlas thought that was too simple, too easy on Tyson. When I asked him if he had overreacted when he held the gun to Tyson's head, he said, "This was a kid who did not hesitate to tear out the soul of another human being. He completely violated other people. And then he just moved on.

"Mike is very selfish. He was bred to be selfish. I remember sitting in the kitchen once at Cus's place and there were two plates of spaghetti, one for Mike and one for some other kid, another fighter, who hadn't sat down yet. Tyson went to take the other kid's food, too, and Camille"—D'Amato's companion—"said, 'Mike, no, don't take it.' But Cus said, 'No, go ahead, take it. You're gonna be the next champion of the world. Eat it.' Tyson was just fifteen or sixteen, and it was the wrong lesson. Listen, there are plenty of kids from Brownsville with that background and some of them are great people, people who find something in themselves to trigger a sense of accountability, the sense that someone else in the universe matters."

Atlas said Tyson was a fighter who depended solely on fast hands and the image of extreme violence. Nearly all his opponents were beaten before they ever got in the ring. Tyson never fought a truly great heavyweight (as Tunney fought Dempsey, as Ali fought Joe Frazier), and on the two occasions when an opponent stood up to him he lost: first to Buster Douglas in Tokyo in 1990, and then to Holyfield last November.

"You can lie to yourself in the ring in a hundred different ways," Atlas said. "You can quit by degrees. You can stop punching, with the idea, crazy as it sounds, that the other guy will stop if you do. Then you can make excuses to yourself, and the people around you will echo the excuses, and everything will seem to be all right. You can even foul and then claim you would have won, given the chance. Remember, this is a kid who used to hide between the walls of condemned buildings to make sure he wouldn't get beaten up. When you live like that, you learn to lie, to coax people that you are the toughest—you learn to scare people, to manipulate them. And when you can't do it you're lost.

"When I see Tyson, I see a guy who's scared, a guy who can't do it on the up and up. In his world, he was never allowed to be scared, or even honest, and so he is neither of those things. He is lost. When Tyson is alone with himself, I don't know if he believes there is one single person around him who is there because of his merits as a person. I don't even know that the women would be around without his ability to raise money. He'd have to show something independent of the ring and of his ability to send people on two-hundred-thousand-dollar shopping sprees."

On the day of the fight, I wandered the Strip. Earlier in the week, the casinos in hotels like the MGM Grand, New York New York, and Excalibur—the new family-friendly places—had been jammed with middle-class parents pushing strollers past the blackjack tables at midnight. Las Vegas is a better deal than Disney World. In Las Vegas, you can get a cheap hotel room, visit the Sphinx (at the Luxor), have your picture taken with a stuffed movie character, induce nausea on the rides, and be in the pool by lunchtime. But at the end of the week (when my room rate shot up from seventy-nine dollars per night to three hundred and ninety-nine) all the strollers were gone. The planes out at McCarron International Airport disgorged high rollers from New York, Tokyo, Taipei, and Beijing, athletes and gang-bangers, movie stars in Armani and hoochie girls in Moschino. The mind reeled—and the neck swiveled—at the effect of health clubs and silicone on the American form at century's end. All that hard work and earnest surgery. From the looks of the women at the luggage belts, there could not have been a single hooker left in the greater Los Angeles area. They had all flown in for the fight.

At the instigation of my friend Michael Wilbon, a sports columnist for *The Washington Post*, I spent the afternoon roaming the most expensive stores in town. Fight day, Wilbon instructed me, is a big shopping day, and many of the key stores—Neiman Marcus, Versace, Escada, Gucci, Armani—signed up extra seamstresses and tailors to get things ready for the evening. You don't buy a three-thousand-dollar suit and then not wear it to the main event. Even if you didn't have tickets—and that meant the vast majority who had "come in for the fight"—you showed up in the casinos looking dowdy at your peril.

At Neiman Marcus, I watched Louis Farrakhan take the Italian boutique by storm. While half a dozen of his bodyguards assumed positions near the ties and the shirt racks, the minister tried on a fine pair of mustard-colored slacks. Zegna is evidently one of his favorite designers. I watched him try on slacks for the better part of half an hour. When I asked one of his guards whether it might be possible to interview him, the guard took off his sunglasses and blinked. I took this to mean no.

The Forum Shops at Caesars Palace proved to be a nice place to hang out, too. The ceilings are painted like a cerulean sky with perfect Biblical clouds, and there is a fountain outside the Versace store that is better than the Trevi Fountain in Rome in that the Las Vegas Rome is air-conditioned.

Versace seemed to be the appointed headquarters of Tyson fans, and even of Tyson himself. Before the first Holyfield fight, the managers shut down the store for Tyson. "He bought real good," a manager told me, but he declined to be more specific. The mythical figure among the boxing writers was that Tyson dropped a hundred and fifty thousand there last time. While I was fingering a blouse worth more than a decent used car, a guy with some major forearms and a purposeful stare came in: Tyson's bodyguard. Even if one did not know him by his face, there were hints: a "Team Tyson" tattoo on his arm and a "Team Tyson Rules" bomber jacket. The manager spotted him and raced over to serve. He actually rubbed his palms. Within seconds, the bodyguard was handed a suit bag. "Mike says thanks," the bodyguard said. He used his phone to order "immediate pickup" and walked out.

The fight crowd was not always thus. In the films of the big fights of the fifties and sixties, you can see that the ringside seats were taken up mainly by boxy white men in boxy blue suits—mobsters, like Blinky Palermo and Frank Carbo, or, on a slightly higher plane, Rat Pack members. When Ali returned from exile in 1971 to fight Jerry Quarry in Atlanta, the fight crowd changed: suddenly, there were blacks at ringside. They held the same reputable and disreputable jobs as their white predecessors, but the plumage was different. The style of the hustler had shifted from Carbo's dour wool (he was known as Mr. Gray) to the iridescent suits of his black inheritors. It was as if a row of sparrows had flown the wire, to be replaced by a flock of cockatoos.

There were still plenty of white big shots around, plenty of pompadours and big-guy rings. One night at dinner at an Italian place, Trevesi, at the MGM Grand, a woman tossed her glass of wine at her big-guy boyfriend. Then she rose from her chair and, after a second of real consideration, took her glass and smashed it over the boyfriend's head. At which point there was blood on the boyfriend's skull and slivers of glass in the capellini of the woman at the next table. That would turn out to be the cleanest blow of the week.

It is customary at a big fight to surround the ring with press people, anonymous high rollers, and, most of all, "luminaries from the world of sports, politics, and the entertainment industry." In the press section, we were handed an alphabetized list of celebrities in attendance: Paul Anka, Patricia Arquette, Stephen Baldwin, Matthew Broderick, Albert Brooks, James Caan, John Cusack, Rodney Dangerfield, Lolita Davidovich, Ellen DeGeneres, Larry Flynt, Michael J. Fox, Cuba Gooding, Jr., etc. This, of course, was "subject to change," the King people warned us.

It is also customary at big fights to come late, to ignore the undercard. But I had seen about as many vermilion leather vests, chartreuse pants, and siliconed bodies as I wanted to see, and headed into the MGM Grand's arena. King had told everyone that the fight was "the greatest boxing event of all time." It was a wonder, then, why he put together one of the grimmest undercards of all time. The highlight was surely the one women's bout, which left the canvas spotted with bloody pools. The woman in the pink shorts, Christy Martin, won the match. She had acquired all the best habits of boxing. She taunted her opponent, Andrea DeShong, at the pre-fight press conference, by saying she was glad DeShong had finally worn a dress. "It's the first time I've seen you look respectable, like a woman," Martin said, thus proving her . . . manhood.

By eight-thirty, the seats were filled and the place buzzed, loud and nervous, a sound peculiar to the mass anticipation of violence, a more manic buzz than at a basketball playoff game or a political convention. Don King opened the proceedings by having the ring announcer tell us that the fight was dedicated to the memory of Dr. Betty Shabazz and to "the many, many innocent victims of crime and violence." We all stood, and the timekeeper sounded the bell ten times, boxing's equivalent of a twenty-one-gun salute.

Tyson, the challenger, came into the arena to the sound of gangsta rap. In the bowels of the arena, he had complained that he could hear Holyfield's music—electric Jesus music—and couldn't Holyfield turn it down? Tyson, as always, wore his warrior look: black trunks, black shoes, no socks. He came surrounded by Giachetti and Horne and Holloway and Crocodile and a dozen other men, all of them strung out on self-importance. They tried very hard to look dangerous.

Then Holyfield, with a far smaller entourage, came down the aisle toward the ring. He wore purple-and-white trunks with the logo "Phil. 4:13" ("I can do all things through Christ which strengtheneth me"). While Tyson assumed his death mask, his intimidator's face, Holyfield was smiling. He mouthed the words to a gospel song that only he could hear. Tyson paced, and Holyfield stood in his corner, satisfied to jiggle the muscles in his arms and legs. One of his seconds massaged the ropes of muscle in his neck.

In the casino, Tyson was the favorite. You had to bet a hundred and eighty dollars on him to win a hundred. Those odds were based almost entirely on Tyson's Kid Dynamite reputation. Holyfield, however, was the pick on press row by a wide margin. And yet we knew why we were here. It was not to listen to Holyfield sing "Nearer My God to Thee."

Mills Lane, a bald and mumbly judge from Reno, was the referee. At the center of the ring, Lane reminded both fighters of their obligations to the law, to boxing, and to the Nevada State Athletic Commission, and both men nodded assent. They would, of course, not dream of trespass. So said their quick nods, the touch of the gloves.

At the opening bell, Tyson came out bobbing and weaving, but with a certain self-conscious air. He had lost the first fight not least because he had forgotten his old defensive moves. For months, Giachetti, his trainer, had been pleading with him to move his head, to jab, to forget about the one-punch knockout. But within half a minute Tyson was back to where he'd been before, throwing one huge hook at a time. Holyfield ducked the hooks easily and then held on, muscling Tyson around the ring. Last time, we had been amazed that Holyfield was stronger than Tyson, that he could push Tyson back on his heels, that he could grab Tyson's left arm in the clinches and save himself untold trauma to the kidneys and the temple. And now it was happening again. All the training, all the instructions were coming to nothing. Tyson could not intimidate Holyfield—he could not, as he had done to so many others before, terrify his man into dropping his guard, into committing a kind of boxing suicide. Holyfield had every intention of winning again, and he took the first round by controlling the pace and scoring big with two left hooks and then a right hand to Tyson's jaw.

Between rounds, as Tyson drank some water and spat in the bucket, Giachetti told him to take his time.

"Jab for the throat!" he said.

Tyson nodded, but who could tell what he was hearing—what inner voice?

In the second round, the pattern was much the same. Holyfield scored left hooks to the meat of Tyson's flank and shoved him around and back toward the ropes. Tyson jabbed occasionally, but more often he threw big, dramatic punches, and Holyfield smothered them, ducked them. Then came the crucial moment of the round— the moment that set off in Tyson some torrent of rage that would, in the end, botch the fight and possibly ruin his career. As the two men wrestled, Holyfield unintentionally rammed his skull into the sharp brow above Tyson's right eye. Within seconds, there were rivulets of blood running down the side of Tyson's face, and in the clinch he looked up at Lane and said, "He butted me." The physical side was bad enough: the gash was sure to bother Tyson throughout the fight. The blood would run in his eyes, and Holyfield, sensing his advantage, would work over the cut—punch at it, grind his head into it in the clinch—and try to win on a technical knockout. What was worse for Tyson was the tremendous fear the butt stirred up in him, the way the blunt pain on his brow summoned up the last fight, his humiliation. Last time, the two men had butted heads inside, two berserk rams, and Tyson had come away the injured one, dazed and bleeding. It was as if his nightmare had come true. It was all happening again. He was in the ring, bleeding, and facing an opponent who would not back down.

Lane warned both men against excessive "roughhousing" (imagine!), but he didn't deduct any penalty points. Now, in the clinch, Tyson grew more desperate. He shoved a forearm into Holyfield's throat. But his punches, his big punches, were still missing, and they were coming in single volleys rather than in combination. Again, Holyfield won the round because of his superior strength, his ability to waltz Tyson around the ring, and the efficiency of his blows. What he threw, for the most part, landed. All three judges scored the first two rounds for Holyfield, ten to nine.

After the bell, a plastic surgeon worked on Tyson's cut.

As the doctor held a compress to Tyson's brow, the fighter jerked back.

"Aaahhh!" Tyson moaned.

"I'm sorry," the doctor said.

Tyson was breathing hard now—harder than he should have been after six minutes in the ring and months of roadwork. He said nothing. He gave no hint to anyone that something was wrong—that something had "snapped," as he put it days later. Tyson got off his stool and waited for the bell. As the two fighters stood facing each other, Holyfield suddenly pointed to his mouth, reminding Tyson that his corner had not put in his mouthpiece. Tyson walked back to Giachetti and opened his jaws; Giachetti put the mouthpiece in.

At the bell for the third round, Tyson stalked forward, and it was clear that he was enraged, desperate to end the fight before his eye failed him. He was relatively controlled at first, throwing his first sharp hooks of the fight. Holyfield was standing up to the blows and was still moving forward, crowding Tyson, but he was suddenly no longer in command. For more than two minutes of fighting, Tyson showed that he was capable of reviving his old style. Now his punches came in combinations. He kept his head moving, side to side, up and down, making it impossible for Holyfield to flick the jab at his gash. In the clinches, however, Holyfield was still in control. He seemed to be telling Tyson that, while he could win the round, he could not win the fight, and Tyson seemed to see the sense in that. And with about forty seconds left in the round, as Holyfield was steering him around the center of the ring, Tyson suddenly spat out his mouthpiece and started gnawing on Holyfield's right ear. For a second, Holyfield seemed not to feel this lunatic attack, but then the sting hit him. He backed away, jumping up and down, pointing to his ear and the blood that now bathed it. At the same time, Tyson turned his head at an angle and spat out a half-inch chunk of ear. Lane called a time-out. Holyfield headed for his corner. Tyson chased him down and shoved him. Holyfield seemed almost to ham it up, to bounce crazily on the ropes, as if to highlight the madness of it all.

Don Turner, Holyfield's trainer, told his man to keep cool, to think about Jesus, just stay calm.

Lane said to a Nevada State Athletic Commission official at ringside that he was ready to disqualify Tyson—and he certainly would have been within his rights to do so—but first he invited the ring doctor, Flip Homansky, onto the canvas to have a look at Holyfield's ear. Homansky gravely inspected the ear and, presumably in the interests of Nevada and boxing's good name, pronounced Holyfield able to continue. Lane went to both corners and explained to the assembled handlers what had happened. He told Giachetti that Tyson "bit him on the ear."

"No, I didn't," Tyson said.

"Bullshit," Lane replied. He had already examined the ear, the teeth marks. "I thought my ear had fallen off!" Holyfield said later. "Blood was all over!" Lane deducted two points from Tyson—one for the bite, one for the shove—and, or so he claimed in a post-fight interview, warned Tyson that if he did it again the fight was over.

The time-out had lasted more than two minutes, long enough for the crowd to see replays of the incident on the big screens around the arena and start booing, enough time for Tyson to decide whether he had "snapped" or would do it again, and more than enough time for the jokes to begin sweeping through the press section: "Tyson's a chomp," "He's Hannibal Lecter," "a lobe blow," "pay per chew," "If you can't beat 'em, eat 'em." There would be a hundred of them.

Finally, Lane cleared the ring and resumed what little was left of the third round. The crowd, which had been fickle, swerving between chants first for Holyfield, then for Tyson, was now greatly affronted. They booed wildly. We were, of course, all prepared to see one fighter deliver a subconcussive blow to the other's brain, but a bite on the ear was beyond imagining. We were offended, disgusted, perhaps even a little thrilled. Boxing is a blood sport. Now there was blood.

Holyfield was intent on following his corner's plea to keep his cool. He marched in and connected with a stiff hook to Tyson's face. His message was delivered thus: you can do what you want, you can foul, you can threaten, you can even quit, but you will not intimidate me.

The fighters clinched again. There were about twenty seconds left in the round. And, incredibly, Tyson once more nuzzled his way into

Holyfield's sweaty neck, almost tenderly, purposefully, as if he were snuffling for truffles. He found the left ear and bit. Once more, Holyfield did his jumping dance of rage and pain. The bell sounded.

Tyson's handlers now wore guilty looks; their eyes shifted. They knew what was coming.

Holyfield was not quite so sure. "Put my mouthpiece in," he told his cornermen. "I'm gonna knock him out."

But Lane could not let this go on: "One bite is bad enough. Two bites is the end of the search."

"I had to do some thinking," Lane said, reasonably, later on. "I thought about it and thought about it, and decided it was the right thing to do. Let the chips fall where they may." Tyson was disqualified. Holyfield was declared winner and "still heavyweight champion of the world." Subsequently, Tyson said that he had been forced to retaliate for the butt in the second round. After all, he said righteously, "This is my career. . . . I've got children to raise."

In the mayhem that followed Lane's announcement—Tyson still going berserk in the ring, pushing at the police, and then fans raining down ice cubes and curses as he headed for the locker room—in all that, one bit of business was almost forgotten. A hotel employee named Mitch Libonati found the chunk of ear that belonged to Evander Holyfield. He found it on the ring mat, wrapped it in a rubber glove, and delivered it to the champion's locker room.

"At first, they looked at me like I was pulling a prank, but I told them I had a piece of Evander's ear, and I thought he would want it," Libonati said. "It wasn't really bloody, actually. It was like a piece of sausage."

After leaving the arena and press tent, I walked through the MGM Grand casino toward the elevators. I wanted to drop off some things in my room before heading back out to the Strip. How could you miss the victory parties? But just as I was passing some slot machines I saw a stampede of twenty or thirty people running straight at me. There were screams: "Get down!" and "There's shooting!" and "They got guns!" I had already seen some fistfights between Tyson's fans and Holyfield's fans. It was not beyond reckoning that some of the visitors could be armed. I dived behind a bank of slot machines, feeling at once terrified and ridiculous.

"Keep down!"

"Ya hear the shots!"

People were face down on the carpet, ducking under blackjack tables, roulette tables. And then it was quiet. No shots—not that we could hear, anyway. It seemed safe to walk to the elevators.

But then, as the doors opened, more people started dashing around, ducking behind slot machines and into the elevators. I went up to the fourteenth floor and then went back down in a service elevator. I had to get to the bank of elevators that would get me to the twenty-fifth floor. As I was getting out of the service elevator, Jesse Jackson and a team of police were getting in.

"It's sad. The whole thing is sad," Jackson said. "That's the one word I can think of to describe it. It's a tragedy that no one can explain. As far as Tyson is concerned, I guess the butting triggered something in him. I focus on him and what's going on in his head. And now this. They're out there shooting with Uzis, these bad boys."

It was never entirely clear whether there had been any shooting. I doubt it. But the Nevada Highway Patrol did shut down the Strip from Tropicana Avenue to Koval Lane. No one wanted a repeat of the action after the Tyson–Seldon fight last September, when the rap star Tupac Shakur was shot to death in a car.

The rumors of Uzi fire did little to help the gambling receipts at the MGM Grand, but elsewhere on the Strip the high rollers were happy. We had all been witness to a spectacle—to the unraveling of Mike Tyson. In the days to come, he would apologize. He would reach out "to the medical professionals for help." But who now cared about him? In the ring, at his moment of greatest pressure, he had lost everything: he had proved himself to be what in gentler times would have been called a bum. Biting is certainly not unheard-of in boxing—Holyfield himself once bit Jakey Winters in an amateur bout when he was eighteen—yet Tyson had done it not once but twice, in a championship fight seen by "three billion people," or however many Don King had managed to attract. The abysmal and lonely end that he had seemed to predict for himself had come so soon.

"It's over," he said in the locker room. "I know it's over. My career is over."

No one had envisioned this end more clearly than Tyson himself.

On the day before the fight, he had gone out to a cemetery near the airport and laid a bouquet of flowers on the grave of Sonny Liston. The music ahead for Tyson would be not rap but something more mournful. "Someday they're gonna write a blues song just for fighters," his role model, Liston, once said. "It'll be for slow guitar, soft trumpet, and a bell."

Katherine Dunn

Katherine Dunn (b. 1945) caught the literary world by surprise in 1989 with a left hook of a novel called *Geek Love*. It was the tale of carnival freaks trapped on society's outermost edge, with a hump-backed albino dwarf for a narrator, and Dunn's deft mixture of revulsion and compassion proved impossible to ignore. Readers of her boxing coverage for Portland's *Willamette Week*—and for magazines ranging from *Vogue* to *Playboy*—were well acquainted with her ability to apply artistry to subjects that could be as compelling as they were grotesque. In this 1998 essay, Dunn painted a compassionate portrait of Lucia Rijker, deemed the world's best female prizefighter (though she never fought her nemesis, Christy Martin). Rijker went on to achieve a kind of ignominy by playing the villain in the Oscar-winning 2005 boxing movie *Million Dollar Baby*. It was based on the short stories of F.X. Toole (real name Jerry Boyd), a been-around-the-block guy who didn't begin working as a cut man until he was in his late forties and didn't become a published author until he was sixty-nine. In one of those sad twists that would have been perfect for a story he or Dunn wrote, Toole died before the movie came out.

The Knockout: Lucia Rijker

In the summer of 1998 Women's Sports & Fitness *magazine asked me to identify and write about the "best" professional woman boxer in the country. "Best" is a word that starts many an argument, but in this case I decided it was probably Lucia Rijker. I spent time chasing around Los Angeles, and then Foxwoods Casino in Connecticut, after the most dangerous woman on the planet. She was as courteous as a queen.*

THE huge blue Suburban swoops out of the white haze of the L.A. heat and pulls to the curb. The door opens and the world's most dangerous woman flashes a devilish grin and invites you in.

Lucia Rijker is running late for an appointment with her hair stylist and she's in a hurry. To make room she shoves aside a translation

461

of "The Art of War" by the ancient Chinese military strategist Sun Tzu. The battered paperback is always with her lately, in the car, in her gym bag. "It's complicated," she says. "I have to read it carefully." When she tells you to buckle up you obey.

Driving, she explains why she admires her hair stylist, what a serious person he is, and a dedicated artist who works with an impressive list of movie stars. She met him at a photo shoot when she first moved to Los Angeles from her native Amsterdam. "If I were rich," she says, "I'd fly him in to do my hair for every fight." The light Dutch accent shifts her snappy American toward the exotic.

She doesn't look at you as she talks. Her whole body is absorbed in muscling the borrowed van around. She likes the van's power and size, and the view from up high. Her eyes assess all 360 degrees of traffic. Swift reflexes respond smoothly to every opening or threat. By the time she parks and cuts the engine you've decided that only world-class athletes should be allowed to drive.

When you mention reflexes she nods. "You know what I notice? How guys have a tendency to reach to touch your face or your head, like to cuddle? Right away my head jerks away, ducks, whup, whup. And they say what's up with you? And I say I can't help it, it's a reflex. When something comes toward my face, I move away. There was this police officer in Holland who got hit and paralyzed by a guy and she didn't see it coming because she was looking at her notebook. I would feel it coming and would move without looking. That's why I want to train the police. Because they have a gun they think they can deal with anything. I think they should train in kickboxing and boxing so they will know what another human being is capable of physically. And so they know what they themselves are capable of."

She slips into the salon the back way, through a dim tropical lanai where slim young men relax, smoking, talking quietly in the shadows. Phillip, her stylist, hugs her, scolds her for being late.

They gossip cheerfully as the scissors fly. She could be any chic female in a hair salon except that he is asking her advice about his workout, his diet. When he steps away for a moment, she leans back in the chair, stretches her arms and briefly flexes the monumental shoulders under her snug T-shirt, the biceps carved out of velvet oak. The frail creatures around her stop for an instant, and stare.

Movie boxers are never as gorgeous as the real thing. Actors aren't graceful enough. Or fast enough. The fluid density of muscle isn't there, and the eyes are never right. Mere Hollywood magic can't compete with the luminous intensity honed by a life of fear for breakfast, sweat for lunch, and pitched battle before supper.

After twenty-four years of combat sports, thirty-year-old Lucia Rijker looks like she sees through brick walls. Picture her zapping the forces of evil and dancing on the bar in triumph till the cops arrive to beg for her autograph.

The T-shirts sold at the Wildcard Boxing Gym where Rijker trains in Los Angeles show her in a superhero pose. The shirt calls her "Lightning Lucia." Monikers have always been part of boxing and the hypesters can't resist heaping labels on Rijker (rhymes with "hiker" and "biker"), the Women's World Champion boxer in the 139-pound division. They call her the most dangerous woman on the planet. The Women's International Boxing Federation dubbed her "Pound for Pound the Best Female Boxer in the World." She doesn't like the tag "Lady Tyson." She doesn't mind "Lady Ali," even considers it appropriate because she, like Muhammad Ali, sees her mission as larger than the boxing ring.

Rijker is sharply conscious of her role in the new wave of serious women in a sport that has traditionally marginalized females as titillating novelty acts. The bets are still being laid on whether female fighters are a passing fad in this controversial sport, but so far Rijker's skills stand up to the scrutiny of the critics, and the probing fists of her opponents.

Born and reared in the Netherlands, Rijker says she learned to fight at her mother's knee. "My mother is a fighter," says Rijker. "She was one of the first white women to marry a black man in Holland and she had to fight for her marriage and for her children. I respect that."

Still, by Rijker's lights, she has not suffered from discrimination. She has a sophisticated view of her own novelty. "Being a woman, being bi-racial, and being an athlete competing in a 'man's' sport have all been advantages for me."

Her mother was a waitress in Amsterdam, her father a mechanic. The youngest of the family's four children, Lucia has two older sisters but is closest to her brother. She started judo at the age of six, karate at nine. At thirteen, she took up fencing and became the Netherlands' junior champion.

She was fourteen when Holland was swept by a mania for Bruce Lee. "My brother came home with stories of Bruce Lee, and started practicing kickboxing. He dragged me to the gym. After my first lesson I thought Wow! This is tough! But I liked it. So I went back."

Competing while she finished high school, she wove her life around the sport. She now calls her kickboxing career "semi-pro" because the pay was never enough to live on. She held four women's World Championships. She smashed bones, noses, and careers, sending at least one former champ into retirement. She had a record of 36 victories and no defeats. Her only loss was in an exhibition match with a bigger male opponent. She stretched her income by managing the gym where she trained, working on tournament promotions, and teaching kickboxing.

Her coach, a powerful figure in European martial arts circles, taught her to teach by sudden immersion. Announcing that he had to leave town, he'd tell her she had to teach his class the next day. The first time it happened she spent a tormented night figuring out how to conduct the class. She came to love teaching.

After twelve years of kickboxing she was fed up. There were injuries, and extended periods of recuperation. She felt trapped by her contract with the coach who was also her manager. In 1993 she took her first vacation, coming to Los Angeles to visit friends. After years of rigid scheduling around training times, the freedom was intoxicating.

"I made a call and said I'm not coming back," she says. Her friends and family were shocked, "but I just cut it all off and started all over."

She took up teaching martial arts classes in some of L.A.'s tonier private schools and health clubs. "I had to learn to talk with women, to teach women. I had spent my life in gyms working with men and this was a new thing for me. Very interesting."

Rijker speaks what she calls "three and a half languages: Dutch, German, English, and enough French to survive." She studied English in school in the Netherlands, but she learned her California style "on the street. I had to teach to make a living so I have to be able to communicate." She took some time to consider who she was and what she wanted to do.

In the United States the Eastern martial arts have been open to women since the 1950s. The USA fields women's judo and Tae Kwon Do teams in the Olympics. But the western martial art—boxing—was different.

Boys who want to box learn the sport the same way they learn to play baseball—in amateur programs that allow them to compete from the age of eight on. Most professional boxers have had years of amateur training and dozens or even hundreds of amateur bouts. Right-to-work laws have allowed women to box professionally for decades in the United States, but American women were flatly forbidden to participate in amateur boxing. It was the equivalent of trying out for the Olympic swim team if you've never been allowed in the pool, or trying out for the Yankees when you've never been permitted to throw a ball.

Then, in 1993, a bright Seattle teenager named Dallas Malloy sued the national amateur association, U.S. Amateur Boxing, Inc., in Federal Court for gender discrimination and won. When the new ruling went into effect in October of 1993, women and girls began trickling into boxing gyms all over the nation. In 1995, Lucia Rijker became one of them.

"A lot of people had talked to me about going into boxing," she explains. "Finally one guy said 'Give me two weeks, let me train you for two weeks. See how you like it.' I realize that my whole identity, all my life has been as a warrior, a fighter. In kickboxing I had done everything I could do. This was a new sport. It was a challenge to learn. I decided to give it a try."

The female amateurs attracted media attention, which prompted promoters of small professional shows in clubs and casinos to scour the bushes for women boxers. Few of the new amateurs were ready to try the pro ranks. But women had already been fighting professionally for years in obscurity.

The earliest documented boxing matches between American women took place in the 1880s. Some legitimate competition has persisted in fits and starts ever since. But most women boxers were circus or variety performers playing rigged exhibitions in saloons and theaters.

In the 1950s the 110-pound Barbara Buttrick started out in the boxing booths at fairs in her native England where she fought any woman, and a few men, who stepped up with the ticket price. Buttrick came to the United States, where some professional matches were taking place, and fought for ten years, racking up a record of 24 wins, one loss and one draw. She retired in 1959 as the most famous female boxer of her day.

The 1970s produced a brief flurry of female ring activity, which subsided for lack of numbers. With only a hundred or so women competing nationwide, matches were rare and difficult to make. Still, the women never went away completely.

While they were banned from entering the sport as amateurs, women discovered alternate routes to the ring. Some started out in the "tough woman" competitions that grew as part of "tough man" tournaments. Derived from the early "boxing booths" at fairs and carnivals, these "tough man" shows featured untrained citizens, from college students to truck drivers, who plunked down their twenty-five dollar entry fee for a chance to step into the ring with another untrained character and brawl and sprawl their way through a three round bout. The winners advanced, fighting each other, with the last one standing collecting a purse that might be a hundred or a thousand dollars or more. The winners were often inspired to hit the gym and practice up for the next "Tough" contest.

Some women as well as men have used this route into the professional game. The other back door to the pros was through training in the Asian martial arts. Kickboxers switch sports or compete in both because boxing pays more.

The new demand for women in the 1990s means these novice pros are better paid than men starting off in the sport. While a male boxer fights his first few bouts for a standard hundred dollars per round, the women sometimes get twice as much.

The fight crowds loved them. At first there was the raw shock of seeing women fighting. Then there was the energy they brought to it. Few had any defensive skills. All offense and fury, they were the most entertaining bouts on many a small card. When USA Cable TV offered its first women's bout on a televised show, an audience poll showed 85 percent of viewers wanted to see more women's bouts.

In 1993, former boxer Barbara Buttrick, now widowed and the mother of grown children, founded the Women's International Boxing Federation, an organization which lists and ranks professional women boxers and sanctions championship titles in all weight classes, from flyweight to heavyweight.

In April of 1997, a promotional company called Event Entertainment created a rival sanctioning organization, the International Female Boxing Association, to add the luster of "championship bouts" to its all-woman boxing shows. Pay-per-view shows with titles like "Lips of Rouge, Fists of Fury" and "Leather and Lace" followed.

The much-touted "male bastion" has been breached. Boxing trainers and managers all over the country are on the lookout for female talent. In such an eager atmosphere, Lucia Rijker, the world champion kickboxer, had major advantages. Her first boxing trainer was the famed Joe Goosen, head of the Ten Goose Boxing Club in L.A. She sparred with highly skilled men such as Gabe and Rafael Ruelas.

The rigorous regimen appealed to her. "I love the lifestyle, the discipline, the training, the atmosphere of the gym and the challenge of learning a new sport." She won all five of her amateur boxing matches by knockout.

Then, on March 16, 1996, what had been an underground movement exploded in front of a massive, worldwide television audience. The event was the Don King–produced Mike Tyson vs. Frank Bruno heavyweight championship bout. But the main event was eclipsed when the show opened with the gutsy slugger, Christy Martin, "The Coal Miner's Daughter" from West Virginia, punching her way into the public eye with a bloody win over "Dangerous" Deirdre Gogarty of Ireland. The Martin–Gogarty bout out-clashed and out-classed the men's bouts.

Martin, the former Tough Woman, landed on the cover of *Sports Illustrated* and high on the national talk-show and headline circuit. In that one match, Martin and Gogarty ripped down the cutesy veil that had relegated women boxers to the foxy-boxing fringes of the sport. Overnight the sturdy, powerful, and ferociously aggressive Martin became the highest paid and most famous female boxer the world has ever known.

Just five days later, on March 21, 1996, Lucia Rijker made her debut as a professional boxer by knocking out Melinda Robinson in the first round. Robinson, who had previously lost to Martin, claimed that Rijker's lightest punches were heavier than Martin's hardest.

Boxers are matched by weight classes. Christy Martin, who started out in Tough Gal tournaments, and Lucia Rijker, the martial artist, fall into the same general weight range—135 to 140 pounds. The experts predict a collision.

The back of that "Lightning Lucia" T-shirt reads, "You Can't Hide Forever." It's a message to Christy Martin. In this one-on-one dueling sport quality cannot be measured by the clock or by the number of points scored or yards gained. A fighter's quality is defined by the quality of her opponents. Martin is the biggest target for the ambitious young guns. The ring logic is that the woman who defeats her will have a chance to inherit the limelight and the substantial paydays that only Martin has earned so far. The challengers are lining up in hopes of getting a crack at her. They include big banger Kathy Collins of New York, who is fresh from the amateur ranks, and Michigan's fast, smart Tracy Byrd, who grew up in boxing gyms with her gifted heavyweight brother, Chris Byrd.

Rijker is first in line because of her experience, her genuine skills and media appeal, and because the hefty weight of promoter Bob Arum is behind her. She is being schooled and honed for the ultimate purpose of meeting Martin. As one Rijker fan puts it, "Lucia is a bullet with Christy Martin's name etched in the steel."

Of course, 30 other women have already failed to put the kibosh on Martin. Putting Rijker into the ring with her is no guarantee at all of who comes out the other side. The attraction for the fans is that the pairing would almost certainly be a great fight. But in the flaming business of boxing, simply getting the two together is a major battle.

The ritual pissing match is in full swing. Martin's acid remarks about other female boxers have earned her a caustic tag in some circles as "the Tonya Harding of women's boxing." The plump Martin announced early on that she wouldn't fight the lean, muscular Rijker unless Rijker passes medical tests to prove she's a woman. According to Martin, Rijker could be a male transsexual or be pumped up on steroids, so it wouldn't be a fair fight.

The Rijker camp says Lucia will happily take any tests necessary to prove her unalloyed femininity. They say Martin is ducking a fight with Lucia because she knows Rijker would beat her. Claiming that Deirdre Gogarty was seventeen pounds lighter than Martin, these critics claim most of her other recent opponents have been under-skilled and over-matched. They sneer that Martin's honorary title of World Boxing Council champion is a sham because the WBC, a major sanctioning body for male boxers, has no female rankings, and Martin did not win the gaudy belt in a title bout. It was simply presented to her for the benefit of her powerful promoter, Don King.

Rijker won the WIBF European championship by stopping Irma Verhoef in the Netherlands in the fourth round in February of 1997. She won the WIBF World Championship on November 20, 1997, with a devastating knockout of German Jeannette Witte in the Los Angeles Olympic Forum in front of a global pay-per-view television audience.

The Martin fans claim that Rijker doesn't deserve a shot at Martin because Rijker has only had eight professional bouts and five amateur bouts as a boxer, while Martin's record is 34 wins, one loss. The Rijker fans reply that her 35 kickboxing victories are more legitimate than the many tough woman bouts included in Martin's record.

Pissing and hissing aside, the real question is whether Martin's promoter Don King will risk putting his leading lady into the ring against Rijker, who is promoted by his archrival Bob Arum. These decisions aren't sentimental and have nothing to do with the integrity of the sport. The issue is money. If the fight will sell enough tickets, the two businessmen will make it happen.

The dreamers say it could be the first female main event on a major pay-per-view card. The scowlers say it will never happen, that Martin will retire rather than face Rijker. The media momentum is growing.

Fox Sports boxing expert Rich Marotta named Rijker–Martin as one of the ten most interesting matches of 1998. *The Ring* magazine, known as "The Bible of Boxing," flagged its story on Rijker as "The Woman Who's Gonna Kick Christy's Butt!" The HBO broadcasters who first applauded Christy Martin are now asking when she will take Rijker on.

Rijker, a dreamer, has a gut feeling that she will meet Martin in the ring. "I will fight her. I know it. Either she will retire or I will fight her."

The Wildcard Boxing Gym is on the rough edge of Hollywood, upstairs in a shabby strip mall that features a laundromat, a Thai language newspaper office, and a Hispanic alcohol rehab center. A steep staircase leads up to the open door. The gym is clean, bright, and discreetly ornamented with fight posters. The door and a wall of windows yawn open to let the hot, dry Santa Ana winds blow through.

In one corner a tough handful of Russian immigrants are practicing footwork under the tutelage of a former Russian Olympic star. The speed bags across the room are doing drum rolls under the flying hands of a Mexican featherweight and a black middleweight television producer working back to back.

The Wild Card's owner and chief trainer, 34-year-old Freddie Roach, is a lean redhead with scholarly glasses, a soft voice and a notable head-knocking career as a boxer behind him. Over the past ten years he's trained serious contenders, and a few marginal champions. He also serves as a boxing consultant for movies and television. When actor Mickey Rourke wanted to become a boxer, Roach trained him. Other actors come into the gym to work. It's a funny world where the actors want to box because it makes them feel real, and the boxers want to act because the pay is so much better. Occasionally Roach helps a fighter get bit parts.

In the ring, a powerful bear of a man finishes trying to rip holes in the reluctant belly of his sparring partner and steps out, sweating happily. With the helmet and gloves removed, the bear is Sam Simon, producer of the TV show *The Simpsons* among others. Simon is the one who introduced Lucia Rijker to Roach in 1996.

"I was thinking about doing a boxing bit on the show," Simon remembers. "She was teaching at Bodies In Motion (a health club) and I heard somebody mention her at a party." He called her. They met and he watched her videotapes.

"It's obvious that she's a star," Simon shrugs. "She's a tremendous fighter and she's got movie star looks. She can do anything." Simon asked Roach to meet her. "Freddy didn't want to. He was strictly, 'No chicks!'"

Roach nods, and explains. "People had come to me about women before and they'd always say, 'She can fight.' But they could fight 'for a girl.' One round on the mitts with Lucia convinced me she could fight for anybody. A lot of guys her weight she could knock out. Maybe most of them."

Rijker says she switched trainers despite her respect for Joe Goosen and the serious intensity of his gym. "Freddie taught me things I could use in our very first lesson. He explains the why of what I'm doing and I need that."

With just one pro win under her belt at the time, Rijker did not have a manager, so Roach introduced her to his friend Stan Hoffman. The cheerful "not so silent" partner of the famed Gleason's Gym in New York, Hoffman managed another of Roach's students, light heavyweight James Toney, and a Dutch fighter named Rogelio Tuur. Hoffman's experience in Holland helped him hit it off with Rijker and they agreed to work together.

Roach also took Rijker to see promoters Don King and Bob Arum. King had already signed Christy Martin and was looking seriously at women's boxing, but Rijker didn't like the terms of the contract. Visiting Arum on the same day in Las Vegas, she encountered exactly the opposite attitude. Arum has frequently made it clear that he does not approve of women boxing.

"He was polite," Rijker recalls, laughing. "But he wasn't interested." She insisted that he look at a tape of her fighting. He didn't want to. She said she would not leave the office until he watched it. "So he put on the tape and all of a sudden he was shouting, 'She can punch! This girl can really punch!' and calling for the people in his office to come and see."

Arum agreed to promote Rijker, but he still tells reporters, "I am promoting Lucia Rijker. I am not promoting women's boxing."

So you're a fifty-year-old chainsmoker on a strict sugar and caffeine diet, but you've seen Rijker's javelin jab smack the chops of gritty Dora Webber under the lights at Foxwoods Casino and you have a nagging curiosity about what that fist looks like, coming at you. Freddie Roach is known for his courtesy as well as his ring wars, and he chats amiably while perched on a stool behind the gym's counter. You ask if you might possibly, maybe, spar, for just one round, with Rijker. His answer is fast and final.

"That would not be a good idea. Lucia is training for a fight and she's very aggressive. She does not mess around. She's very focused."

Focus is the word. She's already done her long morning run when she marches through the gym door at the stroke of noon, nods briskly to an acquaintance, and ducks into the women's dressing room. She emerges in sweats and ring shoes and pauses, carefully wrapping her hands in yards of protective white gauze bandage. She's always regal, and she's imposing when she wants to be, but this silence surrounds her with a solid wall.

There are other boxers beating the bags and jumping rope. A few loungers watch the action, socializing and joking as they lean against the office counter. But Rijker acts like she's in an empty room. She launches directly into her workout and for two solid hours does not stop moving. The other boxers stop their own training to watch her but she speaks to no one, seems to see no one except her trainer, Freddie Roach.

She stretches in front of the big wall mirror, and then climbs into the ring to warm up with round after round of furiously fast shadow boxing. Her hands punch the air in flashing combinations as she swivels, circles, and advances against an invisible opponent. Roach crouches, watching and brooding just outside the ring.

The many brutal fights Roach endured have left him with Parkinson's syndrome. He has a limp, a heel that won't touch down, and a kink in his neck that hoists one shoulder toward his ear. Except in the ring. The minute he steps through the ropes his body changes, legs steady, shoulders relaxed, as though the fighter in him overrides all that's gone wrong, making him whole again.

He climbs into the ring wearing big leather catching mitts and guides Rijker through a long, grueling lesson. He asks her for particular combinations of punches and her gloved fists batter his padded hands with a sound like gunfire. Roach was right. You wouldn't want to be on the receiving end of those punches.

It is six weeks from her next bout and soon she will add daily sparring sessions to her routine. For now she moves from the ring to the punching bags, pounding three different sizes of bag in different patterns and rhythms, and then to skipping rope followed by wrenching floor exercises. Only at the end, as she is finishing a balance exercise in agonizing slow motion, only then does someone speak to her. A small boy watching her poised on her toes on the edge of a platform, demands to know what she's doing.

She laughs delighted, her sober face transformed in impish merriment. She hops down to explain and soon has the boy trying it. She positions his feet, helps align his posture, and steps back to watch, encouraging him. "You can do it." He topples off balance howling, "It's hard!" She rumples his hair and gets him to try again.

An hour or so later, freshly showered in tight white jeans and spike heeled sandals, stoked on lamb chops and iced tea, Rijker glows in the vine-shaded terrace of a nearby Greek restaurant. The waiters hover worshipfully. She triggers male stares and double takes even on Sunset Boulevard where the starlets promenade. But she is busy talking about being held a virtual prisoner in Tokyo by a kickboxing promoter. She is a lively storyteller, mimicking different voices and accents, acting out the body language of shock or fear or disdain.

Describing Yakuza involvement in some areas of the Asian martial arts, she comments coolly that she admires the simple ethics of organized crime. "You screw up, off with your finger. You screw up again, your throat is slit. It's tough but you know the rules." She contrasts this clear cause and effect with the murky doings of the straight world, where right or wrong is often a matter of who has the most expensive lawyer.

Turning to practical matters, she interrogates her manager, Stan Hoffman, on the relative merits of leasing or buying a car to replace her own worn-out heap.

She grills anyone she runs into who strikes her as having experience or knowledge on a topic that interests her. She asks endless, probing questions. Later she will ask others the same questions and compare the answers.

She's working to be smart about the intricate processes of the boxing industry. "I have to learn this business, and it's tough! Sometimes I wonder what I've gotten myself into," she says.

She uses the same technique in figuring out her financial situation. She spent days questioning a financial advisor.

"So many boxers end up broke. I don't want that. A few weeks ago I saw a beautiful house by the sea with beige pink marble floors and brown-gold tinted mirrors. I wanted it. I always fought to be the best, to win, for fame. Now I will add money to my goals—to build something secure so I can have that house and not have to worry about rent. So I can teach and start camps for kids, run a gym, whatever."

While female novice boxers are paid more than men, the advantage does not continue as they gain experience. No women's bout has yet been featured as the main event on a televised card that includes males. Christy Martin has a contract with Don King that reportedly guarantees her $100,000 per fight and several fights a year. Rijker and all the other women boxers earn much less. Rijker earned $5,000 each for most of her bouts. The bout against Andrea DeShong was on a large pay-per-view show so she was paid $20,000. But, as with all boxers, a substantial percentage of her purse goes to her trainer and to her manager before taxes. Even fighting five times a year as she did in 1997, Rijker is not yet earning an opulent living.

She's careful with her health, tuning her workouts with an inner ear trained over a fighting lifetime. She rearranged her already healthy diet with help from sports nutritionists. Learning about the potential damage caused by her occasional dehydrating fasts to make weight, she ditched the practice. "I don't want to end up with Parkinson's like Freddie. He's a warning to me."

The apartment tour takes ten seconds. The place is small, sparsely furnished, and immaculate—a Dutch stereotype of cleanliness. Once, describing training camp digs she shared with a group of slobby male boxers, she said, "If it would make me a better fighter to clean the entire house from top to bottom, I would do it." Serving as a scrub-woman in camp didn't strike her as useful, but keeping her own place squeaky clean obviously does. She remarks on the mess if a magazine stack is slightly askew.

The only clutter is corralled on one small bulletin board beside the kitchen door. It is thick with mementos, photos of friends and family. A snapshot of a newborn infant Lucia is taped to an old news clipping about a boxer killed in the ring. The inked word "remember" is scrawled in the margin. She says, "I keep it to remind me that's not what I was born for, to die in the ring. This is serious, what I do.

"And this is my meditation altar, where I chant."

It's a low table set with candles and flowers, a small rug in front. She learned to chant Sanskrit prayers years ago from athlete friends. The process worked for her, helped her relax and concentrate on her performance. She adopted it.

Arriving in Los Angeles, the Mecca of personal exploration, where Asian religions are the core of the fermenting new age mysticism, Rijker decided to study the Buddhist traditions behind the medita-tion techniques.

"Buddhism," says Rijker, "acknowledges cause and effect. It recog-nizes that you have your life in your hands."

She attends a meditation center regularly. When a friend from the center was recovering from surgery this summer, Rijker visited to help her chant and meditate. Through meditation, she says, "You can get in touch with your heart. It's a survival mechanism to close off my heart because I'm alone, far from home, cut off from my family. If I allowed myself to feel I might cry for ten days without stopping."

One whole wall of the apartment is covered with rows of Rijker's unframed pastel drawings. They are abstract color studies in strong, angular compositions.

One drawing is different, almost childlike—a volcano spewing tears. "I did that one when my dog died," she explains. The dog lived and traveled with her for many years, an emotional anchor in an often solitary life, a responsibility to keep her from running wild, staying out late, or not coming home at all. "I always had to come home to walk the dog, to feed her and care for her. Taking care of her was also taking care of myself."

She talks about presenting a strong, independent image although she knows she's emotional and sensitive. "But I always have to be tough in the gym. If you show vulnerability there, those guys will walk all over you."

The phone rings and she is instantly absorbed in the friend on the other end. At one point she says, "I guess I have to learn to live with celibacy."

Rijker has recently broken off with her boyfriend—an actor and part-time boxing trainer. The rigors of her training, she says, made her demanding and self-centered. She is moody and tense as a fight looms nearer. She didn't feel she could give enough to the relationship.

"I wouldn't advise anyone to become a professional athlete," she says. "It is an isolated, grueling life and there are many negative aspects. But there is an up side. I saw a special little piece on TV—a collage of little girls saying 'sports make me feel strong, make me feel confident, teach me to keep going.' All these positive things about sports. Little girls saying 'let us play.' And there is me among the other women athletes shown as role models. I am so glad to be part of something like that. I asked one little girl, the daughter of a friend, what she wanted to be when she grew up and she said 'a soccer player, or maybe a boxer.' And it was just so natural for her. But ten years ago that would have been impossible."

And there are other pleasures. "The day of a fight the world is mine. Everything has to go my way and everyone does what I tell them. It's a very powerful day. You're like a queen because you're there to do a job. You are important that day. And everyone is there to help you win. To perform. I love that feeling."

She also loves knocking people out. "It is such a feeling of power. There she is, stretched out on the floor, and I am still standing."

Rijker could not afford to go away to a training camp before her September fight, so she did the next best thing and moved away from her telephone. She borrowed a small house from friends while they were out of town. Except for her time in the gym each day she stayed secluded, preparing her own meals and tightening her focus.

The September 13, 1997 bout was supposed to be a world title fight. The WIBF 135-pound championship was held by a Don King fighter named Nieves Garcia. Since King would not agree to a Rijker challenge for Garcia's title, the obliging WIBF created a new weight class, the 139-pound division, especially for Rijker. The 139-pound championship was declared vacant. Rijker was ranked number one in the class, and a German kickboxer named Jeannette Witte was ranked number 2. Rijker and Witte were to fight for the title on the undercard of the huge September 13 pay-per-view show in which promoter Bob Arum matched his "Golden Boy," the WBC welterweight champion Oscar De La Hoya, against the aging wizard, Hector "Macho" Camacho.

But Jeanette Witte was unable to get her U.S. travel visa in time and the championship match had to be postponed until November. Just days before the September bout, Rijker learned that she would not be fighting Witte, whose light-fisted, jab-and-run style she had been training for. Instead she would meet the most experienced boxer she had ever faced, the heavy punching Andrea DeShong.

A former tough woman fighter from Mingo Junction, Ohio, DeShong is a professional masseuse and the only woman to defeat Christy Martin. She fought Martin three times, winning once and losing twice. In their last encounter Martin stopped her in the seventh round. DeShong is a wily, ring-wise veteran with 13 wins, five losses, and one draw on her record. Judging by the size of her belly, DeShong never seems to be in top-notch condition, but she is always relaxed and is apparently unimpressed by hoop-lah.

Arriving in Las Vegas days before the fight, Rijker was inundated by hoop-lah. Television crews followed her into the gym, videotaping as she worked out. She was interviewed and photographed whenever she poked her head out of her room. In a formal press conference the day before the fight, she sat on a dais with her manager Stan Hoffman as he said, "In all my years in boxing, this is the first time I ever had to make a hair appointment for my fighter."

Her hair looks fine. She charms a cluster of cynical boxing reporters with her looks, articulate remarks, and a modesty that is alien to this sport. How would she describe her style? "I have no style yet. I'm still learning. You have to know this game well before you can develop an individual style."

Nobody asked about DeShong. They asked about Christy Martin. She refused to make nasty remarks about Martin, but said she hopes to fight her some day.

No one asked her about Martin's demand that she prove she's female. They waited until she was gone and promoter Bob Arum was answering questions.

"All I can say is, when she was fighting in Biloxi in June, we had to get a special medical clearance for her to fight because she was menstruating," says Arum. It's probably the first time Arum ever used that word at a press conference. From the pink faces of the hardnosed reporters, it might be the first time they'd heard it out loud.

Rijker had talked about the Biloxi fight while she was back in L.A. She usually takes birth control pills to make sure she won't be menstruating when she has to fight. That time she'd accidentally left the pills behind. "I'll never do that again," she said. "I got so tense that I went into the shower after the fight and just stood there and screamed at the top of my lungs." That was after she stopped Gwen Smith with a picture-perfect left hook in the fourth round.

Rijker met DeShong for the first time at the weigh-in the night before. They shook hands and wished each other good luck. Rijker says, "She's a nice girl. Very polite."

The Thomas & Mack Center, Las Vegas, 6 P.M., September 13, 1997.

The arena is jammed and roaring with De La Hoya fans eager for the main event. An audience of millions is tuned in via worldwide pay-per-view television. But the opening act has its own excitement.

The black-clad Rijker is grimly serious entering the ring, eyes down, listening only to the murmuring Freddie Roach, who sticks close by her. The cheerful DeShong mugs for the camera. The fight is scheduled for eight rounds, each lasting two minutes. The referee tells the two fighters, "I want good sports-ladylike conduct."

It's clean and fierce. Rijker comes out in her textbook stance, dancing forward and jabbing her left fist into DeShong's face. DeShong uses her left to distract Rijker while swinging her wrecking ball right hand. The right catches Rijker high on the head and a snaking DeShong hook lands on Rijker's temple. Rijker jabs her way in and slams her own right to DeShong's soggy belly. By the third round Rijker's fast fencer's jab dominates DeShong's every move. The canny DeShong is backing up but switching from a right-handed to left-handed stance, trying to confuse Rijker. She does it once too often. Rijker times her and catches her with her arms spread too wide to defend herself. Rijker's right hand slams under DeShong's rib cage. All the air explodes from DeShong's lungs. Her arms drop to her sides and she falls back against the ropes, gasping. The ref jumps in to stop the action. One look at DeShong's stunned face and he signals that the fight is over. Rijker has stopped DeShong in the third round. Rijker's fiercely serious face breaks into a broad grin and she throws her arms into the air, dancing on her toes in jubilation.

In the drab grey dressing room afterwards, Rijker was still smiling, relaxed as she dressed to go out to sit with her friends and watch the rest of the fights. Manuel Diaz, the cut man who worked her corner, hands her an ice pack to press against her temple where a slight reddening is visible. Diaz is wearing a black "Rijker" shirt, but has occasionally worked for Christy Martin and worn her pink ring colors. Rijker tells him, "I think you look better in black than in pink." A well-wisher congratulates her on the win and her face becomes almost childlike with wonder. "I dreamed I would stop her in the third round," she says. "I dreamed it and it was true."

In DeShong's dressing room the excitement was still high. The still wet DeShong bounced out of the shower wrapped in a white towel to talk enthusiastically about Rijker.

"She caught me switching. She timed me right and caught me

with a good one. I couldn't breathe," she laughed. A gleaming, irides-cent shiner was coming into bloom over DeShong's right eye.

"She doesn't punch as hard as Christy but she's a much better boxer. She'd beat Christy today. Right this minute. And . . ." DeShong's merry eyes lit with inspiration, "I could teach her some things. If I could train her for just two weeks, she'd be the world champion for twenty years."

Two months later, on November 22, Lucia Rijker knocked out German Jeanette Witte in the third round, to win the 139-pound women's world championship. Her manager, Stan Hoffman, says he is hoping for a bout with Christy Martin in the spring or summer of 1998.

Edward Hoagland

Though revered as the author of widely praised travel-themed books (*Walking the Dead Diamond River*, *Red Wolves and Black Bears*), Edward Hoagland originally aspired to a career as a writer of fiction. A summer job with the circus provided the background for his first novel, *Cat Man* (1955), which he completed while still a Harvard undergraduate. His second, *The Circle Home* (1960), was hailed by Pete Hamill as "the best novel written by anyone about the world of professional boxing." Although Hoagland (b. 1932) never boxed himself, he immersed himself in the sport during a two-year Army hitch that gave him weekends free to hang around boxing gyms in New York and Philadelphia. Almost half a century later, in his 2001 memoir *Compass Points*, Hoagland recalled the wonderful world of Stillman's Gym during this era of postgraduate research at what A. J. Liebling called "The University of Eighth Avenue."

---

from

Compass Points: How I Lived

IN the *Daily Mirror* I read a piece about Stillman's boxing emporium, near the old Madison Square Garden on Eighth Avenue in the fifties, where I was at home anyway from working in the circus. And so I went, and went (you paid a quarter to get in to watch), gradually choosing this new form of risky showmanship as the setting for my second novel. But again I focused on a loser, not a champ. My fighter was overmatched by his manager, deliberately manipulated in the gym as a kind of unpaid sparring partner against opponents who were too strong for him. I rather liked the trainers that I saw, in fact, but did despise most of the managers, although it took hundreds of hours of observation over the next three years to put this all together. As a choice of subject matter, the gym was too close to my first novel for somebody who aspired perhaps to be a great novelist, and played too much to my previous strengths in style and observation. But I was instead in embryo an essayist—a witness and describer—and boxing was good early training for that. Right and wrong, mixed motives and irrational punishment, honorable defeat and corrupt victory, brute suffering and innate equilibrium. Grace and coordination: yet the resilience to take a punch. All the misery, cruelty, humiliation of such a sport: and yet delight. [. . .]

Contenders like Joey Giardello and Isaac Logart trained at Stillman's Gym for a chance at a title while I was haunting the place. Logart was a fancy dan, a lithe, bolo-punching welterweight, one of a series of whizzing Cubans who came to America to find their fortunes. Kid Gavilan and Emile Griffith were others, and were better. Though Logart was very stylish, his punches were weak. He never got above number four in the world ratings, but coincided with the time that I was paying attention, and I liked his peppy grace.

Joey Giardello was a slugger, all heart and swarming arms and slurpy mouthpiece. Briefly, he became the Middleweight Champion, in 1963, after he had changed managers and got connected to Frankie Carbo, the Mafia don who ran all big-time boxing in this era for the mob. Giardello was a Philadelphia fighter who soon moved north to New York and to my 1960s neighborhood, around Tenth Street and First Avenue, when he began to be allowed to have some money bouts. "Philadelphia" was such a synonym for heartbreak in boxing because fighters like George Benton and Harold Johnson, no matter how good they were (and Johnson—whom I watched train in a hole-in-the-wall down there—like Benton, was far better than any fighter at Stillman's), so often were only matched with journeymen, or else with spoilers, who hopelessly beat on them. Joey, too, had been shut out because he might endanger the trajectory of the Cosa Nostra boxers, but now with his new sponsors could see light at the end of the tunnel. He was exuberant, and clusters of well-wishers accompanied him to the speed bag and heavy bag for his sessions at punching, and then watched the couple of rounds that he sparred with a paid opponent in the practice ring in Lou Stillman's loftlike walkup room. Joey was white, which already was unusual, and not stuck-up—a good, brave, slouching, street-fight brawler who punched through the other guy's attack and defenses. He didn't bother much with a strategy or parrying anything. Somebody more vital could beat him, but he wouldn't have to knock Joey silly to do it, and at that happy point in his life, he didn't think anyone could.

The managers connived at the row of pay phones on the back wall while their fighters trained. A suit-jacket pocket for phone numbers might be all the office that they had, and Lou Stillman, spitting on the floor when he yelled at them—the most sardonic, eruptive man there, tougher than any *fighter*—ruled the place with his sneers and kicks-in-the-pants and threats of exile. But my favorites were also his, I think: the cornermen and cutmen, like Whitey Bimstein and Chickie Ferrara, Charlie Goldman, Freddie Brown, and Dan Florio. They were the good guys who saw each fighter through his bout, win or lose. Nobody was a "bum" to them. Whitey and Charlie were teeny, wizened family men, veterans of the ring, whose own noses had been rearranged in their previous careers. Chickie, Freddie, and Dan were more mundane in height and build, but Chickie was high-strung and snappish, whereas Freddie and Dan had a calming, fatal-istic, even avuncular air. Hundreds and hundreds of passionately hopeful, macho souls had flailed through their patient hands, but by and by had been smashed.

I was a baseball fan, for entertainment. Its multiple heroes, com-plex rituals, and intricate elegance can't be topped. But boxing is the ultimate sport, where you leave your unconscious opponent for dead if you win, and next month may be derided as a broken-down pug yourself. It's combat, not diffused into a team sport such as football where the officiating is more solicitous and the pain is blurred, or gen-trified like tennis or golf. It is conflict with no drinks together after-wards. I never thought boxing entertaining, and stopped following it when I had finished my book, in contrast to other subjects—such as my beloved Alaskan-Canadian wilderness, or Ringling Bros., or cen-tral Africa—which I've done books on. And, while I rooted for home-run hitters like DiMaggio, Williams, and Hank Greenberg, in Yankee Stadium, and Stan Musial, Johnny Mize, and Ralph Kiner, at the Giants' Polo Grounds, I didn't go to championship boxing bouts at all, and never saw Rocky Marciano, Ezzard Charles, or Jersey Joe Walcott, who were the reigning heavyweights in this period. Instead of Madison Square Garden, I went to club fights, as they were called, the minor leagues of boxing, at the St. Nicholas Arena on Manhattan's Upper West Side, or at the Sunnyside Gardens in Queens, where young fighters fought old fighters to make a name by tearing apart a faltering head, torso, and reputation. My heavyweight was poor Hurricane Jackson, a Stllman's fighter who trained endlessly, skipping rope, punching the light and heavy bags, but was treated as a sort of inside joke—somebody's cash machine. He seemed to function as a clumsy punching bag for favored heavyweights who needed a winning payday on TV, yet brought in money for his owners in the match and was named "Hurricane" for how he windmilled, as part of the hype.

Prizefighters brutalized themselves for cash, like an extravagant paradigm of what warehousemen hefting hundred-pound loads all day, steel puddlers, hod carriers, and stoop laborers did for no glory and less pay. Like a male equivalent of the strippers I'd watched on the vaudeville stage at the Old Howard Theater in Scollay Square in Boston, they displayed their topless chests as public bodies (with the extra titillation of bleeding). And from my viewpoint, the grungy club boxer or workaday stripper was more affecting and representative than movie stars and headline athletes who take off their clothes for the crowd for lots more bucks. I'd learned on the highway and in the circus, in the army, and at boxing gyms that even if you have a cutman in your corner to stanch the blood, it doesn't obviate the need for stamina, self-reliance, and keeping oriented to what I think of as the earth's magnetic field. You can have allies, mentors, be married, but still you're going to be alone most of your life and, if you run off the rails, you had better be good company for yourself. You've got to be able to take a punch and get up after you're knocked down—the cutman doesn't do that for you—not feel sorry to be alive and mark time, nor accept the idea that only the rich can be mobile.

Carlo Rotella

Carlo Rotella (b. 1964) came to boxing by way of his academic interest in the decline of America's Rust Belt cities. A native of Chicago's South Side, he was teaching at Lafayette College when he befriended a young fighter and decided to write about the life experience he could get in the gym and never in a million years find on campus. The result was an essay called "Cut Time," which became the foundation for his much-praised 2003 book of the same name. Rotella is currently director of the American Studies Program at Boston College and a frequent contributor to *The New Yorker*, *The New York Times Magazine*, and *The Washington Post Magazine*, where the following essay was published in 2002. To call the subjects of his essays eclectic would be understatement. Musicians, politicians, clergymen, blue-collar workers—he has written about them all. But his most memorable subject thus far remains Larry Holmes, whom he met at the end of the former heavyweight champion's career and who provides the ultimate truth about the sport: "People talk about 'I love boxing.' That's bullshit. Boxing is bidness, that's what it is. Bidness."

Champion at Twilight

T HE main event had gone the distance. Afterward, there was a press conference at which the loser had half-graciously accepted defeat and the winner had managed to half-insult the loser every time he tried to say something nice about him. The combatants and their supporters then repaired to a nearby nightclub for the postfight party.

Upstairs at the club, big, once-famous middle-aged men in suits gathered at a table. Earlier they had been lined up at ringside like decommissioned battleships in port: the former heavyweight champions Joe Frazier and Leon Spinks; Earnie Shavers and Gerry Cooney, booming punchers who had both challenged for the title and lost; the former Dallas Cowboys lineman Ed "Too Tall" Jones, who had dabbled in pugilism; and Darryl Dawkins, the former Philadelphia 76er, who never boxed but who once dunked a basketball so hard that he shattered the backboard and (he half-believes) the life of the man he dunked on, who later killed himself.

These dreadnoughts of the 1970s and 1980s were appropriate semi-celebrities for a nontitle bout with mostly nostalgic and novelty appeal. There had been no currently hot stars at ringside, no big-time rappers or supermodels, no Sopranos. But the bruisers in suits were an accomplished and physically impressive crew, all the more so for their advanced ages and filled-out frames. They had all been famous for beating other good big men—for pushing around and knocking down guys who were used to pushing around and knocking down other people.

When Larry Holmes, who held the heavyweight championship from the late 1970s to the mid-1980s, appeared at their table in casual street clothes and with a longneck beer bottle in hand, he instantly became the center of attention. The other big men called out his name, gestured for his attention, and raised their drinks to toast him. He had beaten Spinks, Cooney and Shavers (twice). He had held his own as a novice when he sparred with Frazier in his prime, and he had destroyed Frazier's son Marvis in less than one round in 1983. Holmes had never had the chance to beat up Jones and Dawkins, both of whom were much bigger than he, but next to him the two giants looked harmless. Holmes looked eminently capable of doing harm, as always. Hard-handed, resilient, solid through the body but light on his feet, he looked good for a 52-year-old man with 75 professional fights to his credit—even better when one considered that he had fought the 75th that very evening, the 10-round main event that went the distance.

The other veterans had retired long ago. Shavers, who had moved to England, worked the after-dinner speaking circuit. Cooney hawked memorabilia and was trying to start up a fund for former boxers on the skids. Spinks, who never recovered from winning the heavyweight title in his eighth professional bout and losing it in his ninth, had spent most of the evening cadging drinks. Frazier, who was there because his 40-year-old daughter had fought on the undercard, had politely asked the fellow next to him at ringside what town he was in. They were all done. It could be that Holmes, too, was finally done now.

Holmes's opponent, a strong fat man named Eric "Butterbean" Esch, never made it upstairs at the club. He was waylaid near the foot of the stairs by an excited, good-looking, overweight couple who repeatedly assured him that he was the man. While they were talking, more flushed, soft-bodied people collected around them, drinks in hand, until Butterbean stood with his broad back to the wall at the center of a crowd. There were fresh cuts and livid red marks around his left eye. Women kept trying to hug him, and everybody kept telling him how great he was. He was one of them, a regular guy with outsize dreams, and they were proud of him. That was not some bum he had just fought; that was Larry Holmes.

A week or so earlier, during the last phases of the buildup to the fight, Holmes and Butterbean were busy expressing personal dislike for each other in interviews. The promoter's tag line for the event was "Respect: One will give it, one will get it," and he hoped to present their encounter as a grudge match, rather than, say, a fight between an old guy and a fat guy. On the phone with me from his office in Easton, Pa., Holmes tried to do his part to keep up prefight appearances. "He wants to be the man," he said of Butterbean. "He wants to run the show, and make out like I'm the punk kid. I'm a long way from being a punk kid. I beat guys he can't even dream of getting to know, let alone fight."

Holmes had been the best heavyweight in the world in his prime. He had come up through the ranks as a sparring partner for Frazier, Shavers and Muhammad Ali, then he had beaten most of his former employers and a whole generation of promising contenders. Having held the title for seven years and 20 successful defenses, a reign second only to that of Joe Louis, Holmes ranked high on all-time lists of heavyweight champions. He kept company in these rankings with Rocky Marciano, Jack Dempsey, Jack Johnson—the big boys. His exact place depended on the subjective judgment of the list-maker, but only Ali and Louis were unfailingly rated above him.

Butterbean was a novelty act. At 35, he stood 5 feet 11 and usually weighed between 310 and 350 pale, hairless, near-neckless, jiggle-breasted, spherically distributed pounds. He once weighed in at 373 pounds for a fight. He came up in the early 1990s via Toughman competitions, messy affairs resembling reality TV as much as boxing, in which brawlers off the street exchange roundhouses like drunks in an alley. Butterbean eventually graduated to real boxing, although of a bottom-feeding variety. For most of the past decade, he campaigned as the King of the Four-Rounders, beating butchers, stiffs and outright patsies in brief dust-ups. The appeal of these spectacles resided mostly in Butterbean's girth and potency. People enjoyed watching him club down an opponent with crude blows after walking unhurt through the other man's punches, like a monster in an old movie advancing upon a disbelieving victim who fires until his gun is empty, looks wildly at the useless weapon, and then throws it at the monster in a final act of desperation before being devoured.

One principal mission of the buildup to the Holmes–Butterbean bout was to present the combatants as evenly matched, a grand old man against a young lion. On the phone, Holmes tried to say the right things about his opponent—"Never take anybody lightly," and "They say he's tough and he hits so hard"—but his heart wasn't in it. "Look, I won't lie to you," he said, interrupting this train of promotional sweet nothings. "He ain't somebody I should be afraid of. I can't see that man getting inside on me. Maybe he lands a lucky punch, but I don't believe in luck. Not that kind." Now that Holmes was speaking his mind, a passionate note entered his voice. "Look, man, he cain't fight and I'm a kick his ass." So much for marketing double talk.

When I called Butterbean at his prefight hideaway, a casino on the Gulf Coast of Mississippi, he pushed the personal grievance line with greater conviction. "I don't like the man," he said of Holmes in his high, energetic, Alabama-accented voice. "He runs his mouth." This was in part a reaction to a crack Holmes made in his autobiography to the effect that Butterbean was a "circus attraction" and "a fat slob impersonating a fighter." Holmes claimed that his collaborator, a sportswriter, had put the words in his mouth, but he wasn't taking them back, either.

Asked to explain why he was fighting Holmes, Butterbean said, "One, I don't like him, and two, it's the fights after this one, after I beat Holmes, that matter. There's not a lot of money in a Holmes fight"—although Butterbean would make about $100,000, his biggest payday ever—"but people are already calling about the next one." He saw Holmes as a gatekeeper blocking his path not only to big-money fights, but also to legitimacy. Hidden somewhere in the breast of every good-natured buffoon is an aspiration to be taken seriously, and Butterbean, having reached his mid-thirties, was no longer satisfied to be a novelty act.

As a novelty act, though, Butterbean was gradually attaining the kind of celebrity for which most legitimate boxers, even distinguished champions, can only wish. He had already had a triumphant cameo in a Wrestlemania broadcast, and an adept agent should have no trouble working him into the TV mainstream with appearances on talk shows, reality shows, advertisements, perhaps an animated Saturday morning show. Butterbean vs. Mr. T? It could happen. He's a natural for sitcoms, too. The King of the Four-Rounders clocks the King of Queens—ha ha. An overprotective dad meets his daughter's new boyfriend, and it's *Butterbean*—hee hee. Butterbean might spend many years in that kind of limelight, and he was already well on his way to entering it, but now he wanted to be accepted by fight people as a real boxer, too. He could begin to win their acceptance by flattening Holmes.

The fight was held on July 27 in Norfolk, a Navy town that has seen more prosperous days and hopes to see them again in the near future. Some elements of a downtown revitalization are already in place. The USS Wisconsin, a decommissioned battleship, has been converted into a museum. There's a semi-high-end mall named for Douglas MacArthur at the lower end of Granby Street, the old central shopping artery. Farther up Granby, the desolate serenity of a supplanted downtown is relieved by the presence of a couple of places to eat and drink and dance. The Scope, the arena where the fight would take place, is just off Granby, closer to the bus station than to MacArthur Center.

Larry Holmes's locker room in the Scope was big and stark: white tile floor, white cinder-block walls, buzzing fluorescent lights set into the low off-white ceiling, a row of mirrors framed by naked incandescent bulbs. Holmes, big and stark himself in white boxer-briefs and a red polo shirt, sat in a folding chair an hour before fight time. A half-dozen seconds and close associates were in the room with him, most of them wearing matching red-and-white athletic suits of a stiff synthetic fabric that whisked and crackled whenever they moved.

The state boxing commission's doctor came in to take Holmes's blood pressure and to ask ritual questions while Holmes put on socks and laced up and tied his white boots. Any cuts or knockdowns suffered in the gym? No. Any recent operations? No. Any eye operations, in particular? No. There was an ugly mouse under Holmes's right eye, which has given him serious trouble for years, but he didn't intend to let Butterbean hit him in the eye anyway. The doctor chose not to press the matter. On his way out, the doctor passed the referee coming in to go over the rules. Holmes, who has been boxing since the late 1960s, knows the rules.

When the referee left, Cliff Ransom from Holmes's corner started working on his boss's right hand. First he rubbed it thoroughly, working it into suppleness, then he wrapped it in gauze and fitted cotton pads over the punching surface of the knuckles. Next came the bandage-like wrap, over and around and over and around, then a cocoon of tape. Holmes helped him by flexing the hand and making a fist, testing the job at each stage. When Ransom was finished, Holmes smacked the newly wrapped hand into his left palm a few times to test it. One of his cornermen called out, "Big Jack!"—an old nickname for Holmes—"Knock 'em out so they *don't* come back."

Ransom started on the left hand, which required special attention because Holmes lands 10 times as many punches with it as he does with the right. While Ransom worked, Holmes said, "He said he takes a good punch. We'll find out how good." When it was all done, Holmes didn't like the way it felt, so Ransom cut the entire wrap job off with scissors and started from scratch. The second time felt better. Holmes held his hands out to a representative from Butterbean's corner who had come in to observe the wrapping, as mandated by the rules of boxing. The representative nodded, then a neutral party, a fellow who worked for the arena, signed both wrap jobs with a black marker. Holmes got up and began stretching and shadowboxing. After a while, he sat down again and watched the undercard fights on a muted television monitor. He sang snatches of songs, lustily if not well. First, "Thin Line Between Love and Hate," then "Stand by Me," then "You Send Me," to which he improvised a new set of bawdy lyrics.

All this time, his cornermen were mostly standing around and watching him. This is what cornermen do, an ancient routine enacted under buzzing fluorescents in cinder-block rooms all over the world. They have duties to perform during training, and there are times during a fight when they must perform decisively under pressure to close a cut, propose a tactical adjustment, or save their fighter from serious harm, but mostly they watch and wait and offer their warm, breathing presence. An old pro like Holmes no longer needs or asks for much advice, so his cornermen didn't even get to take pleasure in passing on their hard-won experience. There was an easy, sprung rhythm to their routine. At any given moment, most of them would be still, but one or two would be in motion—pacing, or triple-checking a detail like the supply of bottled water and Vaseline. When one stopped, another would start. Every once in a while, somebody would call out something encouraging—"Undisputed champion of the world!" "Seven years!" "Big Jack!"—and the others would nod and murmur. Then the round of movement and stillness would start up again.

"Old" and "fat" are not the disqualifying absolutes for professional athletes that they might seem to be. Watching a cleanly contested tank-town bout between an old guy and a fat guy can turn out to be a lot more interesting than watching two-muscleheads clinch and roll around in a marquee title fight. And by any reasonable standard, both Holmes and Butterbean were in good shape, despite the failure of their bodies to conform with the ripped-and-cut conventions currently in vogue. Holmes was nowhere near as quick as he had been in his prime, but he was still very quick for a big man, and he made up in experience some of what he had lost in reflexes. Speed is power, as fight people say, and knowing from long practice when to throw a punch or block one is a form of speed. For his part, Butterbean was not fast but he was strong. Most of that strength was locked up inside him in raw form, inexpressible because he did not have the technical ability to put it to work as leverage, but he was still hard to move, hard to hurt, hard to stop.

Still, sports commentators and editorialists, when they noticed the upcoming Holmes–Butterbean bout at all, generally took the position that it was meaningless, or worse: a farce, joke, meaningful only to the extent it proved that people will pay to see any freak show. These pious responses made me all the more curious about what the fight might actually mean to Holmes, who appeared to have relatively little to gain and much more to lose.

In the days before the bout, he was still trying to talk himself into believing that whupping Butterbean would matter to him and to others. When I asked him, on the phone, why he was fighting Butterbean, he said, "A carpenter don't have to retire when he's 52. Why do I?" A good question, but not a satisfying answer to mine. He was sitting in his office in the L&D Holmes Plaza, a pair of brick-and-glass office buildings with a fine view of the riverfront, on Larry Holmes Drive in Easton. He was rich and comfortable and accomplished enough to suit almost any son of the working class made good. Why, really, was he fighting Butterbean, and why was he fighting at all at his age?

To begin with, Holmes stood in line for government cheese as a boy, which means that he always finds it hard to pass up a payday, even when he doesn't really need the money. And, while earning a quarter-million dollars for an hour's work, he wanted to show people that he was still good at his job. He had been having trouble finding anybody to fight, though. Titleholders, contenders and those with even an outside chance of becoming contenders would no longer have anything to do with him, since he could only make them look bad. Holmes could still find an opponent's flaws, and getting beaten by a 52-year-old would ruin a career. A good fighter could probably defeat him just by staying busy in every round, but there would be little glory in it for the victor. That left one potential big-money opponent: George Foreman, a contemporary who—like Holmes—had fought on into middle age. Foreman had made a fortune and—unlike Holmes—achieved ubiquity on television as a boxing commentator and a pitchman for cooking implements, car repairs and fast food. Holmes had been trying for years to coax him into the ring, but it appeared that Foreman had grown too rich and fallen too far out of shape to take the risk. If Foreman wouldn't fight, Holmes would settle for Butterbean.

Finding a notable opponent was part of Holmes's continuing effort to extract his due from a public that, he feels, has never offered it in full. His comparing himself to a carpenter, a steady working man, was telling. He has always been a businesslike worker, rather than a crowd-pleasing showman, in the ring. His pragmatic boxing style, founded on the left jab and good defense and the timeless premise of hitting without being hit, never made much concession to popular taste. Posterity unfairly tends to reduce him, perhaps the finest technical boxer on the short list of heavyweight all-timers, to the champion who, in one writer's words, "made boxing seem strictly an act of commerce." Bracketed in history by the two premier celebrity boxers of the television age—Ali, who made boxing seem like political theater, and Tyson, who makes boxing seem like nonconsensual sex—Holmes has been partially eclipsed.

For Holmes, a respectable payday for an easy fight and a chance to show his skill at center stage in front of 7,000 fans in a packed arena and a pay-per-view television audience were reasons enough to take the fight, but he offered yet one more. While I was asking him about how much money he would make, he blurted out a seeming non sequitur: "Let me ask you this: Who you think is the greatest of all time?" I asked if he seriously thought that fighting on into his fifties against increasingly unimpressive opponents would eventually place him above Muhammad Ali and Joe Louis on all-time lists. Holmes said, wonderingly, "I didn't even know I was going to say that. It just came out."

But he did have a point, sort of. He has held up much better than Ali and Louis, both of whom faded badly in the twilight phase of their careers. Ali, at the age of 38, was barely able to defend himself when Holmes put him out to pasture in 1980; Louis, comebacking at 37, was knocked through the ropes and into retirement by Marciano in 1951. Since turning 40, by contrast, Holmes had won 20 fights and lost only three. In 1992, at the age of 42, he fought consecutive 12-rounders in which he first scored a heroic victory over Ray Mercer, who was at the time the most feared heavyweight contender, and then lost a closely contested title fight by decision to Evander Holyfield. In the latter fight, Holmes wore a contact lens to protect his right eye, on which he had recently had surgery for a detached retina. Always confident of his defensive ability, he had the gall to be genuinely exasperated—like a guy on a big date—when it popped out in the third round.

Butterbean would indeed gain some credibility as a boxer if he beat Holmes, but he had almost no chance of winning. For Holmes's part, beating Butterbean was certainly not going to leapfrog him past Ali and Louis in the all-time rankings, and it wouldn't remove him from the media shadow of Ali and Tyson. Holmes enjoyed unimpeachable legitimacy; Butterbean enjoyed growing celebrity. Each craved what the other had, and each saw beating the other as a way to get it. In that sense both were probably fighting in vain.

The gloves, red Everlasts, arrived in Holmes's locker room. Holmes said, mostly to himself, "Better get myself together." He stood up, stepped into his foul protector, and stripped off the red polo shirt. He had weighed 254 pounds, 30 to 40 pounds above his fighting weight during his reign as undisputed champion. Even in his prime, Holmes always had a can-do working man's build, not an ultra-developed anatomical model of a body like Holyfield's or Ken Norton's. Now, well into middle age, his chest and stomach sagged and there was a broad layer of suet around his middle, but his comparatively slender legs were still strong, and he still had the labor-thickened shoulders and arms of a plasterer. The muscles, big but not cut, moved smoothly beneath the skin.

Holmes, still standing, put on his white trunks. Ransom applied Vaseline to his torso and then his face. One of his cornermen was intoning a mantra: "Take control. Take control. In the ring. Take control." Even if Butterbean was not a real boxer, Holmes had a fight to win in front of an audience.

Somebody opened the locker room door for a moment to call out, "Five minutes." Time to put on the gloves—left first, then right, with white tape at the wrists to cover the laces and secure the fit. The neutral party signed the tape. Ransom put on a pair of practice mitts and Holmes banged them for a while, getting the gloves properly settled onto his hands, then went into a familiar shadowboxing sequence: left jab, left jab, right cross, more lefts, grunting and circling first one way and then the other as he threw punches. He looked so utterly competent, sagging middle and all, that it was hard not to sympathize at least a little with his complaint that he could still fight and nobody worthwhile would fight him.

In the ring, a woman was singing the national anthem with the requisite soulful flourishes and quavers. Strains of it echoed down the backstage hallways and filtered through the closed door of Holmes's locker room. Inside, Holmes's crew collected near the door, readying themselves for the ring walk. Holmes, still warming up, did a tricky crabwise shuffle and threw a combination. He reached down with a glove to adjust his protective cup. "Got to protect my future," he said, grinning. "Oh, I forgot. I don't got no future."

The national anthem was over, and Butterbean's ring walk music, "Sweet Home Alabama," was playing. The door opened, and word came from the hallway that Butterbean had made his entrance. Holmes left off warming up, slipped into the red-and-white robe that someone held for him, and went through the doorway without breaking stride, his crew stepping aside to admit him into their midst and then gathering around him in motion. In a tight mass, the group went down the hall to the heavy black curtains that masked the entrance to the arena proper. They paused here, waiting in the backstage twilight, eager to enter the loud brightness on the other side. Smoke from a special-effects machine drifted in thick skeins, catching stray bars of light that stabbed through small gaps where the curtains did not meet flush.

Now Holmes's familiar ring walk music began: "Ain't No Stopping Us Now," the old Philadelphia soul anthem. Everybody in the crew stood up a little straighter. Functionaries pulled aside the curtains, and Holmes and his people went through into the light and the roar of acclamation that greeted his appearance. This might be the last time.

After the usual prefatory huffing and puffing, the bell rang and the combatants got down to it.

In the opening minutes of a fight, Holmes looks as if he is in trouble. He backs away from an advancing opponent, stiff-legged and blinking, arms extended in what seems like a desperate attempt to save himself from incoming blows. Far from denoting a steely determination to prevail, his manner seems to say, "Hey! Watch it with those fists!" A naive spectator would think that Holmes, realizing he can't cope with his opponent, has panicked. Actually, Holmes is taking measurements of the other man's style, using his long arms as calipers to calculate the distance between them at which he can hit without being hit in return. The more straightforward the opponent's style, the sooner Holmes gets inside it and figures it out. Then he settles down to the grind of winning rounds.

It took Holmes less than one round to parse Butterbean. That done, he ceased retreating and set himself up at medium-long range, jabbing and making small, well-timed changes in the space between the fighters to maintain his advantage in leverage. He began landing punches with the straight-and-true authority of a master carpenter driving nails. His arm-extended defense now revealed itself as a form of command rather than submission. He does not wait for punches to be thrown before he blocks them, preferring to reach into his opponent's space and smother punches before they take final form. When he had found his defensive rhythm against Butterbean—when he had figured out and entered Butterbean's rhythm—he stymied developing punches like a parent taking food out of the hands of an enormous baby who is rearing back to throw it.

Butterbean, by contrast, comes out for a first round as if he could punch a hole in the universe. His size and fierce demeanor can briefly distract a spectator from recognizing that he takes forever to load up leverage for a punch and then bring it around his keg-shaped torso in a wide arc, that he has a rudimentary understanding of footwork and feinting and self-defense, and that he doesn't know much about how to hit somebody who knows how to defend himself. In the first round he charged Holmes a few times, stamping and throwing outsize blows, a couple of which landed, but not flush. Holmes shook them off.

By the second round, the two men had tacitly worked out the terms under which they would contest the rest of the bout. The pace was steady, if slow, and there was very little clinching. Holmes stood in the middle of the ring in his characteristic fighting posture, head cocked, frowning intently, like a dog catcher extricating a foaming stray from under a porch. Butterbean tried to get at him, but not with the sustained free-swinging gusto he typically displays in four-rounders. Feeling the pressure of having to go 10 rounds for the first time, facing a skilled boxer who would make him pay for his mistakes, he tried to pace himself and grew over-careful. He threw left hooks, but Holmes smothered them or swayed out of their path. Butterbean had trouble getting into position to throw a right, and when he did manage to throw one, it fell short. Holmes, seeing it coming, had already stepped away. While Butterbean was thinking of what to do next, Holmes would step in and jab a couple of times, perhaps following up with a right. Sometimes, Holmes would throw the right hand all by itself, a crisp shot that jarred Butterbean's big head back against the roll of flesh that padded his squat neck.

Butterbean, frustrated, did not land many punches. He hurt Holmes only once, by accident, when the fighters clashed heads near the end of the fifth round. Butterbean's head, which resembles a marble dome, makes an ideal instrument for butting. When the bell rang to end the round, Holmes, in a daze, mistakenly visited a neutral corner and was headed for Butterbean's when he finally located his own. It took him most of the minute between rounds to recover, but he came out clearheaded for the sixth.

By then, both men already knew how the fight would turn out. Butterbean's left eye, the one closer to Holmes when they were in boxing position, had been reddening and swelling as Holmes pounded it with jabs, and in the middle rounds a cut opened in the eyelid and began to bleed. The blood on Butterbean's face seemed to be satisfying to both men: Holmes was outboxing a man 17 years his junior; Butterbean was taking his medicine, going the distance against the odds.

Murray Sutherland, Butterbean's cut man, yelled at his fighter to keep his left hand up and punch to the body—to protect the eye and take away Holmes's legs—but Butterbean, who flinched whenever Holmes feinted a left jab, wouldn't or couldn't do what he was told. Expecting Butterbean to suffer a terrible beating, Sutherland had brought along an extra-large supply of cut solution, topical thrombin in a 1/1000 mixture, to control the bleeding. Sutherland, who was a light heavyweight contender in the 1980s and who now supervises Toughman competitions, understood the difference between the combatants.

Holmes, with a good sweat going and the fight well in hand, made in-the-rhythm whooping noises when he punched—*Yoop! Hughgh! La-yoop!*—and let his gloves drop down out of defensive position. He was now dismissing Butterbean's punches with slight head movements and nuances of footwork. This was disheartening for the younger man because it seemed that Holmes no longer needed to bother blocking his punches or even to think about them. Butter-bean's best shots were minor distractions from the more engrossing task of punching Butterbean in the eye.

Before the 10th and last round, Butterbean's seconds told him—as they had been telling him all evening—that he had to turn the box-ing match into a brawl. "Three minutes," said one. "You stay right on his case. You're gonna get hit, but . . ." There was no other way to get inside Holmes's long arms.

Butterbean rediscovered his abandon and did what he could to make the fight messy, hoping to create a chance to land a lucky knockout punch. He had no success until, in the round's wan-ing seconds, he threw a left hook that glanced off the outside of Holmes's right shoulder. It looked like nothing, a missed blow, but Holmes stumbled backward and sort of sat on the lower strands of the ropes for a moment before getting up. The referee called it a knockdown. Holmes stood, looking disgusted, while the referee counted to eight.

The final bell sounded a few seconds later. Functionaries and cor-nermen climbed through the ropes and filled the ring as Holmes grimaced into a ringside camera to indicate his displeasure with the referee. Butterbean went around with his right glove raised high to the crowd until Sutherland corraled him. Sutherland smiled as he tended to Butterbean's mangled left eye. His boy had gone the distance with Larry Holmes, and the record would show for pos-terity that he had scored a knockdown. That was something.

The judges all scored the fight in Holmes's favor by a wide margin, and most people in the crowd saw it the same way, but there were exceptions. A young couple in ringside seats repeated the usual two-syllable protest in unison, giving it their shouting, red-faced best, as if they were only two among thousands of enraged chanting partisans. A curiously archaic-looking fellow—dark suit, slicked-back hair, pen-cil mustache—wandered along press row saying, "*Holmes* won that fight? He just walked *around*." Somebody else yelled, "You da man, Butterbean," but the sentiment hung awkwardly in the air. Butter-bean was clearly not the man that night.

When I called Butterbean three days after the bout, he still didn't understand exactly what Holmes had done to him. He hesitated and second-guessed himself on the phone just as he had in the ring. "If we done it over," he said, "I'd go all-out in the middle rounds, just go at him and keep going at him like I used to do." Then, as if disagreeing with something somebody else had just said, he added, "Yeah, but maybe if I'd gone out in my old way, I'd a got knocked out."

He was certain, though, that fighting Holmes had been a mistake. "I took the wrong guy for my first 10-round fight. He's too slick." Butterbean wanted to fight another real boxer, but he wanted to fight one who wasn't so slick, a brawler who would consent to stand directly in front of him and trade punches.

Why had Butterbean made the unwise leap directly from four rounds to 10, and against a great technical boxer? Because, he said, he had been in a hurry to prove that he was a real heavyweight. "I wanted to prove the critics wrong. I wanna be taken serious. There's always that little bit in me that says, 'I'll show you.' That's the move I'm making now. It's the path that'll quiet a lot of the people who say I'm not a real boxer."

I asked if perhaps the most insistent voice Butterbean was trying to silence was in his own head. "Yeah," he conceded, "it might be that I want to prove it to myself. It may not be nothin' to prove *but* to myself." There was a pause in which I could hear him breathing into his phone, then his marketing instincts returned to him in the way that a fighter's senses return to him after a hard shot scatters them. "Hey, when I write my book, it'll make a good chapter."

"Everybody's calling, saying they're surprised Larry looked so good at 52," said Jay Newman, Holmes's publicist, when I called him in Easton after the fight. I asked if that response was giving Holmes any crazy ideas about continuing his latest comeback. "It gives *me* crazy ideas," admitted Newman, but he didn't really expect Holmes to fight again. "Not unless there was a million dollars in it for him," and that seemed unlikely. "It makes no sense to fight again for less."

After a pause, Newman added, "And even if Larry's not feeling like he's done, the guys in his corner have been with him a long time. They're starting to get tired." Holmes's crew had lived significant portions of their lives vicariously through the body of their boss, watching him stretch and work out and shadowbox and spar; worrying about his meals and digestion, his bad eye and breakable right hand; making the ring walk at his side and dutifully urging him on from ringside as his weigh-in figures went up and down. That was a heavy burden of lives and aspirations for one body to carry—too heavy, perhaps, for a 52-year-old body, even one that had retained a large measure of its competence and force. There were other, easier ways to make money.

Newman said, "The niche marker for us right now is grand openings. A Champs, a Circuit City, they fly Larry in, he signs some autographs, gets his fee, and that's it." A former champion of Holmes's stature can work this circuit in perpetuity—not just in-store appearances, but also conventions, corporate functions, after-dinner speaking, motivational gigs. He moves through a landscape of hotel ballrooms, airport concourses, parking lots with grand-opening banners and knots of balloons fluttering in the breeze. He tells stories about forcing a way against adversity, about taking care of your assets. He laughs, he gets laughs; because he's a boxer, it's often okay if he tells an off-color anecdote or cusses a little. When he appears at ringside as a distinguished retiree, he's announced to the crowd, which gives him a respectful hand. And if he's Larry Holmes, he's sizing up the young men in the ring and telling himself, with pride and regret, that he could still whup them.

Sources and Acknowledgments

Great care has been taken to locate and acknowledge all owners of copyrighted material included in this book. If any such owner has inadvertently been omitted, acknowledgment will gladly be made in future printings.

The texts of the original printings chosen for inclusion here are presented without change, except for the correction of typographical errors. Spelling, punctuation, and capitalization are often expressive features and are not altered, even when inconsistent or irregular.

Sherwood Anderson, Brown Bomber: *The Sherwood Anderson Reader*, ed. Paul Rosenfeld (Boston: Houghton Mifflin, 1947). Copyright © 1937 by Sherwood Anderson. Copyright renewed 1965 by Eleanor Copenhaver Anderson. Reprinted by permission of Harold Ober Associates Incorporated.

James Baldwin, The Fight: Liston vs. Patterson: *Antaeus*, Spring 1989. Originally published in *Nugget*, copyright © 1963 by James Baldwin, and collected in *The Cross of Redemption: Uncollected Writings*, published by Pantheon Books, 2010. Reprinted by arrangement with the James Baldwin Estate.

Bill Barich, Never Say Never: *Missouri Review*, Summer 1986. Copyright © 1986. Reprinted courtesy of the *Missouri Review*.

Heywood Broun, The Orthodox Champion: *Pieces of Hate and Other Enthusiasms* (New York: George H. Doran, 1922).

Jimmy Cannon, Archie: *Who Struck John?* (New York: Dial Press, 1956). Copyright © 1956 the Estate of Jimmy Cannon. Reprinted with permission.

Irvin S. Cobb, Cobb Fights It Over Again: *New York Times*, July 3, 1921.

Bob Considine, Louis Knocks Out Schmeling: International News Service syndicated column, June 22, 1938. Reprinted by permission of the Hearst Corporation.

Pete Dexter, from *Paper Trails*: *Paper Trails* (New York: HarperCollins, 2007). Reprinted by permission of International Creative Management, Inc.

Katherine Dunn, The Knockout: Lucia Rijker: *One Ring Circus* (Tuscon,

AZ: Schaffner Press, 2009). Copyright © 2009 by Katherine Dunn, permission courtesy of Schaffner Press and Inkwell Management, LLC.

Gerald Early, Ringworld: *Tuxedo Junction* (Hopewell, NJ: Ecco, 1989). Copyright © 1989. Reprinted courtesy of Gerald Early.

Joe Flaherty, Amen to Sonny: *Chez Joey* (New York: Coward, McCann, & Geoghegan, 1974). Copyright © 1974. Reprinted with permission of *The Village Voice*.

Paul Gallico, Pity the Poor Giant: *Farewell to Sport* (New York: Knopf, 1938). Reprinted by permission of Harold Ober Associates Incorporated. Copyright © 1937, 1938 by Paul Gallico. Copyright renewed 1964, 1965 by Paul Gallico.

Leonard Gardner, Sweeter than Sugar: Originally appeared in *Inside Sports*, August 31, 1980. Copyright © 1980 by Leonard Gardner. Reprinted with permission of Lescher & Lescher, Ltd.

Frank Graham, As It Was in the Long Ago: *New York Journal-American*, June 18, 1954. Copyright © 1954. Reprinted by permission of the Hearst Corporation.

Pete Hamill, Up the Stairs with Cus D'Amato: *Village Voice*, November 19, 1985. Copyright © 1985 by Pete Hamill. Reprinted by permission of International Creative Management, Inc.

Thomas Hauser, from *The Black Lights*: *The Black Lights* (New York: McGraw-Hill, 1986). Copyright © 1986 by Thomas Hauser. Reprinted with permission of McGraw-Hill.

W. C. Heinz, Brownsville Bum: *What a Time It Was: The Best of W. C. Heinz on Sports* (San Francisco: Da Capo Press, 2001). Copyright © 2001 by W. C. Heinz. Reprinted by permission of Da Capo Press, a member of the Perseus Books Group.

Edward Hoagland, from *Compass Points: How I Lived*: *Compass Points: How I Lived* (New York: Pantheon, 2001). Copyright © 2001 by Edward Hoagland. Used by permission of Pantheon Books, a division of Random House, Inc.

Richard Hoffer, Still Hungry After All These Years: *Sports Illustrated*, July 17, 1989. Copyright © 1989. Reprinted courtesy of *Sports Illustrated*.

Jerry Izenberg, My Friend, My Teacher: *Newark Star-Ledger*, March 8, 1994. Copyright © 1994 by *The Star-Ledger*. All rights reserved. Used by permission and protected by the copyright laws of the United States. The printing, copying, redistribution, or retransmission of the material without express written permission is prohibited.

Murray Kempton, The Champ and the Chump: *Rebellions, Perversities, and Main Events* (New York: Times Books, 1994). Copyright © 1994 by

Murray Kempton. Used by permission of Times Books, a division of Random House, Inc.

George Kimball, Leonard–Hagler: The Fight and Its Aftermath: *Come Out Writing*, ed. Bill Hughes and Patrick King (London: Queen Anne Press, 1991). Copyright © 1991 by George Kimball. Reprinted with permission.

Mark Kram, "Lawdy, Lawdy, He's Great": *Sports Illustrated,* October 13, 1975. Copyright © 1975. Reprinted courtesy of *Sports Illustrated*.

Mark Kriegel, The Great (Almost) White Hope: *Esquire*, November 1996. Copyright © 1991. Reprinted with permission of Vigliano Associated.

John Lardner, Down Great Purple Valleys: *The World of John Lardner* (New York: Simon & Schuster, 1961). Copyright © 1961. Reprinted courtesy of the Estate of John Lardner.

A. J. Liebling, Kearns by a Knockout; Ahab and Nemesis: *The Sweet Science* (New York: Viking, 1956). Copyright © 1965 by the Estate of A. J. Liebling. Reprinted by permission of North Point Press, a division of Farrar, Straus and Giroux.

Robert Lipsyte, Pride of the Tiger: *The Atlantic*, September 1975. Copyright © 1975. Permission courtesy of Robert Lipsyte.

Jack London, Johnson vs. Jeffries: *Jack London Reports*, ed. King Hendricks and Irving Shepard (New York: Doubleday, 1970).

Mike Lupica, Donfire of the Vanities: *Esquire*, May 1991. Copyright © 1991 by Mike Lupica. Reprinted by permission of International Creative Management, Inc.

Norman Mailer, from *The Fight*. *The Fight*: (Boston: Little, Brown, 1975). Copyright © 1975 by Norman Mailer. Reprinted with permission.

H. L. Mencken, Dempsey vs. Carpentier: *A Mencken Chrestomathy* (New York: Knopf, 1949). Copyright © 1916, 1918, 1919, 1920, 1921, 1922, 1924, 1926, 1927, 1929, 1932, 1934, 1942, 1949 by Alfred A. Knopf, a division of Random House, Inc. Used by permission of Alfred A. Knopf, a division of Random House, Inc.

Larry Merchant, Beethoven to Boxing: *New York Post,* August 9, 1968. Copyright © 1986 by Larry Merchant. Reprinted with permission of International Creative Management, Inc.

William Nack: "The Fight's Over, Joe": *My Turf* (New York: Da Capo Press, 2003). Originally published in *Sports Illustrated*, September 30, 1996. Copyright © 1996. Reprinted courtesy of *Sports Illustrated*.

Barney Nagler, from *James Norris and the Decline of Boxing*: *James Norris and the Decline of Boxing* (Indianapolis: Bobbs-Merrill, 1964). Copyright © 1964 by Barney Nagler. All rights reserved. Reprinted with the permission of Scribner, a Division of Simon & Schuster, Inc.

Joyce Carol Oates, Rape and the Boxing Ring: *Newsweek*, February 24, 1992. Copyright © 1992 by Ontario Review. Reprinted with permission.

George Plimpton, Miami Notebook: Cassius Clay and Malcolm X: *Harper's,* June 1964. Copyright © 1964 by George Plimpton, renewed 1992 by George Plimpton. Reprinted by permission of Russell & Volkening as agents for the author.

Pat Putnam, Eight Minutes of Fury: *Sports Illustrated*, July 17, 1989. Copyright © 1989. Reprinted courtesy of *Sports Illustrated*.

David Remnick, Kid Dynamite Blows Up: *Reporting* (New York: Picador, 2006). Copyright © by David Remnick. Reprinted by permission. Originally published in *The New Yorker*. All rights reserved.

Carlo Rotella, Champion at Twilight: *Washington Post Magazine*, November 17, 2002. Copyright © 1992. Reprinted courtesy of Carlo Rotella.

Dick Schaap, Muhammad Ali Then and Now: *The Best of Sport* (Toronto: Sport Classic Books, 2003). Copyright © by Dick Schaap. Reprinted courtesy of Trish McLeod Schaap.

Budd Schulberg, The Fight (The King Is Dead): *New York Post*, October 3, 1980. Copyright © 1980. Reprinted courtesy of Betsy Schulberg. From *Moving Pictures*: *Moving Pictures* (New York: Stein & Day, 1981). Copyright © 1981 by Budd Schulberg. Reprinted by permission of Miriam Altshuler Literary Agency, on behalf of Budd Schulberg.

John Schulian, Nowhere to Run: *Writers' Fighters* (Kansas City: Andrews and McMeel, 1983). Copyright © 1983 by John Schulian. Reprinted with permission.

Red Smith, Night for Joe Louis: *The Red Smith Reader*, ed. Dave Anderson (New York: Random House, 1982). Copyright © 1982 by Random House, Inc. Used by permission of Random House, Inc.

Gay Talese, Floyd Patterson: *The Overreachers* (New York: Harper & Row, 1965). Copyright © 1964 by Gay Talese. Originally published in *Esquire*. Reprinted by permission of the author.

Gene Tunney, My Fights with Jack Dempsey: *The Aspirin Age 1919–1941*, ed. Isabel Leighton (New York: Simon & Schuster, 1949). Reprinted with permission of Jay Tunney.

Ralph Wiley, Then All the Joy Turned to Sorrow: *Classic Wiley* (New York: Hyperion, 2005). Copyright © 1982. Reprinted courtesy of *Sports Illustrated*.

Richard Wright, High Tide in Harlem: *New Masses*, July 28, 1938. Copyright © 1938 by Richard Wright. Reprinted by permission of John Hawkins & Associates, Inc.

Vic Ziegel, Roberto Duran's New York State of Mind: *Inside Sports,*

June 20, 1980. Copyright © 1980 by Vic Zeigel. Reprinted courtesy of Roberta Zeigel.

The editors would like to acknowledge the following for their intellectual and spiritual support:

Sam Abrams, David Amram, Amiri Baraka, Alex Belth, Ira Berkow, Bridget Bower, Tom Cannon, Bill Caplan, Farley Chase, Darrell Christian, Gene Collier, Nigel Collins, Jorge Costales, Dr. Tony Cucchiara, Dan Cuoco, Tom Cushman, Steve Davis, Lou DiBella, Ray Didinger, Eric Fettman, Jeanine Johnson Flaherty, Rob Fleder, Bill Gallo, Brenda Galloway, Patrick Goldstein, Bob Goodman, Pete Hamill, Gayl Heinz, Chris Hunt, John Jeansonne, Dan Jenkins, Michael Katz, Dave Kindred, Don Kloss, Mark Kram Jr., Susan Lardner, James Lawton, Steve Lott, Michael Lynch, Kathy Mann, Chris Mannix, David Markson, Linda McCoy- Murray, Hugh McIlvanney, Joel Minor, John Mosedale, Patrick Myler, Thomas Myler, Bill Nack, Peter O'Brien, Richard O'Brien, Sandy Padwe, Vincent Patrick, Colleen Putnam, J. Russell Peltz, Bonnie Raitt, Ron Rapoport, Ray Ratto, Ray Robinson, Tom Russell, Bob Ryan, Lee Samuels, Jeremy Schaap, Budd Schulberg, Benn Schulberg, Ken Solarz, Andy Thibault, Dave Smith, Terry Smith, George Solomon, Fred Sternberg, Glenn Stout, W. K. (Kip) Stratton, Quincy Troupe, George Vecsey, John Walsh, Dick Waterman; and the New York Public Library, Schomburg Center for Research in Black Culture and Library for the Performing Arts, and Lincoln Center.

Portions of the preface originally appeared in slightly different form on Alex Belth's *Bronx Banter Blog*, http://bronxbanterblog.com/.

Index

PETE AYRTON was born in London in 1943. After studying and briefly teaching philosophy, a period of left-wing tourism in France and Italy led to his learning to read and converse in these languages, and to take part in the intense, opaque discourses of Marxism. A period of work as translator led to a job as editor with Pluto Press and to his founding in 1986 of Serpent's Tail. Two First World War classics published by Serpent's Tail, Frederic Manning's *Her Privates We* and Gabriel Chevallier's *Fear*, are included in *No Man's Land*.

Praise for *No Man's Land*

'Splendid ... what a cast Ayrton has assembled ... The war, in all its calculated cruelty, its human impact, its formidable weapons of death and destruction and – yes – its futility, is captured brilliantly in this remarkable, wide-ranging anthology' *Herald*

'Trailblazing ... even avid readers of First World War prose will find eye-opening discoveries here' Boyd Tonkin, *Independent*

'The essential collection of writing from the First World War ... wonderfully wide-ranging' *The Times*

'Handsomely produced ... impressive ... intriguing ... Ayrton's volume will undoubtedly send people in search of the books from which he has drawn such enticing extracts. It also stands as a tribute to the art of translation ... This marvellous book truly lives up to its subtitle' Peter Parker, *Times Literary Supplement*

'Every week, of every year, literary editors find among the haul of new books at least two about the world wars of the last century. In this centenary year the proportion has dramatically increased. This book, however, is different. If you want to know what the Great War of 1914–18 was really like, you need read no other. Peter Ayrton has collected the best prose about that war ... Every extract rings with authenticity ... He makes us understand that it was, truly, a world war ... Ayrton's .... extracts from man ...

'The real strength of *No Man's Land* is the sheer diversity of the voices it offers, especially those from fronts often overlooked or considered peripheral ... All told, writers from twenty countries are represented ... A broad canvas to paint the biggest picture possible' Larry Rohter, *New York Times*